Photoshop Elements 6

for Mac

THE MISSING MANUAL

*The book that
should have been
in the box*®

Photoshop Elements 6

for Mac

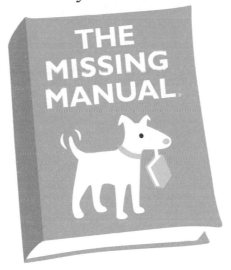

Barbara Brundage

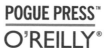

POGUE PRESS™
O'REILLY®

Beijing · Cambridge · Farnham · Köln · Paris · Sebastopol · Taipei · Tokyo

Photoshop Elements 6 for Mac: The Missing Manual

by Barbara Brundage

Copyright © 2008 Barbara Brundage. All rights reserved.
Printed in Canada.

Published by O'Reilly Media, Inc., 1005 Gravenstein Highway North, Sebastopol, CA 95472.

O'Reilly books may be purchased for educational, business, or sales promotional use. Online editions are also available for most titles (*safari.oreilly.com*). For more information, contact our corporate/institutional sales department: (800) 998-9938 or *corporate@oreilly.com*.

Printing History:

March 2008:   First Edition.

ISBN: 978-0-596-51936-0
[F]

Table of Contents

Part Three: Retouching

Part Six: Additional Elements

Part Seven: Appendixes

The Missing Credits

About the Author

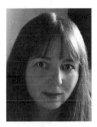 **Barbara Brundage** is the author of *Photoshop Elements 5: The Missing Manual,* an Adobe Community Expert, and a member of Adobe's prerelease groups for Elements 3, 4, 5, and 6. She's been teaching people how to use Photoshop Elements since it first came out in 2001. Barbara first started using Elements to create graphics for use in her day job as a harpist, music publisher, and arranger. Along the way, she joined the large group of people finding a renewed interest in photography thanks to digital cameras. If she can learn to use Elements, you can, too! You can reach Barbara at *bbrundage@mac.com.*

About the Creative Team

Dawn Frausto (editor, copy editor) is assistant editor for the Missing Manual series. When not working, she likes rock climbing, playing soccer, and causing trouble. Email: *dawn@oreilly.com.*

Peter Meyers (editor) is the managing editor of O'Reilly Media's Missing Manual series. He lives with his wife, daughter, and cats in New York City. Email: *peter. meyers@gmail.com.*

Nellie McKesson (production editor) is a graduate of St. John's College in Santa Fe, NM. She currently lives in Cambridge, MA, where her favorite places to eat are Punjabi Dhaba and Tacos Lupita. Email: *nellie@oreilly.com.*

Raymond Robillard (technical reviewer) likes the Montral Canadiens hockey team, his Macintosh, playing video games, and computer graphics programs, especially Photoshop Elements. He's been teaching people how to use Photoshop Elements and Macs for over five years in forums, online classes (*www.eclecticacademy.com*), and in person.

Acknowledgements

Many thanks to Ray Robillard and Dawn Frausto for reading this book and giving me the benefit of their advice and corrections. I'm also grateful for the help I received from everyone at Adobe, especially Karina Buettner, Florian Baeckermann, Hinnerk Schmidt do Rega Sliva, and Mark Dahm.

Special thanks also to graphic artist Jodi Frye (*www.frontiernet.net/~jlfrye/Jodi_Frye*) for allowing me to reproduce one of her Elements drawings to show what can be done by those with more artistic ability than I have. My gratitude also to Florida's botanical gardens, especially McKee Botanical Garden (*www.mckeegarden.org*), Historic Bok Sanctuary (*www.boktower.org*), Heathcote Botanical Gardens (*www.heathcotebotanicalgardens.org*), and Harry P. Leu Gardens (*www.leugardens.org*), for creating oases of peace and beauty in our hectic world. Finally, I'd like to thank everyone in the gang over at the Adobe Photoshop Elements support forum for all their help and friendship.

The Missing Manual Series

Missing Manuals are witty, superbly written guides to computer products that don't come with printed manuals (which is just about all of them). Each book features a handcrafted index; cross-references to specific pages (not just chapters); and RepKover, a detached-spine binding that lets the book lie perfectly flat without the assistance of weights or cinder blocks.

Recent and upcoming titles include:

Access 2007: The Missing Manual by Matthew MacDonald

AppleScript: The Missing Manual by Adam Goldstein

AppleWorks 6: The Missing Manual by Jim Elferdink and David Reynolds

CSS: The Missing Manual by David Sawyer McFarland

Creating Web Sites: The Missing Manual by Matthew MacDonald

Digital Photography: The Missing Manual by Chris Grover and Barbara Brundage

Dreamweaver 8: The Missing Manual by David Sawyer McFarland

Dreamweaver CS3: The Missing Manual by David Sawyer McFarland

eBay: The Missing Manual by Nancy Conner

Excel 2003: The Missing Manual by Matthew MacDonald

Excel 2007: The Missing Manual by Matthew MacDonald

Facebook: The Missing Manual by E.A. Vander Veer

FileMaker Pro 8: The Missing Manual by Geoff Coffey and Susan Prosser

FileMaker Pro 9: The Missing Manual by Geoff Coffey and Susan Prosser

Flash 8: The Missing Manual by E.A. Vander Veer

Flash CS3: The Missing Manual by E.A. Vander Veer and Chris Grover

FrontPage 2003: The Missing Manual by Jessica Mantaro

GarageBand 2: The Missing Manual by David Pogue

Google: The Missing Manual, Second Edition by Sarah Milstein, J.D. Biersdorfer, and Matthew MacDonald

The Internet: The Missing Manual by David Pogue and J.D. Biersdorfer

iMovie 6 & iDVD: The Missing Manual by David Pogue

iMovie '08 & iDVD: The Missing Manual by David Pogue

iPhone: The Missing Manual by David Pogue

iPhoto 6: The Missing Manual by David Pogue

iPhoto '08: The Missing Manual by David Pogue

iPod: The Missing Manual, Sixth Edition by J.D. Biersdorfer

Mac OS X: The Missing Manual, Tiger Edition by David Pogue

Mac OS X: The Missing Manual, Leopard Edition by David Pogue

Microsoft Project 2007: The Missing Manual by Bonnie Biafore

Office 2004 for Macintosh: The Missing Manual by Mark H. Walker and Franklin Tessler

Office 2008 for Macintosh: The Missing Manual by Jim Elferdink

Office 2007: The Missing Manual by Chris Grover, Matthew MacDonald, and E.A. Vander Veer

PCs: The Missing Manual by Andy Rathbone

Photoshop Elements 6: The Missing Manual by Barbara Brundage

PowerPoint 2007: The Missing Manual by E.A. Vander Veer

QuickBase: The Missing Manual by Nancy Conner

QuickBooks 2006: The Missing Manual by Bonnie Biafore

QuickBooks 2008: The Missing Manual by Bonnie Biafore

Quicken 2008: The Missing Manual by Bonnie Biafore

Switching to the Mac: The Missing Manual, Leopard Edition by David Pogue

Switching to the Mac: The Missing Manual, Tiger Edition by David Pogue and Adam Goldstein

Wikipedia: The Missing Manual by John Broughton

Windows 2000 Pro: The Missing Manual by Sharon Crawford

Windows XP Home Edition: The Missing Manual, Second Edition by David Pogue

Windows Vista: The Missing Manual by David Pogue

Windows XP Pro: The Missing Manual, Second Edition by David Pogue, Craig Zacker, and Linda Zacker

Word 2007: The Missing Manual by Chris Grover

The "For Starters" books contain only the most essential information from their larger counterparts—in larger type, with a more spacious layout, and none of the more advanced sidebars. Recent titles include:

Access 2003 for Starters: The Missing Manual by Kate Chase and Scott Palmer

Access 2007 for Starters: The Missing Manual by Matthew MacDonald

Excel 2003 for Starters: The Missing Manual by Matthew MacDonald

Excel 2007 for Starters: The Missing Manual by Matthew MacDonald

PowerPoint 2007 for Starters: The Missing Manual by E.A. Vander Veer

Quicken 2006 for Starters: The Missing Manual by Bonnie Biafore

Windows Vista for Starters: The Missing Manual by David Pogue

Windows XP for Starters: The Missing Manual by David Pogue

Word 2007 for Starters: The Missing Manual by Chris Grover

Introduction

Mac-loving photo enthusiasts, rejoice! It's been a long, long wait, but Adobe has *finally* released a new Mac version of Photoshop Elements. (It's been two whole years since Elements 4 came out, and Adobe skipped version 5 for Macs.) Why is that a big deal? Because if you're a digital photographer, there's simply nothing like a Mac for editing your photos and creating projects with them, so a Mac with Elements is a match made in heaven.

Digital cameras give you instant gratification—you can preview your photos as soon as you take them, and there's no more wondering how many duds you're going to get back from the photo store. You save a bundle on printing, too, since you can pick and choose which photos to print. Or perhaps you're thinking that printing's pretty 20th century. Maybe you want to post your photos on a Web site, email them to friends, or create a really cool slideshow with fancy transitions and music.

If the digital camera bug has bitten you, you're probably aware of something else: The image-editing and picture-organizing software that comes with most cameras is pretty limited when it's time to spruce up your digital photos. Even if you're scanning in old prints and slides, you'll want a program that helps you rejuvenate these gems and eliminate the wear and tear of all those years.

Enter Photoshop Elements 6 for Mac. There's no more elegant, fun tool for working with images than a Mac running OS X, and now Elements 6 gives you an amazingly powerful—yet inexpensive—tool for improving your photos and using them in a variety of fun projects. If you've used Elements before, you'll be blown away by all the new features in Elements 6. If you've never tried Elements, you're in for a real treat.

Why Photoshop Elements?

Adobe's Photoshop is the granddaddy of all image-editing programs. It's the Big Cheese, the industry standard against which everything else is measured. Every photo you've seen in a book or magazine in the past 10 years or so has almost certainly passed through Photoshop on its way to being printed. You just can't buy anything that gives you more control over your pictures than Photoshop does.

But Photoshop has some big drawbacks—it's darned hard to learn, it's horribly expensive, and many of the features in it are just plain overkill if you don't plan to work on pictures for a living.

For several years, Adobe tried to find a way to cram many of Photoshop's marvelous powers into a package that normal people could use. Finding the right formula was a slow process. First there was PhotoDeluxe, a program that was lots of fun but came up short when you wanted to fine-tune *how* the program worked. Then Adobe tried again with Photoshop LE, which many people felt just gave you all the difficulty of full Photoshop but still too little of what you needed to do top-notch work.

Finally—sort of like "The Three Bears"—Adobe got it just right with Photoshop Elements. It took off like crazy because it offers so much of the power of Photoshop in a program that almost anyone can learn. With Elements, you, too, can work with the same wonderful tools that the pros use.

Elements 6 is a big jump forward, bringing you all the new tools that Windows folks got in both versions 5 and 6, as well as some new features to make it easier for beginners to get started editing photos. It's also optimized to take advantage of the latest Mac hardware and most recent versions of OS X.

With the earliest versions of Elements, there was something of a learning curve. It was a super program but not one where you could just sit down and expect to get perfect results right off the bat. In each new version, Adobe has added lots of push-button-easy ways to correct and improve your photos, but the tradeoff for the extra features is that it's become more and more complicated to find what you want. In Elements 6, Adobe has made a big effort to streamline things and make it easier for you to find your way around.

You'd think that with such a long hiatus between versions, some sort of serious competitor to Elements would have appeared in the Mac software arena. But despite the few programs that have tried, there's still nothing you can buy that gives you as much editing power for so little money as Elements does.

What You Can Do with Elements 6

The list of what you can do with Elements is pretty impressive. You can:

- Enhance your photos by editing, cropping, and color correcting them, including fixing exposure and color problems.

- Add all kinds of special effects to your photos, like turning a garden-variety photo into a drawing, painting, or even a tile mosaic.

- Combine photos into a panorama or a montage.

- Move someone from one photo to another, and even remove people (your ex?) from last year's holiday photos.

- Repair and restore old and damaged photos.

- Use Adobe Bridge to organize your photos and assign keywords to them so you can search by subject or name.

- Add type to your images and turn them into things like greeting cards and flyers.

- Create digital artwork from scratch, even without a photo to work from.

- Create and edit graphics for Web sites, including making animated GIFs (pictures that move animation-style).

- Create wonderful collages that you can print or share with your friends digitally. Scrapbookers—get ready to be wowed.

- Create Web galleries and slideshows, and email your photos (although you've already got pretty good tools for doing all this with OS X and the programs that came with your Mac).

It's worth noting, though, that there are still a few things Elements *can't* do. While Elements handles text quite competently, at least as photo-editing programs go, it's still no substitute for Quark, InDesign, or any other desktop publishing program. And Elements can do an amazing job of fixing problems in your photos, but only if you give it something to work with. If your photo is totally overexposed, blurry, and the top of everyone's head is cut off, there may be a limit to what even Elements can do to help you out. (C'mon, be fair.) The fact is, though, you're more likely to be surprised by what Elements *can* fix than by what it can't.

What's New in Elements 6

The first thing you'll notice about Elements 6 is the program's snazzy new darker color scheme to give it a more professional look. But that's not all that's new in Elements 6:

- **Compatibility.** Elements 6 is a universal application, which means it's designed to give you top performance on whatever hardware you've got, whether you have a newer Mac with an Intel processor (like a Macbook or recent iMac), or one of the older Power PC Macs (with a G4 or G5 processor). If you've got an Intel Mac, Elements 6 runs at full speed—it's not using Rosetta, the program that lets you run Power PC programs, although they usually run slower than programs designed for Intel processors. (Page 46 has more about Rosetta.) Elements 6 is fully optimized for Leopard (Mac OS X 10.5), too. It'll run on Tiger

(Mac OS X 10.4), but you need at least 10.4.8, and will be happier with Elements' performance if you update to 10.4.11. For Leopard, you'll get the best results if you have 10.5.2 or higher.

- **Guided Edit.** If you're just starting out with Elements, you now get a special editing mode, Guided Edit, which walks you through many basic editing tasks, like cropping a photo or adjusting its exposure (page 29).

- **Photomerge.** Elements has always had a panorama maker (called Photomerge), but in Elements 6 it gets a complete makeover. It's gone from being one of the weakest parts of Elements to one of the best. You'll find it incredibly easy to make beautiful panoramas in Elements 6 (page 289), with no more tweaking and patching afterward to hide the seams. For a lot of people, this feature alone is worth the price of the program.

- **Faces and Group Shot** (page 296). In Elements 6, Photomerge isn't just for panoramas anymore. You get two new variations: Faces and Group Shot. Faces is just a fun way to combine parts of different faces for caricatures and amusing effects, but Group Shot is a solution to the old problem of taking several photos of a group of people and having one person spoil the best shot by closing his eyes or looking away from the camera. Group Shot makes it easy to move that person over from another photo where he was behaving himself.

- **Improved RAW conversion.** If you shoot photos in RAW format, you'll be happy to know that the RAW Converter in Elements 6 has a number of new features, like the ability to apply your settings to many photos at once and new tools for activities like straightening right in the Converter. You can use the RAW Converter to edit JPEG and TIFF files now, too (page 228).

- **Quick Selection tool.** With the new Quick Selection tool, it's incredibly easy to make complex selections with just a quick drag over the area you want (page 116).

- **Refine Edge.** If you've used Elements before you understand how important it is to have good edges on objects you plan to cut out or move to another photo. With Refine Edge, it's easy to create clean edges that blend seamlessly into other images (page 119).

- **Quick CD/DVD burning.** In Elements 6, you can easily burn photos or projects to a disc for sharing right from Elements (page 60).

- **True black-and-white conversion.** Elements has always let you remove color, but Elements 6 can create truly stunning black-and-white shots from your color photos (page 271).

- **Curves.** Not a drawing tool, but one of the most sophisticated color-correction tools from Photoshop. It's arrived in Elements in a simpler, easy-to-use form (see page 254).

- **Fix Lens Distortion.** With the new Correct Camera Distortion Filter, you can quickly fix problems caused by your camera's lens, like barrel or pincushion distortion (see page 300).

- **Dozens of new graphics, frames, and special effects** to jazz up your photos (Chapter 15), and new alignment tools to position them just so (page 161).

- **Professional-looking new photo collages** (page 405). Other great new projects include DVD cover inserts and CD/DVD labels.

- **Multi-page documents.** For the first time, you can create Elements files that are more than one page long (see page 410).

If you've used Elements before and you're not sure which version you've got, a quick way to tell is to look for the version number on the disc. If the program is already installed, see page 16 for help figuring out which version you have.

Incidentally, all the versions of Elements are totally separate programs, so you can run all of them on the same computer if you like, as long as your operating system is compatible. (You can even have more than one version open at a time, as long as you open the older version first.) So if you prefer the older version of a particular tool, you can still use it. As a matter of fact, if you're experienced in Elements and addicted to the many add-on tools and actions for Elements 3 and earlier versions, you definitely want to keep your old Elements around. (Adobe has taken steps to make sure that most of those tools *can't* work in Elements 4, 5 and 6; more details in Chapter 18.) If you've been using one of the earlier versions, you'll still feel right at home in Elements 6. You'll just find that it's easier than ever to get stuff done with the program.

> **NOTE** The official system requirements for Elements 6 specify at least 64MB of video RAM. If you have a computer, like some G4 iBooks, which meets the requirements in other ways but doesn't have that much video RAM, Elements 6 may run, but it'll probably be slow and things may not render completely. You may be happier with Elements 4 till you get a new Mac.

Mac vs. PC

In Elements, Adobe has departed from its longstanding policy of making the Mac and Windows versions of its programs as similar as possible. The Mac version of Elements 6 is pretty different from its Windows counterpart. You should understand the differences in case you ever want to follow tutorials or videos written for the Windows version.

The good news is that photo editing is pretty much the same on both platforms. If you want to follow a Windows demonstration about editing with Elements 6, just substitute ⌘ for Ctrl and Option for Alt, and you should be fine.

Where the platforms diverge is in the features for organizing your files. The Windows version includes the Organizer, whereas Mac users get Adobe Bridge. That's actually a good thing—Bridge is the professional-level browser program included with the full version of Photoshop. Bridge is really useful, particularly if you shoot in RAW format (see Chapter 8 to learn all about RAW)—Bridge is much better than the Organizer at dealing with RAW files. Bridge also has the advantage that you don't have to use it much at all, especially if you already use iPhoto, Aperture, or another program to organize your photos. (In Windows, it's darned hard to work around the Organizer if you don't like it.)

What you don't get in the Mac version of Elements is the fancy slideshows and Web galleries that come with the Windows version. You still get slideshows and Web galleries, but they're the same ones you get with Photoshop—more of a convenience, not a major feature of the program. But you've got lots of other ways to create slideshows on your Mac—and Web galleries, too, if you have iWeb or use .Mac. And you get a much more robust picture package (page 434) and contact sheet (page 432) than in Elements for Windows.

The bottom line is that both platforms get the same editing features (the heart of the program), but the extras are a bit different.

> **NOTE**   If you're using Windows, there's a separate edition of this book specifically for the Windows version of Elements 6. You can find it on *missingmanuals.com*.

Elements vs. Photoshop

It's easy to get confused about the differences between Elements and the full version of Adobe Photoshop. Because Elements is so much less expensive, and because many of its more advanced controls are tucked away, a lot of Photoshop aficionados tend to view Elements as some kind of toy version of their program.

They couldn't be more wrong. Elements is Photoshop, but it's Photoshop adapted for use with a home printer and for the Web. The most important difference between Elements and Photoshop is that Elements doesn't let you work or save in CMYK mode, which is the format used for commercial color printing. (CMYK stands for Cyan, Magenta, Yellow, and blacK. Your inkjet printer also uses those ink colors to print, but it expects you to give it an RGB file, which is what Elements creates. This is all explained in Chapter 7.)

Elements also lacks several tools that are basic staples in any commercial art department, like Actions or scripting (to help automate repetitive tasks), the extra color control you can get from Selective Color, and the Pen tool's special talent for creating vector paths. Also, for some special effects, like creating drop shadows or bevels, the tool you'd use—Layer styles—doesn't have as many settings in Elements as it does in Photoshop. The same holds true for a handful of other Elements tools.

And although Elements is all most people will need to create graphics for the Web, it doesn't come with the advanced tools in Photoshop, which let you do things like automatically slice images into smaller pieces for faster Web display. If you use Elements, you'll have to do those tasks manually or look for another program to help out.

The Key to Learning Elements

Elements may not be quite as powerful as Photoshop, but it's still a complex program, filled with more features than most people will ever end up using. The good news is that the Quick Fix window (Chapter 4) lets you get started right away, even if you don't understand every last option that Quick Fix presents you with. And in Elements 6, you also get the Guided Edit mode (page 29), which provides a step-by-step walkthrough for some popular editing tasks, like sharpening your photo or cropping it to fit on standard photo paper.

As for the program's more complex features, the key to learning how to use Elements—or any other program, for that matter—is to focus only on what you need to know for the task you're currently trying to accomplish.

For example, if you're trying to use Quick Fix to adjust the color of your photo and to crop it, don't worry that you don't get the concept of "layers" yet. You won't learn to do everything in Elements in a day or even a week. The rest will wait until you need it. So take your time and don't worry about what's not important to you right now. You'll find it much easier to master Elements if you go slowly and concentrate on one thing at a time.

If you're totally new to the program, you'll find only three or four big concepts in this book that you really have to understand if you want to get the most out of Elements. It may take a little time for some concepts to sink in—resolution and layers, for instance, aren't the most intuitive concepts in the world—but once they click, they'll seem so obvious that you'll wonder why things seemed confusing at first. That's perfectly normal, so persevere. You *can* do this, and there's nothing in this book that you won't be able to understand with a little bit of careful reading.

The very best way to learn Elements is just to dive right in and play with it. Try all the different filters to see what they do. Add a filter on top of another filter. Click around on all the different tools and try them. You don't even need to have a photo to do this. See page 47 for how to make an image from scratch in Elements, and read on to learn about the many downloadable practice images you'll find at this book's companion Web site, *www.missingmanuals.com*. Get crazy—you can stack up as many filters, effects, and Layer styles as you want without crashing the program.

About This Book

Elements is such a cool program and so much fun to use, but figuring out how to make it do what you want is another matter. Elements only comes with a brief quickstart guide, not a full manual, although the Help files are available as a PDF file. The PDF is very good, but of course you need to know what you're looking for to use them to your best advantage.

Which is where the Missing Manual comes in. This book is intended to make learning Elements easier by avoiding technical jargon as much as possible, and explaining *why* and *when* you'll want to use (or avoid) certain features in the program. That approach is as useful to people who are advanced photographers as it is to those who are just getting started with their first digital camera.

What's more, this is a whole book just for you Mac folks. You won't have to waste time skipping over huge chunks of text about features you don't have or mentally substituting keystrokes in every list of instructions. Everything in this book is specific to the Mac version of Elements 6—it's all Mac, all the time.

> **NOTE** This book periodically recommends *other* books, covering topics that are too specialized or tangential for a manual about Elements. Careful readers may notice that not every one of these titles is published by Missing Manual parent O'Reilly Media. While we're happy to mention other Missing Manuals and books in the O'Reilly family, if there's a great book out there that doesn't happen to be published by O'Reilly, we'll still let you know about it.

You'll also find tutorials throughout the book that refer to files you can download from the Missing Manual Web site (*www.missingmanuals.com*) so you can practice the techniques you're reading about. And throughout the book, you'll find several different kinds of sidebar articles. The ones labeled "Up to Speed" help newcomers to Elements do things or explain concepts that veterans are probably already familiar with. Those labeled "Power Users' Clinic" cover more advanced topics that won't be of much interest to casual photographers.

> **NOTE** The new darker look of Elements 6 is very cool but you may find the program's solid background very un-Maclike. Not to worry: You can turn it off and have the sort of floating Mac interface you're used to (see page 22). If you have trouble seeing highlighted text because there's not enough contrast, you can do what was done for this book and just go to System Preferences → Appearance and choose a different color. Keep in mind that his change affects all your programs, so you may need to experiment to find a color you like in Elements and your other programs.

About the Outline

This book is divided into six parts, each focusing on a certain kind of task you may want to do in Elements:

Introduction to Elements

The first part of this book helps you get started with Elements. Chapter 1 shows you how to navigate Elements' slightly confusing layout and mishmash of programs within programs. You learn how to decide which window to start from, as well as how to set up Elements so it best suits your own personal working style. You also learn about some important basic keyboard shortcuts and where to look for help when you get stuck. Chapter 2 covers how to get photos into Elements, the basics of using Bridge, and how to open files and create new images from scratch, as well as how to save and back up your images. Chapter 3 explains how to rotate and crop your photos, and includes a primer on that most important digital imaging concept—resolution.

Elemental Elements

Chapter 4 tells you how to use the Quick Fix window to dramatically improve your photos. Chapters 5 and 6 cover two key concepts—making selections and layers—that you'll use throughout the book.

Retouching

Having Elements is like having a darkroom on your computer. In Chapter 7, you'll learn how to make basic corrections, such as fixing exposure, adjusting color, sharpening an image, and removing dust and scratches. Chapter 8 covers topics unique to people who use digital cameras, like RAW conversion and batch processing your photos. In Chapter 9, you'll move on to some more sophisticated fixes, like changing the light, using the clone stamp for repairs, making a photo livelier by adjusting the color intensity and light and shadows in an image. Chapter 10 shows you how to convert your photos to black and white, and how to tint and colorize black-and-white photos. Chapter 11 helps you to use Elements' Photomerge feature to create a panorama from several photos and to make perspective corrections to your images.

Artistic Elements

This part covers the fun stuff—painting on your photos and drawing shapes (Chapter 12), using filters and effects to create a more artistic look (Chapter 13), and adding type to your images (Chapter 14).

Sharing your images

Once you've created a great image in Elements, you'll want to share it, so this part is about how to get the most out of your printer (Chapter 16), how to create images for the Web and email (Chapter 17), how to make slideshows (Chapter 15) and Web Galleries with your photos (Chapter 17), and all the fun projects you can create with Elements 6 (Chapter 15).

Additional Elements

There are literally hundreds of plug-ins and additional styles, brushes, and other fun stuff you can get to customize your copy of Elements and increase its abilities; the Internet and your local bookstore are chock-full of additional information. Chapter 18 offers a look at some of these, as well as information about using a graphics tablet in Elements and some resources for after you've finished this book.

For Newcomers to Elements

There's a lot of information in this book, and if you're new to Elements you don't need to try to digest it all at once, especially if you've never used any kind of photo-editing software before. So what do you need to read first? Here's a simple five-step way to use the book if you're brand-new to photo editing:

1. **Read all of Chapter 1.**

   That's important for understanding how to get around in Elements.

2. **If you aren't sure how to get photos onto your Mac, or if you want to organize your photos or assign keywords to them, read about Bridge in Chapter 2.**

   That chapter also tells you how to open photos in Elements, if you're unsure about it.

3. **When you're ready to edit your photos, read Chapters 3 and 4.**

   Chapter 3 explains how to adjust the view of your photos in the Editor. Chapter 4 shows you how to use the Elements Quick Fix window to easily edit and correct your photos. Guided Edit (page 29) can also be very helpful when you're just getting started. To understand your options for saving your photos, go back and read the section of Chapter 2 that explains them (page 56).

4. **When you're ready to print or share your photos, flip to the chapters on sharing your images.**

   Chapter 16 covers printing, both at home and from online services. Chapter 17 explains how to email photos and put them online.

That's all you need to get started. You can come back and pick up the rest of the information in the book as you get more comfortable with Elements and want to explore more of the wonderful things it can do for your photos.

The Very Basics

This book assumes that you know how to perform basic activities on your computer like clicking and double-clicking and dragging objects onscreen. Here's a quick refresher:

Since you have a Mac, you have a choice between using a one-button mouse or a two-button mouse. (If you have the Apple Mighty Mouse that comes with recent Macs, you can use it either way: Go to → System Preferences → Keyboard & Mouse → Mouse to set your mouse's behavior.) You can do all the same things with a one-button mouse that you can do with a two-button mouse. Here's the lowdown:

To click means to move the point of your mouse or trackpad cursor over an object on your screen and press the left (or only) mouse or trackpad button once. To double-click means to press the left (or only) mouse or trackpad button twice, quickly, without moving the cursor between clicks. To drag means to click an object and use the mouse or trackpad to move it while holding down the mouse or trackpad button (let go of the button when you're done moving the object).

For two-button mousers, to right-click means to press the right mouse button once. For one-button folks, holding down the Control key while you click does the same thing as right-clicking, so you'll see "right-click (Control+click)" in the instructions in this book. Right-clicking typically calls up a menu of options you can choose from.

Most selection buttons onscreen are pretty obvious, but you may not be familiar with *radio buttons*: To choose an option, you click one of these little empty circles that are arranged like a list. If you're comfortable with basic concepts like these, you're ready to get started with this book.

In Elements, you'll often want to use keyboard shortcuts to save time, and this book gives keyboard shortcuts when they exist (and there are a lot of them in Elements). So if you see "Press ⌘+S to save your file," that means to hold down the ⌘ key while pressing the S key.

> **NOTE** In this book, you'll see Leopard (OS X 10.5) screenshots, but nearly everything in Elements is exactly the same whether you use Leopard or Tiger (OS X 10.4). In the one or two places where things are different, you'll find directions for both operating systems, or a note that a particular feature is only available in Leopard.

About → These → Arrows

Throughout *Photoshop Elements 6: The Missing Manual* (and in any Missing Manual, for that matter) you'll see arrows that look like this: "Go to Filter → Artistic → Paint Daubs."

This is a shorthand way of helping you find files, folders, and menu choices without having to read through excruciatingly long, bureaucratic-style instructions. So, for example, the sentence in the previous paragraph is a short way of saying: "Click the Filter choice in the menu bar. In that menu, choose the Artistic section, and then go to Paint Daubs in the pop-out menu." Figure I-1 shows you an example in action.

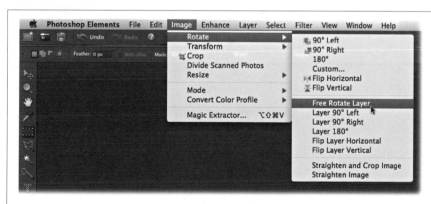

Figure I-1:
In a Missing Manual, when you see "Image → Rotate → Free Rotate Layer," that's a quicker way of saying "Go to the menu bar and click Image, and then slide down to Rotate and choose Free Rotate Layer from the pop-up menu."

About MissingManuals.com

If you head on over to the Missing Manual Web site (*www.missingmanuals.com*), you can find links to downloadable images for the tutorials mentioned in this book, if you want to practice without using your own photos. (Or maybe you never take pictures that need correcting?)

A word about the image files for the tutorials: To make life easier for folks with dial-up Internet connections, the file sizes have been kept pretty small. This means you probably won't want to print the results of what you create (since you'll end up with a print about the size of a match book). But that doesn't really matter because the files are really meant for onscreen use. You'll see notes throughout the book about which images are available to practice on for any given chapter.

At the Web site, you can also find articles, tips, and updates to the book. If you click the Errata link, you'll see any corrections to the book's content, too. If you find something you think is wrong, feel free to report it by using this link. Each time the book is printed, we'll update it with any confirmed corrections. If you want to be certain that your own copy is up to the minute, this is where to check for any changes. And thanks for reporting any errors or suggesting corrections.

Safari® Books Online

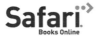 When you see a Safari® Books Online icon on the cover of your favorite technology book, that means the book is available online through the O'Reilly Network Safari Bookshelf.

Safari offers a solution that's better than e-books. It's a virtual library that lets you easily search thousands of top tech books, cut and paste code samples, download chapters, and find quick answers when you need the most accurate, current information. Try it for free at *http://safari.oreilly.com*.

Part One: Introduction to Elements

1

Finding Your Way Around Elements

Photoshop Elements lets you do practically anything you want to your digital images. You can colorize black-and-white photos, remove demonic red-eye stares, or distort the facial features of people who've been mean to you. The downside is that all those options can make it tough to find your way around Elements, especially when you're new to the program.

This chapter helps get you oriented in Elements. You'll learn about what to expect when you start up the program and how to use Elements to fix your photos with just a couple of keystrokes, as well as how to use the new Guided Edit mode to help you get started editing your photos. Along the way, you'll find out about some of Elements' basic controls and how to get hold of the program's Help files if you need them.

The Welcome Screen

To launch Elements for the first time, you need to go to your Applications folder and open the Adobe Photoshop Elements 6 folder you find there. Double-click the Photoshop Elements icon to start the program (it's the blue circle icon with the silver camera on it). When you do so, the Elements icon appears in your Dock. (To keep Elements in your Dock when you quit the program, right-click [Control+click] the icon and choose "Keep in Dock".)

> **NOTE** Elements will take a while to start up the first time you launch it, because it's building a database for the Content and Effects palettes. Don't be concerned if the program seems to hang—just give it a minute to finish. Once Elements creates the database, it'll launch much more quickly in the future.

Which Version of Elements Do You Have?

This book covers the Mac version Photoshop Elements 6. If you're not sure which version of Elements you have, the easiest way to find out is to look at the program's icon (the file you click to launch Elements). The icon for Elements 6 is quite distinctive–it's a silver camera in a blue circle. But if you're still not sure, just check in your Applications folder–Elements is listed there as "Adobe Photoshop Elements" followed by the version number.

You can use this book if you have an earlier version of Elements because a lot of the basic editing procedures are

the same. But getting around in Elements is a little different in Elements 6, so you'll see lots of references to screen features and tools you don't have. There are *Missing Manuals* for Elements 3 and 4, too, and you may prefer to track down the right book for your version of Elements. If you have Elements 6 for Windows, there's a separate edition of this book for that version, which has very different tools for organizing and sharing photos, although editing them is pretty much the same on both platforms.

When you first launch Elements, you get a veritable smorgasbord of options, all neatly laid out for you in the Welcome Screen (Figure 1-1). It offers you no less than four options for where to start:

- **Start from Scratch.** This brings up the New File dialog box, where you set your options for a new, blank file. You can read more about your choices in this window on page 47.

- **Browse with Adobe Bridge.** Choose this option and Elements launches Adobe Bridge, a second program you got with Elements that lets you look through your photos and choose one to work on. Bridge does lots of other things, too; there's more about it on page 17.

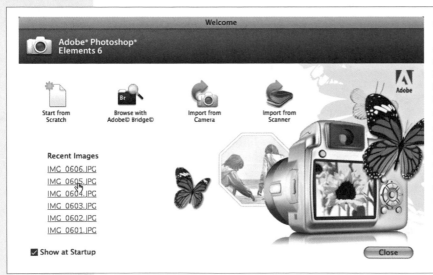

Figure 1-1:
The Elements Welcome Screen gives you four icons to click for different starting points. If you've opened Elements before, the Welcome screen remembers the images you've opened most recently. To work on one of them, just click its name in the list. Elements opens your file and closes the Welcome window.

NOTE   If you use iPhoto, you shouldn't use Bridge to try to see into your iPhoto library. See the
next section for more about why not.

- **Import from Camera.** You got yet another extra program with Elements: the
  Adobe Photo Downloader. If you click this button on the Welcome Screen, Elements sends you over to Bridge and launches the Photo Downloader. However,
  you may not want to do this, especially if you use another program like iPhoto
  to organize your photos, or if you use another download program like Canon's
  ImageBrowser. There's more about the Downloader on page 19.

- **Import from Scanner.** If your scanner driver allows you to scan directly into
  Elements, click this button and, in the window that appears, select your scanner from the pull-down menu. Of course, you need to have your scanner driver
  and any necessary Photoshop plug-ins (page 45) for your scanner installed or
  this won't get you anywhere. (Many scanners come with software that lets you
  scan and save your scan. You can then open the resulting file in Elements like
  any other image, as long as you saved it in a format that Elements can read—see
  page 57.) If you have a Mac with an Intel processor and your scanner plug-in is
  old, when you launch Elements, you may see a message about plug-ins not
  loading. See page 46 for what to do about that.

NOTE   If Elements doesn't recognize your scanner but you know you should be able to scan
into Elements, try reinstalling your scanner driver and any scanner plug-ins.

If this isn't the first time you've launched Elements, you'll also see a list of recently
opened files in the lower-left part of the window. Click a photo's name to open it.

You don't have to choose any of these options if you don't want to. Just click the
Close button in the lower right and you'll find yourself in Elements, free to do
whatever you want. You can even turn off the Welcome screen altogether if you
want to, as explained in the box below.

FREQUENTLY ASKED QUESTION

Say Goodbye to the Welcome Screen

How do I get rid of the Welcome screen?

If you get to feeling like you've been welcomed
enough, you can turn off the Welcome screen. Then
you don't have to click through it every time you start
the program.

It's super easy to put the Welcome screen away permanently. Just turn off the little checkbox in the lower-left corner of the window that says "Show at Startup". If you want
to bring the Welcome Screen back again, go to Window →
Welcome, and then turn the checkbox back on. The next
time you launch Elements, it'll be there to greet you.

Adobe Bridge—Decisions, Decisions

When you first start using Elements 6, you have a decision to make: How do you
want to organize and search for your photos?

Of course, you can decide not to organize your photos, but it sure can make them hard to find. These days, everyone has lots of photos to deal with, whether you take them with your camera or cellphone or you're busy scanning in old prints. Most people want to organize photos so they can easily find particular photos when they need 'em.

With that in mind, Adobe gives you Bridge CS3, the image browser that comes with full Photoshop and the other Creative Suite programs. (You can see Bridge in Figure 1-2.) In some ways, this is a big step up from the File Browser in early editions of Elements or the Organizer that comes with the Windows version, especially if you shoot RAW. (Chapter 8 has info about RAW formats.) You can use Bridge to search for, move, and assign keywords and ratings to your photos, and to get tons of detailed information about them.

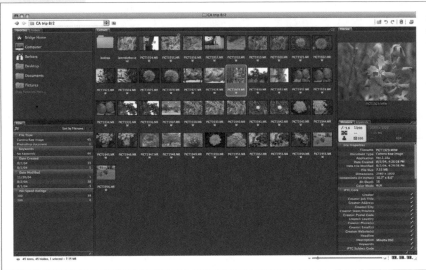

Figure 1-2:
Adobe Bridge makes it easy to find photos to work with in Elements. You can see all kinds of info about your photos in the Metadata panel in the lower right, and assign keywords to your images using the Keywords panel (hidden here).

But if you're like a lot of Mac folks, you already use some kind of photo organizer. iPhoto, which comes with all new Macs, is by far the most popular, but Apple's Aperture and Adobe's Lightroom also have big followings. If you use one of these programs, you probably don't want to use Bridge most of the time. For one thing, trying to get into your photo database (like the iPhoto library file, for example) from Bridge or any application other than the program that created it can make bad things happen. The iPhoto library file, in particular, is prone to corruption if you mess with it from outside iPhoto, and that can cause big problems.

The good news is that you can send your photos directly to Elements from within any of these organizer programs (page 43 has the details). So for most tasks, it's best to avoid Bridge entirely.

However, if you want to make any of the online projects that are built into Elements (see page 419), you'll get bounced over to Bridge during the process, so you'll need to deal with Bridge a little bit, even if it's not your main way of organizing photos. Page 44 gives you a rundown of the Bridge basics you need to know.

If you're not already locked into another photo organizer, Bridge lets you do a lot of useful things with your photos, like rate them, move and rearrange them, and assign metadata keywords to them that lots of programs can understand. For many people, Bridge can be a valuable tool, especially if you prefer your own folder structure. You may find that Bridge is all you need for organizing your photos. There's lots more about it on page 37.

The Photo Downloader

Along with Bridge, you get the Adobe Photo Downloader. You can use the Downloader to get photos from your camera, but in OS X, you already have Image Capture that handles that part for you, and does a fine job. For most people, the Downloader isn't terribly useful, and Adobe makes it easy to forget it even exists, since you can only launch it from Bridge or Elements. (It's not a standalone program like the Downloader that comes with the Windows version of Elements, although you can set it launch automatically any time you connect a camera or card reader, even if Bridge and Elements aren't running.)

> **NOTE** Although both the Mac and Windows versions of Elements include a Photo Downloader, there are a number of differences between the two. The Mac version doesn?t let you choose among different types of media to view and import, or let you correct red eye or create automatic stacks as you download your photos.

Few Mac people use the Downloader at all, but it can be useful in a few situations:

- **Convert to DNG.** If you shoot RAW files (page 213) and you want to convert them to DNG files as you import them, the Downloader can do this automatically. (Page 230 has info about the DNG format.) You can convert to DNG in a couple of other ways in Elements, though, as Chapter 8 explains.

- **Add Metadata.** This is the most important feature of the Downloader. As you import your photos, you can tell the Downloader to add an author or copyright holder to the photo's information. Or you can create your own custom metadata template (a list of info about the picture that gets stored as part of the file, like who took it or a keyword to help you find the photo by searching) and apply it to every photo you import. (There's lots more about metadata on page 52.) You can also use Bridge to add or edit metadata (even for batches of pictures), if you prefer—see page 52.

You can launch the Downloader at any time if you want to check it out. In Elements, go to File → Adobe Photo Downloader; in Bridge it's File → Get Photos from Camera. (Since most people with Macs aren't too interested in the Downloader, it's not covered in depth in this book. If you want to know more about how to use it, you'll find detailed Downloader instructions on this book's Missing CD page at *www.missingmanuals.com*.)

Page 33 talks more about getting photos into Elements, including some of the nifty new ways of browsing through your pictures in Leopard (OS X 10.5) right in the Finder.

Editing Your Photos

The main component of Elements is the Editor (Figure 1-3), where you get to edit, adjust, transform, and generally glamorize your photos, and where you can create original artwork from scratch with the drawing tools and shapes.

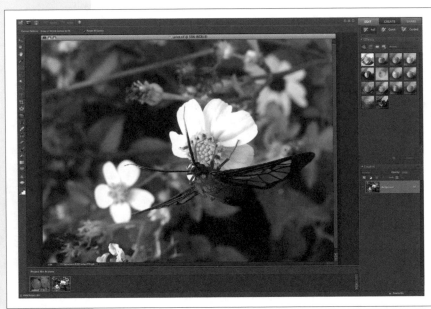

Figure 1-3:
The main Elements editing window, which Adobe calls Full Edit. In some previous versions of Elements it was known as the Standard Editor, something you might want to remember in case you ever try any tutorials written for Elements 3 or 4.

You can operate the Editor in any of three different modes:

- **Quick Fix.** For many beginners, Quick Fix (Figure 1-4) ends up as your main workspace. Adobe has gathered together the basic tools you need to improve most photos. It's also one of the two places in Elements where you can choose to have a before-and-after view while you work. (Guided Edit, described below, is the other.) Chapter 4 gives you all the details on using Quick Fix.

- **Full Edit.** The Full Edit window gives you access to Elements' most sophisticated tools. You have far more ways to work on your photo in Full Edit than in Quick Fix, and if you're fussy, it's where you'll do most of your retouching work. Most of the Quick Fix commands are also available via menus in the Full Edit window.

- **Guided Edit.** This is new in Elements 6, and it can be enormously helpful if you're a newcomer to Elements. Basically, it provides a step-by-step walk-through for popular projects such as cropping your photos and removing blemishes from them. Like Quick Fix, Guided Edit offers a before-and-after view of your photo as you work on it. Guided Edit is explained on page 29.

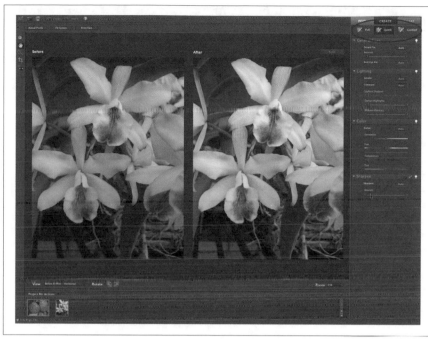

Figure 1-4:
The Quick Fix window (shown here) and Guided Edit are the only places in Elements where you can see a before-and-after view of your photo as you work. Use the navigation buttons at the top of the screen (circled) to navigate from Full Edit to the Quick Fix window (and to Guided Edit, if you like) and back again.

There are also tabs for making projects (Create) and sharing files (Share). You'll learn about working in these tabs in Chapters 15 through 17.

The rest of this chapter covers some of the basic concepts and key tools you'll come across in Elements.

Your Elements Tools

Elements gives you an amazing array of tools to use when working on your photo. You get almost two dozen primary tools to help you select, paint on, and otherwise manipulate your photos, and many of the tools have as many as six subtools hiding beneath them (see Figure 1-5). Bob Vila's workshop probably isn't any better stocked than Elements' virtual toolbox.

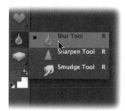

Figure 1-5:
Like any good toolbox, the Elements Toolbox has lots of hidden drawers tucked away in it. Many Elements tools are actually groups of tools, which are represented by tiny black triangles on the lower-right side of the tool icon (you can't really see the triangle in the illustration because the pop-out menu obscures it). Holding the mouse button down as you click the icon brings out the hidden subtools. The little white square next to the Blur tool means it's the active tool right now. (It looks black here because it's highlighted.)

Feeling Surrounded?

One of the first things you'll notice about Elements 6 is the way it takes over your entire screen when you launch it, putting a solid dark gray background between you and the other things on your desktop. If you're a recent convert from Windows, you'll probably love this. If you're a longtime Mac fan, you probably won't.

Luckily, there's a checkbox in Elements' preferences (Photoshop Elements → Preferences → General, and turn off Fill Workspace Background) where you can turn the background off so that Elements looks like a normal Mac program, with menu bars and toolbars floating over your desktop. (This preference only changes Full Edit, Create, and Share. Quick Fix and Guided Edit will still show the background even if you turn it off.)

No matter which view you choose, you can't resize the Elements window. If you've used other versions of Elements or Photoshop for Mac, you have to say goodbye to using the Tab key to hide the toolbars and menu bars—it won't work in Elements 6. Tabbing only hides palettes that are out of the Palette bin on your Elements desktop. (See page 23 for more about bins and palettes.)

To hide Elements completely (including your open images), press ⌘+Control+H. Elements vanishes until you call it back by clicking its icon in the Dock. (You can't use the standard Mac ⌘+H keystroke combo to hide Elements because those keys are used to hide *selections* [see Chapter 5] in the photo you're working on.)

Here's another trick: If you keep the Elements icon in your Dock, when Elements is hidden or isn't running, drag a photo to the Elements icon in the Dock. Let go of the mouse button and Elements pops up with your photo open and ready to edit.

TIP When you want to explore every cranny of Elements, you need to open a photo (choose File → Open). Lots of the menus are grayed out if you don't have a file open.

The long, skinny strip on the left side of the Full Edit window is the main Elements Toolbox, as you can see in Figure 1-5. It stays perfectly organized so that you can always find what you want without ever having to lift a finger to tidy it. And what's more, if you forget what a particular tool does, then hold your mouse over the tool's icon and a label (called a tooltip) appears. To activate a tool, click it. Any tool that you select comes with its own collection of options, as shown in Figure 1-6.

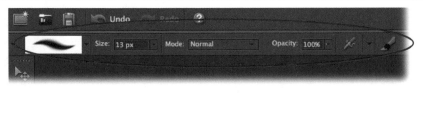

Figure 1-6:
When a tool is active, the Options bar changes to show its available settings (circled). Elements tools are highly customizable, letting you do things like adjust a brush's size and shape. Here you see the options for the Brush tool. (The caterpillar-like thingy at the left is a sample of the stroke you'd get from the current brush settings.)

Incidentally, in Elements 6 your screen size determines the number of rows in the Toolbox. If you have a small screen, you have a double-column Toolbox. If your screen is large enough to show all the tools in one long column, that's how your Toolbox appears. (Nearly all recent Mac monitors show the single column.) If you'd rather have a more compact Toolbox, see the box "Doubling Up."

POWER USERS' CLINIC

Doubling Up

If you have a single column Toolbox and you'd prefer the double-columned Toolbox (maybe you think it would be more efficient not to have your tools spread out so much, for example), good news—you can tear the Toolbox loose from its moorings and collapse it into a double column by grabbing its top edge and pulling it off the Options bar. But keep in mind that a double-columned Toolbox isa bit quirky. When you put it too close to the left edge of the screen, it springs back to its original form.

Unfortunately, while pressing the Tab key hides a floating Toolbox in the *Windows* version of Elements, it doesn't work in Elements 6 for Mac.

Other windows in Elements, like Quick Fix and the RAW Converter (see page 213), also have toolboxes, but none is as complete as the one in Full Edit.

> **NOTE** If you've used Elements before, you'll find an important difference in getting to subtools in Elements 6. The only way to choose a tool from a group in Elements 6 is by using the tool's pop-out menu in the Toolbox. You can't switch from one tool in a subgroup to another in the Options bar anymore.

Don't worry about learning the names of every tool right now. It's easier to remember what a tool is once you've used it. And don't be concerned about how many tools you have available. You probably have a bunch of Allen wrenches in your garage toolbox that you don't use more than a couple of times a year. Likewise, you'll find that you tend to use certain Elements tools more than others.

> **TIP** You can activate any tool with a keyboard shortcut, thereby saving a *ton* of time, since you don't have to interrupt what you're doing to trek over to the Toolbox. To see a tool's shortcut key, hover your mouse over the icon. A tooltip (page 28) pops up that tells you the shortcut key (it's the letter in parentheses).

Panels, Bins, and Palettes

No matter which editing mode you're in, the right side of your screen is always pretty busy. Adobe calls this area the *Task panel*. You use it to select different modes, like whether to edit a photo or use it in a project.

Once you click a tab, you see your choices for that tab: the different editing modes under the Edit tab, for instance, or a list of projects you can make with the Create tab. You can collapse the main part of the Task panel to get it out of your way by clicking its left edge, but the main tabs are always visible. Click the edge again to bring the panel back.

The Project bin

The long narrow photo tray hogging the bottom of your screen is called the *Project bin* (Figure 1-7). It shows you what photos you currently have open, and offers you a shortcut to the Create and Share modes.

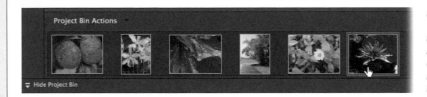

Figure 1-7:
The Project bin runs across the bottom of your screen. It holds a thumbnail of every photo you have open. If you have more photos than the bin can display at once, use the scroll bar on the right (where the cursor is in the figure) to see the rest of your photos. To change the active photo, double-click the thumbnail of the one you want and it moves to the front and becomes the active image.

You can drag your photos' thumbnails in the bin to rearrange them if you want to use the photos in a project. Using the Project bin's pull-down menu, you can:

- **Create.** Use your photos in one of Elements' built-in projects in the Create Tab, like a Photo Collage or DVD label. See Chapter 15 for more about creating projects.

- **Share.** This menu option takes you to the Share tab, where you can email your photos or create a Web gallery for them. There's more about the Share tab in Chapter 17.

- **Print Project Bin Files.** You can start a picture package (page 434) right from this menu, if you like.

All these options are also available in other places, so you don't need to keep the bin around just for them.

The Project bin is a useful feature, but if you have a small monitor, sometimes you may prefer to have the space for your editing work. If you don't want to see the bin all the time, you can collapse and expand it. To close the bin, click the Hide Project Bin arrow at the lower left of your screen. Click the arrow again when you want the Project bin to reappear.

> **NOTE**   If it bothers you to have multiple photos open in the Full Edit workspace, click the yellow minimize buttons on the photos you want to move out of your way. They'll glide offscreen into your Dock. You can bring them back into the Elements workspace by double-clicking them in the Project bin, or clicking them in the Dock.

The Palette bin

When you're in Full Edit, the Task panel displays the Palette bin. Elements stores *palettes* in this bin, letting you do things like keep track of what you've done to your photo (Undo History palette) and apply special effects to your images (Effects palette and Content palette).

With most recent Mac monitors, the Palette bin is no problem—your Mac's widescreen monitor gives you plenty of space for it. If you don't have a large monitor, you may find it wastes too much desktop acreage, and in Elements, you need all the working room you can get. Fortunately, you don't have to keep your palettes in the bin; you can close the bin and just keep your palettes floating around on your desktop, or you can minimize them.

You open and close the bin by clicking the Palette bin button at the bottom of your screen (below the bin), or you can click the Palette bin's left edge (anywhere along the thin vertical bar). You can also pull palettes out of the bin by dragging the name bar of any palette. Figure 1-8 shows how to make your palettes even smaller once they're out of the bin. Freestanding palettes can also be combined with each other, as shown in Figure 1-9.

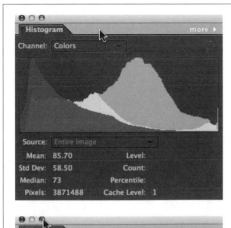

Figure 1-8:
You can free up even more space by collapsing your palettes, accordion-style, once they're out of the bin.

Top: To collapse a palette, double-click the palette's top bar. You can also toggle back and forth between expanded and contracted views by clicking the green button on the palette.

Bottom: A shrunken palette.

Only two palettes are in the Palette bin to start with: Layers and Effects. To see how many more palettes Elements actually gives you, check out the Editor's main Window menu (the one at the top of your screen). When you select a new palette, it appears floating on the desktop. If you want to put a palette into the bin, click the little double arrow at the upper right of the palette and choose "Place in Palette Bin when Closed", and then click the Close button. The palette jumps into the bin. To take a palette out of the bin, drag it out, and then go back to the menu and deselect "Place in Palette Bin when Closed." The next time you close the palette, it disappears and you have to choose it from the Window menu to see it again.

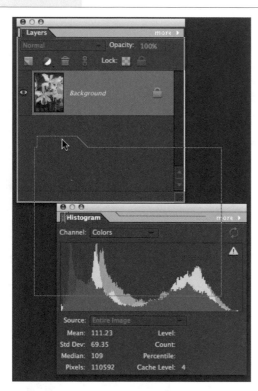

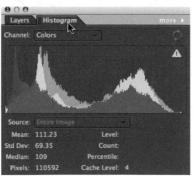

Figure 1-9:
You can combine two or more palettes once you've dragged them out of the bin.

Top: The Histogram palette is being pulled into, and combined with, the Layers palette. To combine palettes, drag one of them (by clicking on the palette's name bar) and drop it onto the other palette (notice the white line that appears around the Layers palette, signaling it's "ready" to accept the Histogram palette).

Bottom: To switch from one palette to another after they're grouped, just click the tab of the one you want to use. To remove a palette from a group, simply drag it off the palette window. If you want to return everything to how it looked when you first launched Elements, go to Window → Reset Palette Locations.

NOTE   If you've been going crazy because you're trying to get rid of one of the bin's original palettes (either the Layers or Effects palette), but every time you close it, it just hops back into the bin, click the More button in the upper-right corner of the palette and turn off "Place in Palette bin when Closed." Next time you close the palette, it goes away and won't return till you choose it again from the Window menu.

Special palettes

As Adobe adds more and more goodies to Elements, organizing everything so that you can get to it quickly has become something of a problem. To help reduce the clutter in Elements 6, Adobe has come up with a couple of new palettes, and new ways to navigate some old friends.

When you first launch Elements, you see the Effects palette as one of the palettes in the bin. The Effects palette lets you add special effects to your images. It gives you access to filters (page 350), Layer styles (page 366), and Photo Effects (page 364). To use it, click the icon for the main type of effect you want, as explained in Figure 1-10, and then use the pull-down menu to choose a category. You apply the effect by double-clicking its thumbnail or clicking the thumbnail once, and then clicking Apply, or just by dragging the thumbnail onto your photo.

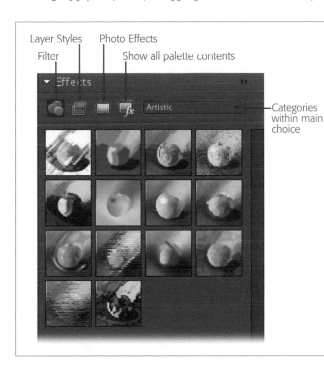

Layer Styles   Photo Effects
Filter   Show all palette contents
Categories within main choice

Figure 1-10:
Use these buttons to choose what you see in the Effects palette: Filters, Layer Styles, Photo Effects, or all three.

> **NOTE**   Both the Effects and Content palettes have a little trash can at the bottom of the window. Be careful: Clicking it deletes the selected palette item *permanently* until you reinstall Elements. It's for getting rid of palette content you're sure you don't want (the Layer style, say, or the Background graphic), not for removing something from your current image. Don't use it to remove an effect or piece of artwork—use one of the escape routes described on page 31 instead.

The other special palettes are the Content palette and the Favorites palette. They're actually loaded when you first start Elements, but you don't see them because they're hidden away in the Create tab. To see them, click Create. Just below the main Create tab, you'll see two sub-tabs. When you enter Create for the first time, Projects is the active tab. If you click the Artwork sub-tab, the Task panel switches over to show you the Content and Favorites palettes.

The Content palette holds backgrounds, frames, graphics, shapes, text effects, and themes to use in your projects. The Favorites palette provides a convenient parking space for everything from the Effects and Content palettes that you use all the time and want to keep handy. You can read more about how to use these palettes on page 413.

The Content and Favorites palettes tend to resist if you try to haul them out of the bin when you're in the Create tab's Artwork mode. If you want one (or both) of them on your desktop in Full Edit, it's easiest to start by going to the Window menu and choosing the palette there. Then you can dock it in the Palette bin if you like, or keep it free floating by using the methods described above. (They still appear in Artwork even when you set them to show in Full Edit, too.)

> **NOTE**   Elements has one palette-related quirk. In the Window menu, visible palettes should have a checkmark next to their names. (Palettes that are open in another tab but not currently visible have a dash next to their names.) But if you collapse a palette, even though the palette's name stays on your desktop, it remains unchecked in the Window menu. If you lose a collapsed palette (they occasionally get hidden behind the Options bar when you switch back and forth from Full Edit to Quick Fix), just select the palette's name in the list again to bring it back to the front where you can reach it. If all else fails, choosing Reset Palette Locations in the Window menu puts everything back in its original position.

Getting Help

Wherever Adobe found a stray corner in Elements, they stuck some help into it. You can't move anywhere in this program without being offered some kind of guidance. Here are some of the ways you can summon assistance if you need it:

- **Help menu.** Choose Help → Photoshop Elements Help. Elements launches the Adobe Help Viewer and you'll see the Elements Help files displayed there. (There are separate Help files for Bridge and for Elements, so you may need to choose the correct program from the pull-down menu in the upper left of the Help Viewer window.) In the Help Viewer, you can search or browse a topic list and glossary. If you're using Mac OS X Leopard, you'll also see a Search box where you can type in a search term. This doesn't search the Elements Help files, but rather lets you search the Elements menus, a very cool feature, as explained in Figure 1-11.

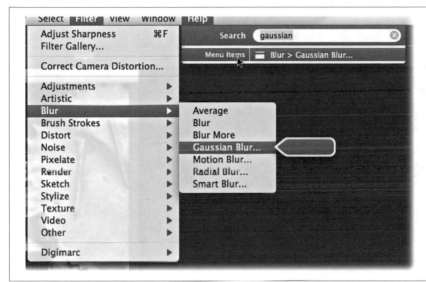

Figure 1-11:
In Leopard (OS X 10.5), you can easily find Elements menu items by typing the name of what you're looking for into this search box. For instance, if you don't know where the Gaussian Blur filter (page 362) is located, enter the term "Gaussian", and then click the file path that appears below the search box. Leopard expands your menus and displays a big floating arrow to show you where to find it.

- **Tooltips**. The text that pops up under your mouse as you move around Elements is linked to the appropriate section in Elements Help. Click a tooltip for more information about whatever your mouse is hovering over.

- **Dialog box links**. Most dialog boxes have a few words of bright blue text somewhere in them. That text is actually a link to Elements Help. If you get confused about what the settings for a filter do, for instance, then click the blue text in the settings dialog box for a reminder.

Guided Edit

If you're a beginner, your biggest help in Elements may be the new Guided Edit feature, shown in Figure 1-12. Guided Edit walks you through a variety of the editing tasks you're likely to want to do, like cropping, sharpening, correcting colors, and removing blemishes.

Guided edit is really easy to use:

1. **Go to Guided Edit.**

   Click the Edit tab → Guided.

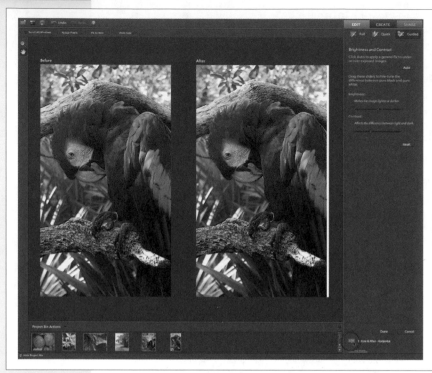

Figure 1-12:
Guided Edit gives you step-by-step help with basic photo editing. Just use the tools that appear in the task panel once you choose an activity. After you've selected a task, you can change the view of your photo to Before and After. Keep clicking the little blue button (circled) at the bottom of the window to toggle views between After Only, Before & After—Horizontal, and Before & After—Vertical.

2. **Open a photo.**

   Press ⌘+O and choose your photo in the window that appears. If you already have a photo open, it appears in the Guided Edit window automatically. If you have several photos in the Project bin, you can switch images by double-clicking the thumbnail of the one you want to work on.

3. **Choose what you want to do.**

   Your options are grouped into major categories like Basic Photo Edits and Color Correction, with a variety of individual projects under each heading. Just click the specific task you want in the list on the right side of the window. The Task panel switches to show you the buttons and/or sliders you need to use.

4. **Make your adjustments.**

   Just move the sliders and click the buttons till you like what you see. If you want to start over, click Reset. If you change your mind about the whole project, click Cancel.

   If there are several steps (like there are in "Guide for Editing a Photo", for instance), Elements will show you just what you need to use for the current step, then switch to a new set of choices for the next step as you go along.

5. **Click Done to finish.**

   If there are more steps, you may see another set of instructions. If you see the main list of topics again, you're all through. Don't forget to save your changes (page 35). To close your photo, press ⌘+W, or leave it open and switch to another tab to share it or use it in a project.

If you need to adjust your view of your photo while you work on it, Guided Edit has a little toolbox with the Hand (page 81) and Zoom (page 79) tools to help you out.

> **NOTE**   Guided Edit shows you quick and easy ways to change your image, but you won't always get the best possible results. It's a great tool for starting out, but don't make the mistake of thinking what you see here is the best you can possibly do for your images. Once you're more comfortable in Elements, Quick Fix (Chapter 4) is a good next step.

Escape Routes

Photoshop Elements has a couple of really wonderful features to help you avoid making permanent mistakes: the Undo command and the Undo History palette. After you've gotten used to them, you'll probably wish it were possible to use these tools in all aspects of your life, not just Elements.

Undo

No matter where you are in Elements, you can almost always change your mind about what you just did. Press ⌘+Z and the last change you made goes away. Pressing ⌘+Z works even if you've just saved your photo, but only while it's still open. (If you close your picture, your changes are permanent.) Keep pressing ⌘+Z and you keep undoing your work, step by step.

If you want to redo what you just undid, just press ⌘+Y. These keystroke commands are great for toggling changes on and off while you decide whether you really want to keep them.

> **TIP**   You do have some control over the key combination you use for Undo/Redo, if you don't like the ⌘+Z combination. Go to Photoshop Elements → Preferences → General. Elements gives you two other choices, both of which involve pressing the Z key in combination with the ⌘, Option, and Shift keys. You can't just assign any key combination you like because you're used to it in another program.

Undo History palette

In the Full Edit window, you get even more control over the actions you can undo, thanks to the Undo History palette (Figure 1-13), which you open by choosing Window → Undo History.

This palette holds a list of the changes you've made since the last time you opened your image. Just push the slider up and watch your changes disappear one by one as you go. Undo History even works if you've saved your file: As long as you

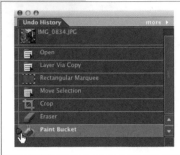

Figure 1-13:
For a little time travel, just slide the pointer up and watch your changes disappear one by one. You can only go back sequentially. Here, for instance, you can't go back to Crop without first undoing the Paint Bucket and the Eraser. Slide the pointer down to redo your work. You can also move to a different point in your work by just clicking the place in the list where you want to go, instead of using the slider.

haven't closed your file, the palette tracks every action you take. You can also slide the other way to redo changes that you've undone.

Be careful, though. You can back up only as many steps as you've set Elements to remember. Elements lets you keep track of as many as 1,000 actions. You can regulate this number in Preferences, as explained in Figure 1-14.

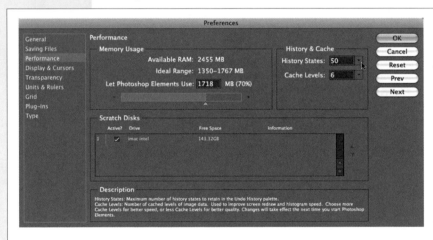

Figure 1-14:
You can set the number of steps the Undo History palette remembers in Edit → Preferences → Performance → History & Cache. Elements initially sets it to 50, but you can set it as high as 1,000. Beware, though— remembering even 100 steps may slow your system to a crawl if you don't have a superpowered processor, plenty of memory, and loads of disk space. If Elements runs slowly on your machine, then reducing the number of history states it remembers (try 20) may speed things up a bit.

The one rule of Elements

As you're probably beginning to see, Elements lets you work in lots of different ways. What's more, most people who use Elements approach projects in different ways. What works for your neighbor with her pictures may be quite different from how you would choose to work on the very same shots.

However, you'll hear one suggestion from almost every Elements veteran, and it's an important one: *Never ever work on your original. Always, always, always make a copy of your image and work on that.* (If you use a program like iPhoto, it can make a *version set* for you. In other words, you can tell it to remember one edited version plus your original. See page 43 for more about version sets.)

> **TIP** You can easily make a copy of a file in the Finder before you even launch Elements. Click the file once to select it, and then press ⌘+D, or Option+drag it away from the original and then let go of the mouse button. Either way, the new file automatically gets a name that lets you know it's not the original, one ending in "copy" or "2," for example.

Follow these steps to make a copy of your image in Elements:

1. **Go to File → Duplicate.**

   You can also right-click (Control-click) the photo's Project bin thumbnail and choose Duplicate there.

2. **Name the duplicate, and click the red close button on the original.**

   Now the original is safely tucked out of harm's way.

3. **Save the duplicate using ⌘+S.**

   Choose Photoshop (.psd) as the file format when you save it. (You may want to choose another format after you've read Chapter 3 and understand more about your different format options.)

Now you don't have to worry about making a mistake or changing your mind, because you can always start over if you want to.

> **NOTE** Elements doesn't have an autosave feature, so you should get into the habit of saving frequently as you work. Read more about saving on page 56.

Getting Started in a Hurry

If you're the impatient type, and you're starting to squirm because you want to be up and doing something to your photos, here's the quickest way to get started in Elements: Adjust the brightness and color balance all in one step.

1. **Open a photo.**

   Press ⌘+O and navigate to the image you want, and then click Open.

2. **Press Option+⌘+M.**

   You've just applied Elements' Auto Smart Fix tool (Figure 1-15).

Voilà! You should see quite a difference in your photo, unless the exposure, lighting, and contrast were almost perfect before. The Auto Smart Fix tool is one of the many easy-to-use features in Elements. (Of course, if you don't like what just happened to your photo, no problem—simply press ⌘+Z to undo it.)

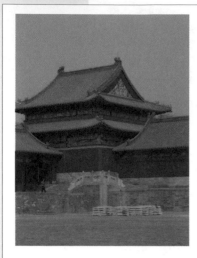
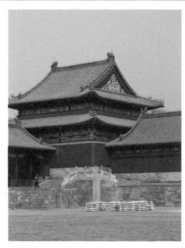

Figure 1-15:
Auto Smart Fix is the easiest, quickest way to improve the quality of your photos.

Top left: The original, unedited picture.

Top right: Auto Smart Fix makes quite a difference, but the colors are still slightly off.

Bottom: By using some of the other tools you'll learn about in this book (like Auto Contrast and Adjust Sharpness), you can make things look even better.

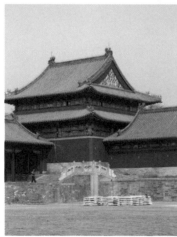

If you're the really impatient type, you can jump right to Chapter 4 to learn about using the Quick Fix commands. But it's worth taking the time to read the next two chapters so you understand which file formats to choose and how to make some basic adjustments to your images, like rotating and cropping them.

Don't forget to give Guided Edit a try if you see what you want to do in the list of topics. Guided Edit can be a big help when you're first learning your way around.

Importing, Managing, and Saving Your Photos

Now that you've had a look around Elements, it's time to start learning how to get photos *into* the program, and also how to keep track of where these photos are stored. As a digital photographer, you may no longer be facing shoeboxes stuffed with prints, but you've still got to face the menace of photos piling up on your hard drive. Fortunately, Elements gives you some great tools for organizing your collection and quickly finding individual pictures.

In this chapter, you'll learn how to import your photos from cameras, memory card readers, and scanners. You'll also find out how to import individual frames from videos, how to open files that are already on your computer, and how to create a new file from scratch. After that, you'll learn how to use Adobe Bridge to sort and find your pictures once they're on your Mac. Finally, you'll learn how to save the work you create in Elements and how to make backups.

> **NOTE** In addition to the info about Bridge in this chapter, Appendix C (page 501) contains a complete listing of all Bridge's menu items and what they mean.

Importing from Cameras

You have four basic ways of getting photos from your camera or memory card reader onto your computer:

> **NOTE** Take a moment to carefully read the instructions from your camera manufacturer. Those directions should always take precedence over anything you read here that suggests doing something differently.

• **iPhoto.** Your Mac comes set up to launch iPhoto whenever it detects incoming photos from a camera or card reader, and that's convenient—if you want to use iPhoto. But if you prefer another program for organizing your photos, or if you just like to be disorganized, you don't have to use iPhoto.

• **Apple's Image Capture program.** OS X also has a built-in downloading program called Image Capture, which you can set to open any program you like (you can have it open Bridge, for instance, if you want to first sort through your photos there).

To choose the program that Image Capture launches, start up Image Capture when you don't have a camera or card reader connected (go to Applications → Image Capture). Then go to Image Capture → Preferences → Camera and use the pull-down menu to browse to the program you want to use. You don't have to use any application to download photos, though, as explained below in "Drag and drop."

NOTE If you're downloading directly from a camera, always be sure your camera is set to the correct mode for transferring files before you connect it to the computer. It's not a bad idea to use a card reader: It's slightly safer than getting photos directly from your camera and, if your camera has a USB 1.0 port, a USB 2.0 or Firewire card reader will also be much faster. In addition, card readers hardly ever have trouble getting computers to recognize them, a problem people occasionally have with direct camera connections.

• **Adobe Photo Downloader.** You got this program along with Elements, and it's set up to grab your photos and launch Bridge so you can sort through them. (The Downloader isn't really an independent program, though—you have to launch it from Elements or Bridge, at least the first time you use it.) But, as with Image Capture, you can set the Downloader not to open Bridge (turn off the checkbox in the Downloader window). However, for most people most of the time, the Downloader isn't very useful, and you can safely ignore it. The situations where the Downloader offers you an advantage are outlined on page 19. If the Downloader interests you, you'll find detailed instructions on how to use it on this book's Missing CD page at *www.missingmanuals.com*.

• **Drag and drop.** You don't actually need to use any program to get your photos onto your Mac. Dragging and dropping files is a popular method with people who don't always want to launch a program to view newly downloaded images. To set things up this way, just follow the directions given for Image Capture above, only instead of selecting a program, choose "No application". That way, the next time you plug in your card reader, it will appear on your desktop like a removable drive and you can just drag the folder containing your photos to wherever you want to put it. (This method works much better with a card reader than with a direct camera download.)

Once you've downloaded your photos, always be sure to eject the card before unplugging your card reader from the computer, as explained in Figure 2-1.

(Applications like iPhoto have an Eject button or command right in the program.) Incidentally, it's best to let your camera erase photos from your memory card, rather than using your computer to do that, since your camera understands its own file structure better than any computer does.

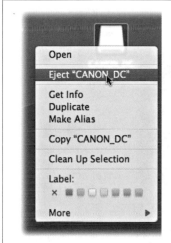

Figure 2-1:
If you prefer to drag your photos from the memory card instead of using Image Capture, be sure to properly remove your card or camera when you're done. Don't just yank it out of the port. First, right-click (Control+click) its icon on your desktop, and then choose Eject, or use the Eject button next to its name in a Finder window. Failing to do this may damage the card.

Opening Photos in Elements

Now that you've got your photos onto your Mac, you need to get them into Elements so you can work on them. This section explains the many ways to open files in Elements. One option is to use Bridge, Adobe's browsing program that you got with Elements, but you can do lots of things with Bridge besides open photos in Elements (see page 49) You'll also learn how to send photos to Elements from other programs, like Aperture or iPhoto.

> **NOTE**   If you have Leopard, you can also browse for files to open in Elements without using any special programs like Bridge or iPhoto, as Figure 2-2 explains.

Bridge Basics

Instead of the Organizer that comes with the Windows version of Elements, you get Adobe Bridge, you lucky Mac person. Bridge is the ultra-deluxe file browser that comes with Photoshop CS3. You can use Bridge to view and organize your picture files—and other kinds of files, if you want. (See the box on page 39 for the differences between the Elements and Photoshop versions of Bridge.) You can do a ton of different things with your photos in Bridge: browse, arrange, categorize, delete, search, apply keywords, view, edit, and apply metadata information (page 52). But this section just explains the minimum you need to know to find your way around Bridge. The more advanced features are discussed later in this chapter, beginning on page 49.

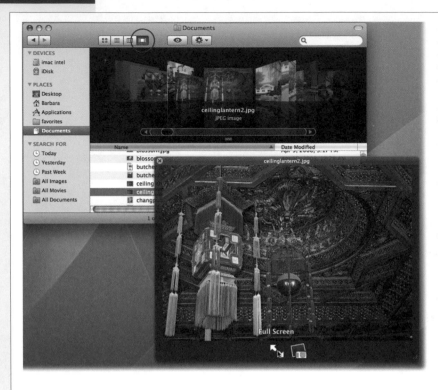

Figure 2-2:
In Leopard (OS X 10.5), the Finder makes a handy photo browser. First, open a Finder window (click once on your desktop and then press ⌘+N) and click the button for Cover Flow view (circled). In the top of the Finder window, you can quickly scroll through thumbnails of the contents of any folder. To get a closer look at a photo, right-click (Control+click) its name in the list in the bottom half of the window, and then choose Quick Look. A larger view of your image appears, without actually opening the file. You can even get a full-screen view of it by clicking the arrows at the bottom of the preview window (where the cursor is here). Click the arrows again to close the full-screen view. To close the preview, click the X in the upper left of the window (or at the bottom of the window if you're in full-screen view).

If you're already in Elements, you can launch Bridge by going to File → "Browse with Bridge", or by clicking the little dark red folder next to the New File button in the Shortcuts bar (in the upper-left part of your screen, just above the Options bar). If Elements isn't running, go to Applications → Adobe Bridge CS3 and double-click Bridge CS3.

The Bridge window

If you launch Bridge from Elements, Elements gets whisked out of sight and the Bridge window appears. If you used the old File Browser that came with early versions of Elements, you should understand the Bridge layout right away, and it's pretty straightforward even for newbies.

Bridge: Elements vs. Photoshop

Do I really get the full *version of Adobe Bridge with Elements?*

Almost. You get pretty nearly every useful feature from the more exalted Photoshop version of Bridge, minus a few not very critical ones. For instance, you don't get the meetings feature, which lets graphics pros collaborate on projects, but that isn't a big deal for most Elements folks.

There is one fairly major feature missing from Elements Bridge, though: the ability to apply camera RAW settings to groups of photos and to call up the RAW Converter right from Bridge. (Chapter 8 tells more about RAW conversion.) In Elements Bridge, you can select RAW files for editing, but they open in the Converter in Elements. (You can rename and apply metadata to groups of photos in Elements Bridge, though.)

The folks at Adobe did this because they reasonably figured that if you're processing so many photos that you need to set Bridge to work on your RAW files while you keep editing photos, you really need Photoshop instead of Elements.

Incidentally, if you happen to have both Elements and Photoshop CS3 installed on your Mac, when you install Elements, you automatically get access to all the Creative Suite 3 features, whether you access Bridge from Photoshop or from Elements.

Like the windows in your house, the Bridge window is divided into panes, which are similar to the bins in Elements. Within each pane are tabbed panels, which are something like Elements' palettes—you can move and combine them, but they never come out of the panes (you can drag a panel from one pane to another, though).

On the left you see the Favorites panel, a Folders panel (which is covered by the Favorites panel; it gives you a folder view of your hard drive), and a Filter panel, which you can use to set search criteria (it's blank until you select a photo). The middle area—the Content panel—shows all the folders and images at the level of your hard drive selected in the Favorites or Folders panel. The upper right of the Bridge window shows a larger preview of any image(s) you select, and the bottom right has panels for keywords and metadata (these are explained on page 52).

You aren't stuck with this view, though. You can totally customize Bridge's layout (called your *workspace*), as explained below. For now, what you need to know is that to see the contents of a folder, you just click its thumbnail (double-click in the Content Pane, single click in Favorites or Folders), or use the clever tool shown in Figure 2-3. You can see any folder on your hard drive by selecting it in the Folders or Favorites panel.

Use the slider at the bottom right of the window to change the size of the thumbnails. If you want to see even more detail, in the Preview panel, just click the area of your photo you want to examine. Bridge presents a cool loupe view that ultra-magnifies the area where you clicked. (A loupe is the kind of magnifying glass jewelers use.) Click another spot, and the loupe moves to that location. You can also drag the loupe around in your photo. This feature is great for checking for things like the best focus from a group of similar shots.

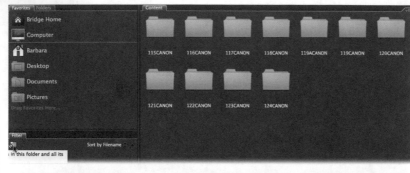

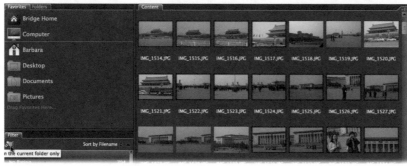

Figure 2-3:
Top: Feeling too lazy to open all those folders to see what's in them? No problem.

Bottom: Click the little folder icon just under the word "Filter" on the Filter panel (where the cursor is here), and Elements automatically shows you the contents of all the folders and subfolders currently in the Content panel.

To see more than one photo at a time in the Preview panel, just select all the photos you want to view. You can have a separate loupe on each photo so you can compare the differences between shots. Click on a loupe to make it go away.

You can use the left- and right-facing arrows at the top left of the Bridge window (or the pull-down menu next to them that shows the current folder name) to move backward and forward through the folders you've been looking in. Click the little folder icon with the upward-pointing arrow on it to go up one level in your folder structure.

You can also browse through all the photos in a folder as a slideshow (go to View → Slideshow). Press Escape to leave Slideshow view. You can change the settings for Slideshow view in View → Sideshow Options. (This is just a way of browsing through your photos—you can't save a slideshow from this menu choice. See page 420 for info about creating slideshows you can save and share.)

You can rearrange the Bridge window in a number of ways, but before you do that, there's one very important task you need to perform: choosing your file associations.

Setting file associations

If you've already played around with Bridge, you may have encountered one of those "What the…?" moments. Say you found a JPEG file you wanted to edit, confidently double-clicked it, and the photo opened right up in…Preview? Yes, you've learned the hard way that Bridge is not wedded to Elements even though it comes with Elements. It's a general file browser, and it can send photos to lots of different programs. It was designed for use with Adobe Creative Suite, where you might use it to send TIFF files to Photoshop, Illustrator files to InDesign, and so on.

> **NOTE** Bridge isn't just for photos. You can see all kinds of files in Bridge, and even watch movies from your digital camera in the Preview panel.

In order to have Bridge open your photos in Elements, you may have to tell Bridge that's what you want. (Bridge should come already set up to open most graphics formats in Elements, but you may want to change how it behaves.) Go to Bridge CS3 → Preferences → File Type Associations. That brings up a window with an impressive list of *all* the file types that Bridge can recognize. Next to each type is the application that Bridge will use to open files of that type. What you need to do is to go through the list and tell Bridge to open your image files in Elements (see page 57 for more about file formats).

To do that, skim through the list and, for the file types that aren't set properly, just click the current program for a pull down menu where you can choose Elements. Note that this only changes where Bridge opens a file. If you normally open JPEGs from the Finder in Preview, say, that won't change because of what you do here. It's a bit of a nuisance to have to do this, but you only have to do it once—Bridge remembers your choices.

You don't need to do anything about file types you won't open, or won't open in Elements (like .cda files from compact disk recordings, for instance). Likewise, if you have a Nikon camera, you don't care about the file associations for Canon RAW files (.crw). If you just stick to the file types you expect to use, it doesn't take long to go through the list.

> **TIP** You can speed things up by turning on the Hide Undefined File Associations checkbox at the bottom of the Preferences window before you start, since the undefined file types are all pretty unlikely formats to use in Elements.

Customizing your Bridge workspace

You may not be thrilled with the basic view you get when you first launch Bridge: There's a limit to how large you can make the thumbnails, and the Preview panel isn't very big. Not to worry—you can adjust your view (a.k.a. your *workspace*) in all sorts of ways. To start, go to Window → Workspace.

This gives you a choice of no less than 6 different layouts. You can choose Horizontal Filmstrip, for instance, to see a large Preview panel with the Content panel as a scrolling line of thumbnails across the bottom of the window. There are keystroke shortcuts for changing workspaces, too, which you can see next to their names in the menu. Your workspace options are described in detail in Appendix C (page 513).

What's more, you can move the panels around to suit you, and hide ones you don't want:

- **Move a panel.** Drag it by the top tab (the one that says Content or Preview or whatever) to where you want it. You can combine panels to make a multi-tabbed panel, just like you can do with Elements palettes (see page 26). Panels never float, though—they always have to be in one of the panes.

- **Add or remove a panel.** Go to the Window menu and select a panel you want to appear in Bridge. Select it again to turn it off. (Visible panels have checkmarks next to their names.)

- **Collapse a panel.** If you want to temporarily get a panel out of your way, double-click its tab and it collapses, just like a palette. Double-click the tab again to expand it. (You can also double-click the edge of a pane to collapse it, and then double-click it again to bring it back.)

After all that work customizing Bridge, you'll be pleased to know you can save your workspace just the way you arranged it, as explained in Figure 2-4.

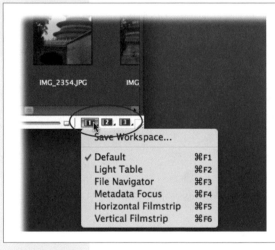

Figure 2-4:
Once you've gotten your workspace set up just so, save it by going to Window → Workspace → Save Workspace, or by clicking and holding down one of the three buttons in the lower-right corner of the Bridge window (circled) and choosing Save Workspace from the pop-up menu. You can save up to three custom workspaces, and quickly switch from one to another by clicking the button for the workspace you want.

There's more about Bridge's many other features later in this chapter, starting on page 49.

> **TIP** Like iTunes, Bridge has a compact mode, which turns it into a smallish window that doesn't take up much of your desktop. In Bridge, press ⌘+Return, or go to View → Compact Mode to shrink Bridge. Do the same thing to return it to full size.

Opening Stored Images

There are several different ways to open photos in Elements:

- **From the Finder.** If the image is one whose file type is set to automatically open in Elements, just double-click the filename and Elements launches (if it's not already open) and your image appears in the main editing window. If it's a file that's not set to open in Elements, simply right-click (Control+click) the photo's icon, and then go to Open With → Adobe Photoshop Elements, or just drag it to the Elements icon in the Dock.

TIP   To change which application opens files of a particular type, in the Finder, find a file of that type. Click once to select it, and then press ⌘+I. This brings up the Get Info window, which has lots of info about your file. Expand the Open With section by clicking the flippy triangle next to it, and then choose the program you want from the pull-down menu. Then click the Change All button. Voilà—from now on, all files of that type will open in the program you chose.

- **From Adobe Bridge.** Click once on a thumbnail to select it, or select multiple thumbnails by Shift+clicking (to select a range) or ⌘+clicking (to select scattered files). Then press ⌘+O, double-click (if the photo is a file type you've set to open in Elements—see page 40), or go to File → Open. Your photos open in Elements, as long as you've set the Bridge file associations for them to do so (see page 40).

- **From Elements.** Press ⌘+O or go to File → Open and navigate to the file you want to open. If you'd rather choose your photos in Bridge, click the "Browse with Bridge" icon (circled in Figure 2-5) in the upper-left part of the Elements window or use one of the other methods described in Figure 2-5.

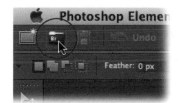

Figure 2-5:
The easiest way to call up Bridge from Elements is to click this icon, but you can also go to File → "Browse with Bridge". Select the photo(s) you want to work on, and then double-click them to open them in Elements.

Sending Images from Other Programs

If you use a program other than Bridge to keep track of your photos (like iPhoto or Lightroom) but you want to open them in Elements, it's best to send your photos from that program over to Elements rather than trying to find them using Elements or Bridge.

There are two reasons for this. First, you can corrupt your library file—the program's database of your photos—by poking around in it from outside the program that owns it. (This is especially true of the iPhoto library file—*never* try to see into that file from outside iPhoto.) Secondly, most photo organizing programs can create *version sets* if you send photos over for editing in a way they can understand. A version set means that iPhoto, say, keeps a record of your original image *and* the saved, edited version you create in Elements, as long as you don't change the filename. iPhoto only keeps one version plus the original (the next time you edit, the previously saved version is lost), but other programs can keep more.

To send a photo to Elements:

- **From iPhoto.** Go to iPhoto → Preferences → General → Edit Photo → In Application, and then choose Elements from the list. After that, when you want to edit a photo in Elements, you just double-click it in iPhoto and iPhoto automatically sends your photo over for editing. When you're done, just save your changes and iPhoto remembers them (*don't* use the Save As command and rename your file or iPhoto won't create a version set for it—see above).

- **From Aperture.** Pretty much the same as iPhoto: In Aperture's preferences, choose Elements as your external editor, and then right-click (Control+click) a thumbnail and select "Open with External Editor".

- **From Lightroom.** Go to Lightroom → Preferences → External Editor tab, and then browse to Elements. Then, when you're in the Edit or Library modules, right-click (Control+click) a thumbnail and choose the external editor.

There are lots of other programs you might be using to manage your files, and the majority of them will have similar options.

> **TIP** Another way to send photos to Elements is to use your organizing program's Export command (it's usually under File → Export) to send them to your desktop, then open them in Elements, save them under a new name, and then import the edited files back into whatever program you started in. This is a bit more of a nuisance to do, but it has the advantage of letting you save as many different edits of your photo as you like, as long as you give each version a new name.

INFORMATION STATION

Bridge for People Who Don't Use Bridge

As stated on page 43, if you already use another program to organize your photos (like Aperture, iPhoto, or Lightroom, for example), most of the time you're better off sending your photos directly to Elements from within your organizing program. One of the nice things about Bridge is that, unlike the Organizer in the Windows version of Elements, Bridge doesn't care whether or not you use it.

However, you may want to check out some of the online components in Elements that only work from Bridge. Or maybe you occasionally want to use Bridge, the way some people only go to iPhoto to create projects like slideshows. For example, Bridge can be very helpful for tracking down photos that never made it into your regular organizing program.

There are a few Bridge basics you should understand even if you don't plan to use it much. They're explained in the "Bridge Basics" section on page 37. At the very least, you should set the file associations for Bridge in case you ever want use it for anything, and while you're there you might want to set up your workspace to suit you (see page 41).

Working with PDF Files

If you open a PDF file in Elements, you'll see the Import PDF dialog box (Figure 2-6), which gives you lots of options for how you want Elements to treat your file. You can choose to import whole pages or just the images on the pages, you can import multiple pages (if the PDF is more than one page), and you can choose the color mode (page 48) and the resolution, as well as whether or not you want anti-aliasing (page 125).

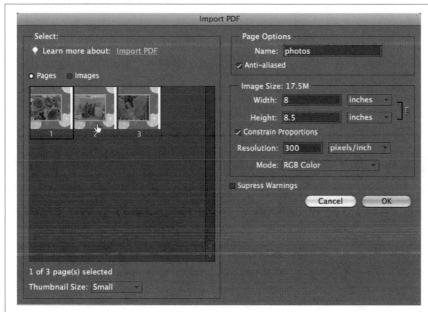

Figure 2-6:
You can open multipage PDF files in Elements. If you want to open just one page of the file, double-click the thumbnail of the page you want, and Elements opens it right up. To open multiple pages of the file, Shift+click to select the pages you want before you double-click to open them.

Scanning Photos

Elements comes bundled with many scanners because it's the perfect software for making your scans look their best. You have two main ways of getting scans into Elements. Some scanners come with a *driver plug-in*, a small utility program that lets you scan directly into Elements. Look on your scanner's installation software for information about Elements compatibility or check the manufacturer's Web site for a Photoshop plug-in to download. (If you can scan into Photoshop, you should be able to scan into Elements.) You may also be able to scan into Elements if your scanner uses the *TWAIN interface*, which is an industry standard used by many scanner manufacturers.

If you don't have an Elements plug-in for your scanner and the Adobe TWAIN driver doesn't work for you, you'll need to use the scanning program that came with your scanner. Then, once you've saved your scanned image in a format that Elements understands, like TIFF (.tiff, .tif) or Photoshop (.psd), open the file in Elements like any other photo.

To control your scanner from within Elements, go to File → Import, and you'll see your scanner's name on the list that appears. If you have a Mac with an Intel processor and your scanner driver (the software that lets it talk to your computer) is old, you may see the message shown in Figure 2-7 when you start up Elements.

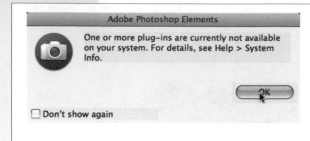

Adobe Photoshop Elements

One or more plug-ins are currently not available on your system. For details, see Help > System Info.

OK

☐ Don't show again

Figure 2-7:
If you have an Intel Mac and an older scanner driver, this warning may appear when you launch Elements. It means that Elements found something that isn't designed to run on an Intel Mac. But don't worry—you can still scan. You just need to force Elements to run under Rosetta, the built-in OS X emulator for older Power PC systems.

It's less complicated than it sounds. Simply quit Elements (⌘+Q), and then go to the Applications folder and find the program (Applications → Adobe Photoshop Elements 6 → Adobe Photoshop Elements). Click once on the program's icon, then press ⌘+I to bring up the Get Info window. Turn on the checkbox next to "Open using Rosetta," and then relaunch Elements. Note that Elements probably won't be as zippy as it is when it's not running in Rosetta, so you most likely only want to do this when you need to scan. To return things to normal, head back to Elements' Get Info window and turn off the "Open using Rosetta" checkbox.

TIP If you do a lot of scanning, check out the Divide Scanned Photos command (page 63) for helpful tips on how to quickly scan in lots of photos at the same time. Also, you can save yourself a lot of drudgery in Elements if you make sure that both your scanner glass and the prints you're scanning are as dust-free as possible before you start.

Capturing Video Frames

Elements lets you capture a single frame from a video and use it the way you would any still photo. This feature only works for videos that are already on your computer (as opposed to streaming video from the Internet, for example).

Elements can open video files in most formats your Mac can open. But Elements *can't* open Windows Media files (.wmv files), or any video files that include DRM (digital rights management, which is code that restricts who can view the file).

NOTE The video capture tool in Elements isn't really designed for use with long movies. You'll get the best results with clips that aren't more than a minute or two long.

To import a video frame, go to File → Import → Frame From Video, and then in the Video import dialog box:

1. **Find the video that contains the frame you want to copy.**

   Click the Browse button and navigate to the movie you want. After you choose the movie, the first frame should appear in the window in the Frame From Video dialog box.

2. **Navigate to the frame you want.**

   Either click the Play button or use the slider below the window to move through the movie until you see what you want.

3. **Copy the frame you want by clicking Grab Frame.**

   You can grab as many frames as you want. Each frame shows up in the Elements Editor as a separate file.

4. **When you have everything you need, click Done.**

   While grabbing video frames is a very fun thing to be able to do, it does have certain limitations. Most important, your video is going to appear at a fairly low resolution, so don't expect to get a great print from a video frame.

Creating a New File

You can create a new blank Elements document. You may want to create a new blank document when you're using Elements as a drawing program or when you're combining parts of other images together, for example.

To create a new file, go to File → New → Blank File (or press ⌘+N) to bring up the New File dialog box. You have lots of choices to make each time you start a new file; they're all covered in the following sections.

Picking a File Size

The first thing you need to decide, logically enough, is how big you want your document to be. In Elements 6, there are two ways to do this:

- **Start with a Preset**. Preset, the first menu item in the New File window, lets you choose the general kind of document you want to create. If you want to create a file for printing, pick from the second group in the menu. The third group contains choices for onscreen viewing. Once you make a selection in this menu, the next menu—Size—changes to show you suitable sizes for your choice. Figure 2-8 shows you how it works.

- **Enter the numbers yourself**. Just ignore the Preset and Size menus and type in what you want. You can choose inches, pixels, centimeters, millimeters, points, picas, or columns as your unit of measurement. Just pick the one you want in the Width and Height pull-down menus and then enter a number.

Choosing Resolution

If you decide not to use one of the presets, you need to choose a resolution for your file. You'll learn a lot more about resolution in the next chapter (page 82), but a good rough guide is to choose 72 pixels per inch (ppi) for files that you'll look at only on a monitor, and 300 ppi for files you plan to print.

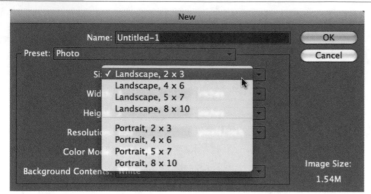

Figure 2-8:
Elements helps you pick an appropriate size when you use the Preset Menu. Choose a general category—here, Photo is the choice. The Size menu then changes to show you standard sizes for photo paper, each available in either landscape or portrait orientation. The size that Elements automatically selects is 6" × 4" at 300 pixels per inch, which works well if you're just playing around and trying things out.

Choosing a Color Mode

Elements gives you lots of color choices throughout the program, but Color Mode is probably your most important one because it determines which tools and filters you can use in your document. There are three choices available in the Color Mode menu:

- **RGB Color.** Choosing RGB (red, green, and blue) means that you're creating a color document, as opposed to a black-and-white one. You'll probably choose RGB Color mode most of the time, even if you don't plan on having color in your image, because RGB gives you access to all of Elements' tools. Page 198 has lots more about picking colors. You can use RGB Color mode for black-and-white photos if you like, and many people do, since it gives you the most options for editing your photo.

- **Bitmap.** Every pixel in a bitmap mode image is either black or white. Use Bitmap mode for true black-and-white images—shades of gray need not apply here.

- **Grayscale.** Black-and-white photos are called *grayscale* because they're really made up of many shades of gray. In Elements, you can't do as much editing on a grayscale photo as you can in RGB (for example, you can't use some of the filters on a grayscale photo).

NOTE Sometimes you may need to change the color mode of an existing file to use all of Elements' tools and filters. For example, there are quite a few things you can do only if your file is in the RGB color mode. So if you need to use a filter (page 350) on a black-and-white photo and your choice is grayed out, go to Image → Mode and select RGB Color. Choosing RGB Color won't suddenly colorize your photo; it just changes the way Elements handles the file. You can always change back to the original color mode when you're done. If you use the "Convert to Black and White" feature in Elements (page 271), you still have an RGB mode photo afterward, not a grayscale mode.

If you have a 16-bit file (page 228), you need to convert it to 8-bit color or you won't have access to many of the commands and filters in Elements. Make the change by choosing Image → Mode → 8 Bits/Channel. You're most likely to have 16-bit files if you import your images in RAW format (page 213); some scanners also offer you an option of creating 16-bit files. JPEG photos are always 8-bit.

Choosing Your File's Background Contents

The last choice you have to make when you start a new file is the *background contents* of the file. Choosing your file's background contents is where you tell Elements the color to use for the empty areas of the file, like the background. You can be a traditionalist and choose white (almost always a good choice), or else choose a particular color or transparency. More about transparency in a minute.

If you want to choose a color other than white, use the Foreground/Background color squares to do so, as shown in Figure 2-9.

Figure 2-9:
To choose a new Background color, just click the Background color square (the green one shown here) to bring up the Color Picker. Then choose the color you want. Your new color appears in the square, and the next time you do something that involves using a Background color, that's the shade you get. The whole process of picking colors is explained in much more detail on page 198.

Transparency is the most interesting option. To understand transparency and why it's such a wonderful invention, you need to know that every digital image, every single one, is either rectangular or square. A digital image *can't* be any other shape.

But digital images can *appear* to be a different shape—sunflowers, sailboats, or German Shepherds, for example. How? By placing your object on a transparent background so that it looks like it was cut out and only its shape appears, as shown in Figure 2-10. The actual photo is still a rectangle, but if you placed it into another image, you'd see only the shell and not the surrounding area, because the rest of the photo is transparent.

To keep the clear areas transparent when you close your image, you need to save the image in a file format that allows transparency. JPEGs, for instance, automatically fill transparent areas with solid white, so they're not a good choice. TIFFs, PDFs, and Photoshop files (.psd), on the other hand, let the transparent areas stay clear. Page 440 has more about which formats allow transparency.

The Many Uses for Bridge

Earlier in this chapter, you learned the very basics of finding photos with Adobe Bridge. But you can do lots more with Bridge than just that: You can use Bridge to organize your photos; search for photos; assign keywords, labels, and ratings to them; and create and edit their metadata (page 52).

Before you do anything in Bridge, there's one important thing you should understand: When you move or delete a file in Bridge, you're moving or deleting *the original*. Bridge doesn't keep copies of your images or need to have a perfect database of them all the time. It's a just browser for, well, browsing files, not an asset management program.

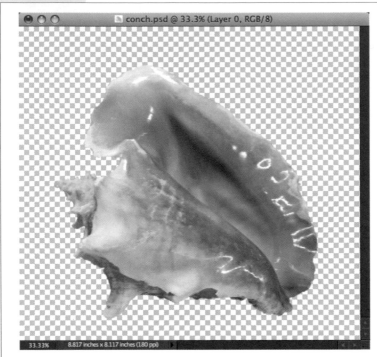

Figure 2-10:
The checkered background is Elements' way of indicating that an area is transparent. (It doesn't mean you've somehow selected a patterned background.) If you place this photo into another image, all you'll see is the seashell itself, not the checkerboard or the rectangular outline of the photo. When you don't like the size and color of the grid, you can adjust them in Edit → Preferences → Transparency.

One benefit of this is that Bridge doesn't care what you do to your photos when you're not in Bridge. Unlike iPhoto or the Organizer in the Windows version of Elements, which want you to use them for all photo moving, Bridge just shows you your files and folders as they are right now. If you move a file from the Finder, Bridge won't complain that it can't find that file anymore, the way other organizing programs do when you don't use them for every move you make with the photos you've catalogued with them.

Moving and Organizing your Photos

Bridge is great for arranging your photo collection. In Bridge, you can:

- **Move a Photo or Folder.** To move a photo, just drag it to where you want it. Use the Folders panel (page 39) to find the folder you want to put it in (just keep clicking the flippy triangles to expand your view down to the folder you want), and then drag the photo's thumbnail to the folder's icon. You can move folders by dragging, too.

  You can also drag a photo, a group of photos, or a folder right out of Bridge onto the OS X desktop. Then you can drag it into another program from the desktop, or just store it there. Option+dragging a file copies it to the new location instead of moving the original.

- **Create a new folder.** In the Folders panel, click where you want your folder to appear, and then go to File → New Folder or click the New folder icon (in the upper right of the Bridge window) and then name your folder.

- **Delete a photo.** Click to select a photo (or photos), and then press the Delete icon (the little trash can in the upper right of the Bridge window). Bridge sends your selection to the OS X trash, so if you change your mind, you can retrieve it as long as you haven't emptied the trash. You can also select a photo and press Delete to bring up a window that lets you delete the photo (send it to the trash) or assign it the Reject rating (page 52).

- **Rename photos.** Click a thumbnail, and then click its name and type the new one. You can also batch rename in Bridge (see page 237 to learn how).

- **Sort Photos.** Select a group of photos and right-click (Control+click) one for a pop-out menu. Choose Sort from the menu and you get a submenu offering a long list of sorting options, like Date created, File size, and Filename. You can also choose to sort in ascending or descending order.

- **Stack Photos.** If you want to tidy things up, you can group related photos into *stacks* so that you only see one image from the group unless you expand the stack. To create a stack, select the photos you want to include, and then press ⌘+G or go to Stack → Group as Stack. The photos group together so they only take up as much space as one unstacked photo, and you see the distinctive icon shown in Figure 2-11, which explains how to expand stacks. To unstack photos, expand the stack, select all the images in the stack, and then press Shift+⌘+G.

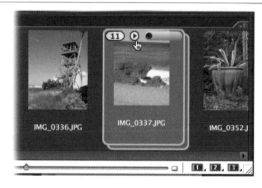

Figure 2-11:
When you stack photos in Bridge, you see this distinctive icon with the number of photos in the stack in the upper-left corner. To expand the stack and see all the photos, press ⌘+ the right arrow key. To collapse it again, use ⌘+ the left arrow key. If you double-click a stack, you open all the photos in the stack in Elements (or whatever program you've set for that file type—see page 40).

If you have at least ten photos in a stack, you can click the stack to see the controls shown here. Press the play button to see your photos one after the other in a sort of animated preview, or use the slider (the black circle in the gray bar) to scroll through the stack.

Rating and labeling photos

In Bridge, you can assign star ratings and labels to your photos to make it easier to sort through them and find the photos you want. Here's how:

- **Ratings.** Click a photo, and then press ⌘+the number of stars you want to give it (between 1 and 5), or go to the Label menu and choose a rating there. To change a rating, just apply a different one, or pressing ⌘+0 to unrate your

Metadata and Metadata Templates

The information about a photo that is stored in the image file itself is called *metadata*. Metadata includes your *EXIF* (Exchangeable Image Format) data, which is info your camera stores about your photo, including what camera you used, when you took the picture, the exposure, file size, ISO speed, aperture setting, and much more. By paying attention to your EXIF data, you can learn a lot about what makes for good shots—and what doesn't. Bridge displays some of your EXIF in the *metadata placard*, the little yellowish-gray rectangle at the top of Bridge's Metadata panel that displays the shooting settings (the aperture, the shutter speed, and so on) the way you'd see it on your camera's LCD.

There are lots of kinds of metadata besides camera info, and Bridge gives you a lot of control over your metadata. For instance, you can add metadata—like a description of your image or copyright info—right into the file itself. One way to do this is in the Metatdata panel. Scroll down it, and you see a huge list of metadata types. The categories you can edit a tiny pencil icon

to the right of them. Click in that area, and suddenly you can type in any of the boxes. This is a great way to add metadata to a single photo, but Bridge also lets you apply metadata to a bunch of files at once. (For RAW files, since Bridge can't write to the file, your metadata gets stored in a separate XMP format file in the folder with the image. See page 213 for more on RAW files.)

While creating a metadata template sounds really technical and scary, it's actually an easy and useful thing to do. You can create a metadata template that lists you as the author of a photo, the terms under which people can use it, your contact info, and your Web site's URL—all right into the file. To create a metadata template in Bridge, go to Tools → Create Metadata Template, and you'll see the window in Figure 2-12.

You can also view metadata in Elements and add metadata to a single file by going to File → File Info, or pressing Option+Shift+⌘+I.

photo. Once your photos are rated, you can go to the Filter panel (explained below) and search for photos with specific ratings. You can also assign a special red Reject tag to photos you're displeased with by pressing Option+Delete. This doesn't delete them, it just marks them so you can find them easily later. (You can show or hide your rejected files using the View menu.)

- **Labels.** You can assign labels to photos, which appear as colored bars beneath the thumbnails. You get five label colors to use, four of which have keyboard shortcuts assigned to them (⌘+ a number from 6 to 9). If you go to the Label menu, you can see how Adobe pre-assigned the labels. But head to Bridge → Preferences → Labels and you can enter any label text you want, and it will appear in the Label menu instead. You can also use labels as criteria in the Filter panel (page 55). To remove a label from a photo, select the photo, and then go to Labels → No Label.

Keywords

One of the most useful things you can do in Bridge is assign descriptive keywords to your photos to help you find them. These keywords get written right into the file's metadata (see the box above) so that any program that understands metadata—and there are a lot of them—can read them. So, for instance, you can use Spotlight in OS X to search for the keywords in your files, even when Bridge

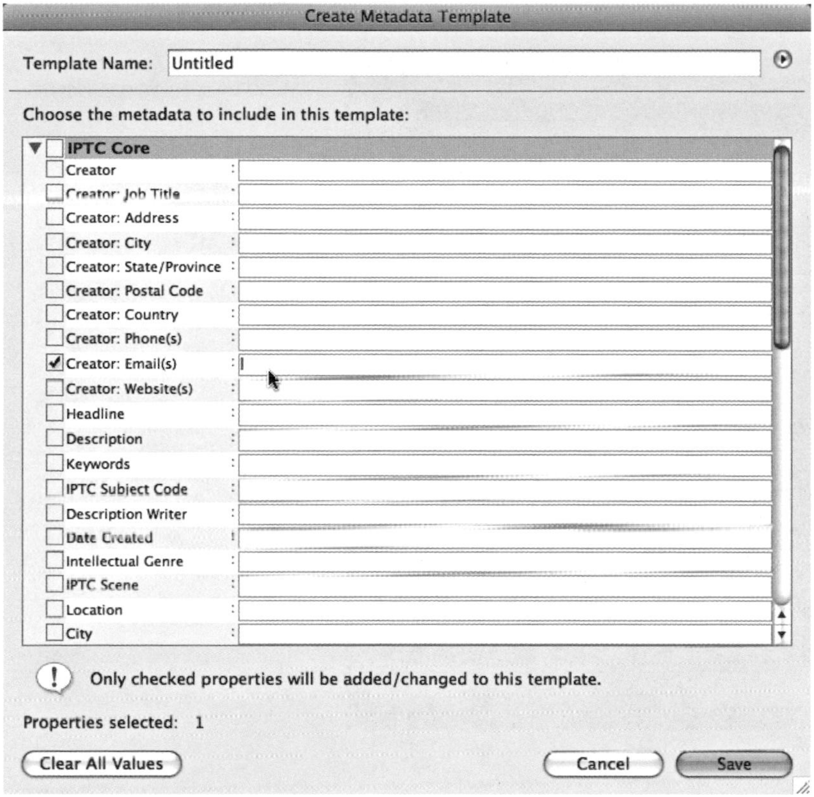

Figure 2-12:
To add metadata to your images, just type the info you want to include in this window, name the template, and then click Save. Now when you want to add that template info to photos, just select them in Bridge and go to Tools → Append Metadata and choose the template you want (you can create as many metadata templates as you want). Be sure not to choose Replace Metadata, since that will obliterate all the existing metadata in your file(s).

and Elements aren't running. Moreover, when you send photos to other people, they can see the keywords in Elements, Photoshop, or any other application that displays metadata. Once you've assigned keywords, it's easy to search by keyword in Bridge, as explained in the next section. Here's how to assign and work with keywords in Bridge:

- **Assign a keyword.** First make sure the Keywords panel shown in Figure 2-13 is visible (if it's not, go to Window → Keywords Panel). Select a photo, and then click the plus-shaped New Keyword button at the bottom of the panel. Or you can click the tiny icon on the upper right of the panel and, from the pop-out menu that appears, choose New Keyword. Either way, enter your keyword in the text box that appears and turn on the checkbox next to it to assign it to your photo. Once you've created a keyword, you can assign it to several photos at once by selecting them and then turning on the keyword.

- **Remove a keyword from a photo.** Select the photo and turn off the checkbox next to the keyword you want to remove.

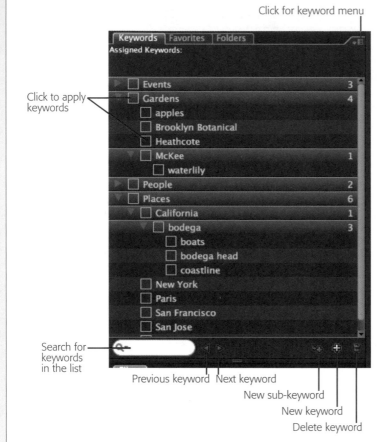

Click for keyword menu

Click to apply keywords

Search for keywords in the list

Previous keyword   Next keyword

New sub-keyword

New keyword

Delete keyword

Figure 2-13:
While you can use menu commands to create new keywords, the simplest way is to use the little icons shown here. (The Delete Keyword button just removes the keyword from the list of keywords, not from your photos. Just turn it off in the photo's Metadata panel to get rid of it.) The search box isn't for finding images tagged with a particular keyword. It's for keyword mavens who create so many keywords that they need a way to find a particular keyword in the Keyword panel's list. The arrows to the right of the search box let you navigate forward and back through keywords in the order you've used them. The number to the right of a keyword tells you how many of your visible photos have that keyword assigned to them.

- **Remove multiple keywords from a photo.** Select the photo, display the Keywords panel's pop-out menu by clicking the tiny icon in the panel's upper left, and then choose Remove Keywords.

- **Delete a keyword.** Click an item in the Keyword panel list to highlight it, and then click the Delete icon (the trash can) in the bottom-right corner of the panel or go to the panel's menu and choose Delete. This doesn't remove it from your photos, only from the list. You need to remove it from individual files, too, to really get rid of it.

- **Change a keyword.** Click it in the Keyword panel list, and then go to the panel's menu (click the icon in the upper right), choose Rename, and then type the new keyword.

You can also create as many hierarchical levels of keywords as you want by creating sub-keywords. To do that, click a keyword in the Keyword panel list, and then click the New Sub Keyword icon at the bottom of the panel. You can also drag an existing keyword onto another one to make it a sub-keyword of the target keyword.

COMMUNICATION STATION

Bridge, Keywords, and Other Programs

What happens when you have photos that you assigned tags or keywords to in a program other than Bridge, or when you want to share your Bridge keywords with people using a different program?

You might run into this situation if you're a switcher from Windows and you used the Windows version of Elements to tag your photos. How can you bring that info into the Mac version? Easy: In Windows, before you copy your photos to your Mac, just go to Organizer → File → "Write Tags and Properties to file(s)". (The exact wording of the command depends on which Windows version of Elements you were using.) That turns your tags into metadata keywords that Bridge can see. (Unfortunately, if you have RAW files—page 213—it doesn't work very reliably, but it works fine for other formats.) You'll lose any categories you assigned in Windows, though, so it's best to assign those as tags before writing the tags to the files. In

Bridge, you'll need to re-establish any hierarchies you had by creating sub-keywords (page 54).

If you use a recent version of iPhoto, the program should find your Bridge keywords automatically, and display them in the iPhoto Keywords area. However, this is a one-way street: iPhoto uses a proprietary tag system that Bridge can't understand, but if you do a search on Google, you can find scripts that will write the iPhoto keywords as metadata keywords.

If you import photos from other programs, you'll notice that their keywords may not want to fit into your keyword hierarchies. To tell a keyword that now it's *your* keyword, highlight it in Bridge's Keywords panel and choose Persistent. Then you can move it around and make it a sub-keyword and so on, just like the Bridge keywords you create yourself (see page 52).

Searching and filtering

Now that you've assigned all these keywords and metadata, they're not much use unless you can find them again. Luckily, Bridge gives you two different ways to do just that: filtering and finding.

There's a Filter panel right in Bridge, which lets you restrict what you see in the thumbnails section using a variety of different criteria. You can view only photos with three-star ratings, for instance, or photos taken at ISO 200. The actual filtering options available to you are restricted to whatever is currently in the Bridge content area. So, for instance, if you have photos with the keywords "sports," "heli-skiing," and "broken leg" in the content area, those keywords appear as filter criteria. If, on the other hand, you're looking at a folder of photos of your nephew's cello recital, you'll see different keywords listed.

You also get a more specific way to search: the Find window shown in Figure 2-14. To call it up, go to Edit → Find, or press ⌘+F. Here you can do a customized search. Start by telling Bridge where to search. Then you can choose from a variety of criteria, ranging from the document type (JPEG, or TIFF, for instance) to the color space (page 184), or even the camera's white balance setting. You can also tell Bridge to exclude certain criteria.

You can also save your search results as a collection. To do that, click the "Save as Collection" button at the bottom left of the Find Window, and then enter a name for your collection and choose where to save it (you can save it anywhere you like).

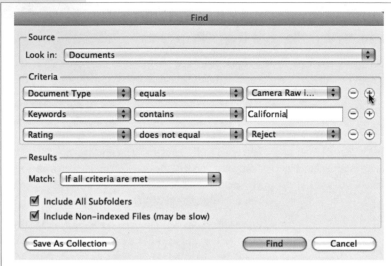

Figure 2-14:
To add additional criteria to a search, just click the plus button to the right of a search term (where the cursor is here). To remove a criterion, click the minus button next to it. (You can set up to 13 criteria.) The search is set to look in the Documents folder for all RAW files with the keyword "California" that don't have Reject ratings.

If you turn on "Add to Favorites", it appears in the Bridge Favorites panel, and you can see that group of pictures again by clicking it there. You can create as many collections as you like.

Saving Your Work

After all your editing, keywording, and resizing effort, you want to be sure you don't lose any of those files you've worked so hard on. Saving your work is just as easy in Elements as in any other programs. (Bridge automatically saves what you do there, like your keywords and ratings—there's no need to do anything special.) The Save As dialog box in Elements has a few settings you don't see in other programs, though. Press ⌘+S to bring it up.

In addition to the standard Save As settings you'd find in any program (format, location, and so on), Elements also gives you these saving options:

- **As a Copy.** When you save an image as a copy, Elements makes the copy, names it "[OriginalFileName] copy," and puts the copy away. The original version remains open. If you want to work on the copy, you must open it. Sometimes Elements forces you to save as a copy—for instance, if you want to save a layered image and you turn off the layers option. (See Chapter 6 for more about layers.)

- **Layers.** If your image has layers, then turn on this checkbox to keep them. When you turn off this setting, Elements usually forces you to save as a copy. To avoid having to save as a copy, flatten your image (page 168) before saving it. Remember that once you close a flattened image, you can't get your layers back again—flattening is a permanent change.

- **Embed Color Profile.** You can choose to keep a color profile in your image. Page 184 explains color profiles.

The File Formats Elements Understands

Elements gives you loads of file format options. Your best choice depends on how you plan to use your image.

- **Photoshop (.psd, .pdd).** It's a good idea to save your files as .psd files—the native file format for Elements or Photoshop—before you work on them. A .psd file can hold lots of information, and you don't lose any data by saving in this format. Also, it allows you to keep layers, which is very important, even if you haven't used them for much yet.

- **Photo Project (.pse).** This is a new format, only for multipage Elements photo creations (see Figure 2-15 as well as page 413).

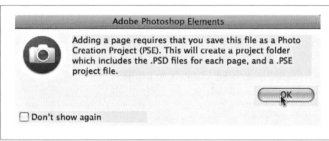

Figure 2-15:
If you add pages to a file (page 410), you see this warning message box. Elements is telling you it needs to save your multipage project in a format that almost no other programs can open. To learn more about working with this format, and how to get your project out of Elements for online printing or use by other programs, see the box on page 413.

UP TO SPEED

File Formats

After you've spent hours creating a perfect image, you want other people to be able to see your picture, too. If everyone who wanted to view your images needed a copy of Elements, you probably wouldn't have a very large audience for your creations. So, Elements lets you save in lots of different *file formats*.

What does that mean? It's pretty simple, really. A file format is a way in which your computer saves information so that another program or another computer can read and use the file.

Because there are many different kinds of programs and several different computing platforms (Windows, Linux, and Mac, for example), the kind of file that's best for one use may be a really poor choice for doing something else. That's why many programs, like Elements, can save your work in a variety of different formats, depending on what you want to do with your image. There are many formats, like TIFF and JPEG, that many different programs can read. Then there are other formats, like the .pages files that Pages creates—which are easily read only by the program that created them.

- **TIFF (.tif, .tiff).** This is another format that, like the Photoshop format, preserves virtually all of your photo's information and allows you to save layers. And like Photoshop files, TIFF files can be very large. TIFFs are used extensively in print production, and some cameras allow you to choose TIFF as a shooting option.

- **JPEG (.jpg, jpeg, .jpe)**. Almost everyone who uses a computer has run into JPEGs at one time or another. Most digital cameras offer the JPEG format as an option. Generally, when you bring a JPEG into Elements, you want to use another format when you save it, to avoid data loss. Keep reading for more about why.

- **JPEG 2000 (.jpf, .jpx, .jp2)**. This newer variation of the JPEG format makes small files without losing any data, and it also supports transparency. There aren't many Web browsers that can display these files, though, so this format is not a good choice for the Web.

- **PDF (.pdf, .pdp)**. Adobe invented PDF, or Portable Document Format, which lets you send files to people with Adobe Reader (formerly Acrobat Reader) so they can easily open and view the files. Elements uses PDF files to create presentations like slideshows.

- **CompuServe GIF (.gif)**. (Everywhere except this menu, this format is known simply as GIF. CompuServe gets added here because they invented and own the code for the format.) This format is used primarily for Web graphics, especially files without a lot of subtle shadings of color. For more on when to choose GIFs, see Chapter 17. GIFs are also used for Web animations; see page 446 for help creating animated GIFs.

- **PICT (.pct)**. PICT is an older Mac format that's still used by some applications. AppleWorks, for example, handles PICTs better than any other graphics format. Also, sometimes larger file formats like Mac-created TIFFs generate their thumbnail previews as PICT Resource files (the type of PICT used within the TIFF file).

- **BMP (.bmp)**. This format is an old Windows standby. It's the file format used for many graphics tasks by the Windows operating system.

- **PNG**. Here's another Web graphic format, created to overcome some of the disadvantages of JPEGs and GIFs. It has its own disadvantages, though. See page 440 for more about these files.

- **Photoshop EPS (.eps)**. EPS (Encapsulated PostScript) format is used to share documents among different programs. You generally get the best results when the documents go to a PostScript printer (laser printers are usually PostScript printers, and inkjets usually aren't).

- **Digital Negative (.dng)**. Elements can't save files in this format (except in the RAW converter), but it can open DNG files. DNG is a format developed by Adobe to create a more universal way to store all the different camera RAW file formats. You can download a special DNG Converter from the downloads area of Adobe's support Web site (*www.adobe.com/downloads*); it lets you convert your camera's own RAW formatted photos into DNG files. DNG files aren't ready to use the way JPEG or TIFF files are—you still need to run your DNG files through the RAW Converter before you can use them in projects. See page 230 for more about DNG.

The not-so-common file formats

Besides the garden-variety formats in the previous list, Elements lets you save in some formats you may never have heard of. Here's a list, and then you can forget all about them, probably.

Opening Obscure File Formats

Once in a while, you may run into a file that was created in a format that Elements doesn't understand. Sometimes you can fake Elements out and con it into opening the document by changing the file extension to a more common one.

For the few file formats that make even Elements throw up its hands in despair, try Graphic Converter (*www.lemkesoft.com*), a wonderful little program that can open darn near anything. It does great batch conversions, too, and even offers some basic image editing features. You may have gotten it bundled with your Mac, if your computer isn't very new. Graphic Converter is shareware, with a very generous demo period, but it's worth every penny.

Very rarely you'll run across a file that makes even Graphic Converter give up. If that happens, try a Google search. (Use the file's three- or four-letter extension as your search term.) It's unlikely to help you open it, but if you can figure out what it is, you can probably figure out where it came from and ask whoever sent it to you to try again with a more standard format.

- **PIXAR.** Yup, *that* Pixar. This is the special format for the movie studio's high-end workstations, although if you're working on one of those, it's extremely unlikely that you're reading this page.

- **Scitex CT.** This format is used for prepress work in the printing industry.

- **Photoshop Raw.** No, it's not the same as your camera RAW file, but rather an older Photoshop format that consists of uncompressed data.

- **Targa TGA,** or Targa. Developed for systems using the Truevision video board, this format has become a popular graphics format, especially for games.

- **PCX.** This format was very popular for graphics back in the days of DOS (remember PC Paintbrush?). Nowadays it's mostly used by some kinds of fax systems and a few document management programs.

About JPEGs

In the next chapter, you'll read about how throwing away pixels can lead to shoddy-looking pictures (page 88). Well, certain file formats were designed to make your file size as small as possible. They make the file smaller by throwing out information by the bucketful. These formats are known as *lossy* because they throw out, or lose, some of the file's data every time you save it, to make the file as small as possible.

Sometimes you want that to happen, like when you want a small-size picture for a Web site. Therefore, many of the file formats that were developed for the Web, most notably JPEG, are designed to favor smallness over any other quality. They compress the file sizes by allowing some data to escape.

> **NOTE** Formats that preserve all your data intact are called *lossless*. (You may also run across the term *non-lossy*, which means the same thing.) The most popular file formats for people who are looking to preserve all their photos' data are Photoshop and TIFF.

If you save a file using the JPEG format, every time you hit the Save button and close the file your computer is squishing some of the data out of the photo. What kind of data? It's the information needed for displaying and printing the fine details. You don't want to keep saving your file as a JPEG over and over again. Every time you do, you lose a little more potential detail from your image. You can usually get away with saving as a JPEG once or twice, but if you keep it up, sooner or later you start to wonder what happened to your beautiful picture.

It's OK that your camera takes photos and saves them as JPEGs. Those are pretty enormous JPEGs, usually. Just importing a JPEG won't hurt your picture. But once you get your files into Elements, save your pictures as Photoshop or TIFF files while you work on them. When you want another JPEG as the final result, change the format back to JPEG *after* you're done editing it.

> **TIP** Your camera may give you several different JPEG compression options to help you fit more pictures on your memory card. Always choose the *least* compression possible. Your photo file sizes are slightly larger, but the quality is much, much better. It's worth sacrificing the space.

Changing the File Format

It's very easy to change the format of a file in Elements. Just press ⌘+Shift+S or go to File → Save As and, from the Format pull-down menu, select the format you want. Elements makes a copy of your file in the new format and asks you to name it.

Burning CDs and DVDs

Elements 6 makes it super easy to burn your photos to discs right from Elements. (Not that it's hard to burn a disc in the Finder, but maybe you're more likely to burn a backup CD if you don't have the extra step of leaving Elements first.) You can burn discs to back up your latest photographic *magnum opus*, or just to share with your friends. You can burn both photos and the projects you'll learn how to create later in this book.

To burn a disc:

1. **Choose your files.**

   You can start from either Elements or Bridge. It's probably best to start from Bridge if you want to back up a lot of files, since you can select as many as you want without opening them. If you start from Elements, you'll back up all your open files—you can't choose which files to include. (If you want to burn images that are open in Elements, save your changes before you start.)

2. **Tell Elements or Bridge you want to burn a CD/DVD.**

   In Elements, go to Share → CD/DVD. In Bridge, go to File → Burn CD (the menu says "CD," but if you have a drive that burns DVDs, too, you can burn either kind of disc). Wherever you start, Elements comes to the front for the actual burning.

3. **Put a disc in your drive.**

   If there isn't already a blank disc in your drive, Elements asks for one. (If you have more than one disk-burning drive, like an external DVD burner, Elements shows you a list of all your available drives.) Put a disc in and make any changes to the burn settings, if you like (see Figure 2-16).

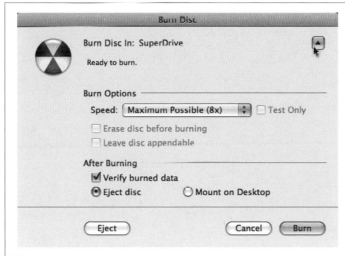

Figure 2-16:
You generally don't need to adjust your burn settings, but if you want to make changes, click this button to expand the Burn Disc window, as shown here. You can change the burn speed, choose settings for erasing rewritable discs, and tell Elements what you want it do with the disc when it's done burning.

4. **Click Burn.**

   Elements burns the disc. (CDs and DVDs that Elements creates can be read by both Macs and Windows computers.)

Burning discs in Elements rather than in the Finder is quick and easy, but there's one disadvantage: You can't choose a name for your disc. It's going to be called Photo CD0000, like it or not. The next disc you burn in Elements will be Photo CD0001, and so on.

BETTER SAFE THAN SORRY

Making Backups

If you're like most people, your photographs are among your most precious possessions. When trouble strikes, the family photo albums are the usually among the first things people grab. It's important to keep a good backup of your digital photos, too, so you don't lose them.

If you have Leopard, Apple's Time Machine application is great for keeping a backup of your computer's files. But disks can fail, and prudent people like to keep a backup copy away from where the computer is located, so that it's safely out of harm's way should something happen. Burn copies of your important photos and give the discs to a friend to keep for you, or put them in your safe deposit box for peace of mind.

Adobe also offers a paid online backup service through *Ironmountain.com*, which you can access right from Bridge (go to Tools → Photoshop Services → Online Backup). You may think it's kind of expensive after the 30-day trial expires, though. Remember that .Mac also offers online backups. Careful folks prefer not to trust an online service as their only backup, though, even if they use it regularly. The bottom line: The more backups, the better.

Rotating and Resizing Your Photos

In the last chapter, you learned how to get your photos *into* Elements. Now it's time to look at how to trim off unwanted areas and straighten out crooked photos. You'll also learn how to change the overall size of your images and how to zoom in and out to get a better look at things while you're editing.

Straightening Scanned Photos

Anyone who's scanned old photos can testify about the hair-pulling frustration when your carefully placed pictures come out crooked onscreen. Whether you're feeding in your precious memories one at a time or scanning batches of photos to save time, Elements can help straighten things out.

Straightening Two or More Photos at a Time

If you've got a pile of photos to scan, save yourself some time and lay as many of them as you can fit on your scanner. Thanks to Elements' wonderful Divide Scanned Photos command, you'll have individual images in no time.

Start by scanning in the photos (Figure 3-1). The only limit is how many can fit on your scanner at once. It doesn't matter whether you scan directly into Elements or use your scanner's own software. (See page 45 for more about scanning images into Elements.)

> **TIP** Sometimes it pays to be crooked. Divide Scanned Photos does its best work if your photos are fairly crooked, so don't waste time trying to be precise when placing your pictures on the scanner.

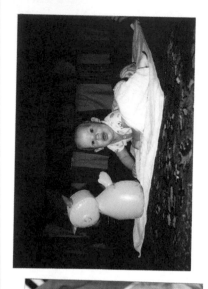
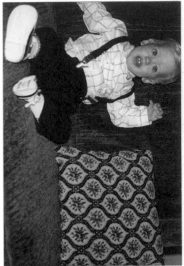
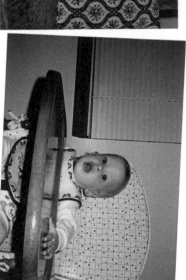

Figure 3-1:
*Consumer-grade flatbed
scanners are generally
pretty slow, so it's a huge
timesaver if you can scan
four or even six photos at
a time. Elements can
automatically separate
and straighten individual
photos in a group thanks
to the Divide Scanned
Photos command.*

When you're done scanning, follow these steps:

1. **Open your scanned image file.**

   It doesn't matter what file format you use when saving your scanned group of photos: TIFF, JPEG, PDF, whatever. Elements can read 'em all.

2. **Divide, straighten, and crop the individual photos.**

   Go to Image → Divide Scanned Photos. Sit back and enjoy the view as Elements carefully calculates, splits, straightens out, and trims each image. You'll see the individual photos appear and disappear as Elements works through the group.

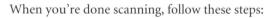

3. **Name and save each separated image.**

When Elements is done, you'll have the original group scan as one image and a separate image file for each photo Elements has carved out. Be sure to save the cut-apart photos with individual names.

Elements usually does a crackerjack job splitting your photos, but once in a while it chokes, leaving you with an image file that contains more than one photo. Figure 3-2 shows you what to do when Elements doesn't succeed in splitting things up.

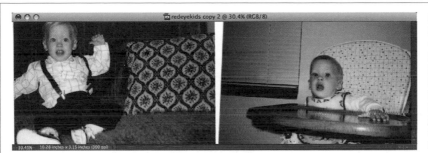

Figure 3-2:
Sometimes Elements just can't figure out how to split up your photos, and you wind up with something like these two not-quite-split-apart images. Rescan the photos that confused Elements, but this time, make sure they're more crooked on the scanner and leave more space between them. Elements should then be able to split them correctly.

TIP Occasionally you may find that Elements can't accurately separate a group scan, no matter what you do. In that case, use the Marquee tool (page 113) to select each individual image, paste it into its own document (File → New → "Image from Clipboard"), and then save it.

Straightening Individual Photos

Elements can also straighten out and crop (trim) a single scanned image. Simply choose Image → Rotate → "Straighten and Crop Image", and Elements tidies things up for you. You can also choose just Straighten Image if you'd rather crop the edges yourself. Better still, you can use Divide Scanned Photos on a single image, as explained in the previous section. (Cropping is explained on page 71.)

Rotating Your Images

Owners of print photographs aren't the only ones who sometimes need a little help straightening their pictures. Digital photos sometimes need to be rotated, because some cameras don't include data in their image files that tells Elements (or any other image-editing program, for that matter) the correct orientation. Certain cameras, for example, send portrait-orientated photos out on their sides, and it's up to you to straighten things out.

Fortunately, Elements has rotation commands just about everywhere you go. If all you need to do is get Dad off his back and stand him upright, here's a list of where you can perform a quick 90-degree rotation on any open photo:

- **Quick Fix** (page 93). Click either of the Rotation buttons at the bottom of the preview area.

- **Full Edit.** Go to Image → Rotate → 90° Left (or Right).

- **Project bin.** Right-click (Control+click) a thumbnail and choose Rotate 90° Left (or Right).

- **RAW Converter** (page 213). Click the left or right arrow at the top of the Preview window.

Those commands all get you one-click, 90-degree changes. But Elements has all sorts of other rotational tricks up its sleeve, as explained in the next section.

Rotating and Flipping Options

Elements gives you several ways to change the orientation of your photo. To see what's available, go to Image → Rotate. You'll notice two groups of Rotate commands in this menu. For now, it's the top group you want to focus on. (The second group does the same things, only those commands work on layers, which are explained in Chapter 6.)

In the first group of commands, you'll see:

- **90° Left** or **Right**. These commands produce the same rotation as the rotate buttons explained earlier. Use these commands for digital photos that come in on their sides.

- **180°**. This turns your photo upside down and backward.

- **Custom**. Selecting this command brings up a dialog box where, if you're mathematically inclined, you can type in the precise number of degrees to rotate your photo.

- **Flip Horizontal**. Flipping a photo horizontally means that if your subject was gazing soulfully off to the left, now she's gazing soulfully off to the right.

- **Flip Vertical**. This command turns your photo upside down without changing the left/right orientation (which is what Rotate 180° does).

> **NOTE** When you're flipping photos around, remember you're making a mirror image of everything in the photo. So someone's who's writing right-handed becomes a lefty, any text you can see in the photo is backward, and so on.

Figure 3-3 shows these commands in action.

If you want to position your photo at an angle on a page (as you might in a scrapbook), use Free Rotate Layer, described on page 69.

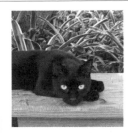
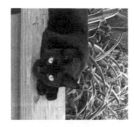
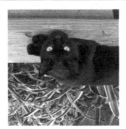
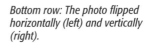
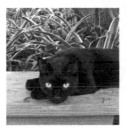
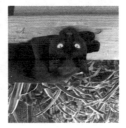

Figure 3-3:
Even the most uncooperative cat will turn somersaults for you if you use the rotate commands.

Top row: From left to right, you see the original, the photo rotated 90 degrees to the right, and the photo rotated 180 degrees.

Bottom row: The photo flipped horizontally (left) and vertically (right).

Straightening the Contents of Your Image

What about all those photos you've taken where the content isn't quite straight? You can flip those pictures around forever, but if your camera was off-kilter when you snapped the shot, your subjects will lean like a certain tower in Pisa. Elements has planned for this problem, too, by including a nifty Straighten tool that makes adjusting the horizon as easy as drawing a line.

> **TIP** About 95 percent of the time, the Straighten tool will do the trick. But for the few cases where you can't get things looking perfect, you can still use the old school Elements method—the Free Rotate command, described on page 69.

Straighten Tool

If you can never seem to hold a camera perfectly level, you'll love the Elements Straighten tool. It lives just below the Cookie Cutter tool in the Full Edit Toolbox. To straighten a crooked photo:

1. **Open the photo, and then activate the Straighten tool.**

   Its icon is two little photos, one crooked and one not. Or, on the keyboard, just press P.

2. **Make any changes to the Options bar settings for the Straighten tool before you use the tool.**

   Your choices are described in a moment.

---

3. **Tell Elements where the horizon is.**

Drag to draw a line in your photo to show Elements where horizontal *should* be. Figure 3-4 shows how. Your line appears at an angle when you draw it. That's fine, because Elements is going to level out your photo, making your line the true horizontal plane in the image.

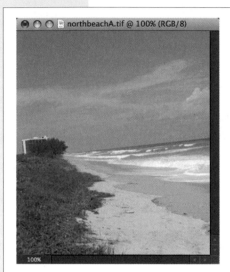 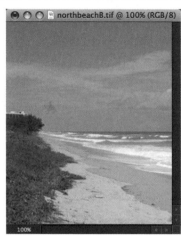

Figure 3-4:
Left: To correct the crooked horizon in this photo, just draw a line along the part that should be level. It's easiest to do this by choosing a clearly marked boundary like the horizon in this photo, but you can actually draw a line across anything you want to make level.

Right: Elements automatically rotates the photo to straighten its contents. In this case, you see the results of selecting "Crop to Remove Background" (in the Options bar), which trims off all the ragged edges for you.

4. **Elements responds by automatically straightening your photo. It also crops the photo if you chose that setting in the Options bar.**

If you don't like what Elements did, press ⌘+Z to undo it and draw another line. If you're happy, you're all done, except for saving your work (⌘+S).

> **TIP** If you have a photo of trees, sailing ships, skyscrapers, or any other subject where you'd rather straighten vertically than horizontally, just hold down ⌘ while you drag. The line you draw determines the vertical axis of your photo.

The Options bar gives you some choices about how to handle the edges of your newly straightened photo. Once your picture's straightened, the edges are going to be a bit ragged, so you can choose what you want Elements to do about that:

- **Grow or Shrink Canvas to Fit.** Elements adds extra space around the edges of your photo to make sure that every bit of the original edges is still there. It's up to you to crop your photo afterward (page 71).

- **Crop to Remove Background.** Elements chops off the ragged edges to give you a nice rectangular image.

- **Crop to Original Size.** Elements makes sure the dimensions of your photo stay exactly the same—even if that means including some blank spaces along the perimeter.

If your photo has layers (see Chapter 6), you can use the Straighten tool to straighten only the active layer (page 146) by going to the Options bar and turning off Rotate All Layers. If you want Elements to straighten your whole photo, leave this checkbox turned on.

The Straighten tool is best for photos where you were holding the camera crooked. If you try it and it makes things look very odd in your photo, perhaps straightening isn't really what you need. Architectural photos, for instance, may look a bit crooked before you use this tool—but a lot worse afterward. If that house is *still* leaning, even though you're sure the ground line has been leveled correctly, then most likely your real problem is *perspective distortion* (a visual warping effect). To fix that, use Correct Camera Distortion (page 300).

> **TIP** In Elements 6, you can also straighten photos right in the RAW Converter. There's a Straighten tool in its toolbox, right between the Crop tool and the Red Eye tool. You use it just like Full Edit's Straighten tool. Page 67 tells you more.

Free Rotate

You can also use the Rotate commands to straighten your photos, or to turn them at angles for use in scrapbook pages or album layouts you create. The rotate command that's best for this use is Free Rotate Layer, which lets you grab your photo and spin it to your heart's desire. And if you aren't sure where straight is, Elements gives you some help figuring it out, as shown in Figure 3-5.

All the rotate commands are also available for use on individual layers, incidentally. (Chapter 6 tells you all about layers, but you don't have to understand layers to use the Free Rotate Layer command.)

To use Free Rotate Layer:

1. **Go to Image → Rotate → Free Rotate Layer.**

   Elements asks you if it should "make this background a layer." Say OK. (Again, Chapter 6 tells you everything you need to know about layers.)

2. **Name the layer if you want to.**

   A dialog box appears, giving you a chance to name the layer. Do so if you want, then click OK.

3. **Use the curved arrows to adjust your photo (Figure 3-6).**

   Your picture may look kind of jagged while you're rotating. Don't worry about that—Elements smoothes things out once you're done.

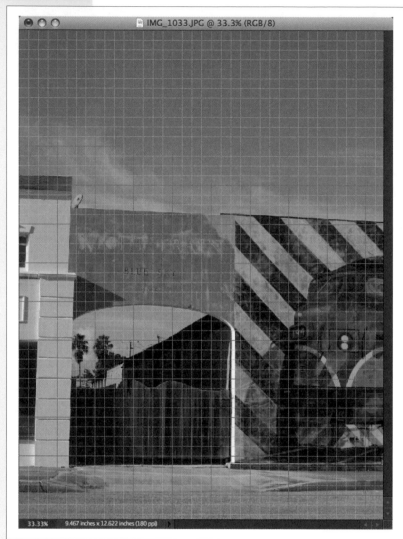

Figure 3-5:
If you need some help figuring out where straight is, in the Editor, go to View → Grid to toggle these handy guidelines on and off. You can adjust the grid spacing in Edit → Preferences → Grid. For a photo like this one, you could also change the color of the grid to make it show up better. To do that, click the color square in the grid preferences window and choose a color from the Color Picker (page 199).

4. **When you've got your image positioned where you want it, click the green OK checkmark or press Return. (If you don't like what you did, press the red "no" symbol to cancel the rotation.)**

Now you've got a nice straight picture, but the edges are probably pretty ragged since the original had slanted, unrotated sides. You can take care of that by cropping your photo, which is covered in the next section.

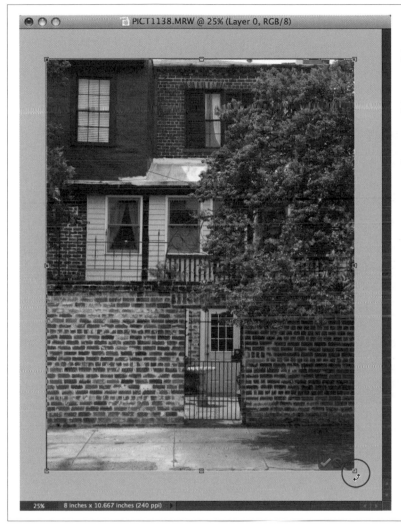

PICT1138.MRW @ 25% (Layer 0, RGB/8)

25%   8 inches x 10.667 inches (240 ppi)

Figure 3-6:
To rotate your photo, just move your cursor close to one of the handles on the photo until it changes into two curved arrows. Then click and drag to adjust your photo the way you'd straighten a crooked picture on the wall. Click the green OK checkmark when you're happy with what you've done, or the red "no" symbol to cancel.

Cropping Pictures

Whether or not you straightened your digital photo, sooner or later you'll probably need to *crop* it—trim it to a certain size. Most people crop their photos for one of two reasons: If you want to print on standard size photo paper, you usually need to cut away part of your image to make it fit on the paper. Then there's the "I don't want *that* in my picture" reason. Fortunately, Elements makes it easy to crop away distracting background objects or people you'd rather not see.

A few cameras produce photos that are proportioned exactly right for printing to a standard size like 4"×6". But most cameras give you photos that aren't the same proportions as any of the standard paper sizes like 4"×6" or 8"×10". (The width-to-height ratio is also known as the *aspect ratio*.)

The extra area most cameras provide gives you room to crop wherever you like. You can also crop out different areas for different size prints (assuming you save your original photo). Figure 3-7 shows an example of a photo that had to be cropped to fit on a 4"×6" piece of paper. If you'd like to experiment with cropping or changing resolution (explained on page 82), download the image in the figure (waterfall.jpg) from the "Missing CD" page at *www.missingmanuals.com*.

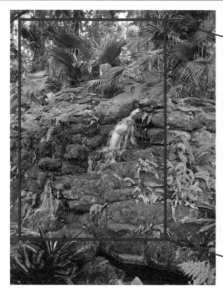
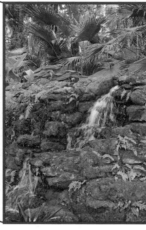

Figure 3-7:
When you print onto standard sized paper, you may have to choose the part of your digital photo you want to keep.

Left: The photo as it came from the camera.

Right: The results of cropping the image to make it the correct shape for a 4"×6" print.

It's best to perform your crops on a copy, since trimming is going to throw away the pixels outside the area you choose to keep. And you never know—you may want those pixels back someday.

Using the Crop Tool

You can use the Crop tool in either the Full Edit or Quick Fix window. The Crop tool includes a helpful list of preset sizes to make cropping easier. If you don't need to crop to an exact size, here's how to perform basic freehand cropping:

1. **Activate the Crop tool.**

   Click the Crop icon in the Toolbox or press C.

2. **Drag anywhere in your image to select the area you want to keep.**

   The area outside the boundaries of your selection is covered with a dark shield. The dark area is what you're discarding. To move the area you've chosen, just drag the bounding box (the outline) to wherever you want it.

   You may find the Crop tool a little crotchety sometimes. See the box on page 75 for help making it behave.

3. **To resize your selection, drag one of the little handles on the sides and corners.**

   They look like little squares, as shown in Figure 3-8. You can drag in any direction, so you can also change the proportions of your crop if you want to.

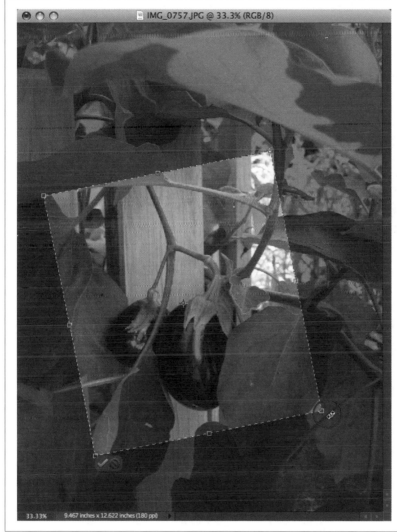

Figure 3-8:
If you want to change your selection from horizontal to vertical or vice versa, just move your cursor outside the cropped area and you'll see the rotation arrows (circled). Grab and rotate them, the same way you would an entire photo. Changing your selection doesn't rotate your photo—just the boundaries of the crop. When you're done, press Return or the green checkmark (for OK) to tell Elements you're satisfied. The red "no" symbol cancels your crop. (The OK and cancel symbols appear when you let go of the mouse.)

4. **If you change your mind, press Cancel (the "no" symbol) on the photo, or press the Escape key.**

   That undoes the selection so you can start over or switch to another tool if you decide you don't want to crop after all.

5. **When you're sure you've got the crop you want, press Return, or press OK (the checkmark) on the photo, or double-click inside the cropping mask, and you're done.**

Cropping Your Image to an Exact Size

You don't have to eyeball things when cropping a photo. You can enter any dimensions you want in the width and height boxes in the Options bar, or, from the Aspect Ratio menu, you can choose one of the Presets, which automatically enters a set of numbers for you. The Aspect Ratio menu offers you several standard photo sizes, like 4"×6" or 8"×10", to choose from. The Use Photo Ratio choice in the Presets list lets you crop your image using the same width/height proportions (the *aspect ratio*) as in the original. Figure 3-9 shows you a timesaver: how to quickly switch the width and height numbers.

> **NOTE**   Although Custom is one of the Aspect Ratio menu choices, there's no reason to select it, since it's there to let you know you've entered a custom size. It selects itself automatically when you enter custom numbers.

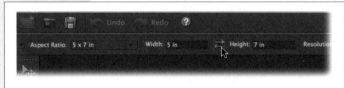

Figure 3-9:
If you want to change which number is the width setting and which is the height, just click these little arrows to swap them. So if you chose 5"×7" from the presets but want to switch to a landscape orientation, click the arrows (shown just above the cursor) to get 7"×5" instead.

> **WARNING**   If you enter a number in the Resolution box that's different from your image's current resolution, the Crop tool resamples your image to match the new resolution. (Resolution is explained in the section on resizing your image that starts on page 82.) See the section on Resampling (page 88) to understand what resampling is and why it isn't always a good thing.

Cropping with the Marquee Tool

The Crop tool is very handy, but it wants to make the decisions for you about several things you may want to control yourself. For instance, the Crop tool may decide to resample the image (see page 88) whether you want it to or not. The Crop tool gives you no warning that it's resampling. It just does it.

For better control, and also for making elliptical crop effects (great for oval vignettes), you may prefer to use the Marquee tool. It's no harder than using the Crop tool, but you get to make all the choices yourself.

There's one other big difference between using the Marquee tool and the Crop tool: With the Crop tool, all you can do to the area you selected is crop it. The Marquee tool, in contrast, lets you make many other changes to your selected area, like adjusting the color, which you may want to do before you crop.

TROUBLESHOOTING MOMENT

Crop Tool Idiosyncrasies

The Crop tool is crotchety sometimes. People have called it "bossy," and that's a good word for it. Here are some settings that may help you control it better.

- **Snap to Grid**. You may find that you just cannot get the crop exactly where you want it. Does the edge keep jumping slightly away from where you put it? Like most graphics programs, Elements uses a grid of invisible lines—called the *autogrid*—to help position things exactly. Sometimes a grid is a big help, but in situations like this, it's a nuisance. If you hold down ⌘, you can temporarily disable the autogrid. You can also get rid of the autogrid or adjust the spacing on it. To turn it off, first make the grid visible by going to View → Grid.

Then you can turn it off by going to Snap to → Grid. (It will stay off after you make the grid invisible by choosing View → Grid again.) You can adjust the grid settings in Photoshop Elements → Preferences → Grid.

- **Clear the Crop Tool**. Occasionally you may find that the Crop tool won't release a setting you entered, even after you clear the Options bar boxes. If the Crop tool won't let you drag where you want and keeps insisting on creating a particular sized crop, you need to reset the Crop tool. Simply click the triangle at the left of the Options bar, and then choose Reset Tool from the shortcut menu, as shown in Figure 3-10.

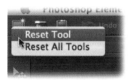

Figure 3-10:
If the Crop tool stops cooperating, there's an easy way to make it behave again. Click this tiny triangle in the Options bar (you can't see it here because it's covered by the pop-up menu), and then choose Reset Tool from the menu that appears. If you want to make sure that all your tools go back to their original settings, choose Reset All Tools.

To make a basic crop with the Marquee tool follow these steps:

1. **Activate the Marquee tool.**

   Click it in the Toolbox (the little dotted square) or press M. Figure 3-11 shows you the shape choices you get within the Marquee tool. For cropping, choose the Rectangular Marquee tool.

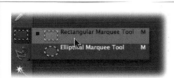

Figure 3-11:
Click the Marquee tool, and you can choose the shape from this shortcut menu. The Toolbox icon shows you the shape that's currently selected.

---

2. **Drag the selection marquee across the part of your photo you want to keep.**

   When you let go, your selected area is surrounded by the dotted lines shown in Figure 3-12. These are sometimes called "marching ants." (Get it? The dashes look like ants marching around your picture.) The area inside the marching

---

ants is the part of your photo you're keeping. (There's a lot more about making selections in Chapter 5.) If you make a mistake, press ⌘+D to get rid of the selection and start over.

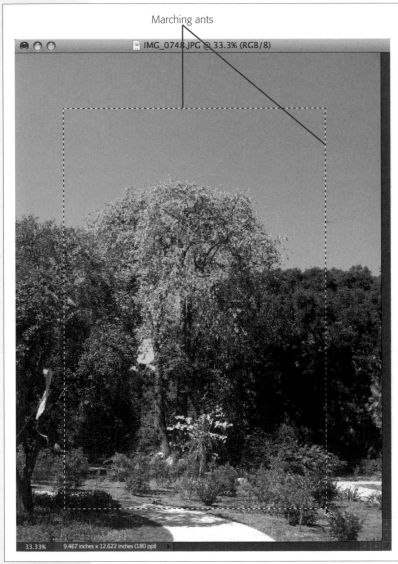

Marching ants

IMG_0748.JPG @ 33.3% (RGB/8)

33.33%   9.467 inches x 12.622 inches (180 ppi)

Figure 3-12:
When you let go after making your Marquee selection, you see the "marching ants" around the edge of your selection. You can reposition the marquee by dragging it. To do so, just put your cursor anywhere inside the selection marquee and then drag it.

3. **Crop your photo.**

   Go to Image → Crop. The area outside your selection disappears, and your photo is cropped to the area you selected in step 2.

If you want to crop your photo to a particular aspect ratio, you can do that easily. Once the Marquee tool is active, but before you drag, go to the Options bar. In the Mode menu, choose Fixed Aspect Ratio. Then enter the proportions you want in the Width and Height boxes. Drag and crop as described earlier. Your photo will end up with exactly the proportions you entered in the Options bar.

You can also crop to an exact size with the Marquee tool:

1. **Check the resolution of your photo.**

   Go to Image → Resize → Image Size and make sure the ppi number is somewhere between 150 and 300 if you plan to print your cropped photo. You'll see that 300 is best, for reasons explained on page 86. If the ppi is OK, click OK and go to step 2.

   If the ppi is too low, change the number in the Resolution box to what you want. Make sure that the checkbox in the Resize dialog box that says Resample Image is turned off, and then click OK.

2. **Activate the Marquee tool.**

   Click the Marquee tool in the Toolbox (the little dotted square) or press M. Choose the Rectangular Marquee tool.

3. **Enter your settings in the Options bar.**

   First, go to the Mode menu and choose Fixed Size. Next, enter the dimensions you want in the Width and Height boxes.

4. **Drag anywhere in your image.**

   You get a selection the exact size you chose in the Options bar.

5. **Crop your Image.**

   Go to Image → Crop.

The Cookie Cutter tool also gives you a way to create really interesting crops, as shown in Figure 3-13.

> **TIP** If you're doing your own printing, there's really no reason to tie yourself down to standard photo sizes like 4" × 6"—unless, of course, you need the image to fit a frame of that size. But most of the time, your images could just as well be square, or long and skinny, or whatever proportions you want. You can be especially inventive when sizing images for the Web. So don't feel that every photo you take has to be straitjacketed into a standard size.

Zooming and Repositioning Your View

Sometimes, rather than changing the size of your photo, all you want to do is change its appearance in Elements so you can get a better look at it. For example, you may want to zoom in on a particular area, or zoom out, so you can see how edits you've made have affected your photo's overall composition.

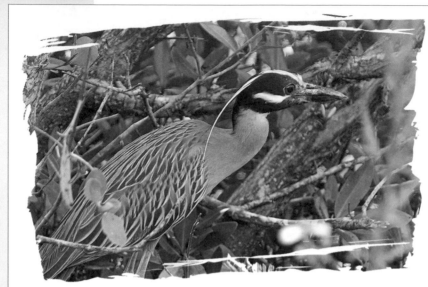

Figure 3-13:
With the Elements Cookie Cutter tool, you don't have to be square anymore. The Cookie Cutter tool lets you crop your images to various shapes, from the kind of abstract border you see here, to heart- or star-shaped outlines. You can read more about how to use the Cookie Cutter tool in Chapter 12.

This section is about how to adjust the view of your image inside Elements. Nothing you do with the tools and commands in this section changes anything about your actual photo. You're just changing the way you see it. Elements gives you lots of tools and keystroke combinations to help with these new views; soon you'll probably find yourself making these changes without even thinking about them.

Image Views

Before you start resizing your view of your photos, Elements gives you several different ways to position your image windows. When you first use Elements, if you have more than one photo open at a time, your photos overlap each other so that you can see as much as possible of the front photo, with only the edges of the photos behind it visible. This is a very efficient way to work, but if you don't like it, you're not stuck with it.

When you go to Window → Images, you get several choices for how you want your image to display:

- **Maximize Mode**. Each photo window takes up the entire Elements desktop.

    NOTE   In Maximize mode, you can only have one photo visible at a time. Switch to Cascade or Tile if you want to work on two or more photos simultaneously.

- **Tile**. Your image windows appear edge to edge so that they fill the available desktop space. With two photos open, each gets half the window; with four photos, each gets one quarter of it, and so on.

- **Cascade**. Your image windows appear in overlapping stacks. Most people find Cascade the most practical view when you want to compare or work with two images.

- **Match Zoom**. All your windows get the same magnification level as the active image window (the photo you're currently working on).

- **Match Location**. You see the same part of each image window, like the upper-right corner or the bottom-left. Elements matches the other windows to the active window.

You also get four handy commands for adjusting the view of your active image window. Go to the View menu, and you see:

- **New Window for**. Choose this command and you get a separate, duplicate window for your image. This view is a terrific help when you're working on very fine detail. You can zoom way in on one view while keeping the other window in a regular view so you don't lose your bearings for where you are in the photo. Don't worry about version control or keeping track of which window you're working in, since both windows just represent different glimpses of the same image.

- **Zoom In/Out**. These are shortcuts for zooming, explained below.

> **NOTE**   You can zoom in or out using the View menu, but it's much faster to learn the keyboard shortcuts for zooming, so you don't have to keep trekking up to the menu. The next section explains the Zoom tool in detail, including how to zoom using the keyboard.

- **Fit on Screen**. This command makes your photo as large as it can be while still keeping the entire photo visible. You can also press ⌘+0 for this view.

- **Actual Pixels**. For the most accurate look at the onscreen size of your photo, go with this option. If you're creating graphics for the Web, this view shows the size your image will be in your Web browser. The keystroke shortcut is Option+⌘+0.

- **Print Size**. This view is really just a guess by Elements because it doesn't know exactly how big a pixel is on your monitor. But it's a rough approximation of the size your image would be if you printed it at the current resolution. (Resolution is explained in the section on resizing your photo, on page 86.)

To adjust the view of a particular image, Elements gives you three useful tools: The Zoom tool, the Hand tool, and the Navigator palette, all of which are explained in the following sections.

The Zoom Tool

Some of Elements' tools require you to get a very close look at your image to see what's going on. Sometimes you may need to see the actual pixels as you work, as shown in Figure 3-14. The Zoom tool makes it easy to zoom your view in and out.

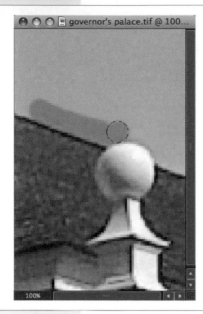

Figure 3-14:
There are times when you want to zoom way, way in when working in Elements. You may even need to go pixel by pixel in tricky spots, as shown here.

The Zoom tool's Toolbox icon is the little magnifying glass. Click it or press Z to activate the tool. Once the tool is active, you see circle icons at the left of the Options bar. If you want to zoom in (to make the view larger), click the one with the + sign on it. To use the Zoom tool, you just click the place in your photo where you want the zoom to focus. The point where you clicked becomes the center of your view, and the view size increases again each time you click.

You can also select the Zoom Out tool in the Options bar, by clicking the magnifying glass with the – sign on it.

> **TIP** If you hold down Option as you click, the selected Zoom tool zooms in the opposite direction; for instance, the regular Zoom tool zooms out rather than in.

The Zoom tool has several Options bar settings you can use as well:

- **Zoom percent.** Enter a number here and the view immediately jumps to that percentage. 1600 percent is the maximum, and 1 percent is the minimum.

- **Resize Windows to fit.** Turn this option on, and your image windows get larger and smaller along with the image size as you zoom. The image always fills the entire window with no gray space around it.

- **Ignore Palettes.** This setting lets windows resize so that they don't stop getting larger when they reach the edge of a floating palette. Instead, they continue resizing *underneath* the palette. This choice This choice is always turned on, unless you turn it off. Frankly, this checkbox doesn't really do anything—Elements ignores palettes anyway, even if you don't want it to.

• **Zoom All Windows.** If you have more than one image window, turn this option on, and the view changes in all the windows in sync when you zoom one window.

> **TIP** If you hold down the Shift key while you zoom, all your windows zoom together. You don't need to go to the Options bar to activate this feature.

The buttons for 1:1 (short for "Actual Pixels"), Fit Screen, and Print Size are the same as the menu commands described in the preceding section, "Image Views" (page 78).

> **TIP** You don't need to bother with the actual Zoom tool at all. You can zoom without letting go of the keyboard by pressing ⌘+= to zoom in and ⌘+ –(that's the ⌘ key plus the minus sign) to zoom out. Just hold down ⌘ and keep tapping the equal or minus sign until the view is what you want. You can also zoom to 100 percent by double-clicking the Zoom tool's icon.
>
> It doesn't matter which tool you're using at the time—you can always zoom in or out this way. Because you'll do a lot of zooming in Elements, this keyboard shortcut is one to remember.

The Hand Tool

With all that zooming, sometimes you can't see your entire image at once. Elements includes the Hand tool to help you adjust which part of your image appears onscreen. It's very easy to use. Just click the little hand in the Toolbox or press H to activate it.

When the Hand tool is active, your cursor turns to the little hand shown in Figure 3-15. Drag with the hand to move your photo around in the window. The hand tool is very helpful when you're zoomed in or working on a large image.

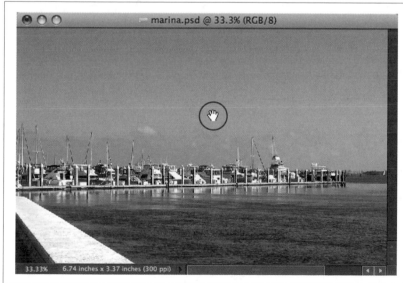

Figure 3-15:
The easiest way to activate the Hand tool is to press the Space bar on your keyboard. You can tell the Hand tool is active by this little white-gloved cursor (circled in red here). No matter what you're doing in Elements, pressing the Space bar calls up the Hand tool and it remains on until you release the Space bar. Then the tool you were previously using returns.

The Hand tool gives you the same "All Windows" option you have for the Zoom tool, but you don't have to use the Options bar to activate it. Just hold down Shift while using the Hand tool, and all your windows scroll in synch. The Hand tool also gives you the same three buttons (Actual Pixels, Fit Screen, and Print Size) that the Zoom tool does. Once again, they're the same as the menu commands described in "Image Views" on page 78.

Figure 3-16 shows the Hand tool's somewhat more sophisticated assistant, the Navigator palette, which is very useful for working in really big photos or when you want to have a slider handy for micro-managing the zoom level. Go to Window → Navigator to call it up.

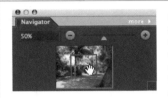

Figure 3-16:
Meet the Navigator. You can travel around your image by dragging the little red rectangle–it marks the area of your photo that you can see onscreen. You can also enter a percent number for the size you want your photo to display at, or move the slider or click the zoom in/out magnifying glasses on either side of the slider to change the view. The Navigator is just great for keeping track of where you are in a large image.

Changing the Size of Your Image

The previous section explained how to resize the view of your image as it appears on your monitor. But sometimes you need to change the size of your actual image, and that's what this section is about.

Resizing your photo brings you up against a pretty tough concept in digital imaging: *resolution*, which measures, in pixels, the amount of detail your image can show. Where it gets confusing is that resolution for printing and for onscreen use (like email and the Web) are quite different.

For example, you need many more pixels to create a good-looking print than you do for a photo that's going to be viewed only onscreen. A photo that's going to print well almost always has too many pixels in it for onscreen display, and as a result, its file size is usually pretty hefty for emailing. So you often need two different copies of your photo for the two different uses. If you want to know more about resolution, a good place to start is *www.scantips.com*.

This section gives you a brief introduction to both screen and print resolution, especially in terms of what decisions you'll need to make when using the Resize Image dialog box. You'll also learn how to add more canvas (more blank space) around your photos. You'd add canvas to make room for captions below your image, for instance, or when you want to combine two photos.

To get started, open a photo you want to resize and go to Image → Resize → Image Size (Figure 3-17).

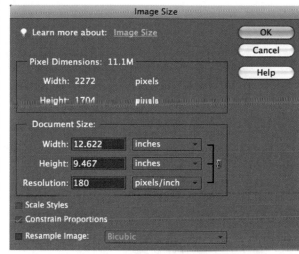

Figure 3-17:
*The Image Size dialog box gives you two different
ways to change the size of your photo. Use the Pixel
Dimensions section when preparing a photo for
onscreen viewing. (The number immediately to the
right of Pixel Dimensions—here, 11.1 M—indicates the
current size of your file in megabytes [as in this
example] or kilobytes.) Before you can make any
changes here, you must turn on Resample Image in
the bottom part of the dialog box, since changing
pixel dimensions always involves resampling (see
page 88). Use the Document Size section to prepare
photos for printing.*

Resizing Images for Email and the Web

It's important to learn how to size your photos so that they show up clear and easy
to view onscreen. Have you ever gotten an emailed photo that was so huge you
could see only a tiny bit of it on your monitor at once? That happens when someone sends an image that isn't optimized for viewing on a monitor. It's very easy to
avoid that problem—once you know how to correctly size your photos for
onscreen viewing.

If you look at the Image Size dialog box, you see two main sections. The top one
says Pixel Dimensions and below that is Document Size. You'll use the Pixel
Dimensions settings when you know your image is only going to be viewed
onscreen. (Document Size is for printing.)

A monitor is concerned only with the size of a photo as measured in pixels, known
as the *pixel dimensions*. On a monitor, a pixel is always the same size (unlike a
printer, which can change the size of the pixels it prints out). Your monitor doesn't
know anything about pixels per inch (ppi), and it can't change the way it displays a
photo even if you change the photo's ppi settings, as shown in Figure 3-18. (It's
true that graphics programs like Elements can change the size of your onscreen
view by, say, zooming in, but most programs, like your Web browser, can't.)

All you have to decide is how many pixels long and how many pixels wide you
want your photo to be. You control those measurements in the Pixel Dimensions
section of the Image Size dialog box.

What dimensions should you use? That depends a little on who's going to be seeing
your photos, but as a general rule, small monitors today are usually 1,024×768 pixels.
Some monitors, like the largest Dell and Apple models, have many more pixels
than that, of course. Still, if you want to be sure that people who see your photo
won't have to scroll, a good rule of thumb is to choose no more than 650 pixels for

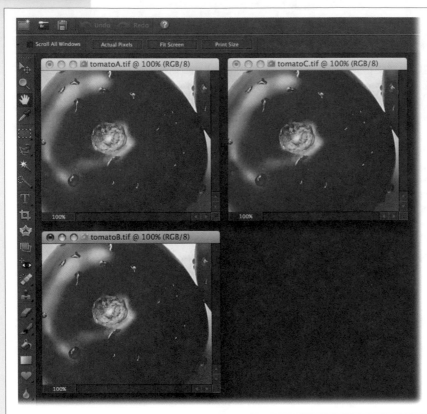

Figure 3-18:
This screenshot demonstrates that your monitor doesn't care about the ppi settings you enter. One of these photos was saved at 100 ppi, the second at 300 ppi, and the last at 1000 ppi. Can you tell which is which? Nope. They all look exactly the same on your monitor because they all have exactly the same pixel dimensions, which is the only resolution setting your monitor understands.

the longer side of your photo, whether that's the width or the height. If you want people to be able to see more than one image at a time, you may want to make your photos even smaller. Also, some people set their monitors to display only 600× 800 pixels, so you may want to make even smaller images to send to them.

> **TIP** To get the most accurate look at how large your photo truly displays on a monitor, go to View → Actual Pixels.

Also, although a photo is always the same pixel dimensions, you really can't control the exact inch dimensions at which those pixels display on other people's monitors. A pixel is always the same size on any given monitor (as long as you don't change the monitor's screen resolution), but different monitors have different sized pixels these days. Figure 3-19 may help you grasp this concept.

> **NOTE** In the following sections, you'll be learning what to do when you want to *reduce* the size of an image. It's much easier to get good results making a photo smaller than larger. Elements does let you *increase* the size of your image, using a technique called upsampling (explained on page 88), but you may get mediocre results. The section on resampling (page 88) explains why.

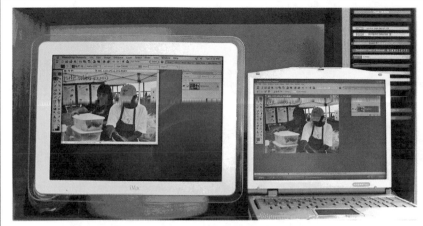

Figure 3-19:
*Both these computers
have a screen resolution
of 1,024 × 768 pixels, and
the photo they're
displaying takes up
exactly the same
percentage of each
screen. But the picture on
the left is larger because
the monitor is physically
larger—in other words,
the pixels are displayed
larger.*

To resize your photos, start by making very sure you're not resizing your original.
You're going to be shedding pixels that you can't get back again, so resize your
photos using a copy (File → Duplicate).

1. **Call up the Image Size dialog box.**

   Go to Image → Resize → Image Size.

2. **In the Pixel Dimensions area, enter the dimension you want for the longer side
   of your photo.**

   Usually you'd want 650 pixels or less. Be sure that pixels show as the unit of
   measurement. You just need to enter the number for one side. Elements automatically figures the dimension for the other side as long as Constrain Proportions
   is turned on down near the bottom of the dialog box. (You need to turn on
   Resample Image before you can change the pixel dimensions.)

3. **Check the settings at the bottom of the dialog box.**

   Constrain Proportions should be turned on. (Scale Styles doesn't matter. Leave
   it off.) Resample Image should be turned on. (*Resampling* means changing the
   number of pixels in your image.) The Resample Image menu lists the different
   resampling methods. Adobe recommends choosing Bicubic Sharper when
   you're making an image smaller, but you may want to experiment with the
   other menu options if you don't like the results you get when using Bicubic
   Sharper.

4. **Click OK.**

   Your photo is resized, although you may not immediately see a difference
   onscreen. Go to View → Actual Pixels, before and after you resize, and you can
   see the difference. Save your resized photo to make your size change permanent.

Sometimes Elements resizes an image automatically—for example, when you use email attachments (see page 448). But the method described here gives you more control than letting Elements make your decisions for you.

> **TIP**   If you're concerned about file size, use "Save for Web" (see page 442), which helps you create smaller files.

Resizing for Printing

If you want great prints, you need to think about your photo's resolution quite differently than you do for images that you're emailing. For printing, as a general rule, the more pixels your photo has, the better. That's the reason camera manufacturers keep packing more megapixels into their new models—the more pixels you have, the larger you can print your photo and still have it look terrific.

> **TIP**   Even before you take your photos, you can do a lot toward making them print well if you always choose the largest size and the highest quality setting on your camera (typically Extra Fine, Superfine, or Fine).

When you print your photo, you need to think about two things: the size of your photo in inches (or whatever your preferred unit of measurement is) and the resolution in pixels per inch (ppi). Those settings work together to control the quality of your print.

Your printer is a virtuoso that plays your pixels like an accordion. It can squeeze the pixels together and make them smaller, or spread the pixels out and make them larger. Generally speaking, the denser the pixels (the higher the ppi), the higher the resolution of your photo, and the better it looks.

If you don't have enough pixels in your photo, the print will appear pixelated—very jagged and blurry looking. The goal is to have enough pixels in your photo so that they'll be packed fairly densely—ideally at about 300 ppi.

You usually don't get a visibly better result if you go over 300 ppi, though, just a larger file size. And depending on your tastes, you may be content with your results at a lower ppi. For instance, some Canon camera photos come into Elements at 180 ppi, and may be happy with how they print. But 200 ppi is usually considered about the lowest density for an acceptable print. Figure 3-20 demonstrates why it's so important to have a high ppi setting.

To set the size of an image for printing:

1. **Call up the Image Size dialog box.**

   Go to Image → Resize → Image Size.

2. **Check the resolution of your image.**

   You want to look at the Document Size section of the dialog box (see Figure 3-17). Start by checking the ppi setting. If it's too low, like 72 ppi, go to

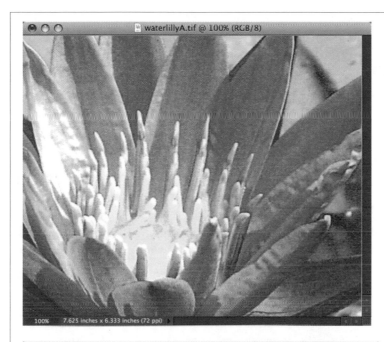

100%   7.625 inches x 6.333 inches (72 ppi) ▶

Figure 3-20:
Different resolution settings can dramatically alter the quality of a printout.

Top: A photo with a resolution of 300 ppi.

Bottom: The same photo with resolution set to 72 ppi. Too few pixels stretched too far causes this kind of blocky, blurry printing. When you can see the individual pixels, a photo is said to be pixelated.

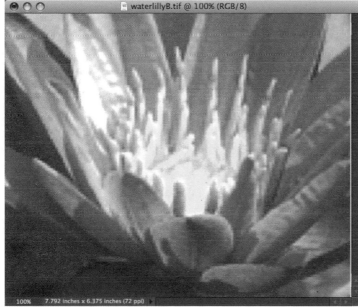

100%   7.792 inches x 6.375 inches (72 ppi) ▶

the bottom of the dialog box and turn off Resample Image. Then enter the ppi you want in the Document Size area. The dimensions should become smaller to reflect the greater density of the pixels. If they don't, click OK, and open the dialog box again.

3. **Check the physical size of your photo.**

   Look at the numbers in the Document Size area. Are they what you want? If so, you're all done. Click OK.

4. **If your size numbers aren't right, resize your photo.**

   If the proportions of your image aren't what you want, crop the photo using one of the methods described earlier, and then come back to the Image Size dialog box. Don't try to reshape an image using the Image Size dialog box.

   Once you've returned to the Image Size dialog box, go to the bottom of the window and turn on Resample Image. Choose Bicubic Smoother in the menu. (This menu choice is Adobe's recommendation, but you may find that you prefer one of the other resampling choices.)

   Now enter the size you want for the width or height. Make sure that Constrain Proportions is turned on. If it is, Elements will calculate the other dimension for you. (Scale Styles doesn't matter. Leave it off.)

5. **Click OK.**

   Your photo is resized and ready for printing.

Resampling

Resampling is an image editing term for changing the number of pixels in an image. When you resample, your results are permanent, so you want to avoid resampling an original photo if you can help it. As a rule, it's easier to get good results when you *downsample*—that is, make your photo smaller—than when you *upsample*, which you do when you want to make your photo larger.

When you upsample, you're *adding* pixels to your image. Elements has to get them from somewhere, so it makes them up. Elements is pretty good at this, but these pixels are never as good as the pixels that were in your photo to begin with, as you can see from Figure 3-21. You can download the figure (russian_box.jpg) from the "Missing CD" page at *www.missingmanuals.com* if you'd like to try this out for yourself. Zoom in very closely so you can see the pixels.

When you enlarge an image to more than 100 percent of its original size, you'll definitely lose some of the original quality. So, for example, if you try to stretch a photo that's 3" wide at 180 ppi to an 8" × 10" print, don't be surprised if you don't like the results.

Elements offers you several resampling methods, and they do a very good job when you find the right one for your situation. You select them in the Resample Image menu in the Image Size dialog box. Adobe recommends choosing Bicubic Smoother when you're upsampling (enlarging) your images and Bicubic Sharper when you're downsampling (reducing) your photos, but you may prefer one of the others. It's worth experimenting with them all to see which you like.

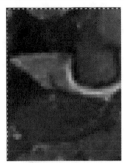  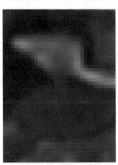

Figure 3-21:
Here's a close-up look at what you're doing to your photo when you resample it.

The photo as it came from the camera.

Downsampled to 72 ppi.

Upsampled back to the original resolution. See how soft the pixels look compared to the original?

Adding Canvas

Just like the works of Monet and Matisse, your photos appear in Elements on a digital "canvas." Sometimes you may want to add more canvas to make room for text or if you're combining photos into a collage.

To make your canvas larger, go to Image → Resize → Canvas Size. You can change the size of your canvas using a variety of measurements. If you don't know exactly how much more canvas you want, choose Percent. Then you can guesstimate that you want, say, 2 percent more canvas or 50 percent more. Figure 3-22 shows how to get your photo into the right place on the new canvas.

> **NOTE** Changing the size of your canvas doesn't change the size of your picture any more than pasting a postcard onto a full-size sheet of paper changes the size of the postcard. In both cases, all you get is more empty space around your picture.

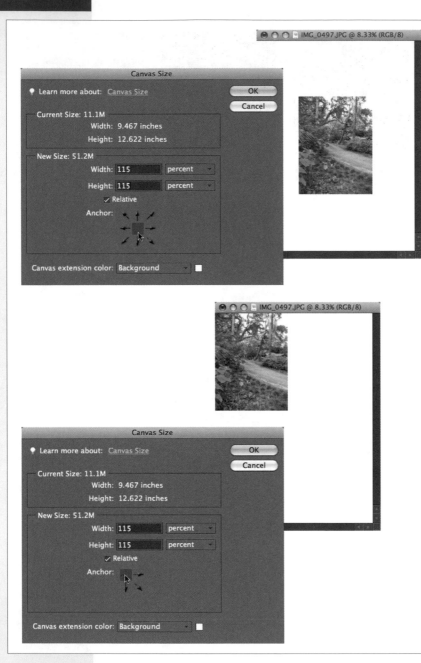

Figure 3-22:
The Canvas Size dialog box isn't as complicated as it looks. The strange little Anchor grid with arrows pointing everywhere lets you decide exactly where to add new canvas to your image. The Anchor box represents your photo's current position, and the arrows surrounding it show where Elements will add the new canvas. By clicking in any of the surrounding boxes, you tell Elements where to position your photo on the newly sized canvas. In the top pair of images, the new canvas has been added equally around all sides of the existing image. In the bottom pair, the new canvas has been added below and to the right of the existing image.

Part Two:
Elemental Elements

2

The Quick Fix

With Elements' Quick Fix tools, you can dramatically improve the appearance of a photo with just a click or two. The Quick Fix window gathers easy-to-use tools that help adjust the brightness and color of your photos and make them look sharper. You don't even need to understand much about what you're doing. You just need to click a button or slide a pointer, and then decide whether you like how it looks.

If, on the other hand, you *do* know what you're doing, you may still find yourself using the Quick Fix window for things like shadows and highlights because the Quick Fix gives you a before-and-after view as you work. Also, the Temperature and Tint sliders can come in very handy for advanced color tweaking, like finessing the overall color of your otherwise finished photo. You even get two tools—the Selection brush and the Quick Selection tool—to help make changes to only a certain area of your photo.

In this chapter, you'll learn how to use all of the Quick Fix tools. You'll also learn about what order to apply the fixes so you get the most out of these tools. If you have a newish digital camera, you may find that Quick Fix gives you all the tools you need to take your photos from pretty darn good (the way they came out of the camera) to dazzling.

> **NOTE** If an entire chapter on Quick Fix is frustratingly slow, you can start off by trying out the ultra-fast Auto Smart Fix—a quick-fix tool for the truly impatient. Page 99 tells you everything you need to know. Also, Guided Edit may give you enough help to accomplish what you want to do (page 29).

The Quick Fix Window

Getting to the Quick Fix window is easy. Just click the Edit tab → Quick button. The Quick Fix window looks like a stripped-down version of the Full Edit window (see Figure 4-1).

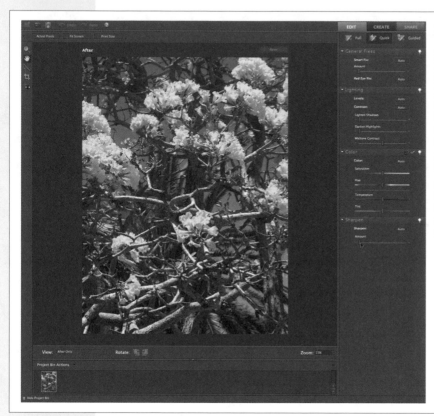

Figure 4-1:
The Quick Fix window. If you have several photos open when you launch the Quick Fix window, you can use the Project bin (page 23) at the bottom of the window to choose the one you want to edit. Just double-click any of the image thumbnails and that photo becomes the active image—the one you see in the Quick Fix preview area in the center of your screen.

NOTE   There's no close button for your photos in the Quick Fix window. To close an image, just use the standard Mac keyboard shortcut (⌘+W) or switch back to Full Edit.

Your tools are neatly arranged on both sides of your image: On the left side, there's a five-item Toolbox; on the right side, there's a collection of quick-edit palettes stored inside the Control Panel. First, you'll take a quick look at the tools Quick Fix provides you with. Then, later in the chapter, you'll learn how to actually use them.

NOTE   If you need extra help, check out Guided Edit (page 29), which walks you step by step through a lot of basic editing projects.

The Quick Fix Toolbox

The Toolbox holds an easy-to-navigate subset of the Full Edit window's larger tool collection. All the tools work the same way in both modes, and you can also use the same keystrokes to switch tools here. From top to bottom, the Quick Fix Toolbox holds:

- **The Zoom tool** lets you telescope in and out on your image so that you can get a good close look at details or pull back to see the whole photo. (See page 79 for more on how the Zoom tool works.) You can also zoom by using the Zoom pull-down menu in the lower-right corner of the image preview area.

- **The Hand tool** helps move your photo around in the image window—just like grabbing it and moving it with your own hand. You can read more about the Hand tool on page 81.

- **The Quick Selection tool** lets you apply Quick Fix commands to select portions of your image. The regular Elements Selection brush is also available in Quick Fix. To get to the Selection brush, in the Toolbox, just click the Quick Selection brush icon and choose the Selection brush from the menu that appears. The difference between the two tools is that the Selection brush lets you paint a selection exactly where you want it (or mask out part of your photo to keep it from getting changed), while the Quick Selection tool makes Elements figure out the boundaries of your selection based on your much less precise marks on the image. The Quick Selection tool is much more automatic than the regular Selection brush. You can read more about these brushes beginning on page 116.

  To get the most out of both these tools, you need to understand the concept of selections. Chapter 5 tells you everything you need to know, including the details of using these brushes.

- **The Crop tool** lets you change the size and shape of your photo, by cutting off the areas you *don't* want (see page 72).

- **The Red Eye tool** makes it a snap to fix those horrible red eyes in flash photos (page 97).

  NOTE If your photo needs straightening (page 67), you need to do that in Full Edit before bringing it into the Quick Fix window, since the Quick Fix Toolbox doesn't include the Straighten tool.

The Quick Fix Control Panel

When you switch to Quick Fix, the Task panel presents you with the Quick Fix Control Panel. The Control Panel is where you make the majority of your adjustments. Elements helpfully arranges everything into four palettes—General Fixes, Lighting, Color, and Sharpen—listed in the order you'll typically use them. In most cases, it makes sense to start at the top and work your way down until you get the results you want. (See page 106 for more suggestions on what order to work in.)

The Control Panel always fills the right side of the Quick Fix screen. There's no way to hide it, and you can't drag the palettes out of the Control Panel as you can in Standard Edit mode. But you can expand and collapse them, as explained in Figure 4-2.

NOTE If you go into Quick Fix mode *before* you open a photo, you won't see the pointers in the sliders, just empty tracks. Don't worry—they'll automatically appear as soon as you open a photo and give them something to work on.

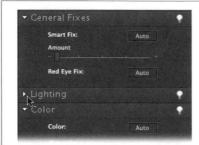

Figure 4-2:
Clicking any of these flippy triangles collapses or expands that section of the Control Panel. If you hardly ever use the tools in the Lighting section, for instance, you can collapse it so it scoots out of the way. If you have a small screen so that that the Sharpen section at the bottom is usually collapsed, there's no need to collapse another section before expanding it—the Color section automatically collapses to make room for Sharpen when you open it.

Different Views: After vs. Before and After

When you open an image in Quick Fix, your picture first appears by itself in the main window with the word "After" above it. Elements keeps the Before view—your original photo—tucked away, out of sight. But you can pick from three other different layouts, which you can choose at any time: Before Only, Before and After—Horizontal, and Before and After—Vertical. The Before and After views are especially helpful when you're trying to figure out if you're improving your picture—or not—as shown in Figure 4-3. Switch between views by picking the one you want from the pop-up menu just below your image.

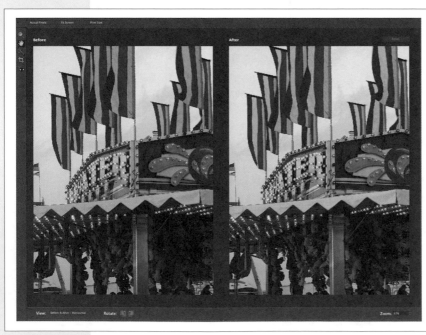

Figure 4-3:
The Before and After view in the Quick Fix window makes it easy to see how you're changing your photo. Here you see Before and After—Horizontal, which displays the views side by side. To see them one above the other, choose Before and After—Vertical. If you want a more detailed view, use the Zoom tool (the magnifying glass icon) to focus on just a portion of your picture.

TIP Quick Fix limits the amount of screen space available for your image. If you want a larger view while you work, click over to Full Edit.

One of the more useful new features in Elements 6 is that you now have access to nearly all the Elements menu items in the Quick Fix window. So if you like having a before-and-after view while you work, you can stay in the Quick Fix while using many of Full Edit's more elaborate commands.

Editing Your Photos

The tools in the Quick Fix window are pretty simple to use. You can try one or all of them—it's up to you. And whenever you're happy with how your photo looks, you can leave Quick Fix and go back to the Full Edit window.

If you want to rotate your photo, you can do so here by clicking the appropriate Rotate button, below the image preview area. (See page 65 for more about rotating photos.) These Rotate buttons only appear when you actually have a photo open in Quick Fix.

NOTE If you click the Quick Fix Reset button, just above your image, you'll return your photo to the way it looked *before* you started working in Quick Fix. This button undoes *all* Quick Fix edits, so don't use it if you want to undo a single action only. For that, just use the regular undo command: Edit → Undo or ⌘+Z.

Fixing Red Eye

Everyone who's ever taken a flash photo has run into the dreaded problem of *red eye*—those glowing, demonic pupils that make your little cherub look like someone out of an Anne Rice novel. Red eye is even more of a problem with digital cameras than with film, but luckily, Elements has a simple and terrific Red Eye tool for fixing it. All you need to do is click the red spots with the Red Eye tool, and your problems are solved.

To use the Quick Fix Red Eye tool:

1. **Open a photo.**

   The Red Eye tool works the same whether you get to it from the Quick Fix Toolbox or the main Toolbox in Full Edit.

2. **Zoom in so you can see where you're clicking.**

   Use the Zoom tool to magnify the eyes. You can also switch to the Hand tool if you need to drag the photo so that the eyes are front and center.

3. **Activate the Red Eye tool.**

   Click the Red Eye icon in the Toolbox or press Y.

4. **Click in the red part of the pupil with the Red Eye tool (see Figure 4-4).**

   That's it. Just one click should fix it. If a single click doesn't fix the problem, you can also try dragging the Red Eye tool over the pupil. Sometimes one method works better than the other. You can also adjust two settings on the Red Eye tool: Darken Amount and Pupil Size, as explained later.

5. **Click in the other eye.**

Repeat the process on the other eye, and you're done.

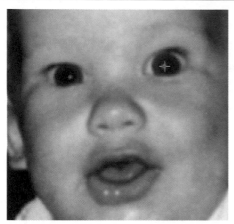

Figure 4-4:
Zoom in when using the Red Eye tool so you get a good look at the pupils. The eye on the left side of the picture has already been fixed. Don't worry if your photo looks so magnified that it loses definition— just make the red area large enough for a bull's-eye. Notice what a good job the Red Eye tool does of keeping the highlights (called catchlights) in the eye that's been treated.

POWER USERS' CLINIC

Another Red Eye Fix

The Red Eye tool does a great job most of the time, but it doesn't always work, and it doesn't work on animals' eyes. Elements gives you a couple of other ways to fix red eye that work in almost any situation. Here's one:

1. Zoom way, way in on the eye. You want to be able to see the individual pixels.

2. Use the Eyedropper tool (page 201) to sample the color from a good area of the eye, or from another photo. Confirm that you've got the color you want by checking the Foreground Color Picker (page 199).

3. Get out the Pencil tool (page 325) and set its size to 1 pixel.

4. Now click the bad or empty pixels of the eye to replace the color with the correct shade. Remember to leave a couple of white pixels for a catchlight.

This solution works even if the eye is *blown out* (that is, all white with no color information left).

If you're a layers fan, you can also fix red eye by selecting the bad area, creating a Hue/Saturation adjustment layer (page 260), and desaturating the red area, but this method doesn't work so well if the eye is blown out.

If you need to adjust how the Red Eye tool works, the Options bar gives you two controls, although 99 percent of the time you can ignore them:

- **Darken Amount.** If the result is too light, increase the percentage in this box.

- **Pupil Size.** Increase or decrease the number here to tell Elements how much area to consider part of a pupil.

NOTE   In Elements 6, you can also fix red eye right in the RAW converter (page 224), if you wish.

Smart Fix

The secret weapon in the Quick Fix window is the Smart Fix command, which automatically adjusts a picture's lighting, color, and contrast, all with one click. You don't have to figure anything out. Elements does it all for you.

You'll find the Smart Fix in the General Fixes palette, and it's about as easy to use as hitting the speed dial button on your phone. Click the Auto Smart Fix button, and if the stars are aligned, your picture will immediately look better. (Figure 4-5 gives you a glimpse of its capabilities. If you want to see for yourself how this fix works, download this photo—finch.jpg—from the "Missing CD" page at *www.missingmanuals.com*.)

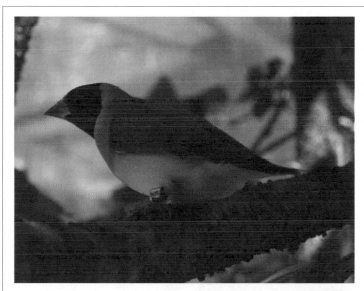

Figure 4-5:
Top: This photo is so dark you may think it's beyond help.

Bottom: The Auto Smart Fix button improved it significantly with just one click. (A click of the Auto Sharpening button, explained later in "Sharpening" [page 105], was added to make it look really spiffy.)

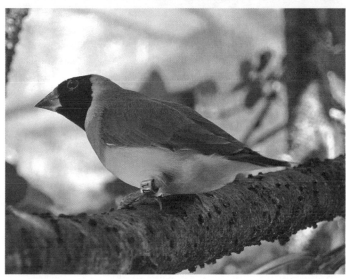

NOTE   You'll find Auto buttons scattered throughout Elements. The program uses them to make a best-guess attempt to implement whatever change the Auto button is next to (Smart Fix, Levels, Contrast, and so on). It never hurts to at least try clicking these Auto buttons; if you don't like what you see, you can always perform the magical undo: Edit → Undo or ⌘+Z.

If you're happy with the Auto Smart Fix button's changes, you can move onto a new photo, or try sharpening your photo a little (see page 105) if the focus appears a little fuzzy. You don't need to do anything to accept the Smart Fix changes. But if you're not ecstatic with your results, take a good look at your picture. If you like what Auto Smart Fix has done, but the effect is too strong or too weak, press ⌘+Z to undo it, and try playing with the Smart Fix Amount slider instead.

The Amount slider does the same thing Auto Smart Fix does, only you control the degree of change. Watch the image as you move the slider to the right. If your computer is slow, there's a certain amount of lag time, so go slowly to give it a chance to catch up. If you happen to overdo it, sometimes it's easier to press the Reset button above your image and start again. Use the checkmark and the cancel button (which appears next to the General Fixes label, as shown in Figure 4-6) to accept or reject your changes.

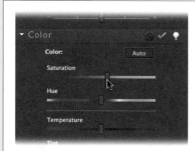

Figure 4-6:
When you move a slider in any of the Quick Fix palettes, the Cancel and Accept buttons appear in the palette you're using. Clicking the cancel symbol undoes the last change you made, while clicking the accept symbol applies the change to your image. If you make multiple slider adjustments, the cancel symbol undoes everything you've done since you clicked Accept. (The little light bulb takes you to the Elements Help Center.)

TIP   Usually you get better results with a lot of little nudges to the Smart Fix slider than with one big sweeping movement.

Incidentally, these are the same Smart Fix commands you see in two places in the Full Edit Enhance Menu: Enhance → Auto Smart Fix (Option+⌘+M), and Enhance → Adjust Smart Fix (⌘+Shift+M).

Sometimes Smart Fix just isn't smart enough to do everything you want, and sometimes it does things you *don't* want. Smart Fix is better with photos that are underexposed than overexposed, for one thing. Fortunately, you still have several other editing choices, covered in the following sections. If you don't like the effect Smart Fix has had, undo it before going on to make other changes.

Adjusting Lighting and Contrast

The Lighting palette lets you make very sophisticated adjustments to the brightness and contrast of your photo. Sometimes problems that you thought stemmed from exposure or even focus may be fixed by these commands.

Levels

If you want to understand how Levels really works, you're in for a long technical ride. On the other hand, if you just want to know what it can do for your photos, the short answer is that it adjusts the brightness of your photo by redistributing the color information; Levels changes (and hopefully fixes!) both brightness and color at the same time.

If you've never used any photo-editing software before, this may sound rather mysterious, but photo-editing pros will tell you that Levels is one of the most powerful commands for fixing and polishing your pictures. To find out if its magic works for you, click the Auto Levels button. Figure 4-7 shows what a big difference it can make. Download this photo (squirrel.jpg) from the "Missing CD" page at *www.missingmanuals.com*, if you'd like to try this out yourself.

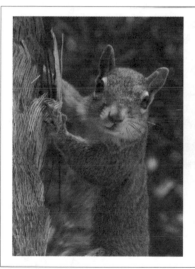 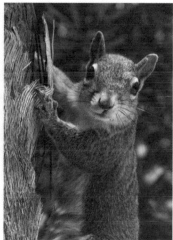

Figure 4-7:
A quick click of the Auto Levels button can make a very dramatic difference.

Left: The original photo of the squirrel isn't bad, and you may not realize how much better the colors could be.

Right: This image shows how much more effective your photo is once Auto Levels has balanced the colors.

What Levels does is very complex. Chapter 7 contains loads more details about what's going on behind the scenes and how you can apply this command much more precisely.

Contrast

The main alternative to Auto Levels in Quick Fix is Auto Contrast. Most people find that their images tend to benefit from one or the other of these options. Contrast adjusts the relative darkness and lightness of your image without changing the

Calibrating Your Monitor

Why do my photos look awful when I open them in Elements?

Do you find that your photos don't look so great on your monitor? Maybe they look muddy or washed out. Or maybe they look great onscreen but terrible when you print them out or post them to a Web site.

If that's the case, you need to calibrate your monitor, as explained on page 184. It's easy to do and it makes a big difference.

Elements is what's known as a *color-managed* program. You can read all about color management on page 183.

Mac OS X has system-wide color management built in via Apple's ColorSync utility. So if you have a problem with your monitor, you'll probably realize it even before you get into Elements. The extra color management options in Elements can be a little more trouble to set up initially, but the truly wonderful results you can get are worth investing a little more time and effort when you're getting started.

color, so if Levels made your colors go all goofy, try adjusting the contrast instead. You activate Contrast the same way you do the Levels tool: just click the Auto button next to its name.

> **NOTE**   After you use Auto Contrast, look closely at the edges of the objects in your photo. If your camera's contrast was already high, you may see a halo or a sharp line around the photo's subject. If you see that line or halo, the contrast is too high and you need to undo Auto Contrast (⌘+Z) and try another fix instead.

Shadows and Highlights

The Shadows and Highlights tools do an amazing job of bringing out the details that are lost in the shadows or bright areas of your photo. Figure 4-8 shows what a difference these tools can make.

The Shadows and Highlights tools are a collection of three sliders, each of which controls a different aspect of your image:

- **Lighten Shadows**. Nudge the slider to the right and you'll see details emerge from murky black shadows.

- **Darken Highlights**. Use this slider to dim the brightness of overexposed areas.

- **Midtone Contrast**. After you've adjusted your photo's shadows and highlights, your photo may look very flat and not have enough contrast between the dark and light areas. This slider helps you bring a more realistic look back to your photo.

> **TIP**   You may think you need only lighten shadows in a photo, but sometimes just a smidgen of Darken Highlights may help, too. Don't be afraid to experiment by using this slider even if you've got a relatively dark photo.

Go easy. Getting overenthusiastic with these sliders can give your photos a very washed-out, flat look.

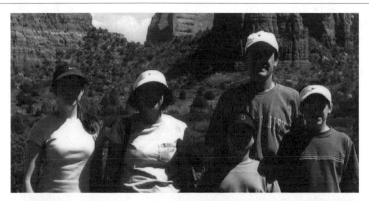

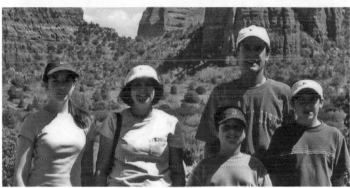

Figure 4-8:
Top: This photo shows a classic vacation picture problem: The day is bright, the scenery's beautiful, but everyone's faces are hidden in the dark shadows cast by their hats.

Bottom: The Shadows and Highlights tools brought back everyone's faces, but now they look a tad orange. Use the color sliders to make them look healthy again.

Color

The Color palette lets you—surprise, surprise—play around with the colors in your image. In many cases, if you've been successful with Auto Levels or Auto Contrast, you won't need to do anything here.

Auto Color

Once again, there's another one-click fix available: Auto Color. Actually, in some ways Auto Color should be up in the Lighting section. Like Levels, it simultaneously adjusts color and brightness, but it looks at different information in your photos to decide what to do with them.

When you're first learning to use Quick Fix, you may want to try all three—Levels, Contrast, and Auto Color—to see which generally works best for your photos. Undo between each change and compare your results. Most people find they like one of the three most of the time.

Auto Color may be just the ticket for your photos, but you may also find that it shifts your colors in strange ways. Give it a click and see what you think. Does your photo look better or worse? If it's worse, just click Reset or ⌘+Z to undo it, and go back to Auto Levels or Auto Contrast. If they all make your colors look a little wrong, or if you want to tweak the colors in your photo, move on to the Color sliders, explained in the next section.

Using the Color sliders

If you want to adjust the colors in your photo without changing the brightness, check out the Color sliders. For example, your digital camera may produce colors that don't quite match what you saw when you took the picture; or you may have scanned an old print that's faded or discolored; or you may just want to change the colors in a photo for the heck of it. If so, the sliders below the Auto Color button are for you.

You get four ways to adjust your colors here:

- **Saturation** controls the intensity of your photo's color. For example, you can turn a color photo to black and white by moving the slider all the way to the left. Move it too far to the right and everything glows with so much color that it looks radioactive.

- **Hue** changes the color from, say, red to blue or green. If you aren't looking for realism, you can have some fun with your photos by really pushing this slider to create funky color changes.

- **Temperature** lets you adjust color from cool (bluish) on the left to warm (orangeish) on the right. Use Temperature for things like toning down the warm glow you see in photos taken in tungsten lighting, or just for fine-tuning your color balance.

- **Tint** adjusts the green/magenta balance of your photo, as shown in Figure 4-9.

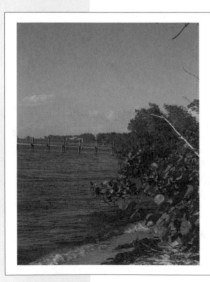 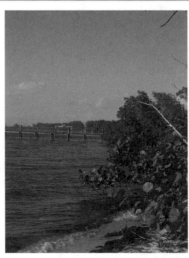

Figure 4-9:
Left: The greenish tint in this photo is a drastic example of a very common problem caused by many digital cameras.

Right: A little adjustment of the Tint slider clears it up in a jiffy. It's not always as obvious as it is here that you need a tint adjustment. If you aren't sure, the sky is often a dead giveaway. Is it robin's egg blue? If the photo's sky is that color and the real sky was just plain blue, tint is what you need.

You probably won't use all these sliders on a single photo, but you can use as many of them as you like. Remember to click the Accept checkmark that appears in the Color palette if you want to accept your changes. Chapter 7 has much more information about how to use the full-blown Editor to really fine-tune your image's color.

> **TIP** If you look at the color of the slider's track, it shows you what happens if you move in that direction. So there's less and less color as you go left in the Saturation track, and more and more to the right. Looking at the tracks can help you know where you want to move the slider.

Sharpening

Now that you've finished your other corrections, it's time to *sharpen* your photo. Sharpening gives the effect of better focus by improving the edge contrast in your photo. Most digital camera photos need some sharpening because the sharpening your camera applies is usually deliberately conservative. Once again, a Quick Fix Auto button is at your service. Give the Auto Sharpen button (located in the Sharpen palette) a try to get things started. Figure 4-10 shows what you can expect.

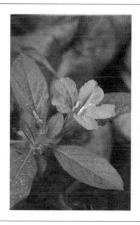 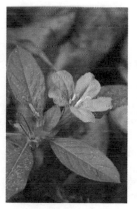 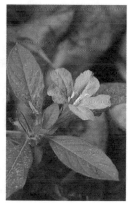

Figure 4-10:
Left: The original image. Like most digital photos, it could stand a little sharpening.

Middle: What you get by clicking the Auto Sharpen button.

Right: The results of using the Sharpen slider to achieve stronger sharpening than Auto was initially willing to perform.

> **TIP** Mac OS X actually has some pretty sophisticated sharpening tools built right in. Preview allows you to apply Luminance Channel sharpening, a complex technique you might like better than the Elements sharpening options. You may want to open a photo in Preview and give it a try to see whether you prefer it to what the Quick Fix can do.

The sad truth is that there really isn't any way to actually improve the focus of a photo once it's taken. Software sharpening just increases the contrast where the program perceives edges, so using it first can have strange effects on other editing tools and their ability to understand your photo.

If you don't like what Auto Sharpening does (you very well may not), you can undo it (press ⌘+Z) and try the slider. If you thought the Auto button overdid things, go very gently with the slider. Changes vary from photo to photo, but usually Auto's results fall at around the 30 to 40 percent mark on the slider.

> **NOTE** If you see funny halos around the outlines of objects in your photos, or strange flaky spots (making your photo look like it has eczema), those are artifacts from too much sharpening.

Always try to view Actual Pixels (View → Actual Pixels) whenever you sharpen because that gives you the clearest idea of what you're actually doing to your picture. If you don't like what the button does, undo it, and then try the slider. Zero sharpening is all the way to the left. Moving to the right increases the amount of sharpening applied to your photo.

As a general rule, you want to sharpen more for photos you plan to print than for images for Web use. You can read lots more about sharpening on page 204.

> **NOTE** If you've used photo-editing programs before, you may be interested to know that the Auto Sharpen button applies Smart Sharpening (page 206) to your photo. The difference is that you don't have any control over the settings, as you would if you applied it from the Enhance menu. But the good news is that if you want it, you can get this control—even from within Quick Fix. Just go to the Enhance Menu and choose Unsharp Mask, or, for even more control, check out the Adjust Sharpness command just below it (page 204).

At this point, all that's left is cropping your photo, if you'd like to reduce its size. Page 71 tells you everything you need to know about cropping.

Quick Fix Suggested Workflow

There are no hard-and-fast rules for what order you need to work in when using the Quick Fix tools. As mentioned earlier, Elements lays out the tools in the Control Panel, from top to bottom, in the order that usually makes sense. But you can pick and choose which tools you want, depending on what you think your photo needs. But if you're the type of person who likes a set plan for fixing photos, here's one order in which to apply the commands:

1. **Rotate your photo (if needed).**

   Use the buttons below the image preview.

2. **Fix red eye (if needed).**

   See page 97.

3. **Crop.**

   If you know you want to crop your photo, now's the time. That way, you get rid of any problem areas before they affect other adjustments. For example, say your photo has a lot of overexposed sky that you want to crop out. If you leave it in, that area may skew the effects of the Lighting and Color tools on your image. So if you already know where you want to crop, do it before making other adjustments for more accurate results.

4. **Try Auto Smart Fix and/or the Smart Fix slider. Undo if necessary.**

   Pretty soon you'll get a good idea of how likely it is that this fix will do a good job on your photos. Some people love it; others think it makes their pictures too grainy.

5. **If Smart Fix wasn't smart enough, work your way down through the other Lighting and Color commands until you like the way your photo looks.**

   Read the sections earlier in this chapter to understand what each command does to your photo.

6. **Sharpen.**

   Try to perform sharpening as your last adjustment because other commands can give you funky results on photos that have already been sharpened.

   TIP   When you're in Quick Fix mode, you can switch back to Full Edit at any point if you want tools or filters not available in Quick Fix. Also, note that there's no Close button in Quick Fix. To close a photo there, use the File menu or ⌘-W.

Adjusting Skin Tones

If you're like most amateur photographers, your most important photos are pictures of people: your family, your friends, or even just fascinating strangers. Elements gives you yet another tool for making fast fixes—one that's designed especially for correcting photos that have people in them. This is the "Adjust Color for Skin Tone" command, available in both the Quick Fix and Full Edit windows.

The name "Adjust Color for Skin Tone" may be a bit confusing. What this command actually does is adjust your *entire* image based on the skin tone of someone in the photo. The idea behind "Adjust Color for Skin Tone" is that you may well be much more interested in the way the people in your photos look than in how the background looks. This command gives the highest priority to creating good skin color. It's an automatic fix, but there's a dialog box where you can tweak the results once you've previewed Elements' suggested adjustments. To use the "Adjust Color for Skin Tone" command:

1. **Call up the "Adjust Color for Skin Tone" dialog box.**

   In either Quick Fix or Full Edit, go to Enhance → Adjust Color → "Adjust Color for Skin Tone". The dialog box shown in Figure 4-11 appears. You may need to move it out of the way of your photo so you can see what's happening.

2. **Show Elements an area of skin to sample for calculating the color adjustments.**

   Once the dialog box appears, your cursor turns to an eyedropper. Just find a portion of your photo where your subject's skin has relatively good color, and click it.

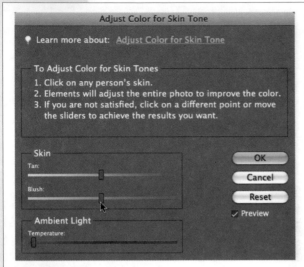

Adjust Color for Skin Tone

💡 Learn more about: Adjust Color for Skin Tone

To Adjust Color for Skin Tones
1. Click on any person's skin.
2. Elements will adjust the entire photo to improve the color.
3. If you are not satisfied, click on a different point or move the sliders to achieve the results you want.

Skin
Tan:
Blush:

OK
Cancel
Reset
☑ Preview

Ambient Light
Temperature:

Figure 4-11:
When this dialog box appears, your cursor turns into a little eyedropper when you move it over your photo. Just click the best-looking area of skin you can find. After Elements adjusts the photo based on your click, you can use the sliders to fine-tune the results. Clicking different spots gives different results, so you may want to experiment by clicking different places.

3. **Tweak the results.**

   Elements is often a bit overenthusiastic in its adjustments. Use the sliders in the dialog box to get a more pleasing, realistic color. The Ambient Light slider works just like the Temperature slider in the Quick Fix control panel (page 104). Blush increases the rosiness of the skin as you move the slider to the right and decreases it to the left. Tan increases or decreases the browns and oranges in the skin tones. You may get swell results with your first click, or you may have to use all the sliders to get a truly realistic result. It all depends on the photo.

   You can preview the changes right in your photo as you work. If you mess up and want to start again, click Reset. If you decide you'd rather be using another tool instead, click Cancel.

   TIP The "Adjust Color for Skin Tone" sliders are like the Quick Fix sliders in that you can get an idea of which way to move them by looking at the colors in the slider tracks in the dialog box.

4. **When you like what you see, click OK.**

   Elements applies your changes. If you want to undo them, press ⌘+Z.

"Adjust Color for Skin Tone" seems to work best on fair skin, and not so well on darker skin tones. And it's most suited for making fairly subtle adjustments, so you may have to reduce the amount of change from what Elements first did.

Also, notice that not only the skin tones are changing. Elements is adjusting *all* the colors in the photo in sync with the skin tones (Figure 4-12). Sometimes you may find you've acquired quite a color cast by the time you've got the skin just right (see page 195). If this bothers you, try a different tool. On the other hand, you can create some very nice late afternoon light effects with this command.

While "Adjust Color for Skin Tone" is really meant as a kind of alternative fast fix, you may find it's most useful for making small final adjustments to photos you've already edited using other tools.

> **TIP**   If you understand layers (explained in Chapter 6), you may want to make a duplicate layer and apply this command to your duplicate. Then you can adjust the intensity of the result by adjusting the layer's opacity (see page 155).

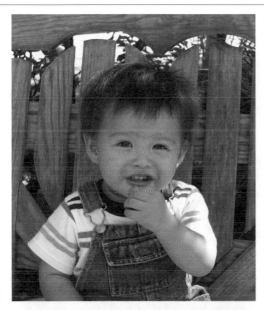

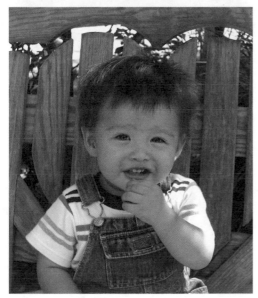

Figure 4-12:
Top: This photo shows a slight greenish cast, giving the little boy a somewhat unappealing skin tone.

Bottom: "Adjust Color for Skin Tone" is able to warm up his skin tones, and it even removes the greenish tinge to the wood of the bench he's sitting on.

Making Selections

One of Elements' most impressive talents is its ability to let you *select* part of your image and make changes only to that area. Selecting something tells Elements, "Hey, *this* is what I want to work on. Just let me work on this part of my picture and don't touch the rest of it." You can select your entire image or any part of it.

By using selections, you can fine-tune your images in very sophisticated ways. You could change the color of just one rose in a whole bouquet, for instance, or change your nephew's festive purple hair color back to something his grandparents would appreciate. Graphics pros will tell you that good selections make the difference between shoddy amateurish work and a slick professional job.

In the past, getting good selections was a time-consuming process. But Elements 6 gives you two great new tools—Adobe sent them over from the full-featured Photoshop—that make the process much simpler. The handy Quick Selection tool (page 116) makes most selections as simple as drawing a line. (If you've used Elements before, you'll see it's a greatly simplified and enhanced version of the Magic Selection brush, and it works much better.) And the Refine Edge command (page 119) gives you far more control over how well your selection blends into another image.

Elements offers you a whole bunch of different selection tools to work with. You can draw a rectangular or a circular selection with the Marquee tools, for instance, or paint a selection on your photo with the Selection brush. When you're looking to pluck a particular object (a beautiful flower, for instance) from a photo, the Magic Extractor works wonders. For most jobs, there's no right or wrong tool; with experience you may find you tend to prefer working with certain tools more than others. Often you'll use more than one tool to create a perfect selection. Once you've read this chapter you'll understand all the different selection tools and how to use each one.

TIP It's much easier to select an object that's been photographed against a plain background. So, if you know you're going to want to select a bicycle, for example, shoot it in front of a blank wall rather than, say, a hedge.

Selecting Everything

Sometimes the only thing you want to do is select your entire photo. For instance, if you want to copy and paste your whole photo, you need to select all of it. Elements gives you some useful commands to help you make basic selections in a snap:

- **Select All** (Select → All or ⌘+A) tells Elements to select your entire image. You'll see the "marching ants" (shown around the outline of the bell in Figure 5-1) around the outer edge of your entire picture.

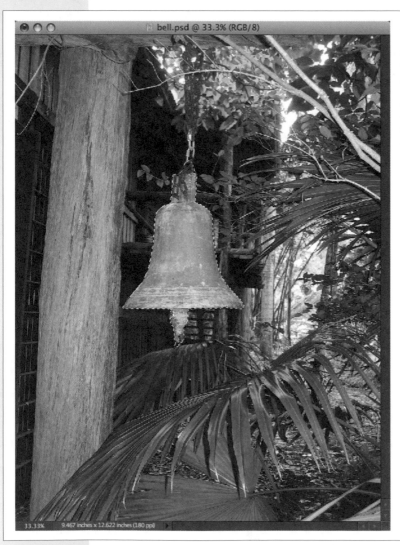

Figure 5-1:
The popular name for these dotted lines is "marching ants" because they march around your selections to show you where the edges lie. When you see the ants, your selection is active, meaning what you do next happens only to the selected area.

If you want to copy your image into another picture or program, performing a Select All is the fastest way to select the entire image. If your photo contains layers, which you'll learn about in Chapter 6, you may not be able to get everything you want with the Select All shortcut. In that case, the section about merging layers on page 166 explains what to do.

TIP   If you're planning on copying an image to another program, like Microsoft Word or Pages, make sure you've got Export Clipboard turned on in Photoshop Elements → Preferences → General.

- **Deselect Everything** (Select → Deselect, Escape, or ⌘+D) removes any current selection. Remember the keystroke combination because it's one you'll probably use over and over again in Elements.

- **Reselect** (Select → Reselect or Shift+⌘+D) tells Elements to reactivate the selection you just canceled. Use Reselect if you realize you still need a selection you just got rid of. Or you can just press ⌘+Z to back up a step.

- **Hide a Selection** (⌘+H) keeps your selection active while hiding its outline. Sometimes the marching ants around a selection make it hard to see what you're doing, or they can be distracting. To see the ants again, press ⌘+H a second time.

NOTE   Sometimes it's easy to forget you have a selection. When a tool acts goofy or won't do anything, start your troubleshooting by pressing ⌘+H to be sure you don't have a hidden selection you forgot about.

If you want to quickly select an irregular area, try the Quick Selection tool, explained on page 116.

Selecting Rectangular and Elliptical Areas

Selecting your whole picture is all well and good, but many times your reason for making a selection is precisely because you *don't* want to make changes to the whole image. How do you select just part of the picture?

Well, the easiest way is to use the Marquee tools. You already met the Rectangular Marquee tool back in Chapter 3, in the section on cropping (page 74). If you want to select a block of your image or a circle or an oval from it, the Marquee tools are the way to go. As the winners of "Most Frequently Used Selection Tools," they get top spot in the Selection area of the toolbox. You can modify how they work, like telling them to create a square instead of a rectangle, as explained in Figure 5-2.

To use the Marquee tools to make a selection:

1. **Press M or click the Marquee tool's icon in the Toolbox to activate it.**

    The Marquee tool is the little dotted square right below the Eyedropper icon. (Or it may appear as a little dotted oval, if you used the Elliptical Marquee tool last.)

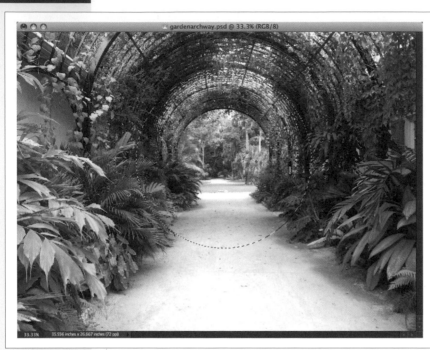

Figure 5-2:
To make a perfectly circular or square selection, hold down the Shift key while you drag. You can reposition your selection after it's drawn by using the arrow keys, or by dragging it.

2. **Choose the Shape you want to draw: rectangle or ellipse.**

   In the Toolbox pop-out menu for the Marquee tools, choose the rectangle or the ellipse to set the shape.

3. **Choose a feather value if you want one.**

   Feathering makes the edges of your selection softer or fuzzier for better blending. See the box on page 125 for a look at how feathering (and anti-aliasing) work.

4. **Drag in your image to make your selection.**

   Wherever you initially place your mouse becomes one of the corners of your rectangular selection or a point just beyond the outer edge of your ellipse (you can draw perfectly circular or square selections, as shown in Figure 5-2). The selection outline expands as you drag your mouse.

   If you make a mistake, just press the Escape key. You can also press either ⌘+D to get rid of all current selections, or ⌘+Z to remove the most recent selection.

The mode choices in the Options bar give you three ways to control the size of your selection: Normal lets you manually control the size of your selection; Fixed Aspect Ratio lets you enter proportions in the Width and Height boxes; and Fixed Size lets you enter specific dimensions in these boxes. The Anti-alias checkbox is explained in the box on page 125. Once you've made your selection, you can move the selected area around in the photo by dragging it (see page 76), or you can use the arrow keys to nudge your selection in the direction you want to move it. Changing the size of a Marquee selection once you've made it is pretty tricky, and it's far easier to just start over again, but you can add to or subtract from any selection you make in Elements. The next section tells you how.

Paste vs. Paste Into Selection

Newcomers to Elements are often confused by the fact that there are two Paste commands in Elements: Paste and Paste Into Selection. Knowing what each one does will help you avoid problems.

- **Paste**. 99 percent of the time, Paste is the one you want. This command simply places your copied object wherever you paste it. Once you've pasted your object, you can move whatever you've pasted by moving the selected area.

- **Paste Into Selection**. This is a special command for pasting a selection into *another* selection. Your pasted object appears only *within* the bounds of the selection you're pasting into.

When you use Paste Into Selection, what you paste can still be moved around, but it won't be visible anywhere outside the edges of the selection you're pasting into. Paste Into Selection is very handy if you want to do something like putting a beautiful mountain view outside your window. Select the window, copy the mountain (⌘+C), and then use Paste Into Selection to add the view. You can maneuver the mountain photo around till it's properly centered. And if you move it outside the boundary of your window selection, it just disappears. Once you deselect, your material is permanently in place; you can't move it again.

Selecting Irregularly Sized Areas

It would be nice if you could always get away with making simple rectangular or elliptical selections, but is life really ever that neat? You aren't always going to want to select a geometric-shaped chunk of your image. If you want to change the color of one fish in your aquarium picture, selecting a rectangle or square isn't going to cut it.

Thankfully, Elements gives you other tools that make it easy for you to make very precise selections—no matter their size or shape. In this section, you'll learn how to use the rest of the selection tools. But first you need to understand the basic controls that they (almost) all share.

Controlling the Selection Tools

If you're the kind of person who never makes a mistake and you also never change your mind, you can skip this section. If, on the other hand, you're human, you need to know about the mysterious little squares you see in the Options bar when the selection tools are active (Figure 5-3).

These selection squares don't look like much, but they tell the selection tools how to do their job: whether to start a new selection with each click, to add to what you've already got, or to remove things from your selection. They're available for

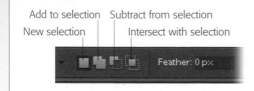

Add to selection   Subtract from selection

New selection   Intersect with selection

Feather: 0 px

Figure 5-3:
These cryptic squares can save you hours of time once you understand how to use them to tell the selection tools how to behave.

all the selection tools except the Selection brush and the Quick Selection tool, which have their own sets of options. From left to right, here's what they do:

• **New Selection** is the standard selection mode that you'll probably use most of the time. When you click this button and start a new selection, your previous selection disappears.

• **Add to Selection** tells Elements to add what you select next to what you've already selected. Unless you have an incredibly steady mouse hand, this option is a godsend because it's not easy to get a perfect selection on the first try. (Holding down the Shift key while you use any selection tool is another way to add to a selection.)

• **Subtract from Selection** removes what you select next from any existing selection. (By holding down Option while selecting the area you want to remove, you can accomplish the same thing.)

• **Intersect with Selection** is a bit confusing. It lets you take a selected area, make a new selection, and wind up with only the area where the selections overlap, as shown in Figure 5-4. (The keyboard equivalent is Option+Shift.)

Figure 5-4:
"Intersect with Selection" lets you take two separate selections and select only the area where they intersect. If you have an existing selection, when you select again your new selection includes only the overlapping area. Here, the top blue rectangle is the first selection, and the bottom purple square is the second. The light area shows the final selection after you let go of the mouse button.

Selecting with a Brush

Elements also gives you two very special brushes to help you make selections. The Selection brush has been part of this program since Elements 2, so if you've used Elements before, you probably know how useful it is. In Elements 6, you also get the amazing new Quick Selection tool, which makes even the trickiest selections as easy as doodling.

The Quick Selection tool and the Selection brush are grouped together in the Toolbox, and they appear in both Full Edit and Quick Fix because they're so useful. You may well find that with these two tools you rarely need the other selection tools anymore.

It couldn't be easier to use the Quick Selection tool:

1. **Activate the Quick Selection tool.**

   Click it in the Toolbox or press A, and then choose it from the Toolbox pop-out menu. It shares a Toolbox slot with the regular Selection brush. Their icons are very similar, so look carefully—the Quick Selection tool looks more like a wand than a brush and it points up, while the regular Selection brush points down.

2. **Drag in your photo.**

   As you move the mouse, Elements calculates where it thinks the selection edges should be, and the selection outline jumps out to surround that area. It's an amazingly good guesser. There's no need to try to cover the entire area or to go around the edges of your object—Elements does that for you.

   There are a few Options bar controls, which are explained below, but you mostly won't need to think about them, at least not till you make your selection. Then you'll probably want to try Refine Edge (explained in the next section).

3. **Adjust the selection.**

   Odds are that you won't get a totally perfect selection that includes everything you wanted on the first click. To increase the selection area, drag in the direction where you want to add to the selection. A small move, and the selection jumps outward to include the area that Elements thinks you want, as shown in Figure 5-5.

   To remove an area from the selection, hold Option and drag or click in the area you don't want.

   Once you're happy with your selection, that's all, unless you want to tweak the edges using Refine Edge (see the next section)—and you probably do.

This new tool in your Toolbox is something like the Magic Selection brush that appeared in the past couple of versions of Elements, except that it's much, much smarter. It's not nearly as likely to get befuddled by complex backgrounds, for example.

The Quick Selection tool does have a few Options bar choices, but you really don't need most of them:

- **Brush.** You can make all kinds of adjustments to your brush by clicking this pull-down menu, including many of the Brush Dynamics palette options (see page 319). However, 99 percent of the time you don't even need to adjust the size of the brush since Elements does all the work for you.

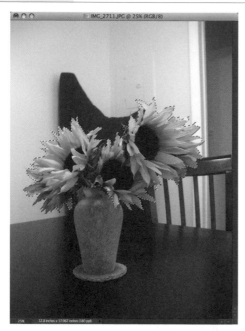

Figure 5-5:
Top: It would be a nuisance to select these sunflowers so that you could use them in a project, because of the many pointy-edged petals. A click and a couple of short drags produced this selection. Notice how well the tool found the edges of the petals.

Bottom: It took only a tiny downward movement of the mouse to tell Elements to select the vase as well. The whole selection took less than 5 seconds to complete.

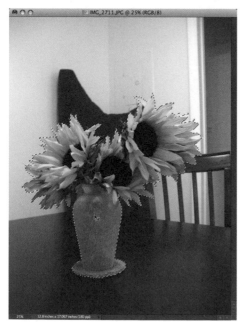

- **New Selection, Add to Selection, Subtract from Selection.** These three brush icons work just like the equivalent selection squares in selection tools (page 115), but you don't need to use them. The Quick Select tool automatically adds to your selection if you drag toward an unselected area. Shift+drag to select multiple areas that are not contiguous. Option+drag to remove areas from your selection.

- **Sample All Layers**. Turn this on, and the Quick Selection tool selects from all the visible layers of your image, rather than just the active layer.

- **Auto-Enhance**. This tells Elements to automatically smooth out the edges of the selection. It's a more automated way to make the same sort of edge adjustments that you make manually with Refine Edge.

- **Refine Edge**. A terrific new feature that also appears for some of the other selection tools in Elements 6. It's explained in the next section.

Refine Edge

This is another great new feature in Elements 6. It allows you to create smooth, feathered, plausible edges on any selection. It appears in the Options bar for some of the tools that allow you to make irregular selections (like Quick Selection), or you can use it on any active selection by going to Select → Refine Edge. To use it, first make a selection, and then:

1. **Call up Refine Edge.**

   If it's not currently available from the Options bar (it's not there when you use the Magnetic Lasso tool, for example), go to Select → Refine Edge to bring it up.

2. **Adjust the edges of your selection.**

   Use the sliders, explained in the list that follows, to tweak and polish the edges of your selection. Use the view buttons to see your selection in different ways, and zoom to 100 percent or more so you can see exactly how you're changing the image.

3. **When you like what you've done, click OK.**

   If you decide not to refine your edges, then click Cancel. To start over, Option+click the Cancel button to turn it into a Reset button. If you play with the sliders and then decide you want to put them back where you started, click Default.

You get three sliders in Refine Edge, and you may need to use only one, or any combination of them to improve your selection. Your choices are:

- **Smooth**. This removes the jagged edges around your selection. Set a value in pixels or use the slider (move it to the right for more smoothing, to the left for less). Be careful: You can go as high as 100 pixels, which is almost certain to be much more smoothing than you need.

- **Feather**. Feathering is explained on page 125.

- **Contract/Expand**. You can use this to adjust the size of your selection. Move the slider to the left to contract the selection, or to the right to expand it outward.

It's easy to refine your selection to the point where it begins to look melted if you get too enthusiastic with Refine Edge, so go in small increments and keep checking your selection.

Adobe makes it simple to check your selection by giving you a choice of views. The buttons at the bottom of the dialog box give you two different ways to see your selection:

- **Standard** shows the regular "marching ants" around your selection.

- **Custom Overlay** shows the red mask overlay you'd get when using the Selection brush in Mask mode (see below). The red area is not part of your selection. Using this view is a good way to check for holes and jagged edges.

    TIP   Double-click the Custom overlay button and you can change the color and opacity of the overlay. You can hide the selection altogether by pressing X. Press X again to bring back the mask or the marching ants, and press F to toggle between Standard and Overlay views.

You also get icons for the Zoom (page 79) and Hand (page 81) tools, so that you can adjust the view to see as much detail as you need.

The Quick Selection tool doesn't work every time for every selection, but it's a wonderful tool that's worth grabbing first for any irregular selection. You can use the Selection brush or one of the other selection tools to clean up afterward, if needed.

The Selection Brush

The Selection brush is one of the greatest tools in Elements. Making complex selections and cleaning up selections are really, really easy with the Selection brush. You can use it on its own or as a complement to the Quick Selection tool, described in the previous section.

With the Selection brush, you simply paint over what you want to select by dragging over that area. You can let go, and each time you drag again, you automatically add to your selection. There's no need to change modes in the Options bar or hold down the Shift key the way you do with the other selection tools.

Not only that, but the Selection brush also has a Mask mode, in which Elements highlights what *isn't* part of your selection. The Mask mode is great for finding tiny spots you may have missed and for checking the accuracy of your selection outline. In Mask mode, anything you paint over gets *masked* out; in other words, it's protected from being selected.

Masking is a little confusing at first, but you'll soon see what a useful tool it is. Figure 5-6 shows the same selection made with and without Mask mode.

The Selection brush is pretty simple to use:

1. **Click the Selection brush in the Toolbox or press A.**

    The Selection brush is located in the Toolbox with the Quick Selection tool. The Selection brush is the brush that looks like it's painting—the brush points down.

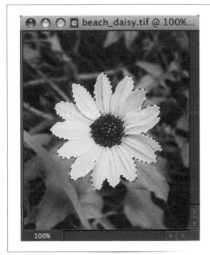
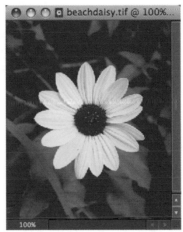

Figure 5-6:
*Left: A selection made with the
brush in Selection mode. It looks
like a completed selection that
you can make using any of the
selection tools.*

*Right: The same selection in
Mask mode. The red covers
everything that's not part of your
selection.*

2. **In the Options bar, choose either Selection mode or Mask mode and the brush
   size you want.**

3. **Drag over the area you want.**

   If you're in Selection mode, the area you drag over becomes part of your selection.
   If you're in Mask mode, the area you drag over is excluded from becoming part of
   your selection.

The Selection brush gives you several choices in the Options bar:

- **Brush.** You can use many different brushes depending on whether you want a
  hard- or soft-edged selection. If you want a different brush, just choose it from
  the menu here. (For more about brushes, see page 314.)

- **Size.** To change the brush size, type a size in the box, click the arrow, and then
  use the slider. Or just press the close bracket key (]) to increase the size (keep
  tapping it until you get the size you want). The open bracket key ([) decreases
  the size of your brush. You can also just put your cursor on the word Size and
  scrub to the left or right to make the brush smaller or larger. (Don't know how
  to scrub? For more on this Elements feature, see page 316.)

  TIP   The bracket key shortcut works with any brush, not just the Selection brush.

- **Mode.** This option is where you tell Elements whether you're creating a selection
  (Selection) or excluding an area from being part of a selection (Mask).

- **Hardness.** This option controls the sharpness of the edge of your selection. See
  Figure 5-7.

Switching between Selection and Mask mode is a good way to see how well you've
done when you finish making your selection. In Mask mode, the parts of your

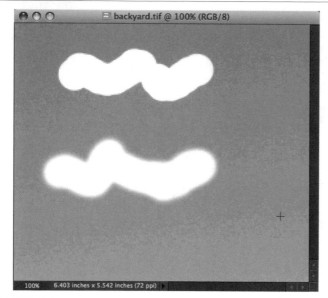

Figure 5-7:
These two Selection brushstrokes show the way the Hardness setting affects the edges of your selection. Here, two different selections were made in the sky. The top selection was made at 100-percent hardness, and the bottom one is at 50 percent. (The selected area was then deleted to show you the outline more clearly.)

image that are *not* part of your selection have a red film over them, so that you can clearly see the selected area.

> **TIP** You don't have to live with the red mask color if you don't want to. To change the color of the mask, click the Overlay Color box in the Options bar while the Selection brush is active and in Mask mode. Use the Color Picker (page 199) to choose a color you prefer. You can also use the Overlay Opacity setting to adjust how well your image shows through the mask.

You can temporarily make the Selection brush do the opposite of what it's been doing by holding down Option while you drag. For example, if you're in Selection mode and you've selected too large an area, Option+drag over the excess to remove it. If you're masking out an area, Option+drag to add an area to the selection. This may sound confusing, but some things are easier to learn just by doing them.

> **TIP** The Selection brush is great for fine-tuning selections made with the other selection tools. Quickly switching to the Selection brush in Mask mode is a great way to check for spots you may have missed—the red makes it really easy to spot them.

The Magic Wand

The Magic Wand is a slightly temperamental—and occasionally highly effective—tool for selecting an irregularly shaped, but similarly colored, area of an image. If you have a big area of a particular color, the Magic Wand can find its edges in one click. It's not actually all that magical: All it does is search for pixels with similar color values. But if it works for you, you may decide it should keep the "magic" in its name because it's a great timesaver when it cooperates, as Figure 5-8 shows.

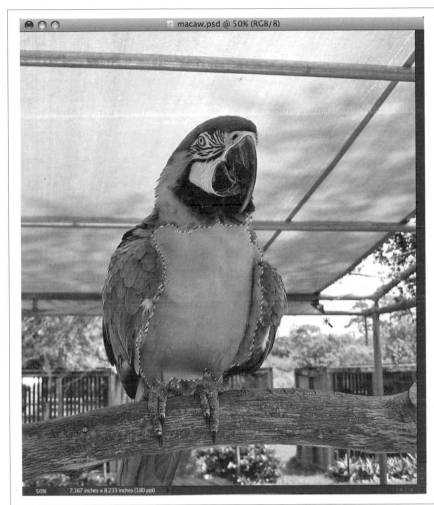

Figure 5-8:
*Just one click with the
Magic Wand created this
selection. If there isn't a
big difference between
the color of the area you
want to select and the
colors of neighboring
areas, the Wand isn't as
effective as it is here.*

Using the Magic Wand is pretty straightforward. You just click anywhere in the
area you want to select. Depending on your *tolerance* setting (explained in the fol
lowing bullet list), you may nail the selection at once, or it may take several clicks
to get everything. If you need to click more than once, remember to hold down
Shift so that each click adds to your selection.

The Magic Wand does its best job when you offer it a good solid block of color
that's clearly defined and doesn't have a lot of different shades in it. But it's frustrating when you try to select colors that have any shading or tonal gradations. You
have to click and click and click. Elements gives you two special Options bar settings
that you can adjust to help the Wand do a better job:

- **Tolerance** adjusts the number of different shades that the tool selects at once. A
  higher tolerance includes more shades (resulting in a larger selection area),

while a lower tolerance gets you fewer shades (and a more precise selection area). If you set the tolerance too high, you'll probably select a lot more of your picture than you want.

• **Contiguous** makes the Magic Wand select only color areas that actually touch each other (see Figure 5-9). It's on by default, but sometimes you can save a lot of time by turning it off.

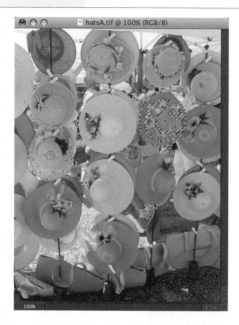

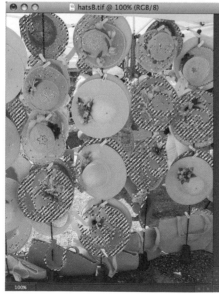

Figure 5-9:
In the top photo, the Contiguous checkbox has been turned on. By turning it off, as in the bottom photo, you can select all the orange hats with just one click. If you want to quickly clean up the selection afterward, use the Selection brush (which is covered on page 120).

UP TO SPEED

Feathering and Anti-Aliasing

If you're old enough to remember what supermarket tabloid covers looked like before there was Photoshop, you probably had many a laugh at the obviously faked photos. Anyone could see where the art department had physically glued a piece cut from one photo onto another picture.

Nowadays, of course, the pictures of Elvis's and Cher's vampire baby from Mars are *much* more believable looking. That's because with Photoshop (and Elements) you can add *anti-aliasing* and *feathering* whenever you're making selections.

Anti-aliasing is a way of smoothing the edges of a digital image so that it's not jagged-looking. When you make selections, the Lasso tools and the Magic Wand let you decide whether to use anti-aliasing. It's best to leave anti-aliasing on unless you have a reason to want a really hard-looking edge on your selection.

Feathering blurs the edges of a selection. When you make a selection that you plan to move to a different photo, a tiny feather can do a lot to make it look like it's always been part of the new photo. The selection tools, except for the Selection brush, let you set a feather value before you use them. Generally a 1- or 2-pixel feather gives your selection a more natural-looking edge without visible blurring.

If you apply a feather value that's too high for the size of your selection, you see a warning that reads "No pixels are more than 50% selected." Reduce the feather number to placate it.

A larger feather gives a soft edge to your photos, as you can see in Figure 5-10.

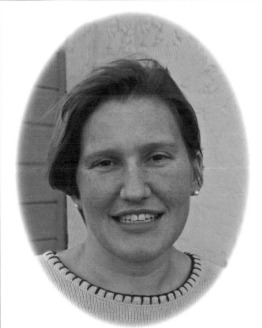

Figure 5-10:
Old-fashioned vignettes like this one are a classic example of where you'd want a fairly large feather. In this figure, the feather is 15 pixels wide. The higher the feather value, the softer the edge effect is.

You also get access to the new Refine Edge command for fixing up the edges of your selection, as explained on page 119.

The big disadvantage to the Magic Wand is that it tends to leave you with un-selected contrasting areas around the edge of your selection that are a bit of a pain to clean up. You may want to try out the Quick Selection tool (page 116) before trying the Magic Wand, especially if you want to select a range of colors. If you put a Magic Wand selection on its own layer (see Chapter 6 to understand how layers work), you can use Refine Edge (page 119) or the Defringe command (page 516) to help clean up the edges.

The Lasso Tools

The Magic Wand is great, but it works well only when your image has clearly defined areas of color. A lot of the time, you'll want to select something from a cluttered background that the Magic Wand just can't cope with. Sometimes you may think the easiest way would be if you could just draw around the object you want to select.

Enter the Lasso tool. There are actually three Lasso tools: the Lasso tool, the Poly-gonal Lasso tool, and the Magnetic Lasso tool. Each tool lets you select an object by tracing around it.

You activate the Lasso tools by clicking their icon in the Toolbox (it's just below the Marquee tool) or by pressing L, and then selecting the particular variation you want in the Toolbox pop-out menu. You then drag around the outline of your object to make your selection. The following sections cover each Lasso tool.

The basic Lasso tool

The theory behind the basic Lasso tool is very simple. Click the tool, and your cursor changes to the lasso shape shown in Figure 5-11. Just click in your photo, and then drag around the outline of what you want to select. When the end of your selection gets back around to join up with the beginning, you've got a selection.

In practice, it's not always so easy to make an accurate selection with the Lasso, especially if you're using a mouse. A graphics tablet is a big advantage when using this tool, since tablets let you draw with a pen-shaped pointer. (There's more about graphics tablets on page 457.) But even if you don't happen to have a graph-ics tablet lying around, you can make all the tools work just fine with your mouse once you get used to their quirks.

It helps to zoom the view way in and to go very slowly when using the Lasso. (See page 77 for more information on changing your view.) Many people use the regular Lasso tool to quickly select an area that roughly surrounds their object, and then go back with the other selection tools, like the Selection brush or the Magnetic Lasso, to clean things up.

The end of the rope controls
where your selection gets drawn

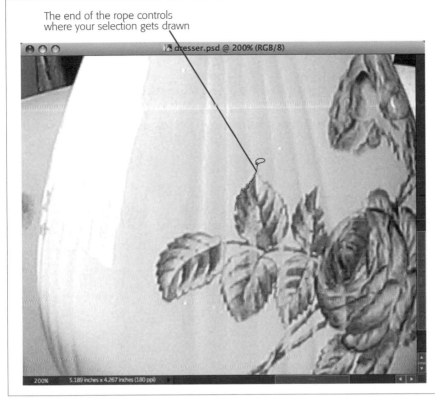

*Figure 5-11:
The end of the rope,
and not the lasso loop,
is the working part of
the basic Lasso tool. If
the cursor's shape
bothers you, you can
change it to crosshairs
by pressing the Caps
Lock key anytime as
you select.*

TIP   If you want to save time when you need to draw a straight line for part of your border, hold down Option and click the points where you want your straight line to start and end. So if you're selecting an arched Palladian window, for instance, once you get around the curve at the top of the window and reach the straight side, press Option and click at the bottom of the side to get the straight part of the side all in one go.

If you want to get out of the Lasso tool before finishing your selection, press Escape. Once you've created a selection, you can use the new Refine Edge command from the Options bar to adjust and feather the edges (see page 119). Press Escape or ⌘+D to get rid of your selection if you decide you don't want it anymore.

The Magnetic Lasso

The Magnetic Lasso is a very handy tool, especially if you were the kind of kid who never could color inside the lines or cut paper chains out neatly. The Magnetic Lasso snaps to the outline of any clearly defined object you're trying to select, so you don't have to follow the edge exactly.

As you might guess, the Magnetic Lasso does its best work on objects with clearly defined edges. You won't get much out of it if your subject is a furry animal, for instance. The Magnetic Lasso also likes a good strong contrast between the object and the background. (You can change the cursor shape with the Caps Lock key, just as with the basic Lasso.)

Click to start a selection. Then move your cursor around the perimeter of what you want to select; click again back where you began to finish your selection. You can also ⌘+click at any point, and the Magnetic Lasso will immediately close up whatever area you've surrounded. You can also adjust how many points the Magnetic Lasso puts down and how sensitive it is to the edge you're tracing, as shown in Figure 5-12.

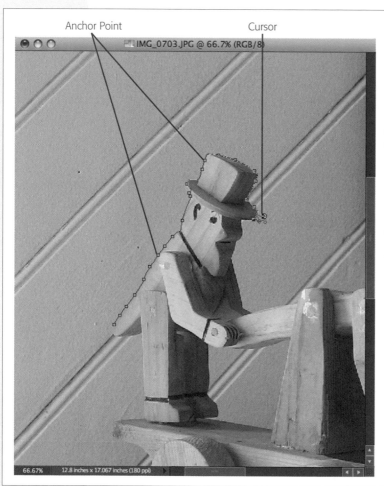

Anchor Point   Cursor

IMG_0703.JPG @ 66.7% (RGB/8)

66.67%   12.8 inches x 17.067 inches (180 ppi)

Figure 5-12:
One nice thing about the Magnetic Lasso is that it's easy to back up as you're creating your selection. As you go, it lays down the tiny boxes, called anchor or fastening points, shown in this figure. If you make a mistake with the Magnetic Lasso, pressing Delete takes you back one point each time you press the key. (If you want to completely get rid of a Magnetic Lasso selection you've begun but not completed, just press Escape.) If the Magnetic Lasso skips a spot or won't grab onto a spot where you want it to, you can force it to put down an anchor point by clicking once where you want the anchor to appear.

The Magnetic Lasso comes with four additional settings in the Options bar:

• **Width** tells the Magnetic Lasso how far away to look when it's trying to find the edge. The value is always in pixels, and you can set it as high as 256.

- **Edge Contrast** controls how sharp a difference the Magnetic Lasso should look for between the outline and the background. A higher number looks for sharper contrasts, and a lower number looks for softer ones.

- **Frequency** controls how fast Elements puts down the fastener points you see in Figure 5-12.

- **Use Tablet Pressure to Change Pen Width**—the little button with a pen at the right of the Options bar—only works if you have a graphics tablet. When you turn this setting on, how hard you press controls how Elements searches for the edge of objects you're trying to select. When you bear down harder, it's more precise. When you press more lightly, you can be a bit sloppier and Elements will still find the edge.

Many people live full and satisfying lives paying no attention whatsoever to these settings, so don't feel like you have to fuss with them all the time. You can usually ignore them unless the Magnetic Lasso misbehaves.

> **TIP** You get better results with the Magnetic Lasso if you go more slowly than if you speed around the object. Like most people, the Magnetic Lasso does better work if you give it time to be sure where it's going.

The Polygonal Lasso

At first, this may seem like a totally stupid tool. It works something like the Magnetic Lasso, but it creates only perfectly straight segments. So you may think, "Well that's great if I want to select a Stop sign, but otherwise, what's the point?"

Actually, if you're one of those people who just plain *can't* draw, and you even have a hard time following the edge of an object that's already on the screen, this is the tool for you. The trick is to use very short distances between clicks. Figure 5-13 shows the Polygonal Lasso in action.

The big advantage of using the Polygonal Lasso over the Magnetic Lasso is that it's much easier to keep it from getting into a snarl. Your only options for this tool are Feathering and Anti-aliasing, which are explained in the box on page 125, and Refine Edge (page 119).

Removing Objects from an Image's Background

Ever feel the urge to pluck an object out of your photo's background? For example, maybe you want to take an amazing shot you got of the moon and stick it in another photo. The traditional procedure is to make your selection, invert it (page 135), and then delete the rest of the image. But Elements streamlines this process with yet another "magic" tool—the Magic Extractor. It works much like the Quick Selection tool in that you just give Elements a few hints and let the program do the rest. When the Magic Extractor's done, your selection is isolated in all its

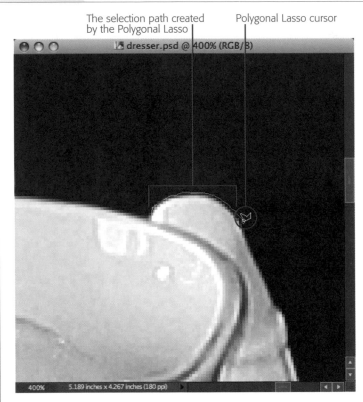

The selection path created by the Polygonal Lasso

Polygonal Lasso cursor

Figure 5-13:
If you have limited dexterity, the Polygonal Lasso tool and a lot of clicks eventually get you a nice accurate selection. You need to zoom way, way in to use this tool to select an object that doesn't have totally straight sides. Here, the Polygonal Lasso easily made it around the curve of the handle by clicking to make extremely short segments.

lonely glory, surrounded by transparency and ready for use on its own. Like the Quick Selection tool, this tool does a surprisingly good job—most of the time. To conduct your own experiments, download the practice photo (coralbean.jpg) from the "Missing CD" page at *www.missingmanuals.com*.

> **TIP**   In Elements 6 you may find it faster to use the Quick Selection tool (page 116), followed by inverting and deleting the background area as explained on page 135. If that doesn't work, then it's time to try the Magic Extractor.

The Magic Extractor has an elaborate dialog box with tools not found elsewhere in Elements. To see it, go to Image → Magic Extractor (see Figure 5-14). You see a full-screen dialog box, including a Toolbox on the left side, instructions across the top, a preview of your image, and a set of controls at right. It looks complicated, but it's really just a bunch of easy-to-use options for tweaking what you've got before Elements extracts your object for you. Here's how to use this timesaving tool:

1. **Go to Image → Magic Extractor, or press Option+Shift+⌘+V.**

   Your image appears in the preview area of the Magic Extractor window (Figure 5-14).

TIP   The Magic Extractor sometimes has problems with very large files. If you need to extract an object from a hefty image, you may get better results if you crop away any large, unnecessary areas first. See page 71 for more about cropping.

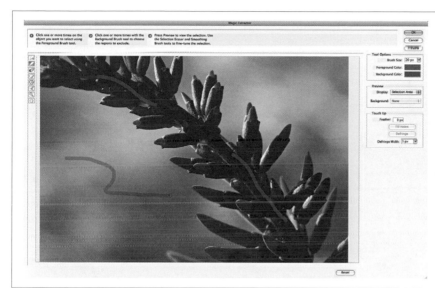

*Figure 5-14:
Manually removing this
spray of coral bean from
its background would be
a mighty long process.
With the Magic Extractor,
these few marks are all
the help Elements needs
to make the selection for
you. (Because the
blossom is red, this
picture shows blue as the
Foreground brush color
and red as the
Background brush color.
That's reversed from the
usual marker colors.)*

2. **If necessary, change the marker colors.**

   On the right side of the window, you see two color squares. Usually, you'll see red for the Foreground brush (the one you use to mark what to keep) and blue for the Background brush (the one that tells Elements what to discard from your image). To make the brush tools easier to see, you can click the squares for the Color Picker (page 199), and choose new colors.

3. **Use the Foreground brush to tell Elements what you want to extract.**

   Make some marks on the object you want to include. You can draw lines, as shown in Figure 5-14, but making dots on your object may work just as well. With a little practice, you'll soon get the hang of knowing what kind of marks you need for each object.

4. **Click the Background brush and tell Elements what to exclude.**

   Similarly, make some marks in the areas you *don't* want Elements to include in your selection.

5. **Click the Preview button.**

   The Preview area shows what Elements thinks you want to do. If what you see isn't even close, press Reset and start over.

6. **If necessary, use the various tools to help Elements adjust the boundaries of your selection.**

   For example, if Elements left off an area you want, usually just one click with the Foreground brush is enough to tell Elements what you want to add. If there are spots missing within the selection, click the Fill Holes button. If you need to get a better view of your work, use the Zoom and Hand tools (both of these tools are explained in more detail beginning on page 79).

7. **Fine-tune the edges of your selection, if you wish.**

   Add a feather (page 125), defringe (page 134), or smooth the edges of the selection with the Smoothing brush.

8. **When you like what you see, click OK.**

   If you want to give up and try another method, click the Cancel button instead. Figure 5-15 shows what the Magic Extractor can do.

   TIP   Once you understand layers (see Chapter 6), you'll know that the Magic Extractor works only on the active layer of your photo. If you want to extract an object without wrecking the rest of your photo, make a duplicate layer (page 151) and work on that new layer.

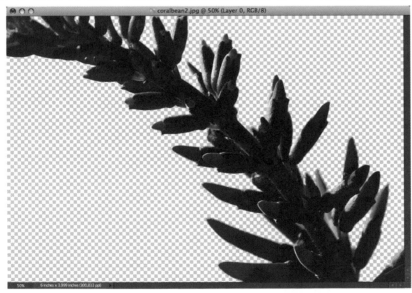

Figure 5-15:
Just the few marks you saw in Figure 5-14 produce this perfectly extracted selection, all ready to move to another image.

The Magic Extractor gives you lots of ways to make sure that you get a perfect selection. The Toolbox contains a whole set of special tools just for the Extractor, as you can see in Figure 5-16. Each has its own keyboard shortcut to make it easy to switch tools while you work (given in parentheses after the tool's name in the list below). From top to bottom, you get:

- **Foreground brush** *(Keyboard shortcut: B)*. Use this brush to mark what you want to include in your extracted object. You can change the brush color by choosing a different foreground color in the square on the right side of the window.

- **Background brush** *(P)*. This brush tells Elements what you want to cut away from your selection. Like the Foreground brush, this brush has a color square on the right side of the window where you can choose a different marker color.

- **Point Eraser tool** *(E)*. If you mark something by mistake with the Foreground or Background brush, use this tool to erase the marks.

- **Add to Selection tool** *(A)*. Use this tool to add to the selection you already have.

- **Remove from Selection tool** *(D)*. Whatever you paint over gets removed from your selection.

- **Smoothing brush** *(J)*. Once you've previewed your selection, you can use this brush to even out any ragged edges. Try the Touch Up commands from the right side of the window first because you may not need this brush.

- **Zoom tool** *(Z)* **and Hand tool** *(H)*. These are the same trusty standbys you use to adjust your view elsewhere in Elements. See page 79 for more about using the Zoom tool and page 81 for the Hand tool.

TIP   Some of the fine-tuning tools, like the Smoothing brush, work much better if you zoom in pretty close before using them.

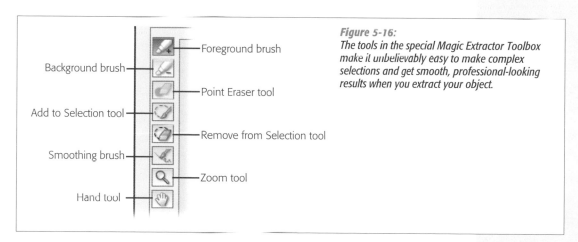

Figure 5-16:
The tools in the special Magic Extractor Toolbox make it unbelievably easy to make complex selections and get smooth, professional-looking results when you extract your object.

So you can see exactly what you're doing, Elements gives you several ways to adjust the tools and also your view of the image. These are found on the right side of the window:

- **Tool Options**. You can use the color squares to choose different colors for the Foreground and Background brushes by clicking these squares and using the Color Picker (page 199). You can also adjust the brush size, but that's hardly ever necessary, unless the brush is too big for the area you want to select.

- **Preview**. Choose whether to see just the selected area or your entire image. You can also choose what kind of background you want to see your selection against to get a clearer view. For example, you can choose None (the standard transparency grid), or a black, gray, or white matte, which puts a temporary solid background to make it easier to check the edges of your selection. Mask is just like working with the Selection brush in Mask mode (page 120). You can paint more of a mask or remove the mask to reveal a larger selection. (Remember that what's masked *isn't* selected.)

Once you've previewed your selection, you also get some very helpful options for making sure your selection is absolutely perfect. Most of these options are on the right side of the dialog box, under Touch Up.

- **Feather**. Enter the amount, in pixels, to feather the edge of your selection. (Page 125 explains feathering.)

- **Fill Holes**. If Elements left some gaps in your selection, you may be able to fill them by clicking this button. This tool works only for holes that are completely surrounded by selected material, though. If the edges of your selection have bites out of them, use the Smoothing brush instead, or paint over the area with the "Add to Selection" brush.

- **Defringe**. If your selection has a rim of contrasting pixels around it, this command can usually eliminate them. Figure 5-17 shows what a difference defringing can make. You can choose a different number of pixels for Elements to consider when defringing, but the standard setting is usually fine.

> **NOTE**   If you've used the Magic Extractor in Elements 4, you'll be pleased with how much more cleanly Elements 6 makes its extractions. You don't need to defringe nearly as often in this version.

Extracting objects used to be a very time-consuming process, often involving expensive third-party plug-ins to make the job easier. But now the Magic Extractor is all you need in most situations.

> **TIP**   If the edges of your selection are ragged but not contrasting, or if defringing alone doesn't clean things up enough, try the Smoothing brush (page 129). Just run it along the edge of your selection to polish it until it's smooth.

Changing and Moving Selections

Now that you know all about how to make selections, it's time to learn about some of the finer points of using and manipulating them. Elements gives you several handy options for changing the areas you've selected and for actually moving

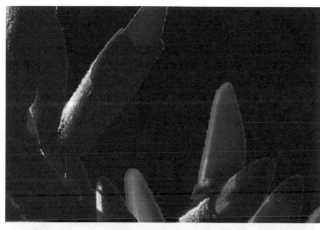

Ragged, messy edges

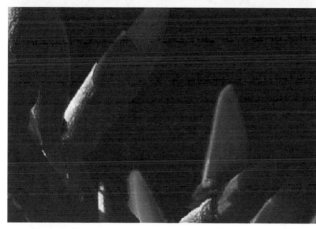

Smooth, neat edges

Figure 5-17:
Defringing is a huge help in cleaning up the edges of your selections.

Top: Here's a closeup of the extracted coral bean blossom. The black matte background makes the ragged edges stand out. If you look closely, you can see the ragged edges of the flower. If you place this image into another graphic, it will look like you cut it out with very dull nail scissors.

Bottom: The edges will blend into another image much more believably after you apply defringing. Here you can see how much softer the edges are after defringing. Now you can place the flower into another file without getting the cut-out effect.

images around once they're selected. You can even save a tough selection so you don't have to do *that* again.

Inverting a Selection

One thing you often want to do with a selection is *invert* it. That means telling Elements, "Hey, you know the area I've selected? Well, I want you to select everything *except* that area."

Why would you want to do that? Well, sometimes it's easier to select what you *don't* want. For example, suppose you have an object with a complicated outline, like the group of buildings shown in Figure 5-18. Say you want to put this building on your letterhead. It may be difficult to select. But the sky is just one big block of color. It's a lot faster to select the sky with the Magic Wand than to try to get an accurate selection of the building itself.

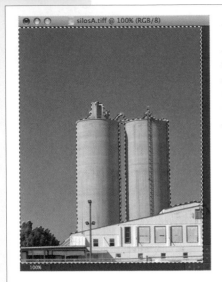

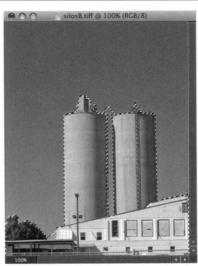

Figure 5-18:
Left: Say you want to make some adjustments to just the building in this photo. You could spend half an hour meticulously selecting it, or instead just select the sky with a click of the Magic Wand and invert your selection to get the silos. Here, the sky has the marching ants around it to show that it's the active selection—but that's not what you want.

Right: Inverting the selection (Select → Inverse) gives you the ants around the buildings without the trouble of tracing out all the ladders and pipes on the silos.

To invert a selection:

1. **Make a selection.**

   Usually, you first select what you *don't* want if you're planning to invert your selection. You can select with any tool that suits your fancy.

2. **Go to Select → Inverse, or press Shift+⌘+I.**

   Now the part of your image that you *didn't* select is selected.

Making a Selection Larger or Smaller

What if you want to tweak the size of your selection? Sometimes you may want to move the outline of a selection outward a few pixels to expand it. Figuring out how to do so confuses people because Elements offers two similar-sounding ways to do it: Grow and Expand. They sound like they should do the same thing, but there's a slight but important difference between them.

- **Grow** (Select → Grow) moves your selection outward to include more similar contiguous colors, no matter what shape your original selection was. Grow doesn't care about shape; it just finds more matching contiguous pixels.

- **Expand** (Select → Modify → Expand) preserves the shape of your selection and just increases the size of it by the number of pixels you specify.

- **Similar** (Select → Similar) does the same thing as Grow but looks at all pixels, not just the adjacent ones.

- **Contract** (Select → Modify → Contract) shrinks the size of a selection.

So what's the big difference between Expand and Grow? Look at Figure 5-19 to see how differently they behave.

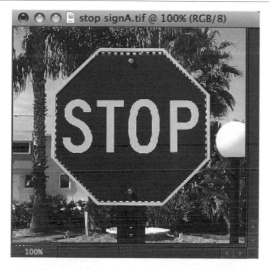

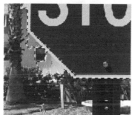
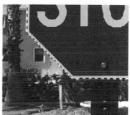

Figure 5-19:
Top: In the original selection, everything in the Stop sign has been selected except the small white border on the outside of the sign.

Bottom left: If you use Grow to enlarge the selection, you also get parts of the building that are similar in tone. As a result, your selection isn't shaped like a Stop sign anymore.

Bottom right: But if you use Expand instead, the selection still has the exact shape of the sign, only now the edges of the selection move outward to include the sign's white border area.

Moving Selections

Often you make selections because you want to move objects around—like putting that dreamboat who wouldn't give you the time of day next to you in your senior year class photo. You can move a selection in several ways.

Here's the simplest, tool-free way to move something from one image to another:

1. **Select it.**

   Make sure you've selected everything you want. It's really annoying when you paste a selection from one image to another and find you missed a spot.

2. **Press ⌘+C to copy it.**

   Or you could use ⌘+X if you want to cut it out of your original. Just remember that Elements leaves a hole if you do it that way.

Smoothing and Bordering

You'll probably use Refine Edge most of the time in Elements 6, but Adobe still includes some alternative ways to tweak the edges of your selections.

- **Smoothing** (Select → Modify → Smooth) is a sometimes-dependable way to clean up ragged spots in a color-based selection (like you'd make with the Magic Wand, for instance). You enter a pixel value, and Elements evens out your selection based on the number you entered, by searching for similarly colored pixels.

    For example, if you enter 5 pixels, Elements looks at a 5-pixel radius around each pixel in your selection. In areas where most of the pixels are already selected, it adds in the others. Where most pixels aren't selected, it deselects the ones that are

selected to get rid of the jagged edges and holes in the selection.

This is handy, but smoothing is sometimes hard to control, and it doesn't affect only the edge of your selection. Usually it's easier to clean up your selection by hand with the Selection brush than to use Smoothing.

- **Bordering** (Select → Modify → Border) adds an anti-aliased, invisible border to your selection. You might say it selects the selection's outline. You would use it when your selection's edges are too hard and you want to soften them. Choose a border size and click OK. Only the border is selected, so you can also apply a slight Gaussian blur (see page 362) to soften it more if you like.

TIP   If you copy and paste a selection, and you see it's got partially transparent areas in it, back up and go over your selection again with the Selection brush using a hard brush, and then copy and paste again.

3. **If you want to dump the selection into its very own document, choose File → New → "Image from Clipboard".**

    Doing so creates a new document with just your selection in it. If you want to place the selection into an existing photo, follow the instructions in the next step.

4. **If you want to add the selection to another photo, then just use ⌘+V to paste it into another image in Elements.**

    Once your selection is where you want it, you can use the Move tool to position it, rotate it, or scale it to fit the rest of the photo. You can even paste your selection into a document in *another* program. Just be sure you've turned on Export Clipboard in Photoshop Elements → Preferences → General.

The Move tool

You can also move things around *within* your photo by using the Move tool, which lets you cut or copy selected areas. Figure 5-20 shows how to use the Move tool to conceal distracting details in photos.

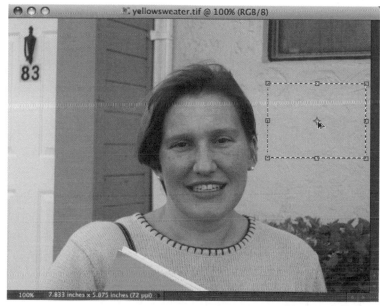

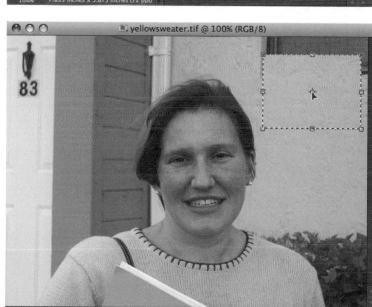

Figure 5-20:
Top: Here's the original version of the photo used for the feathered vignette on page 125. Let's say you wanted to get rid of the window in the upper-right corner of the top photo. By copying and moving a piece of the wall, you can cover up the window and create a simpler background to put the focus on the woman rather than the building. You select the area prior to moving it.

Bottom: Hold down the Option key while using the Move tool to copy a selected area. The piece of wall slides into its new position as a window hider. (If you use the Move tool without holding down the Option key, Elements cuts away the selection, leaving a hole in your photo.)

The Move tool lives at the very top of the Standard Edit Toolbox. To use it:

1. **Make a selection.**

   Make sure your selection doesn't have anything in it that you don't want to copy.

2. **Switch to the Move tool.**

   Click the Move tool or press V. Your selection stays active but is now surrounded by a rectangle with box-shaped handles on the corners.

3. **Move the selection and press Return when you're satisfied with its position.**

   As long as your selection is active, you can work on your photo in other ways and then come back and reactivate the Move tool. If you're worried about losing a complex selection, save it as described in the next section. If you're not happy with what you've done, just press ⌘+Z (as many times as needed) to back up, and you can start over again.

You can move a selection in several different ways:

- **Move it.** If you just move a selection by dragging it, you leave a hole in the background where the selection was. The Move tool *truly* moves your selection. So unless you have something under it that you want to show through, that's probably not what you want to do.

- **Copy it and move the copy.** If you press the Option key as you're moving, you'll copy your selection, so your original remains where it was. But now you'll have a duplicate to move around and play with.

- **Resize it.** You can drag the Move tool's handles to resize or distort your copy, which is great when you need to change the size of your selection. The Move tool lets you do the same things you can do with Free Transform (see page 309).

- **Rotate it.** The Move tool lets you rotate your selection the same way you can rotate a picture using Free Rotate (see page 69). Just grab a corner and turn it.

   TIP   You can save a trip to the Toolbox and move selections without activating the Move tool. To move a selection without copying it, just place your cursor in the selection, hold down ⌘, and move the selection. To move a copy of a selection, follow the same procedure but hold down the Option key as well. You can drag the copy without damaging the original. To move multiple copies, just let go, then press ⌘+Option again and drag once more.

The Move tool is also a great way to manage and move objects that you've put on their own layers (Chapter 6). Page 160 explains how to use the Move tool to arrange layered objects.

Saving Selections

You can tell Elements to remember the outline of your selection so that you can reuse it again later on. This is a wonderful timesaver and easy to do, too.

   NOTE   Elements' saved selections are the equivalent of Photoshop's *alpha channels*. Keep that in mind if you decide to try tutorials written for the full-featured Photoshop. Incidentally, alpha channels saved in files in Photoshop show up in Elements as saved selections, and vice versa.

To save a selection:

1. **Make your selection.**

2. **Choose Select → Save Selection, name your selection, and save it.**

   When you want to use the selection again, go to Select → Load Selection, and there it is, waiting for you.

   > **TIP**   When you save a feathered (page 125) selection, use the new Refine Edge command (page 119) if you change your mind later on about how much feather you want. You can also save a hard-edged selection, load it, and then go to Select → Feather to add a feather if you need one. That way you can change the amount each time you use the selection, as long as you remember not to save the change to the selection.

Making changes to a saved selection

It's probably just as easy to start your selection over if you need to tweak a saved selection, but it is possible to make changes if you want. This can save you some time if your original selection was really tricky to create.

Say you've got a full-length photo of somebody, and you've created and saved a selection of the person's face (called, naturally enough, "Face"). Now, imagine that after applying a filter to the selection, you decide it would look silly to change only the face and not the person's hands, too.

So you want to add the hands to your saved selection. There are a couple of ways to do this.

The simplest is just to load up "Face," activate your selection tool of choice, put the tool in "Add to Selection" mode, select the hands, and then save the selection again with the same name.

But how about if you've already selected the hands and you want to add *that* new selected area to the existing facial selection? Here's what you'd do:

1. **Go to Select → Save Selection.**

   Choose your saved "Face" selection. All the radio buttons in the dialog box become active.

2. **Choose "Add to Selection".**

   What you just selected is added to the original selection and saved, so now your "Face" selection also includes the hands.

Layers: The Heart of Elements

If you've been working mostly in the Quick Fix window so far, you've probably noticed that once you close your file, the changes you've made are permanent. You can undo actions while the file's still open, but once you close it, you're stuck with what you've done.

In Elements, you can keep your changes (most kinds, anyway) and still revert to the original image if you use *layers*, a nifty system of transparent sheets that keeps each element of your image on a separate sliver that you can edit. Layers are one of the greatest image editing inventions ever. By putting each change you make on its own layer, you can constantly rearrange the composition of your image and add or subtract changes whenever you want.

If you use layers, you can save your file and quit Elements, and then come back days or weeks later and still undo what you did or change things around some more. There's no statute of limitations for the changes you make when using layers.

Some people resist learning about layers because they fear they're too complicated. But they're actually very easy to use once you understand how they work. And once you get started with layers, you'll realize that using Elements without them is like driving a Ferrari in first gear. This chapter gives you the information you need to get comfortable working with layers.

Understanding Layers

Imagine you've got a drawing of a room you're thinking about redecorating. Say the drawing features a few items in the room: the walls, the windows, and a piece of furniture or two. To get an idea of your different decorating possibilities, imagine that you've also got a bunch of transparent plastic sheets, each of which has some image on it that changes the room's look: a couch, a few different colors for the carpet, a standing lamp, and so on. Your decorating work is now pretty easy, since you can add and remove, and mix and match the transparencies with ease.

Layers in Elements work pretty much the same way. With layers, you can add and remove objects and also make changes to the way your image looks. And with any of these changes, you can modify or discard them later on.

If you look at Figure 6-1, you can see an Elements file that includes layers. Each object in that flyer is on a different layer, so you can easily remove or rearrange things. (If you want to follow along with a layers-heavy file, you can download a small version of this file from the "Missing CD" page at *www.missingmanuals.com*. Look for harvestfestsmall.psd.)

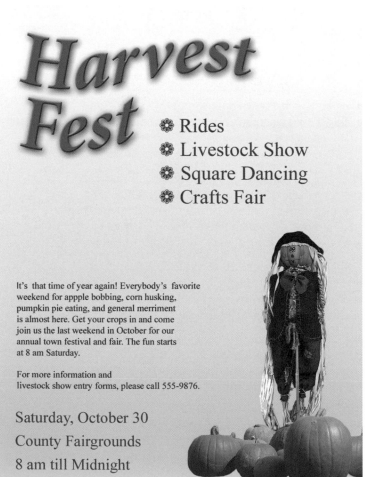

Figure 6-1:
Every object in this flyer—the background, the scarecrow, the pumpkins, each block of text—is on its own layer, which makes changing things a snap. Want to change the background, get rid of the pumpkins, or change the phone number? With layers, it's easy to do any of these things.

You can also use layers for many adjustments to your photos, giving yourself the chance to tweak or eliminate those changes later on. For instance, say you used Quick Fix's Hue slider but then decided the next day you didn't like what you did—you're stuck (unless you can dig out a copy of your original). But if you'd used a Hue/Saturation Adjustment *layer* to make the change, you could just throw out that layer and keep all your other changes intact (you'll learn about Adjustment layers later in this chapter). You can also use layers to combine parts of different photos together, as shown in Figure 6-2.

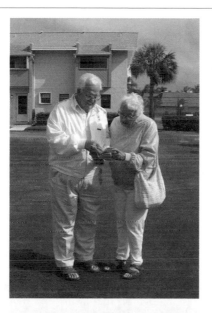

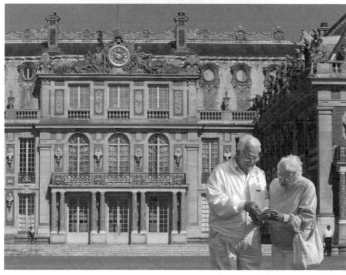

Figure 6-2:
Layers make it easy to combine elements from different photos. You may not be able to afford to send your grandparents on a real trip to Europe, but once you understand layers, you can give them a virtual vacation.

Once you understand how to use layers, you'll feel much more comfortable making radical changes to an image because mistakes are much easier to fix. Not only that, but by using layers, you can easily make lots of very sophisticated changes that are otherwise very difficult and time-consuming. But the main reason to use layers is for creative freedom. Layers make it easy to create lots of special effects that would be very difficult otherwise.

> **NOTE** Along with goodies like graphics and frames, the Content palette contains a number of *smart objects*. These objects take on special powers when you add them to a layered file. For example, if you choose a new background from the palette, it automatically zips down to the bottom of the stack to replace your existing background, no matter which layer was active when you applied the new background. Page 411 explains how smart objects work.

The Layers Palette

The Layers palette is your control center for any kind of layer-related action you want to perform, like adding, deleting, or duplicating layers. Figure 6-3 shows you the Layers palette for an image that already has lots of layers.

It's important to have access to the Layers palette whenever you work with layers, not only for the information it gives you, but because you can generally manipulate layers more easily from the palette than directly in your image. There are many changes, like renaming a layer, that you can do only in the palette.

Each layer displays its name and a little thumbnail icon in the palette showing the layer's contents. You can adjust the size of the icon or turn it off altogether if you prefer, as shown in Figure 6-4.

The Layers palette usually contains one layer that's *active*, meaning that any action you take, like painting, is going to happen on that layer (and that layer only). The active layer is a lighter gray so that you can see which one it is.

> **NOTE** If you use the layer selection options described on page 162, you can wind up with multiple active layers or none, but for general working purposes, usually you want to have only one active layer.

When you look at an image that contains layers, you're looking down on the stack of layers from the top, just the way you would with overlays on a drawing. The layers appear in the same order in the Layers palette—the top layer of your image is the top layer in the stack in the Layers palette. (Layer order is important because whatever is on top can obscure what's beneath it.)

Elements lets you perform lots of different maneuvers right in the Layers palette. You can make a layer's contents invisible and then visible again, change the order in which layers are stacked, link layers together, change the opacity of layers, add and delete layers—the list goes on and on. The rest of this chapter covers all these options and more.

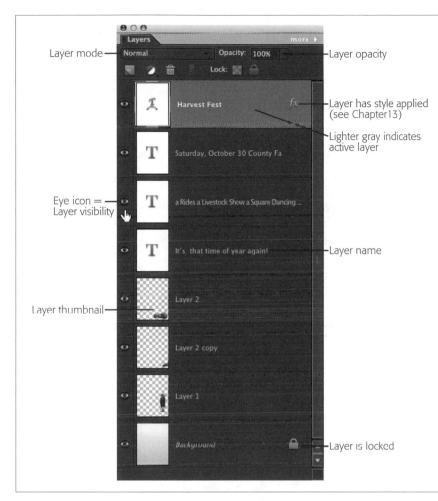

Layer mode

Layer opacity

Layer has style applied (see Chapter13)

Lighter gray indicates active layer

Eye icon = Layer visibility

Layer name

Layer thumbnail

Layer is locked

Figure 6-3:
The Layers palette for the illustration in Figure 6-1 looks like this. Each row lists a separate layer. An eye icon indicates that a layer is visible. To hide a layer so you can see what you're doing while working on other layers, click the eye. When you want to make the layer visible again, click the spot where the eye was.

The Background

The bottom layer of any image is a special kind of layer called the *Background*. If you bring any image or photo into Elements, the first time you open it, you'll see its one existing layer is called Background. (That's assuming that nobody else has already edited the file in Elements and changed things.) The name Background is only logical because whatever else you do will be on top of this layer.

> **NOTE**   There are two exceptions to the first-layer-is-always-the-Background rule. First, if you create a new image by copying something from another picture, you'll just have a layer called "Layer 0." Second, Background layers can't be transparent, so if you choose the Transparency option when creating a file from scratch, you'll have a Layer 0 instead of a Background layer.

As for content, the Background can be totally plain or busy, busy, busy. A Background layer doesn't mean that it literally contains the background of your photograph—your entire photo can be a Background layer. It's entirely up to you to

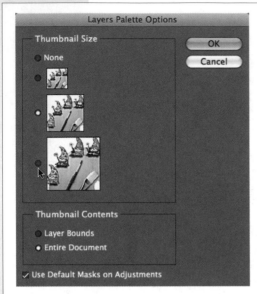

Layers Palette Options

Thumbnail Size

○ None

Thumbnail Contents

○ Layer Bounds
● Entire Document

☑ Use Default Masks on Adjustments

OK
Cancel

Figure 6-4:
If you want to change the size of the thumbnail icons in the Layers palette, click the arrows (or the More button, if the palette is out of the bin) in the palette's upper-right corner to open the pop-out menu. At the bottom of the menu, choose Palette Options, and the dialog box shown here appears. In this case, the medium-size icon is selected.

A TIDY WORKSPACE

Managing the Layers Palette

On most Mac monitors, you have plenty of room to get a good look at the Layers palette in the Palette bin. But on laptops and older Macs, you may find that it's hard to see all your layers in a many-layered file while the palette is in the bin.

The Layers palette is important, so you probably want to get it out where you can see it all the time, at least while you're working with layered files. To do so, just grab the top bar of the palette near the name and pull it out of the bin onto your desktop. (For tips on keeping track of the Layers palette once it's out of the bin, look at page 25.)

You can collapse the Layers palette once it's on the desktop, but Elements gurus usually like to keep it easily accessible.

If you have a big monitor and room to keep the Palette bin open while you work, it's fine to leave the Layers palette in the bin if you prefer. You can drag the Layers palette up or down in the bin to put it in the most convenient position. The idea is to get that palette where you can see it all the time and easily get to it with your mouse.

---

decide what's on your Background layer and what you place on other, newly added layers. A common strategy for photographs is to keep your photo's image on the Background layer, and then perform adjustments and embellishments (like adding type) on other layers.

You can do a lot to Background layers, but there are a few things you *can't* do: If you want to change a Background layer's blending mode (see page 157), opacity (page 155), or position in the layer stack, you need to convert that Background into a regular layer.

TIP   The Background and Magic Erasers automatically turn a Background layer into a regular layer when you click a background with them. If you have a single object on a solid background and you want transparency around the object, one click with the Magic Eraser turns your background into a layer, eliminates a solid-colored background, and replaces it with transparency. (There's more on the Eraser tools on page 334.)

You can change a Background layer to a regular layer by double-clicking the Background layer in the Layers palette. Or, if you try to make certain kinds of changes to the background (like moving its position), Elements will prompt you to change the Background layer to a regular layer.

You can also transform a regular layer into a Background layer if you want. One reason to do this is to send a layer zipping down to the bottom of the stack in a many-layered file. To do so:

1. **In the Layers palette, click the layer you want to convert to a Background layer.**

2. **Select Layer → New → "Background from Layer".**

   It may take a few seconds for Elements to finish calculating and to respond after you tell it what to do. The layer you've changed moves down to the bottom of the layer stack in the Layers palette and automatically gets renamed "Background."

   NOTE   You can't have more than one Background layer in an image. So what do you do if you want to change a regular layer to a Background layer and you've already got a Background layer? Well, you need to change the existing Background layer into a regular layer first. Otherwise, the command is unavailable. (If you add a background from the Content palette, it automatically replaces the contents of your current background layer.)

COMPATIBILITY

Which File Types Can Use Layers?

You can add layers to any file you can open in Elements, but not every file format lets you *save* those layers for future use.

For instance, if your camera shoots JPEGs, you can open the JPEG in Elements and create lots of layers, but when you try to save the file, you'll get the Save As dialog box, and when you turn off the option to save layers, a warning reminds you that you can't have layers in a JPEG file.

Usually you'll want to choose either Photoshop (.psd) or TIFF as your format when saving an image with layers, because they both let you keep your layers for future use. PDF files can also have layers.

If someone using the full-featured Photoshop sends you an image that has layers, you'll see them in the Layers palette when you open the file in Elements. Likewise, Photoshop can see layers you create in Elements.

If you open a Photoshop file with a layer that says "indicates a set" when you mouse over it, you have what Photoshop calls a Layer Group or *layer set* (a way to group *layers* into what are essentially folders in the layers palette), depending on the version of Photoshop that created the file. Elements doesn't understand those, so ask the sender to expand the layer sets and send you the file again, or you can use Layer → Simplify to convert the set to an uneditable single layer.

Creating Layers

Your image doesn't automatically have multiple layers. Lots of newcomers to Elements expect the program to be smart enough to put each object in a photo onto its own layer. It's a lovely dream, but even Elements isn't that brainy. To experience the joy of layers, you first need to add at least one layer to your image, which is what you'll learn how to do in the next few sections.

> **TIP**   It may help you to follow along through the next few sections if you get out a photo of your own or create a new file to use for practice. Or, you can download either the harvestfestsmall.psd or leaves.jpg file from the "Missing CD" page at *www.missingmanuals.com*. (See page 47 for details on how to create a new file; if you do so, choose a white background.)

Adding a Layer

Elements gives you several different ways to add new layers. You can use any of the following methods:

- Select Layer → New → Layer.

- Press Shift+⌘+N.

- In the Layers palette, click the "Create a new layer" icon (the little square shown in Figure 6-5).

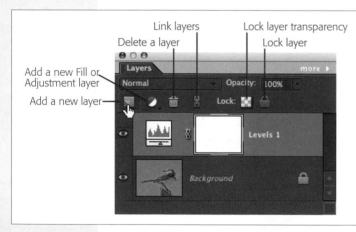

Figure 6-5:
More controls on the Layers palette. Click the little "Create a new layer" icon on the left side of the Layers palette when you want to quickly add a new layer.

When you create a new layer using any of these commands, the layer starts out empty. You won't see a change in your image until you use the layer for something (for example, pasting something into the empty layer or painting on it). If you look at the Layers palette, you'll see that any new layer you add appears just above the layer that was active when you created the new layer.

NOTE The only practical limit to the number of layers your image can have is your computer's processing power. But if you find yourself regularly creating projects with upward of 100 layers, you may want to upgrade to Photoshop, which has tools that make it easier to manage large numbers of layers.

Some actions create new layers automatically. For instance, if you drag an object in from another photo (see page 172 for instructions) or add artwork from the Content palette, the object automatically comes in on its own layer. And that's very handy for arranging the new item just where you want it, without disturbing the rest of your composition.

Deleting Layers

It's very easy to delete layers. Figure 6-6 shows the simplest way.

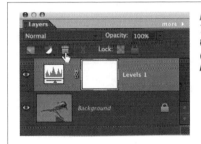

Figure 6-6:
To make a layer go away, you can either drag the layer to the trashcan icon on the Layers palette or, after selecting the layer, just click the "Delete layer" icon (the trashcan). Elements responds by asking if you want to delete the active layer. Say yes, and it's history. Once you delete a layer, it's gone forever.

Elements also gives you a few other ways to delete a layer. You can:

- Select Layer → Delete Layer.
- Right click (Control-click) the layer in the Layers palette and choose Delete Layer from the pop-up menu.
- Click the More button on the Layers palette and choose Delete Layer from the pop-up menu.

Duplicating a Layer

Duplicating a layer can be very useful. Many Elements commands, like filters or color modification tools, won't work on a brand-new *empty* layer. This poses a dilemma because if you apply those changes to the layer containing your main image, you'll alter it in ways you can't undo later. The workaround is to create a *duplicate layer* and make your changes on that new layer. Then you can ditch the duplicate later if you change your mind, and your original layer is safely tucked away unchanged.

If all this seems annoyingly theoretical, try going to Enhance → Adjust Color → Adjust Hue/Saturation, for example, when you're working on a new blank layer, and see what happens. You'll see the helpful dialog box shown in Figure 6-7 if you try to work on a blank layer.

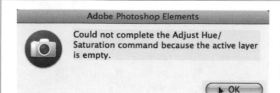

Figure 6-7:
Elements 6 is usually pretty helpful when you try to do something that just isn't going to work, like applying a Hue/ Saturation adjustment to an empty layer. The solution here is just to switch the Layers palette focus to a layer that has something in it.

NOTE Very rarely, you may still encounter the dreaded "no pixels are selected" warning in Elements 6. There are several possible causes, but the most common are too large a feather value on a selection (see the box on page 125), or trying to work in the empty part of a layer that contains only objects surrounded by transparency.

Elements gives you a few ways to duplicate an existing layer and its content. Select the layer you want to duplicate to make it the active layer, and then do one of the following:

- Press ⌘+J.

- Choose Layer → Duplicate Layer.

- In the Layers palette, drag the layer you want to copy to the "Create a new layer" icon.

- Right-click (Control+click) the Layer in the Layers palette and choose Duplicate Layer from the pop-up menu.

- Click the More button on the Layers palette and choose Duplicate Layer.

Creating a new layer using any of these methods copies the entire contents of the active layer into the new layer. You can then mess with the duplicate as much as you want without damaging the original layer.

Copying and Cutting from Layers

You can also make a new layer that consists only of a *piece* of an existing layer. But first you need to decide whether you want to *copy* your selection or *cut* it out and place it on the new layer.

What's the difference? It's pretty much the same as copying versus cutting in your word-processing program. When you make a "New Layer via Copy," the area you select appears in the new layer while remaining in place in the old layer, too. On the other hand, "New Layer via Cut" removes the selection from the old layer and places it on a new layer, leaving a corresponding hole in the old layer. Figure 6-8 shows the difference.

Once you've selected what you want to move or copy, your new layer is only a couple of keystrokes away.

- **New Layer via Copy**. The easiest way to copy your selection to a new layer is to press ⌘+J. You can also go to Layer → New → "Layer via Copy". Whichever you

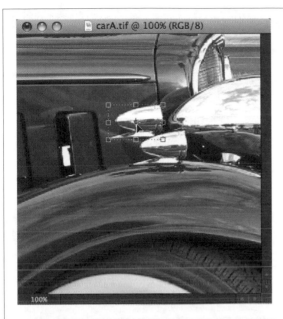

Figure 6-8:
The difference between "New Layer via Copy" and "New Layer via Cut" becomes obvious when you move the new layer so you can see what's beneath it.

Top: With "New Layer via Copy," the original light is still in place in the underlying layer.

Bottom: When you use "New Layer via Cut," the light leaves a hole behind.

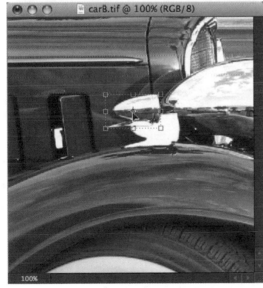

use, if you don't select anything before you use these keystrokes, your whole layer gets copied, so it's also a good shortcut for making a duplicate layer.

- **New Layer via Cut.** To cut your selection out of your old layer and put it on a layer by itself, press Shift+⌘+J, or go to Layer → New → "Layer via Cut". Just remember that you'll leave a hole in your original layer when you do this.

If for some reason you want to cut and move the entire contents of a layer, you can press ⌘+A first, although usually it's easier just to move your layer instead.

Naming Layers

You might have noticed that Elements isn't terribly creative when it comes to naming your layers. You get Layer 1, Layer 2, and so on. Fortunately, you don't have to live with those titles. It's quite easy to rename your layers in Elements.

Maybe renaming layers sounds like a job for people with too much time on their hands, but if you get started on a project that winds up with many layers, you may find that you can pick out the layers you want more quickly if you give them descriptive names.

Incidentally, you can't rename a Background layer. You have to change it to a regular layer first. Also, Elements helps you out with Text layers (see page 383) by naming them using the first few words of the text they contain. To rename a layer:

1. **Double-click its name in the Layers palette**.

   The name turns to an active text box.

2. **Type in the new name**.

   You don't even need to highlight the text—Elements does that for you automatically.

As with any other change, you have to save your image afterward if you want to keep the name.

> **TIP**   If you want to use a layer as the basis for a new document, Elements gives you a quick way to do so. Instead of copying and pasting, you can create a new document by going to Layer → Duplicate Layer. You get a dialog box containing a pull-down menu that gives you the option of placing the duplicate layer into your existing image, into any currently open image, or into a new document of its own. (This maneuver only works from the menu. ⌘+J doesn't bring up the dialog box.)

Managing Layers

The Layers palette lets you manipulate your layers in all kinds of ways, but first you need to understand a few more of the palette's cryptic little icons. Some of the things you can do with layers may seem tiresomely obscure when you first read about them, but once you're actually using layers, you'll quickly see why many of these options exist. The next few sections explain how to manipulate your layers in several different ways: how to hide them, how to group them together, how to change the way you see them, and how to combine layers together.

Making Layers Invisible

You can turn the visibility of layers off and on at will. This feature is tremendously useful, if you think about it. If the image you're working on has a busy background, for example, it's often hard to see what you're doing when you're working on a particular layer. Making the background invisible can really help you focus on the layer you're interested in. To turn off visibility, in the Layers palette, click the eye icon to hide the layer. Click the eye once more to make the layer visible again.

> **TIP**   If you have a bunch of hidden layers and you decide you don't want them anymore, go to Layers Palette → More → Delete Hidden Layers to get rid of them all at once.

Adjusting Transparency

Your choices for layer visibility aren't limited to on and off. You can create immensely cool effects in Elements by adjusting the *opacity* of layers. In other words, you can make a layer partially transparent so that what's underneath it shows through.

To adjust the opacity of a layer, click the layer in the Layers palette and then either:

- Click in the Opacity box and type in the percentage of opacity you want.

- If you'd rather make the adjustment visually (as opposed to entering numbers), click the triangle to the right of the Opacity percentage and adjust the pop-out slider, or just put your cursor on the word Opacity and scrub left for less opacity and right for more. (Figure 6-9 explains the advantage of scrubbing.) (You can download leaves.jpg from the "Missing CD" page at *www.missingmanuals. com*, if you'd like to experiment with creating Fill and Adjustment layers [page 170] and changing their modes and opacity.)

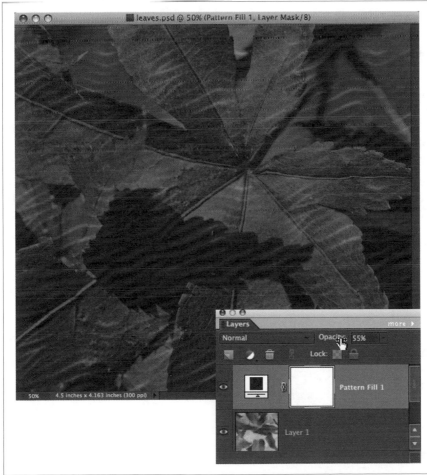

Figure 6-9:
You can watch the opacity of your layer change on the fly if you scrub your mouse back and forth on the word Opacity. Different blend modes (see page 157) often give the best effect if you adjust the opacity of their layers.

When you create a new layer using either the keyboard shortcut (Shift+⌘+N) or the menu (Layer → New → Layer), you can set the opacity right away in the New Layer dialog box. If you create a new layer by clicking the New Layer icon in the Layers palette, you need to Option+click the New Layer icon—the New Layer dialog box appears and you can change the opacity.

> **NOTE** You can't change the opacity of a Background layer. You have to convert it to a regular layer first.

POWER USERS' CLINIC

Fading in Elements

One great thing you get in the full-featured Photoshop that Elements lacks is the ability to *fade* special effects and filters. Fading gives you great control over how much these tools change an image. (Often, filters generate harsh-looking results, and Photoshop's fade command helps adjust a filter's effect until it's what you intended.)

In Elements, you can approximate the Fade tool: First, apply filters, effects, or layer styles to a duplicate layer. Then, reduce the layer's opacity till it blends in with what's below (and change the blend mode if necessary) to get exactly the result you're looking for.

Locking Layers

You can protect your image from yourself by *locking* any of the layers. Locking keeps you from changing a layer's contents. You can also lock just the transparent parts of a layer if you want. When you do that, the transparent parts of your layer stay transparent no matter what you do to the rest of it (see Figure 6-10). (You're actually locking the pixels' current transparency level, so if you have pixels that are only partly transparent, they'll stay at their current transparency level, too.)

To lock the transparent parts of a layer, select the layer and then click the little "Lock transparent pixels" checkerboard in the Layers palette. It works like a button, and it's grayed out if you have no transparency in your photo. When you lock your transparency, a light gray padlock appears in the layers palette on the right side of the layer. To unlock, just click the checkerboard again.

To lock the contents of a whole layer so that no changes can be made to it, click the "Lock all" icon (the dark gray padlock) in the Layers palette next to the checkerboard. A dark gray padlock appears in the layers palette at the right of your layer and the "Lock all" icon shows a dark gray outline around it. Now if you try to paint on that layer or use any other tools, your cursor turns into the shape of the universal "no" symbol (circle with a diagonal line through it) as a reminder that you can't edit that layer. You'll also see a Lock icon next to the layer name in the Layers palette. To unlock the layer, just click the "Lock all" icon once more.

> **NOTE** Locking only preserves the layer from edits. It doesn't keep the layer from being merged into another layer or flattened, and it won't keep your image from being cropped.

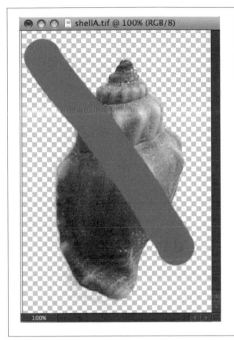 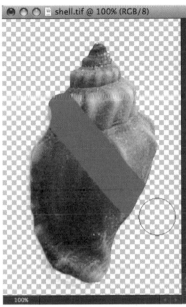

Figure 6-10:
After you've isolated an object on its own layer, sometimes you want to paint only on the object—and not on the transparent portion of the layer. Elements lets you lock the transparent part of a layer, making it easy to paint only the object itself.

Left: On a regular layer, paint goes wherever the brush does.

Right: With the layer's transparency locked, the stroke stops at the edge of the seashell, even though the brush (the circle) is now on the transparent portion of the layer.

Blend Mode

You also see another little menu in the Layers palette that says "Normal" or, in the New Layer dialog box, "Mode: Normal." This is the setting for your *blend mode*. When used with layers, blend modes control how the objects in a layer *blend* with the objects in the layer beneath it. By using different blend modes, you can make your image lighter or darker, or even make it look like a poster, with just a few bold colors in it. Blend modes can also control how some tools—those that have Blend Mode settings—change your image. Changing a tool's blend mode can sometimes dramatically change the results you get.

Blend modes are an awful lot of fun once you understand how to use them. You can use them to fix under- or overexposed photos, or to create all kinds of special visual effects. You can also use some of the tools, like the Brush tool, in different blend modes to achieve different effects. The most common blend mode is Normal, in which everything you do behaves just the way you would expect: An object shows its regular colors, and paint acts just like, well, paint.

Page 329 has lots more about how to use blend modes. For now, take a look at Figure 6-11, which shows how you can totally change the way a layer looks just by changing the layer's blend mode.

The blend modes are grouped together in the menu in categories according to the way they affect your image, but not every mode makes a visible change in every circumstance. Some of them may seem to do nothing—that's to be expected. It just means that you don't have a condition in your current image that's responding to

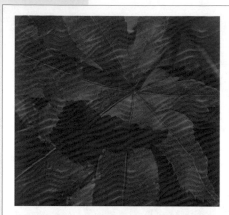

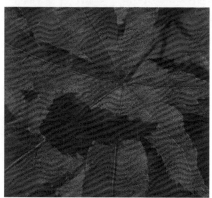

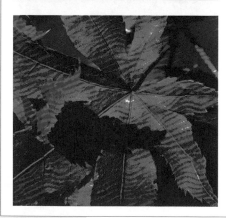

Figure 6-11:
This photo of some leaves has a Pattern Fill layer over it, showing three different modes. In normal mode at 100-percent opacity, the pattern would completely hide the leaves, but by changing the blend mode and opacity of the pattern layer, you can create very different looks. (There's more about Pattern layers on page 170.) From top to bottom, the modes are Normal, Dissolve, and Hard Mix. Notice how dissolve gives a grainy effect and hard mix produces a vivid, posterized effect.

that particular mode change. See page 210 for one example of a situation where a mode change makes an enormous difference.

> **NOTE**   In Elements 6, you get two new blend modes, courtesy of Photoshop CS3: Lighter Color and Darker Color. Darker Color compares the values of all the pixels in your image and displays only the lowest (darkest) values. Lighter color compares the values and displays only the highest values.

Rearranging Layers

One of the truly amazing things you can do with Elements is move your layers around. You can change the order in which layers are stacked so that different objects appear in front of or behind each other. For example, you can position one object behind another if they're both on their own layers. Just grab the layer in the Layers palette and drag it to where you want it to be.

> **NOTE** Remember, you're always looking down onto the layer stack when you look at your image, so moving something up in the list moves it toward the front of the picture.

Figure 6-12 shows the early stages of the flyer for a Fall Harvest Festival (originally shown in Figure 6-1). The pumpkins are already in place, and the scarecrow was dragged in from another image. The scarecrow comes in at the top of the stack, in front of the pumpkins. You can put the scarecrow behind the pumpkins by simply dragging the scarecrow layer beneath the pumpkin layer in the Layers palette.

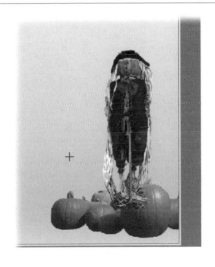
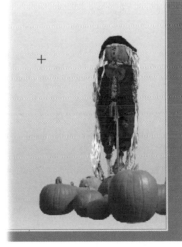

Figure 6-12:
Left: When you bring a new element into an image, it comes in at the top of the layer stack, making it the front object, like the scarecrow here.

Right: Move the new layer down in the stack, and the new object appears behind the existing content, just as the scarecrow moves behind the pumpkins here.

> **NOTE** The only kind of layer you can't move is a Background layer. If you want to bring a Background layer to another spot in the layer stack, first convert the Background layer to a regular layer (page 147), and then you can move it.

You can also move layers by going to Layer → Arrange and choosing the command of your choice:

- **Bring to Front** (Shift+⌘+]) sends the selected layer to the top of the stack so the layer's contents appear in the foreground of your image.

- **Bring Forward** (⌘+]) moves the layer up one level in the Layers palette, so it appears one step closer to the front of your image.

- **Send Backward** (⌘+[) moves the layer down one level so it's sent back one step in the image.

- **Send to Back** (Shift+⌘+[) puts the layer directly above the Background layer so it appears as far back as you can move anything.

- **Reverse** (no keystroke shortcut) switches two layers' locations in the stack, but you must select two layers in the palette (by ⌘+clicking, for example) before this command becomes available.

> **NOTE** These commands (except Reverse) are now also available from the Move tool's Options bar or by right-clicking (Control+clicking) in your photo when the Move tool is active. As a matter of fact, the Move tool can be a great way to rearrange layers in your image, as the next section explains.

Arranging layers with the Move tool

Using the Move tool, you can locate and arrange layers right in your image window, without trekking all the way over to the Layers palette. (If you need a refresher on Move tool basics, check out page 138.)

To arrange layers with the Move tool:

1. **Activate the Move tool.**

   Click its icon in the Toolbox or press V.

2. **Select the layer(s) you want to move.**

   As soon as you activate the Move tool, you see the bounding box (the dotted lines) around the active layer in the Layers palette. As you move your cursor over your image, you see a blue outline around the layer that the cursor is over, no matter how far down the layer stack the object is, as shown in Figure 6-13. When you click to select the layer you want to move, the bounding box then appears around that layer. Shift+click to select multiple layers, and the bounding box expands to include all that you've selected.

3. **Move the Layer.**

   For example, choose Layer → Arrange, or click the Arrange Menu in the Options bar, or right-click (Control+click) inside the bounding box in the image. You see the same choices (Bring to Front, Bring Forward, and so on) described in the previous section, except for Reverse, which is only available from the Layer menu. You can also use keystroke shortcuts (again, except for Reverse).

   > **NOTE** If you selected multiple layers, you may find that some of the commands are grayed out (that is, you can't select them). If that's a problem, just click elsewhere in the image to deselect the layers and then send them one at a time instead of as a group.

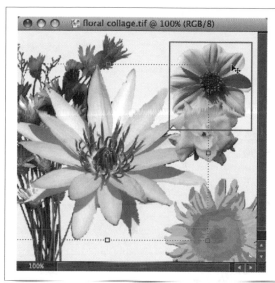

Figure 6-13:
The Move tool lets you select objects from any layer, not just the active one. When you move the cursor over any object, you see the blue outline around its layer. Here, the water lily is the active layer (you can see the bounding box around it), but the Move tool is ready to select the pink flower, even though it's not on the active layer. If all these outlines annoy you, you can turn them off in the Options bar (via the Show Bounding Box or "Show Highlight on Rollover" checkbox). If you want to force the Move tool to concentrate only on the active layer, turn off Auto Select Layer.

Aligning and Distributing Layers

Elements makes it easy to align objects in your image, thanks to the Move tool. The Move tool's *aligning* feature arranges the objects on each layer so that they line up straight along their top, bottom, left, or right edges, or through their centers. So, for example, if you align the top edges of your objects, Elements makes sure that the top of each object is exactly in line with the others.

Evenly distributing the *space* between multiple objects is also a breeze. The Move tool's *distributing* feature spaces out the distance between objects, also letting you choose edges or centers as a guide. If you distribute the top edges, for example, Elements makes sure that there's an even amount of space from the top edge of one object to another.

> **TIP** Distributing objects in this way is especially handy when you're creating projects like those described in Chapter 15.

Aligning and distributing layers with the Move tool works much like rearranging layers:

1. **Activate the Move tool.**

   Click its icon in the Toolbox or press V.

2. **Select the objects you want to align.**

   This maneuver works only if each object is on its own layer. If you have multiple objects on one layer, move them to their own layers, one at a time, by selecting each object and then pressing ⌘+Shift+J.

   Shift+click inside the blue outline to select each layer you want to work with, or select the layers in the Layers palette.

3. **Choose how you want to align or distribute the objects by selecting from the Options bar menus.**

   As shown in Figure 6-14, the Align and Distribute menus both give you the same choices: Top Edges, Vertical Centers, Bottom Edges, Left Edges, Horizontal Centers, and Right Edges.

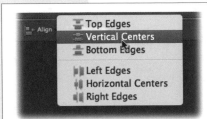

Figure 6-14:
You may get a little confused by the various ways you can arrange objects with the Move tool. The best way to find the choice you want is to look at the little thumbnails next to each label—they show you exactly how your objects will line up. This is a picture of the Distribute menu, but you can't tell because it pops up to hide the word "Distribute" in the Options bar. The Distribute and Align menus both give you the same list of choices.

TIP If you're confused about what the Align and Distribute menus do, just look at the thumbnails next to each menu item. You can apply as many different commands as you like, as long as the layers are still inside the bounding box. Figure 6-15 also gives you an example of how these commands work.

STAYING ORGANIZED

Selecting Layers

You can quickly target multiple layers when you want to manage them, like linking, moving, or deleting your layers. For your quick-selection pleasure, Elements gives you a whole group of layer selection commands, which you'll find in the Select menu. Here's what they do:

- **All Layers**. Choose this command and every layer except the Background layer gets selected. Even if you've turned off visibility (page 154) on a particular layer, that layer still gets selected.

- **Deselect Layers**. When you're done working with your layers as a group, you can choose this option and you won't have any layers selected until you click one.

- **Similar Layers**. This command is the most useful. Choose this option, and every layer of the same type

gets selected, no matter where it is in the stack. So, for example, if you have a Text layer as your active layer when you choose Similar Layers, all your Text layers get selected. If, on the other hand, you had an Adjustment layer active, all your Adjustment layers get selected. You may use this command to quickly select a stack of Adjustment layers you want to drag to another image, for instance, using the technique on page 172.

You can also Shift+click to select multiple layers that are next to each other in the palette, or ⌘+click to select layers that are separated. That way you can avoid the menu altogether. Once you're done, you can either use the Deselect Layers command from the menu, or just click another layer to make it the active layer.

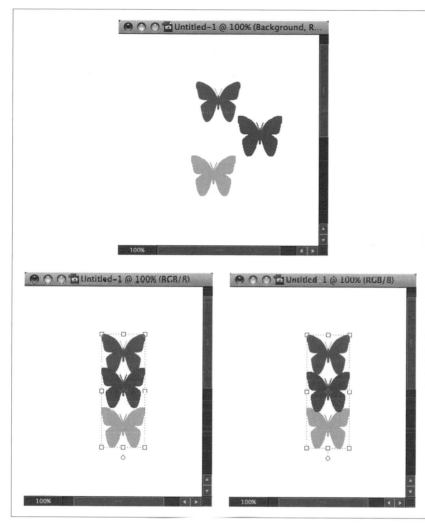

Figure 6-15:
Top: Each of these butterflies is on its own layer, but they need to be tidied up if you want them in a neat stack.

Bottom left: The result, after selecting the butterflies with the Move tool, and then picking Align → Horizontal Center. As you see, the centers of the butterflies are now aligned, but they're not distributed evenly.

Bottom right: The butterflies after adding a trip to Distribute → Vertical Centers. Note that they're evenly spaced but still pretty close together. That's because Distribute doesn't add any additional space between the outermost objects. If you want wider spacing between the shapes, make sure they're farther apart before you distribute them.

Grouping and Linking Layers

What if you want to move several layers at once? For instance, in the Harvest Festival image there are two layers with pumpkins on them. It's kind of a pain to drag each one individually if you need to move them in front of the scarecrow, for instance. Fortunately, you don't have to; Elements gives you a way to keep your layers united.

Linking layers

You can *link* layers together, and then they'll travel as a unit, as shown in Figure 6-16.

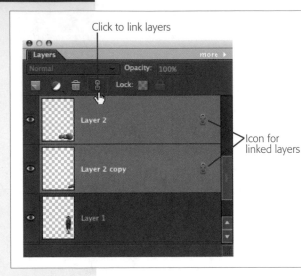

Click to link layers

Figure 6-16:
Shift+click to select the layers you want to link, and then click the little chain (where the hand appears in the figure) to link two layers together. The chain icon appears to the right of each layer name to indicate that the chosen layers will now move as a group.

Icon for linked layers

If you want to remove a link between layers, select the linked layers by clicking one and then clicking the same chain icon to turn it off again. You can always merge the layers (covered in the next section) into one layer if you want. Sometimes, though, you'll want to keep layers separate, while still being able to move the layers as a group. Linking is the way to do that. You can also use the layer selection choices, described in the box page 162, and skip the linking. As long as your layers all stay selected, they'll travel as a group. The advantage to linking is that your layers stay associated until you unlink them. There's no need to worry about accidentally clicking somewhere else in the palette and losing your selection group.

> **NOTE**   The chain icon at the top of the Layers palette doesn't behave quite the same way as the transparency buttons do. You click the chain icon to link your layers, but it doesn't look any different once you've got some layers linked together. The Linked layer chain next to the layer name is the only hint you get that a layer is linked.

Grouping layers

An even more powerful way to combine separate layers is to *group* them. Grouping allows you to let one layer influence the other layers it's grouped with. Grouping layers isn't at all the same as linking them. It's probably easiest to understand grouping by looking at the example shown in Figure 6-17, which shows how you can crop an image on one layer using the shape of an object on another layer. (This kind of grouping is also called a *clipping mask* in Photoshop, and sometimes in Elements.)

> **NOTE**   If you group two layers together, the bottom layer determines the opacity of both layers.

Once the layers are grouped, you can still slide the top layer around with the Move tool to reposition it so that you see exactly the part of it that you want. So in

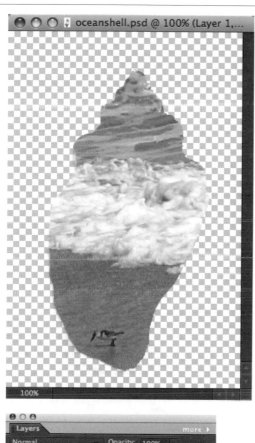

Figure 6-17:
This image began with a picture of a seashell on one layer and a beach scene on the layer above it. At first, the beach image totally hid the seashell, but interesting things happen when you group the layers. The beach layer automatically gets cropped to the shape of the bottom layer, the seashell. The minute little downward-bent arrow (visible just above the cursor) in the Layers palette indicates the beach layer is grouped.

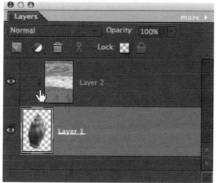

Figure 6-17, the beach layer was maneuvered around till the sandpiper showed in the bottom of the shell shape.

To group two layers together, make the top layer (of the two you want to group) the active layer. Then choose Layer → "Group with Previous". You can also group layers using the keyboard. First, make sure the top layer is the active layer, and then press ⌘+G. Another way to group is to do it right in the Layers palette.

Hold down Option, and in the Layers palette, move your cursor over the dividing line between the layers. Click when you see two linked circles appear by your cursor. Now your layers are grouped.

If you get tired of the layer grouping or you want to delete or change one of the layers, select Layer → Ungroup or press Shift+⌘+G to remove the grouping.

> **TIP** There's an even easier way to group layers. In the New Layer dialog box, there's a checkbox for "Group with Previous Layer." Turn it on, and your new layer is pre-grouped with the layer below it.

Merging and Flattening Layers

By now, you've probably got at least an inkling of how useful layers are. But there is a downside to having layers in your image: They take up a lot of storage space, especially if you have lots of duplicate layers. Layers make files bigger. Fortunately, you aren't committed to keeping layers in your file forever. You can reduce your file size quite a bit—and sometimes also make things easier to manage—by merging layers or flattening your image.

Merging layers

Sometimes you may have two or more separate layers that really could be treated as one layer, like the pumpkins shown in Figure 6-18. You aren't limited to linking those layers together; once you've got everything arranged to your satisfaction, you can merge them together into one layer. Also, if you want to copy and paste your image, many times the standard copy and paste commands (page 115) will copy only the top layer. So it helps to get everything into one layer, at least temporarily.

You'll probably merge layers quite often when you're working with multi-layered files (for example, when you've got multiple objects that you want to edit simultaneously).

To merge layers, you have a few different options, depending on what's active in your image at the time. You can get to any of the following commands from the Layers menu, or from the More button on the Layers palette.

- **Merge Down**. This combines the active layer and the layer immediately beneath it. If the layer just below the active layer is hidden, you won't see this option in the list of choices.

- **Merge Visible**. This combines all the visible layers into one layer. If you want to combine layers that are far apart, just temporarily turn off visibility (by clicking the Eye icon) for the ones in between and for any other layers that you don't want to merge.

- **Merge Linked**. Click any of your linked layers and you see this command, which joins the linked layers into one layer.

- **Merge Clipping Mask**. You need to select the bottom layer of a layer group to see this command. Choose it, and the grouped layers join into one layer.

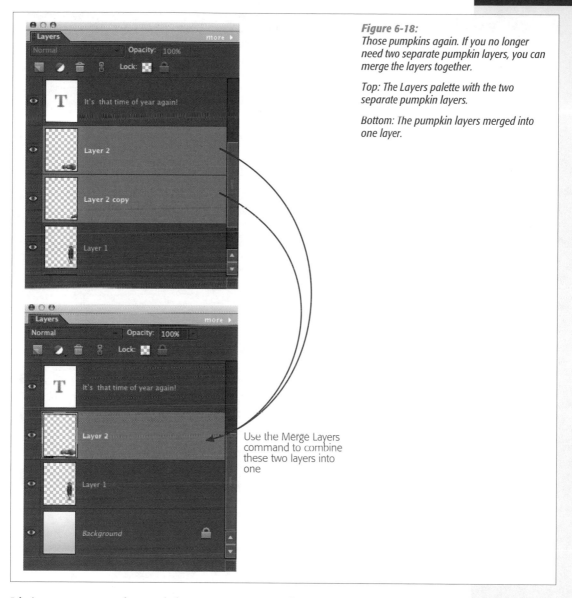

Figure 6-18:
Those pumpkins again. If you no longer need two separate pumpkin layers, you can merge the layers together.

Top: The Layers palette with the two separate pumpkin layers.

Bottom: The pumpkin layers merged into one layer.

Use the Merge Layers command to combine these two layers into one

It's important to understand that once you merge layers and save and close your file, you can't just un-merge them again. While your file is still open, of course, you can use any of the undo commands (page 30), but once you've gotten past the undo limit you've set in Preferences (page 30), you're stuck with your merged layers.

TIP The box on page 168 shows you another way to combine all your layers, while still keeping a separate copy of the individual layers.

Stamp Visible

There are times when you want to perform an action on all the visible layers of your image without permanently merging them together. You can easily do this—and quickly, too, even if you have dozens of layers in your file—by using what Adobe calls the Stamp Visible command. The Stamp Visible command combines the contents of all your layers into a new layer at the top of the stack.

Stamp Visible lets you work away on the new combined layer while still preserving your existing layers untouched, in case you want them back later on. To use Stamp Visible, first create a new blank layer and make it the top layer of your image.

Next, either press ⌘+Shift+Option+E or hold down Option while selecting the Merge Visible command from the Layers menu (or from the More menu in the Layers palette). You'll see the top layer fill itself with the combined contents of all your other layers.

If you want to keep a layer or two from being included in this new layer, just turn off the visibility of those layers you don't wish to include before using the Stamp Visible command.

If you have enough dexterity, you can even skip the layer creation step and press ⌘+Shift+Option+N+E to make the new layer and fill it at the same time.

Sometimes if your layer contains type or shapes drawn with the Shape tool, you won't be able to merge the layer right away. Elements asks you to *simplify* the layer first. Simplifying a layer means that you've converted its contents to a *raster object*. In other words, now it's just a bunch of pixels, subject to the same resizing limitations as any photo would be. So, for example, if you have a type layer, you can still apply filters to the type or paint on it, but you can no longer edit the words. (See page 341 for more about simplifying and working with shapes, and see Chapter 14 for working with type.)

Flattening an image

While layers are simply swell when you're working on an image, they're a headache when you want to share your image, especially if you're sending it to a photoprinting service (their machines usually don't understand layered files). And even if you're printing at home, the large size of a layered file can make it take forever to print. Also, if you plan to use your image in other programs, very few non-Adobe programs are totally comfortable with layered files, so you may get some odd results if you feed them a layered file.

In these cases, you may want to squash everything in your picture into a single layer. It's very easy to do this in Elements. You simply flatten your image. Do so by going to Layer → Flatten Image, or on the Layers palette, choose More → Flatten Image. Or, to keep your original intact, save as a copy and turn off Layers in the Save As dialog box.

TIP   Saving your image as a JPEG file automatically gets rid of layers, too.

There's no keystroke shortcut for flattening, because it's something you don't want to do by accident. Like merging, flattening is a permanent change. Many cautious Elements veterans always do a Save As, instead of a plain Save, before flattening. That way you have a flattened copy and still have your working copy with the layers intact, just in case.

> **NOTE** Flattening creates a background layer out of the existing layers in your image, which means that you lose transparency, just as with a regular background layer. If you want to create a single layer with transparency, use Merge Visible instead of Flatten Image.

Fill and Adjustment Layers

Fill layers and *Adjustment layers* are special types of layers. Adjustment layers let you manipulate the lighting, color, or exposure of the layers beneath them. If you're mainly interested in Elements to spruce up your photos, you'll probably use Adjustment layers more than any other kind of layer. Adjustment layers are great because they give you the ability to undo or change your edits later on if you want to.

You can also use Adjustment layers to take the changes you've made on one photo and reapply those changes to another photo (see the box below). And after you've created an Adjustment layer, you can limit future edits so they affect only the area of your photo covered by the Adjustment layer.

You'll find out much more about all the things you can do with Adjustment layers in the next few chapters. For now, you just need to learn how to create and manipulate them.

Fill layers are just what they sound like: layers filled with a color, a pattern, or a gradient (a rainbow-like range of colors). There's more about gradients on page 370.

> **TIP** Digital photographers should check out the Photo Filter Adjustment layers. They let you digitally make the sort of adjustments that you used to do by attaching a colored piece of glass to the front of your camera's lens. You can read more about what you can do with photo filters on page 231.

GEM IN THE ROUGH

Adjustment Layers for Batch Processing

Page 233 shows you how to perform *batch* commands: simultaneously applying adjustments to groups of photos, using the Process Multiple Files tool. The drawback with Process Multiple Files is that you have access only to some of the auto commands there—your editing options are very limited. So what do you do if you're a fussy photographer who's got 17 shots that are all pretty much the same and you'd like to apply the same fixes to all of them? Do you have to edit each one from scratch?

Not in Elements. You can open the photos you want to fix and then drag an Adjustment layer from the first photo onto each of the other photos (page 172 shows you how to drag layers between images). The new photo gets the same adjustments at the same settings. It's not as fast as true batch processing, but it saves a lot of time compared with editing each photo from scratch.

Adding Fill and Adjustment Layers

Creating an Adjustment or Fill layer is easy. In the Layers palette, just click the black-and-white circle, as shown in Figure 6-19. The button displays a menu of all the Adjustment and Fill layer choices in one list (the first three choices are Fill layers; the rest are Adjustment layers).

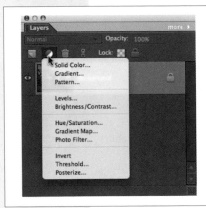

Figure 6-19:
To create a new Adjustment or Fill layer, click the black-and-white circle to get a drop-down menu that lets you choose the type of Adjustment or Fill layer you want. If you'd rather work from the menu bar, go to Layer → New Adjustment Layer (or Layer → New Fill Layer) and choose the layer type you want.

Whichever type of layer you choose, you get a dialog box that lets you tweak the layer's settings (the exception is Invert, which doesn't give you any choices). After you make your choices, click OK, and the new layer appears.

Elements gives you three Fill layer choices: Solid Color, Gradient (a rainbow-like range of colors), and Pattern. There's more about patterns on page 252 and about gradients on page 370.

The kinds of Adjustment layers you can select from are:

- **Levels.** This is a much more sophisticated way to apply Levels than using the Auto Levels button in Quick Fix or the Auto Level command from the Enhance menu. Page 188 has more information about using Levels. For most people, Levels is the most important Adjustment layer.

- **Brightness/Contrast.** This does pretty much the same things as the Quick Fix adjustment (covered on page 101).

- **Hue/Saturation.** Again, it's very much like the Quick Fix command (page 104), only with slightly different controls.

- **Gradient Map.** This is very tricky to understand and is explained in detail on page 379. It maps each tone in your image to a new tone based on the gradient you select. That means you can apply a gradient so that the colors aren't just distributed in a straight line across your image.

- **Photo Filter.** Use Photo Filter to adjust the color balance of your photos by adding warming, cooling, or special effects filters, just like you might attach to the lens of a film camera. See page 231.

- **Invert.** This reverses the colors of your image to their opposite values, for an effect similar to a film negative. See page 267.

- **Threshold.** Use this to make everything in your photo pure black and pure white. See page 267.

- **Posterize.** Reduces the numbers of colors in your image to give a poster-like effect. See page 267.

You can change the settings for a Fill or Adjustment layer by highlighting the layer in the Layers palette, and then going to Layer → Layer Content Options, or by double-clicking the left icon for the layer in the Layers palette. The layer's dialog box reappears, and you can adjust its settings. Deleting Fill and Adjustment layers is a tad different from deleting a regular layer, as explained in Figure 6-20.

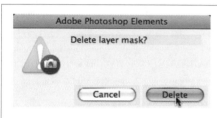

Figure 6-20:
When you click the Layers palette Delete icon, Elements asks you if you want to "Delete layer mask?". Click Delete. Then you have to click the trashcan icon again to fully delete the layer. If you want to get rid of the layer in one step, you've got a few choices: Use the Layer menu, right-click (Control+click) the layer in the Layers palette, or use the More button to delete it. In each case, you should see a Delete Layer choice. There's more about layer masks in the next section.

Layer Masks

Adjustment and Fill layers use something called a *layer mask*, which dictates which parts of the layer are affected when you make your changes (see Figure 6-21). By changing the area covered by the layer mask you can control which part of your image the layer adjustments affect.

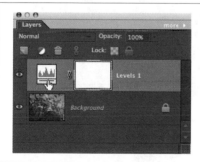

Figure 6-21:
Adjustment and Fill layers, like the Levels 1 layer shown here, always have two icons in the Layers palette: the left side shows what kind of adjustment the layer is making (Levels, in this case). You can double-click that icon to bring up the dialog box to make changes to your settings after the layer is in place. The right icon is for the Layer Mask, and you can use it to control the area that is covered by the adjustment.

Full Photoshop uses layer masks for many other purposes, but in Elements, Adjustment and Fill layers are the only place you encounter a layer mask. The great thing about layer masks is that you can edit them by painting on them, as explained on page 279. In other words, you can go back later and change the part of your image that the Adjustment layer affects.

Incidentally, the term layer *mask* may be a bit confusing if you're thinking about masking with the Selection brush. With the Selection brush, masking prevents something from being changed. A layer mask really works the same way, but by definition, it starts out empty; in other words, the mask can be used to prevent your adjustment from affecting parts of the layer, but not until you mask out parts of your image by painting on the layer mask. So to begin with, your entire layer is affected by your change. You can learn how to edit layer masks on page 279.

Moving Layers Between Images

If you use layers, it's extremely easy to combine parts of different photos together. Just put what you want from photo A into its own layer and then drag it onto photo B. The trick is that you have to drag the layer *from the Layers palette*. If you try to drop one photo directly onto another photo's window, you'll just wind up with a lot of windows stacked on top of each other (unless you activate the Move tool, described on page 147). Figure 6-22 shows you the correct way to move a layer between photos.

NOTE   In an earlier version of Elements you could also drag a photo directly from the Photo bin into another image. That no longer works in Elements 6.

Photo B   Photo A

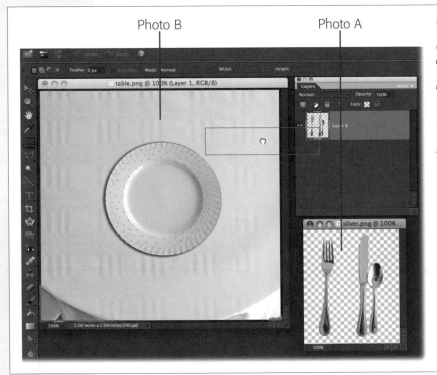

Figure 6-22:
This figure shows how to move objects from one photo to another, working from the Layers palette. Here, the goal is to get the silverware from photo A (whose Layers palette is visible) onto the tablecloth in photo B (whose image is visible). You always drag from the Layers palette onto a photo window when you combine parts of different images into a composite. (If you try to drag from a photo to a photo, it won't work unless you click the Move tool first.) Use the Move tool to adjust your object's placement once you've dropped it into the image.

Here are a few points to keep in mind when you're copying a layer from one image to another:

- **Watch out for conflicting resolution settings** (see page 86). The bottom image (that is, the one receiving the moved layer) controls the resolution. So if you bring in a layer that's set to 300 pixels per inch (ppi), and place it on an image that's set to 72 ppi, the object you're moving will now be set to 72 ppi.

  NOTE You can't work with multiple images when you have your Elements screen view set to Maximize mode. Instead, go to Window → Images and choose Tile or Cascade. Cascade gives you the most flexibility for positioning your photos.

- **Lighting matters.** Objects that are lit differently will stand out if you try to combine them. If possible, plan ahead and choose similar lighting for photos you're thinking about combining.

- **Center your moved layer.** If you want your layer to center itself in the new image, Shift+drag the layer.

- **Feather with care.** A little feathering (page 125) goes a long way toward creating a realistic result.

  NOTE If you'd like more practice using layers, visit the "Missing CD" page at *www. missingmanuals.com* and download the Table Tutorial. It walks you through most of the basic layer functions.

Part Three: Retouching

3

Basic Image Retouching

You may be perfectly happy using Elements only in Quick Fix mode. And that's fine, as long as you understand that you've hardly scratched the surface of what the program can do for you. Sooner or later, though, you're probably going to run across a photo where your best Quick Fix efforts just aren't good enough. Or you may just be curious to see what else Elements has under its hood. That's when you finally get to put all your image-selecting and layering skills to good use.

Elements gives you loads of ways to fix your photos beyond the limited options in Quick Fix. This chapter guides you through fixing basic exposure problems, shows you new ways of sharpening your photos, and most important, helps you understand how to improve the colors in your photos.

If you want to get the most out of Elements, you need to understand a little about how your camera, computer, and printer think about color. Along with resolution, color is the most important concept in Elements. After all, almost all the adjustments that image-editing programs make consist of changing the color of pixels. So quite a bit of this chapter is about understanding how Elements—and by extension, you—can manipulate your image's color.

> **TIP** Most of Elements' advanced-fixes dialog boxes have a "preview" checkbox, which lets you watch what's happening as you adjust the settings. It's a good idea to keep these checkboxes turned on so you can decide if you're improving things. And for a handy "before" and "after" comparison, toggle the checkbox on and off.

Fixing Exposure Problems

Incorrectly exposed photos are *the* number one problem all photographers face. No matter how carefully you set up your shot and how many different settings you try on your camera, it always seems like the picture you really, really want to keep is the one that's over- or underexposed.

The Quick Fix commands (page 97) can really help your photo, but if you've tried to bring back a picture that's badly over- or underexposed, you've probably run into the limitations of what Quick Fix can do. Similarly, the Shadows/Highlights command (page 181) can do a lot, but it's not intended to fix a photo whose exposure is totally botched—just ones where the contrast between light and dark areas needs a bit of help. And if you push Smart Fix to its limits, your results may be a little strange. In those situations, you need to move on to some of Elements' more powerful tools to help improve your exposure.

> **NOTE** In this section, you'll learn about the more traditional ways of correcting exposure in Elements. But also be sure to check out the improved Camera RAW Converter (page 213), which can now help with your JPEG and TIFF photos, too. Your results with non-RAW photos may vary, but the RAW Converter just might turn out to be your best choice.

UP TO SPEED

Understanding Exposure

What exactly *is* exposure, anyway? You almost certainly know a poorly exposed photo when you see it: It's either too light or too dark. But what exactly has gone wrong?

Exposure refers to the amount of light your film (or the sensor in your digital camera) received when you released the shutter.

A well-exposed photo shows the largest amount of detail in *all* parts of your image—light and dark. In a properly exposed photo, shadows aren't just pits of blackness, and bright areas show more than washed-out splotches of white.

Deciding Which Exposure Fix to Use

When you open a poorly exposed photo in Elements, the first thing you need to do is figure out what's wrong with it, just like a doctor diagnosing a patient. If the exposure's not perfect, what exactly is wrong? Here's a list of common symptoms to help you figure out where to go next:

- **Everything is too dark**. If your photo is really dark, try adding a Screen layer, as explained on page 179. If it's just a bit too dark, try using Levels (see page 188).

- **Everything is too light**. If the whole photo looks washed out, try adding a Multiply layer (explained on page 179). If it's just a bit too light, try Levels (page 188).

- **The photo is mostly OK, but your subject is too dark or the light parts of the photo are too light**. Try the Shadows/Highlights adjustment (page 181).

Of course, if you're lucky (or a really skilled photographer), you may not see any of these problems, in which case, skip to page 188 if you want to do something to make your colors pop.

> **NOTE** You may have noticed that you didn't see Brightness/Contrast mentioned anywhere in the previous list. A lot of people tend to jump for the Brightness/Contrast controls when facing a poorly exposed photo. That's logical—after all, these dials usually help improve the picture on your TV. But in Elements, about 99 percent of the time, you've got a whole slew of powerful tools—like Levels and the Shadows/Highlights command—that can do much more than Brightness/Contrast can. However, in Elements 6, Brightness/Contrast is much improved from earlier versions, so feel free to give it a try when you only need to make very subtle changes.

Fixing Major Exposure Problems

If your photo is completely over- or underexposed, you need to add special layers to correct the problems. You follow the same steps to fix either problem. The only difference is the layer blend mode (page 157) you choose: *Multiply layers* darken your image's exposure while *Screen layers* lighten it. Figure 7-1 shows Multiply layers in action (and also gives you an idea of the limitations of this technique if your exposure is really far gone). You can download the file window.jpg from the "Missing CD" page at *www.missingmanuals.com* if you'd like to try the different exposure fixes for yourself.

Be careful, though. If your entire photo isn't out of whack, using Multiply or Screen layers can ruin the exposure of the parts that were OK to start with, because they'll increase or decrease the exposure on the entire photo. Your properly exposed areas may blow out (see page 183) and lose the details if you apply a Screen layer, for example. So, if your exposure problem is spotty (as opposed to problems that affect the entire image), try Shadows/Highlights (page 181) first. If your whole photo needs an exposure correction, here's how to use layers to fix it:

1. **Create a duplicate layer.**

   Open your photo and press ⌘+J or go to Layer → Duplicate Layer. Check to be sure the duplicate layer is the active layer.

2. **In the Layers palette, change the mode for the new layer in the pop-up menu.**

   Choose Multiply if your photo is overexposed, or Screen if it's underexposed. Make sure you change the mode of the duplicate layer, not the original layer.

3. **Adjust the opacity of the layer if needed.**

   If the effect of the new layer is too strong, in the Layers palette, move the Opacity slider to the left to reduce the new layer's opacity.

4. **Repeat as necessary.**

   You may need to use as many as five or six layers if your photo is in really bad shape. If you need extra layers, you'll probably want them at 100 percent opacity, so you can just keep pressing ⌘+J, which will duplicate the current top layer.

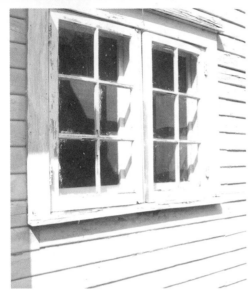

Figure 7-1:
For those who think photographically, each Multiply layer you add is roughly equivalent to stopping your camera down one f-stop, at least as far as the dark areas are concerned.

Top: This photo is totally overexposed, and it looks like there's no detail there at all. Multiply layers darken things enough to bring back a lot of the washed-out areas. This technique can bring out the detail quite a bit.

Bottom: As you can see in the corrected photo, even Elements can't do much in areas where there's no detail at all.

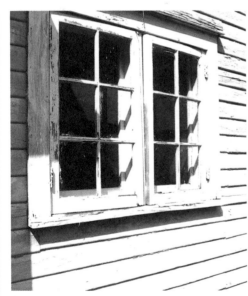

You're more likely to need several layers to fix overexposure than you are for underexposure. And, of course, there are limits to what even Elements can do for a blindingly overexposed image. Overexposure is usually tougher to fix than underexposure, especially if the area is blown out, as explained in the box on page 183.

The Shadows/Highlights Command

The Shadows/Highlights command is one of the best features in Elements. It's an incredibly powerful tool for adjusting only the dark or light areas of your photo without messing up the rest of it. Figure 7-2 shows what a great help it can be.

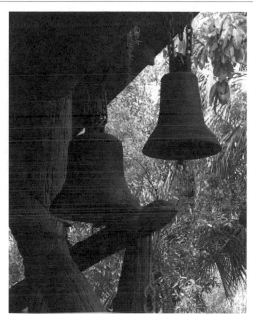

Figure 7-2:
The Shadows/Highlights command can bring back details from photos where you were sure there was no information at all.

Top: The original photo suffers from a severe case of extreme backlighting.

Bottom: The Shadows/Highlights tool brings out the hidden detail and reduces the background glare. If you look closely at the mouths of the bells and the wooden supports just below them, you can see the kind of noise (graininess) that often lurks in underexposed areas. Those problems mean you may need to apply noise reduction (page 357) and tweak the saturation.

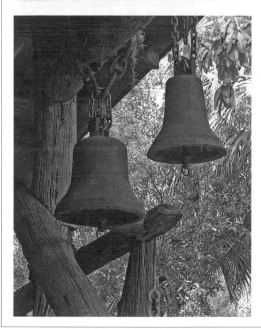

The Shadows/Highlights command in Full Edit works pretty much the same way it does in Quick Fix (page 102). The single flaw in this great tool is that you can't apply it as an Adjustment layer (page 169), so you may want to apply Shadows/Highlights to a duplicate layer. Then, later on, you can discard the changes if you want to take another whack at adjusting the photo. In any case, it's not difficult at all to make amazing changes to your photos with Shadows/Highlights.

Here's how:

1. **Open your photo and duplicate the layer (⌘+J) if you want to.**

   Duplicating your layer makes it easier to undo Shadows/Highlights later if you change your mind.

2. **Go to Enhance → Adjust Lighting → Shadows/Highlights.**

   Your photo immediately becomes about 30 shades lighter. Don't panic. As soon as you select the command, the Lighten Shadows setting automatically jumps to 25 percent, which is way too much for most of your photos. Just shove the slider back to 0 to undo this change before you start making your corrections.

3. **Move the sliders around until you like what you see.**

   The sliders do exactly what they say: Lighten Shadows makes the dark areas of your photo lighter, and Darken Highlights makes the light areas darker. Pushing the slider to the right increases the effect for either one.

4. **Click OK when you're happy.**

The Shadows/Highlights tool is a cinch to use because you just make decisions based on what you're seeing. Keep these tips in mind:

- You may want to add a smidgen of the opposite tool to balance things out a little. In other words, if you're lightening shadows, you may get better results by giving the Darken Highlights slider a teeny nudge, too.

- Midtone Contrast is there because your photo may look kind of flat after you're done with Shadows/Highlights, especially if you've made big adjustments. Move the Midtone Contrast slider to the right to increase the contrast in your photo. It usually adds a bit of a darkening effect, so you may need to go back to one of the other sliders to tweak your photo after you usc it.

- You can overdo the Shadows/Highlights tool. When you see halos around the objects in your photo, you've pushed the settings too far.

> **TIP** If the Shadows/Highlights tool looks like it washed out your photo's colors—making everyone look like they've been through the laundry too many times—you can adjust the color intensity with one of the Saturation commands, either in Quick Fix or in the Full Editor (as described on page 260). Watch people's skin tones when increasing the saturation—if the subjects in your photo start looking like sunless-tanning lotion disaster victims, you've gone too far. Also check out the Vibrance slider in the Raw Converter (page 225), or you can try adjusting colors with Elements' Color Curves feature (page 254).

Controlling the Colors You See

You want your photos to look as good as possible and to have beautiful, breathtaking color, right? That's probably why you bought Elements. But now that you've got the program, you're having a little trouble getting things to look the way you want. Does this sound familiar?: Your photos look great onscreen but your prints are washed out, too dark, or the colors are all a little wrong.

What's going on? The answer has to do with the fact that Elements is a *color-managed* program. That means that Elements uses your monitor for guidance when deciding how to display images. Color management is the science of making sure that the color in your images is always exactly the same, no matter who opens your file or what kind of hardware they're viewing it on or printing it from. If you think of all the different monitor and printer models out there, you get an idea of what a big job this is.

Graphics pros spend their whole lives grappling with color management, and you can find plenty of books about the finer points of color management. On the most sophisticated level, color management is complicated enough to make you curl up, whimpering, into the fetal position and swear never to create another picture.

Luckily for you, Elements makes color management a whole lot easier. Most of the time, you have only two things to deal with: your monitor calibration and your color space. The following pages cover both.

> **NOTE** There are a couple of other color-related settings for printing, too, but you can deal with those when you get ready to print. Chapter 16 explains them.

IN THE FIELD

Avoiding Blowouts

An area of a photo is *blown out* when it's so overexposed that it appears as just plain white—in other words, your camera didn't record any data at all for that area. (Elements isn't all that great with total black, either, but that doesn't happen quite so often. Most underexposed photos have some tonal gradations in them, even if you can't see them very well.)

A blowout is as disastrous in photography as it is when you're driving. Even Elements can't fix blowouts because there's no data for it to work from. So, you're stuck with the fixes discussed in this chapter, which are never as good as a good original.

When you're taking pictures, remember that it's generally easier to correct underexposure than overexposure. Keep that in mind when choosing your camera settings. If you live where there's extremely bright sunlight most of the time, you may want to make a habit of backing your exposure compensation down a hair. Depending on your camera, your subject, and the average ambient glare, you should try starting at −.3 and adjusting from there.

You can also try *bracketing* your shots—taking multiple shots of exactly the same subject with different exposure settings. Then you can combine the two exposures for maximum effect (the box on page 232 explains how to combine images).

Calibrating Your Monitor

Most of your programs pay no attention to what your monitor thinks, but a color-managed application like Elements relies on the *profile*—the information your computer stores about your monitor's settings—when it decides how to print or display a photo onscreen. If that profile isn't accurate, neither is the color in Elements.

So, you may need to *calibrate* your monitor, which is a way of adjusting its settings. A properly calibrated monitor makes all the difference in the world in getting great-looking results. If your pictures in print don't look anything like they look onscreen, you can start fixing the problem by calibrating your monitor.

Getting started with calibrating

Calibrating a monitor sounds intimidating, but it's actually not that difficult—some people think it's even kind of fun. You get an extra added benefit in that your monitor may look about a thousand times better than you thought it could. Calibrating may even make it easier to read text in Word, for instance, because the contrast is better.

Your options for calibrating your monitor are:

- **Use a colorimeter.** This method may sound disturbingly scientific, but it's actually the easiest. A *colorimeter* is just a hardware device with special software that does your calibration for you. The device is much more accurate than calibrating by eye. For a long time, only a pro could afford one, but these days if you shop around you can find the Pantone Huey or the Spyder2Express for about $70 or less. More pro-oriented calibrators like the Eye One Display 2 or the Monaco Optix Spyder are about $200 or less. If you're serious about controlling your colors in Elements, hardware is by far your best option for calibrating.

  NOTE Your calibration software probably asks you to set the brightness and contrast before you begin, even though most newer LCD monitors don't have adjustable dials for these anymore. If you're happy with your monitor's current brightness and contrast, you can safely ignore this step. And unless you have a reason to choose differently, for an LCD monitor you usually want to set your white point to 6500 (Kelvin) and your gamma to 2.2. (Yes, 2.2 is called "PC gamma" sometimes, but it's the native gamma setting for any LCD monitor, including Apple's.)

- **Use your Mac's built-in calibrator.** If you go to → System Preferences → Displays → Color → Calibrate, you can use the Apple Calibration Assistant to calibrate your monitor-sort of (see Figure 7-3). There are also a number of calibration programs you can download from the Internet, but most of them aren't much, if any, better than the Assistant.

If your photos still look a little odd even after you've calibrated your monitor, you may need to turn on the Ignore EXIF setting in Elements' preferences; see Figure 7-4.

Choosing a Color Space

The other thing you may need to do to get good color from Elements is to check the *color space* Elements is using. Color space refers to which standard (out of several

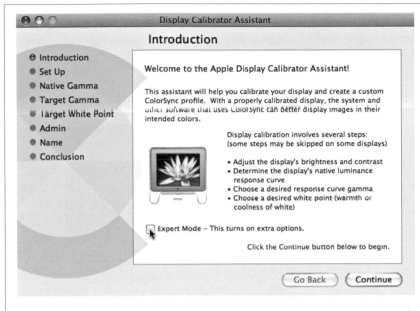

Figure 7-3:
Using the Display Calibrator Assistant is pretty simple. You have two choices: You can do a very basic calibration that just lets you set your gamma and white point, or you can turn on the Expert mode checkbox for a more elaborate color balancing process. In Expert mode, you look at a series of apples (of course!) on a striped background and adjust things till the apples blend into the background.

The problem is that it's almost impossible to get accurate results from a visual calibration. The Calibrator Assistant is better than nothing, but a colorimeter is a much better choice.

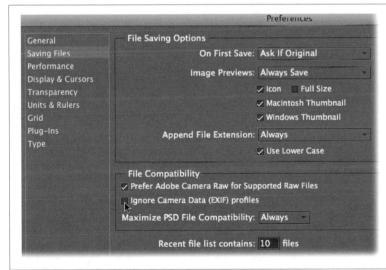

Figure 7-4:
If you still see a funny color cast (usually red or yellow) on all your digital camera photos, go to Photoshop Elements → Preferences → Saving Files and turn on "Ignore Camera Data (EXIF) profiles." Some cameras embed nonstandard color information in their files, and Elements' Ignore EXIF utility just tells Elements to pay no attention to it, allowing your photos to display and print properly.

possibilities) Elements uses to define your colors. Color space can seem pretty abstruse the first time you hear about it, but it's simply a way of defining what colors mean. For example, when someone says "green," what do you envision: a lush emerald color, a deep forest green, a bright lime?

Choosing a color space is a way to make sure that everything that handles a digital file—Elements, your monitor, your printer—sees the same colors the same way. Over the years, the graphics industry has agreed on standards so that everyone has the same understanding of what you mean when you say red or green—as long as you specify which set of standards you're using.

Elements only gives you two color spaces to pick from: *sRGB* (also called *sRGB IEC61966-2.1* if you want to impress your geek friends) and *Adobe RGB*. When you choose a color space, you tell Elements which set of standards you want it to apply to your photos.

If you're happy with the color you see on your monitor in Elements and you like the prints you're getting, you don't need to make any changes. If, on the other hand, you aren't perfectly satisfied with what Elements is giving you, you'll probably want to modify your color space, which you can do in the Color Settings dialog box. Go to Edit → Color Settings or press Shift+⌘+K. Here are your choices:

- **No Color Management**. Elements ignores any information that your file already contains, like color space information from your camera, and doesn't attempt to add any color info to the file data. (When you do a Save As, there's a checkbox that offers you the option of embedding your monitor profile. Don't turn on this checkbox, since your monitor profile is best left for the monitor's own use, and putting the profile into your file can make trouble if you ever send the file someplace else for printing.)

- **Always Optimize Colors for Computer Screens**. Choose this option and you're looking at your photo in the sRGB color space, which is what most Web browsers use, so this is a good choice for when you're preparing graphics for the Web. Many online printing services also prefer sRGB files. (If you've used an early version of Elements, this is the same as the old Limited Color Management option.)

- **Always Optimize for Printing**. This option uses the Adobe RGB color space, which is a wider color space than sRGB. In other words, it allows more gradations of color than sRGB. Sometimes this is your best choice for printing—but not always. So despite the note you'll see in the Color Settings dialog box about "commonly used for printing," don't be afraid to try one of the other two settings instead. Many home inkjet printers actually cope better with sRGB or no color management than with Adobe RGB. (For old Elements hands, this setting used to be called Full Color Management.)

- **Allow Me to Choose**. This option assumes that you're using the sRGB space, but lets you assign either an Adobe RGB tag, an sRGB tag, or no tag at all. If you've selected "Allow Me to Choose," each time you open a file, you see the dialog box shown in Figure 7-5. You can use this dialog box to assign a different profile to a photo. Just save it once without a profile (turn off the Embed Color Profile checkbox in the Save As dialog box), and then reopen it and choose the profile you want from the dialog box. Or there's an easier way to convert a color profile if you need to make a change. See the box on page 187 to learn how.

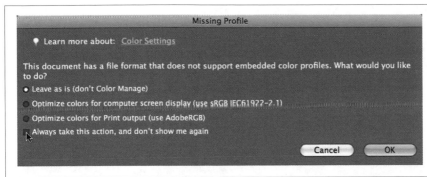

Figure 7-5:
If you select the "Allow Me to Choose" option for color management, you see the Missing Profile dialog box each time you open a previously untagged image. Here's where you can decide whether or not to tag your file and how to tag it.

POWER USERS' CLINIC

Converting Profiles in Elements

If you're a color-management maven, Elements gives you a feature you'll really appreciate—the ability to convert an image's ICC profile from one color space to another. If you've been working in, say, sRGB, and now you want your photo to have the Adobe RGB profile, you can convert it by going to Image → Convert Color Profile and choosing Apply Adobe RGB profile in the pop-out menu.

You can choose to remove a profile, or convert to sRGB or Adobe RGB; your current color profile choice is grayed out (that is, you can't select it).

This is a true conversion. Your photo's colors don't shift the way they might if you just tag a photo with a different profile. Why would you want to perform such a conversion? Well, for example, if you use Adobe RGB when editing your photos, but you're sending your pictures to an online printing service that wants sRGB instead, then you may want to think about converting.

NOTE   Elements automatically opens files tagged with a color space other than the one you're working in without letting you know what it's just done. (Except when you open a file in a color space that Elements can't handle at all, like CMYK. In that case, Elements offers to convert it to a mode you can use.) So, if you have an Adobe RGB file and you're working in "Always Optimize Colors for Computer Screens," Elements doesn't warn you about the profile mismatch the way early versions of the program did—it just opens the file.

So what's your best option? Once again, if everything is looking good, leave it alone. Otherwise, for general use, you're probably best off starting with No Color Management. Then try the others if that doesn't work well for you.

If you choose one of the other three options, when you save your file, Elements attempts to embed the file with a *tag*, or information about the file's color space— either Adobe RGB or sRGB. If you don't want a color tag—also known as an *ICC Profile*—in your file, just turn off the checkbox before you save your file. Figure 7-6 shows where to find the profile information in the Save As dialog box, and how to turn the whole process off.

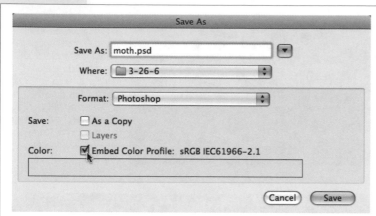

Figure 7-6:
When you save a file, Elements offers to embed the color tag in the file. You can safely turn off the Embed Color Profile checkbox and leave the file untagged. (Assigning a profile is helpful because then any program that sees your file knows what color standards you're working with. But if you're new to Elements, you'll usually have an easier time if you don't start embedding profiles in files without a good reason.)

Using Levels

People who've used Elements for a while will tell you that the Levels command is one of the program's most essential tools. You can fix an amazing array of problems simply by adjusting the level of each *color channel*. (On your monitor, each color you see is composed of red, green, and blue. In Elements, you can make very precise adjustments to your images by adjusting these color channels separately.)

Just as its name suggests, Levels adjusts the level of each color within your image. There are several different adjustments you can make using Levels, from general brightening of your colors to fixing a color cast (more about color casts later in this chapter). Many digital photo enthusiasts treat almost every picture they take to a dose of Levels, because there's no better way to polish up the color in your photo.

The way Levels works is fairly complex. Start by thinking of the possible range of brightness in any photo on a scale from 0 (black) to 255 (white). Some photos may have pixels in them that fall at both those extremes, but most photos don't. And even the ones that do may not have the full range of brightness in each individual color channel. Most of the time, there's going to be some empty space at one or both ends of the scale.

When you use Levels, you tell Elements to consider the range of colors available in *your* photo as the *total* tonal range it has to work with. Elements redistributes your colors accordingly. Basically, you just get rid of the empty space at the ends of the scale of possibilities. This can dramatically readjust the color distribution in your photo, as you can see in Figure 7-7.

It's much, much easier to use Levels than to understand it, as you know if you've already tried Auto Levels in Quick Fix (page 101). That command is great for, well, quick fixes. But if you really need to massage your image, Levels has a lot more under the hood than you can see there. The next section shows you how to get at these settings.

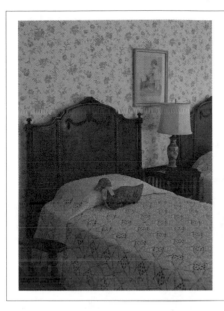 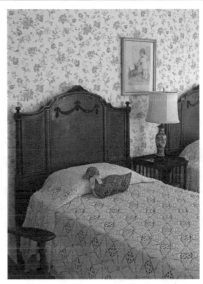

Figure 7-7:
A simple Levels adjustment can make a huge difference in the way your photo looks.

Left: The slight yellow cast to this photo makes everything look dull.

Right: Levels not only got rid of the yellow cast, but the photo also gives the impression of having better contrast and sharpness.

Understanding the Histogram

Before you can get started adjusting Levels, you first need to understand the heart, soul, and brain of the Levels dialog box: the Histogram (shown in Figure 7-8).

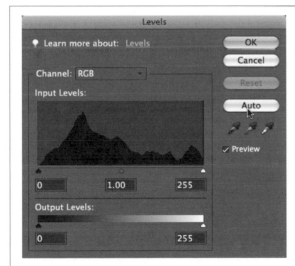

Figure 7-8:
One of the scariest sights in Elements, the Levels dialog box is actually your very good friend. If it frightens you, take comfort in knowing that you've always got the Auto button here, which is the same Auto Levels command as in Quick Fix. But it's worth persevering: The other options here give you much better control over the end results.

The Histogram is the black bumpy mound in the window. It's really nothing more than a bar graph indicating the distribution of the colors in your photo. (It's a bar graph, but there's no space between the bars, which is what causes the mountainous look.)

From left to right, the Histogram shows the brightness range from dark to light (the 0 to 255 mentioned earlier in this section). The height of the "mountain" at any given point shows how many pixels in your photo are that particular brightness. You can tell a lot about your photo by where the mound of color is before you adjust it, as demonstrated in Figure 7-9.

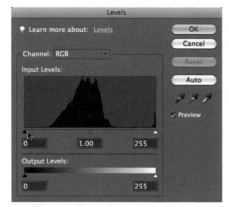

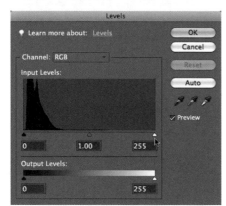

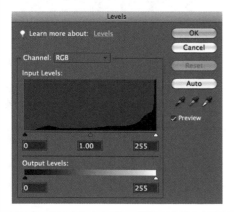

Figure 7-9:
Top: If the bars in your Histogram are all smushed together, your photo doesn't have a lot of tonal range. As long as you like how the photo looks, that's not important. But if you're unhappy with the color in the photo, it's usually going to be harder to get it exactly right compared to a photo that has a wider tonal distribution.

Middle: If all your colors are bunched up on the left side, your photo is underexposed.

Bottom: If you just have a big lump that's all on the right side, your photo is overexposed.

If you look above the Histogram, you can see that there's a little menu that says RGB. If you pull that down, you can also see a separate Histogram for each individual color. You can adjust all three channels at once in the RGB setting, or change each channel separately for maximum control of your colors.

The Histogram contains so much information about your photo that Adobe also makes it available in Full Edit in its own palette; this way, you can always see it and use it to monitor how you're changing the colors in your image. The Histogram palette is shown in Figure 7-10. Once you get fluent in reading Histogramese, you'll probably want to keep this palette around.

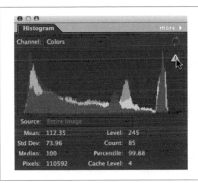

Figure 7-10:
If you keep the Histogram on your desktop, you can always see what effect your changes are having on the color distribution in your photo. To get this nifty Technicolor view, go to Window → Histogram and then choose Colors from the pull-down menu on the palette. To update a Histogram, click the triangle as shown. If you're really into statistical information, there's a bunch of it available from this palette, but if you're not a pro, you can safely ignore these numbers.

The Histogram is just a graph, and you don't do anything to it directly. What you do when you use Levels is use the Histogram as a guide so that you can tell Elements what to consider as the black and white points—that is, the darkest and lightest points, in your photo. (Remember, you're thinking in terms of brightness values, not shades of color, for these settings.)

Once you've set the end points, you can adjust the *gamma*—the tones in between that would appear gray in a black-and-white photo. If that seems complicated, it's not—at least, not when you're actually doing it. Once you've made a Levels adjustment, the next time you open the Levels dialog box, you'll see that your Histogram now runs the entire length of the scale because you've told Elements to redistribute your colors so that they cover the full dark-to-light range.

The next two sections show you—finally!—how to actually adjust your image's Levels.

TIP   Once you learn how to interpret the Histograms in Elements, you can try your hand with your camera's histogram (if it has one). It's really hard to judge how well your picture turned out when all you have to go by is your camera's tiny LCD screen, so the histogram can be a big help. By looking at your camera's histogram, you can tell how well exposed your shot was.

Adjusting Levels: The Eyedropper Method

One way to adjust Levels is to set the black, white, and/or gray points by using the eyedroppers on the right side of the Levels dialog box. It's quite simple—just follow these steps:

1. **Bring up the Levels dialog box by selecting Layer → New Adjustment Layer → Levels.**

   If for some reason you don't want a separate layer for your Levels adjustment, go to Enhance → Adjust Lighting → Levels or press ⌘+L instead. But making the Levels changes on an Adjustment layer gives you more flexibility for making changes in the future.

2. **Move the Levels dialog box out of the way so that you get a good view of your photo.**

   The dialog box loves to plunk itself down smack in the middle of the most important part of your image. Just grab it by the top bar and drag it to where it's not covering up a crucial part of your photo.

3. **In the Levels dialog box, click the black eyedropper.**

   From left to right, the eyedroppers are black, gray, and white.

4. **Move your cursor back over your photo and click an area of your photo that should be black.**

   Should be, not *is*. That's a mistake lots of people make the first time they use the Levels eyedroppers. They click a spot that appears the same color as the eyedropper rather than one that *ought to be* that color.

5. **Repeat with the other eyedroppers for their respective colors.**

   In other words, now find a white point and a gray point. That's the way it's supposed to work, but it's not always possible to use all of the eyedroppers in any one photo. Experiment to see what gives you the best-looking results.

FREQUENTLY ASKED QUESTION

Levels Before Curves

I never know where to start adjusting the colors in my photos. Some photo mavens talk to me about using Levels, others about Curves. Which should I use?

Elements now includes a much requested feature from Photoshop—*Color Curves*. Despite the name, the Curves tool isn't some kind of arc drawing tool. Instead, it's yet another sophisticated method of adjusting the color in your photos. Curves works something like Levels, but with many more available points of correction.

In Elements, you get a simplified version of the Photoshop Curves dialog box, with a few preset settings. Because the Elements version doesn't have quite as many points of adjustment, you get much of the advanced color control of Curves without all the complexity.

Generally speaking, a quick Levels adjustment is usually all you need to achieve good, realistic color. If you still aren't satisfied with the contrast in your image, or you want to create funky artistic effects, check out Color Curves (explained in detail on page 254).

NOTE   You don't always need to set a gray point. If you try to set it and think your photo looked better without it, just skip that step.

6. **When you're happy with what you see, click OK.**

See, it's not so hard. If you mess up, just click the Reset button, and you can start over again.

Adjusting Levels: The Slider Controls

The eyedropper method works fine if your photo has spots that should be black, white, or gray, but a lot of the time, your picture may not have any of these colors.

Fortunately, the Levels sliders give you yet another way to apply Levels, and it's by far the most popular method. The sliders give you maximum control over your colors, and they work great even for photos that don't have a white, black, or gray point to click.

If you look directly under the Histogram, you'll see three little triangles, called *Input sliders*. The left triangle is the slider for setting the black point in your photo, the right slider sets the white point, and the middle slider adjusts your gamma (gray). You just drag them to make changes to the color levels in your photo, as shown in Figure 7-11.

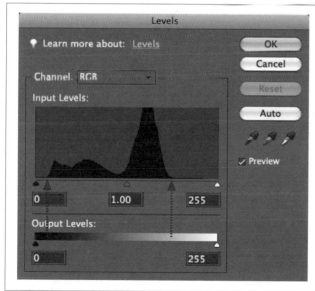

Figure 7-11:
Here's how to use the Levels sliders. You want to move the sliders from the ends of the track until they're under the outer edges of the color data in the graph. If there's empty space on the end, just move the slider until it's under the first mound of data. The red arrows in this figure show where you'd position the left and right sliders for this photo.

When you move the left Input slider, you tell Levels, "Take all the pixels from this point down and consider them black." With the right slider, you're saying, "Make this pixel and all higher values white." The middle slider, the gamma slider, adjusts the brightness value that's considered medium gray. All three adjustments improve the contrast of your image.

NOTE If there are small amounts of data, like a flat line at the ends or if all your data is bunched in the middle of the graph, watch the preview in your photo to decide how far toward the mountain you should bring the sliders. Moving it all the way in may be too drastic. Your own taste should always be the deciding factor when you're adjusting a photo.

The easiest way to use the Levels sliders is to:

1. **Bring up the Levels dialog box.**

   Use one of the methods described in step 1 of the Eyedropper method (page 192).

2. **Move the Levels dialog box so you've got a clear view of your photo and then grab the black Input slider.**

   That's the one on the left side of the Histogram box.

3. **Slide it to the right, if necessary.**

   Move it over until it's under the farthest left part of the Histogram that has a mound of color in it. If you glance back at Figure 7-11, you'd move the left slider to where the left red arrow is. (Incidentally, although you're adjusting the colors in your image, the Levels Histogram stays black and white no matter what you do—you don't get any color in the dialog box itself.)

   You may not need to move the slider at all if there's already a good bit of data at the end of the Histogram. It's not mandatory to adjust everything every time.

4. **Grab the white slider (the one on the right side) and move it left, if necessary.**

   Bring it under the farthest right area of the Histogram that has a mound of data in it.

5. **Now adjust the gray slider.**

   This is called the *gamma* slider, and it adjusts the midtones of your photo. Move it back and forth while watching your photo until you like what you see. Gamma makes the most impact on the overall result, so take some time to play with this slider.

6. **Click OK.**

You can adjust your entire image or adjust each color channel individually. The most accurate way is to first choose each color channel separately from the Channel drop-down menu in the Levels dialog box. Adjust the end points for each channel by itself, and then go back to RGB and tweak just the gamma slider.

TIP If you know the numerical value of the pixels you want to designate for any of these settings— you geek!—you can type that information into the Input Levels boxes. You can set the gamma value from .10 to 9.99. It's set at 1.00 automatically.

The last control you may want to use in the Levels dialog box is the Output Levels slider. Output Levels work roughly the same way as your brightness and contrast controls on your TV. Moving these sliders makes the darkest pixels darker and the lightest pixels lighter. Among pros, this is known as adjusting the tonal range of a photo.

Adjusting Levels will improve almost every photo you take, but if your photo has a bad *color cast*—if it's too orange or too blue—you may need something else. The next section shows you how to get rid of unwanted color.

Removing Unwanted Color

It's not uncommon for an otherwise good photo to have a *color cast*—that is, to have all the tonal values shifted so that the photo is too blue, like Figure 7-12, or too orange.

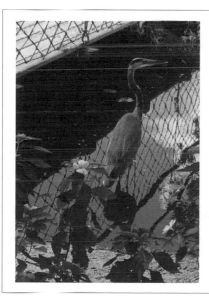
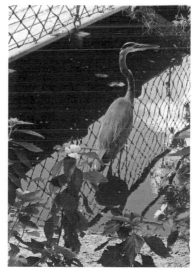

Figure 7-12:
Left: You may wind up with a photo like this one of a heron every once in a while if you forget to change the white balance–your camera's special setting for the type of lighting conditions you're shooting in (common settings are daylight, fluorescent, and so on). This is an outdoor photo taken with the camera set for tungsten indoor lighting.

Right: Elements fixes that wicked color cast in a jiffy. The photo still needs other adjustments, but the color is back in the ballpark.

Elements gives you several ways to correct color cast problems:

- **Auto Color Correction** doesn't give you any control over the changes, but it often does a good job. To use it, go to Enhance → Auto Color Correction or press ⌘+Shift+B.

- **The RAW Converter** may be the easiest way to fix problems, though it works only on RAW, JPEG, and TIFF files. Just run your photo through the RAW converter (page 219) and adjust your white balance there.

- **Levels** gives you the finest control of all the methods in this list. You can often eliminate a color cast by adjusting the individual color channels till the extra color is gone (as explained in the previous section). The drawbacks are that Levels can be very fiddly for this sort of work, sometimes this method doesn't work at all if the problem is severe, and one of the other ways may be much faster at getting you the results you want.

- **Remove Color Cast** is the special command for correcting a color cast with one-click ease. The next section explains how to use this tool.

- **The Color Variations** dialog box is helpful in figuring out which colors you need more or less of, but it has some limitations. It's covered on page 197.

- **The Photo Filter command** gives you much more control than the Color Cast tool, and you can apply Photo Filters as Adjustment layers, too. Photo Filters are covered on page 231.

- **The Average Blur Filter**, used along with a blend mode, lets you fix a color cast. As you'll read on page 363, it's something like creating a custom photo filter.

- **Adjust Color for Skin Tone** lets Elements adjust your photos based on the skin colors in the image. In practice, this adjustment may be more likely to introduce a color cast than to correct one, but if your photo has a slight bluish cast that's visible in the skin of the people in the photo (as explained on page 107), it may do the trick. This option works best for slight, annoying casts that are too subtle for the other methods in this list.

All these tools are useful for fixing a color cast, depending on exactly what your problem is. Usually you'd start with Levels and then move on to the Color Cast tool or the Photo Filter. (To practice any of the fixes you're about to learn, download the photo heron.jpg from the "Missing CD" page at *www.missingmanuals.com*.)

Using the Color Cast Tool

The Color Cast tool is another eyedropper sampling tool that adjusts the colors in your photo based on the pixels you click. In this case, you show Elements where a neutral color should be. As you saw with the heron in Figure 7-12, the Color Cast command can make a big difference with just one click. To use it:

1. **Go to Enhance → Adjust Color → Remove Color Cast.**

   Your cursor should change to an eyedropper when you move it over your photo. If it doesn't change, go to the dialog box and click the Eyedropper icon.

2. **Click an area that should be gray, white, or black.**

   You only have to click once in your photo for this tool to work. As with the Levels eyedropper tool, click an area that *should be* gray, white, or black (as opposed to looking for an area that's currently one of these colors). If several of these colors appear, you can try different spots in your photo, clicking Reset in between each sample, until you find the spot that gives you the most natural-looking color.

3. **Click OK.**

The Color Cast tool works pretty well if your image has areas that should be black, white, or gray, even if they're very tiny. The tricky thing is when you have an image that doesn't have a good area to sample—when there isn't any black, white, or gray anywhere in the picture. If that's the case, consider using the Photo Filter (page 231).

> **TIP** If you generally like what Auto Levels does for your photos, but you feel like it leaves behind a slight color cast, a click with the Color Cast tool may be just the right finishing touch.

Using Color Variations

The Color Variations window (Figure 7-13) is very appealing to many Elements beginners, because it gives you a visual clue about what to do to fix the color in your photo. You just click the little preview thumbnail that shows the color balance you like best, and Elements applies the necessary change to make your photo look like the thumbnail.

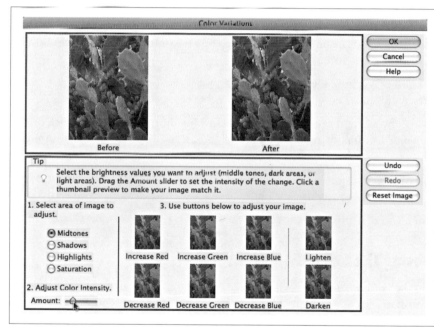

Figure 7-13:
Most of the time, you'll do better using the Quick Fix window to make the kinds of changes you can make with Color Variations, but Color Variations comes in handy when you can see exactly what your photo needs—in this case, a little more blue. The effect is a bit exaggerated here so that you can see it easily. The after photo is bluer than you'd probably want it to be. If that happens to you, click Reset and move the slider (lower left) to the left a bit before you try again.

However, Color Variations has some pretty severe limitations, most notably the microscopic size of the thumbnails. It's very hard to see what you're doing, and even newcomers can usually get better results in Quick Fix (page 104).

Still, Color Variations is useful for those times when you know something is not quite right in your color but you can't figure out exactly what to do about it. And because it's adjustable, Color Variations is good for when you do know what you want but you want to make only the tiniest sliver of a difference to your photo's color.

To use the Color Variations tool:

1. **Open your photo.**

   You may want to make a duplicate layer (page 151) for the adjustments, so that you'll have the option to discard your changes if you're not happy with them. If you don't work on a duplicate, keep in mind that the changes you make here aren't undoable after you've closed the photo.

2. **Go to Enhance → Adjust Color → Color Variations.**

   You see the dialog box pictured in Figure 7-13.

3. **On the lower-left corner of the dialog box (where it says "Select area of image to adjust"), click a radio button to choose whether you want to adjust midtones, shadows, highlights, or saturation.**

   Color Variations begins by selecting midtones, which is usually what you want. But experiment with the other settings to see what they do. The Saturation button works just like Saturation in Quick Fix (page 104).

4. **Use the slider at the bottom of the dialog box to control how drastic the adjustment should be.**

   The farther you push the slider to the right, the more dramatic the change. Usually, just a smidgen is enough to make a noticeable change.

5. **Just below where it says "Use buttons below to adjust your image," click one of the color buttons to make your photo look more like one of the thumbnail photos.**

   You can always Undo or Redo using the buttons on the right side of the window, or use Reset Image to put your photo back to where it was when you started.

6. **When you're happy with the result, click OK.**

Choosing the Color You Want

So far, the color corrections you've been reading about in this chapter have all done most of the color assigning for you. But a lot of the time, you want to be able to *tell* Elements what colors to work with—like when you're selecting the color for a background or Fill layer (page 170), or when you want to paint on an image.

Although you can use any of the millions of colors your screen can display, Elements loads only two colors at a time. You choose these colors using the Foreground and Background color squares at the bottom of the Toolbox (see Figure 7-14).

Foreground and Background mean just what they sound like—use the Background color to fill in backgrounds, and use the Foreground color with the Elements tools, like the Brush or the Paint Bucket. You can use as many colors as you want, of course. The color-picking tools at the bottom of the Toolbox let you control the color you're using in a number of different ways:

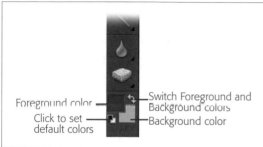

Figure 7-14:
The top square is your Foreground color, and the bottom is your Background color. You can also use keystrokes to reset the standard black and white colors or switch the colors. Either click the two tiny squares at the bottom left or press D to reset your colors to Elements' standard colors of black for the Foreground and white for the Background. Click the curved double-headed arrows or press X to swap the Foreground and Background values.

Foreground color
Click to set default colors
Switch Foreground and Background colors
Background color

- **Reset default colors.** Click the tiny black and white squares to return to the standard settings of black for the Foreground color and white for the Background color.

- **Switch Foreground and Background colors.** Click the little curved arrows above and to the right of the squares, and your Background color becomes the Foreground color, and vice versa. This is very helpful when you've inadvertently made your color selection in the wrong box. (For example, if you've set the Foreground color to yellow, but you actually meant to make the Background color yellow, just click these arrows, and you're all set.)

- **Change either the Foreground or Background color to whatever color you want.** You can choose any color you like for either color square. Click either square to call up the Color Picker (explained later) to make your new choice. There's no limit on the colors you can select to use in Elements. Well, technically there is, but it's in the millions, so you should find enough choices for anything you want to do.

You actually have a few different ways to select your Foreground and Background colors. The next few sections show you how to use the Color Picker, the Eyedropper tool (to pick a color from an existing image), or the Color Swatches palette.

When you're working with some of the Elements tools, like the Type tool, you can choose a color in the tool's Options bar settings. Adobe knows that, given a choice, most people prefer to work with either Color Swatches or the Color Picker, so they've come up with a clever way to accommodate both camps, as shown in Figure 7-15.

The Color Picker

Figure 7-16 shows you the Color Picker. It has an intimidating number of options, but, most of the time, you don't need them all. Picking a color is as easy as clicking wherever you see the color you want.

The Color Picker is actually pretty simple to use:

1. **Click the Foreground or Background color square in the Toolbox.**

   The Color Picker launches. Some other tools—like the Paint Bucket (page 325) and the mask color option for the Selection brush (page 120)—also use the Color Picker. It works the same way no matter how you get to it.

Click here for the Color Picker   Click here for the Color Swatches

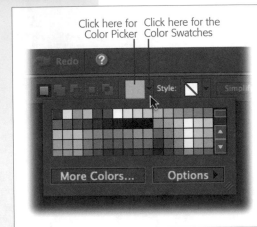

Figure 7-15:
Whether you prefer using Color Swatches or the Color Picker, you can choose your favorite (for most tools) in the Options bar. Click the color sample in the box to bring up the Color Picker, or, if you're a Swatcher, click the arrow to the right of the box to reveal the Color Swatches palette.

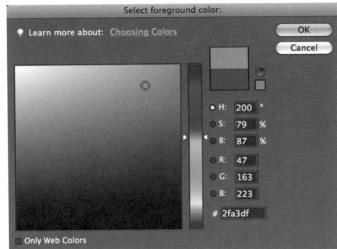

Figure 7-16:
For the majority of beginners, the most important parts of the Elements Color Picker are the vertical rectangular slider in the middle (called, appropriately enough, the Color Slider), and the square box, called the Color Field. Use the Slider to get the general color you want, and then click in the Field on the exact shade.

2. **Choose the color range you want to select from.**

   Use the vertical Color Slider in the middle of the Color Picker. Slide through the spectrum until you see the color you want in the Color Field.

3. **Click the exact spot in the Color Field where you see the particular shade you want.**

   You can keep clicking around to watch the color in the top box in the window change to reflect the color you've chosen. The bottom box continues to show your original color for comparison.

4. **Click OK.**

   The color you selected is now your option in the Foreground or Background square in the Toolbox.

That's the basic way to use the Color Picker. See the box on page 203 for ways to enter a numeric value for your color if you know it, or to change the shades the Color Picker is offering you.

> **TIP** You don't have to use the Elements Color Picker if you don't want to; you can use Mac OS X's color picker instead. To change color pickers, go to Photoshop Elements → Preferences → General.
>
> You might prefer the Apple Color Picker if you like to choose colors from a color wheel. There's even a fun view where you choose colors from a box of crayons. You can also save colors in the Apple Color Picker by dragging them from the color field at the top of the window into the little squares at the bottom. Then just click a square to choose that color the next time you want it.

The Eyedropper Tool

If you've ever repainted your house, you've probably had the frustrating experience of spotting the *exact* color you want somewhere—if only there were a way to capture that color. That's one problem you'll never run into in Elements, thanks to the handy Eyedropper tool that lets you sample any color you see on your monitor and then automatically make it the Foreground color in Elements. If you can get a color into your computer, Elements can grab it.

Sampling a color (that is, snagging it for your own use) couldn't be simpler than it is with the Eyedropper. Just move your cursor over the color you want and click. It even works on colors that aren't already in Elements, as explained in Figure 7-17. Sampling is perfect for projects like scrapbook pages, where you might want to use, say, the color from an event program cover as a theme color for the project. Just scan the program and sample the color with the Eyedropper.

By now, you may be thinking that Elements has more eyedroppers than your medicine cabinet. But this time, the Eyedropper in question is the Official Elements Eyedropper tool that has its own place in the Toolbox. It's one of the easiest tools to use:

1. **Click the Eyedropper in the Toolbox or just press I.**

   Your cursor changes into a tiny eyedropper.

2. **Move the Eyedropper over the color you want to sample.**

   If you want to watch the color change in the Foreground color box as you move the Eyedropper around, hold the mouse button down as you go.

3. **Click when you see the color you want.**

   Your color choice is loaded up, ready to use, as your Foreground color in the Color Squares. To make it a Background color instead, Option+click the color in your source.

If you want to keep your color sample around so that you can use it another time without having to get the Eyedropper out again, you can save your color samples in the Swatches palette. Then you can quickly choose those exact colors again any time you want. See the next section for directions on how to do this.

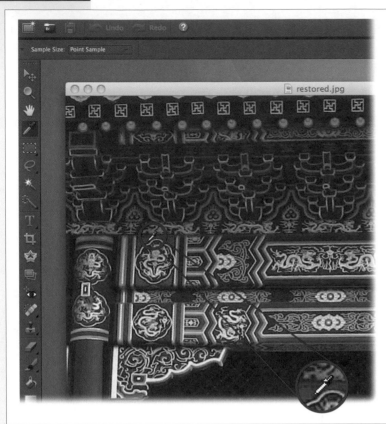

Figure 7-17:
To use the Eyedropper tool to sample colors outside of Elements, start by clicking anywhere inside your Elements file. Then, while still holding your mouse button down, move your cursor over to the non-Elements object (a Web page, for instance), until the eyedropper is over the area you want to sample. Then you can let go, and you'll see the new color in the Elements color squares. If you let go before you get to the non-Elements object, it won't work. Here, the Eyedropper (circled) is sampling the green color from a photo opened in Preview. You can only do this if you've turned off the Elements background (see page 22).

TIP   Since there may be some slight pixel-to-pixel variation in a color, you can set the Eyedropper to sample a little block of pixels and average them. In the Eyedropper Options bar settings, you can choose between the exact pixel you click (point sample), a 3-pixel square average or a 5-pixel square average. Oddly enough, this Eyedropper setting also applies to the Magic Wand. Change it here and you change it for the Wand, too.

The Color Swatches Palette

The Color Swatches palette holds several little preloaded libraries of sample colors for you to use in picking a color. Go to Window → Color Swatches to call up the Color Swatches palette. You can park the Color Swatches palette in the Palette bin just like any other palette, if you like, or leave it floating on your desktop. When you're ready to choose a color, just click the swatch you want, and it appears in the Foreground color square or the color box of the tool you're using.

The Color Swatches palette is very handy when you want to keep certain color choices at your fingertips. For instance, you can put your logo colors into it, and then you always have those colors available for any graphics or ads you create in Elements.

Paint by Number

The Elements Color Picker also includes some very sophisticated controls that most folks can live a long and happy life without ever understanding. For the curious or more advanced, here's what the rest of the Color Picker does.

- **HSB buttons**. These numbers control the hue, saturation, and brightness of your color. The settings control pretty much the same values as the Hue/Saturation adjustment. (See page 260 for more about hue and saturation.)

- **RGB buttons**. The RGB buttons let you specify the amount of red, green, and blue you want in the color you're picking. Each button can have a numerical value anywhere from 0 to 255. A lower number means less of the color, a higher number means more. For example, 128, 128, 128 is neutral gray. By changing the numbers, you can change the blend of the color.

- **Hex number**. Below the radio buttons is a box that lets you enter a special six-character hexadecimal code that you use when you're creating Web graphics. These codes tell Web browsers which colors to display. You can also click a color in the window to see the hex number for that shade.

- **Only Web Colors checkbox**. Turning on this box ensures that the colors you see in the main color box are drawn only from the 216 colors that antique Web browsers can display. For example, if you're creating a Web site and you're really worried about color compatibility with Netscape 4.0, this box is for you. If you see a tiny cube just to the right of the color sample box, the color you're using isn't deemed Web safe.

Elements starts you off with several different libraries (groups) of Color Swatches. Click the pull-down menu on the Swatches palette to see them all. A swatch you create appears at the bottom of the current library, and you can save it there, or you can create your own swatch libraries if you'd rather do that.

Using the Color Swatches to select your Foreground or Background color is as easy as using the Eyedropper tool. Figure 7-18 shows you how.

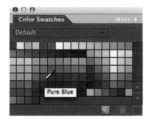

Figure 7-18:
When you move your cursor over the Color Swatches palette, it changes to an eyedropper. Click to select a color. If you're using a preloaded palette you'll see color name labels as you move over each square. If you use the swatches a lot, choose "Place in Palette Bin when closed" from the More menu so the Swatches palette is always there.

To use the Color Swatches palette:

- **To pick a foreground color:** Click the color you want. It appears as the Foreground color choice.

- **To pick a background color:** ⌘+click a color, and Elements makes it the Background color.

You can also change the way the Color Swatches palette displays swatch information, as shown in Figure 7-19.

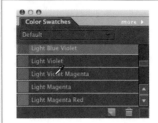

Figure 7-19:
On the Color Swatches palette, click the More button → Small List, and depending on the collection you're using, you can see the names or hex numbers for each color (in addition to a small thumbnail of the color). Some of the tools, like the Type tools, have Options buttons for their swatches viewer instead of the palette's More button.

Saving colors in the Swatches palette

Any colors you've picked using the Color Picker or Eyedropper tool, you can save as swatches. If you don't save them, you lose them as soon as you select a different library or close the palette.

To add a swatch, you can do one of two things:

- **Click the New Swatch icon at the bottom of the Color Swatch palette.** It's the same square that stands for "new" in the Layers palette.

- **Click the More button on the palette, and choose New Swatch.**

In either case, you get a chance to name and save the new swatch. The name shows up as tooltips text when you hover your mouse over the swatch in the palette. (Don't change the save location if you want Elements to continue to recognize it as a swatch.) Your swatch gets saved at the bottom of the current swatch library. To delete a swatch that you've saved, drag it to the Trash icon in the Color Swatches palette, or Option+click the swatch.

You can also create your own libraries, if you want to keep your own swatches separate from the ones Elements gives you. Go to the More button on the palette and pick Save Color Swatches. Then give your new library a name and save it.

> **NOTE** When you save a new swatch library, it doesn't show up in the list of libraries until the next time you start Elements.

Sharpening Your Images

Digital cameras are wonderful, but often it's hard to tell how well you've focused until you download the photos to your computer. And because of the way a camera's digital sensors process information, most digital image data usually needs to be *sharpened*. Sharpening is an image-editing trick that makes your pictures look more clearly focused.

Elements includes some almost miraculous tools for sharpening your images. (It's pretty darned good at blurring them, too, if you want; see page 362.)

NOTE   If you've used early versions of Elements, you may be searching in vain on the Filter menu for the Sharpen filters. It's true—your old friends Sharpen and Sharpen More are gone. In their place, Adjust Sharpness appears at the bottom of the Enhance menu, along with Unsharp Mask. (Both of these features are explained in the following sections.) If you miss the one-click ease of Sharpen and Sharpen More, just go to Enhance → Auto Sharpen to get a similar effect.

Unsharp Mask

Although it sounds like the last thing you'd ever want to do to a photo, Unsharp Mask reigned as the Supreme Sharpener for many generations of image correction, despite the fact that it has the most counterintuitive name in all of Elements.

To be fair, it's not Adobe's fault. *Unsharp Mask* is an old darkroom term, and it actually does make sense if you know how our film ancestors used to improve a picture's focus. (Its name refers to a complicated darkroom technique that involved making a blurred copy of the photo at one point in the process.)

For several versions of Elements, Unsharp Mask ranked right up there with Levels as a contender for most useful tool in Elements, and some people still think it's the best way to sharpen a photo. Figure 7-20 shows how much a little Unsharp Mask can do for your photos.

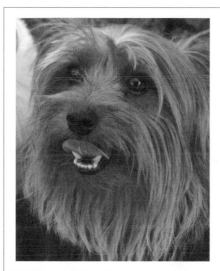 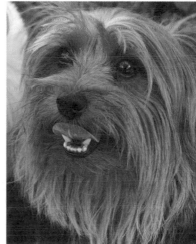

Figure 7-20:
Left: The photo as it came from the camera.

Right: The photo was treated with a dose of Unsharp Mask. Notice how much clearer the individual hairs in the dog's coat are and how much better defined the eyes and mouth are.

To use Unsharp Mask, first finish all your other corrections and changes. Unsharp Mask (or any sharpening tool) can undermine other adjustments you make later on, so always sharpen as the very last step. A good rule to remember when sharpening is "last and once." Repeatedly applying sharpening can degrade your image's quality.

NOTE   An exception to the rule about sharpening only once occurs when you're converting RAW images (page 213). You can usually sharpen both in the RAW converter and then again as a last step without causing problems.

If you're sharpening an image with layers, be sure the active layer has something in it. Applying sharpening to a Levels Adjustment layer, for example, won't do anything. Also, perform any format conversions (page 60) before applying sharpening. Finally, you may want a duplicate layer for the sharpening if you want the ability to undo your changes later on. Press ⌘+J to create the duplicate layer.

> **NOTE** It's helpful to understand just exactly what Elements does when it "sharpens" your photo. It doesn't magically correct the focus. As a matter of fact, it doesn't really sharpen anything. What it does is deepen the contrast where colors meet, giving the impression of a crisper focus. So while Elements can dramatically improve a shot that's just faintly out of focus or a little soft, even Elements can't fix that old double exposure or a shot where the subject is just a blur of motion.

When you're ready to apply Unsharp Mask:

1. **Go to Enhance → Unsharp Mask.**

2. **Adjust the settings in the Unsharp Mask dialog box until you like what you see.**

   Move the sliders until you're happy with the sharpness of your photo. Your adjustment options are explained in the following list. In the Preview window, you can zoom in and out and grab the photo to adjust which part you see.

3. **When you're satisfied, click OK.**

The sliders for Unsharp Mask work very much like the sliders in several of the other tools:

- **Amount** tells Elements how much to sharpen, in percent terms. A higher number means more sharpening.

- **Radius** lets Elements know how far from an edge it should look when increasing the contrast.

- **Threshold** is how different a pixel needs to be from the surrounding pixels before Elements should consider it an edge and sharpen it. If the threshold is left at zero—which is the standard setting—Elements sharpens all the pixels in an image.

There are many, many different schools of thought about which values to plug into each box. Whatever works for you is fine. The one thing you want to watch out for is oversharpening. Figure 7-21 tells you how to know if you've gone too far.

You'll probably need to do a bit of experimenting to find out which settings work best for you. Photos you want to print usually need to be sharpened to an extent that makes them look oversharpened when viewed on your monitor. Therefore, you may want to create separate versions of your photo (one for onscreen viewing and one for printing).

Adjust Sharpness

Unsharp Mask has been around since long before digital imaging. A lot of people (including the folks at Adobe) have been thinking that, in the computer age,

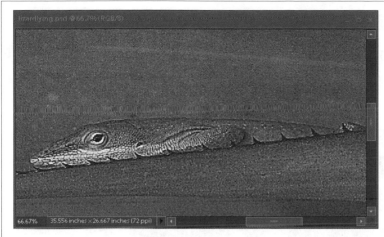

Figure 7-21:
*The perils of oversharpening. This
lizard may have a suspicious
attitude, but he didn't have a skin
condition. The flaky look comes
from overapplying sharpening,
and the white flecks are called
artifacts. If you look very closely,
you can also see how
oversharpening causes a halo
effect around the lizard. The
appearance of halos is often your
first clue that you've
oversharpened your image.*

there's got to be a better way to sharpen, and now there is. The latest tool in the
war on poor focus is Adjust Sharpness.

The Unsharp Mask tool you learned about in the previous section helps boost a
photo's sharpness by a process something like reducing Gaussian blur (page 364).
Problem is, Gaussian blurring is rarely the cause of your picture's poor focus, so
there's only so much Unsharp Mask can fix. In real life, blurry photos usually
come from one of two causes:

- **Lens blur.** Your camera's prime focal point is not directly over your subject. Or
  perhaps your lens is not quite as sharp as you'd like it to be.

- **Motion blur.** You moved the camera—or your subject moved—while you
  pressed the shutter.

Adjust Sharpness is as easy to use as Unsharp Mask, and it gives you settings to
correct all three kinds of blur—Gaussian, lens, and motion. When you first open
the Adjust Sharpness dialog box, its settings are almost identical to Unsharp Mask.
It's the extra things Adjust Sharpness can do that make it a more versatile tool.
Here's how to use it:

1. **Make sure the layer you want to sharpen is the active layer in your photo.**

   See Chapter 6 if you need a refresher on layers.

2. **Go to Enhance → Adjust Sharpness.**

   You can reach this menu item from either Full Edit or Quick Fix.

3. **Make your adjustments in the Adjust Sharpness dialog box.**

   As shown in Figure 7-22, the dialog box gives you a nice big preview. It's usually
   best to stick to 50 or 100 percent zoom (use the plus and minus buttons below
   the preview) for the most accurate view. The settings are explained in detail in
   the list below.

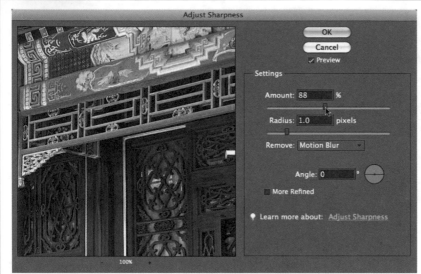

Figure 7-22:
The Adjust Sharpness dialog box shows you a good-sized preview of your image. But it helps if you position the dialog box so you can see the main image window as well. That way you can keep an eye on any changes happening in areas outside the preview frame.

4. **When you like the way your photo is sharpened, click OK.**

The first two settings in the Adjust Sharpness dialog box, Amount and Radius, work exactly the same way they do in Unsharp Mask. Adjust Sharpness also has a couple of additional settings of its own:

- **Remove**. Here's where you choose what kind of fuzziness to fix: Gaussian, lens, or motion blur, as explained on page 206. If you aren't sure which you want, try all three and see which best suits your photo.

- **Angle**. In a motion blur, you can improve your results by telling Elements the angle of the motion. For example, if your grip on the camera slipped, the direction of motion would be downward. Move the line in the little circle or type a number in degrees to approximate the angle. (It's awfully tricky to get the angle exactly right, so you may find it easier to sharpen without messing with this setting.)

- **More Refined**. Turn this checkbox on, and Elements takes a tad longer to apply sharpening since it sharpens more details. Generally you'll want to leave this setting off for photos with lots of little details, like leaves or fur (and people's faces, unless you like to look at pores). But you might want it on for bold desert landscapes, for example, or other subjects without lots of fiddly small parts. Noise, artifacts, and dust become much more prominent when you turn on More Refined, since they get sharpened along with the details of your photo. Experiment, and watch the main image window as well as the preview, to see how it's affecting your photo.

Many people who've used Smart Sharpening in the full-featured Photoshop swear they'll never go back to plain Unsharp Mask. Try out Adjust Sharpness—the Elements version of Smart Sharpening—and see if you agree. To give you an idea of the difference between the two methods, Figure 7-23 shows the dog from Figure 7-20 again, only this time with Adjust Sharpness instead of Unsharp Mask.

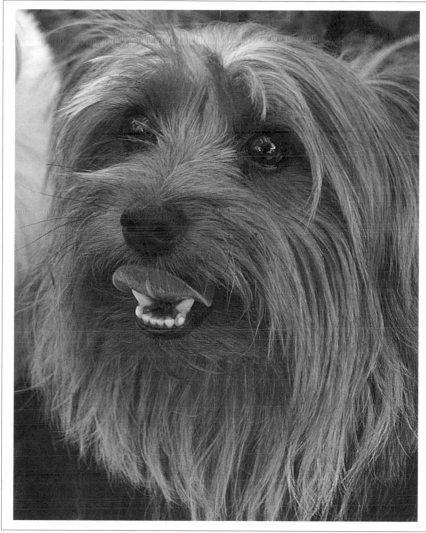

Figure 7-23:
Here's the terrier from Figure 7-20 only this time he's been sharpened using Adjust Sharpness. Notice how much more each hair in his coat stands out, and how much more detail you can see in his nose and mouth.

NOTE Although Amount and Radius mean the same things as they do in Unsharp Mask, don't assume that you can just plug your favorite Unsharp Mask settings into Adjust Sharpness and get the same results. Experiment, and don't be surprised if you prefer very different numbers in these settings for the new tool.

The High-Pass Filter

Unsharp Mask is definitely the traditional favorite, and Adjust Sharpness is the latest thing in sharpening, but there's an alternative method that many people prefer because you do it on a dedicated layer and can back the effect off later by adjusting the layer's opacity, if you like. Moreover, you can use this method to punch up the colors in your photo as you sharpen. It's called *High-Pass* sharpening. All sharpening methods have their virtues, and you may find that you choose your technique according to the content of your photo. Try the following procedure out for yourself by downloading the photo waterlillies.jpg from the "Missing CD" page at *www.missingmanuals.com*.

1. **Open your photo and make sure the layer you want to sharpen is the active layer.**

2. **Duplicate your layer by pressing ⌘+J.**

   If you have a multi-layered image and you want to sharpen all the layers, first flatten your image or use the Stamp Visible command (see the box on page 168), so everything is all in one layer.

3. **Go to Filter → Other → High-Pass.**

   Your photo now looks like the victim of a mudslide, buried in featureless gray. That's what you want for right now.

4. **Move the slider until you can barely see the outline of your subject.**

   Usually that means picking a setting somewhere roughly between 1.5 and 3.5. If you can see colors, your setting is too high. If you can't quite eliminate every trace of color without totally losing the outline, a tiny bit of color is OK. Keep in mind that the edges you see through the gray are the ones that you'll be sharpening the most. Use that as your guide to how much detail to include.

5. **Click OK.**

6. **In the Layers palette, set the blend mode for the new layer to Overlay.**

   Ta-da! Your subject is back again in glowing, sharper color, as shown in Figure 7-24.

   TIP   Elements 6 gives you a new way to create "pop" in your photos. Check out the Clarity setting in the RAW converter (page 226), which sharpens and enhances contrast at the same time. (If you know what "local contrast enhancement" means, this setting does something similar.) You can use it on RAW, JPEG, and TIFF files. It's especially useful for clearing haze from your shots.

The Sharpen Tool

Elements also gives you a dedicated Sharpen tool (Figure 7-25). It's a special brush that sharpens instead of adding color to the areas you drag it over. To get to it, go to the Blur tool or press R, and choose the Sharpen tool from the pop-out menu.

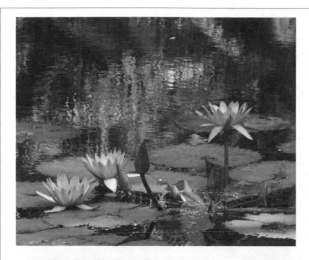

Figure 7-24:
Top: The original photo.

Bottom: High-Pass sharpening using Vivid Light makes the colors more vivid, but the ripples are much harder-edged than they were in the original. For high-pass sharpening, you can use any of the blend modes in the group with Overlay, except Hard Mix and Pin Light. Vivid Light can make your colors pop, but watch out for sharpening artifacts, since they'll be more vivid, too. Overlay gives a softer effect.

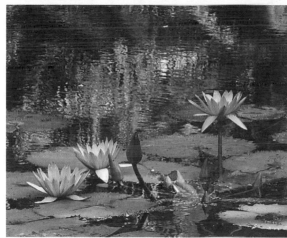

The Sharpen tool has some of the same Options bar settings as the Brush tool (see page 314 for more about brush settings). It also has a couple of settings of its very own:

- **Strength** adjusts how much the brush sharpens what it passes over. A higher number means more sharpening.

- **Mode** lets you increase the visibility of an object's edge by choosing from several different blend modes, but usually Normal gives the most predictable results.

- **All Layers** causes the Sharpen tool to work on all the visible layers in your image. Leave it off if you want to sharpen only the active layer.

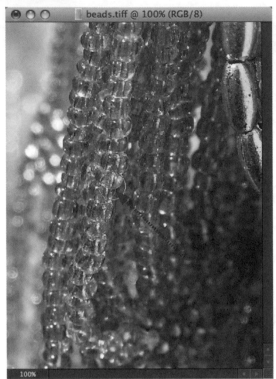

Figure 7-25:
The Sharpen tool isn't meant to sharpen an entire photo, but it's great for detail sharpening. Here, it's being used to bring out the detail in the front strand of beads. (The red arrow helps you find the cursor.) Approach this tool with caution; it's very easy to overdo things with it. One pass too many or a too-high setting, and you start seeing artifacts right away.

Elements for Digital Photographers

If you're a fairly serious digital photographer, you'll be delighted to know that Adobe hasn't just loaded Elements with easy-to-use features, aimed at beginners. Elements is also brimming with a collection of pretty advanced tools pulled straight from the full-featured Photoshop.

Number one on the list is the famous *Adobe Camera RAW Converter*, which takes RAW files—a format some cameras use to give you maximum editing control—and lets you convert and edit them in Elements. In this chapter, you'll learn lots more about what RAW is, and why you may or may not want to use it in your own photography. And the RAW Converter in Elements 6 is just packed with terrific new features, like the ability to work on multiple images at once. Don't go away if your camera shoots only JPEGs, though. Now you can use the RAW Converter to edit JPEG and TIFF images as well as RAW files. This is a very big deal, as you'll see shortly.

You'll also get to know the Photo Filter command, which helps adjust image colors by replicating the old-school effect of placing filters over a camera's lens. And last but not least, Elements includes some truly useful batch-processing tools, including features to help rename files, perform format conversions, and even apply basic retouching to multiple photos.

The RAW Converter

Probably the most useful thing Adobe has done for photography buffs in Elements is include the Adobe Camera RAW Converter. For many people, this feature alone is well worth the price of the program, since you just can't beat the convenience of being able to perform conversions in the same program you use for editing.

If you don't know what RAW is, it's just a file format (a group of formats, really, since every camera maker has its own proprietary RAW format). But it's a very special one. Your digital camera actually contains a little computer that does a certain amount of processing to your photos right inside the camera itself. If you shoot in JPEG format, for instance, your camera has already made some decisions about things like sharpness, color saturation, and contrast before it saves the JPEG files to your memory card.

If your camera lets you shoot RAW files, on the other hand, you get the unprocessed data straight from the camera. Shooting in RAW lets you make your own decisions about how your photo should look, to a much greater degree than you can with any other format. It's something like getting a negative from your digital camera—what you do to it in your digital darkroom is up to you.

That's the big advantage of RAW—total control. The downside is that every camera manufacturer has its own proprietary RAW format, and the format may vary even among models from the same manufacturer. No regular graphics program can edit these files, and very few programs can view them. Instead, you need special software to convert your RAW files to a format that you can work with. In the past, that usually meant you needed to use software from the manufacturer before you could move your photo into an editing program like Elements.

Enter Adobe Camera RAW, which lets you convert your files right in Elements. Not only that, but the Adobe Camera RAW plug-in that comes with Elements lets you make very sophisticated corrections to your photos—before you even open them. Many times, you can do everything you need right in the Converter, so that you're done as soon as you open your converted file. (You can, of course, still use any of Elements' regular tools once you've opened a RAW file.) Using Adobe Camera RAW saves you a ton of time, and it's compatible with most cameras' RAW files.

> **NOTE** Adobe regularly updates the RAW Converter to include new versions produced by different cameras, so if your camera's RAW files don't open, check for a newer version of the plug-in. You can download the latest version by going to *www.adobe.com/downloads* and scrolling down to the section for Photoshop CS3. (Elements and Photoshop use the same plug-in, but you don't see all the features in Elements.) You'll also find a standalone version of the DNG (digital negative) Converter there, which you can use without launching Elements; see page 230.

Using the RAW Converter

For all the options it gives you, the RAW Converter is very easy to use. Adobe has designed it so that it *automatically* calculates and applies what it thinks are the correct settings for exposure, shadows, brightness, and contrast. You can accept the Converter's decisions or override them and do everything yourself—it's your call.

NOTE If you use iPhoto, you may notice that you aren't seeing the RAW Converter when you send your RAW images to Elements. iPhoto normally does the conversion for you and sends a converted file. To tell iPhoto to send the actual RAW files to Elements, go to iPhoto → Preferences → Advanced → RAW Photos, and turn on "Use RAW files with external editor." (This is only in iPhoto 6 and iPhoto '08. Previous versions won't send the RAW file at all.) If you want to convert your RAW files as 16-bit files and save them that way, also turn on the Save → "as 16 bits" option.

To get started, you first need to open your images. You can open RAW files from either Bridge or the Elements. In Bridge, just double-click the thumbnail of the file you want to open. (To open more than one file, select the ones you want, and then double-click any of the selected thumbnails. They'll all open in the Converter in Elements.) If you're starting from Elements, just go to File → Open. In Elements 6, you can work with multiple files in the RAW Converter, as explained in Figure 8-1. If you'd like some practice with RAW, there's a sample image (RAW_practice.mrw) available on the "Missing CD" page (*www.missingmanuals.com*), but be warned: It's a very large file (7.2 MB).

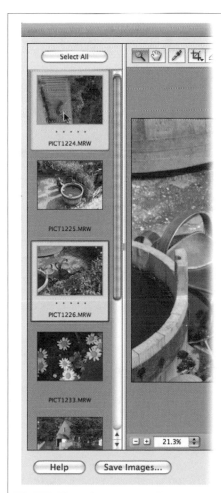

Figure 8-1:
When you open a bunch of files at once in the RAW Converter, you get a handy filmstrip view down the left side of the window. You can select a single image from the group by clicking it, and then your changes apply only to that file. Use Shift+click or ⌘+click to select multiple files (or use the Select All button at the top of the list), and your selected files get changed along with the one in the main preview area. When you finish and click Open, all the files appear in the Project bin. If you want to batch save them in another format, use Process Multiple Files (page 233).

To Shoot in the RAW or Not

Should I shoot my pictures in the RAW format?

It depends. There are pros and cons to using the RAW format. It may surprise you to learn that some professional photographers choose *not* to use RAW. For example, not many journalists use it, and it's not common with sports photographers, either. Here's a quick look at the advantages and disadvantages to help you decide if you want to get involved with RAW.

On the plus side, you get:

- **More control**. With RAW you have a lot of extra chances to tweak your photos, and you get to call the shots, instead of the processing choices made by your camera.

- **More fixes**. If you're not a perfect photographer, RAW is more forgiving—you can fix a lot of mistakes in RAW, although even RAW won't make a bad photo into a great photo.

- **No need to fuss with your white balance all the time while shooting**. However, you'll get better input if your camera's white balance settings are correct.

- **Nondestructive editing**. The changes you make in the RAW Converter don't change your original image one jot. It's always there for a fresh start, if need be.

But RAW also has some significant drawbacks. For one thing, you can't just open a file and start using the photo the way you do with a JPEG file. You always have to convert

it first, whether you use the Elements Converter or one supplied by the manufacturer. Other disadvantages include:

- **Larger file size**. RAW files are smaller than TIFFs, but they're usually much bigger than the highest-quality JPEGs. Consequently, you'll need bigger (or more) memory cards if you regularly shoot RAW.

- **Slower Speed**. It generally takes your camera longer to save RAW files than JPEGs—a significant consideration for action shots. Newer cameras have a buffer that holds several shots and lets you keep shooting while the camera is working, but you may hit the wall pretty quickly if you're using burst (rapid-advance) mode. Then you just have to wait.

- **Worse in-camera preview**. For many cameras, you have some pretty significant limitations for digitally zooming the view in the viewfinder when using RAW.

You may want to try a few shots of the same subject in both RAW and JPEG to see whether you notice a difference in your final results. Generally speaking, RAW offers the most leeway if you want to make significant edits, but you need to understand what you're doing. JPEG is easier if you're a beginner.

It's really your call. There are some excellent photographers who wouldn't think of shooting in anything but RAW, and other excellent photographers who think it's too time consuming.

NOTE OS X has very basic, built-in RAW conversion feature that lets you view your RAW files in Finder windows and in Leopard's Quick Look (see page 38), and open them in Preview. However, you have to take what you get-you can't adjust the conversion settings, and Apple is notoriously slow at adding new camera profiles, so if your camera is a really recent model, you may not be able to open the files outside Elements.

One important point about RAW files: Elements never overwrites your original file. As a matter of fact, Elements can't in any way modify the original RAW file. This means that your original is always there for you if you want to try converting your photo again later on using different settings. It's something like having a negative that you can always get more prints from. This also applies to any image you edit in the RAW Converter in Elements 6, not just RAW files. You can crop a JPEG file here, for instance, and your original JPEG is not cropped, only the copy you open from the Converter. There's more on working with non-RAW files in the Converter on page 228.

Adjusting the view

When the RAW Converter opens, you'll see something like Figure 8-2. Before you decide whether to accept the auto settings that Elements offers or to do your own tweaking, you need to get a good close look at your image. The Converter makes it easy to do this by giving you a large preview of your image and a handful of tools to help adjust what you're looking at.

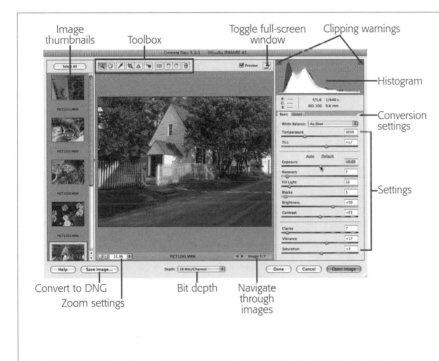

Image thumbnails

Toolbox

Toggle full-screen window

Clipping warnings

Histogram

Conversion settings

Settings

Convert to DNG

Zoom settings

Bit depth

Navigate through images

Figure 8-2:
The Elements RAW Converter packs a number of powerful tools into one window. Besides the large preview window, you get a small tool set (in the upper-left corner) containing some old friends, and a specialized tool for adjusting your white balance (explained on page 219), as well as the panel on the right where you tweak your settings. Below your photo, the Converter gives you a few view-adjusting tools, including a drop-down menu (lower-left) where you can choose zoom settings. If you need to rotate your image, the rotate arrows are above the preview area, on the right side.

- **Hand and Zoom tools.** These tools are in the Toolbox above the upper-left corner of the Converter window. You use them here exactly the same way you would anywhere else in Elements. You'll find more about the Hand tool on page 81; the Zoom tool is described on page 79. The keyboard shortcuts for adjusting the view (page 81) and scrolling (page 82) also work in the RAW Converter.

- **View percentage.** You get a pop-up menu with preset sizes below the lower-left corner of the preview window. Just choose the size you want, or click the + or – buttons to zoom in or out.

NOTE Some adjustments and some of the special views, like the mask views for sharpening, are not available unless you zoom to 100 percent.

• **Full Screen.** If you click the icon that looks like a page with a left-facing arrow on it, just to the right of the preview checkbox above the image area, you can put the RAW Converter window into full-screen view. Click it again to toggle back to the normal view.

• **Histogram.** If you look at the upper-right corner of the Converter, you see a histogram at the top of the window. The Histogram helps you keep track of how your changes are affecting the colors in your photo. (Flip back to page 189 for more on the fine art of reading histograms.)

NOTE Another handy feature in the RAW Converter is the panel just below the Histogram, where you can see important shooting information about your photo, like the aperture and ISO speed (ISO is a digital camera's version of film speed). If you hover your cursor over a pixel in the image, the RGB values for that pixel appear here, as well.

Once you've gotten a good close look at your photo, you need to decide: Did Elements do a good enough job of choosing the settings for you? If so, you're done. Just click Open Image, and Elements opens your photo in the Editor, ready for any artistic changes or cropping. If you prefer to make adjustments to your photo in the Converter, read on. (If you're happy with Elements' conversion, but you want to sharpen your picture, skip ahead to page 226.)

NOTE: Everyone gets confused by the Save Image button. That's actually the DNG Converter (see page 230), and all you can do when you click that button is create a DNG file. To save your edited RAW file, click Done if you just want to save the changes without actually opening the file, or click Open and then save in the format of your choice in the Editor.

Rotating straightening, and cropping

In Elements 6, you can make many basic adjustments to your photo that would have taken a trip to the regular editor in previous versions of Elements. Before you start tweaking your settings, you can make these basic adjustments to your photo right in the Converter:

• **Rotate it.** Click one of the Rotation Arrows above the image preview if you need to rotate your photo.

• **Straighten it.** The RAW Converter now contains its own Straighten tool, which you use just like the one in the Editor's toolbox (page 67), although it has a different icon and cursor. It's just to the right of the Crop tool in the RAW Converter's toolbox.

• **Crop it.** The RAW Converter gives you the same Crop tool you find in the Editor (page 72). Your crop information gets saved to the RAW file's metadata, so the next time you open the file in the Converter, you see the cropped version.

To revert to the uncropped original later, right-click (Control+click) the RAW Converter's Crop tool and choose Clear Crop.

NOTE   You can also fix red eye in the Elements 6 RAW Converter. The Red Eye tool is in the Toolbox just to the right of the Straighten tool, and it works the same way it does everywhere else in Elements (page 97).

Adjusting White Balance

The long strip down the right side of the RAW Converter gives you many ways to tweak and correct the color, exposure, sharpness, brightness, and noise level of your photo. The strip is divided into two tabs. Start with the one labeled Basic, which contains the basic settings for the major adjustments.

The first thing you want to do is to check your white balance, which is at the top of the settings in the Basic tab. Adjusting white balance is often the most important change when it comes to making your photos look their best.

The White Balance control adjusts all the colors in your photo by creating a neutral white tone. If that sounds a little strange, stop and think about it for a minute. The color you think of as *white* actually changes depending on the lighting conditions. At noon there's no warmth (no orange/yellow) to the light because the sun is high in the sky, but later in the day when the sun's rays are lower, whites are warmer. Indoors, tungsten lighting is much warmer than fluorescent lighting, which makes whites rather bluish.

Most digital cameras have a white balance setting on them, although you may have to take your camera out of Auto or Program mode to see it. Your camera's white balance choices are usually something like Auto, Daylight, Cloudy, Tungsten, Fluorescent, and Custom. When you shoot JPEGs, getting the correct setting here really matters, because it's tough to readjust white balance, even in a program like Elements (unless, of course, you open your JPEG with the RAW Converter and tweak it here). With RAW, you can afford to be a little sloppier about setting your white balance, because you can easily tweak it in the RAW Converter.

Getting the white balance right can make a very big difference in how your photo looks, as you can see in Figure 8-3.

Elements gives you several ways to adjust the white balance in your image:

- **Pull-down menu.** The menu just below the Histogram starts out by displaying As Shot, which means Elements is showing you your camera's settings. You can use the menu to change this setting, choosing from Auto, Daylight, Cloudy, and other options. From Daylight down through the other choices on the list, each setting is slightly warmer than the one above it. It's worth giving Auto a try because it picks the correct settings a surprisingly high percentage of the time for many cameras.

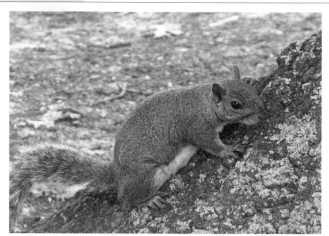

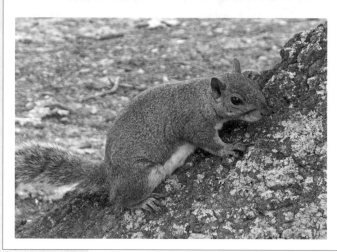

Figure 8-3:

Top: The blue-green color in this photo is typical of photos with poor white balance.

Bottom: By using the tools Elements gives you, you can easily correct the white balance, which also makes your photo appear more vivid and improves the contrast.

- **Temperature.** Use this slider to make your photo warmer (more orange) or cooler (more blue). Moving the slider to the left cools your photo, while moving it to the right warms it. You can also type a temperature in the box in degrees Kelvin (the official measurement for color temperature), if you're experienced in doing this by the numbers. Use the Temperature slider and the Tint slider (described next) in conjunction for a perfect white balance.

- **Tint.** The tint control adjusts the green/magenta balance of your photo, pretty much the way it does in Quick Fix (see page 104). Move it to the left to increase the green in your photo and to the right for more magenta.

- **White Balance tool.** The RAW window has its own special Eyedropper tool. You click a white or light gray spot in your photo with it, and Elements calculates the white balance based on those pixels. This is the most accurate of the methods listed here, but you may have a hard time finding neutral pixels to use it on. You activate the White Balance tool from the Toolbox above the preview area.

If you're a good photographer, much of the time a good white balance and a little sharpening may be all your photo needs before it's ready to go out into the world.

Adjusting Tone

The next group of settings on the Adjust tab lets you make all sorts of changes to the exposure and lighting of your image. In previous versions of Elements, most of these changes happened automatically, but in Elements 6 you can choose how you want Elements to handle things. You also get a bunch of new controls that let you make even finer adjustments to your photos.

At the top of this section of the panel, you see the two words: Auto and Default. They work like hyperlinks on a Web page: click the one that has a blue underline to switch over to it. The one that's grayed out is the one that's active right now (just the way the home page link on a Web site is grayed out if you're on the home page).

- **Auto**. Elements automatically calculates how to adjust your photo for you. If you liked the way earlier versions of Elements made the auto adjustments for you, you can tell Elements 6 to do that, too, as explained in Figure 8-4.

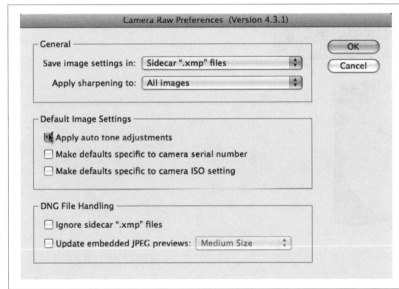

Figure 8-4:
If you want Elements to always open your photos with the auto settings applied, open the RAW Converter's preferences dialog box (it's next to the Red Eye tool in the RAW Converter's Toolbox). Turn on this checkbox for Auto Apply Tone Adjustments, and from now on, the RAW Converter is in Auto mode, at least for the Tone settings.

- **Default**. The RAW Converter contains a database of basic settings for each camera model. If you choose default, you see the baseline settings for your camera, not the auto adjustments Elements makes to your active image by analyzing the image. It's up to you to make the necessary adjustments to your photo. You can set your own camera *defaults* (where the sliders are when your photo opens), too, as explained on page 224. Once you start moving sliders, the word "Default" turns blue. If you want to start over, just give it a click and you're back where you were before you moved anything.

Your choice here determines where you start for all the settings in this section of the panel. You can override any setting by moving the slider yourself. If you go to the trouble of shooting RAW, you may well prefer to make your own settings, as shown in Figure 8-5.

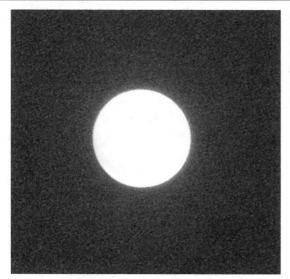

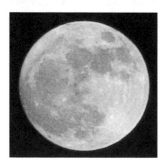

Figure 8-5:
Top: The RAW Converter's suggested settings for this image of the moon. (If you've been wondering what noise is, this is an outstanding example of that annoying problem.)

Bottom: With a little bit of manual adjustment, the photo reveals that the camera actually captured plenty of detail.

There's more about creating and saving your own settings in the next section.

Here's what each of the six settings does for your photo:

- **Exposure.** A properly exposed photo shows the largest possible range of detail. Shadows aren't so dark that all details are lost, and highlights aren't so bright that all you're seeing is white. Move the slider to the left to decrease exposure and to the right to increase it. (The values on the scale are equivalent to f-stops.) Too high a choice here will *clip* some of your highlights. (That is, they'll be so bright you won't see any detail in them.) See Figure 8-6.

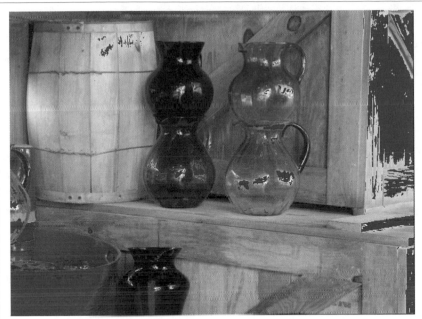

Figure 8-6:
To help you get the Tone settings right, Elements includes two triangles above the ends of the Histogram where you can turn on special masks that show you where your highlights (in red) or your shadows (in blue) lose detail at your current settings. If the photo has no clipping, the triangle for that end of the Histogram is dark. If the triangle is white or colored, you have a problem, so click the triangle to turn the mask on to see the clipping. As you change your settings in the controls, the clipping mask changes to show the current state of your corrections. In this photo, Elements is warning that the areas where you see what looks like red paint will get clipped when you open the photo unless you change the settings.

- **Recovery.** This clever slider brings down overexposed highlights, recovering the details that were lost without underexposing the rest of the photo. Be very careful when using it—a little goes a long way.

- **Fill Light.** If your subject appears backlit, move this slider to the right to bring up the shadowed areas, just the way a photographer's fill light does. The Elements Fill Light is clever enough to bring up the shadowed areas without clipping the highlights in your photos.

- **Blacks.** This slider increases the shadow values and determines which pixels become black in your photo. Increasing the Blacks value may give an effect of increased contrast in your photo. Move the slider to the right to increase shadows or to the left to decrease them. A very little change here goes a long way. Move too far to the right and you'll clip your shadows. (In other words, they'll become plain black, with no details, and your colors may become very funky.)

- **Brightness.** This is somewhat similar to exposure in that moving the slider to the right lightens your image and moving it to the left darkens it. But the Brightness slider won't clip your photo the way the Exposure setting may.

Use this slider to set the overall brightness of your image after you've used the Exposure, Recovery, and Blacks sliders to set the outer range of your photo.

- **Contrast**. The Contrast control adjusts the midtones in your image. Move this slider to the right for greater contrast in those tones and to the left for less. It's usually the last of the sliders to use.

Most of the time, you'll want to use several of these sliders to get a perfectly exposed photo.

Saving your settings

Just below the Histogram, on the far right side of the window, is a small tab with some tiny lines on it. It's really the button for a pull-down menu. Whatever you choose in this menu determines how Elements converts your photo. Here's a look at what the choices mean:

- **Image Settings**. This is the "undo all my changes" option. In other words, if you've made some changes to your photo in the Converter, and you want to revert to the settings Elements presented you with when you first opened the photo, then choose this option.

- **Camera Raw Defaults**. Elements contains a profile of normal RAW settings for your camera model that it uses as its baseline for the adjustments it makes. That's what you get when you pick Camera RAW Defaults.

- **Previous Conversion**. If you've already processed a photo and want to apply the same settings to the photo you're currently working on, choosing this setting applies the settings from the last RAW image you opened (but only if it's from the same camera).

- **Custom Settings**. Once you start changing settings, this choice becomes selected.

Since individual cameras—even if they're the exact same model—may vary a bit (as a result of the manufacturing process), the Camera RAW Defaults settings may not be the best ones for *your* camera. You can override the default settings and create a new set of default settings for any camera.

- **To change your camera's settings**: If you know that you always want a different setting for one of the sliders—like maybe your Blacks setting should be at 13 instead of the factory setting of 9—move any or all of the sliders to where you want them and choose Save New Camera RAW Defaults. From now on, Elements opens your photos with these settings as your starting point.

- **To revert to the original Elements settings for your camera**: If you want to go back to the way things were originally, click the Settings button and choose Reset Camera RAW Defaults.

  NOTE In Elements 6, it's possible to apply changes to multiple photos at once. See page 215 for more on how to do this.

There are also some new preferences for the Elements 6 RAW Converter. To bring up the RAW Converter's Preferences dialog box, click its icon (the three lines) in the RAW Converter's toolbox. You may find these new preferences very useful, especially if you have more than one camera.

- **Make defaults specific to a camera serial number**. Turn this on if you have more than one of a particular camera model; for instance, if you carry two bodies of the same model with different lenses when you shoot, or if both you and your spouse have the same camera model. This setting lets you have a different default for each camera body.

- **Make defaults specific to camera ISO setting**. Since you may shoot very differently at different ISO settings (ISO is something like the digital equivalent of film speed), you can use this to create a default that will only apply to photos shot at ISO 100, or at ISO 1600, and so on.

NOTE If you regularly share photos with people using other programs, you'll be pleased to know that the Elements Camera RAW preferences allow you to choose whether your settings get saved in the Camera RAW database or in a sidecar XMP file that goes along with the image. If you choose the XMP file, your settings become portable along with your photo—that is, if you send the file to someone else, the settings travel along with the photo.

You don't have to create default settings to save the changes you make to a particular photo. If you just want to save the settings for the photo or group of photos you're working on right now, without having to open them all in the Editor and save them in another format, make your changes and click Done to update the settings for the image file(s).

Adjusting Vibrance and Saturation

The final group of settings on this tab controls the vividness of your colors. They don't have auto settings because you may or may not want to use them. Most RAW files have lower saturation to start with than you'd see in the same photo shot as a JPEG, so it's common to want to boost their saturation a bit. Move the sliders to the right for more intense color, and to the left for more muted color. If you know you'll always want to change the intensity of the color, you can change the standard setting by moving the slider until you have the intensity you want and creating a new camera default setting, as described on page 224.

- **Saturation**. The Saturation slider controls how vivid your colors are by applying the same amount of change to the intensity of all the colors in your photo.

- **Vibrance**. While Saturation adjusts all the colors in your photo equally, the nifty new Vibrance slider is much smarter. It increases the intensity of the duller colors, while holding back on those colors that are already so vivid they may over-saturate. If you want to adjust saturation to make your photo pop, this is the slider to try first; it's one of the best features in the Elements 6 RAW Converter.

TIP: You can sometimes create interesting aged or artistic effects by moving the Vibrance slider all the way to the left.

- **Clarity**. This slider appears first, and it's a bit different from the other two. Clarity isn't strictly a color tool, although it is an absolutely amazing new feature. If you're an experienced Elements sharpener, you may have heard of the technique called Local Contrast Enhancement, where you use the Unsharp Mask (page 205) with a low amount setting and a high radius to eliminate haze and bring out details. That's sort of what Clarity does: Through an incredibly sophisticated technique, it creates an edge mask in your photo that it uses to increase detail. It can do wonderful things for many, maybe even most of your photos, to improve contrast and add punch. Give it a try, but be sure to look at your photo at 100 percent or more so you can see how you're changing things.

Adjusting Sharpness and Reducing Noise

Once you've got your exposure and white balance right, you may be almost done with your photo. But in most cases, you'll still want to click over to the RAW Converter's Detail tab to do a little sharpening.

There are two other important adjustments available here as well: *Luminance* and *Color* (both described in a moment), used for reducing noise in your photos. None of the adjustments on this tab have Auto settings, although you can change the standard settings by moving their sliders where you want them and then creating a new camera default, as described earlier.

Sharpening increases the edge contrast in your photo, which makes it appear more crisply focused. The sharpening tools in the RAW Converter also got a recent makeover, but some of the new sliders should be familiar to you if you've done sharpening in Elements before, since they're similar to the settings for Unsharp Mask (page 205) or Adjust Sharpness.

- **Amount** controls how much you want Elements to sharpen. The scale here goes from zero (no sharpening) to 150 (way too much sharpening).

- **Radius** governs how wide an area Elements should consider as an edge to sharpen. Its scale goes from .5 pixels to 3 pixels.

- **Detail** controls how the sharpening is applied to your image. At 100—the far end of the scale—the effect is most similar to Unsharp Mask (in other words, you can overdo it). At zero you shouldn't see any sharpening halos at all.

- **Masking** is a cool new feature that reduces the area where sharpening takes place so that only edges get sharpened. If you find that you are sharpening more details than you like, use this slider to create an Edge Mask that restricts Elements from sharpening areas inside the edges. The farther you move the slider to the right, the more area is protected from sharpening. Masking is doing some amazing behind-the-scenes calculations, so don't be surprised if there's a little lag in the preview when you use this slider.

Masking and Detail work together to create very accurate sharpening, which is why the sliders go so high—you won't like the effect from just one of them set all the way up, but by experimenting with the effect of using both sliders, you can create excellent sharpening for your photo.

You also get a very helpful new view of your image if you hold the Option key as you move the sliders, as explained in Figure 8-7, but only if the view is set to 100%.

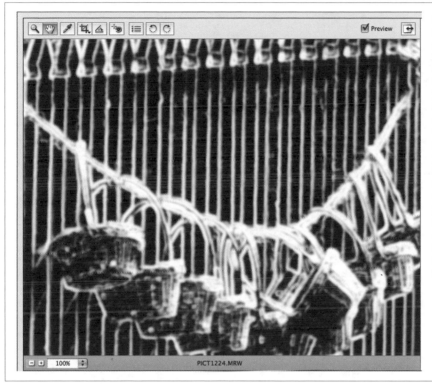

Figure 8-7:
If you've tried High-Pass sharpening (page 210), you won't have any trouble understanding this helpful new view of your image. Set the view to 100 percent and Option+drag any of the sharpening sliders to see this luminance view of your image—very useful, since sharpening doesn't affect the color data, only the luminosity of your photo. If you pay close attention, you get a highly accurate view of exactly what you are doing as you manipulate the sliders.

If you're not planning on making any further edits to your photo when you leave the RAW Converter, go ahead and sharpen it here.

On the other hand, some people prefer to wait to sharpen until they finish all their other adjustments in Full Edit mode, so they skip these sliders. But in fact you can usually sharpen here, and then sharpen again later on, outside the Converter without causing yourself any trouble.

The final two settings on this tab (under Noise Reduction) work together to reduce the *noise* (graininess) of your photo. Noise is a big problem in digital photos, especially with 5-plus megapixel cameras that don't have the large sensors found in true SLR cameras. Elements gives you two adjustments here that may help.

• **Luminance.** This setting reduces grayscale noise, which causes an overall grainy appearance to your photo—something like what you'd see in old newspaper photos. The slider is always at zero to start with since you don't want to use it more than you can help. That's because moving to the right reduces noise, but it also softens the detail in your photo.

- **Color.** If you look at what should be evenly colored areas of your photo, and you see obvious clumps of different-colored pixels, this setting can help smooth things out. Drag the slider to the right to reduce the amount of color noise.

In most cases, it may take a fair amount of fiddling with these sliders to come up with the best compromise between sharpness and smoothness. It helps if you zoom the view up to 100 percent or more when using the sliders.

NEW FEATURE ALERT

Non-RAW files in the RAW Converter

If your camera shoots JPEG files and you've always been curious about what this RAW business is all about, with Elements 6 you can find out for yourself—sort of. Now you can open JPEG or TIFF files with the RAW Converter and process them there. (If you want to try another kind of file, save it as a TIFF, and then open it with the RAW Converter.) This way you can take advantage of the new tools in the Converter, like Vibrance or Clarity, for any photo.

To open non-RAW formats, in Elements use File → Open and choose Camera Raw (*not* Photoshop Raw) as the format before you click Open. Your file opens up in the Converter and you can work on it just like a real RAW file. Actually, it's more accurate to say "almost like a real RAW file." The thing about using other formats in the Converter is this: When your camera processed that JPEG file that it wrote to your memory card, it tossed out the information it didn't need for the JPEG, so Elements doesn't really have the same amount of information to work with

that it has for a true RAW file. The Converter even lets you create a DNG—digital negative—file (page 230) from a JPEG if you wish, but it can't put back the information that wasn't included in the JPEG, so this is of limited usefulness for most people.

This means that your results can be very iffy. You may find that the RAW Converter does a bang-up job on your photo, or you may find that you liked it better before you started messing with it. There are so many variables involved that it's really hard to predict the results you'll get. But it's definitely worth giving it a try to see what you think.

If you find you like using the RAW Converter for JPEGs, you might want to experiment with reducing the saturation, contrast, and sharpening in the camera if you have settings that let you do so. You're more likely to get good results from the RAW Converter if your image is fairly neutral to start with.

Choosing bit depth: 8 or 16 bits?

Once you've got your photo looking good, you have one more important choice to make: Do you want to open it as an 8-bit or a 16-bit file? *Bit depth* refers to the number of pieces of color data, or *bits*, that each pixel in your image can hold. A single pixel of an 8-bit image can have 24 bits of information in it, 8 for each of the three color channels (red, green, and blue). A 16-bit image holds far more color information than an 8-bit photo. How much more? An 8-bit image can hold up to 16 million colors, while a 16-bit image can hold up to 281 *trillion* colors.

NOTE You can adjust 16-bit images with microscopic precision, but in the real world, your home printer only provides 8-bit color anyway. If you want to do all your editing (or at least 90 percent of it) in 16-bit color, consider upgrading to Photoshop.

Most digital cameras produce RAW files with 10 or 12 bits per channel, although a few can shoot 16-bit files. You'd think it makes perfect sense to save your digital files at the largest possible bit depth, but the fact is you'll find quite a few restrictions on how much you can do to a 16-bit file in Elements. You can open it, make some corrections, and save it, but that's about all. You can't work with layers or apply the more artistic filters, or use many of the Auto commands on a 16-bit file.

NOTE Your scanner may say it handles 24-bit color, but this is actually the same as what Elements calls 8-bit. Elements goes by the number of bits per color channel, whereas some scanner manufacturers try to impress you by giving you the total for all three channels ($8 \times 3 = 24$). When you see very high bit numbers—assuming you aren't a commercial printer—you can usually get the Elements equivalent number by dividing by three.

Once you've decided between 8- and 16-bit color, just make your selection in the Depth drop-down menu (in the lower-left corner of the RAW Converter window). The RAW bit-depth setting is "sticky," so if you change it, all your images open in that color depth until you change it again. If you ever forget what bit depth you've chosen, your image's title bar will tell you, as shown in Figure 8-8.

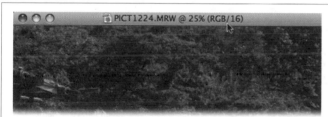

Figure 8-8:
You can always tell an image's bit depth by looking in the title bar of any image window. This image is 16-bit.

TIP If you do decide to create a 16-bit image and you become frustrated by your lack of editing choices, you can convert your image to 8-bit by choosing Image → Mode → 8 Bits/Channel. You can't convert an 8-bit image to 16 bits.

If you want to take advantage of any 16-bit files you might have, you may want to use Save As for the copy you plan to convert to 8-bit. That way you'll still have the 16-bit file for future reference. Incidentally, your Save options are different for the two bit depths. JPEG, for instance, is available only for 8-bit files. If you wonder why you only have choices like JPEG 2000 when you save a file, then you've got yourself a 16-bit file. (Regular JPEGs are always 8-bit files.)

A popular choice when you're thinking about your order of operations (*workflow*, in photo-industry speak) is to first convert your RAW file as a 16-bit image to take advantage of the increased color information while making any basic corrections, and then convert to 8-bit for the fancy stuff like the artistic filters or layer creation.

Converting to DNG

There's been a lot of buzz lately about Adobe's relatively new DNG (digital negative) format, and if you shoot RAW, you should know what's going on. As you read at the beginning of this chapter, every manufacturer uses a different format for RAW files. Even the formats for different cameras from the same manufacturer differ. It's a recipe for an industry-wide headache.

Adobe's solution is the DNG format, which the company envisions as a more standardized alternative to RAW files. Here's how it works. If you convert your RAW file to a DNG file, it still behaves like a RAW file—you can still tweak your settings in the Converter when you open it, and you still have to save it in a standard image format like TIFF or JPEG to use it in a project. But the idea behind DNG is that if you keep your RAW files in this format, then you won't have to worry about whether or not Elements version 35 can open them. Adobe clearly hopes that all camera manufacturers will adopt this standard, putting an end to the mishmash of different formats that make RAW files such a nuisance to deal with. If all cameras used DNG, then every time you bought a new camera you wouldn't have to worry whether your programs could view the camera's images.

You can create DNG files from your RAW files right in the Converter. Just click the Save Image button at the bottom of the window, and you see the DNG Converter, shown in Figure 8-9. Choose a destination, and then select how you want to name the DNG file. You get the same naming options as in Process Multiple Files (page 233), but since you convert only one file at a time here, you may as well keep the photo's current name and just add the .DNG extension.

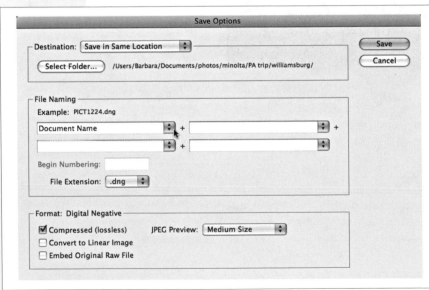

Figure 8-9:
The DNG Converter. The bottom section of the Converter window lets you choose whether or not to compress the file, how to handle the image preview, and whether or not to embed your original RAW file in the new one. Generally, you're best off leaving the settings in this section the way you see them in the illustration.

Of course, the jury is still out on whether DNG is going to become an industry standard, although it does seem to be gaining popularity. There have been other good ideas over the years, like the JPEG 2000 format (see page 58), that never really took off. Whether or not to create DNG files from your RAW files is up to you, but for now, it's probably prudent to hang onto the original files as well, if you decide in favor of DNG.

> **NOTE** If you want to batch convert your RAW files to DNG, the easiest way is to go to Adobe's Web site (*www.adobe.com/downloads* and search for "DNG") and download the standalone DNG Converter, which you can leave on your desktop. Then just drop a folder of RAW images onto its icon, and the DNG Converter lets you process the whole folder at once. (The standalone Converter is part of the RAW Converter update [page 214]. If your RAW Converter is up to date already, just remove the DNG Converter and discard the rest of the download.) You can also batch save images in the RAW Converter itself, by highlighting them in the list on the left side of the window and clicking Save Images.

Photo Filter

The Photo Filter command gives you a host of nifty photo filters that are the digital equivalent of the lens-mounted filters of various colors used in traditional film photography. You can use them to correct problems with your image's white balance, as well as for a bunch of other fixes from the seriously photographic to the downright silly. For example, you can correct a bad skin tone or dig out an old photo of your fifth-grade nemesis and make him green, literally. Figure 8-10 shows the Photo Filter in action.

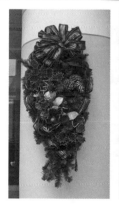 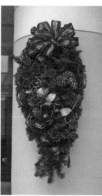

Figure 8-10:
You can use the Photo Filter to correct the color casts you get from artificial lighting.

Left: This photo had a strong bluish tinge from nearby fluorescent lighting.

Right: A Warming Filter (85) took care of it. Use Cooling Filter (80) or Cooling Filter (82) to counteract the orange cast from tungsten lighting. (The numbers stand for the numbers of glass filters you'd use on a film camera.)

Elements comes with 20 Photo Filters, but for most people, the top six are the important ones: three warming filters and three cooling filters. You use these filters to get rid of the color casts that come from a poor white balance (see page 219).

(Faking) HDR/Digital Blending

One of the big new buzz terms in photography recently has been *high dynamic range*, or HDR for short. This technique has been around awhile, but before it was more often called *digital blending*. With most digital cameras, you're likely to hit the clipping point (page 223) in an image much sooner than you want to. If you up the exposure so that the shadows are nice and detailed, about half the time you've blown the highlights. On the other hand, if you adjust your exposure settings down to favor the highlights, your shadows are murkier than an Enron annual report.

HDR/digital blending is a technique photographers use to get around these limitations. To use HDR, you *bracket* your shots. That is, you take two identical shots of your subject at different settings—one exposed for shadows and one for highlights—and then combine them, choosing the best bits of each one. True HDR is a pretty complex process, but you can simulate it, to some extent, in Elements.

That technique is great for landscapes. But if you're shooting hummingbirds, roller-skating chimps, or toddlers, you know it's just about impossible to get two identical shots of a moving subject. And if you're like many amateur photographers, you may not realize you didn't capture what you wanted until you're home and see the shot on your computer.

If you shoot in RAW mode, you can use the Converter to help you fake HDR, sort of. It's not as good as planning ahead, but you can often salvage another stop or two of detail.

Just follow these steps:

1. Run your photo through the Converter twice, one time exposing for the highlights and once for the shadows.

2. Drag one image onto the other—the way you would if you were moving layers between images (page 172).

   Put the image with the largest area that you want to use on top, so you'll have less to change.

3. Use the Eraser tool (page 334) to rub out the bad spots on the top photo, revealing those areas in the bottom layer.

   Figure 8-11 shows this process in action.

When you're done, you can merge the layers (page 166) if you want.

If you'd like to try your hand at the real thing, you'll find an excellent tutorial on Luminous Landscape (*http://luminous-landscape.com/tutorials/digital-blending.shtml*). Every digital photographer should bookmark this site. You're sure to find a ton of valuable information there, including lots of fine tutorials.

You might also want to check out Bracketeer from Pangea (*www.pangeasoft.net*), a very promising, inexpensive, Mac-only program that many people think produces better results than you can get with the HDR feature in full Photoshop.

The filters are an improvement over the Color Cast eyedropper (page 196) because you can control the strength with which you apply them (using the Density slider, explained later). And you can also apply them as Adjustment layers (page 169), so you can tweak them later on.

To apply a Photo Filter:

1. **Open the Photo Filter dialog box.**

   Go to Layer → New Adjustment Layer → Photo Filter, or go to Filter → Adjustments → Photo Filter. The Photo Filter dialog box appears.

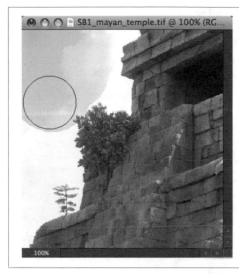

Figure 8-11:
Digital blending (see the box on page 232) in action. Here, the blown-out sky in the top image is being erased to reveal the blue sky in the bottom layer. This maneuver is similar to the technique you'll use for creating spot or accent color, explained on page 275.

2. **Choose a filter from the pull-down list or click the Color radio button.**

   You get two choices. The pull-down list gives you a choice of filters in preset colors. If you want to choose your own custom color, click the Color button instead.

3. **If you chose the Color button, click the color square in the dialog box to bring up the Color Picker (page 199) and choose the shade you want.**

   You can also sample a color from your image. The cursor turns to an eyedropper when you move it from the dialog box into your photo. Just click the color you want for your filter, and that color appears in the color square in the dialog box.

4. **Move the Density slider to adjust the color.**

   Moving the Density slider to the right increases the filter's effect; moving it to the left decreases it. If you leave Preserve Luminosity turned on, the filter won't darken your image. Turn off Preserve Luminosity and your photo gets darker when you apply the filter.

5. **Click OK.**

Processing Multiple Files

If you're addicted to batch processing your photos, you'll love the Elements equivalent: Process Multiple Files. In addition to renaming your files and changing their formats, you can do a lot of other very useful things with this tool, like adding copyright information or captions to multiple files, or even using some of the Quick Fix auto commands.

To call up the batch-processing window, in Elements, go to File → Process Multiple Files. You see yet another of the headache-inducing giant Elements dialog boxes, but this one is actually pretty easy to understand. If you look closely, you see that the dialog box is divided into sections, each with a different specialty (see Figure 8-12). You can also start from Bridge. Go to Tools → Photoshop Elements → Process Multiple Files, and Bridge bounces you back to Elements and opens the same window.

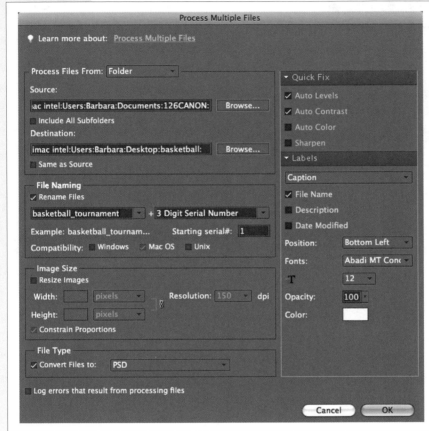

Figure 8-12:
You could also call Process Multiple Files "Computer: Earn Your Keep," because you can make so many changes at once. This dialog box is set up to apply the following changes: Rename every file (from PICT8983 to basketball_ tournament001), change them to the .psd format, apply Auto Levels and Auto Contrast, and add the file name as a caption. You make all that happen by clicking the OK button.

TIP   Process *Multiple* Files is the name of the command, but you can run it on just one photo if you want, although it 's usually easier just to do a regular Save As (see Chapter 2 for more about saving files). Just open your photo, go to File → Process Multiple Files, and choose Opened Files as your source. You can even opt to save the new version to the desktop without overwriting your original.

The following sections cover each main section of the Process Multiple Files dialog box. You have to use the first section (which tells Elements which files you want to process), but you'll probably only want to make use of one or two of the other sections at any one time. (Of course, you can use them all, as shown in Figure 8-12.)

Choosing Your Files

In the first section of the dialog box, in the upper-left corner, you identify the files you want to convert and then tell Elements where to put them once it's processed them. You have several options here, which you pick from the Process Files From pull-down menu. You can choose your currently open files, the contents of a folder, or "Import," which brings up the same options you see when you go to File → Import, like your camera or scanner. Using this option, you can choose to convert your files as you bring them into Elements.

If you want to include files scattered around in different locations on your hard drive, you can speed things up by opening the files or gathering them into one folder. If you have a couple of folders' worth of photos to convert, you can save time by putting all those folders into one folder and using the "include all subfolders" option explained later. Then all the files get converted at once.

Here's how to get started:

1. **Choose the files you want to convert.**

   Use the Process Files From pull-down menu to tell Elements which kind of files you want: opened files, a folder, photos from Bridge, or files imported from your camera or scanner.

2. **If you chose Folder, tell Elements which folder you want.**

   Click the Browse button and, in the dialog box that appears, choose the folder you want. Files for processing must be in a folder if they aren't already open.

   If you have folders within a folder and you want to change all those files, turn on the Include All Subfolders checkbox. Otherwise, Elements changes only the files at the top level of the folder.

3. **Pick a destination.**

   This is where the files will end up once they've been processed. Most of the time, you'll want a new folder for this, so click Browse, and then click New Folder in the window that opens. You can also choose an existing folder in the Browse window if you prefer. You need to be careful about choosing "Same as Source," as Figure 8-13 explains.

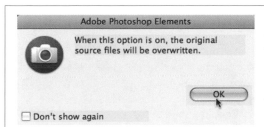

Figure 8-13:
If you turn on the "Same as Source" checkbox, Elements warns that it's going to replace your originals with the new versions. That's a timesaver, but it's dangerous, too. If something goes wrong, your originals can be messed up, so don't choose the "Same as Source" checkbox unless you have backup copies someplace else.

Renaming Your Files

Being able to rename a group of files all in one fell swoop is a very cool feature, but it has a few limitations. Yes, you can rename your files here, but if you think that means you can give each photo a name like "Keisha and Gram at the Park," followed by "Fred's New Newt" for the next photo, you're going to be disappointed. Instead, what Elements offers when you use its file-renaming feature is a quick way of applying a similar name to a group of files. That means it's easy to transform a folder filled with files named DSCF001.jpg, DSCF0002.jpg, and so on, into the slightly friendlier Keisha and Gram001.jpg, Keisha and Gram002.jpg.

To rename your files, turn on the Rename Files option in the dialog box. You then see two active text boxes with pull-down menus next to them (a + sign separates the menus). You can enter any text you like, and it will replace every file name in the group, or you can choose any of the options in the menus. (Both menus are the same.)

The menus offer you a choice of the document name (in three different capitalization styles), serial numbers, serial letters, dates, extensions, or nothing at all (which gives you just the trailing numbers without any kind of prefix). Figure 8-14 shows the many choices you get.

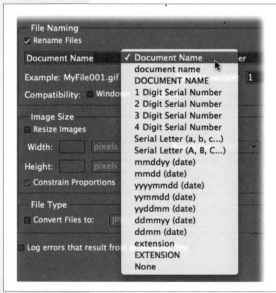

Figure 8-14:
Elements offers lots of naming options to suit whatever you plan to do with your photos. If you select Document Name, for example, your photos retain their original names (plus whatever you choose from the right-side pull-down menu). DOCUMENT NAME gets you the same file names in all capital letters, "1 Digit Serial Number" starts you off with the number 1, and so on.

NOTE If you choose to add serial numbers, there's a box ("Starting serial#") where you can designate the starting number. Your first choice is always 1, which actually shows up as 001 because the leading zeros are needed for your computer to recognize the file order. The tenth figure in your batch would be numbered 010, one hundred would be 100, and so on.

So if you type *tongue_piercing_day* in the text box and choose the three-digit serial number, Elements names your photos tongue_piercing_day001.jpg, tongue_piercing_day002.jpg, and so on.

> **NOTE:** If all you want to do is batch rename your files, you can do that right in Bridge. Select your files, and then go to Tools → Batch Rename. This gives you more naming options than you get in Elements. For instance, you can add multiple text blocks interspersed with numbers.

You also get to designate which operating systems' naming conventions Elements should respect when assigning the new names, as explained in Figure 8-15. If you send files to people or servers using other operating systems, you know how important this is. If you don't, play it safe and turn on all three checkboxes. You never know when you may need to send a photo to your nephew who uses Linux.

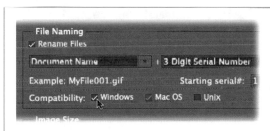

Figure 8-15:
The Compatibility checkboxes tell Elements to watch out for any characters that would violate the naming conventions of the operating systems you check. This is very handy if, say, your Web site is hosted on a Unix server and you want to be sure your file names won't create a problem for it. You can choose to be compatible with either or neither of the other operating systems, but the Mac OS checkbox is always turned on.

Changing Image Size and File Type

The Image Size and File Type sections let you resize your photos and change your images' file formats. The Image Size settings work best when you're trying to reduce file sizes (for example, with a folder of images that you've converted for Web use but found are still too big).

> **NOTE** Before you make any big changes to a group of files, it's important that you understand the concept of how changes in an image's resolution and file size affect its appearance. See page 82 for a refresher.

To apply image size changes, turn on the Resize Images checkbox and then adjust the Width, Height, and Resolution settings, all of which work the same way as those described on page 86.

In the File Type section, you can convert files from one format to another. This is probably the most popular batching activity. If your camera creates JPEGs and you want TIFFs for editing work, you can change an entire folder at once. From the pull-down menu, just select the file type you want to create.

The final setting in the left half of the window is the checkbox for logging errors in processing your files. It's a good idea to turn this checkbox on, as explained in Figure 8-16.

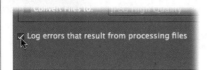

Figure 8-16:
If you turn on "Log errors that result from processing files," Elements lets you know if it runs into any problems while converting your files. You'll find a little text log file in the folder with your completed images, whether there were problems or not. (If nothing went awry, it will be blank.)

Applying Quick Fix Commands

In the upper-right corner of Process Multiple Files, you'll find some of the same Quick Fix commands you have in the regular Quick Fix window. If you consistently get good results with the Auto commands there, you can run them on a whole folder at once here.

You can run Auto Levels, Auto Contrast, Auto Color, Auto Sharpen, or any combination of those commands that you like on all the files in your folder. (Unfortunately, you can't batch run the Auto Smart Fix command from this window.) If you don't see the list, click the flippy triangle next to Quick Fix to expand it. If you need a refresher on what each one does, see Chapter 4, beginning on page 101.

> **NOTE** Don't forget that you can also batch process corrections in the RAW Converter (see page 224), even if your files are TIFFs or JPEGs. Then open the files and use Process Multiple Files to save all the changed files at once.

Attaching Labels

The tools in the Labels section let you add captions and copyright notices, which Elements calls *watermarks*, to your images (see Figure 8-17). Watermarks and captions get imprinted right onto the photo itself. The procedure is the same for both; only the content differs. A watermark contains any text you choose, while a caption is limited to your choices from a group of checkboxes.

First, you need to choose between a watermark and a caption (choose from the pull-down menu right below the Label tab). You can't do both at once, so if you want both, add one, run Process Multiple Files, and then add the other and run Process Multiple Files again on the resulting images. You can download wagonwheels.jpg from the "Missing CD" page at *www.missingmanuals.com* to try adding your own watermarks and captions.

Watermarks

If you want to create a watermark, you first need to enter some text in the Custom Text box. You can enter any text you want. Then choose the position and appearance of your text as explained later.

Text you enter here gets applied to every photo in the batch, so this is a great way to add copyright or contact info that you want on every photo. If you want different text on each photo, check out the Description option for captions, as shown in Figure 8-18.

> **TIP** To type the copyright symbol (©), just hold down Option and then press G.

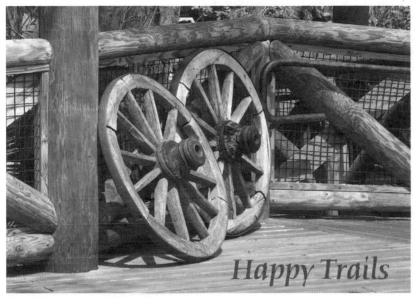

Figure 8-17:
Adobe calls the "Happy Trails" custom text in this image a watermark. Elements is very flexible about the fonts and sizes you can choose for a watermark or caption, but you don't get much say in where it goes on your photo if you use Process Multiple Files. For maximum flexibility, use the Type tool, as explained on page 383. The drawback: You can't batch process using that method.

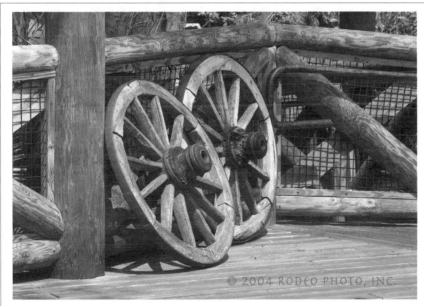

Figure 8-18:
You just can't beat Process Multiple Files for adding quick copyright information to your photo, although there are other methods that give a more sophisticated look, as described in the Tip at the end of this chapter (page 240).

Adding captions

For a caption, you can choose any of the following, separately or in combination:

- **File Name.** You can choose to show the file's name as the caption. If you decide to run the rename option at the same time, you get the new name you're assigning.

- **Description**. Turn this checkbox on to use any text you have entered in the Description section of the File Info dialog box (File → File Info) as your caption. This is your most flexible option for entering text, and the only way to batch different caption text for each photo. Just enter the text for each photo in File → File Info → Description.

- **Date Modified**. This is the date your file was last changed. In practice, that usually means today's date, because you're modifying your file by running Process Multiple Files on it.

Once you've decided what you want your caption to say, you need to make some choices about its position and size. These choices are the same whether you're adding a watermark or a caption, and if you switch from one to the other before actually running Process Multiple Files, your previous choices will appear.

- **Position**. This tells Elements where to put your caption. Your options are Bottom Left, Bottom Right, or Centered. Centered doesn't mean bottom center, incidentally. It puts the text smack in the middle of your image.

- **Font**. From the pull-down menu, choose any font on your system. Chapter 14 has much more information about fonts.

- **Size**. This setting determines the size of your type. Click the menu next to the two little Ts to choose from several preset sizes, up to 72 point.

- **Opacity**. Use this to adjust how solidly your text prints. Choose 100 percent for maximum readability or click the downward arrow and move the slider to the left for watermark type that lets you see the image underneath it.

- **Color**. Use this setting to choose your text color. Click the box to bring up the color picker and make your choice.

> **TIP**　If you want to use a logo as a watermark, the Process Multiple Files tool can't help you. But there is a way to apply a logo to a bunch of images. Here's how. First, create your logo on a new layer in one of the images. Adjust the opacity with the slider in the Layers palette until you like the results. Save the file. Now you can drag that layer from the Layers palette onto each photo where you need it. (To center the logo on your photo, hold the shift key while dragging.) You can also do this with Adjustment layers (page 169) to give yourself a sort of batch-processing capability for applying the same adjustments to multiple files.

Retouching: Fine-Tuning Your Images

Basic edits like exposure fixes and sharpening are fine if all you want to make are simple adjustments. But Elements also gives you the tools to make sophisticated changes that aren't hard to apply, and that can make the difference between a ho-hum photo and a fabulous one. This chapter introduces you to some advanced editing maneuvers that will greatly help you either rescue damaged photos or give good ones that little extra zing.

The first part of the chapter shows you how to get rid of blemishes—not only those that affect skin, but also dust, scratches, stains, and other photographic imperfections. You'll also learn some powerful color-improving techniques, including the Color Curves tool, which gives you a powerful way to improve your image's contrast and color.

Fixing Blemishes

It's an imperfect world, but in your photos, it doesn't have to be. Elements gives you some amazing tools for fixing the flaws in your subjects. You can erase crow's feet and blemishes, eliminate power lines in an otherwise perfect view, or even hide objects you wish weren't in your photo. Not only that, but these same tools are great for fixing problems like tears, folds, and stains—the great foes of photoscanning veterans. With a little effort, you can bring back photos that seem beyond help. Figure 9-1 shows an example of the kind of restoration you can accomplish with a little persistence and Elements.

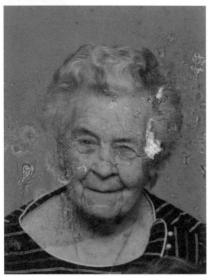

Figure 9-1:
You can do some amazing repair work with Elements if you have the patience.

Top: Here's a section of a water-damaged family portrait. The grandmother's face is almost obliterated.

Bottom: The same image after being repaired with Elements. It took a lot of cloning and healing to get even this close, but if you keep at it, you can do the kind of work that would have required professional help before Elements. If you're interested in restoring old photographs, check out Katrin Eismann's books on the subject. They're written for the full-featured Photoshop, but you can adapt most of the techniques for Elements.

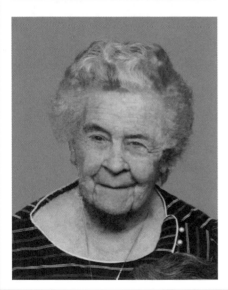

Elements gives you three main tools for this kind of work:

- **The Spot Healing brush** is the easiest way to repair your photo. Just drag over the area you want to fix. Elements searches the surrounding area and blends that information into the troubled spot, making it indistinguishable from the background. It usually works best on small areas, for the reasons explained later.

- **The Healing brush** works much like the Spot Healing brush, only you tell the Healing brush the part of your photo to use as a source for the material you want to blend in. This makes the Healing brush more flexible than the Spot Healing brush, and better suited to large areas, because you don't have to worry about inadvertently dragging in unwanted details.

- **The Clone Stamp** offers another way to make repairs. It works like the Healing brush in that you sample a good area and apply it to the area you want to fix. But instead of blending the repair in, the Clone Stamp actually covers the bad area with the replacement. The Clone Stamp is best for situations when you want to completely hide the underlying area, as opposed to letting any of what's already there blend into your repair (which is how things work with the Healing brushes). The Clone Stamp is also your best option when you want to create a realistic copy of detail that's elsewhere in your photo. You can clone over some leaves to fill in a bare branch, or replace a knothole in a fence board with good wood, for instance.

All three tools work similarly: You just drag each tool over the area you want to change. It's as simple as using a paintbrush. In fact, each of these tools requires you to choose a brush, just like the ones you'll learn about in Chapter 12. But brush selection is pretty straightforward; in this chapter you'll learn everything you need to make basic brush choices.

The Spot Healing Brush: Fixing Small Areas

The Spot Healing brush excels at fixing minor blemishes: pimples, lipstick smudges, stray lint, and so on. You simply paint over the area you want to repair, and the Spot Healing brush automatically searches the surrounding areas and blends that into the spot you're brushing. Figure 9-2 shows what a great job the Spot Healing brush can do. (Download the file radish.jpg from the "Missing CD" page at *www.missingmanuals.com*, if you'd like to try this tool.)

The Spot Healing brush's ability to borrow information from surrounding areas is great, but it's also a drawback. The larger the area you drag the brush over, the wider Elements searches for replacement material. So, if there's contrasting material too close to the area you're trying to fix, it can unintentionally get pulled into the repair. For instance, if you're trying to fix a spot on an eyelid, you may wind up with some of the color from the eye itself mixed in with your repair.

You get best results from this brush when you choose a brush size that just barely covers the spot you're trying to fix. If you need to drag to fix an oblong area, use a brush the minimum width that covers the flaw. The Spot Healing brush also works much better when there's a large surrounding area that looks the way you want your repaired spot to look.

The Spot Healing brush has only three settings in the Options bar. From left to right, they are:

- **Brush.** You can use the pull-down menu to choose a different brush style if you prefer (see Chapter 12 for lots more about brushes), but generally, you're best off sticking to the standard brush that Elements starts out with and just changing the size, if necessary.

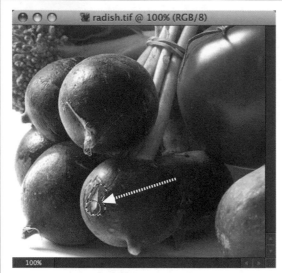

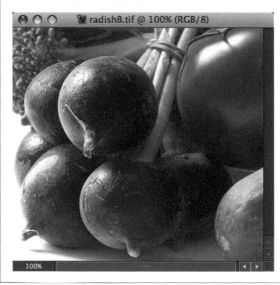

Figure 9-2:
The trick to using the Spot Healing brush is to work in very tiny areas. If you choose too large a brush or drag over too large an area, you're more likely to pick up undesired shades and details from the surrounding area.

Top: The radish in the bottom row has a large gouge in it.

Bottom: By dragging with a brush barely the width of the scar, you can make a truly invisible fix.

- **Size.** Use this slider to set the brush size.

- **Type.** Use these radio buttons to adjust how the brush works. Proximity Match tells the Spot Healing brush to search the surrounding area for replacement pixels, and Create Texture tells it to blend only from the area you drag it over. Generally speaking, if Proximity Match doesn't work well, you'll get better results by switching to the regular Healing brush than by choosing Create Texture.

> **TIP** Adobe suggests that you may like the results you get from Create Texture better if you drag over the spot more than once.

- **All Layers.** Turn this on if you want the brush to look for replacement material in all the visible layers in your photo.

You won't believe how easy it is to fix problem areas with the Spot Healing brush. All you do is:

1. **Activate the Spot Healing brush.**

   Click the Healing brush icon (the Band-Aid) in the Toolbox, and then choose the Spot Healing brush—the one with the dotted selection lines extending from it—from the pop-out menu. (J is the keyboard shortcut.)

2. **Choose a brush size just barely bigger than the flaw.**

   You can choose your brush size from the Options bar Size slider or by pressing] (the close bracket key) for a larger brush or [(the open bracket key) for a smaller brush.

3. **Click the bad spot.**

   If the brush doesn't quite cover the flaw, drag over the area.

4. **When you release the mouse button, Elements repairs the blemish.**

   You won't see any change to your image while you drag, only after you let go.

Sometimes you get great results with the Spot Healing brush on a larger area if it's surrounded by a field of good material that's similar in tone to the spot you're trying to fix. Most of the time, though, you're better off with the regular Healing brush for large areas, as well as for flaws whose replacement material isn't right next to the bad spot.

GEM IN THE ROUGH

Dust and Scratches

Scratched, dusty prints can create giant headaches when you scan them. Cleaning your scanner's glass helps, but lots of photos come with plenty of dust marks already in the print, or in the file itself if the lens or sensor of your digital camera was dusty.

A similar problem is caused by *artifacts*, blobbish areas of color caused by JPEG compression. If you take a close look at the sky in a JPEG photo, for instance, you may see that instead of a smooth swath of blue, you see lots of little distinct clumps of each shade of blue.

The Healing brushes are usually your best first line of defense for fixing these problems, but if the specks are very widespread, Elements offers a couple other options you may want to try.

The first is the JPEG artifacts option in the Reduce Noise filter (page 358). If you're lucky, that will take care of things.

If it doesn't, other possible solutions include the Despeckle filter (Filter → Noise → Despeckle), which is sometimes effective for JPEG artifacts. And if that doesn't get everything, you can undo it and try the "Dust and Scratches" filter (Filter → Noise → "Dust and Scratches"), or the Median filter (Filter → Noise → Median). The Radius setting for these last two filters tells Elements how far to search for dissimilar pixels for its calculations. Keep that number as low as possible. The downside to the filters in this group is that they smooth things out in a way that can make your image look blurred. Generally, Despeckle is the filter that's least destructive to your image's focus.

The Healing Brush: Fixing Larger Areas

The Healing brush lets you fix much bigger areas than you can usually manage with the Spot Healing brush. The main difference between the two tools is that with the regular Healing brush, you choose the area that's going to be blended into the repair. The blending makes your repair look very natural. Figure 9-3 shows what great results you can get with this tool.

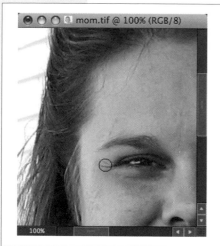
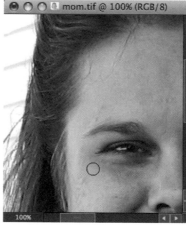

Figure 9-3:
The Healing brush is especially remarkable because it also blends the textures of the areas where you use it.

Left: This photo shows the crow's-foot at the corner of the woman's eye.

Right: The Healing brush eliminates it without creating a phony, airbrushed effect.

The repair material doesn't have to be nearby; in fact, you can sample from a totally different photo if you like. To sample material from another photo, just arrange both photos on the desktop so that you can easily move the cursor from one to the other.

The basic procedure for using the Healing brush is similar to that for the Spot Healing brush: You drag over the flaw you want to fix. The difference is that with the Healing brush, you first Option+click where you want Elements to look for replacement pixels.

The Healing brush offers you quite a few choices in the Options bar:

- **Brush.** Click the brush thumbnail to bring up the Brush Dynamics palette, explained on page 319. This lets you customize the size, shape, and hardness of your brush. But generally, the standard brush works well, so you don't have to change things other than the size if you don't want to.

- **Mode.** You can choose some blend modes (see page 329) here, but most of the time, you want one of the top two options: Normal and Replace. Normal is usually your best choice. Sometimes, though, your replacement pixels may make the area you work on show a visibly different texture than the surrounding area. In that case, choose Replace, which preserves the grain of your photo.

- **Source.** You can choose to sample an area to use as a replacement, or you can blend in a pattern. Using the Healing brush with patterns is explained on page 252.

- **Pattern thumbnails.** If you chose to use a pattern, this box becomes active. Click it to select the pattern you want to use.

- **Aligned.** If you turn on the Aligned checkbox, Elements keeps sampling new material in your source as you use the tool. The sampling follows the direction of your brush. Even if you let go of the mouse button, Elements continues to sample new material as long as you continue brushing. If you leave Aligned turned off, all the material comes from the area where you first defined your source point.

  Generally, for both the Healing brush and the Clone Stamp, it's easier to leave Aligned turned off. You can still change your source point by Option+clicking another spot, but you often get better results if *you* make the decision about when to move on to another location rather than letting Elements decide.

- **All Layers.** If you turn on this option, Elements samples from all the visible layers (page 154) in the area where you set your source point. Turn it off and Elements samples only the active layer.

- **Overlay Options.** Click this icon (the little gray overlapping squares) for a pop-out menu that lets you turn on and adjust a visible overlay for your photo. It allows you to see a floating ghostly overlay of the source area where you're sampling in relation to your original, so you can see exactly how things line up to help you do very accurate healing. You can also adjust the opacity of the overlay or invert it (make the light areas dark and the dark areas light so that you can see details better, if necessary) for a better view. Autohide causes it to disappear at the moment you click so it's not in your way as you work.

  If you're a beginner, you'll probably want to leave this off, but advanced healers may find it very useful. It's also available for the Clone Stamp, and the settings you choose for one tool will appear when you switch to the other tool.

It's almost as simple to use the Healing brush as it is to use the Spot Healing brush.

1. **Activate the Healing brush.**

   Click the Healing brush icon (the Band-Aid) in the Toolbox and choose it from the pop-out menu. (J is the keyboard shortcut.)

2. **Find a good spot you want to sample to use in the repair and Option+click it.**

   When you click the good spot, your cursor temporarily turns into a circle with crosshairs in it to indicate that this is the point where Elements will retrieve your repair material from. (If you want to use a source point in a different photo, both the source photo and the one you're repairing must be in the same color mode. See page 48 for more about color modes.)

---

3. **Drag over the area you want to repair.**

   You can see where Elements is sampling the repair material from: A cross marks the sampling point.

4. **When you release the mouse, Elements blends the sampled area into the problem area.**

   Often you don't know how effective you were until Elements is through working its magic, because it may take a few seconds for the program to finish its calculations and blend in the repair. If you don't like what Elements did, press ⌘+Z to undo and try again.

You can choose to heal on a separate layer. The advantage of doing this is that if you find the end result is a little too much—your granny suddenly looks like a Stepford wife—you can back things off a bit by reducing the opacity of the healed layer to let the original show through. This is a good plan when using the Clone Stamp, too. Just press ⌘+Shift+N to create a new layer and then turn on All Layers in the Options bar.

The Clone Stamp

The Clone Stamp is like the Healing brush in that you add material from a source point that you select. The main difference between the two is that the Clone Stamp doesn't *blend in* when the new material is applied. Instead, the Clone Stamp works by covering up the underlying area completely. This makes the Clone Stamp your tool of choice when you don't want to leave any visible trace of what you're repairing. Figure 9-4 shows an example of when cloning is a better choice than healing.

The choices you make in the Options bar for the Clone Stamp are very important in getting the best results possible.

- **Brush.** You can use the pull-down menu to select a different brush style (see Chapter 12 for more about brushes), but the standard brush style usually works pretty well. If the soft edges of your cloned areas bother you, you may be tempted to switch to a harder brush. But that usually makes your photo look like you strewed confetti on it, because hard edges don't blend well with what's already in your photo.

- **Size.** Choose a brush that's just big enough to get your sample without picking up a lot of other details that you don't want in your repair. While it may be tempting to clone huge chunks at once to get it done faster, most of the time you'll do better using the smallest brush that gets the sample you want.

- **Mode.** You can choose any blend mode (see page 329) for cloning, but Normal is usually your best bet. Other modes can create interesting special effects.

- **Opacity.** Elements automatically uses 100-percent opacity for cloning, but you can reduce opacity to let some details from your original show through.

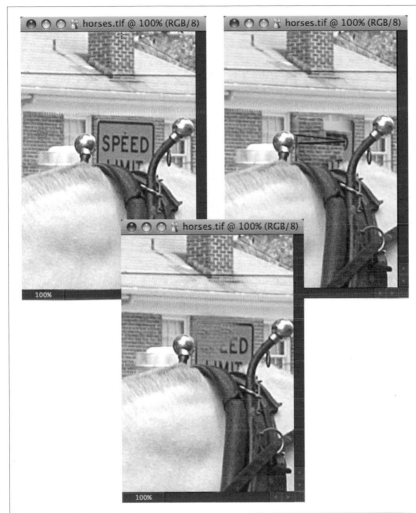

Figure 9-4:
Here's an example of when you'd choose cloning over healing.

Top left: This photo has a very distracting Speed Limit sign just above the horse's collar.

Top right: In this photo, the Healing brush does a lousy job covering up the sign.

Bottom: The Clone Stamp works much better. Only the upper-left corner has been fixed, but you can see how much better the Clone Stamp covers up the sign.

TIP You gain more control by placing your clone on another layer (see page 150) than by adjusting the Clone Stamp's opacity.

- **Aligned.** This setting works exactly the way it does for the Healing brush (described earlier in this chapter). Turn it on and Elements keeps sampling at a uniform distance from your cursor as you clone. Turn it off and you keep putting down the same source material. Figure 9-5 shows an example of when you'd turn on Aligned.

- **All Layers.** When you turn on All Layers, Elements takes its samples from all the visible layers in the area where you set your source point. When it's off Elements samples only the active layer.

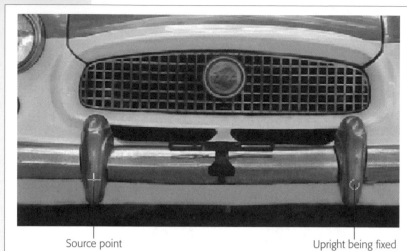

Figure 9-5:
The right-hand upright on this car's bumper was badly damaged. To restore it, the Clone Stamp's Aligned option was used to pull detail from the left bumper, replacing the missing pieces. Dragging with the Clone Stamp in Aligned mode replaces the entire bumper smoothly, rather than in hard-to-align brush-sized samples.

Source point   Upright being fixed

• **Overlay Options.** Click this and choose Show Overlay to turn on a pale overlay that shows the clone source area floating over the original, so that you can see precisely how your possible source material aligns with the original. This is a little confusing at first, but once you get the hang of it, it's very helpful when cloning precise patterns. If you've ever used the Clone Stamp before and had the experience of inadvertently cloning from the wrong spot, or dragging in detail you didn't mean to grab, you'll understand how useful this can be.

The options for adjusting the overlay are the same as for the Healing brush (page 246), which shares this feature. Settings you choose here will appear when you use the Healing brush and vice versa.

The Clone Stamp shares its space in the Toolbox with the Pattern Stamp, which is explained later. (You can tell which is which because the Pattern Stamp icon has a little blue checkerboard to its left.) Using the Clone Stamp is very much like using the Healing brush. Only the result is different.

1. **Activate the Clone Stamp.**

   Press S or click its icon (the rubber stamp) in the Toolbox, and then choose it from the pop-out menu.

2. **Find the spot in your photo that you want to repair.**

   You may need to zoom way, way in to get a good enough look at what you're doing. See page 79 for how to adjust the view.

3. **Find a good spot to sample as a replacement for the bad area.**

   You want an area that has the same tone as the area you're fixing. The Clone Stamp doesn't do any blending the way the Healing brush does, so tone differences are pretty obvious.

Repairing Tears and Stains

With Elements, you can do a great deal to bring damaged old photos back to life. The Healing brush and the Clone Stamp are major players when it comes to restoring pictures. It's fiddly work and takes some persistence, but you can achieve wonders if you have the patience.

That said, if you're lucky enough to have good-size useable replacement sections elsewhere in your photo, you can use the Move tool to copy the good bits into the problem area. First, select the part you want to copy. Then press M to activate the Move tool and Option+drag the good piece where you want it. (There's more about the Move tool on page 138.)

You can use the Rotate commands to flip your selection if you need a mirror image. For example, if the left leg of a chair is fine but the right one is missing, try selecting and Option+dragging the left leg with the Move tool. When it's where you want it, go to Image → Rotate → Flip Selection Horizontal to turn the copied left leg into a new right leg.

If you don't need to rotate an object, sometimes you may be able to just increase the Clone Stamp brush size and clone your object where you need a duplicate. Cloning objects works well only when your background is the same for both areas.

4. **Option+click the spot you want to clone from.**

   When you click, your cursor turns to a circle with crosshairs in it, indicating the source point for the repair. Once you're actually working with the Clone Stamp, you see a cross marking the sampling point.

5. **Click the spot you want to cover.**

   Elements puts whatever you just selected down on top of your image, concealing the original. You can drag with the Clone Stamp, but it acts like it's in Aligned mode (described earlier) when you do, so often it's preferable to use multiple clicks instead for areas that are larger than your sample. (The only difference between real Aligned mode and what you get from dragging is that with dragging, when you let go of the mouse, your source point snaps back to where you started. If you turn on Aligned, your source point stays where you stopped.)

6. **Continue until you've covered the area.**

   With the Clone Stamp, unlike the Healing brush, what you see as you click is what you get. Elements doesn't do any further blending or smoothing.

The Clone Stamp is a very powerful tool, but it's crotchety, too. See the box on the next page for some suggestions on how to make it behave.

You can clone on a separate layer, just as you can with the Healing tool. This lets you adjust the opacity of your repair afterwards. Press Shift+⌘+N to create a new layer and then turn on Sample All Layers in the Options bar. It's almost always a good idea to clone on a separate layer when you can do so, since cloning is so much more opaque than healing. If you use a separate layer, you can adjust the opacity of the cloned area afterwards for a more subtle blend, if necessary.

TROUBLESHOOTING MOMENT

Keeping the Clone Stamp Under Control

The clone tool is a great resource, but it definitely has a mind of its own sometimes.

If you suddenly see spots of a different shade appearing as you clone, take a look in the Options bar at the Aligned box. It has a tendency to insist on staying turned on, and even if you turn it off, it can turn itself back on when you aren't paying attention.

Once in a great while, the Clone Stamp just won't reset itself when you try to select a new sampling point.

Try clicking the tiny down arrow on the extreme left side of the Options bar and choosing the Reset Tool option, as shown in Figure 9-6. If that doesn't do it, exit and restart the Editor and delete Elements' preferences file. Here's how: hold down ⌘+Option+Shift immediately after launching Elements. You get a dialog box asking if you want to delete the Elements settings. Say yes. This returns all your Elements settings to where they were the first time you launched the program. (Resetting the preferences cures about 80 percent of the problems you may run into in Elements.)

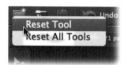

Figure 9-6:
You can reset the Clone Stamp (or, for that matter, any Elements tool) by clicking the tiny arrow at the left end of the Options bar, then choosing Reset Tool. (It's hard to see the little arrow normally, but here you can't really see it at all because the pop-up menu covers it up.) If you want to reset the whole Toolbox, choose Reset All Tools. This clears up a lot of the little problems you may have when trying to make a tool behave correctly.

Applying Patterns

Besides applying solid colors to your images, Elements lets you add patterns to your pictures. You get quite a few patterns with Elements when you buy it, and you can also download more patterns from online sources (see page 459) or create your own. You can use patterns to add interesting designs to your image, or to give a more realistic texture to certain repairs.

You can use either the Healing brush or the Pattern Stamp to apply patterns. The Healing brush has a pattern option in the Options bar. The Pattern Stamp shares the toolbox slot with the Clone Stamp, and it works very much like the Clone Stamp, but it puts down a preselected pattern instead of a sampled area.

> **TIP** Elements actually gives you lots of ways to use patterns, including creating a Fill layer that's entirely covered with the pattern of your choice. Fill layers are covered on page 169.

The tool you choose to apply your pattern makes a big difference, as you can see from Figure 9-7. The next two sections explain how to use both tools.

The Healing Brush

The Healing brush in Pattern mode is great for things like improving the texture of someone's skin by applying just the skin texture from another photo.

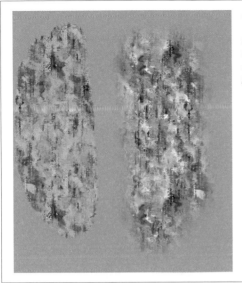

Figure 9-7:
The same pattern applied with the Healing brush (left) and the Pattern Stamp (right). The Healing brush blends the pattern into the underlying color (and texture, when there is any), while the Pattern Stamp just plunks down the pattern as it appears in the pop-out palette.

Using patterns with the Healing brush is just as easy and works the same way as using the brush in normal healing mode: You just drag across the area you want to fix. The only difference is that you don't have to choose a sampling point, since the pattern is your source point. When you drag, the pattern you selected blends into your photo.

Click the Pattern button in the Options bar and then choose a pattern from the palette by clicking the pattern thumbnail. There are more pattern libraries available if you click the right-facing arrow on the Pattern palette, or you can create and save your own patterns. Figure 9-8 explains how to create custom patterns for use with either the Healing brush or the Pattern Stamp.

> **TIP** You can create some very interesting effects by changing the blend mode (page 157) when using patterns.

The Pattern Stamp

The Pattern Stamp is just like the Clone Stamp, only instead of copying sampled areas, it puts down a predefined pattern that you select from the Pattern palette. The Pattern Stamp is useful when you want to apply a pattern to your image without mixing it in with what's already there. For instance, if you want to see what your patio would look like if it were a garden instead, you could use the Pattern stamp to paint a lawn and a flower border on a photo of your patio.

To get started, click the Clone stamp in the Toolbox, and then choose the Pattern Stamp from the pop-out menu. Click the pattern thumbnail in the Options bar. The Pattern palette opens, which is where you choose a pattern. Other options for this brush, like the size, hardness, and so on, are the same as for the Clone Stamp.

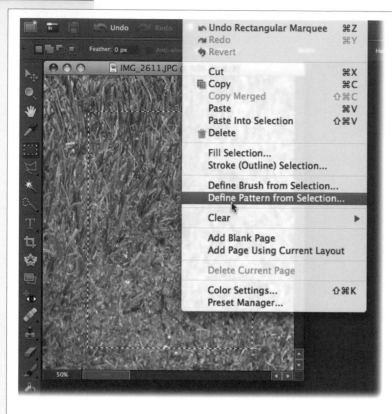

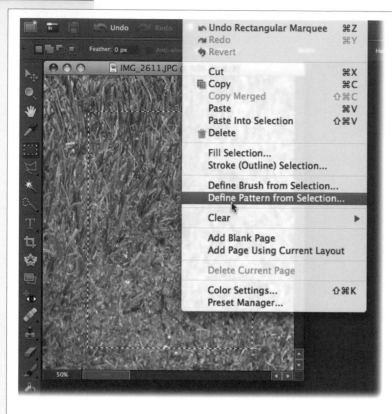

Figure 9-8:
You can create your own patterns very easily. On any image, make a rectangular unfeathered selection, and then choose Edit → "Define Pattern from Selection". Your pattern appears at the bottom of the current pattern palette, and a dialog box pops up and asks you to type a name. To use the whole image, don't make a selection, and go to Edit → Define Pattern. To rename or delete a pattern later, right-click (Control+click) it in the Pattern palette and make your choice. You can also download hundreds of different patterns from various online sources (see page 459).

Note that if you download pattern libraries from the Internet to use in Elements, save them in Applications → Adobe Photoshop Elements 6.0 → Presets → Patterns if you want them to be listed in the Pattern palette's pop-out menu. You can also put patterns in your Home → Library → Application Support → Adobe → Adobe Photoshop Elements 6.0 → Presets → Patterns, but those will only be available to you, not to anyone else who uses your Mac.

The main difference is the Impressionist option demonstrated in Figure 9-9, which is mostly useful for creating special effects.

Once you've selected a pattern, just drag in your photo where you want the pattern to appear.

Color Curves: Enhancing Tone and Contrast

If you hang around photo-editing veterans, you'll hear plenty of talk about how useful the Curves tool is. Contrary to what you might expect, Curves isn't a drawing tool. Instead, it works much like Levels (see page 188), but with many more points of correction. Adobe calls the Elements version *Color Curves* to remind you what it's for. Unlike Levels, in which you set your entire photo's white point, black point, and gamma settings, Curves lets you target specific tonal regions. For instance, Curves lets you make only your shadows lighter or only your highlights darker. Maybe that's why some pros say, "Curves is Levels on steroids." (For advice on when to use Levels and when to use Color Curves, see the box on page 192.)

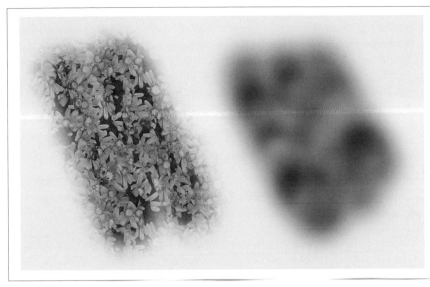

*Figure 9-9:
If you turn on
Impressionist in the
Options bar, your pattern
is blurred, giving an
effect vaguely like an
Impressionist painting.
Here, you can see a
pattern put down with
the regular Pattern
Stamp (left) and the
Impressionist stamp
(right).*

Elements' Color Curves tool is a fairly restricted version of its counterpart (just called Curves) in the full version of Photoshop. In the more powerful Curves tool, you can work on each color channel separately, as you do in the Levels dialog box. You can also drag any point on the Curves graph (like the one you see in Figure 9-10) to manipulate it directly. For example, you can drag to adjust just the middle range of your greens. Elements doesn't give you that kind of flexibility.

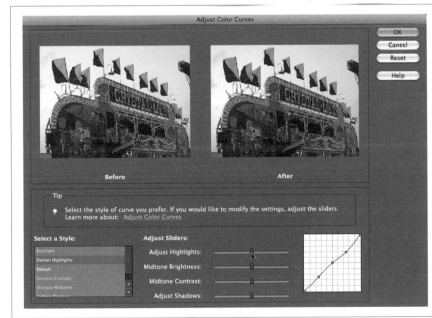

*Figure 9-10:
Elements 6 gives you a
good look at what you're
doing to your photo with
these large before-and-
after previews. Start by
clicking around in the list
of presets on the left, and
then you can use the
sliders in the middle of
the window to fine-tune
the effect if you need to.*

Since Curves, in its original-strength version, is a pretty complicated tool, Adobe makes it easier to use in Elements. To start with, you get a group of preset adjustments to choose from (see Figure 9-10). These presets offer shortcuts to the types of basic enhancements you'll use most often. Just click the one that looks good to you. If you like what it does, you're done. But if you aren't quite satisfied with a preset, you have a simple way to make adjustments in the Adjust Color Curves dialog box's advanced options, to the right of the presets.

Here's how to improve a photo's appearance with Color Curves:

1. **Open your photo and make a duplicate layer.**

   Press ⌘+J or go to Layer → Duplicate Layer. Elements doesn't let you use Color Curves as an Adjustment layer (unlike Photoshop), so you're safer applying it to a duplicate layer in case you want to change something later.

   TIP　If you want to restrict your adjustment to a particular area of your photo, select it first so that Color Curves changes only the selected area. For instance, if you're happy with everything in your shot of your son's Little League game except the catcher in the foreground, select him, and you can do a Color Curves adjustment that affects him alone—not the rest of the photo. See Chapter 5 if you need a refresher on selections.

2. **Go to Enhance → Adjust Color → Adjust Color Curves.**

   The Color Curves dialog box opens. You see your original image in the preview on the left.

3. **Choose a Color Curves preset.**

   Scroll through the list in the lower left of the window and click the preset that seems closest to what you want your photo to look like. Try clicking different presets. (As long as you're just clicking in the list, you don't need to click Reset between each one, since Elements starts from your original each time you click.)

   You can preview the effect right in your image. To do so, drag the dialog box out of the way and check your actual photo to get a closer look at how you're changing things before you make your final choice.

4. **Apply the changes, or tweak them some more.**

   If you're satisfied, click OK. If not, go to the next step. (And if you don't want to apply any Color Curves adjustments at all, click Cancel.)

5. **Make any further adjustments.**

   If you think your photo still doesn't look quite right, use the sliders shown in Figure 9-11 to make any additional changes. (The sliders are described in the list on page 257.) Click Reset if you want to undo any of the changes you make with the sliders.

TIP Easy does it here. Notice how subtle the preset curves are. A tiny nudge of these sliders makes a big difference, so be gentle with the sliders.

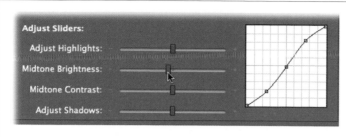

Figure 9-11:
The graph on the right side of the window is where the Color Curves feature gets its name. When you first open the Color Curves dialog box, with no adjustments at all, the graph is a straight diagonal line. The adjustments you make cause the points on the graph to move, resulting in a curved line. Click Reset to go back to the straight line again, or click Default in the list of presets.

6. **When you're happy with your photo's new look, click OK.**

Don't forget to save your changes. If you used the duplicate layer, you can always change your mind about them later on and start over on a fresh layer.

NOTE If you've used Curves add-ons in an old version of Elements (like those from Richard Lynch or Grant Dixon, for example), the Color Curves tool may take some getting used to. (You power user, you!) Unfortunately, those add-ons no longer work in Elements 6. If you want to make the more elaborate adjustments you got from your old add-ons, your only option is to hang on to your copy of Elements 2 or 3 and use it to create Curves Adjustment layers.

Once you've got some Color Curves experience under your belt, you probably won't be satisfied with the results you get from the presets. So don't hesitate to use the sliders to adjust different tonal regions in your photo:

- **Adjust Highlights.** Move the slider to the left to darken the highlights in your photo; move it to the right to lighten them.

- **Midtone Brightness.** If you'd like the middle range of colors to be darker, move this slider to the left. Move it to the right to make the midtones brighter.

- **Midtone Contrast.** This slider works just like the one in the Shadows/Highlights feature (see page 181). Move it to the right to increase the contrast in your photo, and to the left to reduce the contrast.

- **Adjust Shadows.** If you want to lighten shadows, move the slider to the right. To darken the shadow areas of your photo, move it to the left.

As you move the sliders, you can see the point you're adjusting move on the graph and watch the curve change shape. Although it's fun to see what's going on in the graph, you should pay more attention to what's happening in your photo.

Color Curves is such a potent tool, it can change your photo in ways you don't intend. Rather than using Color Curves to make huge adjustments, try another tool first. Then come back and use Color Curves for the final, subtle tweaks. On the other hand, you can also use Color Curves to create some wild special effects, if that's what you're after. See Figure 9-12 for an example.

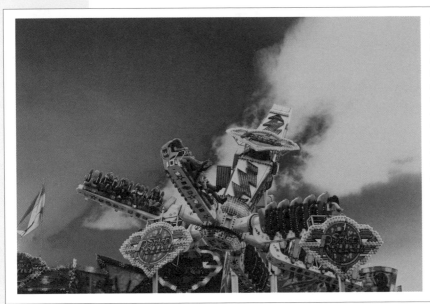

Figure 9-12:
Many people prefer to use Color Curves for artwork and special effects rather than adjusting photos. Jimi Hendrix fans may like the Solarize preset, which Adobe includes to give you a starting point for funky pictures like this one. (Others say this preset should serve as a warning about going overboard with this tool.)

Making Your Colors More Vibrant

Do you drool over the luscious photos in travel magazines, the ones that make it look like the world's full of destinations so vivid they make your regular life seem pretty drab in comparison? What *is* it about those photos that makes things look so dramatic?

Often the answer is the *saturation*, or intensity, of the colors. Supersaturated color makes for darned appealing landscape and object photos, regardless of how the real thing may rate on the vividness scale.

There are various ways to adjust the saturation of your photos. Some cameras offer you settings to help control it, but Elements lets you go even further. For example, by increasing or decreasing a photo's saturation, you can shift the perceived focal point, change the mood of the picture, or just make your photo more eye-catching in general.

By increasing your subject's saturation and decreasing it in the rest of the photo you can focus your viewer's attention, even in a crowded photo. Figure 9-13 shows a somewhat exaggerated use of this technique; you can download the photo (shelf-sitter.jpg) from the "Missing CD" page at *www.missingmanuals.com* to try it out for yourself.

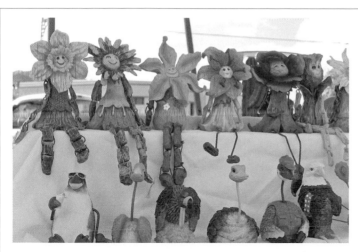

Figure 9-13:
Top: In this photo, all the shelfsitter figures are about equal in brightness.

Bottom: To make one figure stand out from the crowd, the figure was selected and the saturation was increased. Meanwhile, the rest of the photo was desaturated. The effect is exaggerated here, but a subtler use of this technique can work wonders for spotlighting objects in your photos.

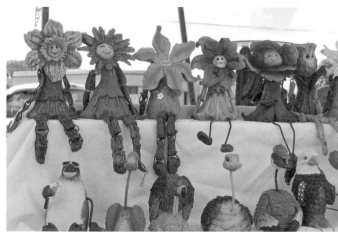

It's quite easy to change saturation. You might want to start out with the RAW Converter's new Vibrance slider if your photo is a TIFF or JPEG (see page 225). If that doesn't work well for you, try using either of the more traditional methods: the Hue/Saturation dialog box or the Sponge tool, which are explained in the following sections. For big areas, or when you want a lot of control, use Hue/Saturation. If you just want to quickly paint a different saturation level (either more or less saturation) on a small spot in your photo, the Sponge tool is faster.

> **NOTE** Many consumer-grade digital cameras are set to crank the saturation of your JPEG photos into the stratosphere. That's great if you love all the color. If you prefer not to live in a Technicolor universe, you may wish to desaturate your photos in Elements to remove some of the excess color.

Using the Hue/Saturation Dialog Box

Hue/Saturation is one of the most popular commands in Elements. If you aren't satisfied with the results of a simple Levels adjustment, you may want to work on the hue or saturation as the next step toward getting really eye-catching color.

Hue simply means the color of your image—whether it's blue or brown or purple or green. Most people use the saturation adjustments more than the hue controls, but both hue and saturation are controlled from the same dialog box. You can adjust both or just one.

In Elements, you can use the Hue slider to actually change the color of objects in your photos, but you probably want to adjust saturation far more often than you want to shift the hue of a photo.

When you use Hue/Saturation, it's a good idea to first make the most of your other corrections—like Levels or exposure corrections (see page 178). When you're ready to use the Hue/Saturation command, just follow these steps:

1. **If you want to adjust only part of your photo, select the area you want.**

   Use whatever selection tools you prefer. (See Chapter 5 for more about making selections.)

2. **Call up the Hue/Saturation Adjustment dialog box.**

   Go to Enhance → Adjust Color → Adjust Hue/Saturation, or go to Layer → New Adjustment Layer → Hue/Saturation. As always, if you don't want to make changes that you can't easily reverse, use an Adjustment layer instead of working directly on your photo.

3. **Move the sliders until you see what you want.**

   If you want to adjust only saturation, you can ignore the Hue slider. Move the Saturation slider to the right to increase the amount of saturation (more color) or to the left to decrease it. If necessary, move the Lightness slider to the left to make the color darker, or move it to the right to make the color lighter. Incidentally, you don't have to change all the colors in your photo equally. See Figure 9-14 for how to focus on individual color channels.

   TIP   Generally speaking, if you want to change a pastel to a more intense color, you'll need to reduce the lightness (move the slider to the left) in addition to increasing the saturation—if you don't want your color to look radioactive.

Adjusting Saturation with the Sponge Tool

The Sponge tool gives you another way to adjust saturation. Although the tool is very handy for working on small areas, all that dragging gets old pretty fast when you're working on a large chunk of your image. For those situations, use the Hue/Saturation dialog box instead.

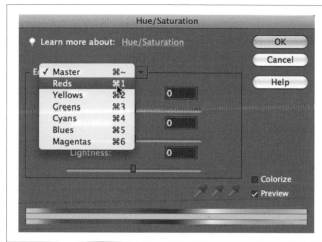

Figure 9-14:
The Hue/Saturation dialog box has a pull-down menu like the Levels dialog box, so you can adjust individual color channels. If only the reds are excessive (a common problem with digital cameras), you can choose to lower the saturation only for the reds without changing the other channels.

Even though it's called a sponge, the Sponge tool works like any other brush tool in Elements. Choosing the size and hardness are just the same as choosing them for any other brush (see page 314). The Sponge has a couple of unique settings of its own as well:

- **Mode.** Choose here whether to saturate (add color) or desaturate (remove color).

- **Flow.** Flow governs how intense the effect is. A higher number means more intensity.

To use the Sponge tool, drag over the area you want to change. Figure 9-15 shows an example of the kind of work the Sponge does.

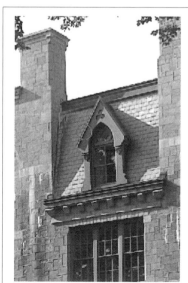

Figure 9-15:
Here, the Sponge tool has been applied to the left side of the window frame and to the roof beside it, increasing the color saturation in those areas. Approach the Sponge tool with some caution. It doesn't take much to cause degradation in your image, especially if you've made lots of other adjustments to it. If you start to see noise (graininess), undo your sponging and try it again at a reduced setting.

You may want to press ⌘+J to create a duplicate layer before you use the Sponge. Then you can always throw out the duplicate layer later on if you change your mind about the changes you made.

1. **Activate the Sponge tool.**

   Press O or click the icon in the Toolbox, and then choose the Sponge from the pop-out menu. Choose the brush size and the settings you want in the Options bar.

2. **Drag in the area you want to change.**

   If you aren't seeing enough of a difference, increase the Flow setting a little. If it's too strong, reduce the number for the Flow.

   TIP   If you have a hard time coloring (or decoloring) inside the lines, you can select the area you want before you start sponging. Then the brush won't do anything outside the selection, allowing you to be as sloppy as you like.

Changing the Color of an Object

In Chapter 4, you saw one way to change the color of an object—select it and use the Hue and Saturation sliders in Quick Fix. Elements also gives you some other ways to do this: You can use an Adjustment layer, the Replace Color command, or the Color Replacement tool.

The method you choose depends to some extent on your photo and to some extent on your own preference. Using an Adjustment layer gives you the most flexibility if you want to make other changes later on. Replace Color is the fastest way to change one color that's widely scattered throughout your whole image, and the Color Replacement tool lets you quickly brush a replacement color over the color you want to change. Whichever method you choose, Figure 9-16 shows the kind of complex color change you can make in a jiffy using any one of these methods.

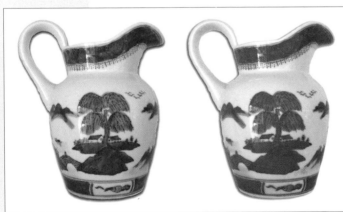

Figure 9-16:
What if you have a blue and white jug, but what you really want is a brown and white one? Just call up the Replace Color tool. Elements actually gives you several ways to make a complicated color substitution like this one, all of which are covered in this section.

Using an Adjustment Layer

You can use a Hue/Saturation Adjustment layer to make the same kind of changes to the color that you saw on page 260. The advantage of the Adjustment layer is that later on, you can change the settings or the area affected by the layer (as opposed to changing your whole image). The procedure is exactly the same as that described in the section "Using the Hue/Saturation Dialog Box," only this time, you start by selecting the object you want to change.

1. **Select the object whose color you want to change.**

   Use any of the Selection tools (see Chapter 5). If you don't make a selection before creating the Adjustment layer, you'll change your entire photo.

2. **Create a new Hue/Saturation Adjustment layer.**

   Go to Layer → New Adjustment Layer → Hue/Saturation. The new layer affects only the area you selected.

3. **Use the sliders in the dialog box to adjust the color until you see what you want, and then click OK.**

   You need to use the Hue slider to start with. Use it to pick the color you want, and when you've gotten that into the ballpark of what you want, use the Saturation slider to adjust the vividness of the new color and the Lightness slider to adjust the darkness.

This method is fine if you have one area of color that's easily selectable. But what if you have a bunch of different areas or you want to change one shade everywhere it appears in your photo? For that, Elements offers the Replace Color command.

Replacing Specific Colors

Take a look at the blue and white pitcher in Figure 9-16 again. Do you have to tediously select each blue area one by one if you want to make a brown and white jug?

You can do it that way, of course, but an easier way is to use the Replace Color command. It's one of those Elements dialog boxes that look a bit intimidating, but it's a snap to use once you understand how it works. Replace Color changes every instance of the color that you select, no matter how many times it appears in your image.

You don't need to start by making a selection when you use Replace Color. As usual, if you want to keep your options for future changes open, make a duplicate layer (⌘+J). When you start, be sure your active layer isn't an Adjustment layer, or Replace Color won't work.

1. **Open the Replace Color dialog box.**

   Go to Enhance → Adjust Color → Replace Color. The Replace Color dialog box in Figure 9-17 appears.

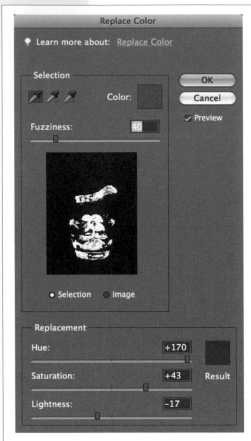

Figure 9-17:
The funny area that looks like a negative in the Replace Color window shows you where the sliders will affect the color. Use the Hue/Saturation sliders to adjust the replacement color (shown in the bottom color square) the way you would with a regular Hue/Saturation adjustment. Fuzziness works like a Tolerance Setting for the Magic Wand, as explained in Figure 9-18. You can watch a live preview of your photo's changes once you've chosen a replacement color.

NOTE If you want to protect a particular area of your chosen color from being changed, paint a mask on it by using the Selection brush in Mask mode (page 120) before you start.

2. **Move your cursor over your photo.**

   The cursor changes to an eyedropper. Take a moment to confirm that the left eyedropper in the Replace Color dialog box is the active one. That's the one without a plus or minus sign.

3. **Click an area of the color you want to replace.**

   All the areas matching that particular shade are selected, but you won't see the marching ants in your image the way you do with the Selection tools. If you click more than once, you just change your selection instead of adding to it, just the way you would with any of the regular Selection tools (see page 115). To add to your selection (that is, to select additional shades), Shift+click in your photo.

   Another way to add more shades is to select the middle eyedropper (the one with the + sign next to it) and click in your photo again. To remove a color, select the right eyedropper (with the minus sign) and click. Alternatively, Option+click with the first eyedropper, and the shade you click is removed from the selection. If you want to start your selection all over again, Option+click the Cancel button to turn it to a Reset button.

4. **When you've selected everything you want to change, move the sliders to replace the color.**

The Hue, Saturation, and Lightness sliders work exactly the way they do in Hue/Saturation (explained earlier in this chapter). Move them and watch the color box in the Replace Color window to see what color you're concocting. You can also click the color box to bring up the Color Picker (see page 199) and choose a color there. If you need to tweak the area of color you're changing, the Fuzziness slider adjusts the range of colors that Color Replacement affects, as shown in Figure 9-18.

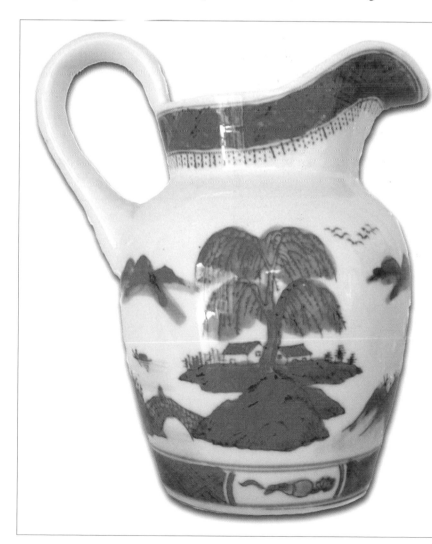

Figure 9-18:
Fuzziness is similar to the Tolerance setting for the Magic Wand (page 122). Take a look at the brown areas of the jug. There's still a lot of blue around them. Set Fuzziness higher to include more shades than you've previously been changing (in this figure, making such a change would cause all the blue to get turned to brown). If you find you're picking up little bits of areas you don't want, set Fuzziness lower. Move the slider to the right for more fuzziness and to the left for less.

Look at your photo after you've chosen your replacement color. If the preview doesn't show the color in all the areas you want, just click the missing spots with the middle eyedropper to fix them.

5. Click OK.

Using a Brush to Replace Colors

The Color Replacement tool gives you yet another way to change the colors in your photo. It lets you brush a replacement color onto the area you want to change, without changing any other colors in your photo except the one you target. Figure 9-19 shows how great this tool is for changing hard-to-isolate areas like feathers.

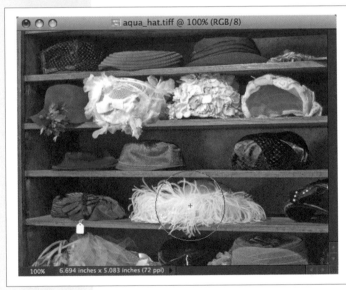

Figure 9-19:
Feathers, hair, and fur are usually exasperating to try to select. But the Color Replacement tool saves you from having to fool with selections. Just move the crosshairs in the cursor over the area you want to change and click or drag. It would have taken hours to get a good selection on this marabou hat, but the Color Replacement tool is smart enough to find all those drifting white areas and change them to aqua—without bleeding the color into other light areas, like the price tag on the adjacent hat.

The Color Replacement tool shares a slot with the Brush tool in the Toolbox. To select it, press B or click the Brush tool, and then choose the Color Replacement tool from the pop-out list.

The Options bar settings make a big difference in the way the Color Replacement tool works:

- **Brush Options.** These settings (size, hardness, angle, and so on) work the same way they do for any brush. See Chapter 12 for more information about brushes.

- **Mode.** This is the blend mode (page 329) the tool uses. Generally you want Color or Hue, although you can get some funky special effects with Saturation.

- **Sampling.** These choices appear as icons in the Options bar. Click one to tell the tool how to look for colors in your image. From left to right, they stand for Continuous, Once, and Background Swatch. If you choose Continuous, the brush changes every color that falls under the crosshairs as you move through your photo. Choosing Once means that no matter how far you travel while holding the mouse button, Elements replaces only the color that was under the crosshairs when you first clicked. Background Swatch means that Elements replaces only the color currently featured in the Toolbox's Background color swatch.

- **Limits**. This setting tells the Color Replacement tool which areas of your photo to look at in its search for color. Contiguous means only areas that touch each other get changed. Discontiguous means the tool changes all the places it finds a color—whether they're touching one another or not.

- **Tolerance**. This is just like the Tolerance setting for the Magic Wand: The higher the number, the more shades of color are affected by the tool. Getting this setting right is the key to getting good results with the Color Replacement tool.

- **Anti-alias**. This setting smoothes the edges of the replacement color. It's best to leave it turned on.

Using the Color Replacement tool is very straightforward:

1. **Pick the color you're going to use as a replacement.**

   Elements uses the current Foreground color as the replacement color. To choose a new Foreground color, click the Foreground color square in the Toolbox and choose a new color from the Color Picker (page 199) when it appears.

2. **Activate the Color Replacement tool and pick a brush size.**

   See Chapter 12 for help with using brushes. Generally for this tool, you want a fairly large brush, as shown in Figure 9-19.

3. **Click or drag in your photo to change the color.**

   Elements targets the color that is under the crosshairs in the center of the brush.

The Color Replacement tool is great for changing large areas of color to an equivalent tone, but if you want to replace dark red with pale yellow you probably won't like the results. It's not great for colors where the lightness is very different.

> **TIP** You may want to use the Color Replacement tool on a duplicate layer (⌘+J) so that you can adjust the layer opacity to control the effect.

Special Effects

Elements gives you some other useful ways of drastically changing the look of your image. You can apply these effects as Adjustment layers (Layer → New Adjustment Layer) or by going to Filter → Adjustments (there's much more about filters in Chapter 13). Either way gives you the same options for their settings. You can see them in action in Figure 9-20.

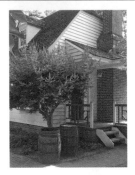
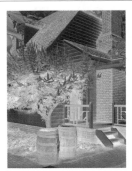
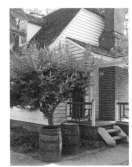
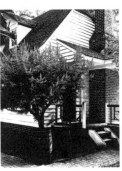
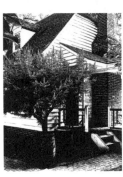

Figure 9-20:
You can get some interesting special effects with the Adjustment commands, whether you apply them as filters or Adjustment layers. If you want to use them as filters, it's not a bad idea to start with a duplicate layer.

Top row (left to right): The original photo, Invert, Equalize.

Bottom row (left to right): Posterize and Threshold.

In most cases, you use these adjustments as steps along the way in a more complex treatment of your photo, but they're effective by themselves, too. Here's what each does:

- **Equalize** makes the darkest pixel black and the lightest white, and redistributes the brightness values for all the colors in a photo to give them all equal weight. When you have an active selection, you see a dialog box that lets you choose between simply equalizing your whole photo and equalizing it based on a selection. It doesn't always work, but sometimes Equalize is great for bringing up the brightness level of a dim photo. This choice is not available as an adjustment layer, only as a filter.

- **Gradient Map** is pretty complicated. According to Adobe, it "maps the grayscale range of an image to the colors of a specified gradient fill." If you want to know what the heck *that* means, turn to page 379. Basically, a gradient map lets you apply a gradient based on the light and dark areas of your photo. The gradient colors replace the existing colors in your photo. There's a lot more to it than that, though.

- **Invert** makes your photo look like a negative. It's so useful in doing artistic effects that Elements also lets you invert in the Editor at any time just by pressing ⌘+I.

NOTE If you think choosing the Invert option sounds like a great way to get your negatives scanned in with a basic flatbed scanner and turned to positive images, sorry, but you need to think again. Color negatives have an orange mask on them that Elements can't easily undo. You're best off with a dedicated film scanner that's designed to cope with negatives, or at least with a scanner that has software designed to deal with the mask.

- **Posterize** reduces the total number of colors in your photo, giving a less detailed, more poster-like effect. The lower the number you enter in the dialog box, the fewer colors you'll get (thus, the more extreme the result). If you want blocky, poster-like edges in your photo, try Filter → Artistic → Poster Edges instead of or in addition to this.

- **Threshold** turns every pixel in your photo to pure white or pure black. You won't find any shades of gray here. Figure 9-21 explains how to adjust the settings for the Threshold command.

- **Photo Filter** makes color corrections, like removing color casts from your photos. You can read about it in detail on page 231.

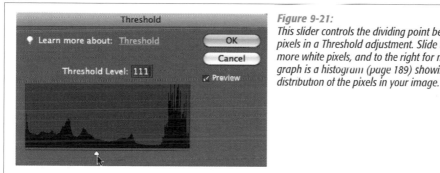

Figure 9-21:
This slider controls the dividing point between black and white pixels in a Threshold adjustment. Slide to the left if you want more white pixels, and to the right for more dark ones. The graph is a histogram (page 189) showing the light to dark distribution of the pixels in your image.

Removing and Adding Color

If you love classic black-and-white photography, or if you yearn to be the next Ansel Adams, then you'll be over the moon with the high-quality black-and-white conversion in Elements. If you can't imagine why anyone would willingly abandon color, consider that in a world crammed full of eye-popping colors, black and white really stands out. Also, you may be planning to have something printed where you can't use color illustrations. And, of course, for artistic photography there's still nothing like black and white, where tone and contrast make or break the photo, without any pretty colors to distract you from the picture's underlying structure.

In this chapter, you'll learn how to make a color photo black and white, and how to create images that are partly in color and partly in black and white. You'll also learn how to colorize a black-and-white image, and, along the way, how to use and edit *layer masks*, an important technique for advanced Elements work.

Method One: Making Color Photos Black and White

A good black-and-white image is so much more than just a color photo without color. Generally, just removing the color from a photo produces a pretty flat-looking, uninteresting image. A good black-and-white photo usually needs more contrast. You can create very different effects and totally different moods in your photo, depending on what you decide to emphasize in the black-and-white version.

Black-and-white conversion has traditionally been regarded as a pretty complicated process. When you do a Google search, you can find literally dozens of different recipes for making conversions. Fortunately for you, Elements makes it really easy to perform these conversions, and even to do sophisticated tweaking of the different color channels. (Read more about conversion below.)

Just follow these steps:

1. **Open the photo you want to convert.**

   If the photo has multiple layers, flatten it (Layer → Flatten Image), or make sure the layer you want to convert is the active layer (click it in the Layers palette). If you want to convert only a part of your photo, then select the area you want to make black and white. (See Chapter 5 for more on selections.) As always, it's best to do this on a copy, not your original photo.

2. **Go to Enhance → "Convert to Black and White".**

   You see the dialog box shown in Figure 10-1.

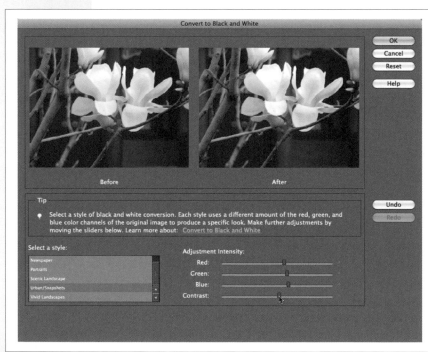

Figure 10-1:
The "Convert to Black and White" dialog box makes it very easy to create effective transformations, even if you don't have any idea what you're doing. First, choose a conversion style from the list on the left, and then use the sliders to tweak your conversion, if necessary.

3. **Choose a conversion style.**

   Elements gives you various preset styles for the conversion. Click a style in the list to apply it to your photo. Try different styles to see which suits your photo best.

4. **Tweak the conversion, if necessary.**

   Use the Adjustment Intensity sliders below the preview area (Red, Green, and so on) to increase or decrease the prominence of each color channel. (These sliders are explained in more detail below.) Watch the preview to see how you're changing your photo. Go gently—it doesn't take much to make quite a difference in your image.

Once you move a slider, Undo and Redo buttons appear. Use them to step backwards and forwards through your changes. If you want to start from scratch, click Reset.

5. **When you're satisfied with how your photo looks, click OK.**

Be sure to examine your actual image carefully. Don't rely on just the smallish preview window. Move the "Convert to Black and White" dialog box around your screen so that you can see all the regions of your photo before you accept the conversion. If you decide against creating a black-and-white image, then click Cancel.

NOTE Very often, you may prefer to emphasize certain details in your photo without making additional changes to the overall tonality. To do that, use the Dodge and Burn tools (page 326), once you've completed your conversion.

While the different conversion styles have descriptive names, like Portraits and Scenic Landscape, don't put too much stock in the names themselves. Instead, test out the various styles to see which best matches your photo. For instance, you may vastly prefer the way Uncle Julio looks when you choose the Newspaper style instead of the Portraits style. Basically, the names are just a less intimidating way of describing preset collections of settings to the color channels in your photo.

But wait a minute: changes to the color channels? That's right. Back in Chapter 7, you read about how your photo consists of three separate color channels: red, blue, and green. What you may not realize is that, in your original camera file, each of these channels is recorded merely as variations in light and dark tones, in other words, a black-and-white image. Your image file tells the computer or printer to make a particular channel all red, blue, or green, and the blending of the three monotone channels makes all the colors you see.

Now when you convert your photo back to black and white, each of these channels contains varying amounts of details from your photo, depending on the color of your original subject. So, the green channel might have more detail from your subject's eyelashes, while the red channel may have more detail from the bark on the tree she's standing under. (Remember, the color channels themselves don't necessarily correspond to the color of the objects you see in your final photo. Or, put another way: Your camera needs to use a mixture of red, blue, and green to create what looks like bark to us humans.) Noise (see page 357) often happens much more in one channel than the others, as well.

The Adjustment Intensity sliders in the dialog box (More Red, More Green, and so on) let you increase or decrease the presence of each color channel. So you can adjust how prominent various details in your photo are by changing the importance of that color channel in the complete photo. These adjustments can greatly change the appearance of the final conversion. The Contrast slider adjusts the contrast for the combined channels.

That's the theory behind those color channel sliders, but fortunately you don't have to understand it to use them effectively. Just be sure you can get a good view of your photo (zoom and, if necessary, move the dialog box around), and slide till you're happy with what you see. If you plan to print your converted photo, read the box on page 275 for some tips on how to get a good black-and-white print from a color inkjet printer.

> **TIP** Elements gives you an easier way to convert your photo to black and white, but it's an all-or-nothing scenario—you don't get any options for adjusting the tones in your image. There's a very nice black-and-white tint effect in the Effects palette. Go to Effects → Photo Effects → Monotone Color and double-click the black-and-white apple to apply the effect. Also, some frames in the Frames section of the Content palette (page 413)—like some of the Color Tint frames—automatically convert your photo to black and white when you place it in the frame. See page 405 for details on how to use these frames.

Method Two: Removing Color from a Photo

Since one size never fits all, Elements gives you a few other, fundamentally different ways to remove the color from your image. Most times, you should follow the instructions in the preceding section to convert your photo to black and white. But if you want to drain the color from a particular part of your photo, or if you're looking to do something artistic, like changing a color photo into a drawing or a painting, then you'll probably want to try one of these three methods:

- **Convert Mode.** You may remember from page 48 that you need to choose a color mode for your photo: RGB, Bitmap, or Grayscale. You can remove the color from your photo by changing its mode to Grayscale. To do this, choose Image → Mode → Grayscale. This method is quick, but it's also a bit destructive, since you can't apply it to a layer: Your entire photo is either grayscale or not.

- **Remove Color.** You can also keep your photo as an RGB file and drain the color from it, by going to Enhance → Adjust Color → Remove Color (or pressing Shift+⌘+U). This removes the color from the active layer only, so if your photo has more than one layer, you need to flatten it first (Layer → Flatten Image), or the other layers keep their color.

    Remove Color is really just another way to completely desaturate your photo as you might when using the Hue/Saturation command (described in the next option). Remove Color is faster but you don't get the control that the Hue/Saturation command gives you. Figure 10-2 shows you the difference between applying the Remove Color command versus converting your entire image to grayscale.

- **Hue/Saturation.** You can also call up the Hue/Saturation dialog box (page 260), and move the Saturation slider all the way to the left, or type "–100" into the Saturation box. The advantage of this method is that if you don't care for the shade of gray you get, you can desaturate each color channel separately by using the pull-down menu in the dialog box. With this method, you can tweak your settings a bit to eliminate any color cast you may get from your printer.

Figure 10-2:
Uncoloring your photo can give you very different results depending on the method you use.

Top: Each star, when first created, has a pure color value of 255. In other words, you're looking at stars that are 100 percent blue, red, and green, with zero as the number for the other two channels.

Middle: The same images with the mode converted to grayscale (Image → Mode → Grayscale).

Bottom: Using the Remove Color command causes a very different change.

OUTSIDE ELEMENTS

Digital Black and White

If you love black-and-white photography, there's good news for you in the digital world. The quality of digital black-and-white printing is improving by leaps and bounds, and now you can get decent black-and-white photos from even some of the lowest-priced printers, if you shop carefully and investigate your options before you buy.

For all the wonders of digitizing, though, there's still nothing that can exactly duplicate the effect of a traditional silver print—although digital printing has made great strides in the past couple of years.

If you want to print black-and-white photos, you may still want to look into a photo printer that allows you to substitute several shades of gray for your color cartridges. The special inks available are constantly improving, and you can get much better prints now than you could even a year or two ago. You can now purchase special grayscale ink cartridge sets for even very inexpensive inkjet printers, and more printer drivers have settings for grayscale printing.

TIP   If you're planning to print the results of your conversion, the paper you use can make a *big* difference in the gray tones you get. If you don't like the results from your usual paper, then try a different weight or brand. You'll need to experiment because the inks for different printer models react differently with different brands of paper.

Creating Spot Color

Removing almost all the color from a photo but leaving one or two objects in vivid tones, called *spot color*, is a very effective artistic device that's long been popular in the print industry. (The term can also have a different meaning among those in the commercial printing business, where it refers to the use of special ink for a particular color in a multicolor image.) Figure 10-3 shows an example of spot color. To practice the maneuvers you're about to learn, download the photo (barn.jpg) from the "Missing CD" page at *www.missingmanuals.com.*

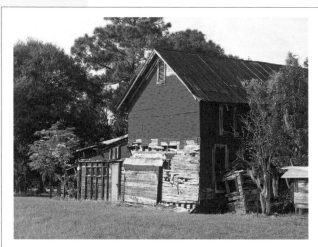

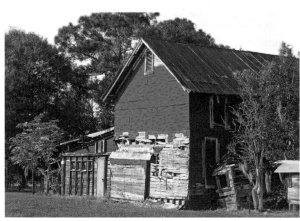

Figure 10-3:
With Elements, you can easily remove the color from only part of an image.

Top: Here, the photo is a regular color image.

Bottom: The color is gone from everything except the barn. You'll learn three easy methods for removing color in this section.

This section walks you through three of the easiest methods. (The fourth and simplest way, explained earlier in this chapter (page 271), is to select the area you want to make black and white and use "Convert to Black and White".) You can erase your way back to color, change only a selected area to black and white, or use an Adjustment layer. In learning to use the last method, you'll also learn how to edit the layer mask of an Adjustment layer so that you can change the area the adjustment affects.

The end result looks the same no matter which of these methods you choose. Just select the one you find easiest for the particular photo you want to change.

TIP   If you have a newish digital camera, check your special effects settings for a spot or accent color setting. Many cameras can now create a black-and-white image with only one shade left in color.

Erasing Colors from a Duplicate Layer

A super simple way to remove colors from parts of your image is to use the Eraser tool. (See page 334 for more about the different Erasers.) When you use this method, you place a color-free layer over your colored original and erase bits of the top layer to let the color below show through.

1. **Make a duplicate layer.**

   Press ⌘+J or go to Layer → Duplicate Layer. This is the layer that's going to be black and white.

2. **Remove the color from the new top layer.**

   Go to Enhance → "Convert to Black and White", or to Enhance → Adjust Color → Remove Color. (Be sure the top layer is the active one before you do this.) You should now see only a black-and-white image.

3. **Erase the areas on the top layer where you want to see color.**

   Use the Eraser tool (page 334) to remove parts of the top layer so the colored layer underneath shows through. Usually you'll get the best results with a fairly soft brush.

If you want to have an image that's mostly colored with only a few black-and-white areas, reverse the technique—remove the color from the bottom layer and leave the top layer in color. Then erase as described above.

When you're finished, you can flatten the layers if you want, but if you do keep them separate, you can always go back and erase more of the top layer later on. And you'll still have the option of trashing the layer you erased and making a new duplicate of the bottom layer, if you want to start over.

Removing Color from Selections

If you don't want to have multiple layers, you can also use "Convert to Black and White" or the Remove Color command on a selection. (See Chapter 5 for more about making selections.) Just make sure you perform this method on a copy. You don't want to risk wrecking your original photo.

The procedure for changing a selected area to black and white is very simple.

1. **Mask out the area where you want to keep the color in your image.**

   Use the Selection brush in Mask mode (see page 120) to paint a mask over the area where you want to *keep* the color, to protect it from being changed in step 2. In other words, you're going to make everything black and white *except* where you paint with the Selection brush.

If you want to keep the color in most of your photo and remove the color from only one or two objects, paint over them with the brush in Selection mode instead of Mask mode, or use the Quick Selection tool.

2. **Remove the color from the selected area.**

Go to Enhance → "Convert to Black and White", or to Enhance → Adjust Color → Remove Color, or press Shift+⌘+U. The color disappears from the areas not protected by the mask, but the area under the mask is untouched. (You can also do this step by going to Enhance → Adjust Color → Adjust Hue/Saturation and moving the Saturation slider all the way to the left.)

You should see a photo with color only in the areas that you didn't select. This method's the least flexible. Once you close your image, the change is permanent and not undoable, which is why you don't want to use this method on your original photo.

SPECIAL EFFECTS

Hints for Coloring Old Photographs

It's easier to put each element of a face that you're going to color—lips, eyes, cheek color, skin—on a separate layer. That way, you can change just one color later without a lot of hassle. You can always merge the layers (Layer → Merge Visible, or Merge Down) later, once you know for sure that you're done.

If you want the effect of a photo that was hand-colored a century ago, paint at less than 100-percent opacity. The tinting on old photos is very transparent.

If you select the area before you paint, you won't have to worry about getting color outside of where you want it, because your paint is confined to your selection.

Skin colors are very hard to create in the color picker. Try sampling skin tones from another photo instead. If it's a family photo, after all, the odds are good that the current generation's basic skin tones are reasonably close to Great-Granddad's.

Using an Adjustment Layer and the Saturation Slider

If you'd like to keep the option of easily changing your mind about which areas keep the color, it's best to remove the color with a Hue/Saturation Adjustment layer. This is your most flexible choice (though it doesn't offer you the tone adjustments you can make when using "Convert to Black and White"). Using an Adjustment layer lets you both add and subtract areas of color later if you like.

1. **Select the area where you want to remove the color.**

Use any Selection tool you like (see Chapter 5 for more about Selection tools). If you think it would be easier to select the area where you want to keep the color, do that, and then press Shift+⌘+I to invert your selection so that the area that's going to lose the color is selected instead.

2. **Create a Hue/Saturation Adjustment layer.**

Go to Layer → New Adjustment Layer → Hue/Saturation, or click the New Adjustment Layer icon on the Layers palette and choose a Hue/Saturation layer.

3. **In the Hue/Saturation dialog box that appears, remove the color.**

Move the Saturation slider all the way to the left to remove the color.

Why is this method better? Well, for one thing, you can always discard the Adjustment layer if you change your mind. But that's not all. You can actually edit the Adjustment layer's layer mask (see page 171 for more about layer masks) so that you can change which parts of your photo are in color, even days or weeks later.

Don't want that tree as well as the vine on the house? Or maybe you wish you'd left all the window frames in color? All are easily fixed by editing the layer mask. The next section tells you how.

Editing a layer mask

Elements gives you the ability to make changes to the layer mask of an Adjustment layer any time you want to—as long as the layer hasn't been merged into another layer and the image hasn't been flattened. You may want to edit your layer mask when you realize your original selection needs some cleaning up, or when you want to make changes to the area the Adjustment layer affects.

> **NOTE** Remember that masking something means it won't be affected by a change. So the area that shows up in black or red on your layer mask is the area that isn't going to be changed by your adjustment. If you don't see any black or red when you look at a layer mask, then the Adjustment layer is going to change your whole photo, because you haven't masked out any parts of your image to protect them from being changed.

You can work on the mask directly in your photo, or you can make the layer mask visible and work on the mask itself. Here's the simplest way to make changes to the area covered by a layer mask:

1. **Make sure the Adjustment layer is the active layer.**

If it isn't, then click it in the Layers palette.

2. **Set your foreground/background colors to black and white.**

Just press D. If you want to paint with white, press X to swap the colors so that white (the background) becomes the foreground color.

3. **Paint directly on your image.**

Use the Brush tool to paint on the image. Paint with black to keep an area from being affected by your adjustment. Paint with white to increase the area affected by the adjustment. In other words, black masks an area, while white increases your selected area.

You can also use the Selection tools (the same way you would on any other selection) to change the mask's area. Just keep in mind that what's selected gets changed by the adjustment, while what's masked doesn't change. See Chapter 5 if you need help making selections. If you watch the layer mask icon in the layers palette, you'll see that it also changes to show where you've painted.

To make a layer mask visible, click it in the Layers palette. Elements gives you a choice of two different ways to see the masked area, as shown in Figure 10-4. You merely Option+click the right thumbnail for the Adjustment layer in the Layers palette, and then you'll see the black layer mask (instead of your photo) in the image window. Add the Shift key when you click to see a red overlay on the photo instead of the black-and-white view. Press the same keys again to get back to a regular view of your image.

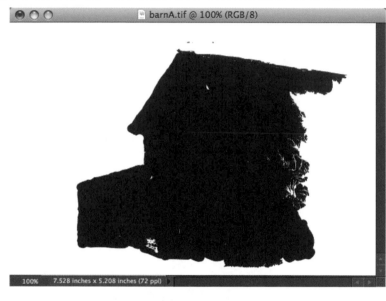

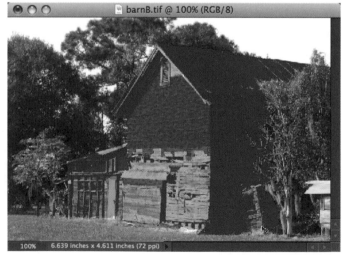

Figure 10-4:
Elements lets you edit your layer mask and also gives you two different ways to see it.

Top: To see the masked area in black, Option+click the right thumbnail for the layer in the Layers palette.

Bottom: To see the masked area in red, Option+Shift+click the layer's thumbnail.

The black mask view shows only the mask itself, not your photo beneath it. This is a good choice when you're checking to see how clean the edges of your selection are. If you're adding or subtracting areas of your photo, then choose the red overlay view so that you can see the objects in your photo as you paint over them. You can use the method described above to paint in either view.

That's all there is to it, but that's not all you can do to edit a layer mask. You can use shades of gray to adjust the transparency of the mask. When you paint on your mask with gray, you can change the opacity of the changes made by the Adjustment layer. You can let a little color show through the mask, for instance, without letting the full vividness of the color come through. Figure 10-5 shows an example of how you'd use this technique.

The lighter the shade of gray you choose, the more color shows through.

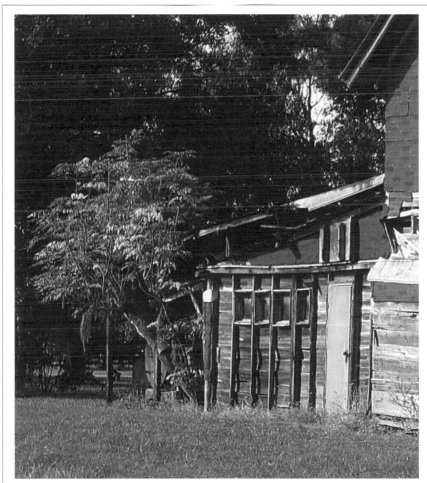

Figure 10-5:
By painting with different shades of gray on the layer mask, you can cause the effect of the adjustment to be partially transparent. Here, a fairly light gray was used to paint over the tree so that a little green shows, but it's not the bright, saturated green of the original photo. Only part of the tree was painted to make it easy to see the contrast with what was there before.

Faking Photoshop

In Chapter 6, you learned the basics of layer masks and how to use a layer as a mask by grouping it with the layer you want to mask (page 164).

If you're trying to follow a tutorial written for the full-featured Photoshop, sometimes you can get closer to the way a layer mask works in that program by placing your mask *underneath* the layer you're grouping it with. If you remember, in grouped layers (page 172), the bottom layer calls the shots for things like visibility and opacity.

If you want to control visibility for parts of the masked layer, put the masking layer (the Adjustment layer) below it and you can adjust what shows and what's hidden on the real layer by painting on the layer mask of the bottom layer.

Both ways (above and below) have their uses, but they give you control in different ways. If you do a little experimenting, it won't take long to develop a sense for which one you want in a particular situation. The simplest way of all, though, is to download one of the many free add-on toolsets that include real layer masks for Elements (see page 459).

Colorizing a Black-and-White Photo

So far, you've read about ways to make all or part of a color photo black and white. But what about when you've got a black-and-white photo and you want to add color to it? Elements makes things easy (or if not easy, then at least possible). For instance, you can give an old photo the sort of hand-tinted effect you sometimes see in antique prints, as shown in Figure 10-6.

You can easily color things with Elements. Before you start tinting your photo, first make any needed repairs. See page 251 for repair strategies. For fixes to the exposure, see page 178.

1. **Make sure your photo's in RGB mode.**

   Go to Image → Mode → RGB Color. Your photo must be in RGB mode or you can't color it.

2. **Create a new layer in Color blend mode.**

   Go to Layer → New → Layer and select Color as the layer mode. By choosing Color as your layer mode, you can paint on the layer and the image details still show through.

3. **Paint on the layer.**

   Use the Brush tool (page 314) and choose a color in the Toolbox's Foreground color square (page 198). Keep changing the foreground color as much as you need to. If the coverage is too heavy, then in the Options bar, reduce the opacity of the brush.

You can also paint directly on the original layer. (Try switching the brush blend mode to Color for this.) But the problem with that is that it's far more difficult to

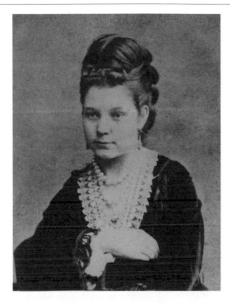

Figure 10-6:
Top: If you decide to color an old black-and-white or sepia photo, put each color on its own layer. That way you can adjust the transparency or change the hue or saturation of one color without changing the other colors, too.

Bottom: A very low opacity is enough for really old photos like this one if you want to give the effect of a print that was hand-colored.

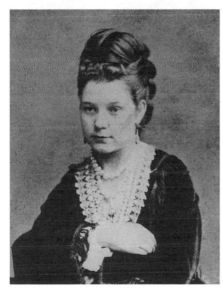

fix things if you make a mistake when you're well into your project. Using the original layer also doesn't give you much of an out if you decide later on that the lip color you painted first doesn't look so great with the skin color you just chose.

Tinting an Entire Photo

You can give an entire photo a single color tint all over, even if the original is a grayscale photo. In fact, you can use tinting to create a variety of different moods.

You have two basic ways to tint your photo. Actually, there are a lot more than two, but two should get you started. The first method (Layer style) described here is faster, but the second (Colorize) lets you tweak your settings more. Figure 10-7 shows the result of using the Layer style method on a color photo. (For a more subtle effect, you can also use Photo Filters, described on page 231.) There are also some terrific monotone tint effects in the Photo Effects, as explained on page 364.

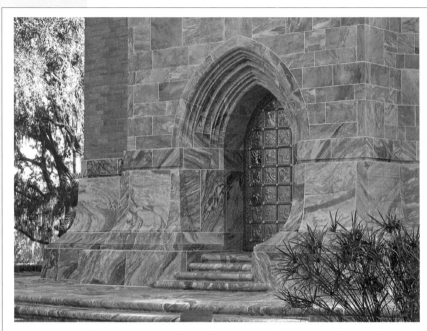

Figure 10-7:
The easiest way to create a monochrome color scheme for your photo is with the Photographic Effects Layer styles, which are explained in Chapter 13. Shown here is the Gray-Green Tone style applied to the original color photo. It removes any existing color and recolors your image in one click. The downside is that you can't edit the color once you're done if you decide you'd rather have, say, orange.

For either method, if you want to keep the original color (or lack thereof) in part of your photo, use the Selection brush in Mask mode (page 120) to mask out the area you don't want to change.

> **NOTE** Some of the frame effects in the Content palette automatically add a tint to your photo when you apply them. There are also some handy monochrome tint effects in the Effects palette among the Photo Effects.

Using a Layer style

Although many people never dig down far enough to find them, Adobe gives you some Photographic Effects Layer styles that make tinting a photo as easy as double-clicking. You'll learn more about Layer styles on page 366, but this section tells you all you need to know to use the Photographic styles. It's a very simple procedure.

1. **Create a duplicate layer.**

   Go to Layer → Duplicate Layer or press ⌘+J. (If you don't create a duplicate layer and your original has only a Background layer, you'll get asked to convert it to a layer when you apply the style. Say yes.)

2. **If necessary, change the mode to RGB.**

   Go to Image → Mode → RGB Color. With this method, it doesn't matter if your original is in color or not. The Layer style gets rid of the original color and tints the photo all at the same time.

3. **Choose a Layer style.**

   Go to the Effects palette → Layer Styles → Photographic Effects. Double-click the style of your choice, drag it to the photo, or click it once in the palette and then click Apply. You can click around and try different styles to see which you prefer. Undo (⌘+Z) after each style that you try.

4. **When you see what you like, click OK.**

   The drawback to this method is that you can't easily go back and edit the color you get from the Layer style. When you call up the Style Settings (see page 369), you won't see any active checkboxes, because these styles don't use those settings. Instead, you'd need to use a Hue/Saturation adjustment (see page 260) or Color Variations (page 197) to go back later and change the Layer style's tint color.

Additional tint effects from the Content palette

The Content palette includes some frames that automatically apply a tint to your photo, as shown in Figure 10-8. These range from simple all-over colors like Sepia, to fading gradients. (See page 370 for more about gradients.)

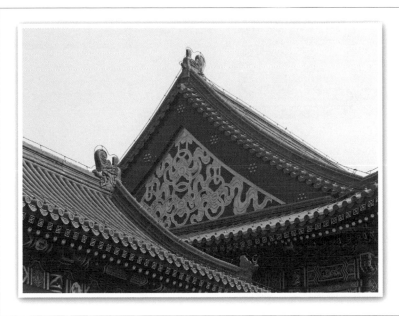

Figure 10-8:
Using the Content palette, you can apply elaborate effects, like this fading gradient, drop shadow, and frame, with just a double-click. The effect used here is the Color Tint Blue Fadeout 20px.

You can read more about using the Frames from the Content palette on page 405. To tint your photo, choose Type → Frames and scroll down towards the bottom of the list of thumbnails.

There are also some very effective color tints in the Photo Effects section of the Effects palette. Read about how to apply Effects on page 364.

Using Colorize

You can use the Colorize checkbox in the Hue/Saturation dialog box to add a color tint to a grayscale photo or to change the color of a photo that already has color in it. With this method, you can choose any color you like, as opposed to the limited color choices of the Layer styles in the previous section. You can also adjust the intensity of the color with the Saturation slider once you've selected the shade you want.

Figure 10-9 explains how the Colorize setting changes the way the Hue/Saturation command works.

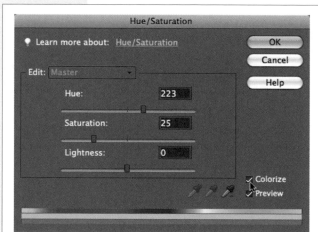

Figure 10-9:
If you want to color something that has no color information in it, like a white shirt or a grayscale image, then in the Hue/Saturation dialog box, turn on Colorize to add color to the image. If you don't turn on the Colorize checkbox, you can adjust the hue, saturation, and lightness of white all day long, and all you'll do is go from white to gray to black because there's no color info there for Elements to work with. Also, if something is pure white (i.e., no color information at all), you may need to darken it—by moving the Lightness slider to the left—before any color will show.

1. **Make sure your photo is in RGB mode.**

   Go to Image → Mode → RGB Color.

2. **Remove the color from your photo, if necessary.**

   Press Shift+⌘+U to remove the color. Do this if the photo has become yellowed or discolored (because of age, for example). If your whites are really dingy, you might want to make a Levels adjustment (page 188) to brighten them back up before removing the color.

3. **Colorize your photo on a new layer.**

   Go to Layer → New Adjustment Layer → Hue/Saturation and turn on the Colorize checkbox. When you turn this setting on, your image becomes filled with the foreground color. If you don't like it, that's fine. You're going to change it right now.

4. **Adjust the color until it looks the way you want it to.**

Move the sliders for Hue, Saturation, and Lightness until you find the look you
want, and then click OK. Figure 10-10 shows the results.

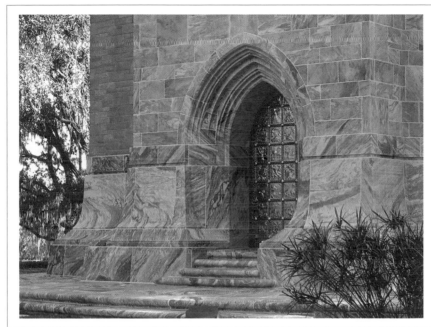

Figure 10-10:
*Here's the photo from
Figure 10-7. It was tinted
with a purple tone by
turning on the Colorize
checkbox in the Hue/
Saturation dialog box.
The door was masked
out so that it stays in full
color.*

If you selected and masked an area, that part should still show the original color.

You can change your mind about the colorizing by double-clicking the left icon on
the layer in the Layers palette. That brings up the controls for the Hue/Saturation
adjustment again so you can change your settings. And you can also edit the layer
mask, as described on page 279, if you want to change the area that's affected by
the Adjustment layer.

When you're done, if you merge layers, or press ⌘+Option+Shift+N+E to produce a
new merged layer above the existing layers, you can use Levels (page 188), Color
Variations (page 197), and the other color-editing tools to tweak the tint effect.

Photomerge: Creating Panoramas, Group Shots, and More

Everyone's had the experience of trying to photograph an awesome view—a city skyline or a mountain range, for instance—only to find the whole scene won't fit into one picture because it's just too wide. Elements, once again, comes to the rescue. With Elements' Photomerge command, you can stitch together a group of photos that you've taken while panning across the horizon. You end up with a panorama that's much larger than any single photo your camera can take. Panoramas can become addictive once you've tried them, and they're a great way to get those wide, wide shots that are beyond the capability of your camera lens.

If you've used Elements before, you may know that in the past you had to do a bunch of tweaking to get a smooth-looking result, but Photomerge got a huge makeover for Elements 6. If you know anyone who's used Photoshop CS3, the latest version of the full Photoshop, you may have heard how terrific its new Photomerge feature is. Now you can try it out for yourself, because Adobe put the same Photomerge (minus a couple of settings) into Elements 6. You won't believe how easy it is now.

Not only that, but Adobe gives you a couple of fun new twists on Photomerge that are unique to Elements: Faces and Group Shot, which let you easily move features from one face to another, and replace folks in a group photo.

If you're into photographing buildings (especially tall ones), you know that you often need some kind of perspective correction: The building appears to be lean-ing backward or sideways as a result of distortion caused by your camera's lens. This chapter shows you how to use the new Correct Camera Distortion filter to straighten things back up. You'll also learn how to use the Transform commands to adjust or warp your images.

Creating Panoramas

In Elements 6, the jazzed-up, improved Photomerge Panorama makes it much, much easier to stitch together several photos into really terrific panoramas.

Making a Panorama

It's incredibly simple to make fabulous panoramas in Elements 6. (If you've used previous versions of Elements, you know that there were lots of other programs that made better, easier panoramas than Elements used to. Not anymore: The Elements 6 Photomerge does an amazing job, totally automatically.) To make a panorama in Elements 6, about 99 percent of the time, you just tell Elements which photos you want to use, and Elements automatically stitches together a perfect panorama. Figure 11-1 shows what a great job it does.

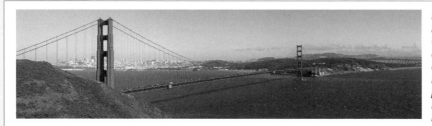

Figure 11-1:
For subjects like the Golden Gate Bridge, you can never capture the entire scene in one shot. Here's a five-photo panorama made with Photomerge. The individual photos had huge variations in exposure and were taken without a tripod. Elements takes the images—straight from the camera with no adjusting—and blends them seamlessly.

Elements can merge as many photos as you want to include in a panorama. The only real size limitation comes when you want to print out your merges. If you create a five-photo horizontal panorama but your paper is letter size, your printout is going to be only a couple of inches high, even if you rotate your panorama to print lengthwise. However, you can buy a printer with an attachment that lets you print on rolls of paper, so that there's no limit to the longest dimension of your panorama. These printers are very popular with panorama addicts. You can also use an online printing service, like the Kodak EasyShare Gallery, to get larger prints than you can make at home. See page 424 for more about how to order prints online.

You'll get the best results creating a panorama if you plan ahead when shooting your photos. The pictures should be side by side, of course, and they should overlap each other by at least 30 percent. Also, you'll minimize the biggest panorama problem—matching the color in your photos—if you make sure they all have identical exposures. While Elements can do a lot to blend exposures that don't match well, for the best panorama, adjust your photos before you begin, as explained in Figure 11-2. (The box on page 296 has more tips for taking merge-ready shots.)

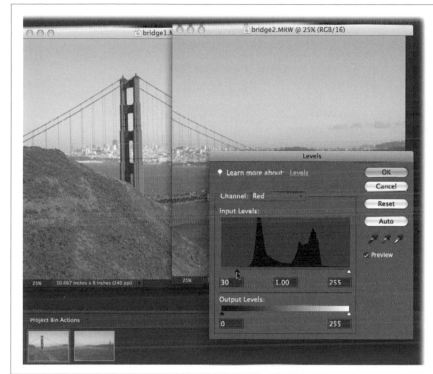

Figure 11-2:
While Elements did a very credible job with the bridge panorama in Figure 11-1 if you look closely you can see that the two end photos were much lighter than the middle ones. For even better results, use Elements to correct your photos so that the colors are as close as possible before beginning your panorama. It helps to keep them side by side so that you can compare them as you work.

When you're ready to create a panorama, just follow these steps:

1. **Start your merge.**

   You can begin from either Full Edit or Bridge. In Elements, go to File → New → Photomerge Panorama. In Bridge, it's Tools → Photoshop Elements ‣ Photomerge Panorama. (In Bridge, you should pre-select at least one photo, or Bridge may try to open all the photos visible in the Content pane.) No matter where you start, you wind up in Full Edit and the Photomerge file selection dialog box appears.

2. **Choose your photos.**

   If the photos you want to include are already open, just click Add Open Files. Otherwise, in the pull-down menu, you can choose individual files, or all the images in a particular folder; then click the Browse button to navigate to the ones you want. As you click them in the window that appears, they get added to the list in the Photomerge window.

You can add more files by clicking Browse again. To remove a file, click it in the list, and then click Remove.

NOTE In Elements 6, you can make a merge directly from RAW files, although of course you won't have any controls for adjusting the file conversions. Photomerge only works with 8-bit files, so if you have 16-bit files it asks if you want to convert them when it begins merging. For faster RAW merges, set the RAW converter to 8 bits (page 234) before you start.

3. **Choose a merge style from the Layout list on the left side of the window.**

   Ninety-nine percent of the time you want to choose Auto, the first Layout option. In Elements 6, that's usually all you need to do. When you click OK, your completed panorama is darned near perfect. You also get some other merge style choices for use in special situations:

   - **Perspective.** Elements adjusts the other images to match the middle image using such methods as skewing and other Transform commands to create a realistic view.

   - **Cylindrical.** Sometimes adjusting perspective can create a panorama that's shaped like a giant bow tie. Cylindrical mapping corrects this distortion. (It's called "cylindrical" because it gives an effect like looking at the label on a bottle—the middle part seems the largest, and the image gets smaller as it fades into the distance (similar to the label wrapping around the sides of the bottle). You may want this style for very wide panoramas.

   NOTE If you choose Auto, Elements may use either Perspective or Cylindrical mapping when it creates your panorama, depending on what it thinks will do the best job for your photos.

   - **Reposition Only.** Elements overlaps your photos and blends the exposure, but it doesn't make any changes to the perspective of the images.

   - **Interactive Layout.** This style allows you to position your images manually. It takes you to a window that's similar to the old Photomerge window in earlier versions of Elements; there's a detailed explanation in the next section.

4. **Click OK to create your panorama.**

   Elements whirls into action, combining, adjusting, looking for the most invisible places to put the seams, and whips up a completed panorama for you. That's all there is to it.

   NOTE Elements has a lot of complex calculations to make when creating a panorama, especially if there are lots of images or big exposure differences between the photos, so it may take awhile. Don't assume that Elements is stuck; give it time to think about what it's doing. It may need a few minutes to finish everything.

You'll probably want to crop your panorama (page 71), but otherwise, you're all done. You can use any of the editing tools on the final panorama once Photomerge is through, if you like. You can do anything to your panorama that you can do to any other photo.

Interactive Layout

If you find that you absolutely must do some manual positioning of your photos, choose Interactive Layout from the Layout list. When you click OK, Elements does its best to combine your photos, and presents them to you in the window shown in Figure 11-3.

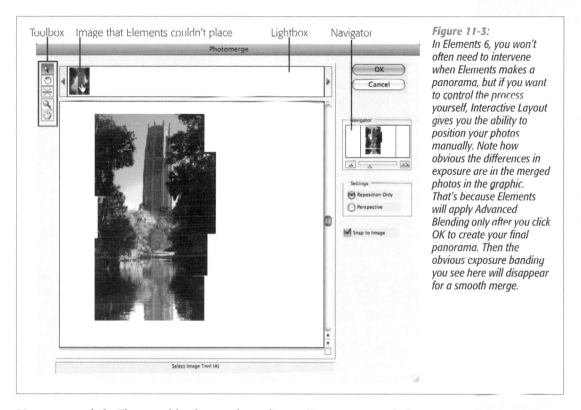

Figure 11-3:
In Elements 6, you won't often need to intervene when Elements makes a panorama, but if you want to control the process yourself, Interactive Layout gives you the ability to position your photos manually. Note how obvious the differences in exposure are in the merged photos in the graphic. That's because Elements will apply Advanced Blending only after you click OK to create your final panorama. Then the obvious exposure banding you see here will disappear for a smooth merge.

Here you can help Elements blend your photos better. Your panorama in its current state appears in the large preview area, surrounded by special tools to help you get a better merge. There's a special toolbox on the left of the window. The Lightbox, which contains the photos that Elements couldn't figure out how to place, is across the top, and there are special controls down the right side. You can use any combination of these features to improve your panorama.

You can manually drag files from the Lightbox into the merged photos and also reposition photos already in your panorama. Just grab them with the Select Image tool (explained below) and drag them to the correct location in the merge.

If you try to nudge the position of a photo and it keeps jumping away from where you've placed it, turn off "Snap to Image" on the right side of the Photomerge window. Then you should be able to put your photo exactly where you want it. However, Elements isn't doing the figuring for you anymore, so use the Zoom tool to get a good look at the alignment afterward. You may need to micro-adjust the photo's exact position.

At the top left of the Photomerge window is a little toolbox. Some tools are familiar; others are special tools just for panoramas:

- **Select Image**. Use this tool to move individual photos into or out of your merged photos or to reposition them. When the Select Image tool is active, you can drag photos into or out of the Lightbox. Press A or click the tool to activate it.

- **Rotate Image**. Elements usually rotates images automatically when merging them, but if it doesn't or if it guesses wrong, press R to activate this tool and then click the photo you want to rotate. You see handles on the image, just the way you would with the regular Rotate commands (page 66). Just grab a corner and turn the photo until it fits in properly. Usually, you won't need to drastically change a photo's orientation, but this tool helps make the small changes often needed to line things up better.

- **Set Vanishing Point**. To understand what this tool does, think of standing on a long, straight, country road and looking off into the distance. The point at which the two parallel lines of the road seem to converge and meet the horizon is called the *vanishing point*. The Vanishing Point tool in Elements tells Photomerge where you want that point to be in your finished panorama. Knowing the vanishing point helps Elements figure out the correct perspective. Press V to activate the *Vanishing Point* tool. Figure 11-4 shows an example of how it can change your results.

- **Zoom tool**. This is the same Zoom tool (page 79) you meet everywhere else in Elements. Click the magnifying glass in the Toolbox or press Z to activate it.

- **Move View tool**. Use the Move View tool exactly the way you'd use the Hand tool (page 81) when you need to scoot your *entire* merged image around to see a different part of it. Click the hand icon in the Toolbox or press H to activate it. When moving an individual photo within your panorama, use the Select Image tool instead of the Hand tool.

To control your onscreen view of your panorama, Elements gives you the Navigator on the right side of the Photomerge window. It works just like the regular Navigator described on page 82. Move the slider to resize the view of your panorama.

Drag to the right to zoom in on one area, or to the left to shrink the view so that you can see the whole thing at once. If you want to target a particular spot in your merge, drag the red rectangle to control the area that's onscreen.

Below the Navigator box you see two radio buttons—Reposition Only and Perspective—that adjust the viewing angle of your panorama. You can choose one or the other, but not both.

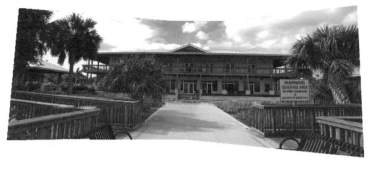

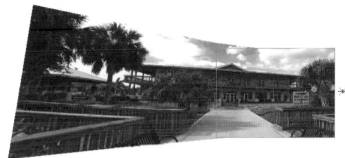

Figure 11-4:
You can radically alter the perspective of your panorama by selecting a vanishing point.

Top: Here you see the result of clicking in the center.

Bottom. Here you see the result of clicking on the right-hand image. Note that the tool selects only a particular image in the merge group, not the actual point within the photo. You can click any photo to put your vanishing point there, but if you subsequently try to tweak it by clicking a higher or lower point within the same photo, nothing happens. To change the Vanishing point you've set, just click a different photo.

- **Reposition Only**. This button merely overlaps the edges of your photos, with no changes to the perspective. If you don't like the way the angles in your panorama look, try clicking Perspective instead. (In Elements 6, Advanced Blending is always on, so Elements always blends the exposure for a smooth transition. You can't turn it off.)

- **Perspective**. If you click this button, Elements attempts to apply perspective to your panorama to make it look more realistic. Sometimes Elements does a bang-up job, but usually you'll get better results if you help it out by setting a vanishing point, as explained earlier. If you still get a totally weird result, go ahead and just create the merge anyway. Then correct the perspective yourself afterward using one of the Transform commands, covered later in this chapter.

Once you get your photos arranged to your satisfaction, just click OK and Elements creates your final panorama.

> **TIP** Elements always creates layered panoramas. If you're sending your panorama out for printing, flatten it (Layer → Flatten Image) before doing so, since most commercial printers don't understand layered files. Also, if you enlarge the view of your layered panorama and zoom in on the seams, you may see what look like hairline cracks. Merging or flattening the layers gets rid of these.

IN THE FIELD

Shooting Tips for Good Merges

The most important part of creating an impressive and plausible panorama starts before you even launch Elements. You can save yourself a lot of grief by planning ahead when shooting photos for a panorama.

Most of the time, you know *before* you shoot that you'll want to try to merge your photos. You don't often say, "Wow, I can't believe I've got seven photos of the Dr. Dre balloon at the Thanksgiving Day parade that just happen to be exactly in line and have a 30-percent overlap between each one! Guess I'll try a merge."

If you know you want to create a panorama, when you're taking pictures, set your camera to be as much in manual mode as possible. The biggest headache in panorama making is trying to get the exposure, color, brightness, and so on to blend seamlessly. Elements is darned good about blending the outlines of the physical objects in your photos. Lock your camera settings so that the exposure of each image is as identical as possible.

Even on small digital cameras that don't have much in the way of manual controls, you may have some kind of panorama setting, like Canon's Stitch Assist mode, that does the same thing.

(To be honest, your camera may make merges itself that work at least as well as what Elements can do, because the camera's doing the image-blending internally. Check out whether your model has a panorama feature.)

The more your photos overlap, the better. Elements does what it can with what you give it, but it's really happy if you can arrange a 30- to 40-percent overlap between images.

It's helpful to use a tripod if you have one, and *pan heads* (tripod heads that let you swivel your camera in an absolutely straight line) were made for panoramas. Actually, as long as your shots aren't wildly out of line, Elements can usually cope. But you may have to do quite a bit of cropping to get even edges on the finished result if you don't use a tripod.

Whether you use a tripod or not, keep the camera—rather than the horizon—level to avoid distortion. In other words, focus your attention more on leveling the body of the camera than what you see through the viewfinder. Use the same focal length for each image, and try not to use the zoom, unless it's manual, so that you can keep it exactly the same for every image.

Merging Different Faces

Merging isn't just for making panoramas anymore. One of the new tools that Elements 6 brings you is Faces, a fun (OK, let's be honest—silly) feature that lets you merge parts of one person's face with another person's face. You can use it to create caricature-like photos, or for things like pasting your new sweetie's face over your old sweetie's face in last year's holiday photo. Figure 11-5 shows an example of what Faces can do. (Elements' other new tool, Group shot, is explained later in this chapter.)

Although you'd be hard put to think of a serious use for Faces, it can be fun to play with, and it's quite simple to use:

1. **Choose the photos to combine.**

   You need to have at least two photos available in the Project bin before you start.

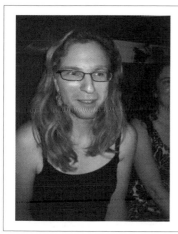

Figure 11-5:
Faces is really just for fun. You can create composite images like this one, and then use the Editor's other tools to make your photo even sillier, if you like.

2. **Call up the Faces feature.**

   You've got lots of ways to find it. You can get to it from File → New → Photomerge Faces, from Guided Edit → Photomerge → Faces, or from Bridge → Tools → Photoshop Elements → Photomerge Faces.

   A dialog box asks you to choose the photos you want to include. In the Project bin, ⌘+click to select the photos you want to use, or choose Open All from the dialog box. Elements then opens the Faces window, which has a preview area on the left and an instruction pane on the right.

3. **Choose a Final photo.**

   This is the main photo into which you're going to paste parts of the face from one or more photos. Just drag a photo from the bin into the Final Image area (on the right-hand preview).

4. **Choose your Source photo.**

   This is the photo from which you're going to copy part of the face to move to the Background Image. Double-click it in the Project bin and it appears in the left-hand preview area.

5. **Align your photos.**

   This step is very important, because otherwise Elements can't adjust for any differences in size or angle between the two shots. Click the Alignment tool button in the Faces pane, and the three little targets shown in Figure 11-6 appear in each image.

   Position the markers over the eyes and mouth in each photo and click Align Photos. (If you need help seeing what you're doing, there's a little Toolbox on the left with your old friends the Zoom [page 79] and Hand [page 81] tools, so you can reposition the photo for the best view.)

   Elements adjusts the photos so they're the same size and sit at the same angle to make a good blend.

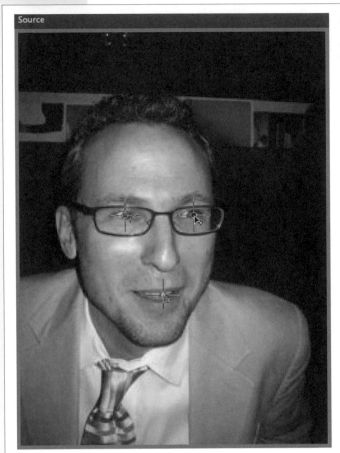

Figure 11-6:
To tell Elements how to align your photos, just drag one of these three little targets over each eye and the mouth in each photo.

6. **Tell Elements what features to move from the Source image to the Final Image.**

Click the Pencil tool in the Faces pane and, in the Source photo, draw over the area you want to move. In a few seconds you should see the selected area appear in the Final photo. It only takes a quick line—don't try to accurately color over all the material you want to move. You can adjust the size of the Pencil tool in the Options bar if it's hard to see what you're doing, or if it's grabbing too much of the surrounding area.

If Elements moves too much material from the Source photo, use the Faces Eraser tool to remove part of your line. Watch the preview in the Final image to see how you're changing the selection.

If you want to start over, click Reset.

7. **When you're happy, click Done.**

Elements creates your merge as a layered file. Now you can edit it using any of the Editor's tools, if you wish. You may want to clean up the edges a bit or to manually clone (page 248) a little more material than Elements moved. And you can make your image even sillier with the Transform commands (page 305), the Liquify filter (page 395), and so on.

There are two settings with checkboxes in the Faces pane:

- **Show Strokes**. If you want to see what you're selecting, leave this on.

- **Show Regions**. Turn this on, and you see a translucent overlay over the Background image, which makes it easier to tell which regions you're copying over from your Source photo. It's something like the overlay option for the Healing brush (page 246) and the Clone Stamp (page 248).

It would be nice if you could use this feature to merge things besides faces, but it doesn't do a very good job at all. Even for faces, if you're doing something important, like repairing an old photo with parts from another picture of the same person, you may prefer to do your own selections and manually move and adjust things (see page 172). However, the alignment tools in Faces can simplify the process enough that it's worth giving it a try to see if it can do what you need.

Arranging a Group Shot

Group Shot is another new kind of merge feature in Elements 6. Have you ever tried taking photos of a whole group of people? Almost every time, you get a photo where everything is perfect, except for that one person with his eyes shut. In another shot, that person is fine, but other people are yawning or looking away from the camera. You probably thought, "Dang, I wish I could move Ed from that photo to this one. Then I'd have a perfect shot."

Adobe hears your wishes, and Group Shot is the result. It's specifically designed for moving one person in a group from one photo to another, similar photo.

You launch Group Shot by going to File → New → Photomerge Group Shot, or Guided Edit → Photomerge → Group Shot.

The steps for using Group Shot are the same as for Faces, except that you don't normally need to align the photos, since Group Shot is intended for those situations where you were saying, "Just one more, everybody—and hold it!" as opposed to moving people from photos taken at different times with different angles and lighting.

But if you do need to align your photos, you can do that in the advanced options. Just place the markers the same way you do in Faces (see page 296). Another advanced option is Pixel Blending, which adjusts the moved material to make it closer in tone to the rest of the Final image.

NOTE   It would be great if you could use Group Shot for things like creating a photo showing many generations of your family by combining images from photos taken over many years. However, Group Shot moves someone from the Source photo and pastes that person into the same spot in the Final photo, and then creates a composite layer in the completed merge. That means the relocated person is merged into the entire Background image, and isn't left as an extracted object, which makes it impossible to put that person in a completely different location. You need to do that the old-fashioned way, by moving each individual onto a separate layer (see page 152) and then repositioning everybody where you want them.

Correcting Lens Distortion

If you ever photograph buildings, you know that it can be tough getting good shots with a fixed-lens digital camera. When you get too close to the building, your lens starts to cause distortion, as shown in Figure 11-7. Special perspective-correcting lenses are available, but they're expensive (and if you have a pocket camera, they aren't even an option). Fortunately, you can use Elements' Correct Camera Distortion filter to fix your photos after you've taken them. It's another very popular Photoshop tool that Adobe transferred over to Elements, minus a couple of advanced options.

Correct Camera Distortion is a terrifically helpful filter, and not just for buildings. You can also use it to correct the slight balloon effect you sometimes see in close-ups of people's faces (especially in shots taken with a wide-angle setting). You can even deploy the filter for creative purposes. For example, you can create the effect of a fish-eye lens by pushing the filter's settings to their extremes.

Here are some telltale signs that it's time to summon Correct Camera Distortion:

- You've used the Straighten tool (page 67), but things still don't look right.

- Your horizon is straight, but there are no true right angles in your photo. In other words, the objects in your photo lean in misleading ways. For instance, buildings lean in from the edges of the frame, or back away from you.

- Every time you straighten to a new reference line, something else gets out of whack. For example, say you keep choosing different lines in your photo that ought to be level, but no matter which one you choose, something else in the photo goes out of plumb.

- If you have a problem with vignetting—a dark, shadowy effect in your photo's corners—you can also fix that with Correct Camera Distortion. You can also *create* vignetting for special effects.

Adobe's made this filter extremely easy to use. Just follow these steps:

1. **Open a photo, and then go to Filter → Correct Camera Distortion.**

    The large dialog box shown in Figure 11-8 appears.

    NOTE   Even though Correct Camera Distortion is in the Filter menu, you can't reapply it using the ⌘+F shortcut, the way you can with most other filters. You always have to select it from the Filter menu.

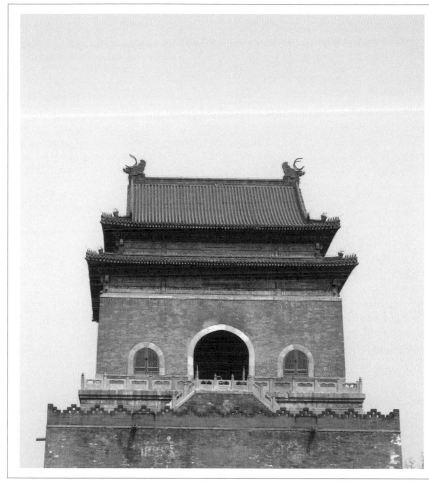

Figure 11-7:
Here's a classic example of a candidate for Elements' Correct Camera Distortion filter. See how the top of the building appears to be leaning away from you? You can fix such problems in a jiffy with the help of this filter.

2. **Use the Hand tool (page 81) to adjust your photo in the window so that, ideally, a line in the photo is along one of the grid lines.**

   If the distortion is very bad, this mission may be impossible, but get at least one line as closely aligned to the grid as you can, so you have a reference for how you're changing the photo. You can also use the usual view adjustment controls (including zoom in and out buttons) in the lower-left corner of the dialog box.

   The Show Grid checkbox lets you turn the grid on and off, but since you're going to be aligning your image you'll almost always want to keep it on. To change the color of the grid, click the Color box next to the Show Grid checkbox.

3. **Make your adjustments.**

   The filter lets you fix three different kinds of problems: barrel/pincushion distortion, vignetting, and perspective problems. These are the most common distortion errors you're likely to run into, and correcting them is as easy as

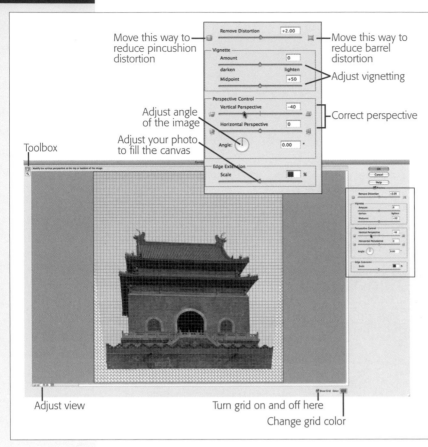

Move this way to reduce pincushion distortion

Move this way to reduce barrel distortion

Adjust vignetting

Adjust angle of the image

Correct perspective

Adjust your photo to fill the canvas

Toolbox

Adjust view

Turn grid on and off here

Change grid color

Figure 11-8:
To use Correct Camera Distortion, look at the little icons next to each slider, which show you what happens when you move the slider toward the icon. For instance, if your photo suffers from barrel distortion (everything bows outwards), move the Distortion slider toward the pinched-in pincushion. The icon illustrates exactly what you want to do to your photo—slim it down.

dragging sliders around. The small icons on each side of some of the sliders show you how your photo will change if you move in that direction. You may only need to make one adjustment, or you may need many (the bulleted list that follows will help you decide which controls to use).

Watch the grid carefully to see how things are lining up. When you get everything straightened to your satisfaction, you're done. If you want to start over, Option+click the Cancel button to change it to a Reset button and return your photo to the state it was in when you brought it into this filter.

4. **Scale your photo, if you wish.**

As you make your adjustments, you'll probably notice some empty space appearing on either side of your canvas (the background area of your file). See Figure 11-8 for an example. That's often what happens when Elements pinches and stretches your photo to correct the distortion. To make things right, you've got two options. You can click OK now and crop the photo yourself (using any of the options you learned about back on page 71). Or, you can stay here and use the Edge Extension slider to enlarge your photo so that it fills up the visible window. If you use this method, Elements crops some of the photo anyway.

NOTE   Edge Extension is handy, but gives you little control over how the photo is cropped. After all the effort you made using this filter, you may as well do your own cropping to get the best possible results.

5. **Click OK to apply your changes.**

If you don't like the way things are turning out, you can reset your photo by Option+clicking the Cancel button. If you just want a quick look at where you started from (without undoing your work), toggle the Preview checkbox on and off.

The Correct Camera Distortion filter gives you a few different ways to adjust your image. Your choices are divided into sections, according to the different kinds of distortion they fix:

• **Remove Distortion.** Use this slider to fix *barrel distortion* (objects in your photo balloon out, like the sides of a barrel, as shown in Figure 11-9), and its opposite, *pincushion distortion* (your photo has a pinched look, with the edges of objects pushing in toward the center). Move the slider to the right to fix barrel distortion and to the left to fix pincushion distortion.

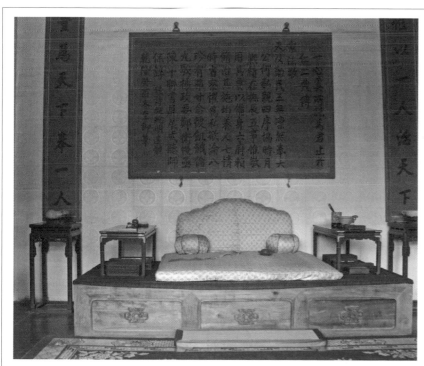

*Figure 11-9:
A classic case of barrel distortion. This photo has already been straightened with the Straighten tool (page 67), but things are still pretty out of plumb here. Notice how the platform seems to sag in the middle and the side banners on the wall lean in toward the top of the photo. Barrel distortion is the most common kind of lens distortion, but fortunately, it's very easy to fix with the Correct Camera Distortion filter.*

TIP Barrel distortion is usually worst when you use wide-angle lens settings, while pincushion distortion generally appears when a telephoto lens is fully extended. Barreling's more common than the pincushion effect, especially when you use a small point-and-shoot camera at a wide-angle lens setting. You can often reduce barrel distortion in a small camera by simply avoiding your lens's widest setting. For instance, if you go from f2.8 to f5.6, you may see significantly less distortion.

- **Vignette.** If you see dark corners in your photo (usually caused by shadows from the lens or lens hood) you need to spend time with these sliders. Vignetting typically afflicts owners of digital SLR (single lens reflex) cameras, or people who use add-on lenses with fixed-lens cameras. Move the Amount slider to the right to lighten the corners, and to the left to darken them. The Midpoint slider controls how much of your photo is affected by the Amount slider. Move it to the left to increase the area (to bring it toward the center of the photo), or to the right to keep the vignette correction more toward the edges. Also consider turning off the Show Grid checkbox, so that you have an unobstructed view of how you're changing the lightness values in your photo. Turn it back on again if you have other adjustments to make afterward.

- **Perspective Control.** Use these sliders to correct objects like buildings that appear to be tilted or leaning backward. It's easiest to understand the sliders by looking at the icons at both ends; Each icon shows you the effect you'll get by moving the slider in that direction. The Vertical Perspective slider spreads the top of your photo wider as you move the slider to the left, and makes the bottom wider as you move it to the right. (If buildings seem like they're leaning backward, move it to the left first.) The Horizontal Perspective slider is for when your subject doesn't seem to be straight on in relation to the lens (for example, if it appears to be rotated a few degrees to the right or left). Move the slider to the left to bring the left side of the photo toward you, and to the right to bring the right side closer.

- **Angle.** You can rotate your entire photo by moving the line in the circle to the angle you want, or by typing a number into the box. A very small change here has a huge effect. The circle tool is easy to work with, but if you prefer, you can type a precise angle, in degrees. Here's how it works: There are 360 degrees in a circle. Your photo's starting point is 0.00 degrees. To rotate your photo to the left (counterclockwise), start from 0.01 and go up in small increments to increase the rotation. To go clockwise, start with 359.99 and then reduce the number. In other words, 350 is further to the right than 355.

TIP Each of the adjustment settings is accompanied by a box where you can type a number instead of using the sliders. If you want to make the same adjustments to many photos, take note of the numbers you used to fix your first photo. Then just plug those numbers into the boxes for the other photos.

- **Edge Extension**. As explained earlier in the step on scaling your photo, when you're done fixing your photo, you're likely to end up with some blank areas along the edge of your photo's canvas, as shown in Figure 11-8. Move the Scale slider to the right to enlarge your photo, thereby getting rid of the blank areas. Moving the slider to the left shrinks your photo and increases the blank areas, but you'll rarely need to do that.

  The Scale slider changes your actual photo, not just your view of it (as would be the case when using the Zoom tool). When you click OK, Elements resizes and crops your photo. If you want the objects in your photo to stay the same size they were, don't use this slider. Instead, just click OK and then crop using any of the methods discussed starting on page 71.

The most important thing to remember when using Correct Camera Distortion is that a little goes a long way. For most of the corrections, start small and work in small increments. These distortions can be very subtle, and it often takes subtle adjustments to correct them.

> **TIP** The Correct Camera Distortion filter isn't just for corrections. You can use it to make your sour-tempered boss look truly prune-y, for example, by pincushioning him (just make sure you do it at home). Or, you can add vignettes to photos for special effects. You can also use the filter on shapes (simplify them first [page 341]), artwork, or anything else that strikes your fancy.

Transforming Images

You'll probably end up using the Correct Camera Distortion filter, as explained in the previous section, for most of your straightening and warp correction needs. But Elements also includes a series of Transform commands that you can use, as shown in Figure 11-10. For example, Transforming comes in handy when you want to make a change to just *one* side of a photo, or for final tweaking to a correction you made with Correct Camera Distortion. You can also apply these commands just for fun to create wacky photos or text effects.

Skew, Distort, Perspective

Elements gives you four commands, including three specialized ones—skew, distort, and perspective—to help straighten up the objects in your photos. While they all move your photo in different directions, the way you use them is the same. The Transform commands have the same box-like handles that you see on the Move tool, for example. You choose the command you want, and then the handles appear around your photo. Just drag a handle in the direction you want your photo to move. Figure 11-11 shows how to use the Transform commands.

To see the list of Transform commands, go to Image → Transform. The first one, Free Transform, is the most powerful because it includes all the others. There's more about Free Transform in the next section.

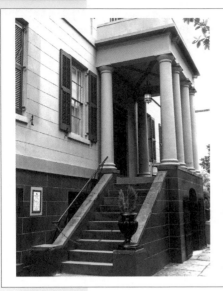
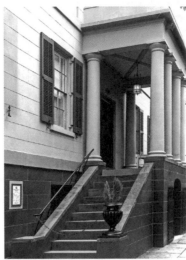

Figure 11-10:

Left: While you'd usually use Correct Camera Distortion (page 300) to straighten a slanting building like this, you can also use the Transform commands. You just have more limited choices with Transform.

Right: Here, it took only a dose of Skew and a bit of Distort to pull the building straight and make it tall again.

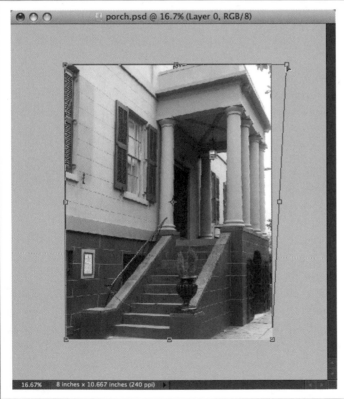

Figure 11-11:

Here's an example of how you'd use the Skew command to pull a building straight upright. The trick to applying the Transform commands is to make sure you can reach the handles on the corners. It helps to enlarge your image window far beyond the size of the actual image to give yourself room to pull. To do that, just drag the window corner, or better yet, click the little square on the far right of the menu bar (to the left of the Edit tab) to get into Maximize view.

NOTE Transform works only on layers or active selections. If you have just a Background layer, Elements offers to turn it to a regular layer so that you can use Transform.

The other Transform commands, which are more specialized, are:

- **Skew** slants an image. If you have a building that looks like it's leaning to the right, you can use Skew to pull it to the left and straighten it back up again.

- **Distort** stretches your photo in the direction you want to pull it. Use it to make buildings (or people) taller and skinnier, or shorter and squatter.

- **Perspective** stretches your photo to make it look like parts are nearer or farther away. For example, if a building in your photo looks like it's leaning away from you, you can use Perspective to pull the top back toward you.

Although Free Transform is the most capable command, it can also be trickier to use. You may find it easier to use one of the one-way commands from the previous list so you don't have to worry about inadvertently moving a photo in an unwanted direction.

> **TIP**   If you have an active selection in your image, you can apply the Transform commands just to the selection, as long as you're not working on a background layer.

All the Transform commands, including Free Transform, offer the same settings in the Options bar, which are shown in Figure 11-12.

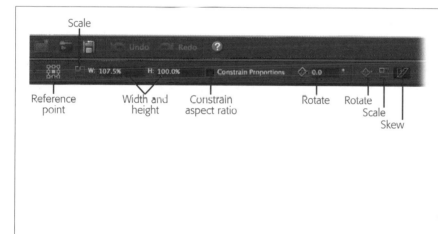

Figure 11-12:
The Options bar for the Transform commands. The width and height boxes let you manually specify dimensions when resizing your image (click the Scale button to their left once you're done entering the numbers). To scale by dragging, click the Scale button towards the right side of the tool options and drag any of the scaling handles (not shown) that appear on the bounding box surrounding your image.

From left to right, the Option bar settings control:

- **Reference Point Location.** This strange little doodad (shown in Figure 11-13) lets you tell Elements where the fixed point should be when you transform something. It's a miniature cousin of the placement grid you see in the Canvas Size dialog box (page 90). The reference point starts out in the image's center, but you can tell Elements to move everything using the upper-left corner or the bottom-right corner as the reference point instead. To do that, click the square you want to use as the reference.

Figure 11-13:
This 9-box icon in the Options bar is where you set the reference point for transformations, which tells Elements the central point for rotations. For example, if you want your photo to spin around the lower-left corner instead of the center, click the lower-left square (where the cursor is). For the Transform commands, this also tells Elements the point to work from.

- **Scale.** You can resize your image by dragging, or enter a percentage in the width or height box here. Turn on the Constrain Proportions checkbox to keep the original proportions of your image.

- **Rotate.** The box next to the little rotated squares (to the right of Constrain Proportions) in the Options bar lets you enter the number of degrees to rotate your image or selection.

- **Rotate.** Click this next pair of rotated squares and you can grab a corner of your image to make a free rotation (see page 69).

> **TIP** If you Shift+drag when turning your image, you force it to turn in 15-degree increments.

- **Scale.** Click here if you want to resize your image by dragging—as opposed to entering numbers in the Scale boxes to the left of the Options bar.

- **Skew.** Click here and you can pull a corner of your image to the left or right, the way you do with the Skew command.

In most cases, you can transform your object without paying much attention to these settings. Truly, the easiest way to transform your photo is to grab a handle and drag. Here's how you can proceed:

1. **Position your image to give yourself room to work.**

   You need to position your photo so that you have room to drag the handles far beyond its edges. Figure 11-11 is a good example of an image window that's sufficiently expanded to make lots of transformations.

2. **Choose how you want to transform your image.**

   Go to Image → Transform and select the command you want. It's not always apparent which is best for a given photo, so you may want to try all three in turn. You can always change your mind and undo your changes by pressing Escape (Esc) before you accept a change, or undo using ⌘+Z once the change has been made.

   You can apply Transform commands only to layers, so if your image has only a Background layer, the first thing Elements does is ask you to convert that layer to a regular layer. Just say yes and go on. Once the Transform command is active, you see the handles around your image.

3. **Transform your image.**

Grab a handle and pull in the direction you want the image to move. You can switch to another handle to pull in a different direction, too. If you decide you made a mistake, just press the Escape key (Esc) to return to your original photo.

4. **When you're happy with how your photo looks, accept the change.**

Click the Commit button (the checkmark) in your photo, or press Return. Click the Cancel button (the "no" symbol) instead if you decide not to apply your transformation to your photo.

TIP Before you click the Commit button, you can switch to another Transform command and add that transformation to your image, too.

Free Transform

Free Transform combines all the other Transform commands into one and lets you warp your image in many different ways. If you aren't sure what you need to do, Free Transform is a good choice.

You use Free Transform exactly the way you use the other Transform tools, following the steps listed earlier. The difference is that with Free Transform, you can pull in *any* direction, using keystroke combinations to tell Elements which kind of transformation you want to apply. Each particular transformation, listed as follows, does exactly the same thing it would if you selected that transformation from the Image → Transform menu:

- **Distort.** To make your photo taller or shorter, ⌘+drag any handle. Your cursor turns into a gray arrowhead.

- **Skew.** To make your photo lean to the left or right, ⌘+Shift+drag a handle in the middle of a side. You cursor is the gray arrowhead with a tiny double-arrow attached to it.

- **Perspective.** To correct the way an object appears to lean away from or toward you, press ⌘+Option+Shift and drag a corner. You see the same gray arrowhead that you see when you're distorting.

The Free Transform command is the most powerful of all the Transform commands, but when you're pulling in several different directions, it's tricky to keep your photo from becoming distorted. Consequently, some people prefer to use the simpler Transform commands and apply multiple transformations instead.

Part Four: Artistic Elements

4

Drawing with Brushes, Shapes, and Other Tools

If you're not of the artistic persuasion, you may feel tempted to skip this chapter. After all, you probably just want to fix and enhance your photos. What do you care about brush technique? Surprisingly enough, you should care quite a lot. In Elements, brushes aren't just for painting a moustache and horns on a picture of someone you don't like, or for blackening your sister's teeth in that old school photo.

Many tools in Elements use brushes to apply their effects. So far, you've already run into the Selection brush, the Clone Stamp, and the Color Replacement brush, to name just a few. And even with the Brush tool, you can paint with lots of things besides color—like light or shadow, for example. In Elements, when you want to apply an effect in a precise manner, you're often going to use some sort of brush to do it.

If you're used to working with real brushes, their digital cousins can take some getting used to, but there are many serious artists now who paint primarily in Photoshop. With Elements, you now have access to most of the same tools as in the full Photoshop, if not quite all the settings available for each tool. Figure 12-1 shows an example of the detailed work you can do with Elements and some artistic ability.

This chapter explains how to use the Brush tool, some of the other brush-like tools (like the Erasers), and how to draw shapes even if you can't hold a pencil steady. You also get some practical applications for your new skills, like dodging and burning your photos to enhance them, and a super-easy way to create sophisticated artistic crops for your photos—a favorite feature for scrapbooking.

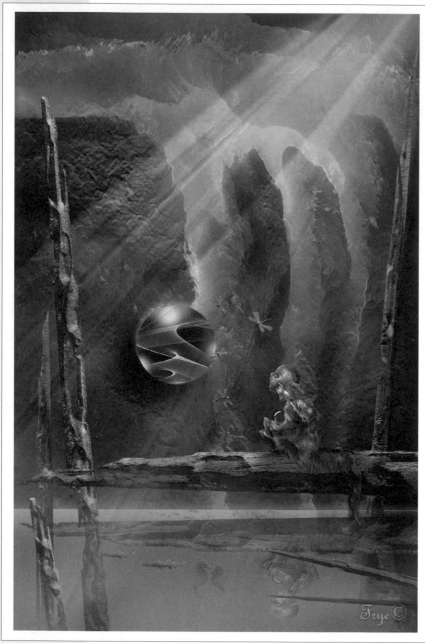

Picking and Using a Basic Brush

If you look at the Toolbox, you'll see the Brush tool icon, which is next to or above the Paint Bucket, depending on whether you have one or two rows of tools.

(Don't confuse it with the Selection brushes, which are up above the Crop or Type tool.) Click the Brush tool's icon or press B to activate it.

The Brush is one of the tools that include a hidden pop-out drawer—you can choose between the Brush, the Impressionist brush, the Pencil tool, and the Color Replacement brush. You can read about the Impressionist brush and the Pencil tool later in this chapter, and about the Color Replacement brush on page 266. This section is about the regular Brush tool.

If you look at the Options bar (Figure 12-2), you can see that the Brush offers you lots of ways to customize the tool.

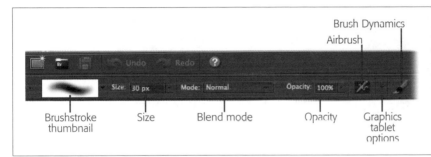

Figure 12-2:
These are the Options bar settings for the Brush tool. By changing the settings shown here, as well as the hidden settings—revealed when you click the Brush Dynamics button—you can dramatically alter the behavior of any brush.

Here's a quick rundown (from left to right) of the available Brush options:

• **Brushstroke thumbnail.** The Options bar displays a thumbnail of the stroke you'd get with the current brush. Click the brushstroke thumbnail to see the Brush palette. Elements gives you a bunch of basic brush collections, which you can view and select here. You can also download many more from various Web sites (see page 459).

> **NOTE** You may think you have a bunch of duplicate brushes in some of the brush libraries (for example, two smiley faces labeled 39 in the Pen Pressure brushes), but if you click the arrows at the upper right of the pop-up menu and choose Stroke Thumbnail view, you'll see that they have different settings for the brushstroke, giving quite different results. (You can change any setting at any time to get just the stroke you want.)

If you click the pull-down menu, you'll see that you get more than just hard or soft brushes of various sizes (see Figure 12-3). You also get special brushes for drop shadows, brushes that are sensitive to pen pressure if you're using a graphics tablet (you can also use them with a mouse, but you don't have as many options), and brushes that paint shapes and designs.

> **TIP** One very cool feature of the brushes in Elements is that any changes you make to a brush are shown in the little brushstroke thumbnail in the Brush palette.

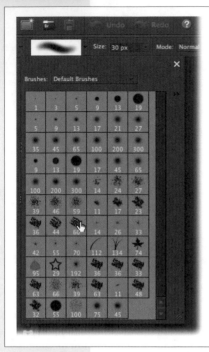

Figure 12-3:
Elements gives you a pretty good list of different brushes to choose from, or you can add your own. You can make brushes, too, as explained on page 323.

- **Size.** This pull-down menu lets you adjust the size of your brush—anywhere from 1 pixel up to sizes that may be too big to fit on your monitor. Or you can just type in a size. Figure 12-4 shows you an easy way to adjust brush size using your mouse. As you're working you can press the close bracket key (]) to quickly increase brush size, or the open bracket key ([) to decrease it.

- **Mode.** Choices in this pull-down menu determine your blend mode. The mode you choose determines how the brush color interacts with what's in your image. For example, Normal simply paints the current foreground color (more about all the Mode choices later).

- **Opacity.** Here's the way to control how thoroughly your brushing covers what's beneath it. You can use the pull-down menu's slider or type in any percentage you like, from 1 to 100. The maximum—100 percent—gets you total coverage. Or you can scrub, as shown in Figure 12-4.

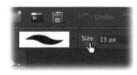

Figure 12-4:
You don't need to open pull-down menus like the one shown here that says "13 px." Just move your cursor onto the word "size" (the word is covered by the hand here), and your cursor changes into a hand-with-double-headed-arrow. Now you can "scrub" back and forth right on the Options bar to make the changes—left for smaller, right for larger. This trick also works anywhere you see a numerical pop-out slider (as in the Layers palette's Opacity menu, for example).

- **Airbrush.** Clicking the little pen-like brush just to the right of the Opacity control lets you use the brush as an airbrush. Figure 12-5 shows you how this works.

- **Tablet Options.** Click the tiny arrow to the right of the airbrush. If you use a graphics tablet, you can use these settings to tell Elements which brush characteristics should respond to the pressure of your stroke. There's more about graphics tablets on page 457.

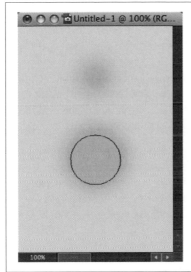

Figure 12-5:
As with real airbrushes, Elements' airbrush option causes Elements to continue to "spray" paint as long as you hold down the mouse button, regardless of whether the mouse is moving or not.

Top: Notice the effect of one click with the brush in Regular mode.

Bottom: Here's the effect of one click with the same brush in Airbrush mode. See how far the color has spread out beyond the actual brush cursor (the circle) when using the airbrush? Not every brush offers the airbrush option.

- **Brush Dynamics.** Clicking this icon gets you the Brush Dynamics palette, which gives you oodles of ways to customize your brush, which are covered in the next section. If you're using your brush for artistic purposes, you should familiarize yourself with these settings, since this is where you can set a chiseled stroke or a fade, for example.

> **TIP** If you ever want to return a brush to its original settings, click the Reset button (the tiny black arrow) on the far left side of the Options bar and then click Reset Tool from the pop-up menu.

To actually use the Brush, you enter your settings—make sure you've selected the color you want in the Foreground color square (page 198)—and then just drag across your image wherever you want to paint.

> **NOTE** If you're used to painting with long, sweeping strokes, keep in mind that in Elements, that technique can be frustrating. That's because when you undo a mistake (by pressing ⌘+Z), Elements undoes *everything* you've done while you've been holding down the mouse button.
>
> In tricky spots, you can save yourself some aggravation by using shorter strokes so you don't have to lose that whole long curve you painstakingly worked on just because you wobbled a bit at the end. (The Eraser tool [page 334] is handy in these situations, too, for tidying up.)

TROUBLESHOOTING MOMENT

What Happened to My Cursor?

One thing that drives newcomers to Elements nuts is having the Brush cursor change from a circle to little crosshairs, seemingly spontaneously. This is one of those "It's not a bug; it's a feature" situations. Many tools in Elements offer you the option of what is called the *precise cursor*, shown in Figure 12-6. There are situations where you may prefer to see those little crosshairs so that you can tell *exactly* where you're working.

You toggle the precise cursor by pressing the Caps Lock key. So, if you hit that key by accident, you may find yourself in precise cursor mode with no idea of how you got there. Just press it again to turn it off.

There's one other way you may wind up with the precise cursor, and this time you have no choice in the matter. It happens when your image is so small in proportion to the cursor that Elements *must* display the crosshairs to show the brush in the right scale for your image. Zooming

the view out usually gets your regular cursor back, unless you're working with a 1-pixel brush, which always uses crosshairs.

There's another wrinkle to the mysterious cursor problem. Your cursor may look like a tiny icon instead of the brush circle. Once again, you can control this by adjusting an Elements preference setting. Go to Photoshop Elements → Preferences → Display & Cursors → Painting Cursors → Normal Brush Tip to get back the normal brush. This preference window also lets you turn off the specialized cursors for tools like the Lasso tools. To do so, in the Other Cursors box, choose Precise.

You can also choose to always see the crosshairs within the regular cursor circle if you want. In the Preferences dialog box, at the bottom of the list of Brush Size options, turn on the checkbox for "Show Crosshair in Brush Tip," and you'll always have a mark for the exact center of your brush.

One of the biggest differences between drawing with a mouse and drawing with a real brush is that, on a computer, it doesn't matter how hard you press the mouse. But if you've got a *graphics tablet*, an electronic pad that causes your pen movements to appear instantly onscreen, you can replicate real-world brushing, including pressure effects. Page 457 tells you all about using a tablet.

> **TIP**   To draw or paint a straight line, hold down the Shift key while you move your mouse. If you click where you want your line to start, and press and hold Shift, and then click at the end point, Elements draws a straight line between those two points. It's important to click first and then press Shift, or you may draw lines where you don't want them.

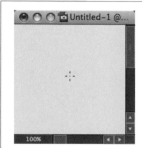

Figure 12-6:
Adobe calls these crosshairs the precise cursor. Elements sometimes makes your tool look like this when you're zoomed way in on an image. To get the normal cursor back, you can zoom out some, and read the box above for further advice.

Modifying Your Brush

When you click the Brush Dynamics button in the Options bar, you'll see a palette that lets you customize the brush in a number of ways. Its official name is the *Brush Dynamics palette*. You'll also run into a version of this palette for some of the other brush-like tools, like the Healing brush. The Brush Dynamics palette lets you change the way your brush behaves in a number of sophisticated and fun ways. Mastering these settings goes a long way toward getting artistic results in Elements.

- **Fade** controls how fast the brush stroke fades out—just the way a real brush does when you run out of paint. Think of the numbers as sort of "how many steps" it would take to run out of paint. A lower number means it fades out very fast (very few steps) while a higher one means the fade happens later (more steps). You can pick a number up to 9999, so with a little fiddling, you should be able to get just what you want. Zero is no fading at all—the stroke is the same at the end as it is at the beginning.

  If the brush isn't fading fast enough, decrease the number. If it fades too fast, increase it. A smaller brush usually needs a higher number than a larger brush does. You may find that you need to set the brush spacing (see below) up into the 20s or higher to make fading show any visible effect.

- **Hue Jitter** controls how fast the brush switches between the background and foreground colors. Some brushes, especially the ones that you'd use to paint objects like leaves, automatically vary the color for a more interesting or realistic effect. The higher the number (percentage) here, the faster the color moves from foreground to background. A lower number means the brush takes a longer distance to get from one color to the other. Brushes that acknowledge hue jitter don't put down only the two colors, but a range of hues in between. Not all brushes respond to this setting, but for the ones that do, it's a pretty cool feature. Figure 12-7 shows you how it works.

- **Scatter** means just what it says—how far the marks get distributed in your brushstroke. If scatter is given a very low number (percentage), you get a dense, line-like stroke, whereas a higher value gives an effect more like random spots.

- **Spacing** controls how far apart the brush marks get laid down when you apply the brush. A lower number makes them close together, a higher number farther apart, as shown in Figure 12-8.

- **Hardness** controls whether the brush edge is sharp or fuzzy. This setting isn't available with all brush types, but when it is, you can choose any value between zero and 100 percent. One hundred percent is the most defined edge, zero the fuzziest.

- **Angle and Roundness**. If you've ever painted with a real brush, you should understand Angle and Roundness right away. They let you create a more chiseled edge to your brush and then rotate it so that it's not always painting with the edge facing the same direction. Painters don't use only round brushes, and you don't have to in Elements, either.

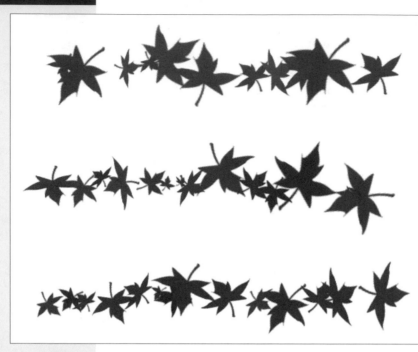

Figure 12-7:
Top: A brushstroke with no hue jitter.

Middle: The same brushstroke with a medium hue jitter value.

Bottom: The same brushstroke with a high hue jitter value. The foreground/ background colors here are red and blue. Notice how the brush automatically does a little shading, even without allowing for jitter. It takes a fairly high number to get all the way to blue in a stroke of this length.

Figure 12-8:
The same brushstroke with the spacing set at 5 percent, 75 percent, and 150 percent (respectively, from top to bottom). You may have been wondering why some of the brush thumbnails look like long caterpillars, when the brush should paint an object, like a star or leaf. The reason? Cramped spacing: The thumbnail shows the spacing as Elements originally sets it. Widen the spacing to see separate objects instead of a clump.

There are some brushes in the libraries that aren't round, like the calligraphy and chalk brushes. But you can adjust the roundness of any brush to make it more suitable for chiseled strokes, as shown in Figure 12-9.

There's also a checkbox ("Keep These Settings for All Brushes") you can turn on if you want to make all your brushes behave exactly the same way.

Saving Modified Brush Settings

If you modify a brush and you like the result, you can save it as a custom brush. You can alter any of the existing brushes and save the result—a great feature if you're working on a project that's going to last awhile and you don't want to have to keep modifying the settings again and again. (Don't worry: When you modify an existing brush, Elements preserves a copy of the original.) To create your own brush, just:

1. **Choose a brush to modify.**

   Select a brush in the Brush palette. You can customize any of the brushes.

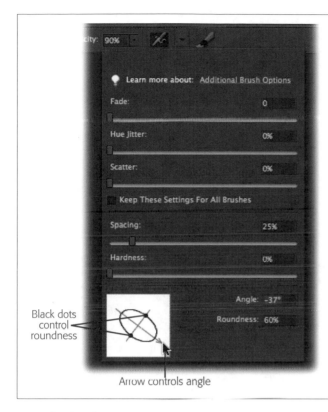

Figure 12-9:
To adjust the angle and roundness of a brush, you push the black dots to make the brush rounder or narrower and then grab the arrow and spin the brush to the angle you want. You can also type a number directly into either the Angle or Roundness box.

Black dots control roundness

Arrow controls angle

2. **Make the changes you want.**

   Change the brush settings until you get what you're after. Watch the brush thumbnail in the Options bar as you go. It changes to reflect your new settings.

3. **Tell Elements you want to keep the new brush.**

   Click the arrow in the upper-right corner of the brush thumbnails palette and choose Save Brush. Elements asks you to name it. You don't absolutely have to, but naming brushes makes them easier to keep track of.

4. **Click OK.**

   The brush shows up in the bottom of your list of brushes.

Deleting brushes is pretty straightforward. You can select the brush in the Brush palette and then choose Delete Brush from the pop-out menu. Or you can Option+click the brush thumbnail. The cursor will change to a pair of scissors when you hold down the key. Clicking with the scissors deletes the brush.

You can also make a selection from an image and save it as a brush, if you like (the next section shows you how). Just remember, though, that brushes by definition don't have color, so you save only the shape of your selection, not the full coloring of it. The color you get is whichever color you choose to apply. If you want to save a full color sample, try saving your selection as a pattern (page 254) or just use the clone stamp repeatedly instead.

The Specialty Brushes

So far you've been reading about brushes that behave pretty much as brushes do in the real world—they paint a stripe of something, whether color, light, or even transparency.

But in the digital world, a brush doesn't have to be just a brush. With some of the brushes included in Elements, you can paint stars, flowers, disembodied eyeballs, gravel, or even rubber ducks with just one swipe of the brush, as shown in Figure 12-10.

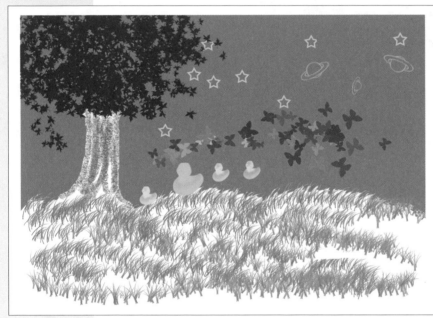

Figure 12-10:
You can digitally doodle using the Elements brushes, even if you can't draw a straight line. Everything in this lovely drawing was done with brushes included with Elements. The leaves were painted with a brush that paints leaves; the yellow ducks come from a brush that paints rubber ducks, and so on.

If you click the arrow next to the brush thumbnail in the Options bar, you'll see the list of brushes in the current category and a pull-down menu that lets you investigate the other brush sets you got with Elements. The brushes used in Figure 12-10, for example, came from several different categories, but you have all of them if you have Elements. Some brushes are sensitive to your pen pressure if you're using a graphics tablet (page 457).

The Specialty brushes respond very readily to changes in the Advanced Brush Options settings (covered earlier in this chapter). Your choices there can make a huge difference in the effect you get—whether you're painting swaths of smooth grass, like a lawn, or scattered sprigs of dune grass, for instance. You get the exact same list of choices described in the previous section on the Advanced Brush Options palette: fade, hue jitter, scatter, and so on.

TIP   If you've tried some of the special effects brushes and found the results rather anemic, you can always go back once you've painted and punch up the color with a Multiply layer, just as you would do for an overexposed photo (see page 179).

Making a Custom Brush

You can turn any picture, or selection within a picture, into a brush that paints the shape you've selected. Figure 12-11 shows what a wreath looks—and behaves like—when it's been turned into a brush.

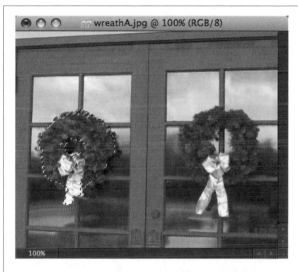

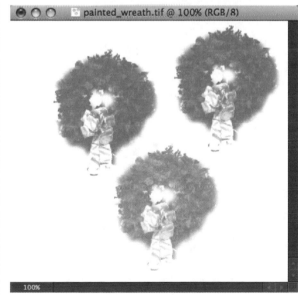

Figure 12-11:
Top: If you want to make a brush to draw holiday wreaths, just select a wreath in a photo and save it as a brush.

Bottom: You can paint better than you thought! Notice, too, that some of the ragged edges of the wreath were left out to improve the shape of the brush.

It's surprisingly easy to create a custom brush from any object you have a picture of.

1. **Open a photo or drawing that includes what you want to use as a brush.**

   You can choose an area as large as 2500 pixels square. (Remember, you can resize your selection once it's a brush, just the way you can resize any other brush, so don't worry if it's a big area.)

2. **Select the object or region you want.**

   Use any of the Selection tools. It's a good idea to check your selection with the Selection brush in Mask mode as a last step (page 120). That's because any stray areas you included by mistake get painted with each stroke—just as if you wanted them to be there.

3. **Create your brush.**

   Go to Edit → "Define Brush from Selection". You see a dialog box showing the shape and asking you to name your new brush. Check the thumbnail to be sure it's exactly what you had in mind. If not, click Cancel and try again. If you like what you've got, click OK.

The new brush shows up at the bottom of your default list of brushes. If you want to get rid of it, highlight the thumbnail in the brush thumbnails, click the arrow on the right side of the palette, and go to Delete Brush, or Option+click the brush thumbnail.

The Impressionist Brush

When you paint with the Impressionist brush, you blur and blend the edges of the objects in your photo, just like an Impressionist painting. At least that's what's *supposed* to happen. This brush is very tricky to control, but you can get some very interesting effects, especially if you paint with it on a duplicate layer and play with the Opacity control (page 155). Usually you want a very low opacity with this brush, or some of the curlier styles will make your image look like it's made from poodle hair.

The Impressionist brush has most of the same options as the regular Brush, but if you click the More Options button (the icon to the right of the Opacity setting), you'll see three new choices:

- **Style** determines what kind of brushstroke effect you want to create.

- **Area** tells Elements the size and number of brushstrokes.

- **Tolerance** is how similar in color pixels have to be before they're affected by the brush.

If you really want to create a hand-painted look, you may prefer the brushstroke filters (Filter → Brush Strokes). Page 350 explains how to use them. The Impressionist brush is really not the best tool for true Impressionist effects, although its blurring qualities can sometimes be useful because it covers large areas faster than the Blur tool. The Smudge tool (page 332) is another excellent, though time-consuming, way to create a painted effect.

The Pencil Tool

Basically just another brush, the Pencil tool shares the Brush tool's slot in the Toolbox. Choose the Pencil from the pop-out menu or press N to activate it.

The Pencil has many of the same setting options as the Brush—like size, mode, and opacity—but it offers only hard-edged brushes. In other words, you can't draw fuzzy lines with the pencil, not even the kind of lines you'd sketch with a soft pencil. The Pencil's lines are always very well defined. It's especially useful when you want to work on a pixel-by-pixel basis.

You use the Pencil tool the same way you use any other brush. The big difference is the Auto Erase option (the checkbox is located in the Options bar). Auto Erase makes the Pencil paint with the background color over areas that contain the foreground color. But if you start dragging in an area that doesn't contain the foreground color, it paints with the foreground color instead. This is really confusing until you try it, but then it's pretty easy to understand. Take a look at Figure 12-12 for some help in understanding what's going on, or better yet, create a blank file (page 47) and try it yourself.

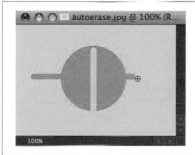

Figure 12-12:
The slightly confusing Auto Erase option, was used to create two lines: a horizontal one consisting of the foreground color (blue) and a vertical one consisting of the background color (pink). The horizontal line was drawn by starting with the cursor in the background (thus, the pencil erased the pink, leaving a blue line across the circle). On the other hand, the pink line was drawn by starting inside the blue circle, causing the background color to be exposed.

The Paint Bucket

When you want to fill a large area with color in a hurry, the Paint Bucket's the tool for you. It's right next to the Brush tool in the Toolbox. If you click it or press K to activate it and then click in your image, the entire available area (either your whole image or the current selection) gets flooded with color. It works something like the Magic Wand: Just as the Magic Wand selects the color you click, the Paint Bucket fills only the color you click.

Use this tool to change the color of a solid layer with one click (so make any tool settings adjustments before clicking in your photo). Most of the Options bar settings for the Paint Bucket are probably familiar:

• **Pattern.** Normally the Paint Bucket fills the area with the foreground color (page 198). Turn this on and it uses a pattern (page 252) instead. You can choose from any of the existing patterns (listed in the Pattern drop-down menu on the Options bar). Or you can create your own, just as you would with the Pattern Stamp (see page 254).

- **Mode.** Use the Paint Bucket in any blend mode, as explained later in this chapter on page 329.

- **Opacity.** 100-percent opacity gives you total coverage; nothing shows through the paint you put down. Lower the percentage for a more transparent effect.

- **Tolerance.** This setting works the same way it does for the Magic Wand (page 122). The higher the number, the more shades the paint fills.

- **Anti-alias.** This setting smoothes the edges of the fill. Leave it turned on unless you have a specific reason not to.

- **Contiguous.** This is another old familiar from the Magic Wand (page 122). If you leave Contiguous on, you change only areas of the chosen color that touch each other. Turn it off, and all areas of the color you click get changed, whether they're contiguous or not.

- **All Layers.** Fills any pixels that meet your criteria, no matter what layer they're on. (The Paint Bucket actually paints on the active layer, but it looks for pixels to change based on all the layers in your image.) To keep out just one layer, click the eye icon on the Layers palette to hide the layer you want to exclude. Turn it back on by clicking the eye after using the Paint Bucket. Don't forget that you can lock the transparent and translucent parts of layers in the Layers palette (see page 156).

You can undo a Paint Bucket fill with the usual ⌘+Z.

> **TIP** You can sometimes improve blown-out skies by using the Eyedropper to select an appropriate shade of blue from another photo and then filling the blown-out areas of your sky using the Paint Bucket at a very low opacity.

Dodging and Burning

Like Unsharp Mask, dodging and burning are old darkroom techniques to enhance photos and emphasize particular areas. Dodging *lightens* and brings out the hidden details in the range you specify (midtones, shadows, or highlights), and burning *darkens* and brings out details (you have the same range choices as for dodging). Both tools live with the Sponge tool in the Toolbox, so you may have run into them while you were using the Sponge.

You may think that since you have the Shadows/Highlights command, you don't have any need for these tools. But they still serve a useful purpose because they let you make selective changes, rather than affecting the entire image or requiring tedious selections, the way Shadows/Highlights does. When you dodge or burn, you just paint your changes. Figure 12-13 gives an example of when you might need to work on a particular area. Of course, you can also make a selection (see Chapter 5) and then use Shadows/Highlights just on that area, which is another technique that you may want to try as well as dodging and burning.

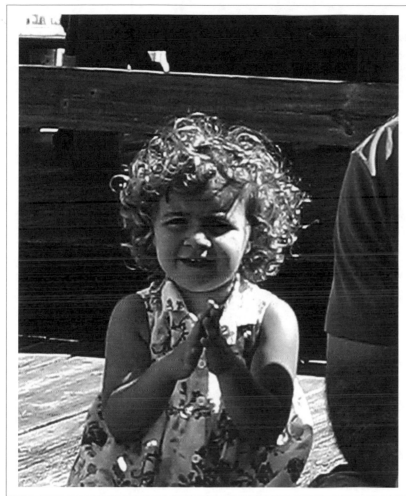

Figure 12-13:
Although the overall shadow/ highlight balance of this photo is about right, the detail in the face of this little concert-goer is obscured by backlighting and by her father's shadow. Careful dodging and burning can really improve these problems, as you can see in Figure 12-14.

Skillful use of dodging and burning can greatly improve your photo, although it helps to have an artistic eye to spot what you want to emphasize and what you want to downplay. When you use the black-and-white conversion feature (page 271), use the Dodge and Burn tools to emphasize certain areas of your photos. The real masters of black-and-white photography, like Ansel Adams, relied heavily on dodging and burning (in the darkroom, in those days) to create their greatest images.

Both the Dodge and Burn tools are really just variants of the Brush tool, except that they don't apply color directly—they just affect the colors and tones that are already present in your photo. Adobe refers to these two as the "toning tools."

One caution about these tools, though—unless you use them on a duplicate layer, you can't undo the effect once you close your photo. So you need to be careful how you use them. Actually, many people prefer to dodge and burn using the method described in the box on page 331, rather than with the actual Dodge and Burn tools, unless they're working on a black-and-white photo.

CHAPTER 12: DRAWING WITH BRUSHES, SHAPES, AND OTHER TOOLS

Dodging

The Dodge tool is used to lighten areas of your image and to bring out details that may be hidden in shadows. You can use dodging to create highlights or to even out areas that have been too deeply shadowed. It's a good idea to create a separate layer (Layer → Duplicate Layer or ⌘+J) when you use this tool, to preserve your image if you go overboard. Be sure you're applying the Dodge tool to a layer that has something in it, or nothing happens.

1. **Activate the Dodge tool.**

   Click the Sponge tool in the Toolbox or press O, and choose the Dodge tool (the lollipop-like paddle) from the pop-out menu. You'll see the usual brush options, but with two differences: a choice of whether the tool should work on highlights, midtones, or shadows, and a setting called Exposure, which determines the strength of the effect.

2. **Drag over the area you want to change.**

   Choose a very low Exposure setting for the Dodge tool (and the Burn tool as well) and drag more than once to get a more realistic result (see Figure 12-14). After you're done, if you think the Dodge tool's effect is still too strong, you can always reduce the opacity of the layer in the Layers palette.

Burning

The Burn tool does exactly the opposite of what the Dodge tool does: It darkens. You can use the Burn tool to make highlights show more details. Of course, there have to be *some* details there for the tool to work. If your photo's highlights are blown out (see page 183), you won't get any results, no matter how much you apply the tool. The Burn tool is grouped with the Sponge and Dodge tools. Its icon is a hand striking a match, logically enough.

The Burn tool is applied exactly the same way as the Dodge tool, and most of the time, you'll probably want to use these tools in combination. They can help draw attention to specific parts of your photo, but they work best for subtle changes. Applying them too vigorously—especially on color photos—gives an obviously faked look to your photo. Black-and-white photos (or color photos converted to black and white) can generally stand much stronger contrasts.

Blending and Smudging

In Elements, you can control how the color you add to your image blends with the colors that are already there. This section takes a look at blending in two different ways—using the Smudge tool to literally mix elements of your image together, and using *blend modes* to determine how the colors you paint change what's already in your image. Blend modes are almost limitless in how you can use them to manipulate your images.

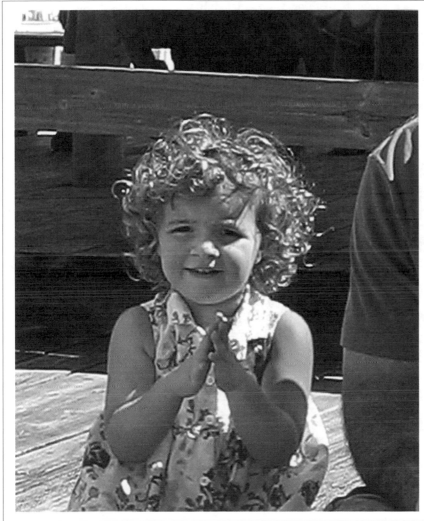

Figure 12-14:
Figure 12-13 after the Dodge and Burn tools did their work. The girl's features are much easier to see, but if you look closely, you can see that the colors in her face are a bit flat. See page 332 to compare a different method for selectively adjusting highlights and shadows. Both solutions have advantages and disadvantages. Things are deliberately a bit too strong in both figures to show you the perils of getting overzealous with either method.

Blend Modes

Blend modes control how the color you add when you paint reacts with the existing pixels in your image—whether you just add color (Normal mode), make the existing color darker (Multiply mode), or change the saturation (Saturation mode).

> **NOTE** Elements 6 gives you two new blend modes with self-explanatory names: Lighter Color and Darker Color, which are available for brushes as well as layers. They appear at the bottom of their respective sections in the Mode menu. Check them out.

Many uses for the blend modes are more advanced and beyond the scope of this book (and would make the book over a thousand pages long). But Figure 12-15 shows a few examples of how simply changing the brush blend mode can radically change your result.

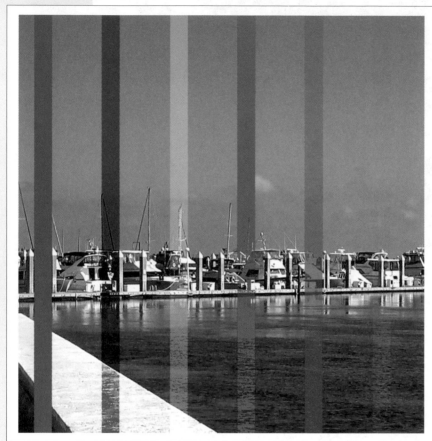

Figure 12-15:
This photo shows the effect of some of the different blend modes when used with the Brush tool. The same color was used for every one of the vertical stripes—you can see how different the result is from just changing the mode.

From left to right, the modes are: Normal, Color Burn, Color Dodge, Vivid Light, Difference, and Saturation.

There are so many ways to combine blend modes that even Elements pros can't always predict the results, so experimenting is the best way to learn about them. Also, many of the more advanced books on Elements include projects that require using the different modes.

Blend modes are grouped according to the effects that they have. The top group in the menu includes what you might call painting modes, followed by modes for darkening, lightening, adjusting light, special effects modes, and adjusting color.

It's also important to be aware that the modes work quite differently with layers than with tools. In other words, painting with a brush in Dissolve mode is going to produce an effect quite different than creating a layer in Dissolve mode and painting on it, as shown in Figure 12-16.

Modes are really cool and very useful once you get used to using them, but if you're just starting out in Elements, there's no need to worry about them right away.

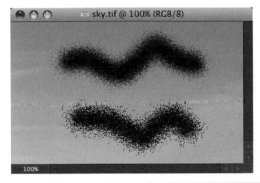

Figure 12-16:
Blend modes behave differently when used in layers than they do when you use a tool in the same mode. Both these strokes were done using Dissolve mode in pure black at 100-percent opacity. The difference is that the top stroke is painted with the Brush tool in Dissolve mode while the bottom one is a brush stroke in normal mode on a Dissolve layer.

NOTE If you'd like to learn more about how each mode works, there are a lot of useful tutorials on the Web. A good place to start is *http://www.photoshopgurus.com/tutorials/t010.html*. (Ignore the section "Additional blend mode information"—that's only for Photoshop.)

POWER USERS' CLINIC

Blend Modes Instead of Dodge and Burn

You can do a lot in Elements without ever getting down and dirty with blend modes, but there are a lot of things you can do more effectively and easily if you take the time to familiarize yourself with them. For instance, you may prefer the effect you get using a layer in Overlay mode to that of the Dodge and Burn tools.

To adjust a photo using an Overlay blend mode layer instead of the Dodge and Burn tools, you first make basic adjustments like Levels or Shadows/Highlights. Then, when you're ready to fine-tune your photo by painting over the details you want to enhance, here's what you do:

1. **Create a new layer**.

   Go to Layer → New → Layer or press ⌘+Shift+N.

2. **Before you dismiss the New Layer dialog box, choose the Overlay blend mode for your new layer**.

   Select Overlay in the Layer mode menu and turn on the box that says "Fill with Overlay-neutral color (50% gray)." You won't see anything happen yet.

3. **Set the foreground and background colors to their original settings**.

   Press D to set the colors in the Foreground/Background squares to black and white.

4. **Activate the Brush tool**.

   Choose a brush (set to Normal mode) and set the opacity very low, maybe 17 percent or even less. You'll need to experiment a bit to see how low a setting is low enough.

5. **Paint on the areas you want to adjust**.

   Paint with white to bring up the detail in dark areas and with black to darken overly light areas. (Remember that you can switch from one to the other by pressing X.) The detail on your photo comes up just like magic.

Figure 12-17 shows the results of using Overlay mode on the image from Figure 12-13 so that you can compare the different results. This method has the added advantage of being adjustable by changing the opacity of the Overlay layer. You can also carry this technique to extremes for very interesting results, when you want an artistic rather than a realistic result.

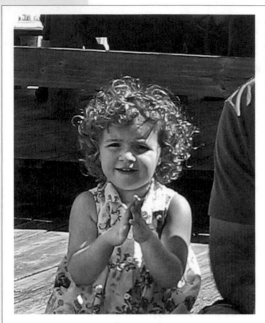

Figure 12-17:
Here's the little girl from Figure 12-13 again, this time after using Overlay blending, as described in the box on page 331. Unlike the results from the actual Dodge and Burn tools, this time the color isn't grayish—as dodging made it—but the contrast where shadowed areas meet bright ones still needs some work.

The Smudge Tool

The Smudge tool does just what its name says. You can use it to smear the colors in your image, just as if you had rubbed them with your finger. You can even "finger paint" with the Smudge tool, if you feel the call of your inner fifth grader. Adobe describes the effect of the Smudge tool as being "like a finger dragged through wet paint." It's sort of like a cousin to the Liquify filter (page 395), but without so many options.

If you're interested in turning your photos into paintings (Figure 12-18), the humble Smudge tool is your most valuable resource. For artistic smudging, you need a graphics tablet so you can vary the stroke pressure. You can use the Smudge tool without a tablet, but you won't get nearly as good an effect. If you'd like to learn more about this kind of smudging, you'll find some excellent tutorials by going to the Retouching forum at *www.dpreview.com* (search for *smudging*). The forums at *www.retouchpro.com* are also a favorite hangout for expert smudgers.

A warning—if you have a slow computer, there's quite a bit of lag time between when you apply the Smudge tool and when the effect actually shows up. This delay makes the tool tricky to control, because you need to resist the temptation to keep going over the area until you see results.

You'll find the Smudge tool hidden under the Blur tool in the Toolbox. Click the Blur tool or press R and, from the pop-out menu, choose the Smudge tool (its icon is a finger that looks like it's painting).

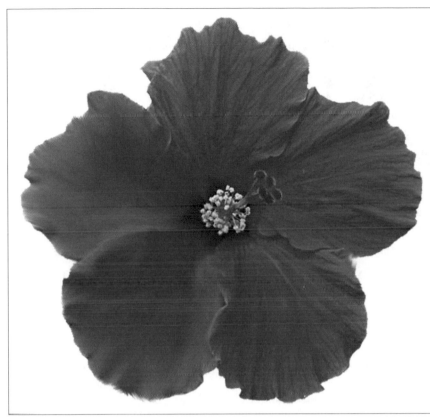

Figure 12-18:
With the help of a graphics tablet, you can join the ranks of the many skilled smudgers who create amazing effects using only this tool. The two petals on the left side of this hibiscus blossom show preliminary smudging results. The brushes you use determine whether the effect is smooth, as you see here, or more heavily stroked. When you want to blend in other colors, use the Finger Painting option. In effect, the Smudge tool lets you turn your photo into a painting.

The Smudge tool offers mostly the same settings as a regular brush, but it also includes the (sample) All Layers option (page 247), like you have for the Healing brush or the Clone Stamp. It also has two additional settings: Strength and Finger Painting.

- **Strength**. This setting means just what it says—it controls how hard the tool smudges the colors together. A higher number results in more blending.

- **Finger Painting**. Turning on this checkbox makes the Smudge tool smear the foreground color at the start of each stroke. When the box is turned off, the tool uses the color that's under the cursor at the start of each stroke. Figure 12-19 helps you understand the difference. This option is very useful for creating artistic smudges. If you want a bit of a contrasting color to help your strokes stand out more, choose a foreground color (page 198) and turn this on.

TIP   Use the Eyedropper (page 201) to sample other areas of your image to add Finger Painting colors that harmonize well with the area you're smudging.

Once you've chosen your settings, smudge away.

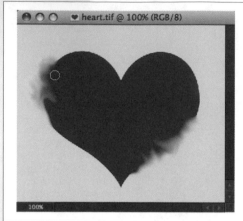

Figure 12-19:
The Smudge tool smears colors together. The stroke on the left was done with the Finger Painting checkbox turned on, which lets you introduce a bit of the foreground color (green, in this case) into the beginning of each stroke. This is very useful for shading or when you need to mix in just a touch of another color. The smudging on the right was done with Finger Painting off, so it uses only the colors that are already in your image.

NOTE When using the Smudge tool, you only see results where two colors come together. It blends together the pixel colors where edges meet. If you use Smudge in the middle of an area of solid color, nothing happens unless you've turned on Finger Painting.

The Eraser Tool

Everyone makes mistakes sometimes. Adobe has thoughtfully included three different mistake-fixers. If you click and hold the Eraser icon in the Toolbox, you'll see the Eraser, the Magic Eraser, and the Background Eraser. You'll probably use all three Erasers at one time or another. You can also activate the Eraser by pressing E.

Using the Eraser

The Eraser is basically just another kind of brush tool, only instead of adding color to your image, it removes color from the pixels. How it works varies a little, depending on where you use it.

If you use the Eraser on a regular layer, it replaces the color with transparency. On a Background layer, or one in which transparency is locked, it replaces whatever color is there with the background color (see Chapter 6 for more about how layers work).

The settings for the Eraser are pretty much the same as for any other brush—including brush style, size, and opacity—but with the Eraser a couple of them work differently:

- **Mode.** For the Eraser, Mode doesn't have anything to do with blend modes (page 329), but rather tells Elements the shape of the eraser you want to work with. Your choices are Brush, Pencil, and Block.

    You can see the difference in how the Eraser is going to work by watching the brush style preview in the Options bar as you change Modes. Picking the Brush or Pencil lets you use the Eraser as you would those tools—in other words, by choosing a brush, you can choose any brush you like. The Brush option lets you make soft-edged erasures, while Pencil mode makes only hard-edged erasures. Choosing Block changes the cursor to a square, so that you can use it just the way you would a regular artist's erasing block—sort of.

- **Opacity** determines how much of the color is removed—at 100 percent, it's all gone (or all replaced with the background).

To use the Eraser:

1. **Activate the Eraser.**

   Click the Eraser tool in the Toolbox or press E. The tool looks like an eraser, so it's easy to find.

2. **Choose your settings.**

   Choose the eraser's size, mode, and opacity. As noted earlier, the mode and opacity settings work differently here than they do for regular brushes.

3. **Drag anywhere in your image to remove what you don't want.**

   You may need to change the size of the Eraser a few times. It's usually easiest to use a small eraser (or the Background Eraser, which is explained later) to accurately clear around the edges of the object you want to keep, as shown in Figure 12-20. Then you can use a larger eraser brush size to get rid of the remaining chunks, once you don't have to worry about accidentally going into the area you want to keep.

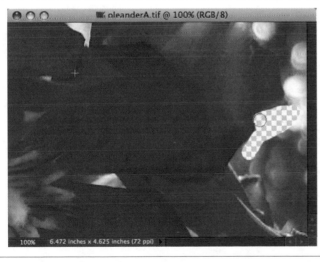

Figure 12-20:
Accurate erasing around an object usually means zooming way, way in so that you can control which pixels the Eraser is changing.

TIP   You can use a selection (see Chapter 5) to limit where the Eraser operates.

It's tedious to erase around a long outline or to remove entire backgrounds, so Elements has two other kinds of Erasers for those situations.

The Magic Eraser

Once you try it, you're likely to wonder why the heck Adobe gave this pedestrian tool such an intriguing name. What's so magic about the Magic Eraser?

Well, not much, really. It's called "magic" because it works very much like the Magic Wand tool (page 122). Use it to select pixels of a single color or range (depending on the tolerance settings). It even has the same little sparklies as the Magic Wand does in its icon to remind you of the relationship.

The problem, as Figure 12-21 shows you, is that the Magic Eraser isn't as clean in its work as the other erasers. Still, it can be a big help in eliminating large chunks of solid color. Moreover, if you're lucky, you may be able to clean the edges right up with Refine Edge (you'll need to make a selection to use it) or the Defringe command (Enhance → Adjust Color → Defringe Layer). There's more about Refine Edge on page 119 and about Defringing on page 135.

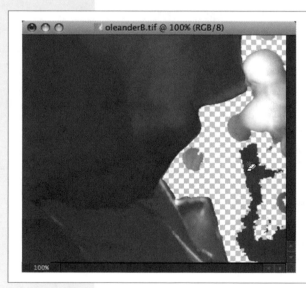

Figure 12-21:
This figure gives you a close-up look at the Magic Eraser at work on the flower petals from Figure 12-20. One click of the Magic Eraser got rid of a bunch of the background, and setting the Tolerance higher would've gotten even more. But if you look closely, you can see the disadvantage of the Magic Eraser: The edges of the flowers are fringed with dark ragged areas it didn't eliminate. The following fixes aren't always 100 percent successful but you may be able to clean up the edges with Enhance → Adjust Color → Defringe Layer (page 516), or the new Refine Edge command (page 119).

It's usually best to use the Magic Eraser in combination with at least one of the other erasers if you're looking to achieve really clean results. One sometimes useful side effect of the Magic Eraser is that if you click your photo with the Magic Eraser, it automatically transforms your Background layer into a regular layer, just the way the Background Eraser does.

The Background Eraser

Lots of people think this eraser deserves the name "Magic" much more than the Magic Eraser does. The Background Eraser is a tremendous help when you want to remove all the background around an object. For example, say you've got a photo of a football and you want to quickly remove the ball from the background.

The Background Eraser erases all the pixels under the brush (but outside the edges of the object) and renders the area it's used on transparent, even if it's a Background layer. (If you click with it on a Background layer, your computer may hesitate initially because it's busy transforming your Background to a regular layer.)

Here's how to use it:

1. **Select the Background Eraser.**

   Press E or, in the Toolbox, click the Eraser icon, then choose the Background Eraser from the pop-out menu. It's the eraser with a pair of scissors next to it.

2. **In the Options bar, choose a brush size.**

   The cursor turns to a circle with crosshairs in it. These crosshairs are important: They're the Background Eraser's "hot spot." Any color that you drag them over is turned to transparency. The circle size changes depending on how large a brush you've chosen, but the crosshairs stay the same size. As you can see in Figure 12-22, with a large brush, there may be a lot of space around the crosshairs, so it's easy to remove big chunks of the background at once, since everything in the circle is going to get eliminated.

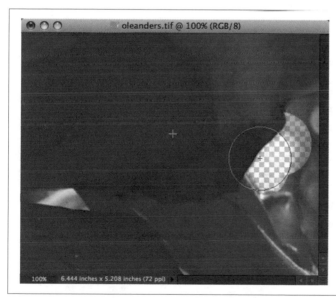

Figure 12-22:
The Background Eraser does a very careful job of separating the flowers from their background. Just be sure to keep the little crosshairs outside the color you want to keep. Here, because the crosshairs are outside the petals, only the background is getting removed. But if you moved the crosshairs into the flower, you'd be biting chunks out of it with the tool.

   If you start seeing *all* your brushes (not just the Background Eraser) as crosshairs, take a look at the box on page 318 to see how to get back to your regular cursor.

3. **Drag in your photo.**

   Move around the edge of the object you want to keep, being very careful not to let the crosshairs move into the object, or else you'll start erasing that, too. If you make a mistake, just use ⌘+Z to undo your actions.

The Background Eraser has three Options bar settings to help you refine how it works:

- **Brush**. If you want a different brush style, choose it from the pull-down menu.

- **Limits**. Do you want the Background Eraser to remove only contiguous color, or all patches of a certain color? This works exactly like the Contiguous setting for the Magic Wand (page 122).

- **Tolerance**. This tells the Background Eraser how similar colors must be for it to remove them, again like the Magic Wand setting (page 122).

However, you may never need to change any of these settings to get the results you want.

If you want to remove the background from around an object, you may find it most effective to start with the Background Eraser around the edge of your object. Then, use the other Erasers to clean up afterward. The advantage of working this way is that you don't have to clean up junk left over from the Magic Eraser. It's also easier to maneuver the Background Eraser than the regular Eraser, especially if you don't have a graphics tablet.

Drawing with Shapes

Wow, so many brush options and Adobe still isn't done—there's yet another way to draw things in Elements. The program includes a Shape tool (actually a group of tools that share one slot in the Toolbox), which lets you draw geometrically perfect shapes, regardless of your artistic ability. And not just simple shapes like circles and rectangles. You can draw animals, plants, starbursts, picture frames—all sorts of things, as shown in Figure 12-23. This tool should appeal to anyone whose grade school masterpieces always seemed to get put up on the wall behind the piano somewhere.

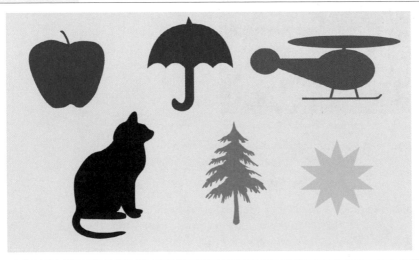

Figure 12-23:
Here are just a few of the shapes that you can draw with Elements, even if you flunked art class in elementary school. These objects look much more impressive once you gussy them up with Layer styles (page 366).

Turning yourself into an artist by using Elements' Shape tool is easy. Just follow these steps:

1. **Open an image or create a new one.**

    You can add shapes to any file that you can open in Elements.

2. **Activate the Shape tool.**

    Click the Shape tool in the Toolbox, or press U. The Shape tool is sometimes a little confusing to newcomers to Elements, because the icon reflects the shape that's currently active—so you may see a rectangle, a polygon, or a line, for instance. (You see a blue heart shape—the Custom Shape tool's icon—before you've used this tool for the first time.)

3. **Select the kind of shape you want to draw.**

    Use the Toolbox menu to choose a rectangle, a rounded rectangle, an ellipse, a polygon, a line, or a custom shape. (If you choose the custom shape, you have many different shapes to choose from. Click the Shape pull-down menu in the Options bar to choose the one you want.) All the shapes, and their accompanying options, are described in the following sections.

4. **Adjust your settings in the Options bar.**

    Choose a color by clicking the color square in the Options bar or use the foreground color (page 198). If you click the Options bar color square, you see the Color Picker (page 199). If you click the arrow to the right of the square, you get the Color Swatches palette instead (page 202).

    If you have special requirements, like a rectangle that's exactly 1"×2", click the downward-facing arrow just to the right of the shape thumbnails for the Shape Options palette and enter the size of your shape.

    There's also an Options bar setting that lets you apply a layer style (see page 366) as you draw your shape. Just click the downward-facing arrow on the right side of the Style box and choose the style you want from the pop-out palette. To go back to drawing without a style, choose the rectangle with the diagonal red line through it.

5. **Drag in your image to draw the shape.**

    Notice that *how* you drag the cursor affects the final appearance of the shape. For example, the way you drag determines the proportions of your figure. If you're drawing a fish, you can drag so that it's long and skinny or short and fat. Even with practice, it may take a couple of tries to get exactly the proportions you want.

    TIP   If you're trying to create exact copies of a particular shape, use the Shape Selection tool, described later, to create duplicates of the first shape.

The Shape tool automatically puts each shape on its own layer. If you don't want to do that, or you need to control how shapes interact, you can use the squares in the middle of the Options bar. They're the same as the ones for managing selections (page 115). Use them to add more than one shape to a layer, subtract a shape from a shape, keep only the area where shapes intersect, or exclude the areas where they intersect.

> **TIP** If you want to draw multiple shapes on one layer, click the "Add to Shape" squares in the Options bar. Then, everything you do is on the same layer. Shapes don't have to touch or overlap to use this option.

You can also turn any shape from a vector image (infinitely resizable) into a raster image (drawn pixel by pixel) by clicking the Simplify button in the Options bar. The box on page 341 tells you everything you need to know about the difference between vector and raster images.

You can also add custom shapes by choosing them in the Content palette. Just double-click the one you want, or click its palette thumbnail and then click Apply.

The following sections describe all of the main shape categories and their special settings.

Rectangle and Rounded Rectangle

The Rectangle and Rounded Rectangle tools work pretty much the same way and are very popular for creating Web page buttons. They both have Shape Options settings in the Options bar pull-down menu for:

- **Unconstrained.** Choose Unconstrained to draw a rectangle of whatever dimensions you want. How you drag determines the proportions of your shape.

- **Square.** To draw a square instead of a rectangle, click this radio button before you start, or just hold down the Shift key as you drag.

- **Fixed Size.** This setting makes Elements draw your shape the size you specify. Just enter the dimensions you want in inches, pixels, or centimeters.

- **Proportional.** Use this setting if you know the proportions you want your rectangle to have, but not the exact size. Just type in the proportions. So if you enter a length of 2 and a height of 1, no matter where you drag, the shape is always twice as long as it is high.

- **From Center.** This setting lets you draw your shape from its center instead of from a corner. It's useful when you know exactly where you want the shape but aren't sure exactly how big it needs to be.

- **Snap to Pixels.** This setting makes sure that the edge of your rectangle falls exactly on the edge of a pixel. You'll get crisper-looking edges with Snap to Pixels turned on. It's available only for the Rectangle and Rounded Rectangle tools.

Rasterizing Vector Shapes

Back in Chapter 3, you read about how the majority of your images (definitely your photos) are just a bunch of pixels to Elements. These images are known as *raster* images. The shapes you draw with the Shape tools work a little differently. They're called *vector* images.

A vector image is made up of a set of directions, specifying what kind of geometric shapes should be drawn. The advantage of vector images is that you can size them way up or down without producing the kind of pixelation you see when you resize a raster image too much.

Your shape keeps its vector characteristics until you *simplify* the layer that it's on. Simplifying, also called *rasterizing*, just means that Elements turns your shape into regular pixels. Once you simplify, you have the same limitations on resizing as you do for a regular photo. For example, you can make your image smaller, but you can't make it larger than 100 percent without losing quality. Sooner or later, you may want to transform your vector image to a regular raster image so that you can do certain things to it, like adding filters or effects.

If you try to do something that requires simplifying a layer, Elements generally asks you to do so, via a pop up dialog box. To rasterize your shape, just click OK, or click the Simplify button in the Options bar. Remember that once you've rasterized a shape, if you try to resize, you won't get the nice, clean unpixelated results that you got when it was a vector image. If you need to resize a shape, it's easiest to start over with a new shape—if that's feasible (which is yet another good reason to use layers).

Also, it may puzzle you that, where at one time you were able to change the color of an existing shape by clicking the color box, now all of a sudden the shape totally ignores what you do in the Options bar. That's because you simplified the shape layer. Simplifying always affects the entire layer—everything on it is simplified, or nothing is. Once your shape is simplified, you have to make a selection and change the color the way you would on any detail in a photo.

The Content palette brings yet another wrinkle to the raster/vector situation—Smart Shapes. The items in the Content palette (the frames, backgrounds, and other doodads) act as vector objects, except that they may seek out a particular place in the layer stack. (See page 411 for more on Smart Shapes.)

Most of the Shape tools have similar options. The Rounded Rectangle has one Options bar setting of its own, though: *Radius*, which is the amount (in pixels) that the corners are rounded off. A higher number means more rounding.

TIP   Looking to add a simple, empty rectangle, square, circle, or ellipse? See the box on page 345.

Ellipse

The Ellipse tool has the same Shape Options as the Rectangle tool. The only difference is that you can opt for a circle instead of a square. The Shift key constrains the Ellipse to a circle.

Polygon

You can draw many kinds of regular polygons using this tool. You set the number of sides yourself in the Options bar.

The shape options in the Options bar pull-down menu are a bit different for this tool:

- **Radius.** This setting sets the distance from the center to the outermost points.

- **Smooth Corners.** If you don't want sharp edges at the corners, choose Smooth Corners. (Actually, you're likely to get something more like a circle than a polygon if you turn this on—it's pretty buggy.)

- **Star.** This setting inverts the angles to create a star-like shape, as shown in Figure 12-24.

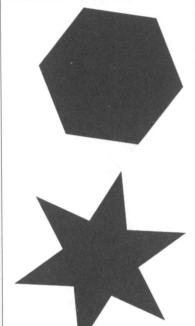

Figure 12-24:
Top: A hexagon drawn with the Shape tool.

Bottom: Turning on the Star option inverts the angles on a polygon, so that instead of drawing a hexagon, you create a star.

- **Indent Sides by.** If you're drawing a star, this sets how much (in a percentage) you want the sides to indent.

- **Smooth Indents.** Use Smooth Indents if you don't want sharp angles on your star.

Line Tool

Use this tool for drawing straight lines and arrows. Specify the weight (the width) of the line in pixels in the Options bar. If you want an arrowhead on your line, the Shape options give you some settings for adding one to your line as you draw:

- **Start/End.** Do you want the arrowhead at the start or the end of the line you draw? Tell Elements your preference with this setting.

• **Width and Length.** This setting determines how wide and how long you want the arrowhead to be. The measurement unit is the percentage of the line width, so if you enter a number lower than 100, your arrowhead is narrower than the line it's attached to. You can pick values between 10 and 5,000 percent. If your length setting is too low, you get a shape that looks more like a T than an arrow.

• **Concavity.** Use this setting if you want the sides of the arrowhead indented. The number determines the amount of curvature on the widest part of the arrowhead. See Figure 12-25. Pick a setting between –50 percent and +50 percent.

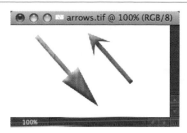

Figure 12-25:
Two arrows drawn with the Line tool. Both arrows have Layer styles applied to them so they don't look so flat. You can read more about how to do that in the next chapter.

Left: An arrow with no concavity.

Right: An arrow with concavity set to +50 percent.

TIP If you prefer fancier arrows, you'll find some in the Custom Shape tool.

The Custom Shape Tool

The Custom Shape lets you draw a huge variety of different objects, as you can see in Figure 12-26. Its icon is the little blue heart in the Toolbox. Click it or press U to activate the Custom Shape tool, and then choose the Custom Shape tool from the pull-down menu.

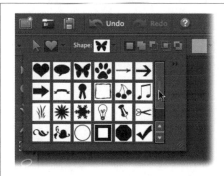

Figure 12-26:
Here's just a small part of the shape library you can choose from in the Shape Picker. To add more custom shapes to your repertoire, you can download and add them to Applications → Adobe Photoshop Elements 6 → Presets → Custom Shapes. Look for the file extension .csh when you want shapes that you can add to your library. Downloaded shapes that you add show up as drawing options when you click the More button on the Shapes palette. See page 464 for more about adding shapes to Elements.

Once the Custom Shape tool is active, if you look in the Options bar, you see a little window labeled Shape with the arrow for a pull-down menu next to it. Click this arrow to bring up the Elements Shape Picker.

Various shapes automatically come up, but if you click the More button at the upper-right corner of the window, you get a menu giving you lots more choices. To scroll through all of them, just choose All Elements Shapes.

> **TIP** There's a copyright symbol available in the custom shapes if you prefer not to use text to create one.

The Custom shape also has a few optional settings, like the other Shape tools. They are:

- **Unconstrained.** Control the proportions of your shape by the way you drag.

- **Defined Proportions.** The shape always has the proportions that the designer who created the shape gave it.

- **Defined Size.** The shape is always the size it was originally created to be—dragging won't make it bigger or smaller. It just plinks out at a fixed size that you can't control, except by resizing after the fact.

- **Fixed Size.** Enter the dimensions you want in inches, pixels, or centimeters.

- **From Center.** Start drawing in the center of the object.

The Shape Selection Tool

The arrow in the Options bar just to the left of the any Shape tool's icon is the Shape Selection tool. This is a special kind of Move tool (page 138) that works only on shapes that haven't been simplified yet, as explained in Figure 12-27. (You can also activate the Shape Selection tool from the Toolbox pop-out menu.)

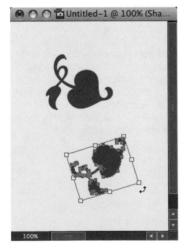

Figure 12-27:
The Shape Selection tool gives you the same kind of bounding box as the Move tool, and it works the same way, but only on shapes that haven't been simplified yet. You can also apply transformations like skewing and rotating (page 305) when the Shape Selection tool is active. Once you've simplified a shape layer, you need the regular Move tool to move it around. You can always use the Move tool, even on shapes that haven't been simplified, where you could use the Shape Selection tool instead.

It may seem unnecessary, but if you're working with shapes, it saves a lot of time not to have to keep switching tools when you want to move one shape.

Click the Shape Selection tool and then move your shape. Your shape doesn't have to be on the active layer. You can also use the Shape Selection tool to combine multiple shapes into one by clicking the Combine button. You also have the other options that you have when using any of the shape tools: add, subtract, intersect, and exclude.

The Shape Selection tool works just like the Move tool. You can drag to move, hold down Option to copy (instead of moving) the original shape, drag the handles to resize the shape, and so on. Unfortunately, you can't align and distribute shapes with this tool the way you can with the Move tool (see page 138). If you need to line things up, use the regular Move tool instead.

WORKAROUND WORKSHOP

Drawing Outlines and Borders

If you've played around at all with the Shape tool, you may have noticed that you can't draw shapes that are just outlines (that is, that aren't filled with color). No matter what you do, your shape is always a solid shape (except for the frame shapes).

Even if you haven't ever touched the Shape tool, you may be wondering how the heck to get a simple plain colored border around a photo.

The easiest way to create an outline is to make a selection using the Marquee tool or other selection tools and then select Edit → Stroke (Outline) Selection. The Stroke dialog box pops up and lets you enter the width of the line in pixels and choose a color.

You'll also see choices for Location, which tell Elements where you want the line—around the inside edge of the selection, centered on the edge of the selection, or around the outside. If you're bordering an entire photo, don't choose Outside, or the border won't show because it's off the edge of your image.

You can choose a blend mode (page 329) if you like and set the opacity. Using a mode can give you a more subtle edge than a normal stroke does. The Preserve Transparency setting just ensures that any transparent areas in your layer stay transparent. When you're finished adjusting the settings in the Stroke dialog box, click OK, turn off your Marquee, and you've got yourself an outlined shape.

Also check out some of the simpler frame designs in the Content palette (page 413). They let you apply a simple border with just a double-click.

The Cookie Cutter

At first glance, you may think the Cookie Cutter is a pretty silly tool. Actually, it's a very handy tool that you may use all the time, once you understand it. The Cookie Cutter creates the same shapes as the Custom Shape tool, but you use it on a photo to crop it to the shape you chose. Want a heart-shaped portrait of your sweetie? The Cookie Cutter is your tool. If you're a scrapbooker, with a couple of clicks you can get results that would have taken ages and a bunch of special scissors to create with paper.

If you're not into that sort of thing, don't go away, because hidden away in the shapes library are some of the most sophisticated artistic crop shapes you can find.

You can use them to get the kinds of effects that people pay commercial artists big bucks to create—like creating abstract crops that give a jagged or worn edge to your photo (a look that's great for contemporary effects).

You can also combine the result with a stroked edge, as explained in the box above, and maybe even a Layer style (page 366). Even without any additional frills, your photo's shape will appear more interesting, as shown in Figure 12-28.

> **TIP** The Frames section of the Content palette also includes a bunch of crops, ranging from simple shapes like stars to elaborate edges that make your photo look like a half-completed jigsaw puzzle.

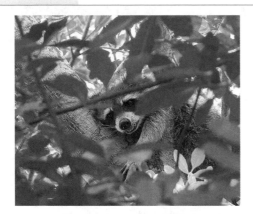

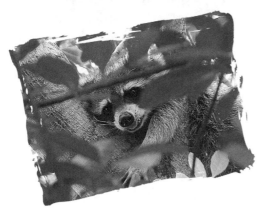

Figure 12-28:
A quick drag with the Cookie Cutter is all it took to create the bottom graphic from the top photo. If you want to create custom album or scrapbook pages, you can rotate or skew your crops before you commit them. See page 305 for how to rotate and skew your images.

You use the Cookie Cutter just like the Custom Shape tool, but you use it to cut a shape from a photo, instead of drawing a shape:

1. **Activate the Cookie Cutter tool.**

   Click the Cookie Cutter in the Toolbox (the icon looks like a star), or press Q.

2. **Select the shape you want your photo to be.**

Choose a shape from the Shapes palette by clicking the down arrow next to the shape display in the Options bar. You have access to all the Custom Shapes, but pay special attention to the Crop Shapes category. Click the More button on the Shape Picker to see all the shape categories it contains, or choose All Elements Shapes.

3. **Adjust your settings, if necessary.**

You have the same Shape Options described earlier for the Custom Shape tool (page 343), so you can set a fixed size or constrain proportions if you want. Click the Shape Options button to see your choices.

You can choose to feather the edge of your shape, too. Just enter the amount in pixels. (See page 125 for more about feathering.) The other option, Crop, crops the edges of your photo so they're just large enough to contain the shape.

4. **Drag in your photo.**

A mask appears over your photo and you see only the area that will still be there once you crop, surrounded by transparency.

5. **Adjust your crop if necessary.**

You can reposition the shape mask or drag the corners to resize it. Although the cropped areas disappear, they'll reappear as you reposition the mask if you move it so that they're included again.

Once you've created the shape, you'll see the Transform options (page 307) in the Options bar (which means that you can skew or distort it if you want) until you commit your shape, as explained in the next step. You can drag the mask around to reposition it if you'd like, or Shift+drag a corner to resize it without altering the proportions. It may take a little maneuvering to get exactly the parts of your photo that you want inside the crop.

6. **When you've gotten everything lined up the way you want, click the Commit button in the image window or just press Return.**

If you don't like the results, click the Cancel button in the window, or press Escape (Esc). Once you've made your crop, you can use ⌘+Z if you want to undo it to try something else.

TIP   The Cookie Cutter replaces the areas it removes with transparency. If the transparency checkerboard makes it too hard for you to get a clear look at what you've done, temporarily create a new white or colored Fill layer (page 169) beneath the cropped layer. You can delete it once you're sure you're happy with your crop.

Filters, Effects, Layer Styles, and Gradients

There's a popular saying among artistic types who use software in their studios: *Tools don't equal talent.* And it's true: No mere program is going to turn a klutz into a Klimt. But Elements has a few special tools—*filters*, *effects*, and *Layer styles*—that can sure help you fool a lot of people into thinking you're a better artist than you actually are. It's amazing what a difference you can make to the appearance of any image with only a couple of clicks.

Filters are a jaw-droppingly easy way to change the appearance of your image. You can use certain filters for enhancing and correcting your image, but Elements also gives you a bunch of other filters that are great for unleashing all your artistic impulses, as shown in Figure 13-1. You'll find the original photos (courthouse.jpg and paulownia.jpg) on the "Missing CD" page at *www.missingmanuals.com*, if you want to play around with these images yourself.

Most filters have settings that you can adjust to control how the filter changes your photo. Because you get more than a hundred different filters with Elements, there isn't room in this chapter to cover each filter individually, but you'll learn the basics of applying filters, and you'll get in-depth coverage of some of the filters you're most likely to use frequently.

Effects are like little macros or scripts, designed to make very elaborate changes to your image, like creating a three-dimensional frame around it or making it look like a pencil sketch or an oil pastel. They're very easy to apply—you just double-click a button—but tweaking their settings isn't as easy to do as it is with filters, since effects are programmed to make very specific changes. (Adobe calls them Photo Effects, but you can apply them to any kind of image, not just a photo.)

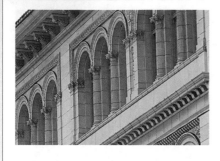
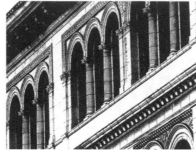
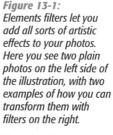
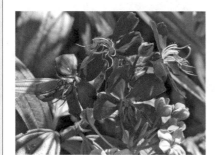
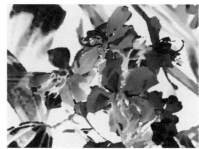

Figure 13-1:
Elements filters let you add all sorts of artistic effects to your photos. Here you see two plain photos on the left side of the illustration, with two examples of how you can transform them with filters on the right.

Top: These figures show how you can make a photo resemble a colored steel engraving.

Bottom: These figures show how you can create a watercolor look. For both images, several filters were applied to build up the effect.

Layer styles change the appearance of just one layer of your photo (see Chapter 6 for more about layers). They're very popular for creating impressive-looking text, but you also can apply them to objects and shapes. Most Layer styles include settings you can easily modify.

You can combine filters, effects, and Layer styles on the same image if you like. And you may spend hours trying different groupings, because it's addicting to watch the often-unpredictable results you get when you mix them up.

The last section of this chapter focuses on *gradients*. A gradient is a rainbow-like range of color that you can use to color in an object or a background. But that's not all gradients are good for. You can also use gradients and *Gradient Maps*—gradients that get distributed according to the brightness values in your photo—for very precise retouching effects.

Using Filters

Filters make it possible for you to change the look of your photos in very complex ways; using them is as easy as double-clicking a button. Elements gives you a huge number of filters, which are grouped in categories to help you choose the one that does what you need. This section offers a quick tour through the filter categories as well as some information about using a few of the most popular filters, like the Noise and Blur filters.

To make it easy to apply filters, Elements presents your filters in two different places: the Filter menu, where you choose them from the list that appears, and the Effects palette. (The menu is the only place where you can see every filter. Some filters, like the Adjustment filters, don't appear in the palette.) There's also a Filter Gallery, a great feature that makes it very easy to get a good idea of how your photo will look when you apply the artistic filters. The next part of this section explains how to use all three methods.

Applying Filters

In the Filter menu, you choose your filter by name from the list. In the Effects palette, thumbnail images give you a preview of what the filters do. The filters do exactly the same thing no matter which way you choose them.

The Filter Gallery gives you a good preview of what a filter looks like when applied to your image. Some filters automatically open the Filter Gallery when you choose them from the menu or the palette. Or you can call up the Gallery itself (without first choosing a filter) by going to Filter → Filter Gallery. Not every filter can be applied from the Gallery—only some of the filters with adjustable settings.

> **TIP** Elements makes it easy to apply the same filter repeatedly. Press the ⌘+F keyboard shortcut, and Elements automatically applies the last filter you used, with whatever settings you last used. The top listing in the Filter menu also shows the name of this same filter (selecting it works the same way as the keyboard shortcut: You get the same settings you just used). Press ⌘+Option+F to bring up the last filter you used, but with the dialog box open in case you want to change your settings.

Filter menu

The Filter menu groups filters into 14 main categories. Correct Camera Distortion (page 300) is all by itself at the top of the list. You'll also see a divider below the bottom category (called Other). When you first install Elements, the Digimarc filter is the only filter below this line, but other filters you download or purchase will appear here, too.

When you choose a filter from the list, one of three things happens:

- **Elements applies the filter automatically**. This happens if the filter's name in the list doesn't have an ellipsis (…) after it. Just look at the result in your photo and undo it (⌘+Z) if you don't like its effect. If you do like it, you don't have to do anything else. If you don't, you have no options for adjusting the settings on these filters.

- **You see a dialog box**. The Elements filters that have adjustable settings have an ellipsis (…) after their names. Some of them (mostly corrective filters) open a dialog box where you can tweak the settings. Set everything as you want it, watching the small preview in the dialog box to see what you're doing. Then click OK.

- **You see the Filter Gallery**. Some of the more artistic, adjustable filters automatically call up the Filter Gallery so that you can get a nice large preview of what you're doing and also so you can rearrange the order of multiple filters before applying them. Applying filters from the Gallery is explained later.

Regardless of how you've applied the filter, once you're done, you can always undo it (⌘+Z) if you're not happy with the effect. If you like it, there's no need to do anything else, except of course to eventually save your image.

> **TIP**   Since there's no way to undo filters after you've closed your image, many people apply filters to a duplicate layer. Press ⌘+J to create a duplicate layer.

Effects palette

If you're more comfortable with visual clues when choosing a filter, you can also find most filters in the Effects palette (Figure 13-2), which is, logically enough, also where you apply effects.

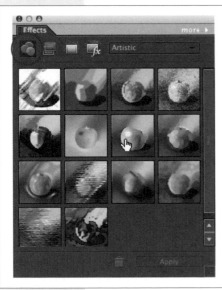

Figure 13-2:
The Effects palette gives you a preview of what every filter looks like when applied to the same picture of a green apple. Click the Filters button (circled), and then choose a category from the pull-down menu. If you know what you want a filter to do but don't know what name to look for, scrolling through these thumbnail images should help you find the one you want. To apply a filter from the palette, double-click the thumbnail, or click the thumbnail once and then click Apply. You can also drag the filter's thumbnail from the palette onto your image.

The Effects palette is one of the palettes in the Palette bin the first time you launch Elements. If it's not there waiting for you, go to Window → Effects, and then click the Filters button. Choose a Filter category from the pull-down menu or choose Show All. The categories are the same ones you see in the Filter menu, except that Adjustments is available only through the menu, and Sharpen appears in the palette but not the Filter menu.

To apply a filter from the palette, double-click its thumbnail, or drag the thumbnail onto your image. If the filter has adjustable settings, you see the same dialog box or Filter Gallery you'd see if you'd applied the filter from the Filter menu, as described earlier.

One small drawback to applying filters from the palette is that you can't tell from the thumbnail whether a filter is one that applies automatically, with no adjustable settings. There's no clue like the ellipsis (...) to tell you which group a filter falls into.

Filter Gallery

The Filter Gallery, shown in Figure 13-3, is one of Elements' more popular features. It gives you a large preview window, a look at all the little green apple thumbnails so you have a visual guide to what your filter will do, and most important it lets you apply filters like layers—you can stack them up and change the order in which they're applied to your image. Changing the order of filters can make some big differences in how they affect your image. For example, you get very different results if you apply Ink Outlines *after* the Sprayed Strokes filter than you do if you apply Ink Outlines first. The Gallery lets you play around and experiment to see which order gives you the exact look you want. The layer-like behavior of the filters in the gallery is only for previewing, though. They don't end up as real layers.

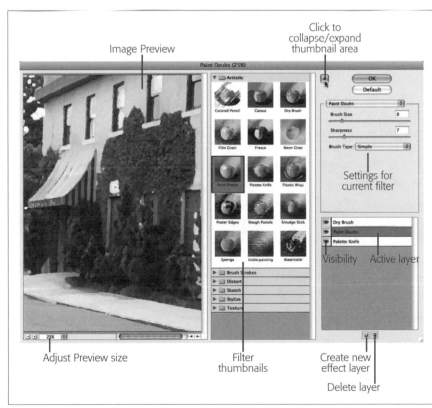

Click to
collapse/expand
thumbnail area

Image Preview

Adjust Preview size

Filter
thumbnails

Create new
effect layer

Delete layer

Settings for
current filter

Visibility   Active layer

Figure 13-3:
The Filter Gallery. If you want an even larger preview, you can click the arrow that the cursor is over in the figure to collapse the thumbnails and regain that entire section for preview space.

The Gallery is more for artistic filters than for corrective filters. You can't apply the Adjustment or Noise filters from the Gallery, for instance. All the Gallery filters are in the artistic, brushstroke, distort, sketch, stylize, and texture categories. (See the next section for an overview of all the filter categories.)

The Filter Gallery is divided into three panes. On the left side is a preview of what your image will look like when you apply the filter. The center holds the thumbnails for the different filters, and the right side contains the settings for the currently chosen filter. At the bottom of the settings pane are your filter layers. You can see what filters you've applied, and add or subtract layers and rearrange their order here.

> **NOTE** Filter layers work something like regular layers (see Chapter 6) with one important difference: Your filter layers are what you might call "working" layers. In other words, you only have separate filter layers until you click OK. Then all your chosen filters get applied to your image at once. You can't close your photo and come back later and still expect to see the filters as individual, changeable layers after you've actually applied the filters. And most important, your filters become part of the layer you apply them to. You aren't creating a new permanent layer when you use the Filter Gallery.
>
> If you've used the latest version of the full version Photoshop, be aware that Elements doesn't create editable smart filters the way Photoshop CS3 does—it handles filters the way the earlier versions of Photoshop did. This is good to keep in mind if you're trying to do something based on instructions written for Photoshop CS3 (instructions you've found online, say).

In addition to letting you adjust the settings for a given filter, the Filter Gallery lets you perform a few other tricks:

- **Adjust the preview magnification of your image.** In the lower-left corner of the Gallery, click directly on the percentage listing or click the arrow next to it for a list of preset sizes to choose from. You can also click the + and – buttons to zoom the view in or out. Easier still, use the ⌘+= (the ⌘ key plus the equal sign key) and ⌘+– (the ⌘ key plus the minus key) shortcuts to zoom in and out from the keyboard.

- **Choose a new filter.** Just click a filter's thumbnail once, and you get the settings for the new filter and the preview image updates right away—usually. (See the box on page 357.)

- **Add a new filter layer.** You can stack up filters in layers in the Filter Gallery the way you would layers in the Layers palette. Each time you click the New Filter Layer icon (see Figure 13-4), you add another filter layer to the ones you already have.

- **Change the position of filter layers.** Just drag them up and down in the stack like regular layers (page 159) to change the order in which they'll get applied to your image.

- **Hide filter layers.** Click the eye next to a filter layer in the filter layer palette to turn off visibility, just like in the regular Layers palette (page 154).

- **Delete filter layers.** Highlight any filter layer by clicking it, and then click the Trash icon to delete it.

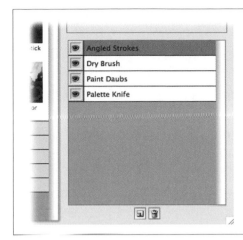

Figure 13-4:
If you've used layers before (see Chapter 6), these little icons should look familiar. In the Filter Gallery, they make new filter layers instead of regular layers. Click the square icon (shown at the bottom of this figure) to add a new filter layer to your image. Click the trashcan icon to delete a filter layer. The eye icons next to your filter layers turn visibility on and off just as they do in the Layers palette. It's true that the filters preview in layers, but they don't show up as real layers in the Layers palette— only in the Filter Gallery.

- **Change the content of a layer.** You can change what kind of filter is in a particular layer. For instance, if you applied, say, the Smudge Stick, and you like all your other changes but wish you had used the Glass filter instead, you don't have to delete the Smudge Stick layer. Instead, just highlight the Smudge layer and click the Glass filter button to change the layer's contents.

TIP ⌘+F reapplies all the filters that were in your last gallery set if you press it again after using the Filter Gallery. ⌘+Option+F brings up the dialog box for the last filter so you can change your settings before you apply it again.

Filter Categories

Elements divides the filters into categories to help make it easier for you to track down the filter you want. Some of the categories, like Distort, contain filters that vary hugely in what they do to your photo. Other categories, like the Brush Stroke filters, contain filters that are all pretty obviously related to one another. Here's a quick breakdown of the categories:

- **Correct Camera Distortion.** This filter lets you correct perspective distortion (think: tall buildings) as well as vignetting (shadows) caused by your camera's lens. It's explained in detail on page 300.

- **Adjustments.** These filters apply some photographic, stylistic, and artistic changes to your photo. Most of the adjustments are explained on page 267, but you can find more information on Photo Filters on page 231.

- **Artistic.** This is a huge group of filters that do everything from making your photo look like it was cut from paper (Cutout) to making it look like a quick sketch (Rough Pastels). You generally get the best effects with these filters by using multiple filters or applying the same one multiple times.

- **Blur.** The blur filters let you soften the focus of your photo and add artistic effects. They're explained later in this chapter.

- **Brush Strokes.** These filters apply brushstroke effects to your photo to give it a hand-painted look.

- **Distort.** These filters warp your image in a great variety of ways. The Liquify filter is the most powerful, and you'll find a tutorial for using it on page 395.

- **Noise.** Use these filters to add or remove grain from your image. They're explained later in this chapter.

- **Pixelate.** The Pixelate filters break your image up in different ways, making it show the dot pattern of a magazine or newspaper's printed image (Halftone), or the fragmented look you see on television when they're concealing someone's identity.

NOTE   The Color Halftone filter makes your photo look like a *halftone,* a one-color image whose dots simulate the shades of gray you see in a black-and-white photo. It's not the same as true halftone screening, which isn't available in Elements. If the print shop you're working with needs a halftone, you either need to use the full-featured Photoshop or ask the printer to do the conversion for you.

- **Render.** This group includes a pretty diverse bunch of filters that let you do things like create a lens flare effect (Lens Flare), transform a flat object so it looks three dimensional (3D Transform), and make an effect that looks like fibers (Fibers) or clouds (Clouds). The Lighting Effects filter, a powerful but confusing filter that's like a whole program in itself, helps you change the way lighting appears in your image. For a full rundown on what this filter does, as well as how to use it, check out the "Missing CD" page at *www.missingmanuals.com.*

- **Sharpen.** Unsharp Mask (page 205) appears in the palette but not the Filter menu. (The sharpening commands are in the Enhance menu.)

- **Sketch.** These filters can make your photo look like it was drawn with charcoal, chalk, crayon, or some other material—and they can also make the photo look like it was embossed in wet plaster, photocopied, or stamped with a rubber stamp.

- **Stylize.** These filters create special effects by increasing the contrast in your photo and displacing pixels. You can make your photo look radioactive, reduce it to outlines, or make it look like it's moving quickly.

- **Texture.** These filters change the surface of your photo to look like it was made from another material. Use them to create a crackled finish (the Craquelure filter), a stained glass look (Stained Glass), or a mosaic effect (Mosaic Tiles).

- **Video.** These filters are for use in creating and editing images for (and from) videos.

- **Other.** This is a group of fairly technical filters that you can highly customize. The High Pass filter is explained on page 210. You can use Offset to shift an image or a layer a little bit, or to position tiled image layers.

- **Digimarc.** Use this filter to check for Digimarc watermarks in photos. Digimarc is a company that lets subscribers enter their information in a database so that anyone who gets one of their photos can find out who the copyright holder is.

You can find a number of filter plug-ins online, ranging from free to very expensive. Page 459 gives you some suggestions for places to start looking. Once you've installed new filters, you access them at the bottom of the list in the Filter menu.

> **NOTE**　Filters are platform specific, so you can't use plug-ins written for Windows if you're using a Mac. Only Mac plug-ins work with the Mac version of Elements.

UNDER THE HOOD

Filter Performance Hints

If Elements could speak, it would say, "Easy for *you*," when it comes to filters and effects. Although you don't have to do much to apply them, Elements has a huge amount of work to do on its end. Elements 6 is pretty fast, but if your computer is slow or memory-challenged, it can take a long time to apply filters and even to update the preview. You can speed things up by applying filters to a selection for previewing. Filters that have their own dialog boxes (as opposed to the Filter Gallery) will show a flashing line under the size percentage below the preview area to indicate the progress they're making. A few other filter-related tips are worth remembering:

- Filters won't do anything if they don't have pixels to work on, so be sure you're targeting a layer with something in it and not an Adjustment layer.

- If you apply a filter to a selection, you'll usually want to feather (page 125) or refine (page 119) the edges a fair amount to help the filter edges blend into the rest of your photo.

- Option+click the Cancel button to turn it into a Reset button. Clicking Cancel makes the window go away, while Reset lets you start over without having to call up the filter again.

- If your filters are grayed out in the Filter menu, check to be sure you're not in 16-bit mode (page 228) or in grayscale, bitmapped, or index color (all these color modes are explained on page 48).

Useful Filter Solutions

This section shows you how to use some of Elements' most popular and useful filters to correct your photos and create a few special effects. You'll learn how to modify the graininess of your photos to create an aged effect or smooth out a repair job. And you'll also see how to blur your photos to create a soft-focus effect, or to make your subjects look like they're moving.

Removing noise: Getting rid of graininess

Noise, the appearance of undesired graininess in an image, is a big problem with many digital cameras, especially those with small sensors and high megapixel counts. It's rare to find a fixed-lens camera with more than 5 megapixels that doesn't have some trouble with noise, especially in underexposed areas. If you shoot using the RAW format, you can correct a fair amount of noise right in the

RAW Converter (page 226). But the RAW Converter may give unpredictable results if you use it on JPEGs. And even RAW files may need further noise reduction once you've edited your photo after converting it.

Elements includes the Reduce Noise filter, which is designed specifically to help you get rid of noise in your photos. To get to it, go to Filter → Noise → Reduce Noise. You get a dialog box with a preview window on the left side and settings adjustments on the right. To use the filter, first use the controls below the preview to set the view to at least 100 percent, or preferably even higher. It's important to be able to see the pixels in your photo so that you can see how the filter is changing them as you adjust the settings.

You get three settings, each of which you control by using a slider:

- **Strength**. This controls the overall impact of the filter. It reduces the same kind of noise as the Luminance Smoothing setting in the RAW converter (page 228). The stronger you set it, the greater the risk of softening your photo.

- **Preserve Details**. Using noise reduction can soften the appearance of your photo. This setting tells Elements how much care to take to preserve the details of your image.

- **Reduce Color Noise**. This control adjusts uneven distribution of color in your image. You can set the slider pretty high without a negative impact on your photo.

There's also a checkbox for minimizing JPEG artifacts, as explained in Figure 13-5.

For each setting, move the slider to the right if you want more and to the left if you want less, while watching the effect in the preview window. You may notice a little lag time before the preview updates. When you see what you want, click OK to apply the filter.

The Elements Reduce Noise filter does an okay job on areas with a small amount of noise, like the sky in many JPEG photos, but it's not one of the strongest tools in Elements. If your camera has major noise problems, you may find you still need third-party noise reduction software. Some of the most popular programs are Noise Ninja (*www.picturecode.com*), Neat Image (*www.neatimage.com*), and Noiseware (*www.imagenomic.com*). All have demo versions you can download to try out the programs. If you search on Google for "noise reduction software," you'll get a variety of other options as well.

Adding noise: Smoothing out repair jobs

Elements also gives you a filter for *creating* noise. Why do that when most of the time you try so hard to get rid of noise? One reason is when you're trying to age the appearance of your photo. If you want to make a photo look like it came from an old newspaper, for instance, you'd add some noise.

The other most common use for noise is to help make repaired spots blend in with the rest of an image. If you've altered part of a photo in Elements, especially by painting on it, odds are that the repaired area is going to look perfectly smooth. That's great if the

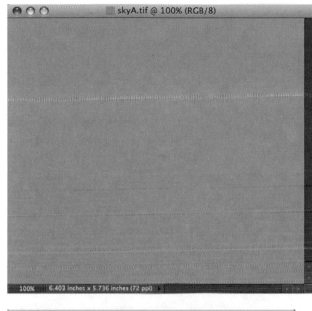

Figure 13-5:
Many JPEG photos have a problem with artifacts, uneven areas of color caused by JPEG compression (see page 59).

Top: Here's an extreme closeup of a JPEG photo. The mottled pattern you see in the pixels in the sky is typical of the kind of artifacts you sometimes get in JPEG photos.

Bottom: Turning on the checkbox in the Reduce Noise filter helps to smooth out the color.

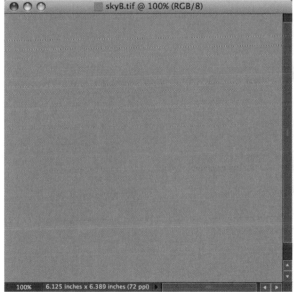

rest of the photo is noise free. But if the rest of the photo is a little grainy, that smooth patch is going to stand out like a sore thumb. Add a bit of noise to make it blend in better with the rest of the photo, as shown in Figure 13-6. Also, if you see color banding when you print, a little noise may help to fix that in your next print.

To add noise to a photo, start by selecting the area where you want to add the noise (unless you want to change your whole photo). Using a duplicate layer

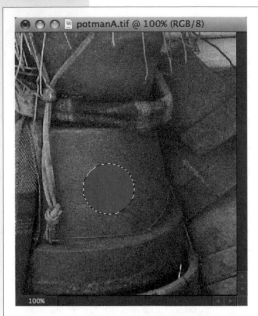

Figure 13-6:
Top: If you use the Average Blur filter in a repair on this noisy photo, the blended area stands out, making your repair obvious.

Bottom: If you add some noise, the changes you've made become much less noticeable.

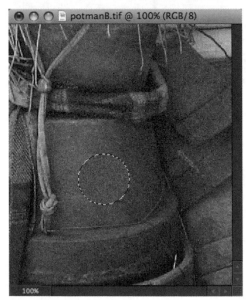

(⌘+J) for the noise is a safe step, since you can always undo your changes if you've got them on a layer.

1. **Call up the Add Noise filter.**

   Go to Filter → Noise → Add Noise to bring up the dialog box with the settings for the filter.

2. **Adjust the settings to your liking.**

   The settings are explained in the following list. Use the preview window in the dialog box to check how the changes are affecting your photo.

3. **When you're satisfied, click OK.**

You have three options in the Add Noise dialog box:

- **Amount.** This option controls how heavy the noise is going to be. Just drag the slider to the right for more noise or to the left for less. You can also type in a number. A higher percentage means more noise.

- **Uniform or Gaussian.** These buttons let you control how the noise gets distributed through your image. Uniform is just what it says—the same all over. Gaussian distributes the noise to produce a more speckled effect.

  If you're adding noise to duplicate existing noise in a grainy photo, you'll probably want a Gaussian distribution. For an old newspaper photo look, try Uniform. In either case, experiment until you get what you want.

- **Monochromatic.** This setting limits you to grayscale noise. Take a look at the middle image in Figure 13-7 and notice how many more colors you can see inside the noise, compared to the solid red of the original. The noise was applied with the Monochromatic setting turned off.

Figure 13-7:
Filters can really spruce up solid objects.

Top: An unfiltered solid red heart, drawn with the Shape tool (page 343).

Middle: Here's the same heart after adding some Uniform noise to it.

Bottom: Adding the Angled Strokes filter gives the heart a hand-painted look. If you didn't add noise before applying the filter, you wouldn't see any texture change from the top graphic when you applied the filter.

Noise can also help you when you want to apply special effects to blocks of solid color, as shown in Figure 13-7. If you try to apply the Angled Strokes filter to a solid color, you won't see the strokes. Adding noise gives the filter something to work on.

Gaussian Blur: Drawing attention to a foreground object

Probably the most frequently used of the Blur filters, the Gaussian Blur filter lets you control how much your image is blurred. Besides using it to blur large areas of your photo, like the background in the bottom photo in Figure 13-8, you can apply the Gaussian Blur filter at a very low setting to soften lines—very useful when you're trying to achieve a sketched effect. If you'd like to try out the different blurs, you'll find the hawk photo (hawk.jpg) on the "Missing CD" page at *www.missingmanuals.com*.

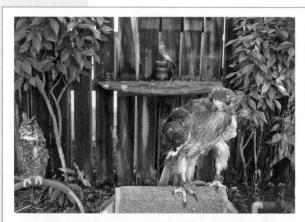

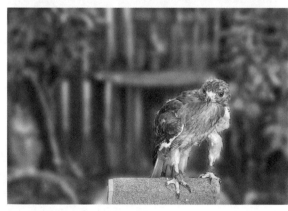

Figure 13-8:

Top: This photo could use some help from the Blur filters. The hawk is hard to distinguish from the rest of the photo; blurring helps center the focus on the hawk.

Bottom: With a Gaussian Blur filter applied to the background, the hawk becomes the clear focal point of the photo.

When you use the Gaussian Blur, you have to set the *radius*, which controls how much you want the filter to blur things. A higher radius produces more blurring; use the filter's preview window to see what you're doing.

Radial Blur: Producing a sense of motion

As you can see in Figure 13-9, the Radial Blur really produces a sense of motion. It has two available styles: Zoom, which is designed to give the effect of a camera zooming in, and Spin, which produces a circular effect around your designated center point.

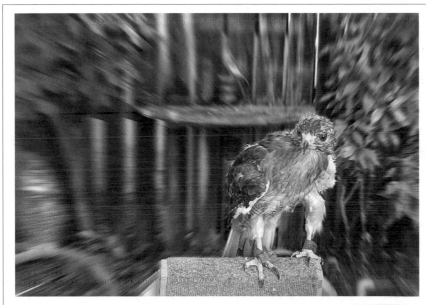

Figure 13-9:
A Radial Blur applied in Zoom mode. As you can see, this filter can produce an almost vertiginous sense of motion. If you don't want to give people motion sickness, go easy on the Amount setting.

The Radial Blur dialog box may look a bit complicated, but it's really not. Unfortunately, you don't get a preview with this filter, because it drains so much processor power. That's why you have a choice between Draft, Good, and Best Quality. Use Draft for a quick look at roughly what you'll get. Then, most of the time, choose Good for the final version. There's not much difference between Good and Best except on large images, so don't feel that you must choose Best for the final version all the time.

Once you've chosen your method (Zoom or Spin), set the amount, which controls the intensity of the blur that's applied. Next, click inside the Blur Center box to identify the point where you want the blur to center, as shown in Figure 13-10. Finally, click OK when you're finished.

Color correcting with the Average Blur filter

If you've already given the Average Blur filter a whirl you may be wondering what on earth Adobe was thinking when they created it. Use it on your entire photo, and your image disappears under a hideous soup, something like what you'd get by pureeing together all the colors in your photo. Oddly enough, this effect makes the filter a great tool for getting rid of color casts (see page 195). You can use the Average Blur to create a sort of custom Photo Filter (see page 231), toned specially

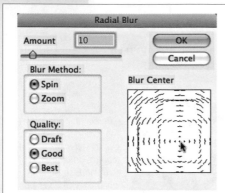

Figure 13-10:
The Blur Center box lets you identify the center point of the Radial Blur's effect (whether you've chosen Zoom or Spin mode). Drag the ripple drawing inside the box in any direction; here, the center point has been moved just to the right and down from its original position in the center of the box.

for the image you use it on. The secret is in using blend modes (page 157). Here's how:

1. **Open your image and make a duplicate layer.**

   Just press ⌘+J, or go to Layer → Duplicate Layer.

2. **Apply the Average Blur filter.**

   Make sure your duplicate layer is the active layer (click it in the Layers palette if it isn't), and then go to Filter → Blur → Average. Your photo disappears under a layer of (probably) very unpleasing solid color, but you'll fix that next.

3. **Change the blend mode of the blur layer.**

   In the Layers palette, choose Color from the Mode pull-down menu. Already things are starting to look better.

4. **Invert the blur layer.**

   Press ⌘+I to invert the colors.

5. **Reduce the opacity of the blur layer, and do other tweaking, if necessary.**

   Use the opacity slider in the Layers palette. Try 50 percent. By now, the color should look right—no more color cast. Tweak if necessary, and save your work.

   You may want to add a Hue/Saturation layer (see page 260) if you find that no matter how you adjust the opacity slider, the photo looks a little flat.

The Average Blur filter is a particularly good way to color-correct underwater photos, where it's very hard to get a realistic white balance using your camera's built-in settings.

Adding Effects

Like filters, effects give you loads of ways to really change the appearance of your photo—from adding green slime textures to surrounding your photos with classy picture frames. Although you apply effects with a simple double-click of your mouse, these clicks actually trigger a sequence of changes that Elements applies to your image. Some of the effects involve many complex steps, although Elements works so quickly you might not even notice all the changes taking place.

Adobe puts effects in two places: in the Effects palette, and in the Content palette. In Elements 6, you'll still find some basic photo effects in the Effects palette, but most of the frames and all of the Text Effects have moved over to the Content palette, which works a bit differently from the Effects palette. Page 413 explains how to use the Content palette, and there's more about Text Effects on page 394. This section is about working with the Photo Effects from the Effects palette.

> **NOTE** You usually can't customize or change an effect's settings. Effects are typically an all-or-nothing deal. For example, if you use one of the Frame effects, you either take the frame size as Elements applies it to your image, or you don't. No need to ask if you can adjust the scale of the frame relative to your photo—you can't. (This is why most of the frames are now Smart Objects [page 411] that you apply from the Content palette.)

You apply effects from the Effects palette (choose Window ▸ Effects, and then click the Photo Effects button). Photo Effects are subdivided into several different categories, but in Elements 6 they're mostly just for tinting your photos, as shown in Figure 13-11, although there are a couple of frames. But there are many more frame styles in the Frames section of the Content palette (see page 413).

Just as with filters, use the pull-down menu on the Effects palette to see all your choices, or pick from only one category. The thumbnail images give you a preview of what the effect will do to your image.

> **NOTE** Effects don't get their own menu the way filters do. The only way to apply them is from the Effects palette.

To apply an effect, double-click its thumbnail in the Effects palette, or click the thumbnail once and click Apply, or just drag the thumbnail onto your photo. That's all there is to it. If you don't like the result, press ⌘+Z to undo it, but there's not much you can tweak in the effects.

Here are a few other effects-related tips to help you get the most out of these nifty-but-quirky features:

- A few effects flatten (page 168) or simplify (page 341) your image. Therefore, it's usually best to make a copy of your image, or wait until you're done making all your other edits, before applying an effect.

- Many effects create additional layers; check the Layers palette once you're done applying them. You may want to flatten your image to reduce the file size before printing or storing it. (See Chapter 6 if you need a refresher on using layers.)

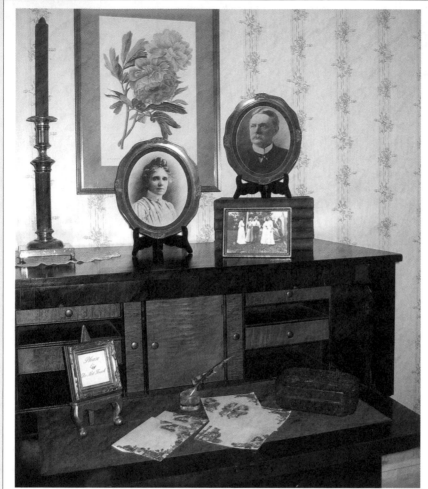

Figure 13-11:
The Effects palette's Photo Effects section lets you age a photo by applying an antique look to it, as shown in this color photo which has the Vintage Photo effect applied.

Adding Layer Styles

Like filters and effects, Layer styles let you transform objects by giving them new characteristics, like Drop Shadows, for instance. Layer styles are especially useful for modifying individual objects, like text and buttons, because you can edit the text and change the button's shape even *after* you've applied the Layer style.

Layer styles, as their name suggests, work on the contents of one layer—rather than on your whole image. That's important. A Layer style affects the *entire* contents of a layer. If you want to apply a Layer style to just one object in your picture, select the object and put it on a layer of its own (⌘+J or Layer → New → "Layer via Copy", or ⌘+Shft+J or New → "Layer via Cut"). Figure 13-12 shows what you can do with Layer styles.

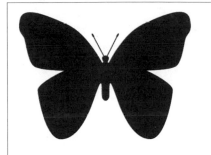 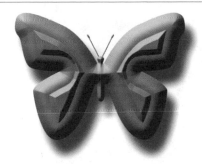

Figure 13-12:
Layer styles are great for making fancy buttons for Web sites. Changing this plain black Custom Shape was as simple as clicking the Sunset Sky Layer style (in Complex Styles), adding a bevel, and then making the bevel bigger. (Keep reading to learn how to edit Layer styles.)

You apply Layer styles from the Effects palette (Window → Effects). Click the Layer Styles button, and then—from the pull-down menu—choose a Layer style category, or choose Show All. Finally, select the layer you want to modify (by highlighting it in the Layers palette), and then click the Layer style you want to use. The box on page 369 shows you how to modify any style's settings.

> **TIP**   Some tools, like the Type tool (see page 383), have an Options bar that lets you choose a Layer style

Here's a quick rundown of the choices available in each Layer style category:

- **Bevels** give objects a 3-D look by making them appear raised from the page or embossed into it. Figure 13-13 shows an example of how combining a bevel and a drop shadow can add a lot of dimension to even a simple shape.

- **Complex** includes a variety of elaborate Layer styles that make an object look like it's made from metal, cactus, or several other materials. These styles are particularly useful for applying to type.

- **Drop Shadows** adds shadow effects that make your object look like it's floating above the page.

> **TIP**   Adding a drop shadow to an entire photo requires adding canvas (see page 89) to give the shadow someplace to fall.

- **Glass Buttons** are supposed to make objects look like glass buttons, but many people think they look more like plastic. They're useful for creating Web page buttons.

- **Image Effects** give you a wealth of ways to transform your photo, including fading it and making it look like the pieces of a puzzle or a tile mosaic.

- **Inner Glow** adds light around the inside edge of your object.

- **Inner Shadows** give your image a hollow or recessed effect by casting a shadow within the object, rather than outside it the way drop shadows do.

Figure 13-13:
Here's the heart image from earlier in this chapter. Adding a bevel and a drop shadow gives it much more dimension and depth.

- **Outer Glows** create the same kind of light effects that Inner Glows do, only they go around the outer edge of your image.

- **Patterns** apply an overall pattern to your image. Want to make something look like it's made from metal or dried mud, or want to fill in a dull background with a really vivid pattern? You'll find lots of choices here.

- **Photographic Effects** include several favorite traditional photographic techniques. You can add a variety of monochrome effects, like good old-fashioned sepia.

- **Visibility** changes the opacity and visibility of your layer. Use them to create a ghosted effect—or when you're applying multiple Layer styles and you want to use the outlined shape of an object without having the object itself visible.

- **Wow Chrome, Neon, and Plastic Styles** make an object look like it's made from shiny chrome, outlined in neon, or made from plastic.

NOTE You can apply Layer styles only to regular layers, so if you try to apply one to a Background layer, Elements will ask you to convert it to a regular layer before the style can take effect.

If someone sends you a file made using Layer styles that you don't have, you can snag them for your own use by highlighting the layer with the styles on it, and then going to Layer → Layer Style → Copy Layer Style. Then, in an image where you want to use the styles, click the layer that you want to modify and then choose Layer → Layer Style → Paste Layer Style. This command applies all the styles used in the original image to the layer you targeted.

Editing Layer Styles

You can create highly customized Layer styles in Elements (see Figure 13-14). Start by applying a Layer style, and then you can edit it as much as you like. Just double-click the Layer Styles icon in the Layers Palette (the little italic "fx") or select Layer → Layer Style → Style Settings.

Once the Style Settings dialog box appears, you can edit your style in many different ways:

- **Drop Shadow**. You can change the shadow's direction, distance, opacity, or even its color. Once the Style Settings dialog box is open, you can drag the shadow around, right in your image window, until it's positioned where you want it.

- **Glow**. You can set the color, size, and opacity for both inner and outer glows, and turn each one on or off individually.

- **Bevel**. Change the size or direction of the bevel.

- **Stroke**. A stroke is a border around the edge of the style (like a line). You can change the color, size, and opacity of the stroke.

With Elements 6, you can customize styles in so many ways that you can practically make your own style from any existing one. There's only one hitch: You can't change the standard settings for each style, so any changes you make only affect the style as you're currently applying it.

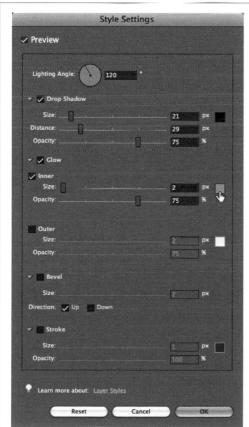

Figure 13-14:
The Style Settings dialog box gives you a lot of choices. Use the flippy triangles on the left to see the settings for a particular style characteristic or to collapse the ones you don't care about to get them out of your way. To apply a new characteristic to a style (like adding a glow to a style that doesn't already have one), just turn on its checkbox. (Turn the box off to remove it.) Click the color squares to the right of the sliders to bring up the Color Picker (see page 199) and choose a new color for that setting.

To remove a Layer style, right-click (Control+click) the layer in the Layers palette and choose Clear Layer Style, or go to Layer → Layer Style → Clear Layer Style. These commands are all-or-nothing: if your layer has multiple styles, they all go away at once. To remove one style at a time, use the Undo History palette (page 31).

> **TIP**   If you want to see what your image looks like without the styles you've applied to it, go to Layer → Layer Style → Hide All Effects.

You can download hundreds of additional Layer styles from the Web (see page 459 for tips on where to look and how to install them). It's easy to get addicted to collecting Layer styles because they're so much fun to use.

Applying Gradients

You may have noticed that a few of the Layer styles and Photo Effects fade out a color at the edges. In fact, Elements lets you fade and blend colors in almost any way you can imagine by using *gradients*. Use gradients to create anything from a multicolor rainbow extravaganza to a single color that fades away into transparency. Figure 13-15 shows you a few examples of what you can do with gradients. The only limit is your imagination.

You can apply gradients directly to your image using the Gradient tool, or you can create *Gradient Fill layers*, which are entire layers filled with—you guessed it— gradients. You can even edit gradients and create new ones using the Gradient Editor. Finally, there's a special kind of gradient called a *Gradient Map* that lets you replace the colors in your image with the colors from a gradient. This section covers the basics of using all these tools and methods.

The Gradient Tool

If you want to apply a gradient to a particular object in your image, the Gradient tool is the fastest way to do it. This tool may seem complicated when you first see it, but it's actually pretty easy to use. Start by activating the Gradient tool in the Toolbox (the yellow and blue rectangle) or by pressing G. Figure 13-16 shows the Gradient tool's Options bar.

Using the Gradient tool is as easy as dragging. Click where you want the gradient to begin and then drag to the point where you want it to stop (you'll see a line connecting your beginning and ending points). When you release the mouse, the gradient covers the entire available space.

For example, say you're using a yellow-to-white gradient. If you click to end the gradient one-third of the way into your photo, the yellow stops transitioning at that point, but the remaining two-thirds of your photo is covered with white. Drag the gradient within a selection if you want to confine the area it covers (see Chapter 5 if you need a refresher on making selections).

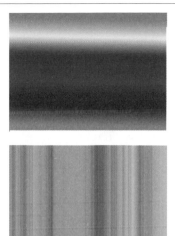

Figure 13-15:
Here are three examples of gradients drawn with the Gradient tool.

Top: This figure shows a gradient that creates a rainbow effect.

Middle: If you play with the Gradient Editor (page 375), you can create all sorts of interesting effects. Here's the gradient from the top figure again, only this time it's applied left to right instead of top to bottom. It looks so different because the noise option was used (see page 378). Click the Randomize button a couple of times for this effect.

Bottom: This figure shows a gradient you can create if you want a landscape background for artwork.

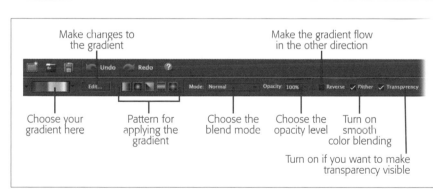

Make changes to the gradient

Make the gradient flow in the other direction

Figure 13-16:
The Gradient tool's Options bar gives you lots of choices for customizing how you apply your gradient.

Choose your gradient here

Pattern for applying the gradient

Choose the blend mode

Choose the opacity level

Turn on smooth color blending

Turn on if you want to make transparency visible

NOTE The Gradient tool puts the gradient on the same layer as the image you apply it to, which means that it's hard to change anything about your gradient after it's applied. If you think you might want to alter your gradient, use the Gradient Fill layer, described later.

Some of the gradients available in Elements use your chosen foreground and background colors as the two colors that generate the gradient. But Elements also offers a number of preset gradients, which are gradients in different color schemes that Adobe has created for you.

Click the arrow to the right of the gradient thumbnail in the Options bar and you'll see a little palette of different gradients, some of which use your selected colors and others that are preset with their own color scheme. The gradients are grouped into categories; you can only work with the gradients in one category at a time.

Click the arrows on the upper-right corner of the gradient thumbnails pop-out menu to see all the available gradient categories. Choose one, and the available gradients change to reflect those in the new category.

You can also download gradients from the Web and add them to your library using the Preset Manager (see page 460), or you can create your own gradients from scratch. (See page 459 for some suggestions of where to look for new gradients.) Creating and editing gradients is explained later, in the section about the Gradient Editor.

You can customize your gradient in several ways, even without using the Gradient Editor. When the Gradient tool is active, you see several choices in the Options bar:

- **Gradient.** Click the arrow to the right of the thumbnail to choose a different gradient than the one displayed.

- **Edit.** Click this button to bring up the Gradient Editor (explained later).

- **Gradient types.** Use this setting to determine the way the colors flow in your gradient. Click a thumbnail to choose how to apply the gradient. From left to right, your choices are: Linear (in a straight line), Radial (a sunburst effect), Angle (a counterclockwise sweep around the starting point), Reflected (from the center out to each edge in a mirror image), and Diamond. Figure 13-17 shows what each one looks like.

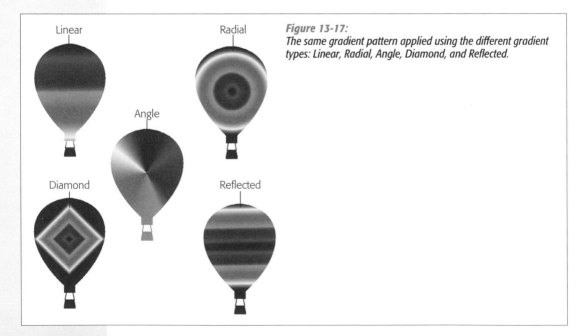

Figure 13-17:
The same gradient pattern applied using the different gradient types: Linear, Radial, Angle, Diamond, and Reflected.

- **Mode**. You can apply a gradient in any blend mode (see page 157).

- **Opacity**. If you want your image to be visible through the gradient, reduce the opacity here.

- **Reverse**. This setting changes the direction in which the colors are applied so that instead of yellow to blue from left to right, you get blue to yellow, for instance.

- **Dither**. Turning on this checkbox uses fewer colors but simulates the full color range using a noise pattern. It can help to prevent banding of your colors, making smoother transitions between them.

- **Transparency**. If you want to shade to transparency anywhere in your gradient, you need to turn Transparency on. Otherwise, the gradient can't show transparent regions.

Using the Gradient tool

To apply a gradient with the Gradient tool, first make a selection if you don't want to see the gradient in your whole image. Then:

1. **Choose the colors you want to use for your gradient.**

   Click the Foreground/Background color squares (page 198) to choose colors. (Some gradient choices ignore these colors and use their own preset colors instead.)

2. **Activate the Gradient tool.**

   Click it in the Toolbox or press G.

3. **Select a gradient.**

   Go to the Options bar and click the Gradient thumbnail and choose the gradient style you want. Then make any other changes to the Options bar settings, like reversing the gradient, if necessary.

4. **Apply your gradient.**

   Drag in your image from the starting point to the ending point, marking where the gradient should run. If you're using a linear gradient, you can make the gradient run vertically by dragging up or down. Or you can make it go left to right by dragging sideways. For Radial, Reflection, and Diamond gradients, try dragging from the center of your image to one edge. If you don't like your results, press ⌘+Z to undo it. Once you like the way the gradient looks in your image, you don't need to do anything special to accept it, except of course to save your image before you close it.

Gradient Fill Layer

You can also apply your gradient using a special fill layer. Most of the time, this is a better choice than the Gradient tool, especially if you want to be able to make changes to your gradient later on.

To create a Gradient Fill layer, go to Layer → New Fill Layer → Gradient. The New Layer dialog box appears, which lets you set the opacity for the layer and choose a blend mode (page 157), if you like. Once you click OK, the new layer immediately fills with the currently selected gradient, and the dialog box shown in Figure 13-18 pops up. You can change many of the settings for your gradient here or choose a different gradient.

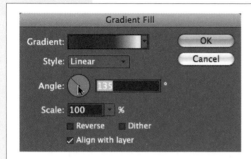

Figure 13-18:
The Gradient Fill dialog box gives you access to most of the same settings you find in the Options bar for the Gradient tool. The major difference is that in the fill layer, you set the direction of your gradient by typing in a number for the angle or by changing the direction of the line in the circle as shown here. You don't get a chance to set the direction by dragging, as you do with the Gradient tool.

The settings in the Gradient Fill dialog box are pretty much the same as those in the Options bar for the Gradient tool:

- **Gradient.** To choose a different gradient, click the arrow next to the thumbnail for the Gradient palette. To choose from a different gradient category, click the arrow on the palette and choose the category you want.

- **Style.** You get the same choices you do for the tool (for example, Linear, Diamond, and so on). In this case, you see only the name of the style. Choose a different style and it previews in the layer itself.

- **Angle.** This setting controls the direction the colors will run. Enter a number in degrees or spin the line in the circle by moving it with your mouse to change the direction of the flow.

- **Scale.** This setting determines how large your gradient is relative to the layer. 100 percent means they're the same size. If you choose 150 percent, the gradient will exceed the size of your layer, which means you'll see only a portion of the gradient in the layer. For example, if you had a black-to-white gradient, you'd see only shades of gray in your image. If you turn off "Align with Layer," you can adjust the location of the gradient relative to your image. Just drag the gradient in your image.

- **Reverse.** Turn Reverse on to make colors flow in the opposite direction.

- **Dither.** Use this setting to avoid banding and create smooth color transitions.

- **Align with Layer.** This setting keeps the gradient in line with the layer. Turn it off, and you can pull the gradient around in your image to place it exactly where you want it.

When you've gotten the gradient looking the way you like, click OK to create your layer. You can edit it later by double-clicking the left icon for the layer in the Layers palette.

Editing a Gradient

The Elements Gradient Editor lets you create gradients that include any color combination you like. You can even make gradients in which the color fades to transparency, or you can modify existing gradients. For instance, you can easily make a two-color gradient where the fade is very one-sided, if you want a large plain area where you can put text (the plain area helps keep the text readable).

The Gradient Editor isn't the easiest tool in the world to use. This section will give you the basics you need to get started. Then, as happens so often with Elements features, a little bit of playing around with the Gradient Editor will help you understand how it works.

The Gradient tool must be active to launch the Gradient Editor. Click the Edit button in the Options bar to see the Gradient Editor (see Figure 13-19).

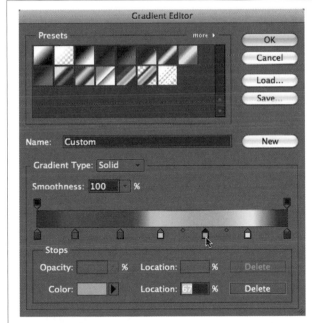

Figure 13-19:
The powerful and complex Gradient Editor. You won't see the little diamonds under the long rectangular Gradient bar until you click a Color Stop (where the cursor's pointed) to edit a color. The black triangle on the Stop is Elements' way of telling you it's the active Stop.

The Gradient Editor opens showing the currently selected gradient. You can choose a different gradient by picking from the thumbnails at the top of the Gradient Editor window, or by clicking the More button to the right and choosing a new category from the list. You'll learn how to save your gradients later in this chapter.

Using the Gradient Editor

To get started using the Gradient Editor, first choose your gradient's type and smoothness settings:

- **Gradient Type**. Your choices are Solid or Noise. Solid gradients are the most common types of gradient; they let you create transitions between solid blocks of color. Noise gradients, which are covered later in this section, produce bands of color, as you might see in a spectrometer.

- **Smoothness**. This setting controls how even the transition appears between colors.

Most of the work you'll do in the Gradient Editor takes place in the *Gradient bar*, the long colored bar where your chosen gradient is displayed. The little boxes (also called *stops*) and diamonds surrounding the Gradient bar let you control the color and transparency of your gradient.

For now, you care only about the stops *beneath* the Gradient bar. Each is a Color Stop; it represents where a particular color falls in the gradient. You always need at least two Color Stops in a gradient.

If you click a stop, the pointed end turns darker, letting you know that it's the active stop. Anything you do at this point is going to affect the area governed by that stop. You can slide the stops around to change where the colors transition in your gradients. The Color Stops let you customize your gradient in lots of different ways. Using them, you can:

- **Change where the color transitions**. Click a Color Stop, and you see a tiny diamond appear under the bar. The diamond is the midpoint of the color change. Diamonds always appear between two Color Stops. You can drag the diamond in either direction to skew the color range between two Color Stops so that it more heavily represents one color over another. Wherever you place the diamond tells Elements the point at which the color change should be half completed.

- **Change one of the colors in the gradient**. Click any Color Stop and then click the color square (at the bottom of the Gradient Editor, in the Stops section) to bring up the Color Picker (page 199). Choose a new color, and the gradient automatically alters to reflect your change. You can also pick a new color by moving your cursor over the Gradient bar. The cursor turns to an eyedropper that lets you sample a color from the bar or from anywhere in your image.

- **Add a color to the gradient**. Click a Color Stop and then click again (not in the bar, but anywhere just beneath it) to indicate where you want the new color to appear. You see a new Color Stop where you clicked. Next, click the color-picking window to choose the color you want to add. The new color appears in the gradient at the new stop. Repeat as many times as you want, adding a new color each time.

• **Remove a color from a gradient**. If there's a gradient that's *almost* what you want but you don't like one of the colors, you don't have to live with it. You can remove a color by clicking its stop to make it the active color. Then click the Delete button to remove that color, or just drag its stop downward off the bar. The Delete button is grayed out if no Color Stop is active.

Transparency in gradients

You can also use the Gradient Editor to adjust the transparency in a gradient. Elements gives you nearly unlimited control over the transparency in your gradients and over the opacity of any color at any point in the gradient. Adjusting opacity in the Gradient Editor works very much like using the Color Stops to edit the colors. Instead of Color Stops, you use Opacity Stops.

> **TIP** Transparency is particularly nice in images for Web use, but remember that you need to save in a format that preserves transparency, like GIF, or you lose the transparency. If you save your file as a JPEG, the transparent areas become opaque white. See page 439 for more about file formats for the Web.

The Opacity Stops are the little boxes *above* the Gradient bar. You can move an Opacity Stop to wherever you want and then adjust the transparency by using the settings in the Stops section of the Gradient Editor. Click the Gradient bar wherever you want to add more Opacity Stops (click above the Gradient bar, rather than in it). The more Opacity Stops your Gradient bar has, the more points at which you can adjust your gradient's opacity.

Here's how to add an Opacity Stop and then adjust its opacity setting:

1. **Click one of the existing Opacity Stops.**

   If the little square on the stop is black, it means the stop is completely opaque. A white square is totally transparent. The new stop will have the same opacity as the stop you click, but you can adjust the new stop once you've created it.

2. **Add a stop.**

   Click anywhere along the Gradient bar where you want to add a stop. If you want your gradient to be precisely positioned, you can enter numbers (indicating percentage) in the Location box below the gradient bar. For example, 50 percent positions a stop at the midpoint of the Gradient bar.

3. **Adjust the new stop's opacity.**

   Go to the Opacity box below the Gradient bar and either enter a percentage or click the arrow to the right of the number and move the slider to change the opacity setting. If you want to get rid of a stop, click its tab and press Delete, or drag it upward away from the bar.

By adding stops, you can make your gradient fade in and out, as shown in the background of Figure 13-20, which shows a simple vertical blue to transparent linear gradient that's been edited so that it fades in and out a few times.

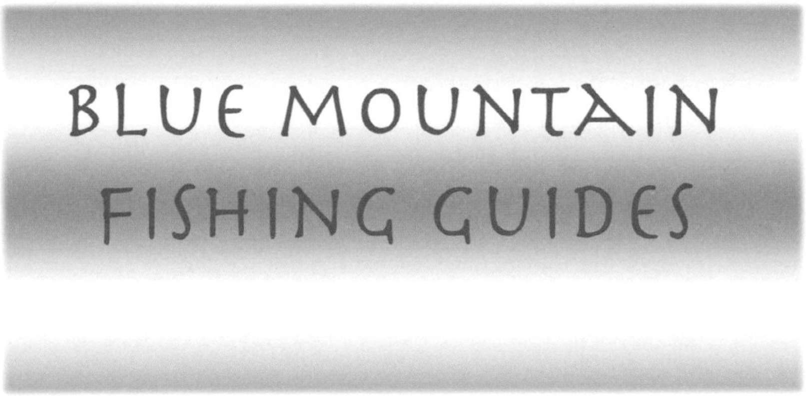

Figure 13-20:
You can make a gradient fade in and out like this background by adding more Opacity stops and reducing the opacity level of each stop.

Creating noise gradients

Elements also lets you create what Adobe calls *noise gradients*. A noise gradient isn't speckled (as you might expect if you're thinking of camera noise). Instead, noise gradients randomly distribute their colors within the range you specify, giving a banded or spectrometer-like effect to the gradient. The effect is interesting, but noise gradients can be a bit unpredictable. The noisier a gradient is, the more stripes of the colors you'll see, and the greater the number of random colors.

You can create a noise gradient by clicking the More button (the arrow at the upper right) on the Options bar gradient pop-out menu and selecting Noise Samples in the pop-out list of categories. Or you can click the Edit button to bring up the Gradient Editor and choose Noise as your Gradient Type.

Noise gradients have some special settings of their own in the Gradient Editor:

• **Roughness** controls how often the gradient transitions (see Figure 13-21).

Figure 13-21:
The amount of noise in a gradient can make quite a difference in the effect you get.

Top: Here's a Solid gradient.

Middle: A gradient with the same colors and 50 percent noise.

Bottom: A gradient with the same colors and 90 percent noise.

- **Color Model** determines which color mode you work in—RGB or HSB. RGB gives you red, green, and blue color sliders, while HSB lets you set hue, saturation, and brightness (see page 203 for more information about these settings).

- **Restrict Colors** keeps your colors from getting too saturated.

- **Add Transparency** puts random amounts of transparency into your gradient.

- **Randomize.** Click this button to add random colors (and transparency if you turned on that checkbox). Keep clicking the Randomize button until you see an effect you like.

Saving Gradients

After all that work, you'll probably want to save your gradient so you can use it again. To save a gradient, you have two options:

- **Click the New button in the Editor.** Enter a name for your new gradient in the Name box first. Your gradient gets added to the current category. Elements creates a new preset gradient for you that's now available in the Gradient thumbnails.

  TIP If you forget and click the New button before naming your gradient, or if you just want to change its name, right-click (Control+click) the thumbnail in the Gradient Editor and choose Rename Gradient.

- **Click Save.** The Save dialog box appears, and Elements asks you to name the gradient. You'll save the new gradients in a special Gradients folder, which Elements automatically takes you to in the Save dialog box. When you want to use the gradient again, click Load, and then select it from the list of gradients that appear.

  TIP You can also save and load gradients from the More menu on the Options bar Gradient pop-out menu.

Gradient Maps

Gradient Maps let you use gradients in nonlinear ways. In other words, instead of a rainbow that shades from one direction to another, in a Gradient Map, the gradient colors are substituted for the existing colors in your image. You can use Gradient Maps for funky special effects or for serious photo corrections.

What Elements does when you create a Gradient Map is map the brightness values of your image to a gradient (light to dark), and then replace the existing colors with the gradient you choose, using the lightness values as a guide for which color goes where.

That may sound complicated, but if you try it, you'll quickly see what's going on. Take a look at Figure 13-22, for instance. Applying a Gradient Map dramatically livens up this really dull photo, but that's not all Gradient Maps are good for. Gradients and Gradient Maps can also be valuable tools for straight retouching. See the box on page 381 for how to use gradients to fix the color in your photo.

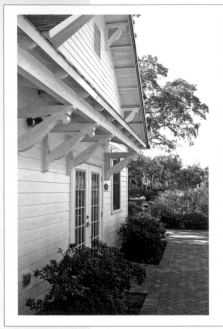
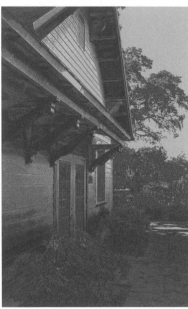

Figure 13-22:
Left: A boring shot with a totally blown-out sky.

Right: The image becomes something altogether different when you apply a Gradient Map adjustment.

You can apply a Gradient Map directly to your image by going to Filter → Adjustments → Gradient Map. But most times, you'll want to use a Gradient Map Adjustment layer, because it's easier to edit after you've created the layer. Here's how:

1. **Create a Gradient Map Adjustment layer.**

   Go to Layer → New Adjustment Layer → Gradient Map. You see the dialog box shown in Figure 13-23.

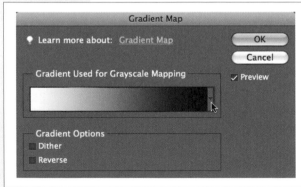

Figure 13-23:
The Gradient Map Adjustment layer dialog box. Clicking the tiny arrow at the right of the thumbnail (where the cursor is in the figure) gives you a drop-down menu showing the available gradient patterns.

2. **Choose a gradient.**

You'll see a gradient in the dialog box. The gradient color is based on your current Foreground/Background colors (see page 198). That's the map of the lightness/darkness values that Elements has made for your image. If you want your image to show color, you need to choose a color gradient. Click the arrow at the right of the Gradient bar and choose a color gradient.

The Dither setting adds a little random noise to make smoother transitions. The Reverse setting switches the direction the gradient is applied to the map. For example, if you chose a red-to-green gradient, reversing it would put green where it would have previously put red, and vice versa. It's worth giving this setting a try—you can get some very interesting effects.

3. **Click OK when you're satisfied with the result.**

Elements automatically replaces the colors in your image with the equivalent values from the gradient you chose.

Remember, too, that you don't have to use your gradient in Normal mode. You can use any blend mode (page 329). You can spend hours playing around with the different effects you can get with the Gradient Map. Other filters and adjustments can produce unexpected results when used with it.

> **TIP** Try Equalizing your image (Filter → Adjustments → Equalize) after applying a Gradient Map adjustment. The colors can shift quite dramatically. Equalize is a good thing to try if you find that your Gradient Map makes your image look dull or dingy. You may need to merge the layers (page 166) to get this command to work though, since you can't equalize an Adjustment layer. (See page 268 for more about the Equalize command.)

POWER USERS' CLINIC

Using Gradients for Color Correction

If your only interest in Elements is enhancing and correcting your photos, you may think that all this gradient business is a big waste of time. But keep in mind that gradients and Gradient Maps aren't just for introducing lurid colors into your photos. They're powerful tools to help you correct your photographs.

For instance, say you've got a photo where one side is much darker than the other. You may want to apply an Adjustment layer so it affects only the dark side of the image.

You can do this by bringing up the layer mask of the Adjustment layer (see page 279) and applying your gradient directly to the mask.

You can also use Gradient Map Adjustment layers in different blend modes to help balance out the colors in your photos, although you may need to use the Gradient Editor to play with the distribution of light and dark values to get the best effect. You can use a gradient map to give you more points of correction that you get in the Elements Color Curves. There's a detailed tutorial about this at *www.kaboom.com* (type *elements curves* in the site's search box to find the tutorial).

Gradient maps are also useful for colorizing skin in black-and-white photos. Set up a gradient based on three or more skin tones, and you can get a more realistic distribution of color tones than you could get by painting.

Type in Elements

If you want to add text to your images, Elements makes it easy. You can quickly create all kinds of fancy text to use on greeting cards, as newsletter headlines, or as graphics for Web pages.

Elements gives you lots of ways to jazz up your text: you can apply Layer styles, special effects, and gradients, or you can warp your type into psychedelic shapes. And the Type Mask tools let you fill individual letters with the contents of a photo. Best of all, most type tools let you change your text with just a few button clicks (see Figure 14-1). By the time you finish this chapter, you'll have learned about all the ways that Elements can add pizzazz to your text.

Adding Type to an Image

It's a cinch to add text to an image in Elements. Just select the Type tool, choose your font from the Options bar, and type away. The Type tool has a Toolbox icon that's easy to recognize: a capital T. Elements actually gives you four different type tools, all of which are hidden behind the Toolbox icon's pop-out menu: the Horizontal Type tool, the Vertical Type tool, the Horizontal Type Mask, and the Vertical Type Mask.

You'll learn about the Type Mask tools later in this chapter (see page 398). To get started, you'll focus on the regular Horizontal and Vertical Type tools. As their names imply, the Horizontal Type tool lets you enter type that runs left to right, while the Vertical Type tool is for creating type that runs down the page.

When you use the Type tools, Elements automatically puts your text on its own layer, which makes it easy to throw out that text and start over again later.

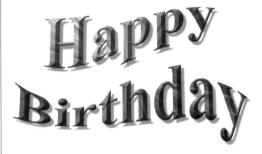

Figure 14-1:
With Elements, you can take basic type and turn it into the kind of snazzy headlines you see on greeting cards and magazine covers. It took only a couple of clicks—a couple of Layer styles (Angled Spectrum and a bevel) and some warping—to turn the plain black type (top) into an extravaganza (bottom). Before you start typing, you can choose a Layer style for your text from the Options bar. If you want to apply Layer styles to text you've already committed, you have to choose the styles in the Effects palette (see page 366).

TROUBLESHOOTING MOMENT

Why Does the Type Tool Turn My Photo Red?

If your image gets covered with an ugly orange-red film every time you click it with the Type tool, you've got one of the Type Mask tools turned on. (Type Masks, covered later in this chapter, are useful when you want to create text that's cut from an image.)

To switch over to the regular Type tools, click the Type tool icon in the Elements Toolbox. Use the pop-out menu to select either of the regular Type tools (horizontal or vertical).

Type Options

Whether you select the Horizontal or Vertical Type tool, the first thing you're going to want to do is take a look at the many settings available in the Options bar (Figure 14-2). These choices let you control pretty much every aspect of your type, including font selection, font color, and alignment.

Your choices from left to right are:

- **Font.** Choose your font, listed here by name. Elements uses the fonts installed on your computer.

    TIP   The font menu displays the word "Sample" in the actual fonts to make it easier for you to find the one you want. To see all your fonts, in the Options bar, click the down arrow to the right of the font name box for a pop-out menu. You can also adjust the size of the preview samples by going to Photoshop Elements → Preferences → Type.

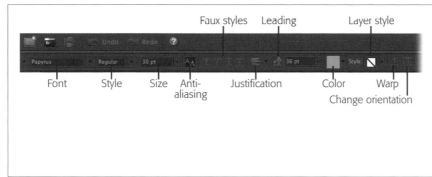

Faux styles   Leading   Layer style

Font   Style   Size   Anti-   Justification   Color   Warp
                      aliasing   Change orientation

Figure 14-2:
*The Type Options bar
lets you control lots of
different settings, most of
which are pretty
standard, like the font
you want to use and the
size of the letters. The
choices toward the right
end–like Warp and
Layer style–are where
the fun begins.*

- **Style**. Here's where you select the styles available for your font, like Bold or Italic.

- **Size**. This is where you choose how big your type should be. Text is traditionally measured in *points*. You can choose from the list of preset sizes in the pull-down menu or just type in the size you want. You aren't limited to the sizes shown in the menu—you can type in any number you want. See the box on page 390 for help understanding the relationship between points and actual size in Elements.

  If points make you nervous, you can change the type measurement unit to millimeters, pixels, or picas in Photoshop Elements → Preferences → "Units and Rulers".

- **Anti-aliasing**. This setting smoothes the edges of your type. Turn it on or off by clicking the little square with the two A's on it. Anti-aliasing is explained later, but usually you want it turned on.

- **Faux Styles**. Faux as in "fake." If your chosen font doesn't have a Bold, Italic, Underline, or Strikethrough version, you can tell Elements to simulate it here by clicking the appropriate icon. (This option isn't available for some fonts.)

- **Justification**. This pull-down menu tells Elements how to align your text, just like in a word processor. If you enter multiple lines of type, here's where you tell Elements whether you want it lined up left, right, or centered (for horizontal type). If you select the Vertical Type tool, you can align top, bottom, or middle.

NOTE   If you choose the Vertical Type tool, your columns of type run from right to left (each time you start a new column) instead of left to right. If you want vertical type columns to run left to right, you need to put each column on its own layer and position them manually. You can use the Move tool's Distribute option to space them evenly (page 161).

- **Leading** (rhymes with "bedding"). This setting controls the amount of spacing between the lines of type, measured in points. For horizontal type, leading is the difference between the baselines (the bottom of the letters) on each line. For vertical type, leading is the distance from the center of one column to the center of the column next to it. Figure 14-3 demonstrates what a difference leading can make in the appearance of your text. The first setting you'll always see is Auto, which is Elements' guess about what looks best. You can change leading by choosing a number from the list or entering the amount you want (in points).

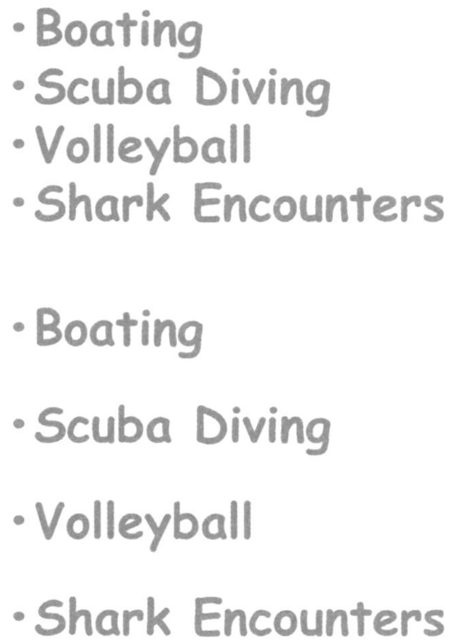

- Boating
- Scuba Diving
- Volleyball
- Shark Encounters

- Boating

- Scuba Diving

- Volleyball

- Shark Encounters

Figure 14-3:
Leading is the space between lines of type.

Top: Here, you see a list with Auto leading.

Bottom: Here's one with the leading number set much higher. (If you change the leading of vertical type, you change the space between the vertical columns of type, rather than the space between letters in an individual column. See the box on page 391 for how to tighten up the space between letters that are stacked vertically.)

- **Color.** Click this square to set the color of your text. Or click the arrow to the right of the color square to bring up Color Swatches (page 202). When you've made your selection, the Foreground color square (page 198) changes to show the new color.

    NOTE   When the Type tool cursor is active in your image, you can't use the keyboard commands to reset Elements' standard colors (black and white) or to switch them. You'll need to click the relevant buttons in the Toolbox instead. (See page 198 for how to use the Toolbox's color picking squares.)

- **Layer style.** You can add funky visual effects to your type with Layer styles (page 366). First, enter some text and then, on the Options bar, click the Commit button (the green checkmark). Next, click the Layer style box and choose a style from the pop-out palette. If you want to remove a style that you've just applied, choose "Clear Layer style" from the More button's menu (on the upper-right corner of the Layers palette).

The next two choices are grayed out until you create some text for them to work on:

- **Warp.** The little T over a curved line hides a multitude of options for distorting your type in lots of interesting ways. There's more about this option on page 390. (The Warp Text command is also available from Layer → Type → Warp Text.)

- **Orientation.** This button changes your text from horizontal to vertical, or vice versa. You can also change type orientation by going to Layer → Type → Horizontal or Vertical.

These two choices don't show up at all until you've typed something:

- **Cancel.** When you add type to your image, the text automatically gets placed on its own layer. Click the Cancel button to delete this newly created text layer. This button works only if you click it before you click the Commit checkmark. To delete text after you've committed it, drag its layer to the Trash in the Layers palette.

- **Commit.** Click this green checkmark after you type on your image to tell Elements that yes, you want the text to remain as it appears. Committing your type gives you access to the other tools again.

If you see either of these buttons, you haven't committed your type, and many menu selections and other tools won't be available until you do. When you see the Cancel and Commit buttons in the Options bar, you're in what Elements calls "Edit mode," where you can make changes to your type, but most of the rest of Elements isn't available to you. Just click Commit or Cancel to get the rest of the program options back.

Creating Text

Now that you're familiar with the choices you've got in the Options bar, you're ready to start adding text to your image. You can add type to an existing image, or start by creating a new file (if you want to create type to use as a graphic by itself). To use either the Horizontal or Vertical Type tools, just follow these steps:

1. **Activate the Type tool.**

   Click the tool in the Toolbox or press T, and then select the Horizontal Type tool or the Vertical Type tool from the pop-out menu.

2. **Modify any settings you want to change on the Options bar.**

   See the list in the previous section for a rundown of your choices. You can make changes after you enter your type, too, so your choices aren't set in stone yet. Elements lets you edit your type until you simplify the layer. (See page 341 for more about what simplifying a layer means.)

3. **Enter your text.**

   Click in your image where you'd like your text to go and then begin typing. The Type tools automatically create a new layer for your text. If you're using the Horizontal Type tool, the horizontal line you see is the baseline your letters sit on. If you're typing vertically, the vertical part of the cursor is the centerline of your character.

   Type the way you would in a word processor, using the Return key to create a new line. If you want Elements to *wrap* your type (adjust it to fit a given space), drag a text box with the Type tool before you start typing. Otherwise, you need to make your returns manually. If you create a text box, you can resize it to adjust the type flow by dragging the handles after you finish typing. This won't work anymore after you simplify the layer.

As noted earlier, if you want to use the Vertical Type tool, you can't make the columns of type run left to right. If you need multiple vertical columns of English language text, enter one column and then click the Commit button. Then start over again for the next column, so that each column is on its own layer.

4. **Move your text if you don't like where it's positioned.**

Sometimes the text isn't placed exactly where you want it. You can move text with the Text tool before you commit it—just grab the little black square at the beginning of the baseline and drag. If you have trouble moving your text, try the Move tool, but note that switching to the Move tool automatically commits your text (see step 5). If you need to move vertical type columns, wait until you've committed the type to rearrange the columns.

5. **If you like what you see, click the checkmark in the Options bar to commit the type.**

When you commit your type, you tell Elements that you accept what you've created. The Type tool cursor is no longer active in your photo once you commit. If, on the other hand, you don't like what you typed, click the Cancel button in the Options bar, and the whole type layer goes away.

Once you've entered type, you can modify it using most of Elements editing tools—you can add Layer styles (page 366), move it with the Move tool (page 138), rotate it, make color adjustments, and so on.

> **TIP** If you try to paste text into Elements by copying it from your word processor, the results are unpredictable. Sometimes things work fine, but you may find the text comes in as one endlessly long line of words. If that happens, it's easier to type your text in Elements from scratch than to try to reformat the text.

Editing Type

In Elements, you can change your text after you've entered it, just like in a word processor. Elements lets you change not only words, but the font and its size, too, even if you've applied lots of Layer styles (see Figure 14-4). You modify text by highlighting it and making the correction or changing your settings in the Options bar.

> **TIP** As mentioned earlier, you can see the word "Sample" in the menu displayed in the actual fonts themselves. Even better, Elements also gives you a quick way to preview what your actual text will look like in other fonts. First, select the text, and then click in the Font box in the Options bar. Use the up and down arrow keys to run down the font list. You'll see your words appear in each font as you go down the list.

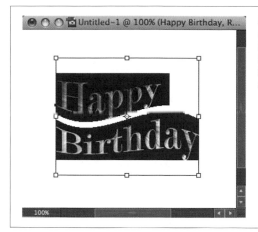

Figure 14-4:
If you change your mind about what you want to say, no problem. Here, the text is highlighted so that the words can be changed. The best part is that you can change the text to say anything, and all the formatting stays exactly the same. You can't do this after you simplify a type layer, though.

You can make all these changes as long as you don't *simplify* your type. Simplifying is the process of changing text from a vector shape that's easy to edit to a rasterized graphic (see the box on page 341). In this respect, text works just like the shapes you learned about in Chapter 12: Once you simplify text, Elements doesn't see it as text anymore, just as a bunch of regular pixels.

You can either choose to simplify text yourself (by selecting Layer → Simplify Layer), or you can wait for Elements to prompt you to simplify, which it will do when you try to do things like apply a filter or add an effect to your type.

> **NOTE** Some text effects automatically simplify your text without asking first. So, make sure you've made all the edits you want to your text before using these effects.

Smoothing type: anti-aliasing

Anti-aliasing smoothes the edges of your type. It gets rid of the "jaggies" by blending the edge pixels on letters to make the outline look even, as shown in Figure 14-5. In Chapter 5 (page 125), you read about anti-aliasing for graphics; anti-aliasing has a similar effect on type.

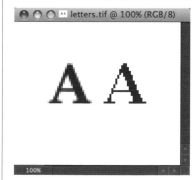

Figure 14-5:
An extremely close look at the same letter with and without anti-aliasing. The left letter A has anti-aliasing turned on, making the edges smooth. If you look at the letter A on the right, you can see how the edges are much more jagged and rough looking.

How Resolution Affects Font Size

It's easy enough to pick the font size in the Text tool's Options bar. But you may find that what you thought would be big, bold, headline-size type is so tiny on your image that you can hardly see it. What gives?

In Elements, the actual size of text in your image is tied to the resolution of your image. So, if you thought that choosing 72-point type would give you a headline that's an inch high, it will, but only if the *resolution* of your file is also 72 pixels per inch (ppi). The more you increase the resolution, the smaller that same type is going to be. If you double the resolution to 144 ppi, your 72-point text prints half an inch high. If you triple it to 216 ppi, it's one-third of an inch high.

If you're working with high-resolution images, you have to increase the size of your fonts to allow for the extra pixel packing that comes from increased resolution.

It's not uncommon to have to choose sizes that are much higher than anything listed in the size menu in the Options bar. Don't be afraid of really big sizes if you need them—just keep entering larger numbers in the size box until the text looks right in proportion to your image.

Another thing that sometimes causes confusion is that Elements is creating the type based on the actual size of your image, not the view size. People often try to put very small type on a very big image and wonder why it looks so bad. If you aren't sure about the actual size of your document, try going to View → Print Size before typing. This view offers only an approximation, but it helps you get a better idea of what your text will look like.

Elements always starts you off with anti-aliasing turned on, and 99 percent of the time you'll want to keep it on. The main reason to turn it off is to avoid *fringing*—a line of unwanted pixels that make it look like the text was cut out from an image with a colored background.

You turn anti-aliasing on and off by clicking the Anti-aliasing button (the two A's) in the Options bar. The button shows a dark outline when anti-aliasing is on. You can also turn anti-aliasing off and on by going to Layer → Type → Anti-Alias Off or Anti-Alias On. Once you simplify type, you can't change the anti-aliasing setting for the type.

> TIP   If you're seeing really jagged type even with anti-aliasing turned on, check your resolution. Type often looks poor at low resolution settings—just as photos do. See page 82 for more about resolution.

Warping Type

With Elements, you can warp the shape of your type in all sorts of fun ways. You can make it wave like a flag, bulge out, twist like a fish, arc up or down, and lots more. These complex effects are really easy, too, and best of all, you can still edit the type once you've applied the effects. Figure 14-6 shows just a few examples of what you can do. If you add a Layer style (explained on page 366), warping is even more effective.

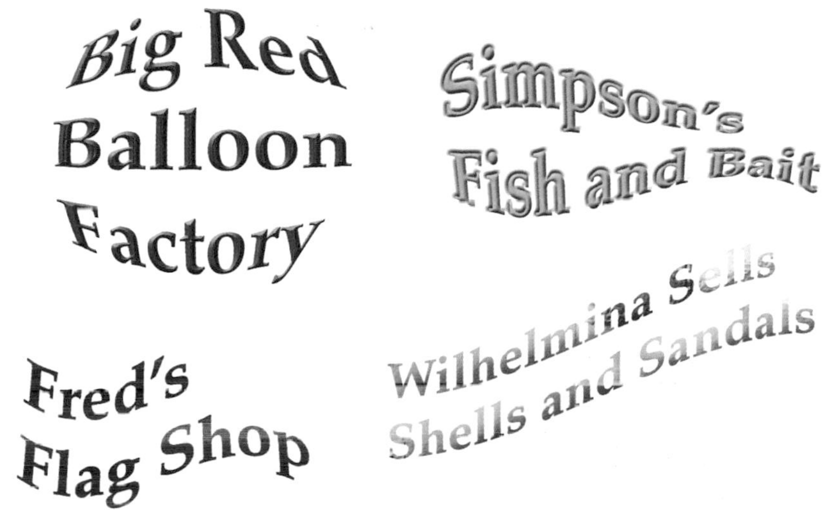

Figure 14-6:
Elements gives you oodles of ways to warp your type. Here are just a few of the basic warps, applied using their standard settings. Clockwise from the upper left: Inflate, Fish, Rise, and Flag. You can tweak these effects endlessly using the sliders in the Warp dialog box. (These examples also have Layer styles applied to them.)

WORKAROUND WORKSHOP

Using Asian Text Options to Control Text Spacing

Getting letters spaced correctly when using the Vertical Type tool can be tough. Elements lets you set the *leading*, but with vertical type, your leading setting affects the spacing between *columns* of letters, not the spacing of the letters within a column.

Also, sometimes you may want to adjust the spacing between letters written in horizontal text. Elements lets you make either of these fixes, but you need to use the Asian Text Options, even if you're writing in English.

To get started, go to Photoshop Elements → Preferences → Type and turn on the checkbox for Show Asian Text Options. Then, the next time you click in an image with the Type tool, you'll see an Asian character in the Options bar, just to the left of the Cancel button.

Click the symbol for a pop-out menu with three options: *Tate-Chuu-Yoko, Mojikumi,* and a pull-down menu with

percentages on it. You want the pull-down menu, which is for *Tsume*, which reduces the amount of space around the characters or letters you apply it to.

To apply Tsume, just highlight the characters you want to change and select a percentage from the pull-down menu. The higher the percentage, the tighter the spacing becomes.

You can select a single letter or a whole word for Tsume. Since it reduces the space all the way around each letter you apply it to, you can use it for either vertical or horizontal text, although for horizontal type, you'd be most likely to use it to tidy up the spacing of just one or two letters. For vertical type, tsume is a great way to tighten up the vertical spacing of your text.

To warp your type, follow these steps:

1. **Enter the text you want.**

   Use the Move tool (page 138) to reposition your text if necessary.

2. **Select the text you want to warp.**

   Make sure the Text layer is the active layer, or you won't be able to select what you typed. Click the Text layer in the Layers palette if it's not already highlighted there.

3. **Click the Create Warped Text button in the Options bar.**

   It's the T with a curved line under it. The Warp Text dialog box, shown in Figure 14-7, appears.

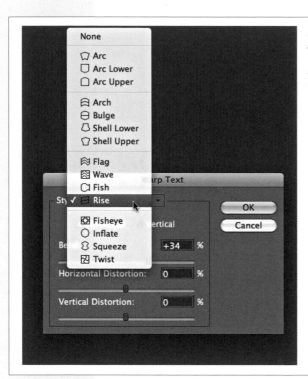

Figure 14-7:
As you can see, you have a lot of choices for how to warp your text. Once you choose a warp style, you see sliders in the dialog box that you can use to further customize the effect.

4. **Tell Elements how to warp your text.**

   Select a warp style from the pop-up list. Next, make any changes you want to the sliders or the horizontal/vertical orientation of the warp. Tweaking these settings can radically alter the effect. Push the sliders around to experiment. You can preview the results right in your image. Your choices are described in more detail in the next section.

5. **When you come up with something you like, click OK.**

   NOTE   You can't warp type that has the Faux Bold style applied to it. If you forget and try to do so, Elements politely reminds you. The program even offers to remove the style and continue with your warp.

Elements gives you lots of different warp styles to choose from, and you can customize the look of each style by using the settings in the Warp Text dialog box, described in the next section.

The Warp Text Dialog Box

The little dialog box that comes up when you click the Create Warped Text button is pretty straightforward. Your setting choices are:

- **Warp Style.** This is where you choose your warp style: Arc, Flag, and so on. To help you choose a style, Elements gives you thumbnail icons demonstrating the general shape of each warp.

- **Horizontal/Vertical.** These radio buttons control the orientation of the warping. Most of the time, you'll want to leave the button the same as the text's orientation, but you can get interesting effects by warping the opposite way.

  A vertical warp on horizontal text gives more of a perspective effect, like the text is moving towards you or away from you. You can get some very funky effects by putting a horizontal warp on vertical text.

- **Bend.** This is where you tell Elements how much of an arc you want. If you want to change the arc from Element's standard setting, type a percentage in the box or just move the slider until you get what you want. A higher positive percentage makes a bigger warp. A negative number makes your text warp in the opposite direction. For example, if you want an inverted arc, choose the Arc style and move the slider into the negative region.

- **Horizontal/Vertical Distortion.** These settings control how much your text warps in the horizontal or vertical plane. Moving the sliders gives you a very high degree of control over just how and where your text warps. They work pretty much the same way as the Bend setting—type a negative or positive percentage or move the sliders.

The best way to find the look you want is to experiment. It's lots of fun, especially if you apply a Layer style first (page 366) to give your type a 3-D look before warping it.

> **TIP**   Many of the warps look best on two lines of type, so that the lines bend in opposite directions. However, you can also get very interesting effects by putting two lines of type on separate layers and applying a different warp to each.

To edit your warp after it's done, double-click the Warp thumbnail icon for the text layer in the Layers palette. Doing that automatically makes the text layer active and highlights the text. Then, click the Create Warped Text button in the Options bar. The Warp dialog box opens and shows your current settings. Make any changes you want or set the style to None to get rid of it.

Adding Special Effects

Besides warping your type, you can apply all kinds of Layer styles, filters, and special Text effects to give your text a more elaborate appearance. You can change the color of your text, make the letters look 3-D, add brushstrokes for a painted effect, and so on. (There's more about Layer styles, filters, and effects in Chapter 13.)

Elements gives you lots of different ways to add special effects to your text. The following sections show you three of the most interesting: applying the Text effects, using a gradient to make rainbow-colored type, and using the Liquify filter to warp your text in truly odd ways.

Text Effects

The Content palette contains an entire category dedicated to special Text effects (Figure 14-8). You apply Text effects just the way you would apply any other effect—make the type layer active and double-click the effect you want.

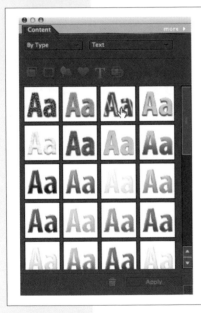

Figure 14-8:
The Content palette includes an entire section for Text effects. Some, like Animal Fur Zebra, are unique to this section. Others, like the Bevel and Drop Shadow, are just shortcuts for effects you could also achieve using Layer styles.

If you already have Layer styles on your text, it's hard to predict how much the effects will respect the Layer palette styles. Some effects build onto the changes you've previously made with Layer styles; most undo anything you've done before. Experimenting is the best way to find out what happens when you combine Layer styles and effects.

Type Gradients

Gradient palette patterns fill your text with a spectrum of color. The simplest way to get these rainbow effects is to apply one of the Layer styles or Text effects that include a gradient. On the other hand, these features give you no control over the colors or direction of the gradient. If you have a specific look in mind, you may have to start from scratch and do it yourself.

The easiest way is to start with a Type Mask, as explained on page 398. But if you already have some existing text, as long as it's not yet simplified, you can easily fill it with a gradient.

> **TIP** A heavier, chunky font shows off your rainbow better than a thin, spidery one. Fonts with names that end in Extended, Black, or Extra Bold are good, like Hoefler Black or Rockwell Extra Bold.

First, make sure you've got some text in your image, and then follow these steps:

1. **Create a new layer for your gradient. Make sure it's directly above your text layer in the Layers palette.**

   You're going to group the two layers, which is why they need to be next to each other. To create the new layer, press ⌘ | Shift+N or go to Layer → New → Layer. In the New Layer dialog box, turn on "Group with Previous Layer".

   Look at the Layers palette to be sure the new layer is the active layer. If it isn't, give it a click in the Layers palette to highlight it.

2. **Activate the Gradient tool.**

   Click the Gradient tool in the Toolbox and choose a gradient style in the Options bar. (See page 370 for more about how to select, modify, and apply gradients.)

3. **Drag across your new layer in the direction you want the gradient to run.**

   Because the layers are grouped, the gradient appears only in your type. If you don't like the effect, press ⌘+Z and drag again until you like what you see. That's all you have to do, except of course, save your work if you want to keep it.

Applying the Liquify Filter to Type

The Create Warped Text button in the Options bar (explained earlier on page 390) gives you lots of ways to reshape your type. But there's an even more powerful way to warp type: the Liquify filter (see Figure 14-9).

> **NOTE** You can actually use the Liquify filter to warp anything in an image—not just text. Use it to alter objects in photographs and drawings, for example. Fix someone's nose, make your brother look like E.T., give a scene a watery reflection, and so on.

To use the Liquify filter, you first need to simplify the layer your text is on (Layer → Simplify Layer, or just click OK when the Liquify filter asks if you want to simplify). (Remember, you can no longer edit your text once you simplify it.) Then,

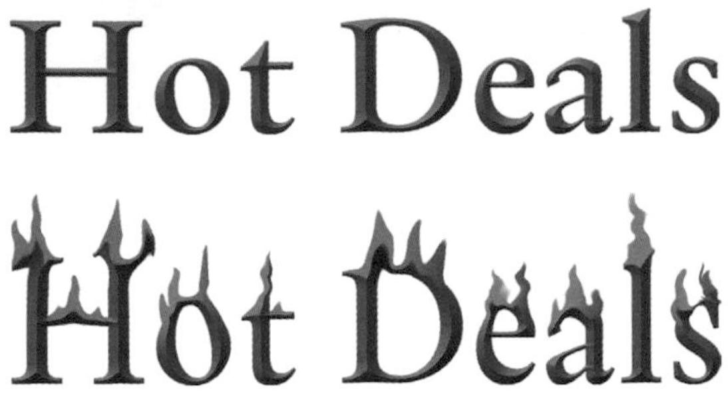

Figure 14-9:
The Liquify filter can reshape text in many different ways, including adding a flame-like effect (shown here), making letters twirl around on themselves, or making text undulate like it's underwater.

Top: Text with a bevel Layer style applied.

Bottom: Use the Liquify filter's Warp tool to pull these little "flames" from the text.

call up the Liquify filter dialog box by going to Filter → Distort → Liquify. You can also get to it by double-clicking the Liquify filter thumbnail in the Distort section of the filters in the Effects palette.

You see yet another large Elements dialog box. Like most of them, it's fairly straightforward once you learn your way around it. In the upper-left corner of the Liquify dialog box is a little toolbox with some very special tools in it (see Figure 14-10).

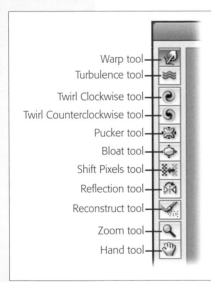

Warp tool
Turbulence tool
Twirl Clockwise tool
Twirl Counterclockwise tool
Pucker tool
Bloat tool
Shift Pixels tool
Reflection tool
Reconstruct tool
Zoom tool
Hand tool

Figure 14-10:
The Liquify dialog box has its own toolbox. Along with the standard Hand and Zoom tools to help you adjust the view as you work, you get highly specialized tools found nowhere else in Elements.

From top to bottom they are:

- **Warp tool.** This lets you push the pixels of your image in whichever direction you want, although it usually takes a fair amount of coaxing to create much of an effect.

- **Turbulence tool.** You can use the Turbulence tool to create clouds and waves. This tool is dependent on the Turbulent Jitter setting on the right side of the window (explained later). A higher number creates a smoother effect.

- **Twirl Clockwise tool.** Hold this tool down on your image, and the pixels under your cursor spin in a clockwise direction. The longer you apply this tool, the more extreme the spin effect.

- **Twirl Counterclockwise tool.** The opposite of the Twirl Clockwise tool, it makes the pixels under the cursor spin counterclockwise.

- **Pucker tool.** This tool makes the pixels under the cursor move toward the center of the brush.

- **Bloat tool.** The opposite of the Pucker tool, it makes pixels move *away* from the center of the brush.

- **Shift Pixels tool.** The pixels you drag this tool over move perpendicularly in relation to the direction of your stroke. For example, if you drag from the top of an image in a straight line down, the pixels you pass over will move to the right. Option+drag to change the direction of the shift.

- **Reflection tool.** Drag to create a reflection of the area the tool passes over. Overlapping strokes create a watery effect.

- **Reconstruct tool.** Pass this wonderful tool over areas where you've gone too far, and you selectively return them to their original condition without wrecking the rest of your changes.

- **Zoom and Hand tools.** These are the same Zoom (page 79) and Hand (page 81) tools you find elsewhere in Elements.

Your image appears in the preview window in the center of the dialog box. You can adjust the view with the Zoom tool or by using the magnification menu in the lower-left corner of the image area.

> **TIP**   It often helps to zoom in very close when using the Liquify filter. If you've added text to a large image, select the text with the Marquee tool (page 113) before activating the Liquify filter. Then you'll see only the selected area in the filter preview, which makes it easier to get a high zoom level.

At the right side of the dialog box are the Tool Options settings:

- **Brush Size.** You can enter a number as low as 1 pixel or as large as 600 in the space provided.

- **Brush Pressure.** This is how much the brush affects the pixels you drag over. The range is from 1 to 100. The higher the pressure, the stronger the effect of the brush. If you're using a graphics tablet, turn on Stylus Pressure so that the harder you press, the more effect you get.

- **Turbulent Jitter.** This controls how smooth your changes look. The higher the number, the smoother the effect you get from your changes.

- **Stylus Pressure**. Turn this on if you're using a graphics tablet (page 457) and you want the tool to be sensitive to how hard you press.

To use the filter, just pick your tool, modify your Tool Options (if you want), and then drag across your image. This is a very processor-intense filter, so there may be a fair amount of lag time before you see results, especially if your computer's slow. Give the filter time to work.

If you like what you see in the preview, click OK and wait a few seconds while Elements applies your transformations. Then you're done. But if you don't like what you see, you can always have another go at it. Use the Revert button, which returns your image to its original condition before you started using the Liquify filter. Another option is to Option+click the Cancel button to turn it to a Reset button (which resets the tool settings as well as your image).

Type Masks: Setting an Image in Type

So far in this chapter, you've been reading about how to create regular type and how to glam it up by applying Layer styles and effects. But in Elements, you can also create type by filling letters with the contents of a photo, as shown in Figure 14-11. (You'll find gourds.jpg, the photo used as the basis for Figure 14-11 and Figure 14-13, on the "Missing CD" page at *www.missingmanuals.com.*)

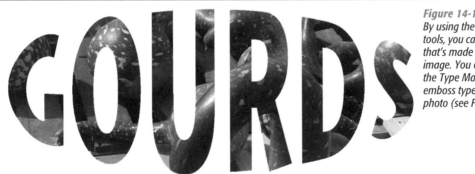

Figure 14-11:
By using the Type Mask tools, you can create type that's made from an image. You can also use the Type Mask tools to emboss type into your photo (see Figure 14-13).

The Type Mask tools work by making a selection in the shape of your letters. Essentially, you're creating a kind of stencil that you'll place on top of your image.

Once you've used the Type Mask to create your text-shaped selections, you can perform all sorts of neat modifications to your text. You can emboss type into your image (which makes it looks like it's been stamped into your image); you can apply a stroke to the outline of your text (useful if your font doesn't have a built-in outline option); or you can copy and move your text to another document entirely.

Using the Type Mask Tools

The following steps show you how to create a Type Mask and lay it over an image so that the letters you create are filled with whatever's in your image:

1. **Open the image that you want to use as your source for creating the text.**

2. **Activate the Type Mask tool.**

   Click the Type tool in the Toolbox or press T. Select the Type Mask tool you want—horizontal or vertical. (Use the pop-out menu.) The Type Mask tools behave just like the regular Type tools—a horizontal mask goes across the page, a vertical mask goes up and down. The Type Mask tool has the same Options bar settings as the regular Type tool, except for Color and Style.

3. **Click your image and start typing.**

   When you click, a red film covers your entire image. The red indicates the area that *won't* be part of your letters. By typing, you're going to cut a visible selection through the red area (see Chapter 5 if you need a refresher on selections).

   When you type, instead of creating regular type, you're creating a type shaped selection. You can see the shape of the selection as you go.

   It's important to choose a very blocky font for the type mask, since you can't see much of the image if you use thin or small type.

   It's hard to reposition your words once you've committed them, so take a good look at what you've got. While the mask is active, you can move the mask by dragging it, as explained in Figure 14-12.

4. **Don't click the Commit button until you're satisfied with what you have.**

   Once you click the Commit button (the green checkmark on the right side of the Options bar), you can't alter your type as easily as you can with the regular Type tool. That's because the regular tools create their own layers, while the Type Mask tools just create selections. Once you commit, your type is just like any other selection— Elements doesn't see it as type anymore, so you can no longer change the size by highlighting the text and picking a different size, for example.

5. **When you're happy with your selection, finish by clicking the Commit button.**

   Once you click the Commit button, you see the outline of your type as an active selection. You can move the selection outline by nudging it with the arrow keys.

6. **Remove the non-text portion of your image.**

   Go to Select → Inverse and press Delete to remove the rest of the image. Or you can copy and paste the selection into another document.

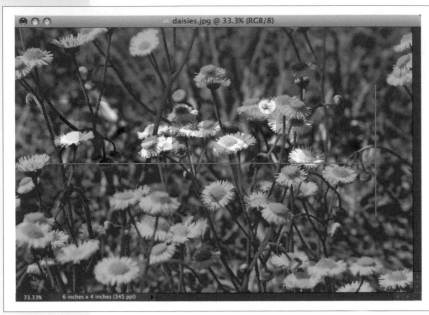

Figure 14-12:
Once you've activated the Type Mask tool and clicked on your image, you'll see a red mask appear over your picture. As you start typing, your text appears, as shown here. To move a selection made with the Type Mask tool, hold down ⌘, and then you can easily drag your selection around in your image as long as you haven't committed it yet.

Figure 14-13 shows the effect of pressing ⌘+J and placing a Type Mask selection on a duplicate layer of its own, and then adding Layer styles (page 366) to the new layer.

Creating Outlined Type

If the font you're using doesn't come with a built-in outline style, there's no one-button option for creating outlined type in Elements (the way you can in Microsoft Word, for example). By using the Type Mask tools, though, you can create outlined text quite easily.

To make a text outline like the one shown in Figure 14-14:

1. **Open your image or create a new one (if you just want the type by itself). Activate the Type Mask tool of your choice.**

    Click the Type tool or press T. Then select either of the Type Mask tools.

2. **Choose your font and size.**

    Use the settings in the Options bar. Outlined type works better with a fairly heavy font rather than a slender one. Bold fonts also work well here, rather than regular fonts.

3. **Enter your type.**

    Type in your image where you want the text to go. If you want to warp your type, do it now, before you commit the type.

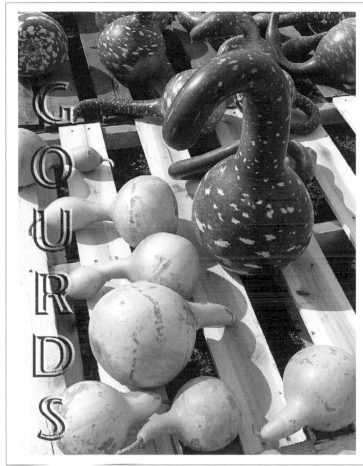

Figure 14-13:
By copying text to another layer, you can bevel or emboss it into your photo. Notice that this photo shows what you need to watch out for—the G is kind of hard to see because it blends right into the image. You may need to place your text a few times before you get it positioned correctly. Or you could also add a colored outline to make it stand out more, as described below.

4. **Click the Commit button (the checkmark).**

   Be sure you like what you've got before you do, because once you commit the text, it changes to a selection that's hard to edit. If you'd rather start over, click the Cancel button (the "no" symbol) instead.

5. **Add a stroke to your outline.**

   Be sure the type selection is active, and then go to Photoshop Elements → Stroke (Outline) Selection. Choose a line width in pixels and the color you want, and then click OK. (There's more about your choices in the dialog box on page 345.) Your selection is now a linear outline of the text you typed.

Outline

Figure 14-14:
By using the Type Mask tools, you can create outlined type almost as quickly as ordinary type.

Part Five: Sharing Your Images

5

Creating Projects

If you're into making scrapbooks, greeting cards, and other photo concoctions, Elements is perfect for you. You can dress up your pictures in all sorts of creative ways without using —or buying—any other software. Elements is crammed with add-on graphics, frames, and other special effects; you can even create multipage documents.

This chapter kicks off with an in-depth look at how to create a Photo Collage. Once you've got those steps under your belt, all the other projects (summarized starting on page 415) use the same basic method. You'll also learn how to create photo books and calendars using Kodak EasyShare, Adobe's online photo-printing partner, and make PDF slideshows to share your photos.

> **TIP** You can also create Online Galleries (photo-filled Web pages) in Elements. Learn all about those projects in Chapter 17.

Photo Collages

The new Create tab helps you create fancy pages featuring your photos, which you can then share either by printing or as digital files. Although Elements gives you lots of preset layouts to start from, you can customize every aspect of these layouts to create projects that are totally your own.

A Photo Collage is a page displaying one or more of your photos, with or without a themed background. (Flip ahead to Figure 15-3 to get a glimpse of what Elements can help you do.) Elements presents you with a series of guided questions that lead you from start to finish. All projects begin with one or more suggested photo placeholders, but you can add or remove photos at will. You can also change the background, frame styles, and other details.

To create a Photo Collage:

> **NOTE** Photo Collages, like all the printable projects on the Create menu, start off at a resolution of 220 ppi. That's perfectly fine for most people's taste. But if you want a higher resolution, your best bet is to cook up your own project from scratch, since increasing the resolution of a pre-built Elements project often throws the layout out of whack. (Photo Books are a little different. If you try to print a single double-paged spread it prints at 72 ppi, unless you first save your book as a PDF.)

1. **Open some photos in the Editor.**

   This step is optional, but if you preselect your photos, Elements automatically places them into your layout for you.

2. **Go to Create → Photo Collage.**

   In Edit or Share mode, if your mouse happens to be down at the bottom of your screen, you can also go to the Project Bin Actions pull-down menu and select Create → Photo Collage (Figure 15-1).

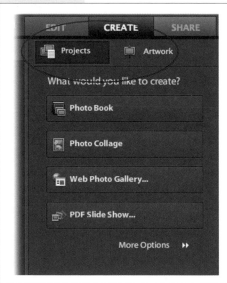

Figure 15-1:
Once you're in the Create pane in the Editor, you have a choice of two tabs (circled). You select and start your project from the Projects tab, and then click the Artwork tab to add frames, graphics, and other doodads to your project.

3. **Choose your page size from the Page Size pull-down menu.**

> **NOTE** Elements gives you a special preferences section that lets you control the measurement units that appear in Create projects. Go to Photoshop Elements → Preferences → Units & Rulers → Photo Project Units, and change the Photo Project Units setting to inches, centimeters, or whichever system you prefer.

4. **From the "Select a Theme" section, if you want, choose a theme.**

   Themes give you coordinated backgrounds and frames for your photos. (You can always choose a different background later if you don't like the one that came with the frame, or a new frame to replace the ones that came with the background.) Click once on a theme to select it, and a larger thumbnail appears just to the left of the Projects pane so you have a closer look at your choice.

   If you choose a theme and then decide you don't want any theme at all, click the upper-left thumbnail in the list of thumbnails (in other words, the first item) to choose No Theme.

5. **Choose a Layout style.**

   Scroll through the thumbnails and click the one you like. You can rearrange your layout after you've chosen it: Add more photos, remove photos, rotate the images, and so on. The layouts are arranged from one picture at the start of the list, to many pictures at the bottom of the group.

6. **Choose from the Additional Options, if desired.**

   If you leave "Auto-Fill with Project Bin Photos" turned on, all your open photos automatically appear in your collage when Elements creates it. If you have photos open and you don't actually want them in your collage, turn off the checkbox.

   There's also a checkbox for having captions you've added to your photos appear in the collage. (You can add text or edit the captions later, so you're not tied to what's in the Caption field of the file's metadata.)

   If you selected some photos before you started, the Number of Pages box tells you how many pages long your creation will be. This number updates to reflect your current Layout choice. So, for example, if you have three photos open and choose a single photo per page, the number of pages is three. If you click a layout that uses three photos per page, the number of pages changes to one. (If you haven't selected any photos yet, you can specify how many pages you want by typing in a number.)

7. **When you've made all your choices, click Done.**

   Elements gets to work creating your collage. You may have to wait a few seconds. If you preselected photos and left autofill turned on, Elements puts your photos right into the frames for you. Your document will have as many pages as needed to place all your photos in the layout you chose. If you didn't select any photos, you see "Click here to add photo or Drag photo here." That's fine, because you can add photos in the next step.

8. **Adjust your photos.**

   If you haven't already picked photos for your project, click a frame and then choose a photo from the dialog box that appears.

NOTE   What you do to photos here doesn't alter your originals in any way, it just changes the way the photos look in this project.

Regardless of how you get your photos into the collage, you can make a number of adjustments to them once they're in. Click once to resize the frame, or double-click any photo and you see the controls shown in Figure 15-2, which let you make a number of different changes to your photo without changing the frame size. Click the green checkmark to apply your changes, or the red Cancel button to get rid of them.

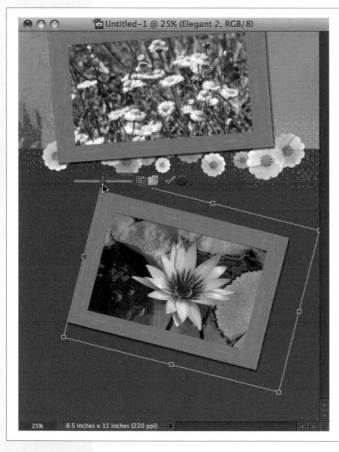

Figure 15-2:
When you double-click a photo, you get controls for adjusting it. To resize your picture, move the slider to the left (smaller) or right (larger). You can rotate your photo by clicking the curved white arrow, or click the folder icon to choose a different photo. You can also drag a corner to resize your photo or do a manual rotation.

You can also change the frame style by clicking a photo, then choosing a new style from the Content palette (page 413). To change to the new frame, double-click the new style, or drag it to the photo, or click it once and then click Apply. The frames wrap around your photo automatically so you don't have to do any juggling in the layer stack.

9. **Customize your collage.**

   Here's the fun part. Click a photo in your collage and drag it into a different position. Drag in art from the Content palette. These graphics are vector images (page 341), which means they'll look great no matter how big or small you resize them. You can also add text to your collage (find out how to do that in Chapter 14). You can change the background by selecting a new one in the Content palette (page 413). You can even flatten your image and use filters on the entire page. Figure 15-3 shows an example of what you can do with a Photo Collage.

   If you click back to Full Edit, you can use any tool or filter on your collage, but you may need to simplify a layer (page 168) or flatten your image first, so save that step till you're sure you like your collage. You can use the Move tool to rearrange your collage layers after you simplify them, but once you simplify layers, you can't make their contents larger than 100 percent without losing quality, just like any normal photo.

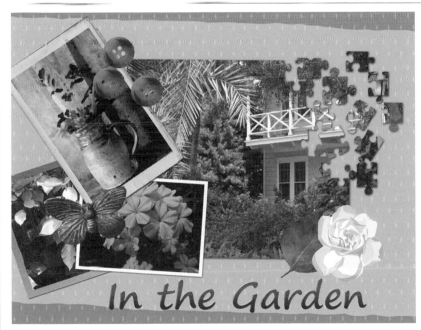

Figure 15-3:
This composition was created as a Photo Collage. Except for the photos themselves, all the additional artwork came from the Content palette. Some of the frames automatically create an aged photo effect, as you see in the photo of the jug of flowers, which also had several filters applied to it first to give a painted effect (see Chapter 13 for more about filters).

10. **Save your collage.**

    When you're done, press ⌘+S to name your project and save it. You can save it in any standard file format if it's a one-page collage, but if you have more than one page you must save it as a PSE file, which is a special format just for multi-page Elements documents.

There's almost no limit to what you can do in a Photo Collage. Anything you've read in the other chapters of this book works here, too. Plus, here are a few special things you can do with photos in a collage:

- **Remove a photo from your collage.** Right-click (Control+click) the photo and choose Clear Photo. To remove the photo's placeholder and frame as well, choose Clear Frame.

- **Make your photo appear without a frame.** Right-click (Control+click) and choose Clear Frame.

- **Resize a frame.** You can resize a frame, either before or after you put a photo into it. Click once on the frame to bring up handles, and then drag a corner of the frame to make it larger. You can also rotate a photo using the handles on the frame.

- **Resize the frame to fit the photo.** If you want to make the frame fit the photo, instead of the other way around, right-click (Control+click) the photo and choose "Fit Frame to Photo."

NOTE   You can do all of the above in Full Edit, too, once your collage is complete, but you need to activate the Move tool first or you won't see correct options when you right-click (Control+click).

- **Add another photo.** Just drag a frame from the Content palette to a blank area in your collage. If you get too close to an existing frame, the new frame may just replace the one on an existing photo. If that happens, just press ⌘+Z to undo it and drag again, more carefully, to another blank spot. You can also drag a photo into your collage from the Project bin.

- **Change your theme.** If you wish you'd gone with a different theme after you've already created your Photo Collage, go to Content → By Type → Themes for a list of all the Create themes. Double-click a thumbnail or drag the new theme to your photo, or click the thumbnail once and then click Apply. Presto—you've got your existing layout with new frames and background.

- **Edit the Layer style of a Frame.** Click the Edit tab to get back to Full Edit, and in the Layers palette, most of the frames have a Layer style icon., Double-click the icon to edit things like the size of the drop shadow on the frame. (See page 369 for more about editing Layer styles.)

What's more, you can add and delete pages from Photo Collages, as explained in the next section.

TIP   You can apply artwork from the Content palette to any image, not just those in Photo Collages and other Create projects.

Creating Multipage Documents

Elements makes it easy to create a file that's more than one page long. A Photo Collage automatically starts with as many pages as needed to hold all your pre-selected

Smart Objects

Smart Objects are one of the ways Adobe makes Elements projects so fun and easy. Like their big-shot cousins in the full version of Photoshop, these objects seem to know where they are and what you're trying to do—and behave accordingly. Here are some of the things that make Smart Objects so smart:

- When you apply a new background from the Content palette, it immediately zooms down to the bottom of the layer stack to replace the existing background, without any assistance from you.

- Similarly, the frames in the Content palette automatically target your photos, but only as long as you're in the Create tab. (Add a frame from the Content palette in Full Edit instead of the Artwork pane and you'll find that it's not so smart. It just sits there on top of your photo, if you have one open, waiting for you to help it out by placing a photo inside it, unless you're adding to an existing Create project.)

- You can resize, transform, or distort objects from the graphics section of the Content palette as much as you want without affecting the image quality. This behavior is something like how vector art works, but what's going on under the hood is quite a bit different. (The preview may appear pixelated if you hugely resize a graphic, but the actual object should be okay once you click the green checkmark.)

Anything you drag from the Project bin into your project while you're in the Create pane will behave like a Smart Object (you can resize it to any size, for instance).

By the way, if you've used Photoshop, you'll find that Smart Objects in Elements don't do nearly as many interesting things as they do in the full version of Photoshop. You can't create linked objects, for instance, where painting on one makes your painting appear on all of them. In fact, if you try to paint on a Smart Object in Elements, you just get the dialog box shown in Figure 15-4.

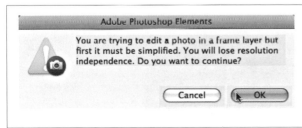

Figure 15-4:
You can enlarge, reduce, transform, and distort Smart Objects, but if you try to paint on them, or to apply filters or effects, you get this message. It's fine to click OK, but once you do, your formerly Smart Object will behave like any other object. (You can't increase its size to more than 100 percent, for instance, or it'll go all pixely on you.)

photos, but you can add pages to any of the Create projects anytime—and remove them, too. (You can also add pages to and remove pages from any Elements file, not just to the Create projects.)

The size and resolution of your existing page determines the size and resolution of pages you add. In other words, if your current file is just a single 3" × 5" photo and you add a page to it, you get a 3" × 5" page. If you want to add a letter-size page to a small photo file, you must first add canvas to the photo (page 89) or resize it. (But check page 88 to see why resizing a small photo to letter size probably won't work well.)

To add a new page to your document, go to the Editor's Edit menu and choose one of the following commands:

- **Add Blank Page**. This command creates a new, totally empty page with the same dimensions and resolution as your existing page.

- **Add Page Using Current Layout**. When you choose this option, Elements creates a page that's exactly like the current state of your existing page, including any changes you've made. Instead of photos, there are placeholders for you to ffsill in. So, for example, if you've changed frame styles and dragged a photo to another position, the new frame and positioning (without the photo) appears in your new page. Any graphics you've added from the Content palette show up as well. This option is a big help when you're making photo books or scrapbooks.

You can navigate through all of the pages in your document using the Project bin, as shown in Figure 15-5. If you decide you've got too many pages, go to Photoshop Elements → Delete Current Page, and the currently active page is history. You can also do any adding and deleting of pages right from the Project bin by right-clicking (Control+clicking)and choosing what you want to do from the pop-out menu, a big help when you're editing a multipage project.

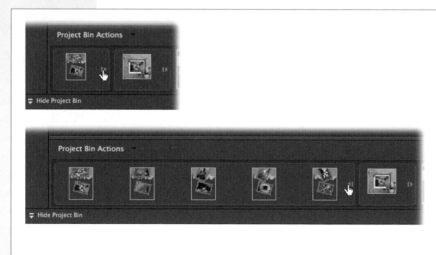

Figure 15-5:
You can expand and collapse the pages of your file so they don't hog all the visible space in the Project bin.

Top: A collapsed multipage Photo Collage and a Photo Book in the project bin. If you look closely, each thumbnail is a miniature of the page, showing every detail of your project exactly as you created it.

Bottom: Here's the expanded thumbnail for the collage, so that you can select a single page to edit. Click the arrow again to collapse the thumbnail.

No matter what kind of file you start with—whether it's from the Create projects or just a regular JPEG—you must save your file as a PSE format file if you add pages to it. Elements reminds you with the dialog box in Figure 15-6. While it's very, very nice to be able to create multipage documents in Elements, the PSE format has some drawbacks, too, as explained in the box on page 413.

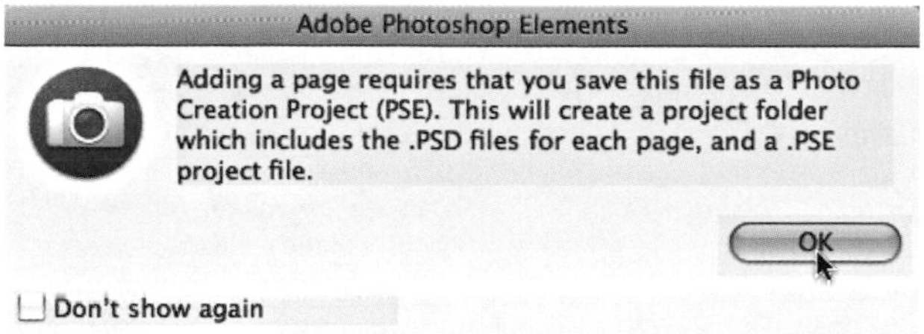

Adobe Photoshop Elements

Adding a page requires that you save this file as a Photo Creation Project (PSE). This will create a project folder which includes the .PSD files for each page, and a .PSE project file.

OK

☐ Don't show again

Figure 15-6:
You can't save a document with multiple pages in common file formats like TIFF or PSD. Your only option is PSE, as this dialog box reminds you every time you add a second page to any document. See the box that follows to learn why PSE is a mixed blessing. You can also save as a PDF, but then you lose some editing features.

TROUBLESHOOTING MOMENT

About PSE Files

Anytime you create a multipage document in Elements, you get one file format choice when it's time to save—PSE. This special new format has both advantages and disadvantages.

When you create a PSE file, you actually create a folder containing a separate .psd file for each page (for each double-page spread for a Photo Book) and the PSE project file, which contains all the information Elements needs to reassemble your document the next time you open it. That's very handy when you're working in Elements, but the drawback is that hardly any other program can read these files. PSE files work just fine if you print at home or use Kodak EasyShare Gallery for online printing. You can send PSE files to EasyShare as easily as you send JPEGs.

The rub comes if you want to use a different printing service. If you make, say, a book that you want to print at Lulu.com or MyPublisher.com, there's no way they can work with your PSE file—at least not at this writing. Most printing services require PDF format files.

Fortunately, you can also save your project as a PDF file, so you should be in good shape for uploading to other printers. But beware: You lose the layers of your project when you make it into a PDF (PDFs can have layers, but your project won't), so you can't edit it anymore. Keep the PSE file, too, at least until you're sure you don't want to change anything else.

Working with the Content and Favorites Palettes

In Elements 6, Adobe gives you a ton of stuff to use for customizing your projects, and a new palette just to hold it all: the Content palette. With Elements 6, you also get a Favorites palette, where you can keep the items you use most often from the Content palette (and from the Effects palette, too).

The Content Palette

This new palette holds backgrounds, frames, graphics, shapes, text effects, and themes to use in projects. At first glance, you'd probably expect the Content palette to work just like the Effects palette, since it has menus and a row of little icons for each of the major categories it contains, as you can see in Figure 15-7. However, the Content palette has its own way of working.

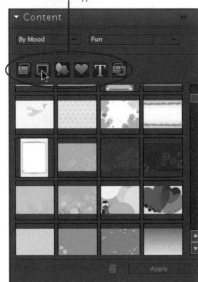

Click a button to exclude content type

Figure 15-7:
Although you'd probably expect that these little category icons are buttons to take you to a particular type of content, that's not how the Content palette works. Click any of the buttons (circled here) to exclude that category from your Content palette search. So here you see the results of searching By Mood → Fun. Click the Frames button (where the cursor is in the illustration) and you won't get any frames in the results visible in the thumbnail area.

Here's how you use the Content palette:

1. **Make the Content palette visible.**

   Go to Create → Artwork. This palette is always visible in the Artwork pane, but you can make it visible in Full Edit, as well, by going to Window → Content. (It still appears in Artwork, even when you make it visible in Full Edit. You can't remove it from the Artwork pane, even if you wanted to.)

2. **Choose how you want to search.**

   In the left-hand pull-down menu, choose to search by type (like backgrounds, frames, and so on), activity, color, event, mood, object, seasons, style, or word, or choose Show All to see everything in the palette.

3. **Refine your search.**

   In the right-hand pull-down menu, choose specifically what you want. The contents of this menu change depending on your choice in the left-hand menu. So if you choose By Type on the left, you see Backgrounds, Frames, Graphics, and so on. If you choose By Mood, the right-hand menu offers you choices like Active, Adventuresome, Fun, Romantic, or Thoughtful.

4. **If you like, filter your results.**

   Here's where those category buttons below the menus come into play. You may still get an awful lot of results from some of your menu choices, so you can use the buttons to filter out items you don't want. If you chose By Seasons and

Winter in the menus but you don't want to see frames, just click the Frames button and frames are excluded from your results. (From left to right the buttons are Backgrounds, Frames, Graphics, Shapes, Text Effects, and Show All.) You can click as many buttons as you want, to exclude as many kinds of content as you like. To bring something you've excluded back into your search results, click its button again.

Of course, if you're like a lot of people, most of the time you'll want to stick with By Type and choose the category you want. In that case the buttons are dimmed out.

5. **Add your choice to your image.**

To use anything from the Content palette, double-click the thumbnail, or drag it to your image, or click once and click Apply.

If that seems like a lot of navigation, check out the Favorites palette (described in the next section) for a faster way to reach Content palette items you use a lot.

The Favorites Palette

If you use the same effects, graphics, and styles over and over, you may find it tedious to keep navigating to them in the Content or Effects palettes. You can make your life simpler by saving your Content and Effects standbys in the new Elements 6 Favorites palette. Then you can get to these items with just a click or two.

To see the Favorites palette, go to Create → Artwork and you should see it at the bottom of the bin. To see the Favorites palette in Full Edit, go to Window → Favorites to bring it up as a free-floating palette. (You can make sure it's always visible in the Palette bin, even when you're not in Artwork mode, by opening it as a floating palette and then choosing "Place in Palette bin when closed.")

To add an item to Favorites, right-click (Control+click) its thumbnail in the Content or Effects palette and choose "Add to Favorites", or just drag its thumbnail to the palette. So, for instance, say you're creating a scrapbook where you're using the Vintage Photo 4 frame on lots of pages. Save the frame as a Favorite, and then you can just go to Favorites → Vintage Photo 4 to apply it, instead of having to scroll all the way to the bottom of the Content palette's Frames section to get to it. The Favorites palette is a big timesaver, especially since you can save art from the Content palette, along with filters, frames, and Layer styles, and have them all in one place to choose from.

To delete a favorite, right-click (Control+click) its thumbnail and choose "Remove from Favorites". If you forget what a thumbnail is for, right-click it and choose Details, and Elements will tell you about it.

Photo Books

Elements lets you create 10.25"×9" pages for use in a bound Photo Book—a very popular gift item. If you wish to order your Photo Book from Kodak EasyShare Gallery (see page 424 to learn how to set up an account), you need at least 20 pages.

Creating a Photo Book is something like creating a Photo Collage; Elements walks you through the process with plenty of hand-holding:

1. **If you want, choose your photos.**

   If you want Elements to automatically place your photos in their slots in the book, make sure you have your photos open in the Project bin and in the correct order before you start. Or if you prefer, you can wait and add each photo manually after you create the book layout.

2. **Start your Photo Book.**

   Go to Create → Photo Book.

   Elements presents your first set of choices for your book.

3. **Choose a title page photo.**

   Photo books usually have a cutout cover through which you can see one large image on the title page. This page has a different layout from the rest of the book. If you're using photos in the Project bin, drag the photo you want for the title page so that it's the first photo in the lineup.

   If you prefer, you can wait and choose your title page photo after you complete the book layout.

   Click Next to go to the next pane.

4. **Choose a layout and theme for your book.**

   You have two choices for your layout:

   • **Random Photo Layout**. Elements makes the decisions for you about how many photos will be on each page, and every page may be different. It's best to avoid this option unless you have a *lot* of photos, since some of the layouts have as many as 20 tiny photos on a page—although, of course, you can edit things later.

   • **Choose Photo Layout**. Click this option and you see a long list of possible page layout thumbnails. Click a thumbnail to select it. You need to pick left- and right-hand page layouts, which can be the same or different, as you prefer. Click Next to return to the main Photo Book pane.

   Now choose a theme. When you click a thumbnail in the theme list, Elements takes a few seconds, and then displays a little thumbnail showing an Adobe-supplied sample image in the selected theme's style.

   Your other choices are the same as for a Photo Collage. "Number of Pages" says 20 when you start your Photo Book; you need to have *between* 20 and 80 pages for a book. If you choose a number outside that range, you'll get a warning. (Actually, the warning pops up as soon as you start typing a number in the box. It doesn't look like there's any way to get rid of it, but if you just pretend it isn't there and finish typing your number, it goes away, as long as the number falls within the allowed page limits.) You don't have to enter a number here, incidentally, if you don't feel like counting. If you have more photos than will fit on 20 pages, the number of pages updates automatically.

5. **Create your Photo Book.**

Click Done, and Elements creates and opens a PSE file for you. You can edit anything in the file, exactly the same way you can change things in a Photo Collage. Once Elements creates your book, you see it, along with some special controls for navigating through your layout, as explained in Figure 15-8.

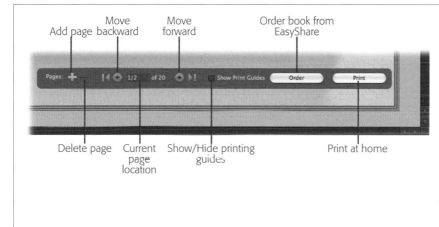

Add page   Move backward   Move forward   Order book from EasyShare

Pages: + −   1/2   of 20   Show Print Guides   Order   Print

Delete page   Current page location   Show/Hide printing guides   Print at home

Figure 15-8:
When you click Done, Elements gives you this helpful view of your Photo Book so that you can make any edits or changes to the layout. The bright aqua lines (not visible here) are the printing guides—they mark the actual page edges, so anything outside them will be cut off when your book is printed. Pay attention to them when moving or resizing your photos. The control strip lets you move through your pages to see each double-page spread, or add or remove pages.

Don't forget to save the PSE file. When you're ready to print, you can upload the book to EasyShare for printing (page 424) right from the Editor by clicking the Order button in the control strip (see Figure 15-8).

If you don't want to order from EasyShare, save your book as a PDF file, since you can send that format to most online book printing services. If you want to easily edit your book again later, just save it as a PSE file. (It doesn't hurt to save it in both formats to keep your options open.) You can also print your book on your home printer, if you like. Just click the Print button and you get the Elements Print dialog box (see page 426). You can choose to print the entire book, or just a page or range of pages.

Pay special attention to the book's page size relative to your paper size. You may not get the best results printing this way (the book's double-page spread may be too big to fit on one sheet of paper when you print full-size, for example), so try a sample page or two before sending the entire book to the printer.

TIP To help keep your pages from getting cut off in printing, in the Print window, click the icon for landscape orientation. (It's the tiny right-hand icon in the lower-left corner of the window that shows a person on his side.)

You can also create a book of photos without using the Elements Photo Book feature at all. You can connect to EasyShare and upload your photos, as explained on page 424, and choose to have EasyShare print them in its own style of photo book. (You don't get any page decorations or layout choices when you use Easy-Share's photo book creator, though.) One thing to keep in mind if you're getting a bound photo book: Whether you order from EasyShare or another publisher, almost all books use only a single photo for the first page because that's what shows through the cover cutout.

Greeting Cards

Adobe calls them "Greeting Cards," but they're more like what *you* call postcards. An Elements Greeting Card is a 4"×6" or 5"×7" single-sided page rather than a folded card. Go to Create → More Options → Greeting Card to get started. The layout and template choices are identical with those offered for Photo Collages, and the procedure is exactly the same, too. Just follow the steps for Photo Collages (page 405).

TIP You can also order greeting cards from Kodak EasyShare Gallery, as explained on page 419.

CD/DVD Jacket

In Elements, you can create CD jewel case inserts or DVD inserts, which appear on the front and back of the case.

To make a CD insert, just go to Create → More Options → CD Jacket, and you get a variety of different templates, all the correct size for use in a CD case.

The steps for creating your CD Jacket are the same as for a Photo Collage, but the layout choices, of course, are different. Pay special attention to the photo placement when choosing your layout: The right side of the layout is the front cover. You can turn Auto-Fill with Project Bin Photos off or on to suit you. (If you have five photos in the Project bin, you don't want to get a five-page CD Jacket.)

Unfortunately, only the "2 Centered" CD insert layout even roughly marks out the approximate spine area, where most CDs display their titles. If you decide to enter text that you want to appear on the spine, click the Horizontal Type tool (page 383), type away, and then go to Image → Rotate → Layer 90° Left. Then use the Move tool to place the text where you want it.

TIP   If you use a theme (page 407) and you want to add spine text, remember that home inkjet printers don't do a good job printing small white type on a dark background. You're better off going with dark type on a light background.

The DVD Jacket wizard (Create → More Options → DVD Jacket) is identical except for the layout choices.

CD/DVD Label

You can create stick-on labels for CDs and DVDs with Elements (Create → More Options → CD/DVD Label) and print them on blank label sheets from any office supply store. Elements gives you templates that create a single label layout, and when you're done, you need to place your work into the template that goes with your brand of labels. (Most CD or DVD labels print two to a page.) The major brands, like Avery (*www.avery.com*) and Neato (*www.neato.com*), have free download-loadable templates on their Web sites to help you position your labels properly on the page.

NOTE   While labels make your discs look great, it's risky to put a stick-on label on any disc you'll use in a computer. If the label gets stuck in the disk drive, you may have to replace the drive. Consider using a marker to label discs for computer use, or buying printable discs if you have a printer that will take them.

Online Creations

Besides what you can do in Elements, you can create a handful of projects online at Kodak EasyShare Gallery (page 424). You can order Kodak greeting cards (using their formats and templates instead of the Elements Greeting Card choices), for example.

You start all online creations from Bridge, not Elements. First, select your photos in Bridge. Then go to Tools → Photoshop Services → Online Photo Printing → Kodak Photo Greeting Cards. Elements automatically uploads your photos, and you see them in the EasyShare window, which walks you through creating and ordering cards. You need to set up an EasyShare account the first time you use the service. Setting up an account and using EasyShare are explained on page 424.

You can also create calendars with EasyShare. Before you start, you must select 12 photos in Bridge. Then go to Tools → Photoshop Services → Online Photo Printing → Kodak Photo Calendars, and Elements whisks you off to EasyShare. If you select fewer than 12 photos, EasyShare nags you to add more, and you don't have the option of using the same photo for each month. (Elements 6 doesn't include templates for creating calendars to print at home or take to your local print shop.)

Another online ordering option is PhotoStamps. This is real, legitimate postage that features the photo of your choice. If you've always wanted to be immortalized on a stamp, here's your opportunity. Select one or more photos if you like (you don't have to preselect your photo[s]), and then go to Tools → Photoshop Services → Online Photo Printing → Photostamps. Elements automatically uploads your photos to Stamps.com. Create an account with Stamps.com, and then you can order your stamps.

> **NOTE**   While PhotoStamps are fun, they're definitely for people with lots of disposable income. Before you spend a lot of time preparing photos, check the price list to see whether you really think the stamps will be worth the cost.

PDF Slideshows

You can create slideshows right in Elements. The Mac version of Elements lets you make exactly the same PDF slideshows you can make in full Photoshop. However, they're pretty basic slideshows, nowhere near as fancy as what you can do in programs like iPhoto, iMovie, or iDVD. Elements slideshows are designed simply to let photographers to present their photos—no music, elaborate graphics, or fancy backgrounds. But they do offer you some security options to make it difficult for folks who receive your slideshow to print out the photos.

To get started:

1. **Call up the slideshow creator.**

   You can start from Elements (File → Automation Tools → PDF Slide Show) or from Bridge (Tools → Photoshop Elements → PDF Slide Show). No matter where you start, you wind up in Elements, looking at the PDF Slide Show dialog box shown in Figure 15-9.

2. **Choose your Photos.**

   Any photos already open in Elements automatically appear in the list of source files. (Photos selected in Bridge don't show up here.) You can remove a photo by highlighting it in the list and clicking Remove. To add more photos, click Browse and find the ones you want. If you want a photo to appear more than once, click Duplicate.

3. **Arrange your photos.**

   If you don't like the order the photos are in, just drag their names in the list to put them where you want them.

4. **Choose your basic settings.**

   Your most important choice is between a multi-page document and a presentation, as explained in Figure 15-9. Your other options are:

   • **Background Color.** Your options are black, white, or gray.

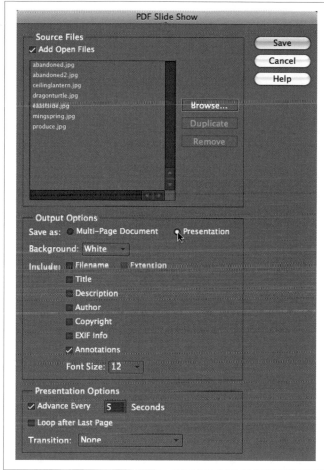

Figure 15-9:
When you start a slideshow, you have to choose whether to create a document or a presentation. If you choose Multi-Page Document, your slideshow opens up just like any other file and viewers navigate through it by moving from page to page. The Presentation option is more what you'd expect: open it in Adobe Reader and you automatically go from one photo to the next in a full-screen window, with transitions between the slides, if you choose to use them.

- **Include.** You can choose to have a variety of metadata appear with your photos: the filename, extension (like .jpg or .tif), title, description, copyright, author, EXIF data (see page 52), or any annotations (created by someone using Photoshop) that might be in the file. Elements pulls these items from the file's metadata (page 52), so if you haven't entered anything there, nothing happens when you check these boxes. You can also choose the font size—but not the font itself—in which this information displays.

- **Presentation Options.** You can only change these settings if you chose to save your slideshow as a presentation. They let you control how long each slide stays onscreen, whether your slideshow repeats in a continuous loop, and whether there are transitions between slides. You've got lots of transitions to choose from, like having one slide dissolve into the next, or having one photo split in half to reveal the next one.

NOTE An Elements presentation only plays like a slideshow if you view it with the free Adobe Reader program for either Mac or Windows (download it from *www.adobe.com*). If you open a presentation in OS X Preview, it appears as a multi-page document. You can make it play like a slideshow in Preview by going to View → Slideshow, but you won't see transitions in any program but Adobe Reader.

5. **Click Save and name your slideshow.**

   Elements brings up a Save dialog box, where you type in a name for you're your slideshow, and then click Save.

6. **Choose your PDF settings and then save your slideshow.**

   After you click the Save button in the Save dialog box, Elements takes you to yet another screen with a bunch more choices, most of which you can totally ignore, although a few may be of great interest to you. Your choices are divided into sections:

   • **General.** The Standard pull-down list lets you set what level of PDF you want. This is a leftover from Photoshop and you can skip it. The Compatibility list lets you choose the earliest version of Adobe Reader that can understand the file. Don't change this if you don't need to. You can leave the Options section alone unless you want to see your slideshow as soon as you finish it—in that case, turn on the "View PDF After Saving" checkbox.

   • **Compression.** You may want to make changes here. You can tell Elements how small you want your images to be, and how large an image should be before Elements resizes it. The standard settings make for are pretty small images. If you plan to keep your slideshow on your computer or burn it to disc, you may want to choose larger settings here. Elements normally converts 16-bit images to 8-bits (see page 228) for slideshows, but you can override that here. The "Convert 16 Bit/Channel Image to 8 Bits/Channel" checkbox is grayed out if you didn't include any 16-bit images.

   • **Output.** This whole screen is pretty irrelevant for Elements slideshows. Unless you're doing prepress work (and you probably wouldn't use Elements for that), just skip it.

   • **Security.** This screen, on the other hand, may be very useful to you. This is where you determine what your viewers will be able to do with your slideshow's photos. You can prevent printing or copying, or require a password to do so, which is handy if you're a wedding photographer sending proofs to a client, for example. You can even require a password just to view the slideshow.

   • **Summary.** This is just a list of all the file's qualities; you can't add or change anything.

7. **When you're done, click Save PDF.**

   Elements *finally* saves your slideshow, and plays it if you selected that option in the General settings.

Printing Your Photos

Now that you've gone to so much trouble making your photos look terrific, you'll probably want to share them with other people. This chapter and the next look at the many different options Elements gives you for sharing your photos with the world at large.

This chapter covers the traditional method: printing your photos. You can print your photos at home on an inkjet printer, take them to a printing kiosk at a local store, or use an online printing service. Elements makes it especially simple to use Kodak EasyShare Gallery, Adobe's online printing partner. You also get an easy connection to several other popular online photo services (page 453). And you're not limited merely to ordinary prints these days: You can create hardcover books, calendars, album pages, and greeting cards, with online services, too.

Getting Ready to Print

Whether you're going to print at home or send your photos out, you need to make sure your image file is set up to give you good-looking prints.

The first thing to check is your photo's resolution, which controls the number of pixels per inch (ppi) in your image. When you don't have enough pixels in your photo, you don't get a good print. (See page 88 for a reminder about why increasing the number of pixels in your photo is usually not desirable.) Three hundred ppi is usually considered optimum, and a quality print generally needs a resolution of at least 150 ppi to avoid the grainy look you see in low-resolution photos (see page 86 for more on setting your photo's resolution).

NOTE Be sure you set your resolution to a whole number—decimals may cause black lines on your prints with some printers. In other words, 247 ppi is fine, but you may have problems if the ppi is 247.32. Older printers are most likely to have problems with decimals.

If you're printing on photo paper or sending your photos out for printing, check to be sure that your photos are cropped to fit a standard paper size. (See page 71 if you need help with cropping.) When you're printing at home, the paper and ink you use make a big difference in the color and quality of your output; you'll get the best results if you use your printer manufacturer's recommended paper and ink.

Ordering Prints

You don't even need to own a printer to print your photos. There's no shortage of companies hoping you'll choose them for the privilege of printing your photos. You can order prints online or use a print kiosk at a local store. Elements makes it very easy to prepare your photos for printing either way. Just save your photos in a compatible file format (see page 57 for more about picking different file formats). The JPEG format is usually your best bet, but always check with the service you plan to use to see if it has any special requirements.

If you plan to physically take your photos in for printing (as opposed to ordering them online), burn the photos to a CD and take that in. You'll have fewer problems than you would if you tried copying your edited photos back onto your camera's memory card.

NOTE You can choose to burn a CD within Elements, and that's fine as long as your photos are already in the correct format. (See page 71.)

Ordering Prints Online

It's a cinch to order prints from Kodak EasyShare Gallery, right from within Elements. EasyShare accounts are totally free—you only pay for the photos you order. (EasyShare used to be called Ofoto.com, so if you had an Ofoto account, you can use that for ordering.) Here's how to place an order:

NOTE Before using any of the online components in Elements, it's a good idea to go to Bridge and select Tools → Photoshop Services → Choose Your Location, since the available services vary by country, and you want to be sure you see the correct options for your location. (EasyShare is available in lots of countries.)

1. **Choose your photos.**

   You can start with your photos open in Elements, or select the ones you want in Bridge.

2. **Go to EasyShare.**

In Elements, go to the Share Tab → Order Prints. In Bridge, it's Tools → Photoshop Services → Online Photo Printing → Kodak EasyShare Gallery Prints. The Adobe Photoshop Services/EasyShare window pops up in Bridge (and Elements hides, if that's where you started).

3. **Log in or create an account.**

If you already have an account, click the "Sign in" link in the upper-left part of the window and then enter your email address and password. (Remember, old Ofoto.com accounts will work.) If this is your first time using EasyShare, fill in your name, email address, and a password to create an account.

4. **Order your prints.**

In the window shown in Figure 16-1, choose the number and size of the prints you want for each photo, and, then enter the recipients and their addresses. (Once you've sent prints to someone, EasyShare remembers their information.) You—or whoever you sent the photos to—will receive the prints in the mail in a few days.

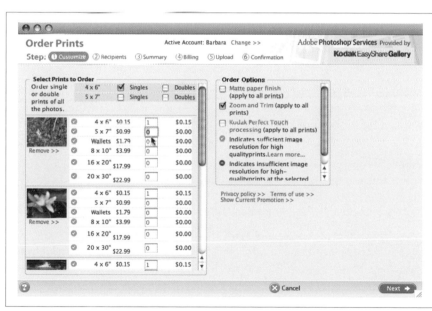

Figure 16-1:
If you decide not to order a photo you've uploaded, you can delete it once you're in EasyShare by clicking the Remove link under its thumbnail on the left side of the window. (You can upload both TIFF and JPEG files to EasyShare, but you'll only see thumbnails of JPEGs.) EasyShare also warns you if your photo's resolution (see page 82) is too low for a good print at the size you've selected.

Elements makes ordering prints from EasyShare very convenient. Of course, you can use EasyShare without Elements, and you can use other online print services like Shutterfly (*www.shutterfly.com*) or Snapfish (*www.snapfish.com*) if you like. (You can also order prints from many online photo-sharing sites. To use them, upload your photos, and then use the site's own instructions to order prints, mugs, tote bags, or whatever other merchandise is offered.)

TIP If you use an organizer program like iPhoto, it probably includes similar features. You might want to compare prices, since they can differ from one program to another—and the price when you go straight to EasyShare in a Web browser (via *kodakgallery.com*), rather than through Elements or iPhoto, may be different still. Shop around for the best prices, especially if you order lots of prints.

Printing at Home

You can also print your photos right from Elements, whether you want to make a single image, a contact sheet with lots of thumbnails, or a picture package that includes different sized prints of one image, like you'd get from a professional photographer.

Before you print anything, go to Page Setup and check the settings. You can get there from File → Page Setup, by pressing Shift+⌘+P, or there's a Page Setup button at the bottom of the Elements Print window once you have that open (File → Print or ⌘+P). Check the following settings:

- **Format for.** Be sure this is set to your specific printer, not Any Printer, or you may have trouble getting the right margins, especially if your printer allows edge-to-edge printing (also called *bleeding*). Moreover, you may not see as many paper size options with the generic setting as you will for your exact printer model.

- **Paper Size.** Make sure this is set to the size you want to print.

You can choose the page orientation (portrait or landscape) either here or in the Elements Print window (where the icons are in the lower left). In either place, just click the icon for the orientation you want.

Print Window

Element's Print window is your control center for printing from Elements. It offers you lots of ways to tweak your prints, from simply positioning your photo correctly to making very sophisticated color adjustments.

Press ⌘+P in Elements to call up the Print window. For simple printing, make sure the photo is properly positioned on the page and click Print. If you're lucky, you'll get a perfect print. If you don't like the color, the next section on color management explains your options.

Don't be intimidated by the Print window, which is shown in Figure 16-2. You probably won't need all the settings every time you print, but each setting comes in handy sooner or later. If you've used Elements before, this window may look more complicated, but it's really not. It's just that now you can see all the extra settings that were hidden in earlier versions unless you went looking for them. It still works pretty much the same as ever.

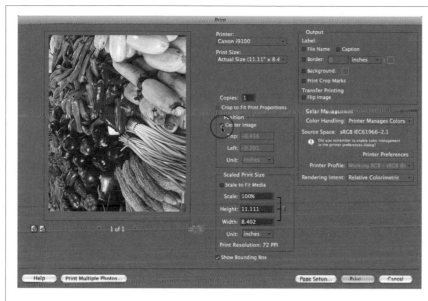

Figure 16-2:
When you begin printing in Elements, you see this dialog box: the Print window, which you can use to print a single image. Turning off the Center Image checkbox (circled) lets you drag your photo around manually so you can position it wherever you like, assuming you've got room on your paper. At the bottom-left corner of the window is a button labeled Print Multiple Photos. Clicking it sends you to the Picture Package dialog box, discussed in the next section.

On the left side of the Print window is an image preview showing the location where your photo will print. Normally, Elements shows a *bounding box*, the black outline with handles on the corners indicating the edges of your photo. Don't worry, the bounding box itself doesn't print along with your photo. The box gives you a way to move and resize your image by dragging the handles. If seeing the bounding box bothers you, then get rid of it by turning off the Show Bounding Box checkbox near the bottom of the window.

The familiar Elements Rotate symbols appear below the right corner of the image window. Use these if you need to change the orientation of your photo. If you need to rotate the paper, use the small white buttons below the lower left corner of the image preview area.

You can resize your photo in the Print window in several ways:

- **Print Size menu.** Choose any print size from the list or enter a Custom Size. Fit On Page changes the size of your image, if necessary, to fit the size of the paper you're using. If you choose a size with a different aspect ratio (different proportions) than your photo, Elements automatically crops your photo to fit, so if you want to control the crop, do it yourself first. If Elements intends to crop your photo, it turns on "Crop to Fit Print Proportions" (explained below) and shows you a preview of what it plans to do.

- **Scaled Print Size.** Resize your photo by entering a percentage or new dimensions here. (If you want a custom size, enter the size here. You don't have to change the Print Size menu, too.) When you turn on "Scale to Fit Media", Elements automatically resizes your photo to fit on the page size you chose in Print Setup.

- **Show Bounding Box.** You can use the bounding box to change the size of your image. Drag one of the handles (they look like tiny white boxes) on any of the bounding box's corners to make your image larger or smaller.

- **Crop to Fit Print Proportions.** If your image has a different aspect ratio (length to width proportions) than the paper you're printing on, and you're feeling lazy, then turn this checkbox on and Elements crops your print for you. Elements turns this box on automatically when you choose a size from the Print Size menu that won't work unless your photo is cropped to fit the aspect ratio.

You need to be cautious about resizing in the Print window, though. Elements resamples your image (page 88) to make it fit the size you choose. Don't go larger than 100 percent, or the quality of your photo starts to deteriorate. Generally, it's better to do most resizing before you get to the Print window, especially when you're making a photo larger. Enlarging your photo in the Print window can make for grainy, poor-quality prints. If you can see pixelation in the preview window, then you know that something's amiss, and you should start by checking your resolution. (Earlier versions of Elements warned you if the resolution was low; in Elements 6, it's up to you to pay attention to the ppi setting in the Scaled Print Size area in the Print window.)

The other setting in the main part of the Print window is:

- **Position.** This setting tells Elements where to put your photo on the page. Elements starts you out with the Center Image checkbox turned on. You need to turn it off before you can reposition your image. To change the location of your photo, either drag its thumbnail or, in the boxes provided, type in the amount of space you want between the photo and the edges of the page, in the measurement of your choice. ("Top" controls how far your image is from the top of the page, and "Left" controls the distance from the left edge of the page.)

The right side of the Print window contains the settings that were hidden in earlier versions of Elements. They're divided into two groups: Output and Color Management. Color Management is explained in the next section. The Output settings give you the following options:

- **Label.** You can print the file name and/or caption directly on your photo by turning on the relevant checkbox. The image preview area shows you where your text gets printed. You can add caption text by going to File → Info or, in Bridge, using the Metadata panel (see page 52).

- **Border.** When you want to add a border to your photo, turn on this checkbox and enter the size you want for your border (in inches, millimeters, or points). Elements shrinks your photo to accommodate the border, even if there's plenty of empty space around the picture, so you may need to resize the photo before you print it to get the size you originally chose. Then click the white square to bring up the Elements Color Picker (see page 199) so that you can choose a color for your border.

- **Background.** If there's empty space on the page and you want to fill it with a background color, turn on this checkbox and choose a color by clicking its color square to bring up the Elements Color Picker.

- **Print Crop Marks.** This setting lets you print guidelines in the margins of your photo to make it easier to trim it exactly. Crop marks are useful mainly for trimming bordered photos so that the borders are exactly even.

- **Flip Image.** Turn this checkbox on to horizontally reverse your image. Use it when printing transfers for projects like T-shirts.

NOTE The Print window isn't *color managed*, which means that what you see in the window isn't meant to show you the exact colors you'll get when you print. Instead, you're looking only at the position of your photo.

WORKAROUND WORKSHOP

Economical Print Experiments

If you've just gone out and bought top-quality photo paper, you may be suffering from a bit of sticker shock and perhaps are even thinking, "Oh yeah, great. Now I'm supposed to use this stuff up experimenting? At that price?"

The good news is, while you have to bite the bullet and sacrifice a sheet or two, you don't need to waste the whole box. Instead, try this: Make a small selection somewhere in a photo you want to print, press ⌘+C, and go to File → New → "Image from Clipboard". You get a new file with only a small piece of your photo in it.

This is your test print. In the Print window, turn off the Center Image checkbox and drag your small photo to the upper-left corner of the page. Try printing the page using Elements' standard settings. If your print looks good, you're ready to print the whole photo.

On the other hand, if you don't like the result, then press ⌘+P to bring up the Print window again. This time, move your test strip over to the right a little bit. Change your settings (keeping note of the changes you've made) and print again on the same piece of paper. Your new test prints out beside the first strip. Keep moving the test area around on the page, and you can try out quite a few different combinations of settings, all on the same sheet of paper.

Color management

Elements gives you several advanced color-related settings in the Print window. If you're content with the way your prints look without adjusting these settings, just be happy and ignore them. But if you don't like the color you're getting from Elements, use these advanced controls to make adjustments.

If you remember from Chapter 7, Elements is a *color-managed* program, which means it tries to coordinate the color settings used by various devices and programs: your photo (which may retain color settings applied by your camera), your monitor, your Elements settings, and your printer. Sometimes you need to step in and help Elements decide which settings are best, since different devices and programs can have different interpretations of what individual colors look like.

The most important choice you need to make is whether you want Elements or your printer to manage your photo's color settings. (It's possible to let both Elements *and* your printer have a say in color management, but that almost always mucks things up.) The good news is that Elements 6 does its best to keep you from making that kind of mistake, and it tries to make managing the color in your prints as painless as possible.

You have four main choices to make in color management:

- **Color Handling.** You decide who's going to be in charge: Elements (Photoshop Elements Manages Colors), your printer (Printer Manages Colors), or nobody (No Color Management). The choice you make here determines your options in the rest of the settings. Elements also gives you some hints about your printer settings, as you can see in Figure 16-3.

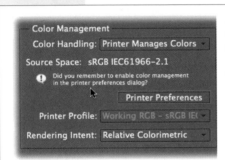

Figure 16-3:
Elements thoughtfully reminds you to turn color management off in your printer when you choose "Photoshop Elements Manages Colors" or "No Color Management", and on for "Printer Manages Colors". The Printer Preferences button just takes you to the Page Setup dialog box.

- **Source Space.** This setting shows you which, if any, color space your file's tagged with (for example, sRGB or Adobe RGB). You don't actually choose a setting here; instead, this line tells you the color space associated with your file. See page 184 for more about color spaces.

- **Printer Profile.** This setting is grayed out unless you chose Photoshop Elements Manages Color in the Color Handling menu. If Elements is managing the color, you can choose the profile you want from a list of all the possible profiles that Elements can find on your computer.

- **Rendering Intent.** You can use this setting to tell Elements what to do if your photo contains colors that fall outside the color range of the print space you're using. Your choices are explained in the box on page 431. When you choose No Color Management for your Color Handling setting, this setting isn't available.

The easiest way to set up color management, and a good way to start, is to choose Printer Manages Color. This means that Elements hands your photo over to your printer and lets your printer take care of the color management duties. Then all you need to do is select the proper paper profile and settings for your printer. More on that in a moment.

TIP   If your camera takes photos in sRGB and you've been editing them in No Color Management or "Always Optimize Colors for Computer Screens," then don't alter your workflow by choosing Adobe RGB for the printer profile. Your colors may shift drastically. If for some reason you want to change the color space for the printer, first go to Image → Convert Color Profile, and then apply the Adobe RGB profile to your photo. If you aren't absolutely sure that your printer understands Adobe RGB (many inkjets don't), and you don't have a compelling reason for changing, then it's best to leave things alone.

There are limitless variations on how you can use the color settings in Elements, and you may need to experiment a bit to find what works best for you. See the box on page 429 for advice on how to cheaply test out a bunch of different print settings. If you go looking around for more information, you'll find that this is a very controversial subject. Everyone has a different approach that's the "right" one. In fact, you have many options that can lead to good results.

When you've made all your adjustments in the Print window, just click Print.

UNDER THE HOOD

What's Your Intent?

The Rendering Intent setting in Elements Print window is the most confusing of the color management options for most people. Here are the basics of what you need to know to choose a setting. Sometimes your photo may contain colors that fall outside the color boundaries of the print space you're using. Intent just tells Elements what to do if that happens. You have four choices:

- **Perceptual** tells Elements to preserve the relationship between the colors in your image—even if that means Elements has to do some visible color shifting to make all the colors fit.

- **Saturation** makes colors very vivid but not necessarily very accurate. This setting is more for special effects than for regular photo printing.

- **Relative Colorimetric** tries to preserve the colors in both the source and the output space by shifting things to the closest matching color in the printer profile's space. Relative Colorimetric is Elements' standard setting, and it's usually what you want because it keeps your colors as close as possible to what you see on your screen

- **Absolute Colorimetric** lets you simulate another printer and paper. This setting is for specialized proofing situations.

The OS X Print Dialog Box

You make your final print setting choices—your paper profile and color management settings—in the OS X system print dialog box. (Your exact paper and color options depend on the kind of printer you have.) First, choose your printer from the top pull-down menu, and then choose your paper and color settings. These settings are well hidden: in Tiger (10.4), you can find them by clicking the text that says "Copies and Pages" for a pull-down menu of print options. In Leopard (10.5), click the blue down arrow button to the right of the printer's name to expand the dialog box, and then choose your paper and color options from the Layout menu.

Selecting a paper profile may sound complicated, but it's usually as simple as selecting the kind of paper you plan to use (Photo Paper Plus Glossy, say) from a list of choices. Setting color options can be as easy as choosing "high-quality photo" from a list of quality settings, and usually you'll have someplace to specify Printer Color Management, although probably not in the same menu item. (Ignore the Color Matching section in the top half of the menu, if it appears—you don't need to do anything there.)

When everything's all set, click Print. If you have an inkjet printer, Elements immediately pops up the mystifying dialog box shown in Figure 16-4. Just turn on the checkbox next to "Don't show again" and then click OK.

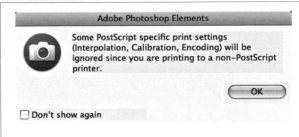

Figure 16-4:
Boy, does this window confuse people. You see it every time you print from a non-Post Script printer, until you turn on the "Don't show again" checkbox. Don't worry: It doesn't mean there's anything wrong with your files, Elements, or your printer. Post Script is simply an Adobe-created language used primarily by higher-quality laser printers. All this dialog box means is that your file contains additional data that isn't relevant to printing to an inkjet printer. Nod, click OK, and forget about it in the future.

Printing Multiple Images

Elements makes it really easy to create and customize contact sheets that show lots of thumbnails on one page. You can also print picture packages with several different sized photos on one page, and you can edit both these layouts to get exactly the arrangement you want.

Contact Sheet II

Contact sheets show a bunch of thumbnails of different photos. You can use contact sheets to keep track of the photos on a CD or as a record of all the photos you took in one shooting session, for example. (In case you were wondering, there's no Contact Sheet I in Elements 6—it was replaced by this one long ago.) The plug-in that comes with Elements (see page 460 for more about plug-ins) makes it a snap to create a contact sheet that's laid out exactly the way you want.

To create a contact sheet:

1. **Organize your photos.**

   You can make a contact sheet of all your open photos, all the photos in a folder, or selected photos in Bridge. So decide which photos you want to use and open them in Elements, put them all in a folder, or open and select them in Bridge.

2. **Call up the Contact Sheet II dialog box.**

In Elements, press Option+⌘+P or go to File → Contact Sheet II. In Bridge, go to Tools → Photoshop Elements → Contact Sheet II. No matter where you start, you end up in Elements, where you create your contact sheet using the dialog box shown in Figure 16-5.

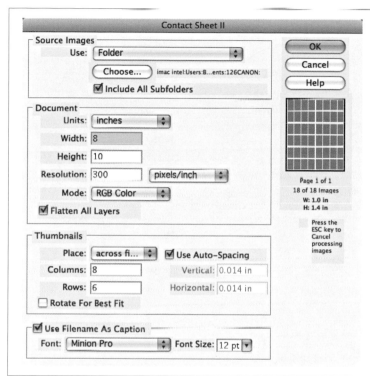

Figure 16-5:
You can customize your contact sheet in many ways, including settings like the amount of space between your thumbnails. As you adjust settings, the layout thumbnail on the right side of the window changes to reflect your choices, and Elements keeps a running tally of the number of pages needed to fit your photos in the current layout.

3. **Choose your settings.**

You've got lots of options:

- **Source Images.** This is where you pick the photos you want to include. You can select the files currently open in Elements, files in a certain folder, or files you selected in Bridge.

- **Document.** This is where you select the overall settings for your page. Set the page size in inches, centimeters, or pixels. Then enter a resolution and choose between RGB color and grayscale for your color mode (see page 48). The "Flatten All Layers" setting doesn't affect your originals—it just creates a contact sheet where text and images are on the same layer. It's best to leave the "Flatten All Layers" checkbox turned on to keep your file size smaller.

- **Thumbnails.** These settings let you control how the thumbnails are laid out. Choose whether you want your pictures to go across the page or down (as they're being laid out), how many columns and rows you'd like, and whether you want Elements to figure out the spacing between images or whether you want to set the spacing yourself. Turning on the "Rotate For Best Fit" checkbox turns the thumbnails so they fit on the paper most efficiently. If you don't like having photos improperly oriented, leave this checkbox off.

- **Use Filename As Caption.** Use this setting if you want the name of each photo to appear as a caption. Your font choices are Myriad Pro, Minion Pro, or Lucida Grande. Getting a font size you like may take some experimenting.

4. **Click OK to create your contact sheet.**

Elements goes to work, and you see your images flash back and forth. If you watch the contact sheet thumbnail in the Project bin, you can see it update to show each new photo as Elements places it. If you change your mind about making a contact sheet while Elements is working, press the Escape key.

5. **Save or print your contact sheet.**

Your finished contact sheet is just like any other file. You can save it in the format of your choice, print it out, burn it to disc along with the photos it contains (see page 60), whatever. If you included so many photos that they don't all fit on one page, each page is a separate document.

Picture Packages

You can also print a group of pictures, called a picture package, on one page. You can make packages that features one photo printed in several different sizes, or create a picture package that includes more than one photo. Here's how:

1. **Start your package.**

You can start a picture package from Elements (File → Picture Package, or click the Print Multiple Photos button in the Print window [⌘+P]), or from Bridge (Tools → Photoshop Elements → Picture Package). You don't need to select any photos first, unless you want to. The Picture Package dialog box opens in Elements, even if you start from Bridge.

2. **Choose your photo(s).**

The Use drop-down menu lets you choose the pictures you want to appear in your package. If you choose lots of files, Elements uses as many pages as necessary to fit them all in. You can use a single file, a folder of photos, the frontmost open photo, pictures you preselected in Bridge, or all open photos. Elements starts by filling the entire layout with copies of one photo, but you can change that in step 4 if you want more than one image per page.

3. **Choose your page size and layout settings.**

Elements gives you lots of options:

- **Document.** This is where you pick the overall settings for your package. You can set the page size (8"×10", 11"×16", or 11"×17"), the layout (how many photos appear on one page and their sizes), resolution, and whether you want to use RGB color or grayscale (see page 48). "Flatten All Layers" works the same way as it does for a contact sheet (see step 3 on page 433).

NOTE   The page size options are all photo paper sizes, but you can print the 8" × 10" layout on standard 8.5" × 11" paper.

- **Label.** This is where you can choose to have text appear on your photos. If you don't want any text, leave Content set to None. If you want text, you can use the filename, copyright, description, credit, or title from the file's metadata (see page 52), or you can enter custom text. The other options are for the text itself: font, size, color, opacity, and position. If you don't want black text, click the Color box to bring up the Color Picker (see page 198). You can tell Elements to rotate the text so that if your photos print sideways, the text still prints right side up on the photo. You can use the Opacity and Position settings to create a watermark, as explained on page 258.

If all these options aren't enough for you, check out the next section, which explains how to customize your picture package even further.

1. **Adjust the placement of your photos.**

   Figure 16-6 explains how to change the contents of a particular placeholder (Adobe calls them *zones*). Keep clicking zones to put as many different shots on a page as you have zones to hold them.

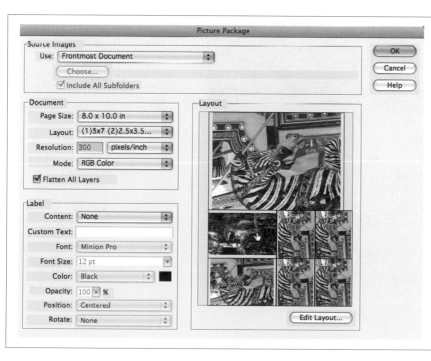

Figure 16-6:
To add a new photo or replace an existing one, click any box in the layout and choose the new photo in the Select an Image File dialog box that appears. (You can't rearrange photos by dragging them from one zone to another.) An even easier way to slot in a new photo is to drag it in from Bridge, iPhoto, or even the Finder, and then drop it in the right zone. Elements opens your image and replaces the existing photo.

5. **When everything's arranged to your liking, click OK to create your package.**

   If your settings required more than one page to accommodate all your photos, each page is a separate file. You can print them or save them in any format that suits you, just like a single photo.

Customizing your picture package

You're not limited to the picture package layouts Elements offers. You can customize a layout in all sorts of ways and then save it to use again. Start by choosing the built-in layout that's closest to what you want. Click the Edit Layout button in the bottom right of the Picture Package window, and the dialog box shown in Figure 16-7 appears.

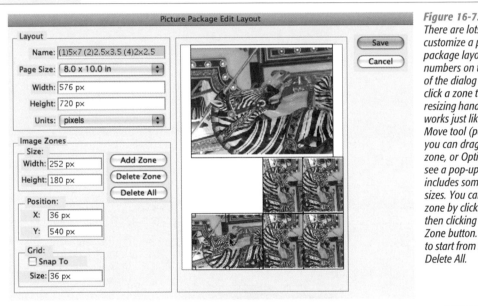

Figure 16-7:
There are lots of ways to customize a picture package layout. Enter numbers on the left side of the dialog box or just click a zone to bring up resizing handles. Resizing works just like using the Move tool (page 138)—you can drag or resize a zone, or Option-click it to see a pop-up menu that includes some standard sizes. You can delete a zone by clicking it and then clicking the Delete Zone button. If you want to start from scratch, click Delete All.

You can choose a preset page size or type in a custom size in inches, centimeters, millimeters, or pixels. As Figure 16-7 explains, you can also change the size and location of the images in your package. (The boxes for typing in custom sizes are grayed out until you select a zone.) If you click a zone and then click Add Zone, Elements creates an additional zone instead of replacing the one you clicked.

If there's no space that's big enough for the new zone, Elements just dumps the new zone on top of the existing layout and leaves you to sort things out. Just delete an existing zone to make room for the new zone. The "Snap to" checkbox in the Grid section helps you line up your zones.

When you're happy with your custom layout, name it by typing something in the Name box, and then click Save. (Be sure to give your layout a new name so you don't overwrite the built-in layout you started with.) Make sure you save it in the folder <your hard drive> → Applications → Adobe Photoshop Elements 6 → Presets → Layouts. That way, your new layout will show up in the list of preset layouts.

If this method of customizing a picture package doesn't meet your needs, the box below explains yet another way to create a custom package.

WORKAROUND WORKSHOP

Creating Your Own Package

You may find that you want a different layout for your picture package than any of the choices that Elements offers. You can make your own picture package from scratch, and it's not hard to do.

1. Save all the photos you want to use at the same resolution.

2. Create a new document (⌘+N or File → New). Make sure it's the size you want your complete package to be. Also make sure it has the same resolution as your photos. (See "Choosing Resolution" on page 47 for more about setting a file's resolution.) You can save time by choosing the Letter preset size from the New file menu. That's already set to 300 ppi.

3. Drag each photo into your new document. Drag the photos from the Layers palette (page 172) and then position them as you wish, or just copy (⌘+C) and paste (⌘+V). You can use the Move tool (page 166) or scale (page 308) to resize them.

When you have all your photos positioned and sized to suit you, save the combined file and print it. You can make the file smaller by flattening the layers first (Layer → Flatten Image). Flatten only if you don't think you'll want to tweak your layout later on.

Elements and the Web

Printing your photos is great, but it costs money, takes time, and doesn't do much to instantly impress faraway friends with your newfound photo prowess. Fortunately, Elements comes packed with tools that make it easy to email your photos, prepare them for posting on the Web, and even create simple Web galleries. You can also upload your photos to popular Internet sites, either to share with your friends or to sell. This chapter gives you the scoop.

Image Formats and the Web

Back in the Web's early days, making your graphic files small was important, because most Internet connections were as slow as snails. Nowadays, file size isn't as crucial; your main obligation when creating graphics for the Web is ensuring they're compatible with the Web browsers people use to view your Web pages. That means you'll probably want to use either of the two most popular image formats, JPEG or GIF, but PNG is also an option:

- **JPEG** (Joint Photographic Experts' Group) is the most popular choice for images with lots of detail and where you need smooth color transitions. Photos are almost always posted on the Web as JPEGs.

  NOTE JPEGs can't have transparent areas, although there's a workaround for that: Fill the background around your image with the same color as the Web page you want to post it on. The background blends into the Web page, giving the impression that your object is surrounded by transparency. See Figure 17-4 for details on how this trick works.

• **GIF** (Graphics Interchange Format) is great for images with limited numbers of colors, like corporate logos and headlines. Text looks much sharper in the GIF format than it does as a JPEG. GIFs also allow you to keep transparency as part of your image.

• **PNG** (Portable Network Graphic) is a Web graphics format that was created to overcome some of the disadvantages of JPEGs and GIFs, and is becoming increasingly popular online. There's a lot to like about PNG files. They can include transparent areas, and the format reduces the file size of photographs without losing data, as happens with JPEG files (see page 59 for more about that). The big drawback to PNG files is that only newer Web browsers deal with them very well. Older Windows versions of Internet Explorer are notorious for not supporting the PNG format, so if you've got potential viewers with ancient computers, you probably won't want to use PNG.

Elements makes it a breeze to save your images in any of these formats. You do so by using the Save For Web dialog box, which is covered in the next section.

Saving Images for the Web or Email

If you plan to email your photos or put them up on your Web site, Save For Web is a terrific tool that takes any open image and saves it in a Web friendly format; it also gives you lots of options to help achieve maximum image quality while keeping file size to a minimum. The goal of Save For Web is to create as small a file as you can without compromising the image's onscreen quality.

Save For Web creates smaller JPEG files than you get by merely using Save As, because it strips out the EXIF data, the information about your camera (see page 52). To get started with Save For Web, go to File → "Save for Web" or press Option+Shift+⌘+S. The dialog box shown in Figure 17-1 appears.

The most important point to remember when saving images for the Web is that the resolution (measured in pixels per inch, or ppi) is completely irrelevant. All you care about are the image's pixel dimensions, such as 400×600. When you have a photo that you've optimized for print, you'll almost certainly need to drastically downsize it. This is easy to do in Save For Web.

Elements gives you a lot of useful tools in Save For Web. In the top-left corner is a Toolbox, featuring the Hand, Zoom, and Eyedropper tools, with a color square below the Eyedropper. The Hand and Zoom work the same way they do elsewhere in Elements. (See page 81 for more about the Hand tool and page 79 for more about the Zoom tool.)

Below each image preview, you'll see the file size and the estimated download time, which you can adjust by modifying your assumptions about your recipient's Internet connection speed, as explained in Figure 17-2. You can also adjust the zoom percentage (using the Zoom menu at the bottom of the window), but usually you'll want to stick to 100 percent because that's the size your image will be on the Web.

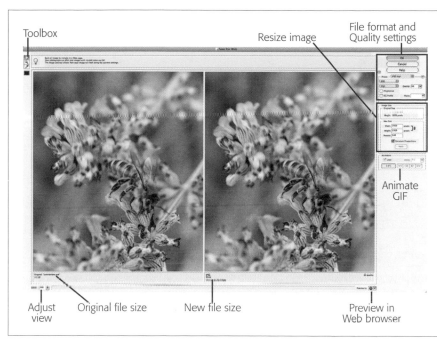

Toolbox

Resize image

File format and
Quality settings

Animate
GIF

Adjust
view

Original file size

New file size

Preview in
Web browser

Figure 17-1:
The Save For Web
dialog box makes it
easy to get the exact
image size and quality
you want. The left side
shows your original
image. The preview on
the right shows what
your newly sized image
will look like at its new
file size.

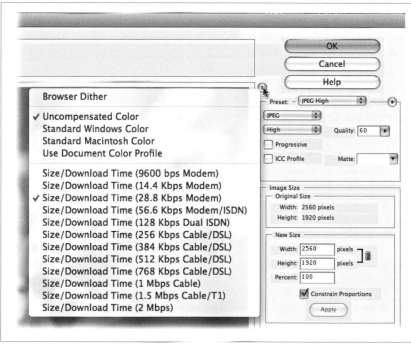

Browser Dither

✓ Uncompensated Color
  Standard Windows Color
  Standard Macintosh Color
  Use Document Color Profile

  Size/Download Time (9600 bps Modem)
  Size/Download Time (14.4 Kbps Modem)
✓ Size/Download Time (28.8 Kbps Modem)
  Size/Download Time (56.6 Kbps Modem/ISDN)
  Size/Download Time (128 Kbps Dual ISDN)
  Size/Download Time (256 Kbps Cable/DSL)
  Size/Download Time (384 Kbps Cable/DSL)
  Size/Download Time (512 Kbps Cable/DSL)
  Size/Download Time (768 Kbps Cable/DSL)
  Size/Download Time (1 Mbps Cable)
  Size/Download Time (1.5 Mbps Cable/T1)
  Size/Download Time (2 Mbps)

OK

Cancel

Help

Preset: — JPEG High

JPEG

High   Quality: 60

☐ Progressive

☐ ICC Profile   Matte:

Image Size
  Original Size
    Width: 2560 pixels
    Height: 1920 pixels

  New Size
    Width: 2560   pixels
    Height: 1920   pixels
    Percent: 100

    ☑ Constrain Proportions

    Apply

Figure 17-2:
The Save For Web window
gives you an estimate of
how long it will take to
download your image. If
you want to change the
download settings (for
example, the speed of the
Internet connection), then
go to the upper-right corner
of the preview area and
click the arrow button for
the pop-out list shown here.

In the upper-right corner of the window are your file format and quality choices. What you see varies a bit depending on which format you've chosen. Below that are your options for resizing your image. If you want to create animated GIFs (those tiny moving images you see on Web pages), then set up the animation at the bottom of the settings panel. How to create animated GIFs is explained later.

Using Save For Web

When you're ready to use Save For Web, follow these steps:

1. **Open the image you want to modify.**

   NOTE   If your camera has more than about 6 megapixels, you're likely to see a warning that your image exceeds the size that Save For Web was designed for. Just click Yes to proceed. Unless you're running Elements on an antique, memory-starved computer, you should be fine.

2. **Launch the Save For Web dialog box.**

   Go to File → "Save for Web" or press Option+Shift+⌘+S. The Save For Web dialog box appears.

3. **Choose the format and quality settings you want for your Web image.**

   Your choices are explained in the following section.

4. **If necessary, resize your image so it fits onscreen without having to scroll.**

   If you want to make sure that anyone can see the whole image, no matter how small their monitor, enter 650 pixels or less for the longest side of your photo in the New Size area. (650 pixels is about the largest size that can fit on small monitors without scrolling, but if you're sending to someone with a *really* old monitor you may want to stay below 500 pixels. If your friends all have big new monitors, you can go much larger.) As long as Constrain Proportions is turned on, you don't have to enter the dimension for the other side of your photo. You can also resize your image by entering a percentage (for example, entering 90 shrinks your image by 10 percent). When you're finished entering the new dimensions, click Apply.

5. **Check your results.**

   Look at the file size again to see if it's small enough, and take a close look at the image quality in the preview area. Use Elements' file size optimization feature, if necessary, as explained in Figure 17-3. You can also preview your image in your actual Web browser (see the section "Previewing Images and Adjusting Color" on page 445).

6. **When everything looks good, click OK.**

   Name the new file and save it to the location of your choice. There's no Undo option in Save For Web, but you can Option-click the Cancel button to change it to a Reset button. If you're processing several photos with the same settings, Option-click the Help button to change it to say Remember. Then next time Save For Web opens, it'll have your current settings pre-selected.

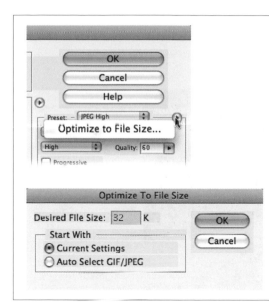

Figure 17-3:
Elements' Save For Web dialog box has a helpful file-size optimization feature for when you need to send a file someplace that puts limits on your total file size.

Top: When you click the triangle next to the Preset menu and choose "Optimize to File Size", Elements gives you a dialog box so you can enter your desired file size.

Bottom: Use K (kilobytes) as your unit of measurement in the Optimize To File Size dialog box. Picking Current Settings tells Elements to start with whatever settings you've entered in the main Save For Web window, like the format and quality. Autoselect GIF/JPEG means you want Elements to decide between GIF and JPEG for you. Once you've finished making your selections, click OK. Elements then reduces your image to the size you requested.

Save For Web file format options

One way to reduce your file size is to reduce the physical size, as explained in step 4. But you can also make your file smaller by adjusting the quality settings. Your quality options vary depending on which format you're using.

- **JPEG.** Elements offers you a variety of basic quality settings for your JPEGs: Low, Medium, High, Very High, and Maximum. You can further adjust the quality by entering a number in the Quality box on the right. A higher number means higher quality. Generally, Medium is usually enough if you're saving for Web use. If you use Save For Web to make JPEG files for printing, then you'll want Maximum.

  If you turn on the Progressive checkbox, your JPEG loads from the top down. This option was popular for large files when everyone had slow dial-up connections, but it makes a slightly larger file, so it's not as popular today. Using the ICC profile checkbox (ICC stands for International Color Consortium), you can keep any color space profile embedded in your image. (See page 184 for more about color spaces.) Few Web browsers understand ICC profiles (Safari is one of the few), so if you use this option, you can expect your photos to look different in color-managed browsers than in, say, Internet Explorer.

  With Matte, you can set the color of any area that's transparent in your original (see Figure 17-4). When you don't set a matte color, you get white. By choosing a matte color that matches the background of your Web page, you can make it look like your image is surrounded by transparency. In Elements, you have three ways to select your color: Click the arrow on the right side of the matte color box and choose from the menu, click the arrow and then sample a color from your image with the eyedropper tool, or click the color square in the matte color box to call up the Color Picker. (See page 199 for more about using the Color Picker.)

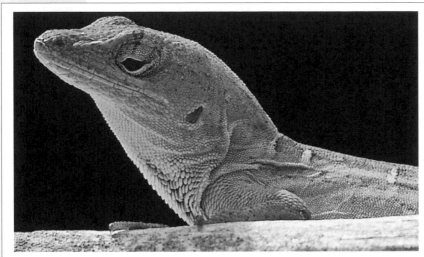

Figure 17-4:
The JPEG format doesn't preserve transparent areas when you save your image. But Elements helps you simulate transparency by letting you choose a matte color, which replaces the transparency. When you choose a matte color that's identical to your Web page's background, you create a transparent effect. The black matte around this lizard will blend into the black background of the page it goes on.

- **GIF.** The fewer colors a GIF contains, the smaller the file. In Elements, GIF format names tell you the number of colors that will be in your GIF. For example, GIF-128 means there are 128 colors, and GIF-32 tells you there are 32 colors. You can also use the Colors box to set your own number of colors. Use the arrows on the left edge of the box to scroll to the number you want, or just type it into the box.

  If you turn on Interlacing, your image will download in multiple passes (sort of like an image that's slowly coming into focus). With today's computers, interlacing isn't as useful as it used to be on slower machines. If you want to keep transparent areas transparent, then leave Transparency turned on. If you don't want transparency, then choose a matte color the way you do for a JPEG. When you create a GIF that you plan to animate, turn on Animate. (You have to have a layered file to make an animated GIF. See page 446 for more about animated GIFs.)

  Dithering is an important setting. The GIF format works by compressing and flattening large areas of colors. When you choose dithering, Elements blends existing colors to make it look like you have more colors than are actually in your GIF. For instance, Elements may mix red and blue pixels in an area to create purple. You can choose how much dither you want. Sometimes you don't want any dithering—it depends on the image.

- **PNG-8.** The more basic of your PNG choices in Elements, PNG-8 gives you pretty much the same options as you get with GIF.

  With both PNG-8 and GIF, you get advanced options for how to display colors (generating the color lookup table if you're a Web-design maven). You can totally forget this option even exists, but if you're curious, these are your choices: Selective, the standard setting, favors broad areas of color and keeps to Web-safe colors; Perceptual favors colors that the human eye is more sensitive to; Adaptive samples colors from the spectrum appearing most commonly in the image; and Restrictive keeps everything within the old 216-color Web palette.

- **PNG-24.** This is the more advanced level of PNG. Technically, both levels of PNG let you use transparency, but more web browsers understand transparent areas in PNG-24 than in PNG-8. Your save options are the same as those for JPEG files.

NOTE   The Elements Color Picker lets you limit your choices to Web-safe colors, if you turn on Only Web Colors. But do you need to stick to this limited color palette for Web graphics? Not really. You need to be seriously concerned about keeping to Web-safe colors only if you know the majority of people looking at your image will be using very old Web browsers. All modern Web browsers have been able to cope with a normal color range for several years now.

Getting colors to display consistently in all browsers is another kettle of fish entirely. See the next section, "Previewing Images and Adjusting Color."

Previewing Images and Adjusting Color

Elements gives you a few different ways to preview how your image will look in a Web browser. You can start by looking at your image in any Web browser you have on your computer (see Figure 17-5).

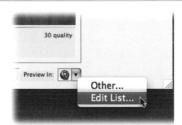

Figure 17-5:
To preview your image in a Web browser, click the Preview In icon to launch your computer's standard Web browser, or click the arrow and choose a browser from the list. The first time you click this icon, you may need to go to Edit List, as shown in the figure, and then click Find All. Elements sniffs out every browser on your computer and automatically adds what it finds to the list of available browsers. The icon you see may vary, because Elements displays your chosen browser's icon (or the last browser you used for previewing in Elements).

To add a new browser, in the Save For Web dialog box, click the Preview In dropdown list and choose Edit List. Then, in the dialog box that appears, click Add Browser and navigate to the one you want. If you want to have all your browsers listed, then click Find All. From now on you can pick any browser from the list. When you do, Elements launches the browser with your image in it.

If you want to get a very rough idea of how your image will look on other people's monitors, click the arrow that's just above the upper-right corner of the right preview window. Above the modem specifications, you see a list of color options:

- **Uncompensated Color.** This option shows colors the way they normally appear on your monitor. This setting makes no adjustment to the color. It's what you usually see.

• **Standard Windows Color.** The Standard Windows Color option shows colors the way they should look on an average Windows monitor.

• **Standard Macintosh Color.** This option shows colors the way they should look on an average Mac monitor.

• **Use Document Color Profile.** If you kept the ICC profile (page 184), this setting tries to match how your image will look as a result.

• **Browser Dither.** If an image contains more colors than a Web browser can display, the browser uses dithering (see page 444) to create the additional colors. Select this option to get an idea of how your image will look if a browser has to dither the colors.

These are all only rough approximations. You need only take a stroll down the monitor aisle at your local electronics chain to see what a wacky bunch of color variations are possible. You really can't control how other people are going to see your image unless you go to their homes and adjust their monitors for them.

> **NOTE** Changing any of these color options affects only the way the image displays on your monitor in Save For Web; it doesn't change anything in the image itself.

Creating Animated GIFs

With Elements, it's simple to create *animated GIFs*, those little animated illustrations that make Web pages look annoyingly jumbled or delightfully active, depending on your tastes. If you've ever seen a strip of movie film or the cels for a cartoon, Elements creates a similar series of frames with these specialized GIFs.

Animated GIFs are made in layers. (If you download an animated GIF and open it up in Elements, it appears as a multi-layered image.) When you create an animated GIF, you make a new layer for each frame. Save For Web creates the actual animation, which you can preview in a Web browser.

> **TIP** It's a shame that you can't easily animate a JPEG the way you can a GIF. Most elaborate Web animations involving photographs are done with Flash, which is another program altogether. If you want to learn about Flash, check out *Flash CS3: The Missing Manual*.

Probably the best way to learn how to create an animated GIF is to make one. Here's a little tutorial on making twinkling stars.

Before you start, set your background color to black and your foreground color to some shade of yellow. (See page 198 if you need help setting your foreground and background colors.)

1. **Create a new document.**

   Press ⌘+N. Set the size to 200 pixels by 200 pixels, choose RGB for the Color mode, and then choose Background Color for your Background Contents.

2. **Activate the Custom Shape Tool.**

   From the Shapes palette (in the Options bar), click the arrow at the upper right of the palette and then select Nature from the menu. Choose the Sun 2 shape, which is in the top row, second from the left.

3. **Draw some stars.**

   Draw one yellow star, and then click the "add to shape area" squares in the Options bar before drawing four or five more stars. (This puts all the stars on the same layer, which is important, since then you won't have a bunch of layers to merge.)

4. **Merge the star layer and the background layer.**

   Choose Layer → Merge Down. You now have one layer containing yellow stars on a black background, like the bottom layer shown in Figure 17-6.

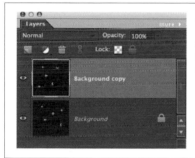

Figure 17-6:
There are only two frames in this animated GIF, which makes for a pretty crude animation. The more frames you have, the smoother the animation. But more frames makes a bigger file, too. On a tiny image like this one, size doesn't matter, but with a larger image, your file can get huge pretty fast.

5. **Duplicate the layer.**

   Choose Layer → Duplicate Layer. You now have two identical layers.

6. **Rotate the top layer 90 degrees.**

   Click any other tool in the Toolbox and then go to Image → Rotate → Layer 90° Left (if the Move Custom Shape tool is active, the Rotate command doesn't work). You should now have two layers with stars in different places on each one, which is why you did the rotation.

7. **Animate your GIF.**

   Go to File → Save For Web and turn on the Animate checkbox. (Select GIF as your Save format if Elements hasn't already done so; you won't see the Animate checkbox for other formats.) You can adjust the time between frames if you want. Leave Loop turned on. That makes the animation repeat over and over. When you turn Loop off, your animation plays once and stops.

   NOTE   Sometimes the Delay box won't let you put your cursor in it to change the number, even though the box looks active. If that happens, you can usually get there by tabbing from one of the boxes in the upper part of the window. Just put your cursor in one of the boxes and keep pressing Tab till you reach Delay, and then you can type a new number.

8. **Preview your animation.**

You can use the arrows in the animation controls to step through your animation one frame at a time, but for a more realistic preview, view the image in a Web browser (explained in the previous section). The stars should twinkle. Well, OK, they flash off and on—think of twinkle lights. Save your animation, if you like, by clicking OK.

ON THE WEB

Creating Web Buttons

Elements makes it a snap to create buttons to use on Web pages. Here's what you need to do:

1. Create a new blank file (File → New → Blank File) choosing one of the Web sizes, and set the background to be transparent.

2. Set the Foreground color square to the color you want to use for your button, and use the Shape tool to draw the shape you want.

   (It helps to choose Actual Pixels for your view size when doing Web work, because that gives you the same size you'll see in a Web browser.)

3. Apply one or more Layer styles (page 366) to make your button look more three-dimensional.

   Bevels, some of the Complex Layer styles, or the Wow Layer styles are all popular choices.

4. Add any necessary text using the Type tool (page 383).

   You may want to apply a Layer style to the text, too.

5. Save as a GIF.

Emailing Your Photos

Elements gives you the ability to send a photo as an email attachment, but it's a pretty limited feature (more of a convenience than anything). You can start from Bridge, Full Edit, or Share. Just follow these steps:

1. **Choose your photo.**

   Open a photo in Elements, or select it in Bridge. (You can only attach one photo per message from Elements. If you have multiple photos selected in Bridge, they all open in Elements, but only the first one gets attached.) If you've made changes to your photo in Elements, you have to save it before you can send it. (Don't worry: Elements reminds you to save if you forget.)

2. **Send your photo.**

   In either Elements or Bridge, go to File → "Attach to Email". If you're in Bridge, you get bounced back into Elements with your selected photo open on the desktop. In Elements, you can also go to Share → Email Attachments. If the file isn't a JPEG, the dialog box in Figure 17-7 pops up.

   You also see this dialog box if the photo is a really big JPEG. And if you're sending something like a large TIFF file, you may even see the dialog box twice: once to convert it to a JPEG, and then again to resize it for emailing.

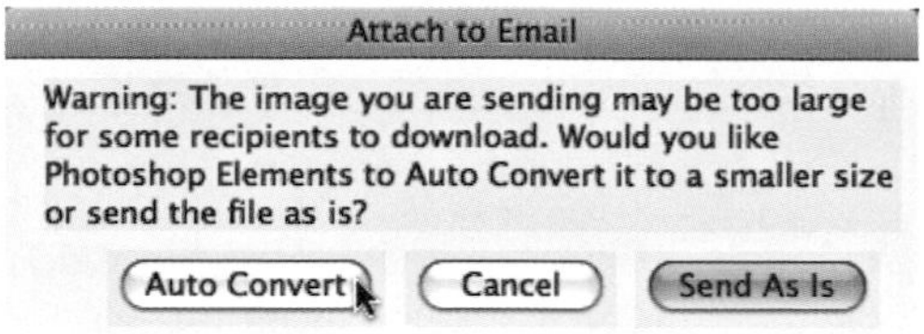

Figure 17-7:
If you try to send a photo in a format other than JPEG, Elements offers to convert it to a JPEG for you. (JPEGs are compact, so they're good for emailing.) Click Auto Convert if you want a JPEG, or click Send As Is if you want to send a large TIFF or PSD, for example. Just be sure your recipient's ISP (Internet Service Provider) allows large files.

After you click through the dialog box (or boxes), Elements pops up your regular email program, with your photo attached to a new message.

It's convenient to send a photo right from Elements, but not many people actually use this feature, since you have no control over how Auto Convert resizes it. (If you start with a really big image, you may still have a large file after Auto Convert is done—maybe too big to send to dial-up users.) You may prefer to use something like Save for Web (page 442) to create a small file, and then use the Attach button in OS X Mail, or whatever email program you use.

TIP   If you're jealous of all the fancy email stationery in the Windows version of Elements, don't be: If you have Leopard (OS X 10.5), just create a new message in Mail and click the Show Stationery button in the top bar of the message window for a bunch of formatting choices, all created by Apple designers.

Creating a Web Photo Gallery

With the Mac version of Elements, you can create the same Web Photo Galleries that you can make with full-blown Photoshop. The gallery styles are pretty basic (they're the same in Photoshop), but if you want to create quick galleries from right in Elements, this feature is a handy tool. You can even add background music to the Flash Gallery styles, if you like, but Elements galleries are only intended to show off your photos, not to be full-blown Web sites. (You can't add large blocks of text, for example.) Here's how to create a gallery:

1. **Start your gallery.**

   In Elements, go to File → Create Web Photo Gallery. In Bridge, go to Tools → Photoshop Elements → Web Photo Gallery. No matter where you start, you wind up in Elements, looking at the Web Photo Gallery window (Figure 17-8).

2. **Choose your settings, and enter a contact email address, if you like.**

   The Web Photo Gallery window gives you tons of options for customizing your gallery. The top sections let you choose:

   • **Styles** lets you select the gallery design you want to use. You get a preview of the selected style on the right side of the window. Unfortunately, the thumbnails are pretty tiny and there's no way to get a closer look except to try one. Some styles have a strip of thumbnails across the bottom of every page, while others just have arrows for navigation.

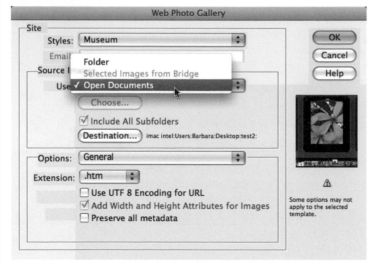

Figure 17-8:
When you create a Web Photo Gallery, either open the photos you want to include so that they're all in the Project bin, or put them all in a folder to simplify the process before you start.

If you start in Elements, Bridge is grayed out in the Source menu, as shown here. If you select photos in Bridge and start your gallery from there, those photos automatically become the contents of your gallery. No matter where you start, the only way to add more photos is to open all the photos you want to include, and then choose Open Documents from the Use menu, as shown here.

Some options may not apply to the selected template.

You'll also see some text beneath the thumbnail for many styles. For instance, you may see a warning like the one in Figure 17-8 that says your chosen style doesn't offer every possible customization option, or you may see info about how to add background music (if you choose a Flash gallery).

- **Email.** Enter an email address here if you want to include it on your Web Gallery.

TIP   Unless you want to get more spam, don't enter an email address in the standard format, like *hpotter@hogwarts.net*. The Web's teeming with programs searching for email addresses (they're called "spambots"). Instead, type something like *hpotterAThogwartsDOTnet*, and tell your friends to replace the AT with @ and DOT with a period.

- **Source Images.** This is where you tell Elements which photos to use in your gallery. You can choose from open files, files preselected in Bridge, or a folder. If you choose Folder, the Browse button becomes active and you can navigate to the folder you want. You can also choose to include the images in any subfolders.

- **Destination.** Tell Elements where you want to save your gallery. It's best to create a new folder for this purpose, since you don't want other files getting mixed up with your gallery when you upload it. To create a new folder, click Destination, navigate to where you want to put the folder, and then click the New Folder button on the bottom-left corner of the dialog box.

The Options section is where you customize the style you picked. The Options pull-down menu gives you several choices (the settings below this menu change depending on which option you select):

- **General.** This option lets you choose whether to use .htm or .html as your extension. (There's no need to change it from .htm, unless you have a reason to.)

If you like, you can opt for UTF 8 encoding for the URL (the online address), which works better for Asian languages but isn't supported by older browsers. You can also add width and height attributes to the HTML code Elements creates for faster downloading (it's best to leave this turned on). Finally, you can tell Elements to preserve the metadata in the files. (See page 52 for more about metadata.)

- **Banner.** Here's where you tell Elements the name you want to use for your site. It appears as a headline across the home page. You can also include the photographer's name and contact info (this can include street address, phone number, and email) and the date (Elements will use today's date, unless you change it). You can also choose the font for this information. The font size setting is for the main banner only.

NOTE If you don't change the existing banner text, your gallery appears with the site name "Adobe Web Photo Gallery."

- **Large Images.** These are the settings for your gallery photos. Turning on the Add Numeric Links checkbox (not available for every style) adds numbers to each image to help you keep track them in a large gallery. You can also set the size of your photos and the image quality (Medium is generally good enough for Web viewing).

  The JPEG Quality box and slider both do the same thing. A higher quality creates bigger files. For some styles, you can set the size of the border around each image. Your title options may include the filename, title, description, copyright, or credits from the metadata. (You don't have access to all these choices in most of the styles.) Font lets you choose the font for displaying this data.

- **Thumbnails.** All the galleries include thumbnails of your images. Some styles let you decide how many rows and columns of thumbnails are displayed, and what size they are. You may have the same choices for borders, titles, and fonts that you do for the large images (see above), depending on the gallery style.

- **Custom Colors.** Some styles let you choose colors for the background, text, links, and banner. For most styles, at least a few of the choices will be grayed out.

- **Security.** This displays text over your images to discourage people from stealing them from your site. You can enter custom text, or tell Elements to use the filename, copyright, description, credits, or title from the photos' metadata. You can choose the font, size, color, opacity, and position for the text.

NOTE You won't see anything for any of the content choices except Custom Text unless you've put something in that field in the photos' metadata. If you haven't entered metadata and you want to display copyright information, just enter it as custom text.

3. **When you've made all your choices, click OK.**

Elements creates your Web Photo Gallery and launches Safari (or whatever your standard Web browser is) so you can preview the site. If you don't like what you see—say you want to try a different gallery style—the easiest thing is to start over. Be careful about re-using the same folder, though, because Elements doesn't always neatly overwrite your previous files. You may get some leftovers from your first try, so create a new folder just to be safe.

4. **When you're happy with your gallery, upload it to your Web space.**

You'll need to use an FTP (File Transfer Protocol) program to do this—you can't upload it directly from Elements. Cyberduck (*http://cyberduck.ch*) is a popular, free Mac FTP program. Of course, you'll also need some Web space where you can put the gallery. Check with your ISP (Internet Service Provider); they may give you some free space. (You can also use your .Mac space, if you have .Mac.) Your Web server administrator can help you with the exact upload settings. Figure 17-9 shows a typical Elements Web Photo Gallery.

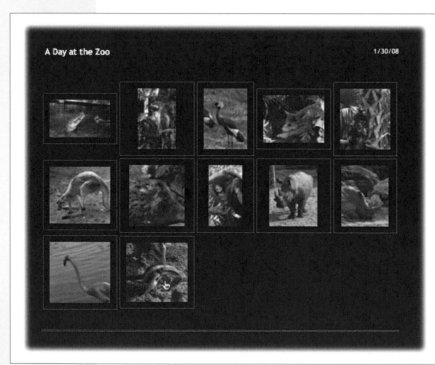

Figure 17-9:
A completed Web Photo Gallery. This is the "Dotted Border–White on Black" style. To see a larger image, you just click one of the thumbnails. Other styles show a large photo with a filmstrip-like view of the thumbnails at the bottom of the page.

If you know HTML, you can edit gallery styles to create one that's uniquely yours. To edit styles, go to Applications → Adobe Photoshop Elements 6 → Presets → Web Photo Gallery and open the style's IndexPage.htm page in an HTML editor or text editor. Duplicate it, make your changes, and then save the edited file back to the

Sharing Photos Online

Elements makes it simple to post your photos to several popular online services, so that your friends can view your photos online. You can quickly send your photos to Kodak EasyShare Gallery, SmugMug, and others. (The list changes depending on Adobe's current partnerships.) Once your photos are posted, you and your friends can order not only prints, but also T-shirts, mugs, bags, and other items with your photos on them. (Merchandise options vary, depending on which service you're using.) Here's a quick rundown of what you can do with each service, and what it'll cost you:

- **Kodak EasyShare**. Besides ordering prints from EasyShare (page 424), you can upload your photos for your friends to view online. Once your friends set up free accounts, they can order prints directly from Kodak. EasyShare also offers a wide variety of gift items with your photos on them, like mugs, bags, shirts, and more. EasyShare's free, except for the cost of what you order.

- **SmugMug**. SmugMug is another online gallery service with a lot of different gift items you and your friends can order. It has a seven-day free trial,

and your friends can order prints and merchandise without a paid account. If you want to maintain a gallery there, however, it's $39.95 a year for a basic account after the trial period expires.

- **MorePhotos.** This service is geared to pros. It allows you to sell your images online, but there is a $200 set-up charge, and a monthly fee of $49 or more. You need to sell quite a few photos to break even here.

You access all these services from Bridge. In Bridge, go to Tools → Photoshop Services. Share Photos Online takes you to the sharing section of EasyShare. You get to the others from "Online Portfolios and Galleries".

You'll be asked to sign in if you already have an account, or to create one if you don't. Each site has a simple-to-use wizard that walks you through the sign-up process, and they also have tours so that you can take a look around before you decide to join.

If you aren't sure which one(s) to try, ask your friends which one they like. Each service has pros and cons. You may want to try them all out before you decide.

same place with a new name. You can duplicate styles and have multiple versions of a style as long as you put them all into the correct folder and give each one a different name.

You don't have to bother with building a gallery if all you want to do is share your photos online. It's easy to upload photos to several popular sites that do the heavy lifting part of the page design and formatting for you (see the box above).

Part Six:
Additional Elements

Chapter 18: Beyond the Basics

6

Beyond the Basics

So far, everything in this book has been about what you can do with Elements right out of the box. But as with many things digital, there's a thriving cottage industry devoted to souping up Elements. You can add new brush shapes, Layer styles, and fancy filters. Best of all, a lot of what's out there is free. And many of the tools are especially designed to make Elements behave more like Photoshop. This chapter looks at some of these extras, how to manage the stuff you collect, and how to know when you really do need the full version of Photoshop instead. You'll also learn about the many resources available for expanding your knowledge of Elements beyond this book.

Graphics Tablets

Probably the most popular Elements accessory is a *graphics tablet*, which lets you draw and paint with a pen-like stylus instead of a mouse. A tablet is like a souped-up substitute for a mouse: you control your onscreen cursor by drawing directly on the tablet's surface—an action that many artists find offers them greater control. If trying to use the Lasso tool with a mouse makes you feel like you're trying to write on a mirror with a bar of soap, then a graphics tablet is for you (Figure 18-1).

> **NOTE** Some deluxe-model graphics tablets act as monitors and let you work directly on your image. But you need to budget a few thousand dollars for that kind of convenience.

Most tablets work like the one shown in Figure 18-1. You use the special pen on the tablet just as you would a mouse on a mousepad; any changes you make appear right on your monitor.

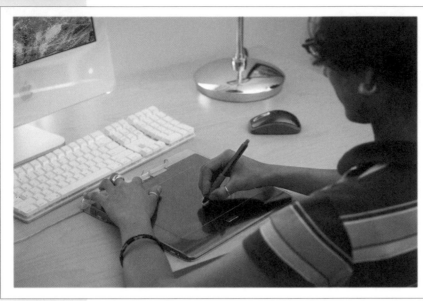

Figure 18-1:
A Wacom Graphire tablet in action. This tablet is 6"×8". The working area is inside the rectangle on the tablet surface. For basic photo retouching, a small size is usually fine once you get used to it. If you want to do more drawing and you generally use sweeping strokes when you draw, then you may want a larger tablet.

For most people, it's much easier to control fine motions with a tablet's pen than with a mouse. Moreover, when you use a tablet, many of the brushes and tools in Elements become *pressure sensitive*—the harder you press, the darker and wider the line becomes. The tablet pen lets you create much more realistic paint strokes, as shown in Figure 18-2.

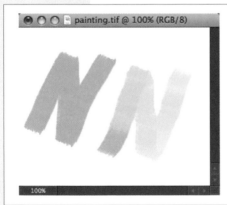

Figure 18-2:
Two almost identical paint strokes, starting with fairly hard pressure and then easing up. Both were made using the identical brush and color in Elements. The only difference is that the stroke on the left was drawn with a mouse, and the one on the right came from a tablet. You can see what a difference the pressure sensitivity makes.

When using the Brush tool, you'll see Tablet Options (it's a tiny black arrow) just to the right of the Airbrush setting in the Options bar. Many brushes and tools are automatically pressure sensitive when you hook up a tablet. You can choose whether to let the pressure control the size, opacity, roundness, hue jitter, and scatter for your brushes. (See page 314 for more about Brush settings.)

With a tablet, you can also create hand-drawn line art—even if you don't have an artistic bone in your body—by placing a picture of what you want to draw on the surface of the tablet and tracing the outline. Also, if you find constant mousing troublesome, you may have fewer hand problems when using a tablet's pen. Most tablets come with a wireless mouse, which works only on the surface of the tablet. Or you can use your regular mouse on a mousepad or your desk the way you always do, if you like to switch back and forth between the stylus and a mouse.

Tablet prices now start at less than a hundred dollars, a big drop from what they used to cost. There are lots of different models, and their features vary widely. Sophisticated tablets offer more levels of sensitivity and respond when you change the angle at which you hold the stylus.

Wacom, one of the big tablet manufacturers, has some pretty nifty tablet demos on its Web site *www.wacom.com*. Check out the tours for the Bamboo and Bamboo Fun tablets. You can't actually simulate what it's like to use a tablet, but the animations give you a good idea of what your life would be like if you went the tablet route.

Free Stuff from the Internet

You have to spend some money if you want a graphics tablet, but there's a ton of free stuff—tutorials, brushes, textures, and Layer styles, for example—available online that you can add to Elements. Most of these add-ons say they work with Photoshop, but since Elements is based on Photoshop, you can use most of them in Elements, too.

Here are some popular places to go treasure hunting:

- **Adobe Exchange** (*www.adobe.com/cfusion/exchange/*). On Adobe's own Web site, you can find hundreds and hundreds of downloads, including more Layer styles than you could ever use, brushes, textures, and custom shapes (to use with the Shape tool). They're all free, once you register. This site is one of the best resources anywhere for extra stuff. About 99 percent of the items listed are made specifically for Photoshop, but Photoshop's brushes, swatches, textures, shapes, and Layer styles work with Elements, too. See the box on page 464 for help with installing your finds in Elements.

- **Creative Mac** (*www.creativemac.com*). It's been sold recently and it's not what it was, but this site is still a wonderful source for specialty brushes, especially for tricky things like hair and skin.

- **MyJanee** (*www.myjanee.com*). You'll find lots of tutorials and free downloads on this site.

- **Sue Chastain** (*http://graphicssoft.about.com*). This is another Web site with lots of downloads and many tutorials.

- **Panosfx** (*www.panosfx.com*). Panos Efstathiadis produces some wonderful actions (see the section "When You Really Need Photoshop," later in this chapter) for Photoshop, and now he's adapted many of them for Elements as well. Most are free; some cost a few dollars.

- **onOne Essentials.** onOne (*www.ononesoftware.com*) makes a suite of plug-ins—add-on utilities—for Elements that's being updated to work with the Mac version of Elements 6. (The new version will be universal and a free upgrade if you already own the older one.) The suites aren't cheap and you can do most of what they do in other ways, but lots of people like the convenience of these plug-ins.

- **ShutterFreaks.** This Web site (*www.shutterfreaks.com*) has a number of Elements add-ons. Some are free, but most cost a few dollars. You'll find tutorials on this site, too.

- **Hidden Elements** (*www.hiddenelements.com*). Richard Lynch has been creating wonderful add-on tools for Elements practically as long as the program has existed. Some are free, many are not, but all are worth the investment.

- **Grant's Tools** (*www.cavesofice.org/~grant/Challenge/Tools/index.html*). Here's another source of popular free tools for Elements, though it may not be updated for Elements 6. But it's well worth checking to find out.

To find other relevant Web sites, just enter what you're looking for as your Google search term, and you're bound to get back lots of search results.

If you're willing to pay a little bit, you've got even more choices. You can find everything from more elaborate ways to sharpen your photos to really cool collections of special edges and visual effects. Prices range from donationware (you pay if you like it) to some quite expensive and sophisticated *plug-ins* that cost hundreds of dollars. (A plug-in is a mini program that expands what Elements can do. You get some plug-ins as part of Elements—like the Save For Web dialog box that's described in "Using Save For Web" (page 442)—and you can add third-party plug-ins, too.) You can also buy books like the *Wow!* series (Peachpit Press), which have very little text and loads of illustrations showing the styles available on the included CD.

> **NOTE**   Elements 6 is based on Photoshop CS3, so CS3 downloads are compatible. Plug-ins and other goodies designed for older versions of Photoshop or Elements usually work with newer versions, but not the other way around. For example, a brush made for Photoshop CS3 works in Elements 6 but may not work in Elements 3.
>
> Windows plug-ins don't work with Macs, and vice versa, but many plug-ins offer two versions, one for each platform. When buying a plug-in, check with the developer to be sure it works with Photoshop Elements. Also, plug-ins written for Mac OS 9 (Classic) won't install in Leopard (10.5) or on Macs with Intel processors. But Intel Macs *can* use plug-ins written for the older PPC chips (like those in G4 or G5 Macs) by forcing Elements to run in Rosetta. Page 46 explains more about Rosetta and how to do this.

With so many goodies available, it's easy to find yourself overwhelmed trying to keep track of everything you've added to Elements. Your best bet is to make backup copies of anything you download so you'll have it if you ever need to reinstall Elements.

Elements also includes a Preset Manager (Figure 18-3) that can help manage certain kinds of downloads. Go to Photoshop Elements → Preset Manager to launch it.

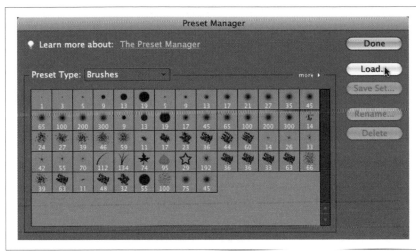

Figure 18-3:
The Elements Preset Manager offers a place to see all your brushes, swatches, gradients, and patterns in one place. You can use it to switch which groups are loaded, to add or remove items, and so on— the same way you do in the main brush window.

When You Really Need Photoshop

You can do an enormous amount with Elements, but some people do need the full version of Photoshop. For example, if you want the ability to write your own *actions* (little scripts, like macros, that automate certain things in Photoshop) or if you have to work extensively in CMYK mode, then you need Photoshop.

CMYK is the color mode used for commercial printing—it stands for Cyan, Magenta, Yellow, and blacK, which are the colors professional printers use. When you send a file to a print shop, the printer usually tells you it needs to be a CMYK file. You can't convert files to CMYK in Elements. If you need CMYK files on a regular basis, it's worth the extra price of Photoshop to avoid the aggravation. If you only occasionally need CMYK, you might just ask your printer about converting the file for you for an additional charge.

> **TIP**   You can technically use Mac OS X's Preview application to convert your photos to CMYK mode, but it's usually best not to. Good CMYK conversion is *device-dependent*, which means you need to know about the machine that's going to print your image and the kind of ink and paper it'll use to know how to adjust your image to get a printed version as close as possible to your original. Preview, just doesn't give you all the tools you need to get optimum results. So, while it's better than no CMYK conversion at all, your best bet is still to talk your print shop about CMYK.
>
> If you have to use Preview to create a CMYK file, here's how: Head to where you image is saved and right-click (Control+click) it and, on the menu that appears, select Open With → Preview. Once you're in Preview, go to Tools → "Match to Profile" → Color Model → CMYK, and then choose the CMYK profile you want.

In Photoshop you get more of everything: more choices, more tools, more settings, more types of adjustment layers, and so on.

POWER USERS' CLINIC

Making Elements Behave More Like Photoshop

While each version of Elements is more talented than its predecessor, there's one thing about Elements 6 that you may not like if you're a longtime member of the Elements community: Some of the tools and actions you find online won't work in Elements 6.

Ever since Elements first came out, there's been quite a cottage industry devoted to figuring out ways to get Elements to behave more like Photoshop. If you've used Elements 3 or earlier versions, the odds are pretty good that you're familiar with the extra tools and action players created by Richard Lynch, Paul Shipley, Grant Dixon, and Ling Nero. Unfortunately, Adobe decided to write Elements 4 in a way that disabled the traditional route used by add-on tools to access some of the underlying Photoshop code needed for these additional features to work,

so many of the existing add-on tools stopped working in Elements 4. For instance, a Photoshop action that calls up a Curves Adjustment layer is going to get confused and stop working in Elements when it reaches that step, since Elements Color Curves doesn't work as an Adjustment layer.

For now, it's best to stick to actions that state they're written for Elements 4, 5, or 6, to be sure they'll work. (See the box on page 464 for more about installing actions.) If you've been using extra tools or actions in Elements 2 or 3, then you may want to keep the older version of the program around just for them. You can have as many different versions of Elements as you like installed on your computer, and even run them at the same time, as long as you open the oldest version(s) before the newer one(s).

Beyond This Book

You can do thousands of interesting things with Elements that are beyond the scope of this book. Bookstores have dozens of titles on Elements and Photoshop, and a lot of things are common to both programs. All kinds of specialized books on everything from color management to making selections to scrapbooking are available.

> **TIP** If you're looking to learn some photo-shooting and -editing techniques from a pro who's been at it since the birth of digital cameras, then check out *Stephen Johnson on Digital Photography* (O'Reilly).

In addition, you'll find hundreds of tutorial sites on the Web. Besides those mentioned earlier in the chapter, other popular sites include:

- **Adobe** (*www.adobe.com*). You'll find plenty of free online training for Elements here.
- **Jay Arraich** (*www.arraich.com/elements/psE_intro.htm*). This longtime Photoshop guru provides lots of Elements information, both basic and advanced.
- **The Graphic Reporter** (*www.graphicreporter.com*). This site, run by iStockphoto maven Lesa King, has a number of excellent tips and tutorials for Elements.

- **Photoshop Elements User** (*www.photoshopelementsuser.com*). This is the Web site for a subscriber-only print newsletter, but it also includes some free online video tutorials, a forum, and a good collection of links. This is the only publication especially for Elements. Read around their forums carefully before you give them any money. They had announced the demise of the magazine, but now they are taking subscriptions again, so check the current status before subscribing.

If you search Google, you're sure to find a tutorial for any project you have in mind, although many of them are written for full Photoshop. In most cases, you can adapt them for Elements. If you get stuck or you need help with any other aspect of Elements, there's a very active online community that's sure to have an answer for you. Besides the sites already mentioned, try:

- **Adobe Support forum** (*www.adobe.com/support/forums/index.html*). Scroll down the page to the Photoshop forums and, in that group, you'll find the Elements User-to-User forum, where you'll find lots of helpful and friendly people. It's your best bet for getting answers without calling Adobe support.

- **Digital Photography Review** (*www.dpreview.com*). You'll find many camera-specific forums on this site. You can also get a lot of Elements answers in the Retouching forum if you specify in your question that you've got Elements rather than Photoshop.

- **Retouch Pro** (*www.retouchpro.com*). The forums here cover all kinds of retouching and artistic uses of Elements and Photoshop.

Many sites are devoted to scrapbooking using Elements. A good place to start is Scrapper's Guide (*www.scrappersguide.com*), a commercial site run by Linda Sattgast.

There are also many sites offering online classes in Elements. Here are two of the most popular, but there are dozens of others:

- **lynda.com** (*www.lynda.com*) is the best-known site for Photoshop courses, and they offer classes in Elements, too. You pay a $25 monthly fee for access to all their offerings instead of a per-class charge. They have free sample tutorials so you can see if you like their courses.

- **Eclectic Academy** (*www.eclecticacademy.com*) offers fun, reasonably priced courses ($30 each) that are extremely popular with Elements fans.

Your local college or university may offer classes in Elements, as well.

No matter what you're looking for—add-ons, tutorials, communities—try a Google search, and you're sure to find a site that has what you want.

There's no question about it: Once you get familiar with Elements, it's addictive. Lots of other folks have found out how much fun this program is, and you shouldn't have any trouble finding the answer to any question you have.

The only limit to what you can do with Elements is your imagination. Enjoy!

Adding Layer Styles, Shapes, and Actions to Elements

Adding your finds to Elements 6 is a good news/bad news situation. The good news is that it's quite easy to add Layer styles, shapes, and actions (see the box on page 462 for more about using actions in Elements). The bad news is that if you want to categorize them or have them show up in your Content palette searches, you're in for a trip through some pretty techie territory.

To add your extras, just put them into the folders described below; the next time you launch Elements, they'll show up in the Show All section of the relevant palette. Here's how to add them:

- **Layer styles**. Just put them into Applications → Adobe Photoshop Elements 6 → Presets → Styles.

- **Actions**. Dealing with actions is a bit more complicated. You need two files for an action: one for the action itself (the .atn file) and one to use as a thumbnail so that you can find the action to launch it. The thumbnail needs to be a 64-pixel-square PNG image with *exactly* the same name as the action (except for the file extension—the part after the period), including spacing, capitalization, and so on. Put both the thumbnail and the .atn file (not in a folder) into <your hard drive> → Library → Application Support → Adobe → Photoshop Elements → 6.0 → Photo Creations → Photo Effects. (Note that you have three Library folders on your hard drive. You want the one that is at the top level of folders on your hard drive, *not* your Home folder → Library or System → Library.)

Once you've put everything in the right place, your Layer style or shape will show up in Show All in the Content

Palette. Actions appear in Effects palette → Photo Effects → Show All. For mere mortals, that's all there is to it, but if you're a techie who understands XML, read on.

You can make your content appear in its own category if you also create an XML file (a little snippet of code that gives Elements directions for how to categorize the file and search for it). The easiest way to do this is to find an XML file for an existing Layer style, photo effect, or whatever you have, duplicate it, and then edit its contents. You can find these XML files in <your hard drive> → Library → Application Support → Adobe → Photoshop Elements → 6.0 → Locale → en_US (this one will have a different name if you aren't in the U.S.) → Photo Creations Metadata.

Regardless of whether you completed the XML steps or not, to remove new content that you've added, just right-click (Control+click) it in the palette and choose Delete Content from the shortcut menu, or click the icon once and then click the trashcan icon at the bottom of the palette. If you created a metadata (XML) file, go dig that out and remove it as well.

XML is pretty intimidating, but it's likely that someone will invent some kind of loader for new content that creates the XML files for you (maybe even by the time you're reading this), so check with your favorite add-on purveyor to see if there's anything available.

After all that, you'll be relieved to know that adding more shapes to the Shape tool is much simpler. Just put your downloaded shapes (which need to have the .csh file extension) into: Applications → Adobe Photoshop Elements 6 → Presets → Custom Shapes.

Part Seven: Appendixes

7

Elements, Menu by Menu

Elements has some pretty complicated menus. All three editing modes—Full Edit, Quick Fix, and Guided Edit—have the same menus, although some choices are grayed out when you're in Quick Fix or Guided Edit mode. When you need a menu item that's unavailable in Quick Fix or Guided Edit, just switch back to Full Edit to use it.

Several of the menus in Elements are dynamic: They change quite a bit to reflect the choices currently applicable to your image. That means the choices you see in this appendix represent only what you *may* see depending on the situation. The Layer menu, for instance, offers you very different options depending on the current state of your image and which layer is active.

> **NOTE**   The leftmost item in your menu bar, the menu, is system-wide and not part of Elements.

Photoshop Elements Menu

These menu choices provide information about Elements, let you adjust some of its settings, and control the program's visibility.

About Photoshop Elements

Choose this to see a window with information about the version of Elements you've got. You'll also see a long list of patents and credits—an impressive testimony to the complexity of the engineering that went into Elements.

About Plug-In

Select this option for a long pop-out menu displaying all the plug-ins (page 460) in your copy of Elements. Choose a plug-in from the list to see its version and date information.

Patent and Legal Notices

This item displays a list of the various patents for Elements, as well as trademark information for some of the components used in the program.

Preferences

This menu item gives you access to the many Elements settings you can customize. You'll find the following preference windows available from this menu:

- **General** (or press ⌘+K)
- **Saving Files**
- **Performance** (where you set the number of history states and assign scratch disks)
- **Display & Cursors**
- **Transparency**
- **Units & Rulers**
- **Grid**
- **Plug-Ins**
- **Type**

Services

This is where you can access the OS X utility programs like Grab (for taking screenshots) or Text Edit (for copying text). Your exact choices in the submenu depend on what programs you have installed on your Mac. It's normal for some to be grayed out. Dictionary, for instance, isn't available unless some text is highlighted.

Hide Photoshop Elements

If you don't want Elements to be visible, choose this or press ⌘+Control+H.

Hide Others

If you want Elements to be your only visible program, choose this or press Option+⌘+H.

Show All

Use this to bring all your hidden programs back into view.

Quit Photoshop Elements

You can shut Elements down by choosing this menu item, or by pressing ⌘+Q.

File Menu

The commands listed here let you create, import, open, save, and print files.

New

Choose this menu item if you want to start a new file in Elements. Your options are:

- **Blank file** (or press ⌘+N).

- **Image from Clipboard.** This automatically pastes anything you've copied into a new file.

- **Photomerge Group Shot.** This new feature lets you move a person from one photo of a group into another photo of the same group (page 299).

- **Photomerge Faces.** Another new feature, this one lets you combine parts of different faces for caricatures and other fun effects (page 296).

- **Photomerge Panorama.** Use this option to combine your photos into panoramas (page 290).

Open

Choose this menu item or press ⌘+O to open an existing file.

Browse with Bridge

Select this, and Elements switches you over to Adobe Bridge, so that you can browse through all your available image files (see page 37).

Open Recently Edited File

Here's you'll find a pop-out list of the most recent files you've had open in Elements.

Duplicate

When you need to make a copy of your photo, choose this option.

Close

To close the active image window, choose this menu item or press ⌘+W.

Close All

To close all your open image windows, choose this option or press Option+⌘+W.

Save

To save your work, select this option or press ⌘+S.

Save As

To save your image under another file name or in a different format, choose this command or press Shift+⌘+S.

Save For Web

To save an image so that it's optimized for posting on a Web page or sending by email, choose this menu item or press Option+Shift+⌘+S. For more on the Save For Web window, see page 442.

Adobe Photo Downloader

If you want to use the Adobe Downloader (page 19) to get photos from your camera or card reader, you can launch it here.

Attach to Email

To send a photo directly from Elements, choose this menu option (see page 448).

Create Web Gallery

If you want to use Elements to make an online gallery, this is where you start (page 449).

File Info

Choose this menu item to bring up the File Info window, which displays general information (file creation date, file format, and so on) about your image. You can also add or edit metadata here (see page 52).

Place

Use this command to place a PDF, Adobe Illustrator, or EPS file into an image as a new layer. When the artwork's larger than the image you place it in, Elements automatically makes it small enough to fit.

Process Multiple Files

This is where you batch process your files to rename them, change their format, add copyright information, and so on (see page 233 for everything that Elements lets you do to groups of files).

Import

This is where you bring certain file formats into Elements. It's also where you can connect to external devices like scanners. (They'll show up in this menu if you install their drivers.) Your basic choices before you connect or install anything are:

- **Anti-aliased PICT.** This is for importing PICT objects created in programs like MacDraw or Canvas. Anti-aliasing makes them appear smooth.

- **PICT Resource.** A type of PICT file used in the resource fork of a Mac file, for things like an application's opening splash screen.

- **Frame from Video** (page 46).

Export

This command is always grayed out. That's normal. Adobe left it in for the benefit of any third-party plug-ins that may need it to be there—but you don't need it in Elements to use the program's standard tools and commands.

Automation Tools

You can make a PDF slideshow here, starting from the pop-out menu (page 420).

Page Setup

This menu option calls up the OS X Page Setup window, where you choose the page size and the orientation of your document and select the printer you wish to format it for. Read more about printing on page 426. Keyboard shortcut: Shift+⌘+P.

Print

Choose this command and you get the Print window, which is discussed in detail in Chapter 16. Keyboard shortcut: ⌘+P.

Contact Sheet II

To make a contact sheet showing thumbnails of many photos (see page 430), choose this menu item.

Picture Package

To print several photos—or multiple copies of one photo—in different sizes on one page (see page 434), choose this command.

Edit Menu

The menu choices listed here let you make changes to your files.

Undo

You can back out of your last action by selecting Undo or by pressing ⌘+Z. You can keep applying this command to undo as many steps as you've set in the Undo History palette preferences (Photoshop Elements → Preferences → Performance → History States). You can also use the Undo button at the top of your screen.

Redo

If you undo something and then change your mind again, redo it here, click the Redo button at the top of your screen, or press ⌘+Y.

Revert

Choose this command to return your image to the state it was in the last time you saved it.

Cut

To remove something from your image and store it on the Clipboard (so that you can paste it into another file), choose this menu item or press ⌘+X.

Copy

To copy something to the Clipboard, highlight it and select this menu item or press ⌘+C. The Copy command copies only the top layer in a file with layers. To copy all the layers in your selected area, use Copy Merged instead.

Copy Merged

To copy all the layers in the selected area to the Clipboard, choose this menu option or press Shift+⌘+C. To copy just the top layer to the Clipboard, use Copy instead.

Paste

Use this command or press ⌘+V to add whatever you have cut or copied into an image.

Paste Into Selection

Use this special command for pasting something within the confines of an existing selection. See page 115 for more on how this command works. Keyboard shortcut: Shift+⌘+V.

Delete

This command removes what you've selected without copying it to the Clipboard—it's just gone. You can press the Delete key to do the same thing.

Fill, Fill Layer, Fill Selection

Choose this menu item to fill your active layer with a color or pattern (page 252). When you make a selection in your image, this menu item changes to "Fill Selection". You can also choose a blend mode and opacity for your fill.

Stroke (Outline) Selection

This command lets you place a colored border around the edges of a selection.

Define Brush, Define Brush from Selection

If you want to create a custom brush from your photo or from an area of your photo, choose this command. The process is explained in detail on page 323.

Define Pattern, Define Pattern from Selection

This command creates a pattern from your image or selection. See page 252 for more about applying patterns.

Clear

Use this command to permanently remove information from the Undo History, Clipboard Contents, or All (both of them). If you have a corrupt image in the Clipboard (or one that's too large), it may cause Elements to slow way down or quit on you. Once in a while, the Clipboard may get stuck, too—you try to copy and paste an item but still get whatever you copied previously. Clear fixes all these problems.

Add Blank Page

This command lets you add a new, blank page to your current project. Find out more about working with multipage files on page 410. Keyboard shortcut: Option+⌘+G.

Add Page Using Current Layout

If you're working with a Photo Collage (page 405) and you want to use that page as a template for new pages, choose this command instead of Add Blank Page. Keyboard shortcut: Option+Shift+⌘+G.

Delete Current Page

If you're working with a multipage document and you decide you want to get rid of your current page, choose this command.

Color Settings

Here's where you choose your color space for Elements (page 184). Keyboard shortcut: Shift+⌘+K.

Preset Manager

This is where you access the window that helps you manage your brushes, swatches, gradients, and patterns. See page 473 for more on how the Preset Manager works.

Image Menu

This menu lets you make changes to your image. Here you can rotate a picture, change its shape, crop or resize it, or change the color mode.

Rotate

Use these commands to change the orientation of your image (page 65). The first group of options applies to your whole image:

- **90° Left**
- **90° Right**
- **180°**
- **Custom**
- **Flip Horizontal**
- **Flip Vertical**

The next group does the same thing but on a layer or selection. The menu choices change depending on whether you have an active selection in your image. If you have a selection, you'll see the word "Selection" instead of "Layer."

- **Free Rotate Layer**
- **Layer 90° Left**
- **Layer 90° Right**
- **Layer 180°**
- **Flip Layer Horizontal**
- **Flip Layer Vertical**

Finally you can choose to:

- **Straighten and Crop Image**
- **Straighten Image**

These last two commands are mostly for use with scanned images when you need to straighten the position of the entire image. To straighten the *contents* of an image, use the Straighten tool (page 67).

Transform

These commands let you change the shape of your image by pulling it in different directions. They're explained in detail on page 305. Your choices are:

- **Free Transform** (⌘+T) incorporates the other three commands.
- **Skew** slants an image.
- **Distort** stretches your photo in the direction you pull it.
- **Perspective** stretches your photo to make it look like parts are nearer or farther away.

   TIP   You might prefer to use the Correct Camera Distortion filter for transforming your images to correct perspective. See page 300.

Crop

Choose this menu item to crop your image to the area you've selected (page 71).

Divide Scanned Photos

You can create a group scan by placing several photos on your scanner glass at once and then choosing this command. Elements then cuts your photos apart and straightens and crops each individual photo. See page 63 for more about how this works.

Resize

Here's where you change the actual size of your image (as opposed to changing the size of the view on your screen). Resizing is explained in Chapter 3. Your choices are:

- **Image Size** (page 82). Keyboard shortcut is Option+⌘+I.
- **Canvas Size** (page 89).
- **Reveal All**. If you drag a layer from another image into your photo and part of the layer falls outside the perimeter of the target image, then use the Reveal All command to see the entire dragged layer. It basically resizes the canvas to fit all of the image(s). Also, some versions of Photoshop hide the area outside a selection when you use the Crop tool. When someone sends you one of these images, use this command to see the area that was hidden by the crop.
- **Scale** (page 308).

Mode

This is where you can change the color mode for your image (page 48). Your choices are:

- **Bitmap**

- Grayscale

- Indexed Color

- RGB Color

You'll find two other commands in this menu:

- **8-bits/Channel** reduces images from 16-bit color to 8-bit (see page 228).

- **Color Table** shows you the color table (the colors of your image as swatches) for an Indexed Color image.

Convert Color Profile

If you need to change the ICC (International Color Consortium) profile of an image, you can do it from this menu, which lets you apply an sRGB or Adobe RGB profile, or you can remove the profile from an image. For more on color profiles, go to page 184.

Magic Extractor

Use this command or press Option+Shift+⌘+V to call up the Magic Extractor window, which automates the process of selecting an object in your photo and removing it from the background. See page 129 for details.

Enhance Menu

This menu contains the commands you use to adjust the color and lighting of your images. The first six options apply changes automatically, and the remainder let you adjust your changes.

Auto Smart Fix

Choose this option or press Option+⌘+M to adjust lighting, color, and contrast at the same time (page 99).

Auto Levels

Use this command or press Shift+⌘+L to adjust the individual color channels of your image (page 101).

Auto Contrast

Choose this command or press Option+Shift+⌘+L to adjust the brightness and darkness of your image without changing the colors (page 101).

Auto Color Correction

Use this option or press Shift+⌘+B to adjust your color in much the same way that Levels does. Auto Color Correction looks at different information in your photo to make its decisions, though (page 103).

Auto Sharpen

This command applies the same one-click sharpening you get when you use the Auto Sharpen button in Quick Fix (page 105).

Auto Red Eye Fix

Use this command or press ⌘+R to automatically fix the red pupils caused by a camera's flash (page 97).

Adjust Smart Fix

This command is the same as Auto Smart Fix, except you get a slider to adjust the degree of change Elements makes to your photo. Keyboard shortcut: ⌘+Shift+M.

Adjust Lighting

Your choices for adjusting the light and dark values in your photos are:

- **Shadows/Highlights** (page 181).
- **Brightness/Contrast** (page 179).
- **Levels.** You can also press ⌘+L to bring up the Levels dialog box (page 188).

Adjust Color

With these settings you can change a color, replace a color, remove a color cast, remove all the color from your image, or add color to a black-and-white photo. Choose from:

- **Remove Color Cast** (page 196).
- **Adjust Hue/Saturation** (page 260). Keyboard shortcut: ⌘+U.
- **Remove Color** (page 274). Keyboard shortcut: Shift+⌘+U.
- **Replace Color** (page 263).
- **Adjust Color Curves** (page 254). The new Color Curves tool lets you adjust the brightness and contrast of specific tonal ranges (like highlights or midtones) in your photo.
- **Adjust Color for Skin Tone** (page 107). This setting adjusts the colors in your image based on the skin tones of someone whom you select in the photo.
- **Defringe Layer** (page 134). This setting gets rid of the rim of contrasting pixels you may get when you remove an object from its background.
- **Color Variations** (page 197).

Convert to Black and White

Use this menu item or press Option+⌘+B to convert a color photo to a black-and-white image (page 271).

Unsharp Mask

This is the most popular traditional method for sharpening your photos (page 205).

Adjust Sharpness

Choose this menu item to use Adobe's newest sharpening tool (page 206).

Layer Menu

Here's where you'll find the commands for creating and managing Layers. (Chapter 6 is all about Layers.) This is the most dynamic menu in Elements—what you see at the bottom of the menu changes depending on the layers in the image that's open and on the characteristics of the active layer. This is a basic rundown of the main menu options you'll usually see if your open image has only a Background layer. (Sometimes you'll see choices visible but grayed out.) The choices for merging and combining layers change the most as your layers change.

New

This is where you create new, regular (as opposed to Adjustment) layers. Your options are:

- **Layer** (or press Shift+⌘+N).

- **Layer from Background**.

- **Layer via Copy** (or press ⌘+J).

- **Layer via Cut** (or press Shift+⌘+J).

If your image doesn't currently have a Background layer, you see "Background from Layer" instead of "Layer from Background."

Duplicate Layer

Use this command to make a duplicate of the active layer. As long as you don't have a selection, you can also use ⌘+J to do the same thing.

Delete Layer

If you want to eliminate a layer, click it in the Layers palette to make it the active layer and choose the Delete Layer command.

Rename Layer

Choose fsthis option to—you guessed it—rename a layer. You can also double-click the layer's name in the Layers palette to rename it.

Layer Style

If a layer has a Layer style applied to it (page 366), you can adjust it here.

- **Style Settings** brings up the dialog box where you can adjust some of the settings of a Layer style. Double-clicking the Layer style icon in the Layers palette brings up the same dialog box.

- **Copy Layer Style** lets you copy any styles applied to a layer to the Clipboard so you can apply them to another image or layer.

- **Paste Layer Style** applies your copied style to a new layer, even in a new image.

- **Clear Layer Style** removes all the styles applied to a layer.

- **Hide All Effects** hides all the styles applied to a layer so that you can see what your image looks like without them. If you hide all the styles, this menu item reads "Show All Effects" instead.

- **Scale Effects** lets you adjust the size of certain aspects of Layer styles.

New Fill Layer

Choose this option to create a layer that's filled with a color, gradient, or pattern. You can also do this from the Layers palette by clicking the Create Adjustment layer icon. Your options are:

- **Solid Color** (page 170)
- **Gradient** (page 373)
- **Pattern** (page 170)

New Adjustment Layer

This command creates a new Adjustment layer (page 169). The types of layers you can create are:

- **Levels** (page 188)
- **Brightness/Contrast** (page 179)
- **Hue/Saturation** (page 260)
- **Gradient Map** (page 379)
- **Photo Filter** (page 231)
- **Invert** (page 268)
- **Threshold** (page 269)
- **Posterize** (page 269)

Change Layer Content

For Adjustment and Fill layers, you can change the type of layer you've got, as long as you haven't flattened your layers. For example, you could change a Levels layer into a Hue/Saturation layer. You can also change an Adjustment layer to a Fill layer, and vice versa. The choices include all the layers listed in the two previous sections.

Layer Content Options

Use this option to bring up the dialog box for an Adjustment or Fill layer. You can also double-click the left icon for the layer in the Layers palette.

Type

This command gives you ways to modify a Type layer, as long as it hasn't been simplified (page 341). You can choose:

- **Horizontal.** Change vertical type to horizontal type.

- **Vertical.** Change horizontal type to vertical type.

- **Anti-alias Off.** Anti-aliasing is explained on page 389.

- **Anti-alias On.**

- **Warp Text.** See page 390.

- **Update All Text Layers.**

- **Replace All Missing Fonts.** When your image is missing fonts, this command replaces them, but you can't choose the replacement. It's usually just as easy to replace fonts by highlighting the text and selecting a new font in the Options bar.

Simplify Layer

The Simplify Layer command rasterizes your layer, turning the layer content from a vector or smart object to one that's built pixel by pixel. See page 341 for more about the difference between vectors and pixels.

Group with Previous

This command links two layers together in such a way that the bottom layer determines the opacity of the upper layer (page 164). Keyboard shortcut: ⌘+G.

Ungroup

This command separates grouped layers so that they're now two unrelated layers. Keyboard shortcut: Shift+⌘+G.

Arrange

Use these commands to change the order of layers in the layers stack, or just drag them in the Layers palette. See page 159 for details on rearranging layers. (Front is the top of the stack, and back is directly above the Background layer.)

- **Bring to Front** (or press Shift+⌘+]).

- **Bring Forward** (or press ⌘+]).

- **Send Backward** (or press ⌘+[).

- **Send to Back** (or press Shift+⌘+[).

- **Reverse.** Select two or more layers, and this command reverses the order in which they appear in the layer stack.

Merge Layers

Choose this command or press ⌘+E to combine multiple layers into one layer. You may also see Merge Down, which merges a layer with the layer immediately beneath it, or Merge Clipping Mask, which merges grouped layers.

Merge Visible

Use this option or press Shift+⌘+E to merge all the visible layers into one layer.

Flatten Image

This command merges all the layers into one Background layer.

Select Menu

Here's where you make, modify, and save selections in your image. See Chapter 5 for more about selections.

All

Choose this command or press ⌘+A to select your entire image.

Deselect

Use this command or press ⌘+D to remove all selections from your image.

Reselect

If you apply the Deselect command, but then want your selection back again, choose this menu item or press Shift+⌘+D.

Inverse

This command switches the selected and unselected areas of your image. The area that wasn't previously selected is now selected, and the previously selected area is now unselected. Keyboard shortcut: Shift+⌘+I.

All Layers

Use this command to select all the layers in your image, including hidden layers.

Deselect Layers

Choose this option to unselect all the layers in your image.

Similar Layers

Use this command to select all the layers of your image that are the same type, such as all Adjustment layers or all regular layers.

Feather

Choose this option or press Option+⌘+D to feather (blur) the edges of a selection (page 125).

Refine Edge

This new command lets you groom the edges of a selection (page 119).

Modify

These commands let you change the size or edges of your selection. They're all explained in Chapter 5.

- **Border** selects the edge of your selection (page 138).
- **Smooth** rounds the corners of selections (page 138).
- **Expand** moves the edge of your selection outward (page 136).
- **Contract** moves the edge of your selection inward (page 136).

Grow

This command expands your selection to include more contiguous areas of similar color (page 136).

Similar

This option expands your selection to include more areas of similar color, but—unlike the Grow command—it doesn't restrict the growth to contiguous areas (page 136).

Load Selection

If you have saved a selection, choose this command to use it again.

Save Selection

If you wish to save a selection so that you can use it another time without recreating it, use this command (page 140).

Delete Selection

Use this command to permanently remove a saved selection.

Filter Menu

Filters let you change the appearance of your image in all sorts of ways. Elements comes with some filters that are mostly for correcting and improving your photos, while others create artistic effects. The filters are grouped into categories to make it easier to find one that does exactly what you want. You can also apply filters from the Effects palette. Learn more about using filters in Chapter 13. Every image responds to filters differently, so the descriptions here are a very rough guide.

Last Filter

The top item in the Filter menu always features the last filter you've applied. Choose it or press ⌘+F to reapply that filter with the exact same settings you previously used. If you want to change the settings, then you need to choose the filter from its regular place in the list of filters or press ⌘+Option+F.

Filter Gallery

This option lets you try the effects of different filters, rearrange them, and preview what they'll look like in your photo (page 353).

Correct Camera Distortion

Use this filter to correct various kinds of lens distortion problems (page 300).

Adjustments

This group of filters is used primarily (but not exclusively) for correcting and enhancing photos. The filters are discussed on page 267, unless otherwise noted.

- **Equalize**
- **Gradient Map** (page 379)
- **Invert** (or press ⌘+I)
- **Posterize**
- **Threshold**
- **Photo Filter** (page 231)

Artistic

Use these filters to apply a variety of artistic effects to your image, ranging from a pencil-sketch look to a watercolor effect.

- **Colored Pencil** makes your photo look like it was sketched with a colored pencil on a solid colored background.
- **Cutout** makes your image look like it was cut from pieces of paper.

- **Dry Brush** makes your photo look like it was painted using dry brush technique.

- **Film Grain** adds grain to make your photo look like old film.

- **Fresco** makes your photo look like it was painted quickly in a dabbing style.

- **Neon Glow** adds vivid color to your image while softening the details.

- **Paint Daubs** gives your photo a painted look.

- **Palette Knife** makes your photo look like you painted it with a palette knife. While you may think of a palette knife as a tool for blending heavy paint daubs, Adobe describes the effect of this filter as looking like a thin layer of paint that reveals the canvas beneath it.

- **Plastic Wrap** makes your image look like it's covered in plastic.

- **Poster Edges** gives your image accented, dark edges while reducing the number of colors in the rest of the photo.

- **Rough Pastels** makes your image look like it was quickly sketched with pastels.

- **Smudge Stick** uses short diagonal strokes that soften the image by smearing the detail.

- **Sponge** paints with highly textured areas of contrasting color like you'd get by sponging on color.

- **Underpainting** makes your image look like it's painted on a textured background.

- **Watercolor** simplifies the details in your image the way they would be if you were creating a watercolor painting.

Blur

Soften and blur your images with these filters.

- **Average** (page 363)

- **Blur**

- **Blur More**

- **Gaussian Blur** (page 362)

- **Motion Blur** (You apply this pretty much the same way as the Radial blur, described on page 363, but it creates a one-way blur, like you'd see behind Road-Runner when he's scooting away from Wile E. Coyote.)

- **Radial Blur** (page 363)

- **Smart Blur** (This filter reduces grain and noise without affecting the edge sharpness of your photo. It's also used for special artistic effects.)

Brush Strokes

These filters give your image a hand-painted look.

- **Accented Edges** emphasizes the edges of objects as though they were drawn in black ink or white chalk.

- **Angled Strokes** creates diagonal brush strokes that all run in the same direction.

- **Crosshatch** creates diagonal brush strokes that crisscross.

- **Dark Strokes** paints dark areas of your image with short, tight, dark strokes, and light areas with long, white strokes.

- **Ink Outlines** makes your image look like it was drawn with fine ink lines.

- **Spatter** gives the effect you'd get from a spatter airbrush.

- **Sprayed Strokes** paints your image with diagonal, sprayed strokes in its dominant colors.

- **Sumi-e** gives the effect of drawing with a wet brush full of black ink, in a Japanese-influenced style.

Distort

These filters warp your image in a variety of ways.

- **Diffuse Glow** makes your image look as though you're viewing it through a soft diffusion filter.

- **Displace** lets you create a map to tell Elements how to distort your image.

- **Glass** makes your image look like you're viewing it through various kinds of glass, depending on the settings you choose.

- **Liquify** (page 395).

- **Ocean Ripple** gives an underwater effect by adding ripples to your image.

- **Pinch** pulls the edges of your photo inward toward the center.

- **Polar Coordinates** lets you create what's called a cylinder anamorphosis. With this kind of distortion, the image looks normal when you see it in a mirrored cylinder.

- **Ripple** creates a pattern like ripples on the surface of water.

- **Shear** distorts your image along a curve.

- **Spherize** makes your image expand out like a balloon.

- **Twirl** spins your photo, rotating a selection more in the center than at the edge, producing a twirled pattern.

- **Wave** creates a rippled pattern but with more control than the Ripple filter gives you.

- **Zigzag** creates a bent, zigzagging effect that's stronger in the center of the area you apply the filter to.

Noise

Use these filters to add *noise* (graininess) to your photos or remove noise from them. (Unless otherwise specified, these filters are explained on page 245.)

- **Add Noise** (page 358)

- **Despeckle**

- **Dust & Scratches**

- **Median**

- **Reduce Noise** (page 357)

Pixelate

These filters break up the appearance of your photo into spots or blocks of various kinds.

- **Color Halftone** adds the kind of dotted pattern you see in commercially printed color.

- **Crystallize** breaks your image into polygonal blocks of color.

- **Facet** reduces your image to blocks of solid color.

- **Fragment** makes your image look blurry and offset.

- **Mezzotint** creates an effect something like that of a mezzotint engraving.

- **Mosaic** breaks your image down to square blocks of color.

- **Pointillize** creates a pointillist effect by making your photo look like it's made of many dots of color.

Render

This is a diverse but powerful group of filters that transform your photo in many ways.

- **3D Transform** makes your image look like it's on a cube, cylinder, or sphere.

- **Clouds** covers your image with clouds using the foreground/background colors.

- **Difference Clouds** also creates clouds, but blends them in your image in Difference mode.

- **Fibers** creates an effect like spun and woven fibers.

- **Lens Flare** creates starry bright spots like you'd get from a camera lens flare.

- **Lighting Effects** is a powerful and complex filter for changing the light in your photo. For an in-depth tutorial on how to use this filter, see the "Missing CD" page at *www.missingmanuals.com*.

- **Texture Fill** lets you use a grayscale image as a texture for your photo.

Sketch

Here's another group of artistic filters. Most of them make your image look like it was drawn with a pencil or graphics pen.

- **Bas Relief** gives your photo a slightly raised appearance, as though it's carved in low relief.

- **Chalk & Charcoal** makes your photo look like it was sketched with a combination of chalk and charcoal.

- **Charcoal** gives a smudgy effect to your image, like a charcoal drawing.

- **Chrome** is supposed to make your image look like polished chrome, but you might prefer the Wow chrome Layer styles in the Effects palette.

- **Conté Crayon** makes your image look like it was drawn with conté crayons (a drawing medium originally made of graphite and wax, now made from chalks, that is used for making bold strokes) using the foreground/background colors.

- **Graphic Pen** makes the details in your image look like they were drawn with a fine pen using the foreground color, with the background color for the paper color.

- **Halftone Pattern** gives the dotted effect of a halftone screen, like you see in printed illustrations. The effect only *looks* like a halftone—this filter doesn't create a true halftone that your print shop might request.

- **Note Paper** makes your image look like it's on handmade paper. The background color shows through in spots in dark areas.

- **Photocopy** makes your photo look like a Xerox copy.

- **Plaster** makes your image look like it was molded in wet plaster.

- **Reticulation** creates an effect you might get from film emulsion—dark areas clump and brighter areas appear more lightly grained.

- **Stamp** makes your image look like an impression from a rubber stamp.

- **Torn Edges** makes your photo look it's made from torn pieces of paper.

- **Water Paper** makes your photo look like it was painted on wet paper, making the colors run together.

Stylize

These filters create special effects by displacing the pixels in your image or increasing contrast.

- **Diffuse** makes your photo less focused by shuffling the pixels according to the settings you choose.

- **Emboss** makes objects in your image appear stamped or raised.

- **Extrude** gives a 3-D effect by pushing some of the pixels in your image up, something like toothpaste squeezed from a tube.

- **Find Edges** emphasizes the edges of your image against a white background.

- **Glowing Edges** adds a neon-like glow to the edges in your photo.

- **Solarize** produces an effect like what you'd get by briefly exposing a photo print to light while you're developing it. It combines a negative and a positive image.

- **Tiles** breaks your image up into individual tiles. You can choose how much to offset them.

- **Trace Contour** outlines areas where there are major transitions in brightness. The result is supposed to be something like a contour map.

- **Wind** makes your image appear windblown.

Texture

These filters change the surface of your photo to look like it was made from another material.

- **Craquelure** produces a surface effect like cracked plaster.

- **Grain** adds different kinds of graininess to your photo.

- **Mosaic Tiles** is supposed to make your photo look like it's made of mosaic tiles with grout in between them.

- **Patchwork** reduces your image to squares filled with the image's predominant colors.

- **Stained Glass** is supposed to make your photo look like it's made of stained glass. The effect's usually more like a mosaic.

- **Texturizer** makes your photo look like it's on canvas or brick. You can select a file to use as a texture.

Video

These filters are for use with video images.

- **De-Interlace** smoothes images captured from video by removing the odd or even interlaced lines.

• **NTSC Colors** restricts your colors to those suitable for television reproduction.

Other

This is a group of fairly technical filters.

- **Custom** lets you create your own filter.

- **High Pass** is discussed on page 210.

- **Maximum** replaces pixel brightness values with the highest and lowest values of surrounding pixels. It spreads out white areas and shrinks dark areas.

- **Minimum** does the opposite of the Maximum filter. It spreads out dark areas and shrinks white ones.

- **Offset** moves your selection by the number of pixels you specify.

Digimarc

Use this filter to check for Digimarc watermarks in photos. Digimarc is a commercial system that lets subscribers enter their information in a database so that anyone who gets one of their photos can find out who the copyright holder is by searching the Digimarc database.

View Menu

This menu features different ways to adjust how you see your image on your screen. For more details on adjusting your view, see page 77.

New Window for...

This command lets you create a duplicate window for your image so that you can see it at two different magnification levels at once. The new window goes away when you close your image—it doesn't create a copy of your photo.

Zoom In

To increase the view size, you can choose this menu item or press ⌘+=. You can also use the Zoom tool (page 79).

Zoom Out

To reduce the view size, choose this menu item or press ⌘+−. You can also use the Zoom tool (page 79).

Fit on Screen

Use this command or press ⌘+0 to make your photo as large as it can be without your having to scroll to see part of it.

Actual Pixels

Choose this option or press Option+⌘+0 to see your image the exact size it would appear on the Web or in other programs that can't adjust view size (as Elements can).

Print Size

Elements makes its best guess as to how large your image would print at its current resolution (page 86).

Selection

When this menu item is turned on, the outlines of your selections are visible. You can toggle the setting off and on here, or by pressing ⌘+H.

Rulers

If you want to see rulers around the edges of your image window, toggle them on and off here, or by pressing Shift+⌘+R. You can adjust the unit of measurement in Photoshop Elements → Preferences → Units & Rulers.

Grid

If you want to see a measurement and alignment grid on your photos, use this setting to toggle it on and off. You can adjust the grid size in Photoshop Elements → Preferences → Grid.

Guide Presets

The preset document sizes for new files include a couple of video sizes with guidelines to help you know the workable areas of the document. The Guide Presets menu item becomes active when you're working with a DV (digital video) file, or if someone sends you a Photoshop file with guides. It's normally grayed out.

Annotations

This command is available only for files that contain voice annotations. Toggle the annotation on and off here. You may get a file with a voice annotation from someone working with Photoshop, which lets you record sound annotations that you can add to your files.

Snap to

If you want to control the Elements autogrid (a hidden system that determines how precisely you can place things when you move them in your images), use these commands.

- **Guides**. When you're working with one of the video document sizes that includes guidelines, or if someone sends you a Photoshop file that includes them, this setting is where you toggle on and off whether you want objects you add to snap to the guidelines.

- **Grid**. When this setting is turned on, Elements automatically jumps to the nearest gridline. If the way your tools and selections keep jumping away from you bothers you, then turn off the Grid here. Then everything stays exactly where you place it. You have to make the Grid visible (View → Grid) before you can change its settings.

Window Menu

This menu controls which palettes and bins you see, as well as letting you adjust how your image windows display. Windows that are currently visible have a checkmark next to their names. A dash next to a name means the window is visible in another pane, but not in the current pane.

Images

Use these commands to control how your images display. The choices are explained in detail on page 78.

- **Maximize Mode**. Each image takes up the entire available space.

- **Tile**. Your images appear edge to edge so that all windows are equally visible.

- **Cascade**. Your image windows appear in overlapping stacks. (Cascade is the usual view when you start Elements for the first time.)

- **Minimize.** You can send the active open image window to the Dock from here or by pressing ⌘+M. Click the image's thumbnail in the dock or double-click it in the Project bin to bring it back.

- **Bring All to Front**. If you've gotten some of your images hidden behind documents from other programs, use this command to bring them forward so that all your open Elements images are the front windows.

- **Match Zoom**. Choose Match Zoom to get the same magnification level in all open windows as in the active image window.

- **Match Location**. When you have only part of a photo visible in a window, choose Match Location to make all open windows display the same part of their images, too, like the upper-left corner, for example.

Tools

The Tools setting hides and shows the Toolbox.

Tool Options

You can show and hide the Options bar by turning it off and on here.

Color Swatches

Use Color Swatches to show and hide the Color Swatches palette (page 202).

Content

The Content palette holds frames, backgrounds, graphics, shapes, themes, and text effects to use in projects. It's always visible in Create → Artwork, but if you want to see it in Edit mode as well, this is where you make it visible. See page 413 for more about how to use this palette.

Effects

Effects shows and hides the Effects palette, from which you apply filters, Photo Effects, and Layer styles. See page 27.

Favorites

You can put your favorite items from the Content and Effects palettes into the Favorites palette for easier access (page 415). Like the Content palette, it's always visible in Create → Artwork, but you can use the setting here to make it visible in Full Edit or hide it again once it's visible.

Histogram

Use the Histogram to show or hide the Histogram in its own palette (page 189).

Info

Use this setting to bring up a palette with information about your photos, like the file size and color value numbers.

Layers

Make the Layers palette visible or hidden by toggling this setting. See page 146.

Navigator

Turn the Navigator off and on here. The Navigator lets you adjust which portion of a large image is visible on your screen and also adjust the zoom. See page 82.

Undo History

The Undo History setting makes the Undo History palette visible or hides it. The Undo History palette shows a record of all the changes to your image up to the number of states you set in Photoshop Elements → Preferences → Performance → History States. See page 31 for more about the Undo History palette.

Palette Bin

This setting minimizes (hides) and maximizes (reopens) the Palette bin (page 25). You can also just click the edge of the bin to hide or expand it.

Reset Palette Locations

Use this command to return all palettes to their original locations.

Welcome

Choose this menu item to see the Welcome window that appears when Elements starts up. You can then use the menu setting to change which Elements component appears when the program starts up.

Project Bin

This setting minimizes (hides) the Project bin. Select it again to maximize (reopen) the bin.

Image Windows

At the bottom of the Window menu you see a list of all the files you have open in Elements. Choose one to bring it to the front as the active window.

Help Menu

The Help menu is where you find the Elements Help files, as well as information about the program itself.

Search Box (Leopard only)

If you have Mac OS X Leopard (10.5), you see a search box as the first item in this menu (it's not visible if you have Tiger [10.4]). This box searches the program menus, not the Elements Help Files. Page 29 has more about this feature.

Photoshop Elements Help

When you call up the Elements Help files here, or press F1, your Web browser launches to show you the Help files.

Glossary of Terms

The Elements Help files include a glossary of terms relating to digital imaging. If you're wondering what a particular term means, choose this menu item and it'll take you to the glossary index so you can look it up.

System Info

Choose this item to see a window showing basic info about your Mac (like the amount of RAM and your serial number), your OS X version, and the plug-ins installed on your computer.

Registration

If you didn't register Elements with Adobe the first time you used the program, you can choose this menu item to bring up the registration window again.

Updates

This is where you check for updates to Elements components. Go to Adobe Updater window → Preferences and you can set your preferences for how you want Elements to handle updates.

Online Support

Choose this option and Elements launches your Web browser and attempts to go to Adobe's support Web site.

Photoshop Elements Online

This menu item takes you to the main product page for Photoshop Elements on Adobe's Web site. As it does with the online support link, Elements launches your browser and offers to connect to the Internet if you're not already online.

Online Learning Resources

Online Learning Resources also takes you to the main product page for Photoshop Elements on Adobe's Web site.

Installation and Troubleshooting

Elements is quite easy to install and is pretty trouble free once it's up and running. This appendix explains a couple of things you can do to ensure that your installation goes smoothly, and it also provides cures for most of the little glitches that can crop up once you're using the program.

Installing Elements

There's not much you need to do prior to installing Elements, but if you have any antivirus software or any Norton/Symantec products, you should disable those before you start. (Be sure to turn them on again when you're through installing Elements.)

You need to install Elements from an administrative user account. (If you have only one user account on your Mac, you're an administrator. If you want to double-check your status, go to → System Preferences → Accounts, and make sure the "Allow user to administer this computer" checkbox is turned on.) Elements won't install (nor run well) from accounts without administrative powers.

You don't have to remove previous versions of Elements to install Elements 6, and the installer won't remove them for you, even if you *do* want to get rid of them. Each version of Elements is a separate, standalone program, and you can have as many versions as you like on one computer. You can even run them simultaneously, provided you launch the older version(s) before the newer one(s). (If you have Leopard—OS X 10.5—Elements 3 is the oldest version that will run on your system.) If you want to remove older versions, just drag their folders from Applications to the Trash.

Make sure you have your Elements serial number handy. You won't be able to run the program without it. If you have a retail version of Elements, the serial number is on the label on the install disc's case. If you got it bundled (when you bought a scanner, for example), you'll usually find the serial number on the paper sleeve the disc's in. (It's not a bad idea to write your serial number right on the disc so that you'll always have it around if you need to reinstall.)

1. **Put the install DVD in your Mac's DVD or combo drive.**

   Double-click the DVD icon to see the disk's contents.

2. **Double-click the Setup icon to launch the installer.**

   Enter your OS X account password when Setup asks for it. The installer may tell you that you need to close other programs, like Word or Safari. Do so, and then click Try Again. (Click Cancel if now's not a convenient time to close all your other programs, and run the installer later.)

3. **Choose a language for the software agreement.**

   Give the agreement a quick read and then click Accept.

4. **Choose a language for Elements.**

   Elements 6 has a multi-language installer. Choose your mother tongue and then click Next to continue.

5. **Choose where you want Elements to install itself.**

   Unless you have a specific reason not to (if you install all your programs on a separate drive, for instance), just agree to the location the installer suggests, which is the main Applications folder on your Mac. Then click Next.

6. **Start the install.**

   Elements displays a summary of your choices (components to install, how much free space will be left on your drive after the install, location, and so on). Unless there's something in the summary that you want to change, just click Install. (If you want to make changes, click Back and keep clicking it till you reach the step you want to change.)

7. **Click Finish to close the Installer.**

   That's it!

The first time you launch Elements, you have to launch it from the Applications folder, and you'll need to enter your serial number before you can use the program. To keep Elements in your Dock, simply click the Dock icon while Elements is running and choose "Keep in Dock". (You can also drag the program—*not* the whole Elements folder—into the Dock when Elements isn't running.) If you add Elements to your Dock and then change your mind, just drag the icon out of the Dock and watch it vanish in a puff of smoke.

Registration

When you first launch Elements, it asks you to register the program. You can run Elements without registering it, but you get a couple of advantages if you register. For one thing, Adobe hangs onto a record of your serial number, so if you ever misplace the number, you can get it from Adobe. Also, when Adobe releases new versions of Elements, there's usually a rebate for registered owners of previous versions. And if you agree to let Adobe send you email, they often offer discounts on other programs, like a big discount on the full version of Photoshop, if you want to move on later.

> **NOTE** In the Registration pull-down menu, you can choose to have Elements remind you to register a week from now, or you can choose not to register. If you choose the latter option and change your mind later on, go to Help → Registration to bring up the Registration window.

Scratch Disks

Elements uses a *scratch disk*—reserve space on a hard drive to supplement your computer's memory—when it's busy making your photos gorgeous. The calculations Elements makes behind the scenes are very complex, and Elements needs someplace to write stuff down while it's figuring out how to make changes to your image. It does so by using a scratch disk if the task at hand is too heavy-duty for your system's main memory alone to cope with.

You probably have just one hard drive in your computer, and Elements automatically uses that drive as the scratch disk. That's fine, and Elements can run very happily without a dedicated scratch disk.

If you're fortunate enough to have a computer with more than one internal drive, you can designate a separate disk as your scratch disk to improve Elements performance. Your scratch disk needs to be as fast as the drive Elements is installed on or there's no point in setting up a special scratch disk. (If you have a USB external drive, for instance, forget it [USB isn't fast enough, even USB 2.0] and just leave your main drive as your scratch disk.)

To assign a scratch disk, go to Photoshop Elements → Preferences → Performance and choose your preferred disk. You can choose up to four disks to use as scratch disks.

Troubleshooting

If Elements behaves badly from the moment you install it, something probably went funky during your installation. That's easy to fix.

You can uninstall Elements and reinstall it, but with Elements 6 you have another option: before uninstalling, you can try reinstalling Elements right over the existing copy, as explained in the list below (which also gives you a couple of other alternatives to uninstalling). If that doesn't help, then your best bet is uninstalling and reinstalling.

One much-requested new feature in Elements 6 is an uninstall utility, which now comes with the program, since Elements installs files in many places around your hard drive, unlike the usual tidy Mac application package. You can uninstall Elements by dragging it to the Trash, but this method might not get rid of all the files that Elements puts on your computer; running the uninstaller should delete 'em all (you might still want to search with Spotlight if the idea of not getting rid of every last little file bugs you).

Here's how to use the uninstaller to get rid of Elements:

1. **Put your Elements install DVD in the drive and launch the uninstaller.**

   Double-click Setup and give the installer (which is also the *uninstaller*) your OS X password, closing any programs if it asks you to.

2. **Uninstall Elements.**

   In the first installer screen, choose "Remove Adobe Photoshop Elements Components," then click Next, and then click Install.

3. **Click Finish to close the Installer.**

However, it's rarely necessary to completely uninstall Elements to fix problems you're having. There are several things you can try before uninstalling:

- **Reset a tool.** If a single tool stops working, go to the far-left part of the Options bar. There's a tiny, black downward-facing arrow there (it's very hard to see). Click it to see a pop-up menu with two items in it. Choose Reset Tool to clear any settings the tool has that may be making it act up.

- **Delete Preferences.** If resetting a tool doesn't solve your problem, or if Elements is generally misbehaving, try resetting your preferences as explained on page 499.

- **Reinstall.** You can also do a Windows-type repair install if you seem to be missing pieces of Elements or if you inadvertently delete part of the program. Just follow the installation instructions in the previous section to run the installer right over your existing installation (in other words, leave Elements installed and run the installer again).

Fortunately, Adobe makes very good software that looks after itself very well. There is, however, one simple procedure you can perform if things start acting funny in Elements: delete your Elements *preferences file*, which is where Elements keeps track of your preferred settings for the program. Deleting it fixes the overwhelming majority of problems you may develop. Elements makes a new fresh copy of the preferences after you delete the old one—it doesn't harm the program to get rid of this file. Incidentally, you don't have a preferences file to delete until you've run the program at least once, so if you've just installed Elements for the first time, you're better off using the reinstall option explained above, rather than trying this.

Here's how to delete your Elements preferences file:

1. **If Elements is currently running, quit the program (⌘+Q).**

2. **Before you restart Elements, press ⌘+Option+Shift and *hold the keys down.***

   This keystroke combination tells Elements you want to delete its preferences.

3. **While still pressing those three keys, launch Elements and keep holding the keys down as the program starts up.**

   After a few seconds, a window should appear asking if you want to delete the Elements Settings File (which stores your preferences). If Elements starts up and you never see this window, quit Elements and pop back to step 2 to try again. (This process generally works pretty well, so if you have trouble, check to be sure you're holding down the right keys.)

4. **Confirm that you want to delete your settings.**

   In the window, click Yes. Elements deletes your settings file and, hopefully, starts behaving itself. (You'll need to redo any changes you'd made to Elements' settings—like turning the background off, for example—after doing this.)

You can use these same keys when starting up Bridge. They bring up a window with checkboxes giving you the option to delete the Bridge preferences, purge the thumbnail cache (for faster thumbnail rendering in the Content panel), or reset the Bridge window (workspace) to look the way it did the first time you opened the program. You can choose to do any or all of these things by turning on the relevant boxes. However, it's not very common to need to delete Bridge's preferences. But for Elements, deleting preferences fixes about 90 percent of the things that can go wrong with the program.

Bridge CS3, Menu by Menu

Bridge CS3 is Adobe's ultra-deluxe file browsing program that you get with the full version of Photoshop and with Elements 6 for Mac (Elements 6 for Windows includes the Organizer instead). Bridge is closely connected with Elements, but it's also a standalone program that lets you browse for photos to edit in Elements, organize your photos, assign keywords to them, rate them, and do some batch processing, like renaming or applying metadata templates to a bunch of images at once. As explained in various chapters, you can start lots of Elements projects by selecting your photos in Bridge. Bridge is also your portal to most of the online components of Elements 6.

> **NOTE** The version of Bridge you get with Elements includes several features that are only useful for the collaborative features of the full Creative Suite, like Version Cue's meetings feature. (You can join a Version Cue meeting from Elements, but you can't start one.) Since these are totally useless to most people who just use Elements, they normally hide so they won't confuse you.
>
> However, it's possible that they might appear in your Bridge menus, especially if you ever have to delete the Bridge preference files. In this appendix, you'll find several references to these normally hidden menu items, just in case. For items like these, this appendix always has a note telling you that this is a feature you normally won't see.

Bridge CS3 Menu

This menu is where you can get information about Bridge, adjust your settings, and control how Bridge interacts with other programs.

About Bridge

This item gives you info about which version of Bridge you have, as well as a long scrolling list of the names of the many, many people who helped develop the program, and a list of patent numbers.

Camera Raw Preferences

You can open the Elements RAW Converter's preferences here. These are the same settings described on page 225.

Preferences

Here's where you adjust your settings for Bridge. Your options are:

- **General**. Use the Appearance sliders to adjust the brightness of the Bridge background, and choose a different text highlight color if you find the color you use elsewhere in OS X too hard to see against Bridge's gray background. This is also where you turn on the Photo Downloader (page 19) if you want it to grab photos any time you plug in a camera or card reader. Finally, you can set the number of files displayed in the Bridge Recent Items menu, and choose what you want to see in the Favorite Items panel (page 39).

- **Thumbnails.** If Bridge seems slow, use the settings in the top half of this window to adjust how the program creates and displays thumbnails. Leave the settings in the top part of the window as they are, unless you have a good reason to change them. With the controls in the bottom half, you can choose to display additional info beneath thumbnails besides the file's name. You have a long list of metadata items (page 52) to select from, and you can add up to four items. You can also control whether you want to see tooltips when you hover your cursor over things (*tooltips* are brief descriptions of whatever your cursor is over).

- **Playback.** If you want to flip through all the photos in a stack (page 61) like an animation, you can choose the frame rate (how long each photo displays) here. Since Bridge also recognizes audio and video files, you have some settings for whether to have these play automatically when you preview them, and whether to have them loop (play continuously) when previewed.

- **Metadata.** This window lets you control the various types of metadata (page 52) from your photos, audio files, and videos that you can view in the Metadata pane. It's also where you turn the Metadata placard (page 52) off and on.

- **Keywords.** If you use Bridge to assign keywords, this window gives you a couple of fairly technical choices about the encoding of hierarchical keywords (keyword and sub-keyword relationships). You can also choose to have Bridge automatically apply parent keywords here (meaning that if you apply a sub-keyword, the keyword it belongs to also gets applied). See page 52 for more about keywords.

- **Labels.** Bridge lets you assign colored labels to your photos (see page 52). This is where you can change what the different colors stand for.

- **File Type Associations.** Choose what program files open in when you double-click them in Bridge (page 40).

- **Cache.** Bridge stores thumbnails and info about your photos (like ratings, for example) in a special cache file. The "Automatically Export Caches To Folders When Possible" checkbox lets you tell Bridge to create caches within the folders where your photos are saved. That way, when you send a folder to someone else, your Bridge information goes along. If you don't care about sharing that info, leave this checkbox turned off, and Bridge saves to one main cache. Sometimes the cache gets so large it impedes Bridge's performance, so you can compact or purge the cache here to speed up Bridge (it rebuilds automatically).

- **Inspector.** This is pretty useless if you only have Elements. It's used for Version Cue projects (Version Cue is part of Adobe's Creative Suite), so it does nothing at all for 99 percent of Elements users. However, if for some reason you need to join a Version Cue project from Elements, you can do so here. This controls the projects that appear in the Inspector panel in Bridge. (You may not see this option—check out the Note on page 501.)

- **Startup Scripts.** Bridge runs special scripts to let it communicate with other programs, to make the Elements options (like the Picture Package) and online components work. You can disable them here, but usually you don't want to do that.

- **Advanced.** Choose your language and your keyboard layout for Bridge here. You can also disable hardware acceleration for previews and Slideshow view, but you don't want to do that unless you understand what that means and have a good reason for changing it.

Services

This is where you can access OS X utility programs like Grab (for taking screenshots) or Text Edit (for copying text). Your actual choices in the sub-menu depend on what programs you have installed on your Mac. It's normal for some to be grayed out. Dictionary, for instance, isn't available unless some text is highlighted.

Hide Bridge CS3

To put Bridge out of sight, choose this item or press ⌘+H.

Hide Others

If you want Bridge to be your only visible program, choose this or press Option+⌘+H.

Show All

Use this to bring back your hidden programs so they're visible on the desktop again.

Quit Bridge CS3

You can shut Bridge down by choosing this menu item, or by pressing ⌘+Q.

File Menu

This menu lets you create new Bridge windows or new folders for your photos, open photos in Elements or other programs, move or delete images, email them, or burn them to CDs and DVDs.

New Window

Choose this or press ⌘+N to open a duplicate Bridge window. You'd do this if you wanted to use two different workspaces at once. For instance, you could have one window in the default thumbnail view and one in Metadata view, so you could see details about the thumbnails you click on.

New Folder

If you're organizing photos in Bridge, choose this command or press ⌘+Shift+N to create a new folder in your current location.

Open

To open a photo in Elements (or whatever program you chose in File Type Associations [page 40]), choose this item, press ⌘+O, or just double-click the photo's thumbnail.

Open With

If you want to open a photo with a different program than you usually use, go here and select the program from the list. Next time, the photo will open with whatever program you normally use.

Open Recent

This item lets you open a photo you've recently opened from Bridge—just pick a photo from the list that appears. If you want to change the number of Recent Items that appear here, in Bridge, go to Bridge CS3 → Preferences → General (page 502).

Close Window

To make the Bridge window go away, choose this option or press ⌘+W. This doesn't close (or quit) the program, just the window.

Move to Trash

Want to say goodbye to one of your photos forever? Select a photo (or photos), and then choose this menu item or press ⌘+Delete. Your photo plunks into the OS X trash, so you can get it back if you change your mind, as long as you haven't emptied the trash.

Eject

If you've been getting photos from a camera, card reader, or CD, you can eject it from here, press ⌘+E, or use the Eject button on your keyboard.

Return to Adobe Photoshop Elements/Photoshop

To go back to Elements without opening a photo, choose this menu item or press Option+⌘+O. If you open Bridge from Elements, this item reads "Photoshop Elements," and that's where it takes you. If you open Bridge another way (double-clicking it in the Applications folder, for instance), it reads "Photoshop," and if you happen to have Photoshop CS3 installed, that's where it'll take you, rather than to Elements.

Reveal in Finder

To bring up the Finder to see where a photo's saved, choose this option.

Reveal in Bridge

This is another leftover from Adobe's Creative Suite. If you're in a Version Cue project, you can use this command on project files to see their locations in Bridge. This is one of the items you generally won't see if you just have Elements (see the Note on page 501).

Get Photos from Camera

This launches the Adobe Photo Downloader (page 19).

Burn CD

Choose this option to make a CD or DVD of your selected Bridge Photos (see page 60).

Attach to Email

Select a photo and choose this to send it to Elements for automatic resizing and attaching to a new email message (see page 448).

Move To

Select a photo or folder and use this command to move it someplace else. The pop-out menu shows a list of your most recently used folders, or you can browse to another location.

Copy To

This works just like Move To, only it makes and moves a copy instead of your original.

Place

This item doesn't give you any submenu options unless you have the full Adobe Creative Suite, in which case you can use it to put a file into a document in another Creative Suite program, like Adobe Illustrator. It's just a useless leftover if you only have Elements. You usually won't see this item if you just have Elements, but it may appear (see the Note on page 501 to learn why).

Add to Favorites/Remove from Favorites

Select an image or a folder and use this command to put into the Favorites panel for fast access, or just drag it to the panel. If an item is a favorite, this option changes to "Remove from Favorites", for when you don't want it in the panel anymore.

File Info

Choose this menu item to bring up the File Info window, which displays general information about your image (file creation date, file format, and so on). You can also add or edit metadata here (see page 52). Option+Shift+⌘+I is the keyboard shortcut.

Edit Menu

You can't really edit photos from this menu, but it contains the usual Mac short-cuts for copying and pasting, and you can rotate and search for images from here.

> **NOTE** Copying and pasting only work within Bridge—you can't copy from Bridge and paste into another program.

Undo

This is actually grayed out much of the time, but for the few things you can undo, this is where you do it, or just press ⌘+Z.

Cut

This command *should* remove a photo from where it is and place it onto the clipboard so you can paste it somewhere else, but this feature doesn't work well in Bridge. (It usually doesn't do anything. If you try it and it doesn't work, just copy the file instead.)

Copy

To copy a photo from Bridge, select it, and then choose this command or press ⌘+C. You can only copy and paste within Bridge, so you could use this command to copy a photo from one folder to another, but not to a Pages or Word document, for example.

Paste

To put something you've copied into another file within Bridge, use this menu item or press ⌘+V.

Duplicate

Choose this item to create a copy of the selected image in the same folder.

Select All

Use this item or press ⌘+A to select all the visible photos in Bridge.

Deselect All

To remove all your current photo selections, choose this menu item or press Shift+⌘+A.

Select Inverse

If you've selected some photos in Bridge and now want to choose all the unselected photos instead, choose this item or press Shift+⌘+I.

Find

Choose this command or press ⌘+F to bring up the helpful Find window, which gives you a bunch of ways to search for photos (see page 55).

Rotate 180°

This turns the selected image(s) upside down (see page 66).

Rotate 90° Clockwise

You can rotate a photo by choosing this command, clicking the right-hand Rotate arrow in the upper-right part of the Bridge window, or pressing ⌘+] (the close bracket key).

Rotate 90° Counterclockwise

Use this command, the left-hand Rotate arrow in the upper-right part of the Bridge window, or press ⌘+[(the open bracket key).

Generate High Quality Thumbnail

This is usually grayed out because Bridge automatically generates high-quality thumbnails of your photos. If you chose to use the next menu item to create lower-quality thumbnails, choose this command or press Shift+⌘+H to recreate high-quality thumbnails.

Generate Quick Thumbnail

If you want lower-quality thumbnails that aren't color managed (see page 183), select the photos you want them for and then choose this or press Shift+⌘+Q. (The only reason to do this is if you have an old, slow computer and Bridge brings your system to a crawl.)

View Menu

This menu controls the various ways of looking at your photos in Bridge.

Compact Mode

Choose this item or press ⌘+Return and Bridge shrinks itself into a much smaller window that you can keep open without losing much desktop space. Choose this item or press the same keys again to return it to Full Mode.

Slideshow

To see a full-screen slideshow of the photos currently visible in Bridge, choose this or press ⌘+L You can't save this slideshow—it's just a view within Bridge.

Slideshow Options

Use this menu item or press Shift+⌘+L to make some choices about how Bridge displays photos in slideshow mode. The Zoom Back And Forth setting, for instance, causes Bridge to zoom in on one slide and zoom back out on the next. You can also control how long each slide appears, choose whether you want transitions, and adjust other aspects of how your images display.

As Thumbnails

Use this menu item and the next to toggle the Content panel view. This option, the way Bridge usually works, shows thumbnails with filenames underneath.

As Details

Instead of just thumbnails and filenames, you also see a list of information about each image. It's the same info you'd see in Metadata view, but it only affects the Content panel.

Show Thumbnail Only

Choose this item or press ⌘+T to hide the filenames under the thumbnails. Repeat to toggle them back on.

Show Reject Files

When this is turned on, you can see photos to which you've given a Reject rating (page 51). To hide them, just turn this setting off.

Show Hidden Files

Bridge normally only displays thumbnails of images, but if you also want to see other files like the .thm files your camera creates for your RAW files, turn this on.

Show Folders

This is usually turned on, but if you don't want to see folders in Bridge, turn them off here.

Sort

If you want to change how Bridge sorts your photos, choose a new criterion from the submenu. You can also choose to sort by ascending or descending order.

Refresh

Press F5 or choose this item and Bridge redraws the thumbnails for your current view. (When you do this, you lose any photo selections you've made.) You can use this command if you find that Bridge has stopped rendering the thumbnails correctly.

Stacks Menu

Bridge lets you group photos into *stacks* (page 51)—you see only one photo as the icon for the whole group—to make it easier to keep track of them. This menu is your command center for creating and managing stacks.

Group as Stack

Select the photos you want to stack, and then use this command or press ⌘+G to corral them into a new stack.

Ungroup from Stack

To remove a photo from a stack, expand the stack, click the photo's thumbnail, and then choose this menu item or press Shift+⌘+G. To totally get rid of a stack, just expand it and select all the photos in it before doing this.

Open Stack

To expand a stack so you can see all the photos in it, press ⌘+the right arrow key, or choose this menu item.

Close Stack

To collapse an expanded stack, use this menu item or press ⌘+the left arrow key.

Promote to Top of Stack

If you'd rather use a different photo from the group as the one visible when the stack is collapsed, expand the stack, click the photo you want, and then choose this item.

Expand All Stacks

If you have multiple stacks and you want to see all the photos in all of them, choose this option or press Option+⌘+the right arrow key.

Collapse All Stacks

To make all your stacks shrink back to single photo view, choose this item or press Option+⌘+the left arrow key.

Frame Rate

You can quickly view all the photos in a stack of ten or more like an animated GIF or a cartoon by pressing the play button that appears when you click on a stack. This menu sets the frame rate, meaning how fast each photo succeeds the next. (The upper numbers are the slowest, the bottom the fastest.)

Label Menu

To help you sort your photos, you can assign labels and ratings to them. See page 51 for more about these features.

Ratings

You can rate photos from one to five stars or mark the ones you don't want with a Reject tag. To rate a photo, select it and then choose your rating from this menu or press ⌘+ the number of stars you want to assign—⌘+3 to assign three stars, for example. Pressing ⌘+0 (the number zero) makes a photo unrated, and pressing Option+Delete assigns the Reject tag.

Label

Bridge lets you assign colored labels to your photos. Adobe gives the various labels default meanings (Select, Second, and so on) but you can assign your own meanings by going to Bridge CS3 → Preferences → Labels and typing in whatever you want. There are keyboard shortcuts for each label, which appear in the Label menu to the right of the labels (⌘+ the numbers 6 through 9). To assign a label, simply select a photo and then choose the appropriate menu item or use the label's keyboard shortcut. (Bridge labels are only visible within Bridge, not in other programs or in the Finder.)

Tools Menu

Here you can rename your files, use them in projects, and add and edit their metadata (page 52).

Batch Rename

Use this command (or press Shift | ⌘ | R) to change the names of several images at once. The resulting window gives you more options for creating custom names than Elements' Process Multiple Files command does (see page 233), including moving the files as you rename them, and preserving the original filename in the metadata (page 52) so you can still search by the old names.

Create Metadata Template

This option lets you create a list of metadata to apply to multiple images, including a huge variety of info like copyright, usage terms, Web site URLs, descriptions, and much more, and then save it as a template to use over and over again. Page 52 has the details.

Edit Metadata Template

To make changes to a template you've already created, choose the template from this item's pop-out list.

Append Metadata

Choose a template from this item's pop-out list, and that template's information gets applied to your selected photos in addition to the metadata they already have.

Replace Metadata

Use this command, and the information in your metadata template overwrites the existing metadata in the files you've selected. You generally don't want to do this because you can lose important information; in most cases, Append Metadata is a better option.

Cache

Bridge stores thumbnails and information about your photos in a file called the cache. This is where you can manage your cache (you can also go to Bridge CS3 → Preferences → Cache). Here you can:

- **Build and Export Cache.** To send cache information along with photos you share, choose the folder the images are in, and then select this menu item.

- **Purge Cache For Folder....** If your cache gets too big, it'll slow down Bridge. Choose this option to force Bridge to create a new cache to speed things up.

Photoshop Elements

Use this menu item to send photos to Elements for use in projects. You can start the following projects from Bridge:

- **Contact Sheet II** lets you print several thumbnails on one page (page 432).

- **PDF Slide Show** creates an Elements PDF slideshow (page 420).

- **Picture Package** lets you print a group of photos of different sizes all on one page (page 434).

- **Photomerge Faces** is a new feature that lets you combine parts of different faces, just for fun (page 296).

- **Photomerge Group Shot** lets you replace just one person in a group photo—the one with his eyes closed or the one in mid yawn (page 299).

- **Photomerge Panorama** is Elements' great revamped feature for stitching together multiple photos for an image wider than you can capture with your camera (page 299).

- **Process Multiple Files** is a way to change the format of many photos at once, resize or rename them, apply some of the auto editing features, or assign captions (page 233).

- **Web Photo Gallery** lets you can create a simple Web gallery to show off your photos (page 449).

Photoshop Services

This is where you find the online projects and sharing options for Elements. (Your actual options here will vary by your location and also by Adobe's current partnerships.)

- **Online Photo Printing.** Get prints, calendars, or photo books from Kodak Easy-Share Gallery (page 424), or order stamps featuring your photos from *photostamps.com* (page 420).

- **Online Portfolios and Galleries.** Send photos to SmugMug so you can share them, or to MorePhotos so you can sell them. (page 453).

- **Share Photos Online.** This sends your photos to the sharing section of Easy-Share (see the box on page 453).

- **Online Backup.** If you want to use the Iron Mountain backup feature (for a fee), this where you get to it (see page 62 for more info).

- **Choose Your Location.** To see the online services available in your area, choose your location here.

- **Automatically Check for Services.** Turn this on, and Bridge will automatically keep your list of online services up to date.

Window Menu

This menu lets you customize the appearance of Bridge.

New Synchronized Window

Choose this command or press Option+⌘+N to create a new window that shows the same photos as your original window. For example, you could have one window in Metadata view so you can see file info about your image, and a second window in one of the Filmstrip views for a large preview. (When you change to viewing another folder in one window, the other window also changes—hence the term "synchronized".)

Workspace

This is where you select the general setup for your Bridge window and save your customized layouts, called *workspaces*. You can choose:

- **Save Workspace**. If you've created a customized workspace, this is how you save it for the future. Then you can choose it from the bottom of the Workspace menu or by clicking one of the buttons at the lower right of the main Bridge window.

- **Delete Workspace**. If you're tired of a saved workspace, this is how to remove it from your list of available workspaces.

- **Reset to Default Workspace**. If things get all confused and you want to go back to what Bridge looked like the first time you opened it, choose this option.

The next part of this menu lists the basic workspace setups that you can customize:

- **Default**. This workspace has a large area for thumbnails in the center, with small panes for the other panels on either side. Keyboard shortcut: ⌘+F1.

- **Light Table**. This workspace only shows thumbnails, with no other panes or panels. Keyboard shortcut: ⌘+F2.

- **File Navigator**. Shows a large thumbnail area with the Folders and Favorites panels on the left. Keyboard shortcut: ⌘+F3.

- **Metadata Focus**. Instead of a grid of thumbnails, you see a list of images with file information below the name. Keyboard shortcut: ⌘+F4.

- **Horizontal Filmstrip**. This workspace has a large preview area with thumbnails in a scrolling filmstrip-like view at the bottom of the window. The left pane appears for navigation and shows the Filter panel. Keyboard shortcut: ⌘+F5.

- **Vertical Filmstrip**. Gives you a large central preview with thumbnails running down the right side of the window. Keyboard shortcut: ⌘+F6.

Folders Panel

This item shows a folder view of your computer you can use to find your photos. Turn it off and on by selecting it here.

Favorites Panel

The Favorites panel holds anything you want to get to quickly. You can drag photos or folders into it so they're always at hand. Use this menu item to show or hide the panel.

Metadata Panel

This is where you can turn on (or off) the panel that shows the metadata in your images (page 52).

Keywords Panel

Turn on this panel here if you want to use Bridge to assign keywords to your photos (page 52).

Filter Panel

This panel lets you set parameters for what photos to view. For instance, you can choose to see only photos with certain ratings or keywords, or only specific file types. It's automatically turned on in some workspaces, but you can turn it off and on here by selecting or deselecting it in the menu. (See page 55.)

Preview Panel

This panel shows a larger view of the selected image(s). It's on for all workspaces, but if you don't like it you can turn it off (or back on again) here.

Inspector Panel

For most people who use Elements, this is a totally useless panel and you'll want to leave it turned off. It would only show anything if you were in a Version Cue meeting with people using Adobe's Creative Suite (Version Cue is part of Adobe's Creative Suite). You won't normally see this item if you just have Elements (see the Note on page 501).

Minimize

To minimize the Bridge window to the Dock, choose this item or press ⌘+M as you would with any program. Click the tiny Bridge window in the dock to bring it back again.

Bring All to Front

This brings all your open Bridge windows to the front on your desktop.

Current Folder Location

The bottom of the Window Menu shows the name of the current folder. If you have multiple views, it shows the location of all windows, so you'll see a folder name repeated if you have two windows open to the same folder.

Help Menu

The Help menu lets you search for information, open the Bridge Help files, and check for updates.

Search Box (Leopard only)

You only see this box if you have Leopard (Mac OS 10.5)—it doesn't appear in Tiger (OS 10.4). You can use this box to search Bridge's menus, as explained on page 29.

Bridge Help

Choose this item to launch the Adobe Help Viewer, where you can browse through the Bridge Help files and search within them.

Updates

Select this option and Bridge searches for updates to all your Adobe programs, not just Bridge. If you want to disable auto-updating, choose this item, click Preferences in the dialog box that appears, and then turn off the checkbox next to "Automatically check for Adobe updates".

Index

PHOTOSHOP ELEMENTS 6 FOR MAC: THE MISSING MANUAL

Colophon

Rachel Monaghan provided quality control for *Photoshop Elements 6 for Mac: The Missing Manual*. Shan Young and Dawn Frausto wrote the index.

The cover of this book is based on a series design originally created by David Freedman and modified by Mike Kohnke, Karen Montgomery, and Fitch (*www.fitch.com*). Back cover design, dog illustration, and color selection by Fitch.

David Futato designed the interior layout, based on a series design by Phil Simpson. This book was converted by Keith Fahlgren to FrameMaker 5.5.6. The text font is Adobe Minion; the heading font is Adobe Formata Condensed; and the code font is LucasFont's TheSans Mono Condensed. The illustrations that appear in the book were produced by Robert Romano and Jessamyn Read using Macromedia FreeHand MX and Adobe Photoshop CS.